# Understanding Data Communications

lbert Held

Boston • Sa

L

Capetown •

For more information, please contact:

Pearson Education Corporate Sales Division

201 W. 103rd Street

Indianapolis, IN 46290

(800) 428-5331

corpsales@pearsoned.com

Visit AW on the Web: www.awl.com/cseng/

ISBN 0-672-32216-1

Text printed on recycled paper

1 2 3 4 5 6 7 8 9 10—CRS—05 04 03 02

First printing, January 2002

**ASSOCIATE PUBLISHER**
*Jeff Koch*

**ACQUISITIONS EDITOR**
*William Brown*

**DEVELOPMENT EDITOR**
*Mark Renfrow*

**MANAGING EDITOR**
*Matt Purcell*

**PROJECT EDITOR**
*Andy Beaster*

**PRODUCTION EDITOR**
*Rhonda Tinch-Mize*

**INDEXER**
*Erika Millen*

**PROOFREADER**
*Suzanne Thomas*

**TECHNICAL EDITOR**
*Mark Hall*

**TEAM COORDINATOR**
*Denni Bannister*

**INTERIOR DESIGNER**
*Anne Jones*

**COVER DESIGNER**
*Aren Howell*

**PAGE LAYOUT**
*Brad Lenser*

# Contents at a Glance

# Table of Contents

## 4  Asynchronous Modems and Interfaces                 129

# About the Author

**Gilbert Held** is an internationally known award-winning lecturer and author. Gil is the author of more than 50 technical books and 400 articles covering the fields of personal computing and computer communications. He is a frequent lecturer at locations ranging from Buenos Aires and Santiago to Helsinki, London, Paris, and Tel Aviv, and he represented the United States at technical conferences in Moscow and Jerusalem. In addition to being the only person to twice win the competitive Karp award for technical excellence in writing, Gil is also the recipient of awards from the American Publishers Association, Federal Computer Week, and Federal Agencies. Gil earned a BSEE from Pennsylvania Military College, an MSEE from New York University, and MBA and MSTM degrees from American University. In his spare time, Gil teaches several courses at Georgia College and State University and likes to restore Corvettes, jog, and climb mountains.

# About the Technical Editors

**Raymond Sarch's** publishing experience includes 13 years with McGraw-Hill as senior technology editor on the staff of *Data Communications* magazine. His book publishing experience includes co-authoring three editions of *Data Communications: A Comprehensive Approach* for the McGraw-Hill Book Company. This text has been adopted by colleges and universities in the United States, England, and other countries. Each chapter is followed by a series of questions that test the reader on what should have been learned in that chapter. Ray has also written the "Data Communications" entry in the *Encyclopedia of Management*. Among the books that Ray has edited for McGraw-Hill are: *Inside X.25: A Manager's Guide*; *Data Network Design Strategies*; *Cases in Network Design*; and *Integrating Voice and Data*.

Since leaving McGraw-Hill, Ray has been freelancing as a writer and editor for publishers such as Van Nostrand Reinhold (which became International Thomson Publishing, Inc.), IEEE (*Spectrum*), Wiley (*International Journal of Network Management*[md]where Ray is a part-time associate editor), and others.

Using his engineering knowledge, Ray has also worked on secondary school electronics and electricity teachers' manuals.

Ray's educational background includes the degree of Bachelor of Electrical Engineering from CCNY in New York City. His engineering background includes employment by RCA, Litton Industries, Reeves Instrument, and Western Union.

**Mark Hall** has been providing technical edits for more than 12 years now with more than 160 titles edited to date. Mark has co-authored three books and written many "How to" primers. Mark has a master's degree in Computer Science Education, a Novell CNE since 1990, and more than 18 years experience as a private network consultant specializing in network design and security.

# Dedication

*To my university students, who provide the challenge to educate.*

# Introduction

## Who This Book Is For

This book was written as a comprehensive guide to the evolution and modern development associated with the various facts of the field of data communications. As such, this book can be used as a textbook both by students and professionals. Each chapter includes a quiz to test your knowledge, and the answers to questions are contained at the back of this book.

## This Book's Approach to Data Communications

The modern society we live in today is a communications-oriented society. Thus, the goal of this book is to assist readers in understanding how this society operates by examining the basic structure of the field of data communications. This book explains how different communications devices operate, describes the different types of transmission facilities used to transport information, and examines such emerging technologies as digital subscriber lines and cable modems that might revolutionize the manner by which we work. For readers who surf the Web with conventional modems, imagine being able to transmit and receive data at a speed several orders of magnitude beyond what we now do. The possibilities for new applications become almost endless. Soon, we will be able to visit museums and join virtual lectures on the style of different artists, and we'll be able to zoom in to see minute details that might previously have required a trip around the world. Soon, we will be able to talk and view our parents, business associates, or pen pals located hundreds or thousands of miles away as if they were in our living rooms or offices, and we will do so not only on our home computer but on our cell phone! So join me in examining the field of data communications as we explore its evolution and the technical aspects of equipment and transmission facilities that make the wonderful world of data communications a reality.

# An Overview of Data Communications

## IN THIS CHAPTER

This book is intended to explain how data communications systems and their various hardware and software components work. To do so, it introduces you to a range of computer and communications technologies you must know in order to understand how data flows between computers connected to the same local area network or computers located at opposite ends of the globe. It is not intended to tell you how to build the equipment, nor will it tell you how to write computer programs to transmit data between two computers. What it can give you is a basis for understanding data communications systems in general. It can also give you some tips for setting up a system to communicate between your personal or professional computer and another personal computer, a database service, an information utility, an electronic bulletin board, or a computer connected to the corporate network or to the Internet.

To understand data communications, you must have some understanding of the telephone channel because it is the medium used by most data communications systems to move information from one place to another. Therefore, part of this book is devoted to describing the public telephone network and the equipment used to interface between it and a computer.

This chapter presents some history of data communications, its expected role in the new millennium, and a general description of a data communications system. Explanations of bits, bytes, two-state communications systems, and codes help lay the foundation for further discussions in the remainder of the book. In the latter half of the chapter, a wholesale grocery example is used to illustrate the changes in and expansion of the role of data communications since the introduction of the computer.

# The Importance of Data Communications

Data communications is the process of communicating information in binary form between two or more points. Data communications is sometimes called computer communications because a majority of the information interchanged today is transferred between computers or between computers and their terminals, printers, or other peripheral devices. The data might be as elementary as the binary symbols 1 and 0 or as complex as the characters represented by the keys on a typewriter keyboard. In any case, the characters or symbols represent information.

The field of data communications represents one of the most rapidly evolving technologies. Through the use of specialized semiconductors developed to perform signal processing and data compression, various multimedia applications are evolving that orient data communications toward the transport of voice, data, and video information.

Today you can talk into a microphone and have your voice conversation digitized, packetized, and transmitted over the Internet without any additional cost beyond your monthly fixed Internet service provider bill. In certain locations throughout the United States and Europe, when communications carriers are conducting field trials of new equipment you can even select a video from your telephone company and access the Internet via your cable television operator. In other locations, cell phones are being developed with miniature charged coupled devices (CCDs) that function as a small video camera, enabling a person to send pictures of a family vacation, a new arrival from the hospital, and similar views in real-time to another party. Thus, the traditional use of data communications as a means of moving data between terminal devices and computers is evolving into a mechanism for moving voice, data, and video.

Although a migration toward the integration of voice, video, and data transmission via packet networks is occurring, it is not problem free. One of the key issues that remains to be resolved concerns what is referred to as *Quality of Service (QoS)*, which enables information to flow end-to-end with minimal delay and consistency in setting up data flows. The development of QoS for packet network transmission is in an evolutionary state and may require several years to evolve to the point where it will enable calls routed over packet networks to consistently produce high-quality reproduced conversations instead of periodic reproductions that sound like a famous mouse whose initials are MM.

It is important for us to understand data communications because of its significance in today's world. Data communications is commonly used in business, and it is being used more and more in homes as well. Whether it is the transmission of bank-account information from a central computer to a convenient electronic teller machine, the selection of a pay-per-view cable TV program, or the downloading of a video game from a computer bulletin board into a home computer, data communications is becoming an integral part of our daily activities. In fact, for many readers, hardly a day goes by that he or she is not the recipient of an activity performed or enhanced through the use of data communications. The more modern a society, the more dependent that society is on data communications.

# The First Data Communications Systems

Modern data communications involves the use of electrical or electronic apparatus to communicate information in the form of symbols and characters between two points. Because electricity, radio waves, and light waves are all forms of electromagnetic energy, it is stretching things only a bit to say that early forms of communication, such as the puffs of smoke from a Native American's signal fire (see Figure 1.1) or reflections of sunlight from a hand-held mirror, also were forms of the same type of data communications. To carry this idea further, think of the puffs of smoke as discrete symbols, just as the symbols used in today's communications systems are discrete.

# Early Uses of Electricity

The discovery and harnessing of electricity introduced many new possibilities for communications codes. One of the early proposals, submitted to a Scottish magazine in 1753, was simple but had profound implications for hardware. This idea was to run 26 parallel wires from town to town, one wire for each letter of the alphabet. A Swiss inventor built a prototype system based on this 26-wire principle, but the technology of wire making at that time eliminated that idea from serious use. The complexity of running 26 wires to denote the 26 letters in the alphabet indicated that a more efficient technique was required.

**FIGURE 1.1**

*The first data communications did not rely on electricity.*

In 1833, Carl Friedrich Gauss used a code based on a 5-by-5 matrix of 25 letters (I and J were combined) to send messages by deflecting a needle from one to five times, right or left. The first set of deflections indicated the row, and the second indicated the column. This technique can be considered equivalent to specifying a column and row to denote a letter, enabling a single line to be used in place of 26 lines.

# The Telegraph

One of the more significant developments in data communications occurred in the 19th century when an American, Samuel F.B. Morse, invented the electric telegraph. Although other inventors had worked on the idea of using electricity to communicate, Morse's invention was by far the most important because he coupled the human mind (intelligence) with the communications equipment, with decoding based on the hearing capability of the person receiving the message as well as his or her knowledge of the code developed by Morse.

A basic telegraph system is diagrammed in Figure 1.2. When the telegraph key at station A was pressed, current flowed through the system, and the armature (a movable part of the electro-mechanical device) at station B was attracted to the coil, clicking as it struck the stop. When the key was released at station A, it opened the electrical circuit, and the armature of the sounder at station B was forced to its open position by a spring, striking the other stop with a slightly different click. Thus, the telegraph sounder had two distinctive clicks. If the time between successive clicks of the sounder was short, it represented a dot, if longer, a dash. Morse developed a code, similar to the one shown in Figure 1.3, to represent characters by a series of these dots and dashes. The transmitting operator converted the characters in the words of a message to be sent into a series of dots and dashes. The receiving operator interpreted those dots and dashes as characters; thus, the information was transmitted from point A to point B.

When Morse developed his code, legend has it that he examined the quantity of type in boxes a typesetter used for storing English characters and digits. Morse assigned short codes to frequently occurring characters and digits and assigned longer codes to less frequently occurring characters and digits. This explains why a dot was assigned to the letter E, which is the most frequently occurring character in the English language, and a dash was assigned to the letter T, which is the second most frequently occurring character.

Morse first developed the telegraph in 1832, but it wasn't until much later that he successfully demonstrated its use. The best-known demonstration took place in 1844, when Morse transmitted over a wire from Washington to Baltimore the message, "What hath God wrought!"

Because mail delivery by the Pony Express was the typical means of communication before the telegraph, the much faster telegraph quickly became a success. The equipment was simple and rugged; the key and the sounder each contained only one moving part. Both the system's strength and its weakness (and its only real complexity) was the human mind—the transmitting and receiving operators. By the time of the Civil War, a telegraph line spanned the continent, crossing the prairies and deserts to connect California with the rest of the United States. It was from this historic technological breakthrough that the Western Union Telegraph Company made its legacy and indeed was named; its line connected the West with the Union. By the time the telephone was invented some 30 years later, the telegraph industry was large and prosperous, with many companies providing service to almost every city and town in the United States. In 1866, the telegraph connected the nations of the world with the laying of the trans-Atlantic cable between the United States and France.

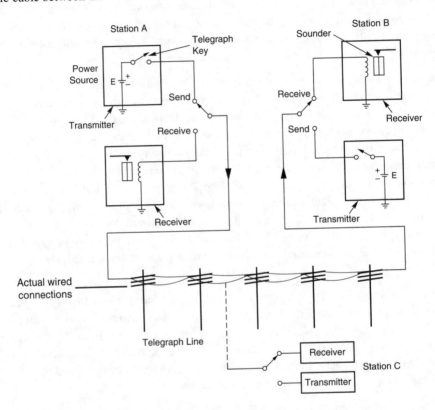

**FIGURE 1.2**

*The basic telegraph system.*

Telegraph Characters

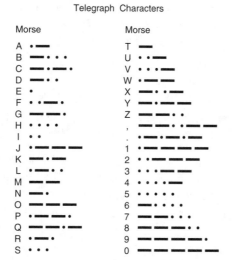

**FIGURE 1.3**
*Much of Morse terminology is still in use today.*

# Two-State Communications Systems

The importance of the Morse telegraph is not just historical. Much of the terminology that developed around the Morse system is still in use today. For example, consider the terms *mark* and *space*. If a device were arranged so that paper continually moved under a pen attached to the telegraph sounder armature, a mark would be made on the paper when the armature was attracted to the coil. Thus, we could refer to the state of current flow in the line as the marking state, and the state of no current flow in the line as the spacing state. Note that this resulted in a two-state device, which can be considered the forerunner of the binary system used to transfer information as well as control the operation of computers. Worldwide standards for data communications today still use the terms mark and space, with the current flow condition on the transmission channel called the *marking condition*.

More important than the terminology, however, was a principle of operation that was derived from the telegraph—the two-state communications system. The telegraph wire (channel) between the operators is in one of two states: current is flowing, or it is not. This simple design has been repeated over and over again in the development of data communications systems. A two-state communications system is the simplest, the easiest to build, and the most reliable. The two states can be on and off (as in the telegraph), plus and minus (with current flowing in opposite directions), light and dark (as in turning a flashlight on and off to send code), 1 and 0 (the concept used in the computer), or some other design with only two possible values. A two-state or two-valued system is referred to as a *binary system.*

## Bits and Bytes

The numbers 0 and 1 are the symbols of the binary system. A binary digit is commonly referred to as a *bit.* The individual line changes in digital data (like the mark and space) are called bits, and each bit is assigned a value of 0 or 1.

The binary system uses positional notation, just as the familiar decimal system does, except that each position has only two possible values, instead of 10. For example, the number 345.27 in decimal means three hundreds plus four tens plus five ones plus two tenths plus seven hundredths. The weight of each position is a power of 10 as indicated here:

```
345.27 = (3 x 100) + (4 x 10) + (5 x 1) + (2 x 1/10) + (7 x 1/100)
       = 3 x 10² + 4 x 10¹ + 5 x 10⁰ + 2 x 10⁻¹ + 7 x 10⁻²
```

Note the use of positive and negative exponents, and remember that any number raised to the zero power is equal to 1. In the decimal system, as shown by the preceding example, 10 is the base, and the weight of each digit position is a power of 10.

Similarly, we can define powers of two in the binary positional system, in which the weight of each position is two times the weight of the one to the immediate right. A table of powers of two can be quite useful when you're dealing with binary numbers because most of us don't want to memorize them. Table 1.1 shows the powers of 2 up to $2^8$, which will be sufficient for this book.

Using this table makes it easy to convert a binary number into its decimal equivalent. For example:

```
1101001 = 1 x 2⁶ + 1 x 2⁵ + 0 x 2⁴ + 1 x 2³ + 0 x 2² + 0 x 2¹ + 1 x 2⁰
        = 64 + 32 + 0 + 8 + 0 + 0 + 1
        = 105 decimal
```

Based on the preceding, another way to convert binary to decimal is to first remember the positional values of each bit in a binary number. For example, if we are working with an eight-bit number, its positional values on a bit by bit basis from most significant to least significant are as follows:

Next, we would simply add the positional values for each set bit (binary 1) in an eight-bit binary number. For example, to convert binary 10010011 to decimal, we would add 128 + 16 + 2 + 1 and obtain 147.

Computers are more efficient if their internal paths and registers are some power of two in length (2 bits, 4 bits, 8 bits, 16 bits, and so on). A commonly used grouping is 8 bits; this 8-bit group is called a *byte* or an *octet*. From Table 1.1, you can see that a byte can represent $2^8$, or 256 unique sequences of ones and zeros.

**TABLE 1.1** The Powers of Two

| Power of Two | Positional Weight | 9-Bit Binary Number |
|---|---|---|
| $2^0$ | 1 | 000000001 |
| $2^1$ | 2 | 000000010 |
| $2^2$ | 4 | 000000100 |
| $2^3$ | 8 | 000001000 |
| $2^4$ | 16 | 000010000 |
| $2^5$ | 32 | 000100000 |
| $2^6$ | 64 | 001000000 |
| $2^7$ | 128 | 010000000 |
| $2^8$ | 256 | 100000000 |

## Bytes and Octets

During the early period of computer design, from the 1950s to the 1970s, different groupings of bits were used to form a computer character. The internal architecture of computers developed during that period used between five and twelve bits to define unique characters or computer bytes. The lack of standards about the number of bits representing a byte resulted in several communications standards, making organizations use the term octet in their literature to reference a grouping of eight bits. Although just about all modern computers are now designed to group eight bits into a byte, most standards-making organizations continue to use the term to reference a group of eight bits. This book uses the terms byte and octet synonymously, even though in the early days of computer design, some engineers would more than likely develop heartburn from this equality.

## Early Communications Codes

A common characteristic of data communications systems is the use of an intelligent device to convert a character or symbol into coded form and vice versa. In the Morse system, the intelligent *devices* were the telegraph operators who converted the characters into dots and dashes.

Skilled telegraph operators were always in short supply, and the work was difficult and exhausting. Therefore an electrical or mechanical means of coding the characters was needed. However, it was essentially impossible to automate the transmitting and receiving operations because of the varying duration of the dots and dashes in the Morse code and the fact that the codes for the characters were made up of different quantities of dots and dashes. Therefore, a code that had the same number of equal-duration, signaling elements for each character, was needed.

## Some Definitions

Before you go any further, learn the following definitions, which you need to know in order to discuss communications codes:

- Codes: Standard (agreed on in advance) interpretations between signaling elements and characters. The key idea is standard. The codes used in data communications systems are already defined, and the code set is built into the equipment. About the only time the user might need to deal with codes is when he or she is interfacing two machines (such as computers and printers) from different manufacturers.

- Characters: The letters, numerals, spaces, punctuation marks, and other signs and symbols on a keyboard. Communication systems use control characters that do not print, but these characters also must be coded. Some of these control characters (such as Carriage Return or Tab) are also on a keyboard, but many are not. For many control characters not directly located on a keyboard, the user can enter their codes from the keyboard by pressing certain pairs of keys. For example, pressing the control (Ctrl) key and the G key at the same time (Ctrl+G) results in the non-printable BEL (bell) key code, which can be used from within a program to transmit an audio alarm to the person operating a terminal or personal computer.

- Signaling elements: Something that is sent over a transmission channel and used to represent a character. The dots and dashes (or marks and spaces) of the Morse code are signaling elements, as are the ones and zeros in this sequence:

  01000001010 0000001011 0111011011 0110001001

  This is the way "A 7#" might look when transmitted between a personal computer and another computer or printer. You will see later that the code is ASCII, with even parity and one start and one stop bit.

The definitions for characters and signaling elements illustrate why machines and people need different ways to represent information. People quickly and reliably recognize printed characters by their distinctive shapes, but that is difficult and expensive for a machine to do. On the other hand, machines can easily handle long strings of two-state signaling elements, such as marks and spaces or ones and zeros, but that is hard for a person to accomplish with any accuracy.

## Baudot Code

As stated before, the Morse code was unsuitable for machine encoding and decoding because of the problems caused by the varying lengths of the codes for the characters. Early in the 20th century, when interest developed in replacing human telegraph operators with machines, several suitable codes already existed. The most prominent of these had been invented in the 1870s by a Frenchman named Emile Baudot. Because Baudot's code, similar to the one shown in Figure 1.4, used the same number of signaling elements (marks and spaces) to represent each character, it was better suited to machine encoding and decoding.

Unfortunately, the number of signaling elements was limited to five by problems in timing the electromechanical devices. The five-bit code could generate only 32 possible combinations—not enough to represent the 26 characters of the alphabet, the 10 decimal digits, the punctuation marks, and the space character. To overcome this limitation, Baudot used two shift-control characters—the letters (LTRS) shift and the figures (FIGS) shift—to enable the code set to represent all the characters that seemed necessary at the time. The shift codes do not represent printable characters; instead, the codes select one of two character sets, each composed of 26 to 28 characters.

Receipt of the letters shift code (11111) causes all following codes to be interpreted as letters of the alphabet; receipt of the figures shift code (11011) causes all the following characters to be interpreted as numerals and punctuation marks. Notice that the LTRS and FIGS codes, as well as the other control codes and the space character, always have the same interpretation, no matter which shift mode the machine is in. Although Baudot's invention did not immediately revolutionize telegraphy (because of the difficulty that human operators had in sending equal-length codes), it did provide a basis for the later development of the teleprinter.

| Start | 1 | 2 | 3 | 4 | 5 | Stop | LTRS Shift | CCITT Standard International Telegraph Alphabet No. 2 Used for Telex | North American Teletype Commercial Keyboard |
|:---:|:---:|:---:|:---:|:---:|:---:|:---:|:---:|:---:|:---:|
| | | | | | | | | FIGS Shift | |
| • Denotes Positive Current | | | | | | | | | |
| • | • | • | | | | • | A | — | — |
| • | • | | | • | • | • | B | ? | ? |
| • | | • | • | • | | • | C | : | : |
| • | • | | | • | | • | D | Who Are You? | $ |
| • | • | | | | | • | E | 3 | 3 |
| • | • | | • | • | | • | F | Note 1 | ! |
| • | | • | | • | • | • | G | Note 1 | & |
| • | | | • | | • | • | H | Note 1 | # |
| • | | • | • | | | • | I | 8 | 8 |
| • | • | • | | • | | • | J | Bell | Bell |
| • | • | • | • | • | | • | K | ( | ( |
| • | | • | | | • | • | L | ) | ) |
| • | | | • | • | • | • | M | . | . |
| • | | | • | • | | • | N | , | , |
| • | | | | • | • | • | O | 9 | 9 |
| • | | • | • | | • | • | P | 0 | 0 |
| • | • | • | • | | • | • | Q | 1 | 1 |
| • | | • | | • | | • | R | 4 | 4 |
| • | • | | • | | | • | S | , | , |
| • | | | | | • | • | T | 5 | 5 |
| • | • | • | • | | | • | U | 7 | 7 |
| • | | • | • | • | • | • | V | = | ; |
| • | • | • | | | • | • | W | 2 | 2 |
| • | • | | • | • | • | • | X | / | / |
| • | • | | • | | • | • | Y | 6 | 6 |
| • | • | | | | • | • | Z | + | " |
| | | | | | | • | | Blank | |
| | • | • | • | • | • | • | | Letters Shift (LTRS) | |
| | • | • | | • | • | • | | Figures Shift (FIGS) | |
| | | | • | | | • | | Space | |
| | | | | • | | • | | Carriage Return | |
| | | • | | | | • | | Line Feed | |

Notes:
1. Not allocated internationally; available to each country for internal use.

**FIGURE 1.4**

*Five-level teleprinter code.*

# Modern Codes

The Baudot code and variations of it were the backbone of communications for almost half a century, but they clearly left much to be desired. Persons in the newspaper industry found the lack of differentiation between upper- and lowercase letters to be a problem. They devised a six-level code to designate the difference between upper- and lowercase letters. This was just one example of general need. Modern communications required a code that could represent all printable characters and still leave room for error checking and format operations. Concerning format operations, a code should support linefeed and carriage-return characters, as well as formfeed and horizontal and vertical tabulation because the use of those characters enables terminal operations to be conveyed as they occur. The code had to enable decoding without reliance on correct reception of previous transmissions, and it also had to enable decoding by machine. Perhaps most important of all, the new code needed to be expandable.

During the 1960s, various data transmission codes were developed. Most of these have fallen by the wayside, leaving three predominant codes:

- CCITT International Alphabet No. 2 is a single five-bit code that is still used for telex transmission.

- The Extended Binary-Coded-Decimal Interchange Code (EBCDIC, pronounced "eb-see-dik"), developed by IBM, is primarily used for synchronous communication in systems attached to large mainframe computers.

- The American Standard Code for Information Interchange (ASCII, pronounced "as-key") was defined by the American National Standards Institute (ANSI) in the United States and by the International Organization for Standardization (ISO) worldwide.

## A Note on the Standards Organizations

Standards can be considered to be the glue that provides the ability to interconnect diverse systems. One of the most important standards-making organizations is the Consultative Committee for International Telephone and Telegraph (CCITT). The CCITT was renamed the International Telecommunications Union (ITU) Standardization Board in the mid-1990s. This standards-making body is a group within the ITU, the latter representing a specialized agency of the United Nations. This group is responsible for developing data communications standards, and its recommendations have the effect of law in some Western European countries; however, its standards are recommendations and are not intended to be mandatory.

The ISO is a nongovernmental entity that has consultative status within the United Nations Economic and Social Council. Membership of the ISO consists of the national standards organizations of more than 100 countries, and its goal according to its charter is to "promote the development of standards in the world with a view to facilitating the international exchange of goods and services." In the United States, ANSI is the principal standards-forming body. This nonprofit, nongovernmental organization represents the United States to the ISO.

# EBCDIC

When a clear need arises for standardization, standards come into existence in two ways. In one way, a single manufacturer (especially a dominant one) can define a standard for its own products, and the rest of the industry can follow. This is what IBM did. It created the EBCDIC eight-bit code, which enabled 256 characters to be represented. The world would probably be better off if EBCDIC had become the standard because it included enough unique characters to allow almost any representation. However, only IBM and firms that build IBM-compatible equipment adopted EBCDIC. Because EBCDIC is primarily used in large IBM-compatible computing systems, it is not used in most of the examples in this book.

# ASCII

The other, more common method of creating a standard is through a committee, which serves as a forum for examination of needs, discussion between interested parties, and compromise. This process produced the ASCII seven-bit code, formally known as ANSI Standard X3.4-1977. ASCII can depict 128 characters, but not all of them represent printed symbols. Included in the character set are all the letters of the English alphabet (both uppercase and lowercase), the numerals 0–9, punctuation marks, and many symbols. This standard code set is used in virtually all small computers and their peripherals, as well as in large computers in most of the world.

Figure 1.5 shows the ANSI Standard ASCII characters and their associated codes. Compare this chart to the Morse code in Figure 1.3 and the five-bit teleprinter code in Figure 1.4. The Morse code had a varying number of elements (dots and dashes) for each character and was quite restricted—only letters, numerals, and a few punctuation marks. The five-bit code had a constant number of elements and a few more special characters, but it still couldn't distinguish between upper- and lowercase letters.

ASCII not only provides for upper- and lowercase letters, but it also has a great deal of regularity that might not be readily apparent. For example, to convert any uppercase alphabetic character (A through Z) to lowercase, it is necessary only to change bit 6 from zero to one. Another feature is that bits 4 through 7 of the numeric characters (0, 1, 2, 3, 4, 5, 6, 7, 8, and 9) are the binary-coded-decimal (BCD) values of the characters. Another advantage of standard ASCII is that 128 different characters can be represented by the seven bits used in the code (as opposed to the 32 characters that can be represented from the five-bit code).

The two leftmost character columns in the chart of Figure 1.5 represent the nonprinting control characters that can be used to control the operation of the receiving device. For example, the control codes for carriage return (CR) and linefeed (LF), which are commonly used on a typewriter, are shown. Other control codes include formfeed (FF), bell (BEL), horizontal tab (HT), and vertical tab (VT). These control codes were designed for printing or display devices,

1

AN OVERVIEW OF DATA COMMUNICATIONS

although some manufacturers have used the control codes for all manner of special functions. Also, some codes control how a receiving device will interpret subsequent codes in a multiple-character function or command. Two shift characters, called Shift In (SI) and Shift Out (SO), are used to shift between ASCII and character sets other than those used in English. ANSI Standards X3.41-1974 and X3.64-1979 expand the definition of the escape (ESC) control code for even greater flexibility. Other control codes delimit text, such as start of text (STX) and end of text (ETX). These codes are used primarily in block or synchronous data transmission. You'll see more of them in later chapters.

A variation of ASCII, commonly referred to as *extended ASCII*, gained wide acceptance with the introduction of the IBM Personal Computer of 1981. The IBM PC and compatible computers support an eight-bit code, with the first seven positions supporting the ANSI standard. The additional bit position extends the computer's ASCII, enabling an additional 128 characters to be represented. This extension enables software developers to use extended codes for such functions as end-of-paragraph markings and bold printing indicators in a word processing system.

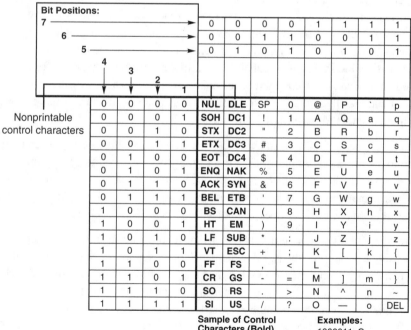

| Bit Positions: | | | | | | | | |
|---|---|---|---|---|---|---|---|---|
| 7 → | 0 | 0 | 0 | 0 | 1 | 1 | 1 | 1 |
| 6 → | 0 | 0 | 1 | 1 | 0 | 0 | 1 | 1 |
| 5 → | 0 | 1 | 0 | 1 | 0 | 1 | 0 | 1 |

| 4 | 3 | 2 | 1 | | | | | | | | |
|---|---|---|---|---|---|---|---|---|---|---|---|
| 0 | 0 | 0 | 0 | NUL | DLE | SP | 0 | @ | P | ` | p |
| 0 | 0 | 0 | 1 | SOH | DC1 | ! | 1 | A | Q | a | q |
| 0 | 0 | 1 | 0 | STX | DC2 | " | 2 | B | R | b | r |
| 0 | 0 | 1 | 1 | ETX | DC3 | # | 3 | C | S | c | s |
| 0 | 1 | 0 | 0 | EOT | DC4 | $ | 4 | D | T | d | t |
| 0 | 1 | 0 | 1 | ENQ | NAK | % | 5 | E | U | e | u |
| 0 | 1 | 1 | 0 | ACK | SYN | & | 6 | F | V | f | v |
| 0 | 1 | 1 | 1 | BEL | ETB | ' | 7 | G | W | g | w |
| 1 | 0 | 0 | 0 | BS | CAN | ( | 8 | H | X | h | x |
| 1 | 0 | 0 | 1 | HT | EM | ) | 9 | I | Y | i | y |
| 1 | 0 | 1 | 0 | LF | SUB | * | : | J | Z | j | z |
| 1 | 0 | 1 | 1 | VT | ESC | + | ; | K | [ | k | { |
| 1 | 1 | 0 | 0 | FF | FS | , | < | L |  | l | \| |
| 1 | 1 | 0 | 1 | CR | GS | - | = | M | ] | m | } |
| 1 | 1 | 1 | 0 | SO | RS | . | > | N | ^ | n | ~ |
| 1 | 1 | 1 | 1 | SI | US | / | ? | O | — | o | DEL |

Nonprintable control characters

Sample of Control Characters (Bold)
STX=Start of Text
EOT=End of Transmission
CR=Carriage Return
HT=Horizontal Tabulation

Examples:
1000011=C
0110011=3
1010000=P
0110000=0 (Zero)
0100000=SP (space)

FIGURE 1.5

*American Standard Code for Information Interchange (ASCII).*

# The Escape Character

The escape (ESC) character designates that the codes that follow have special meaning. Characters received in an escape sequence are not interpreted as printing characters, but as control information to extend the range of the "standard" character set by allowing other definitions. The escape character has the effect of making all character codes available for control of a device. Graphics characters, foreign-language character sets, and special applications sets have been developed that are accessible via escape character sequences; thus, they allow for a much richer variety of displayed symbols than is otherwise normally possible.

The CRT terminal and the personal computer monitor are the two hardware devices that have benefited most from the escape sequence. The serial communications link to these terminals and personal computers is the same as for a teleprinter, and ordinarily, any characters received via this channel are displayed on the terminal or monitor screen, as expected. But the people who developed the ASCII standard did not foresee (and thus did not make provisions for) capabilities for character and line deletion and display enhancements that are available on the CRT terminal and computer monitors, such as inverse video, underlining, and blinking. Unfortunately, little standardization of these sequences existed until the ANSI X3.64 standard came out in 1979. Before then, and without standardization, designers felt free to exercise their creativity. For example, one major feature now found on most video display terminals is absolute cursor positioning. The computer can send a command to the terminal that places the cursor anywhere on the screen. This capability is important for many types of form-filling operations. Unfortunately, there are almost as many escape sequences for cursor positioning as there are terminal manufacturers. Even different models in a manufacturer's line might use different escape sequences to perform the same action.

The result of this "creativity" with the character set is that some manufacturers' equipment will not operate in the same way as most of the rest of the world. An example is a printer that automatically inserts a linefeed after receiving a carriage return. Because most computers send both a carriage return and a linefeed in response to only a carriage return input, the printout will not be spaced as desired because of the extra linefeed supplied by the printer.

To promote compatibility, many terminal and personal computer manufacturers provide implicit or explicit support of the ANSI standard. Explicit support of that standard includes those terminals and personal computers designed explicitly to support the ANSI X3.64 standard. Implicit support is provided by terminals and personal computers that have the capability to load a program and read the contents of a predefined memory area or memory cartridge to enable support of the ANSI X3.64 standard.

Perhaps the most commonly available device capable of supporting the ANSI X3.64 standard is the IBM PC and compatible personal computers. Those computers, which use the Microsoft

MS-DOS or PC DOS operating system as well as different versions of Windows, can be configured to use the device driver ANSI.SYS. ANSI.SYS is a file on the operating system disk that will be loaded into memory during subsequent startups after it's specified. On most MS-DOS or PC DOS computers with a hard drive, you would add the statement DEVICE = C:\DOS\ANSI.SYS (assuming that it is stored under the DOS directory on drive C) to your CONFIG.SYS file to automatically execute the ANSI.SYS device driver on a power-on or system reset. The execution of that file forces the personal computer to function as an ANSI-compatible terminal, including support for standardized escape code sequences. Although teleprinters predate the PC, their operational characteristics highly govern the manner by which PCs operate.

On that note, turn your attention to the operation and utilization of teleprinters.

## Teleprinters

The teleprinter represents the next major step after the telegraph in data communications. Teleprinter equipment has been the backbone of non-voice business communications for more than half a century. As recently as the mid-1970s, a teletypewriter (TTY), which is a teleprinter with a keyboard for input, was the standard terminal for small- and medium-sized computers. Many companies had nationwide and even worldwide private teleprinter networks, although the fax machine and public and private computer-based electronic mail systems brought about the replacement of most of those networks by more modern technology.

Two nationwide public teleprinter networks are the TWX and Telex services; TWX was merged into Telex during the 1980s. Several common carriers will transmit Telex messages to any teleprinter in the United States, and companies called "international record carriers" will deliver them to any teleprinter in the world. Telex, an abbreviation for Teleprinter exchange, is a fully automated real-time service that enables customers to transmit and receive messages in printed form both domestically and internationally among more than 200 connected countries. In 1998, MCI linked access from the Internet to the Telex network with its network MCI Internet Telex service, permitting businesses to instantly transmit Telex messages from any computer with access to the Internet to any terminal device connected to the Telex network. A company's Telex number can be found in a directory similar to a telephone directory.

Like the telegraph, teleprinters are important not only in their own right because they were the principal data communications method for almost 50 years, but also because most of the standards and terminology for low-speed or asynchronous data communications came from the world of teleprinters. Chapter 2, "Terminal Devices," covers asynchronous transmission more thoroughly. For now, it is sufficient to note that the transmission of each coded character begins with a "start" symbol and ends with a "stop" symbol. Although this technique permitted synchronization of teleprinter equipment thousands of miles apart, it also added to the already high overhead (in terms of extra time) required for transmission of each character.

Teleprinter equipment was inherently limited to slow transmission speeds because it was electromechanical: Solenoids had to be energized to attract armatures; motors had to start, turn, and stop; and clutches had to engage and disengage. All of these mechanical operations limited the maximum speed at which teleprinters could operate reliably to fewer than 30 characters per second. International Telex operates even slower—fewer than 10 characters per second! Either speed is much too slow for a computer to communicate efficiently with another computer, even with a modern printer or CRT terminal.

# Data Communications in Computing

Further improvements in data communications were necessitated by the widespread use of electronic computers, introduced in the early 1950s. These computer systems were capable of storing large quantities of information and processing it quickly. Input and output equipment was much improved over the teletypewriter and teleprinter, so it could operate much faster. As more computers were used, it became necessary for computers to communicate with each other. Because this communication did not need any electromechanical equipment, data transfer theoretically could occur at extremely fast rates. Practically, however, data transfer rates are limited by the transmission medium—primarily the public telephone network, and more specifically, the bandwidth or range of frequencies that can be transmitted on that network.

## The 1950s

The typical computer system of the 1950s, shown in Figure 1.6, used punched cards for input, printers for output, and reels of magnetic tape for "permanent" mass storage. There was little or no data communications in these systems because the input devices, output devices, and computer were all located close together and were directly connected by short cables. Information was processed on a "one job at a time" or "batch" basis.

For example, a wholesale grocery company would receive orders by mail and telephone during the day. At the end of the day, these would be collected and punched into cards, which were then assembled as a batch. The data on the cards was read into the computer for processing at night. During the processing, the computer would do such things as check the customer's credit. If the credit was satisfactory, the computer would generate a pick list for the warehouse so that the order could be filled and shipped the next day. The quantity ordered for the different types of items would be deducted from the quantity on hand, and the invoices and various warehouse tickets would be printed. This system worked well except that the person taking the order from the customer during the day, whether on the phone or at the customer's premises, was never certain whether the ordered items were available in the warehouse. Although an updated inventory report was available each morning, a running inventory was not kept during the day as orders were received.

**FIGURE 1.6**

*A typical data processing system of the 1950s.*

## The 1960s

Batch processing systems such as the one just described are the most efficient in the use of computer time and equipment. They are relatively inefficient, however, in the use of the order clerks, salespeople, and other resources of the company. Although the costs of employing people were increasing, the solid-state revolution caused the cost of computer logic and memory to decrease sharply. This meant that companies could invest in more computer equipment to reduce the costs of personnel, as well as to make themselves more competitive.

In the 1960s, batch processing was largely replaced by online processing (see Figure 1.7). In the example of the wholesale grocery company, the clerks took the orders over the phone and used online terminals to enter the orders into the computer at the same time. Some of these terminals were directly connected to the computer by parallel communication channels, but many of the terminals were teleprinter devices that used serial data communications over dedicated private cables to the computer.

As the order was entered, the computer checked the inventory to see whether the goods were on hand. If so, the customer was given a delivery date; if not, he was told that the goods were out of stock and was given the option of placing a back order or selecting another item. Although more expensive than batch processing in terms of computer time and equipment, this method of doing business made the wholesale grocery company more competitive because it gave customers better service.

**FIGURE 1.7**

*A typical data processing system of the 1960s.*

## The 1970s

The 1970s changed this process still further (see Figure 1.8). Other computers, sometimes called minicomputers, could communicate with the larger computer in the wholesale grocer's central office. The online order terminals were not necessarily in the room next to the computer; they were sometimes on a different floor, in a different building, or even in a different city. Toward the end of the decade, even smaller computers, called microcomputers or personal computers, began to be seen not only in the homes of some of the employees, but also on their desks at the office. Sometimes the employees would communicate with the main computer through these smaller computers. The company sales force began carrying portable computer terminals with them on their sales calls. They could enter their orders from the customers' offices directly into the main computer over a standard telephone line.

True data communications was everywhere in the system. There was more equipment around than anyone would have thought possible in the 1950s—more computers, more terminals, more communications channels—and businesses were run more efficiently because of it.

**FIGURE 1.8**

*A typical data processing system of the 1970s.*

## The 1980s

As the wholesale grocery company grew, it decided to produce some of the food products that it sold, so it set up producing operations in California, Texas, and Florida. Because its wholesale business was primarily in the northeast, it had major warehouse facilities in New Jersey, Pennsylvania, and Ohio and sales offices in Chicago, Philadelphia, and New York City. The company headquarters was also in New York City.

With the expansion to the south and west, the company's data communications system also needed expansion. The company decided to use the relatively new satellite communications to tie the New York office with the Texas and California operations. (Satellite communications are discussed in Chapter 7, "Fiber-Optic and Satellite Communications.") The satellite could be used for other points as well, but the company (for various reasons) used leased terrestrial circuits to the Florida, Chicago, and Philadelphia sites. The smaller sales offices in the states where the company operated were tied together with a network of low-speed teletypewriter-like terminals that allowed order entry and some communication with the home office. The company's salesmen still carried portable terminals, but advances in technology had reduced the size of the terminal while increasing its capabilities. A typical terminal used during the 1980s is shown in Figure 1.9.

**FIGURE 1.9**
*A TI 703KSR teleprinter.*

As low-cost personal computers became more widely available during the mid-1980s, many managers acquired them for departmental use. Although the original intention was to use the local processing capability of personal computers for such tasks as budgeting with spreadsheet programs and word processing, corporate management quickly began to integrate personal computers into their company communications networks. Some personal computers replaced CRT terminals and served as both terminals and local processing devices. Other PCs were linked into a local area network (LAN), which enabled users to share peripheral devices and provided the capability of sending electronic messages to other users on the network.

Introduced in mid-1981, more than 10 million IBM PC and compatible computers had been manufactured by 1987, when the Personal System/2 Model 30 computer replaced the original

IBM PC. Figure 1.10 illustrates the major components of an IBM PC computer system. Today, the personal computer is as prevalent in many organizations as the office typewriter once was.

FIGURE 1.10
*A 1980s IBM PC system.*

## The 1990s

The growth in the distribution of personal computers throughout organizations during the 1980s was linked to a requirement to provide communications capability between these devices. In addition, many personal computer users required access to corporate mini- and mainframe computers, further increasing requirements for communications between different types of computers.

For the grocery company previously discussed, personal computers were installed in the sales offices in Chicago, Philadelphia, and New York City. The PCs were initially used for various functions, ranging from what-if computations using spreadsheets to word processing and the maintenance of small databases of sales and marketing information. Eventually, however, it was recognized that productivity could be increased if various PC users within each office could communicate with one another. Through the installation of an appropriate adapter card in each personal computer, as well as cabling and software, local area networks were installed in each sales office. This specialized type of network enabled persons within a building or campus to communicate with one another, share peripheral devices such as laser printers and plotters, and share access to common software programs and database information residing on special types of personal computers known as file servers.

As the grocery company continued to grow, people began to realize that LANs were essentially islands of information isolated from one another. Commencing in the late 1980s and gaining momentum in the 1990s, vendors introduced several internetworking products, consisting of software and hardware, that enabled diverse LANs to be connected to one another. These connections enabled information to flow between devices connected to one another and between devices connected to different LANs and other computer systems. Taking advantage of this technology, the wholesale grocery company installed devices known as gateways, bridges, and routers.

## Gateways

Gateways enable personal computers on selected LANs to access a corporate mainframe computer. Here the corporate mainframe acts as a central repository for large databases and intensive computing programs that are not suitable for execution on personal computers. For example, database information (including inventory, customer accounts, and historical ordering and pricing information) could require hundreds to thousands of billions of characters of storage, whereas most personal computers are limited to a few billions of characters of storage.

Concerning intensive computing applications, the grocery company began to use the mainframe for execution of linear programs that optimized delivery schedules based on an analysis of thousands of variables. Although personal computer users could access the linear programming results produced on the mainframe via gateways, the execution of this type of program on a personal computer might require 10 or 20 hours, whereas the execution might take 15 minutes when performed on a mainframe.

## Bridges

Bridges enable data to be transmitted between two LANs, allowing electronic messages, data files, and programs to be sent between users on different networks. A bridge examines the destination address of data flowing on a LAN to determine whether its destination is on that LAN. If it is, the bridge simply functions as a transparent device and allows the data to continue to flow on the LAN to its destination. If the data destination is a different LAN, the bridge transmits the data via a communications facility to a distant LAN, where another bridge functions in a similar manner.

1

## Routers

With a need to add automation to the company's warehouse facilities, which were also served through the installation of LANs, sales personnel on occasion needed to access information through the use of personal computers connected to warehouse LANs. In fact, the number of LANs installed within the grocery company would have required the establishment of a mesh network with many long-distance lines if only bridges were used. Fortunately, the development of routers, which examine data destination addresses and route data over different circuits based on those addresses, enabled a smaller number of lines to be used to interconnect many LANs.

Figure 1.11 illustrates in a block diagram format the relationship of bridges, routers, and gateways for connecting different networking devices. In this example, a pair of bridges interconnects two sales office LANs, and a router is used to provide a link from one LAN to many warehouse LANs. The gateway provides a mechanism that enables LAN users to access the mainframe computer. In fact, when sophisticated hardware and software are used, it might be possible for a PC user attached to the LAN at the top of Figure 1.11 to be "bridged" to the second LAN and provided, via the gateway, access to the mainframe—a key goal of internetworking.

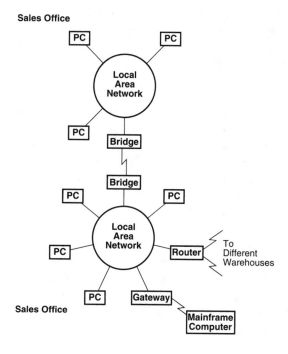

**FIGURE 1.11**

*Internetworking using bridges, routers, and gateways.*

## Terminology Confusion

When LANs were first interconnected, the device that routed data between networks was given the name *gateway*. Today, most references to gateway include the configuration of device addresses under different versions of Windows retain that name even though the device referred to is a router. In comparison, a true gateway performs many types of data conversions to allow PCs to communicate with mainframes. In this book, we will note the operation of both modern gateways and routers and note how PCs are configured to transmit data to devices termed gateways even though they are routers.

## Into the New Millennium

As the grocery company prepared for the new millennium, it recognized the importance of the Internet as a mechanism for both corporate growth and reducing the cost of relatively expensive leased lines used to interconnect geographically separated locations. To enhance recognition of the company, the grocery established a presence on the Internet by adding World Wide Web servers to the LAN at its corporate headquarters and several regional offices, connecting LANs at each location to the Internet. Initially the Web servers simply provided facts about the grocery, listed points of contacts for various regional departments of the company, and allowed current and potential customers to fill out forms to request additional information. As the grocery expanded into wholesale distribution, it recognized that, in an era of extreme business competition, it was necessary to automate as many operations as possible to remain competitive. In addition, the company also recognized that it could take orders via the Internet by adding appropriate software to support electronic commerce on its Web servers.

### Multipurpose Servers

To provide the ability to increase its business, the grocery selected multipurpose servers that could grow as their Internet business increased, similar to the IBM AS/400 E series illustrated in Figure 1.12. The AS/400 is the world's most popular multiuser business computer system, with an installed base of more than half a million computers. The AS/400 E series supports both Internet and PC LAN protocols and also runs Microsoft's Windows NT and Windows 2000 as well as Novell's NetWare operating systems, which enables a common hardware platform to support multiple applications.

### Virtual Private Networks

At first the grocery operated separate networks, with one network of leased lines used to interconnect corporate locations, and a separate network of leased lines used to connect each corporate location to the Internet, enabling both headquarters and regional offices to directly process orders received via the Internet. As the grocery's network manager reviewed monthly bills for leased lines, it became apparent that the maintenance of dual networks was expensive. Because the majority of traffic transmitted over the company's private network of leased lines was time-insensitive traffic such as file transfers and electronic mail, it was recognized that the Internet could be used as a virtual private network (VPN) to interconnect geographically separated locations, support access to the grocery's series of Web servers, and enable employees to surf the Web and perform a variety of Internet-related tasks. Of course, transmitting corporate data over a public network entails a security risk. Thus, any organization considering using the Internet as a private virtual network should consider the use of firewalls with authentication and encryption capability or an appropriate protocol to secure its transmissions through the Internet.

**FIGURE 1.12**

*A scalable computer system permits customers to expand their servers' capability without having to convert previously developed programs. (Courtesy of IBM Corporation.)*

Because most Internet service providers (ISPs) bill their clients based on the operating rate of the connection to the ISP, the use of the Internet represents distance insensitive pricing. In comparison, the monthly cost of private leased lines is based both on their operating rate and distance. Thus, converting the private leased line network into a VPN via the Internet could produce considerable economic savings.

Figure 1.13 illustrates the use of the Internet as a VPN to interconnect geographically separated grocery company locations in Los Angeles and New York. This enables customer and potential customer access to servers located at different company locations.

The Internet is a mesh-structured network that interconnects hundreds of thousands of networks. Data is broken into small units known as *packets* that can flow over different paths or routes from source to destination. Thus, instead of using a fixed route when a private line is routed between two locations, the communications path over the Internet can vary, resulting in the term *virtual* being used to represent a temporary path over the fixed connections formed by leased lines that make up the mesh structure of the Internet. Because any person with Internet access could theoretically attempt to connect to the grocery's computational facilities, they added firewalls to each location as a protection measure. In addition, because traffic over the Internet can be viewed at intermediary nodes, a special feature of the firewall was used to encrypt traffic explicitly routed between different organizational locations yet permit other traffic to traverse the Internet in the clear.

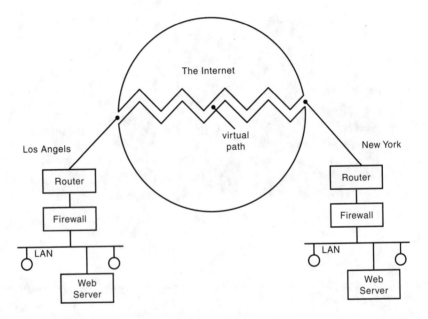

**FIGURE 1.13**
*Using the Internet as a virtual private network (VPN).*

## Voice Over the Internet Protocol

As the grocery plans for communications into the new millennium, its management begins to look at another area that also promises to considerably reduce the cost of communications—voice over the Internet protocol, referred to as VoIP. Introduced as a technology enabling home users to communicate with other online Internet users via voice servers under the name Internet Telephony, this technology is being considered by business, academia, and government as a mechanism to reduce communications costs as well as provide new services. Instead of clicking on an icon to transmit an e-mail to a help desk, customers equipped with multimedia PCs and appropriate software can now click on a telephone icon when accessing certain Web sites and directly talk with a help desk employee, sales associate, or another employee at the Web site they are accessing.

With other software, it is now possible to access voice gateways via the Internet. Those gateways provide a connection between the Internet and the public switched telephone network. This enables a PC user to speak into a microphone, have his or her conversation broken into small samples and digitized by his or her computer, as well as transmitted in packets to the gateway where each packet is converted back into a small period of voice. Although a number of technical issues remain to be resolved before the Internet telephony becomes suitable for business use, the network manager at the grocery company places it on the list of future technologies to investigate.

## The Consumer Revolution

The evolution in communications has not only affected businesses. Over the past few years, there has occurred a literal revolution in the manner by which consumers conduct their daily operations. From sending electronic mail to surfing the Web to paying bills electronically, communications enables consumers to do things faster and usually more economically. For example, you can transmit literally as many e-mails as you want to send each month for a $20 monthly fee that permits you to also surf the Web. In comparison, each first class letter now costs 34 cents in postage and might reach its destination in three to five days, whereas your e-mails are delivered near instantaneously. If you send 59 e-mails a month, or a little more than two per day, the savings on postage allows you to surf the Web free.

As the use of the Internet grew to tens of millions of users, the use of dial modems resulted in the coining of the term "World Wide Wait." The reason for this term was due to the amount of time required to enter a Web address and obtain the display of a Web page that typically contains one or more graphics. Because graphics require the transmission of a large number of characters, the time to display a typical Web page could take 15 to 30 seconds. Recognizing this problem, vendors developed Digital Subscriber Line modems and cable modems. Both devices provide high speed Internet access and are collectively referred to as *broadband modems*.

## The Evolution of the Multifunction Terminal

Another rapidly expanding area concerns the use of the personal computer as a multifunctional terminal. In this role, the addition of hardware and software turns the PC into a LAN workstation, a conventional mainframe computer terminal, a fax machine, or another type of communications device. Through the use of modern graphical user interface (GUI) operating systems, such as Microsoft Windows, you can readily switch from one application to another and execute two or more applications simultaneously. For example, you can execute a spreadsheet program while transmitting or receiving a fax.

The key to the capability of the personal computer to function as a multipurpose terminal was the development of specialized microprocessors and integrated circuits. This technology enabled functions that previously required tens to hundreds of individual computer chips to be performed by one chip or a few chips. This in turn enabled vendors to design adapter cards for insertion into an expansion slot in the system unit of a personal computer, which added the functionality of a standalone device to the PC. Figure 1.14 shows a modem/fax adapter card that enables a personal computer to transmit and receive faxes as well as communicate with other computers, bulletin board systems, and information utilities when it is used as a data modem.

To gain an appreciation for the role of the personal computer as a driving force for the need for speed in the field of data communications, you can examine how its capability has evolved. When the original IBM PC was introduced in 1981, its processor operated at approximately 5MHz, its serial port was capable of transmitting data to an external modem at 9600bps, and the computer stored data on five 1/4-inch floppy disks that had a storage capacity of 360K.

**FIGURE 1.14**
*A fax/modem adapter card for insertion into a PC. (Courtesy of Practical Peripherals, Inc.)*

Today's Micron Electronics Millennium computer can be obtained with an Intel Pentium IV processor operating at 1GHz; its serial port supports data transfers up to 115,200bps; and it contains a hard drive, a 3 1/2-inch floppy drive, and an Iomega Zip drive. The hard drive is capable of storing 20GB of data, the floppy disk can store 1.44MB of data, and the Zip disk can store 250MB of data. The vast increase in processing power and data storage capabilities of personal computers can be considered the driving force behind the need to increase the speed of transmission facilities. Whereas a few years ago a typical word processing document or an e-mail might contain a thousand text characters, today many persons incorporate pictures, art, and other graphics into their documents, which increase data storage requirements by an order of magnitude or more. When such documents are transmitted electronically, the need for speed represents another driving force for faster data transmission facilities.

## Changes in the Industries

The hardware and software developments are not the only things changing. Both the computer industry and the communications industry have changed in ways that would have been unimaginable 20 years ago. The rise of the minicomputer, the microprocessor in personal computers, and programmable controllers for equipment created a situation in which computing power was rather inexpensive. The suppliers of mainframe computers, such as IBM, UNISYS, and Amdahl, were joined by companies such as Texas Instruments, Apple, AST, Compaq, Dell, and Hewlett-Packard that had not previously made computers. As many more computers were used by many more people to create and use much more data, interest in data communications increased. In communications, the advent of satellites, followed by optical-fiber transmission, offered the promise of far greater bandwidths (range of usable frequencies) and thus, faster data transmission speeds.

## The Portable Computer

With the advances in the miniaturization of portable computer components, modern notebook computers offer two to eight GB of disk storage, a color display, and communications support in a package weighing less than four pounds. Fitting into an attaché case, modern notebooks have significantly enhanced the ability of executives, salespersons, students, and teachers to work at home and when traveling, as well as to access information utilities and corporate networks. Looking back at the grocery company previously discussed, sales personnel can now visit clients and check on the status of inventory, place orders, and confirm product shipments during a sales call. Although most notebook computers have a limited expansion capability through the use of a PC Card slot, several vendors recognized the requirements of notebook computer users to communicate both when traveling and when in the office.

Figure 1.15 depicts a combination Ethernet adapter and a data/fax modem PC Card. It is designed for insertion into a PC Card slot like those built into most modern notebook computers. The grocery salesperson, after communicating via the modem portion of the adapter when visiting clients, can return to the office and then connect his notebook to the corporate Ethernet local area network.

**FIGURE 1.15**

*This type of combination adapter has significantly enhanced mobile communications. (Courtesy of Xircom, Inc.)*

## Communications Industry Revolution

The revolution in computing and data transmission was paralleled by an upheaval in the structure of the communications industry. The telephone company's monopoly of almost a century disappeared forever, beginning in the late 1960s and accelerating until the Bell System was broken up in 1984. For the first time, not only could other firms compete with the telephone companies in offering long-distance service, but they also could sell equipment, including data communications devices, to be connected to the telephone network.

These two forces—the advent of the microprocessor-based personal computer and the increase in competition in both the computing and the communications industries—brought about dramatic changes and accelerated technological advances in the communications field. They also brought communications and computing closer together. In the example wholesale grocery company of the 1980s and 1990s, it is hard to say where communications stops and computing begins. Do you classify the salesperson's portable terminal and the manager's personal computer as communications devices or as computers? The answer, of course, is that they are both because they do whatever combination of tasks is required for the job at hand.

As we began to move through the new millennium, salespersons in the wholesale grocery company began to depend on the use of cell phones as they made their rounds. In addition, they would use personal digital assistants (PDAs) to enter their schedule, create "to do" lists, record expenses, and send and receive e-mails through cabling to a cell phone or the use of a separate

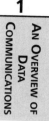

wireless attachment. As you might expect, having to transport two or three separate devices and either perform cabling or attach snap-on products might not be conducive to productivity. Recognizing this, Samsung introduced its PDA Phone during 2001. This cellular phone, which is illustrated in Figure 1.16, supports communications via two types of cellular communications as well as includes the Palm computer Operating System (OS). The latter supports the use of an address book, scheduler, "to do" list, memo pad, scientific calculator, and other features. In addition, the salesman can cable a PC to the PDA Phone, enabling the use of the PC with its larger screen to enter data into the phone.

**FIGURE 1.16**

*The Samsung PDA Phone combines a dual band cellular phone with the features of a Palm PDA. (Photograph courtesy of Samsung USA.)*

# Emerging Technologies

By examining current and evolving computer-based applications, we can predict to a fair degree of accuracy future developments in communications. For example, in a LAN environment, many organizations are replacing mainframe computers through the use of client-server applications, a process referred to as downsizing. In addition, these organizations are adding graphical applications in the form of images stored within a database; using multimedia for training employees in which voice, data, and video are merged for instruction; and using digitized voice messages to add verbal information to electronic mail. Another technology rapidly evolving is the use of intelligent terminals with built-in memory to run different applications via a connection to a network. Referred to as network PCs, these devices can download such diverse data as Java applets or Windows programs and execute the applet or program without the need for a more expensive, conventional PC.

Each of these emerging applications has one common feature: a requirement to transmit and store information many orders of magnitude above what conventional text-based applications require. Thus, a screen filled with text data is represented by 80x24 or 1,920 eight-bit characters, whereas an image on a VGA monitor that is displayed in a resolution of 640x480 pixels in 256 colors would require 640x480x8/8 bits per byte, or 307,200 characters of storage. This means that the transmission of the previously described image would take more than 100 times as long as the transmission of a screen of text data. Because people's patience cannot be expected to grow by a factor of 100 as applications use images and as digitized audio and video are developed, you can reasonably predict the development of new types of communications systems to accommodate emerging computer-based applications.

In fact, this is exactly what is happening in both local and wide area networking. Concerning LANs, the introduction of Fiber Distributed Data Interface (FDDI), Fast Ethernet, and VG-AnyLAN enabled organizations to construct LANs that operate at 100Mbps, in comparison to the current popular operating rates of 10Mbps for Ethernet LANs and 16Mbps for token-ring LANs. The standardization of Gigabit Ethernet in 1998 resulted in another tenfold leap in LAN operating rates. During 2002, 10Gbps Ethernet was being developed that represents another tenfold leap in LAN operating rates. In the wide area networking environment, which can be defined as the infrastructure that connects geographically separated areas, a new technology referred to as Asynchronous Transfer Mode (ATM) gained widespread acceptance.

On the local loop, which connects telephone subscribers to the entry point into the telephone company's public switched telephone network field, trials involving the use of digital subscriber lines (DSL), technology that provides data transfer at an Mbps rate, were successful, resulting in more than five million DSL modems being placed into operation in the United States. Although DSL technology is primarily being advertised as a mechanism to provide residential and business customers with high-speed access to the Internet, it also offers the potential to support the transmission of video on demand to homes, potentially competing with cable television for pay-per-view revenue. Not to be outdone, the cable television industry initiated a series of cable modem trials that would enable subscribers to access the Internet at data rates up to 30Mbps. Successful cable modem trials resulted in the installation of more than seven million cable modems in the United States by 2002. Another technology, Asynchronous Transfer Mode (ATM), is designed to transport voice, data, and video at operating rates of up to 2.488Gbps.

In modern computer-communications systems, you can interconnect equipment of many different sizes and capabilities from various suppliers. One of the purposes of this book is to explain how to interconnect, or interface, these different kinds of equipment so that they all work together in a system.

# General Description of Data Communications Systems

A data communications system can be described simply in terms of three components: the transmitter (also called the source), the transmission path (usually called the channel, but sometimes called the line), and the receiver (occasionally called the sink). In two-way communications, however, the source and the sink can interchange roles; that is, the same piece of equipment can transmit and receive data simultaneously. Therefore, it is easier to think of a data communications system between point A and point B (see Figure 1.17) in terms of the universal seven-part data circuit, which consists of the following parts:

- The data terminal equipment (DTE) at point A
- The interface between the DTE and the data circuit—terminating equipment or data communications equipment (DCE) at point A
- The DCE at point A
- The transmission channel between point A and point B
- The DCE at point B
- The DCE-DTE interface at point B
- The DTE at point B

In the seven-part data circuit, the DTE can be a terminal device or computer part; the DCE can be a modem if an analog channel is used or a Data Service Unit (DSU) if a digital channel is used.

The function of the various parts of the data communications system, both hardware and software, now can be described more easily. The DTE is the source, the sink, or both in the system. It transmits and/or receives data by utilizing the DCE and data transmission channel. Don't be misled by the name "data terminal equipment"; these could indeed be CRT or teletype terminals, but they also might be personal computers, printers, front-end processors for mainframe computers, or any other devices that can transmit or receive data. The whole purpose of the data communications system is to transmit useful information between point A and point B; the information can be used directly by the DTE, or the DTE can process and display the information for use by human operators.

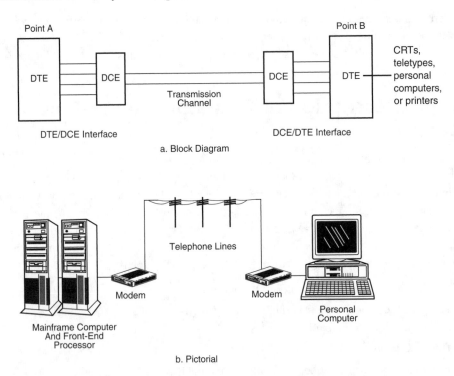

FIGURE 1.17
*The universal seven-part data circuit.*

# The Form and Content of Information

The DCE and the transmission channel perform the function of moving the data from point A to point B. In general, they neither know nor care about the content of the information transmitted; it could be stock market quotations, a display for a video game, or the recipe for Aunt Martha's fudge.

This brings us to an important point about data communications: the difference between the form and the content of the information transmitted. The form of the information might be English language text represented by code for a telegram; the content might advise you that a rich uncle has just left you a million dollars. Clearly, the ordinary user of data communications is much more interested in the content of the information and really is not concerned about the mechanics of the communications process as long as the information is received correctly. It would be rather disappointing if, in fact, your uncle had left you only $100.00, but because of errors in transmission, the telegram you received stated that you had inherited $1,000,000.00.

The data communications system itself is concerned only with the correct transmission between points A and B of the information given it; the system does not operate on the content of the information at all. This means that when this book talks about the "correctness" of the transmitted information, it means only that the information received has the identical form of the information transmitted. If someone gave a message to the telegraph operator stating that your uncle had left you a million dollars when he had left you only a hundred dollars, the inaccuracy of that information would probably not be the fault of the telegraph operator or the data communications equipment.

*Protocol* is the name given to the hardware and software rules and procedures for making sure that any transmission errors are detected. These might be as simple as transmitting an extra bit of information in each character to detect errors, as used with personal computers, or as complex as some systems' use for satellite data communications. The satellite system sends extra information not only to allow the receiver to detect transmission errors, but also to correct the errors and to make the receiver appear to be in the room next to the DTE instead of about 50,000 transmission miles away.

## The DTE-DCE Interface

The DTE-DCE interface has been mentioned several times as though it is something special. It is. The interface consists of the input/output circuitry in the DCE and the DTE, and the connectors and cables that connect them. In most systems, this interface conforms to the RS-232 standard published by the Electronic Industries Association (EIA) in the United States. (The RS-232 and other standard DTE-DCE interfaces are discussed in Chapter 4, "Asynchronous Modems and Interfaces.") The RS-232 interface and other serial interfaces that use some of the RS-232 specification but depart from it in some important way are by far the most commonly used interfaces in data communications. The RS-232 standard specifies the rules by which data is moved across the interface between the DTE and the DCE and, therefore, ultimately from point A to point B. The word serial means that the bits cross the interface one at a time in a series.

The DTE plays a very important part in the process of moving data between points A and B. Basic input and output capabilities are important, but today's intelligent electronic terminals can perform many complex software-driven functions whose goal is to ensure better performance and accuracy of the data transfer. You'll look at these functions in several of the chapters to follow.

Similarly, although a great deal of discussion will be devoted to the interface between the DTE and the DCE, less time will be spent on the interface between the DCE and the communications channel. This is because the latter interface is quite simple (either two wires or four wires, rather than 2–24, as in the RS-232 interface) and because there is not a problem with the sequencing of the electrical signals across this interface.

This chapter doesn't go into great detail discussing the transmission channel either, even though it is obviously crucial to the data communications system. The various electrical characteristics of the channel itself (such as its bandwidth, the relative delay at various frequencies, and other parameters) usually conform to published specifications, and these specifications are often contained in the tariffs published by the telephone companies or other carriers. You have very little control over the transmission channel itself (except to hang up and redial). The equipment used for data communications is tolerant of a wide range of some of the problems; but unless the data transmission rate is at a very high speed, the communications channel usually does not cause any trouble.

So you really don't care much about how the channel works, as long as a standard voice-grade channel between points A and B is available. A standard voice-grade channel is a telephone line that normally would be used for voice communication (that is, a telephone conversation). Thus, a fundamental problem in data communications is that the transmission of digital data must be accomplished over facilities that were designed for voice (analog) communications. The modem, a type of DCE used to convert digital data to an analog form (such as speed or tones) for transmission over the telephone channel, is described in Chapter 4.

## The Effect of Telecommunications Reform

When the AT&T system was broken up in 1984, a total of 160 Local Access and Transport Areas (LATAs) that roughly correspond to metropolitan statistical areas in the U.S. were defined. Local Exchange Carriers (LECs), which include the Regional Bell Operating Companies (RBOCs) resulting from the divestiture of AT&T from its local companies, were given the right to provide intra-LATA local transmission services. Interexchange carriers, such as AT&T, Sprint, and MCI were given the rights to all inter-LATA calls. Prior to that, RBOCs were normally prevented from offering inter-LATA services, and interexchange carriers could not offer local services. These restrictions changed as a result of the Telecommunications Reform Act of 1996. Under this act, interexchange carriers are allowed to provide local telephone service after meeting certain regulatory requirements, and LECs are allowed to provide inter-LATA communications after meeting other regulatory requirements.

A new entity referred to as a Competitive LEC (CLEC) was defined by the reform bill. CLECs can resell any or all services of a LEC's network. Because a CLEC can also construct its own fiber-based network, they can offer end-to-end services. Commencing in the late 1990s, new communications carriers, including Quest, Level 3 Communications, and others, announced plans to install more than 100,000 route miles of fiber-optic cable across North America as the competition heated up for subscribers. Other provisions of this bill allow electric utilities and cable TV companies to offer voice-grade services, and telephone companies will use various technologies to provide high-speed access to the home and office over ordinary twisted-pair wire. In fact, by the time you read this edition, you might be able to obtain video-on-demand movies via your telephone and connect to the Internet via your cable TV operator or electric utility company. The evolution in communications requires one to have a degree of knowledge about the operating characteristics of different transmission media. Those characteristics are described at appropriate points in this book.

## What You Have Learned

Now that the fundamental secrets of data communications have been revealed, briefly review the problem, the terms, and the parts of the system:

- To encode information using some kind of standard code, you must convert it to a form that can be transmitted over the existing telephone network, transmit it between point A and point B without introducing errors, and reverse the process at the receiving end to recover the original information.

- A channel is a transmission facility connecting points A and B. It's usually a voice-grade telephone channel provided by the telephone company. The channel can be established for the duration of a call (dial-up) or from a permanent connection (leased line).

- Data Terminal Equipment (DTE) is composed of the source of the data to be transmitted at one end and the sink that receives the transmitted data at the other end.

- Data Circuit-Terminating (or Communications) Equipment (DCE) refers to conversion equipment between the DTE and the transmission channel. One type of DCE, the modem, converts the data into tones for transmission over the voice channel.

- The RS-232 interface is the interface wiring and electronics between the DTE and the DCE equipment at either end of the system. Although other important interface standards exist, this is the most common.

- The data to be transmitted between points A and B is called information. It could be as simple as a command to turn on an indicator light, or as complex as the commands for drawing a multicolor illustration on a CRT display. In either case, the communications system itself is concerned only about moving the data between A and B without any error. The data communications system does not respond to, nor act on, the content of the data transmitted.

- Internetworking is composed of hardware and software that enables information to flow between devices connected to different LANs and other computer systems.

- Protocol refers to the rules for transmission of information between two points. They include rules for handling such questions as what to do if a transmission error occurs and how to determine whether the receiver is ready to receive the transmission.

- A local area network (LAN) interconnects devices within a building or campus, whereas a wide area network (WAN) interconnects devices within a city or in different cities.

- The 1996 telecommunications reform bill promotes competition by enabling telephone companies to offer video-on-demand and other services traditionally offered by cable TV operators, and those operators can now offer telephone services.

# Quiz for Chapter 1

1. Which is not an example of data communications?
    A. A teletype printing news bulletins.
    B. A computer transmitting files to another computer.
    C. An automatic teller machine checking account balances with the bank's computer.
    D. A salesman telephoning orders to the office.

2. Two-state (binary) communications systems are better than single state systems because
    A. They can interface directly with the analog telephone network.
    B. The components are simpler, less costly, and more reliable.
    C. People think better in binary.
    D. Interstate calls are less costly.

3. Which is not a positional notation system?
    A. Roman (MCMXXXVII)
    B. Binary (01111110)
    C. Decimal (1492)
    D. Hexadecimal (3A2B)

4. What is the decimal equivalent of binary 10110010?
    A. 128
    B. 192
    C. 178
    D. 176

5. Codes are always

   A. Eight bits per character.

   B. Either seven or eight bits per character.

   C. Agreed on in advance between sender and receiver.

   D. The same in all modern computers.

6. The Baudot code

   A. Was invented by the Baudot brothers, Mark and Space.

   B. Requires the escape character to print numbers.

   C. Requires shift characters to provide sufficient combinations.

   D. Is the primary transmission code over PSTNs in Europe.

7. Standard ASCII

   A. Is version II of the ASC standard.

   B. Has 128 characters, including 32 control characters.

   C. Is a subset of the 8-bit EBCDIC code.

   D. Is used only in the United States and Canada.

8. Extended ASCII

   A. Adds extra digits to standard ASCII.

   B. Provides 128 additional character definitions beyond standard ASCII.

   C. Doubles the bit length of each ASCII character.

   D. Provides extra characters that you define.

9. Escape sequences

   A. Use the ESC character to indicate the start of a special control sequence.

   B. Are used to switch (escape) between ASCII and EBCDIC codes.

   C. Are a popular daydream for inmates.

10. The principal difference between batch processing and online processing is that

   A. Computer resources are used more efficiently for online processing.

   B. Teleprinters are used for batch processing; CRTs are used for online processing.

   C. Transactions are grouped for batch processing; transactions are processed as needed for online processing.

11.  The key difference between current and emerging computer-based applications with respect to their communications requirements is that

    A.  Emerging applications will use graphics that require less transmission time.

    B.  The use of voice will reduce the necessity to transmit text.

    C.  Emerging applications will require additional data storage, which will result in additional transmission time.

    D.  The integration of voice, video, and data will reduce transmission time.

12.  The primary function of a bridge is to

    A.  Connect PCs to a LAN.

    B.  Interconnect two LANs.

    C.  Access the corporate mainframe.

    D.  Connect different warehouses in different states.

13.  The technique that converts a private line network to operate over the Internet results in a

    A.  Virtual line.

    B.  Circuit restoration.

    C.  Virtual private network (VPN).

    D.  Firewall.

14.  DCE and DTE

    A.  Are defined as *digital communications equipment* and *digital termination and equipment*.

    B.  Are connected by either two or four wires.

    C.  Refer to the modem and the computer or terminal, respectively.

15.  The correctness and accuracy of the transmitted message content is

    A.  Verified by the modem.

    B.  Determined by the sender and receiver, not by the communications system.

    C.  Ensured by the use of digital techniques.

16.  The Telecommunications Reform Act of 1996 promotes

    A.  Competition among different industry groups.

    B.  Two-wire services.

    C.  The use of digital transmission.

# Terminal Devices

## IN THIS CHAPTER

Various kinds of equipment and software make up a system. This chapter starts with the part of a system that is most visible to the user: the terminal. The great majority of data terminals used through the early to mid-1980s fell into two categories: teleprinter terminals and CRT terminals. Teleprinters are electromechanical devices that transmit and receive data electronically, include a keyboard for data entry, and display data by printing characters on paper fed into the printer portion of the device by mechanically moving a printhead across each line on the paper. In comparison, a CRT terminal has a keyboard and displays information electronically on a display by transmitting electrons to turn on pixels to form characters and symbols.

By the early 1990s, however, more people were using personal computers as terminals than were using teleprinters and CRT terminals combined. By the mid-1990s, advances in the design of semiconductors and disk drives resulted in the manufacture of millions of lightweight notebook and palmtop computers yearly. In fact, the palmtop, which is also often referred to as a personal digital assistant (PDA), may one day become as ubiquitous as a man's wallet or a woman's purse. These devices, as well as conventional desktop personal computers, are modern terminal devices that include an intelligent processing capability. This chapter discusses both the older teleprinter terminals and the newer CRTs, as well as the components of a personal computer that enable desktop, notebook, and palmtop computers to function as multipurpose communications terminals.

# Teleprinters

The device that was invented to replace the Morse telegrapher was called the teleprinter. It was actually a form of specialized telegraph that used the 5-bit character code. Figure 2.1 shows an early teleprinter. The largest manufacturer of teleprinters in the United States was the Teletype Corporation; thus, the word Teletype has been commonly used to refer to any teletypewriter or teleprinter.

A teleprinter can be defined as any device that combines a low-speed printer with a serial communications interface. Although a keyboard is an important component of most teleprinters, it is not required to fit this definition (which is used in the commercial marketplace). Thus, the common line printer qualifies if it has a serial interface.

**FIGURE 2.1**
*An early teleprinter.*

## Communications

Teleprinters use start-stop asynchronous transmission, which is the most widely used method of data communications for a serial interface. It is the simplest technique, but it's also the least efficient (the price paid for simplicity).

Teleprinters transmit at a speed much lower than the capacity of a telephone voice-grade line. Common teleprinter speeds in North America are 75 and 110 bits per second (bps). Common speeds elsewhere in the world are 100 and 200bps. The international teleprinter (Telex) network and many European lines operate at 50bps.

Teleprinters form signals simply by switching an electrical current on and off or by reversing the current's direction of flow. The current is either 20 or 60 milliamperes, and the equipment is called current-loop equipment. Regardless of the method used, switching current on and off or reversing its direction, the result is a two=state binary communications system. One state represents a binary 1, while the other state represents a binary 0, enabling characters to be transmitted and received as a sequence of binary digits. (Most teleprinters today use the RS-232 standard as the external interface, but current-loop circuitry still can be used internally.)

Single-current teleprinter signaling, also known as neutral or unipolar signaling, is common in the United States. Double-current signaling, also called polar or bipolar signaling, is more common in Europe. You'll learn more about current-loop signaling and the RS-232 standard in Chapter 4, "Asynchronous Modems and Interfaces."

# Terminals

Two types of teleprinters are available: those with typewriter-style keyboards (called keyboard send-receive, or KSR), and those without keyboards (called receive-only, or RO). The typical teleprinter is capable of printing from 10 to 30 characters per second (cps), or from 100 to 300 words per minute (wpm), which is much faster than any typist types. However, because much of the terminal's time might be devoted to printing output from a computer instead of entering data, it is usually desirable to have the fastest possible printing mechanism. Thus, teleprinters are available with printing speeds of up to 120cps.

In the usual operation of a teleprinter, a user enters inputs to the computer via the keyboard. The inputs are transmitted back (in what is called an echo) from the computer, character by character, to the printer and are printed to verify receipt. Output originating in the computer or another source is printed as it is received. Thus, a hard copy of both the inputs and the outputs is available. Although many teleprinters are used in this way, some are strictly online printing devices and thus don't require a keyboard.

## Common Applications

The classic and perhaps best application for teleprinter terminals is in interactive sessions with a computer, such as time-sharing or bulletin boards. The slow speed of operation is not as noticeable as in other applications because much of the operator's time is spent thinking rather than waiting for output.

From the 1960s through the 1970s, teleprinters were popularly used in regional weather information networks. In this type of network, weather forecasts and related information were broadcast from a central computer to teleprinters connected to the computer via the installation of leased lines. The transmission of information was always from the computer to the teleprinter, and no response was required or sought, so this was one of the primary applications for the use of RO teleprinters.

## Modern Teleprinters

More modern teleprinters, such as the one shown in Figure 2.2, use various printing techniques and operate at many print speeds. They provide features such as programmable format control, adjustable forms control, upper- and lowercase printing, interchangeable character styles (fonts), bidirectional printing and paper feeding, selectable character and line spacing, status indicators, portability, and additional keys (such as a numeric keypad).

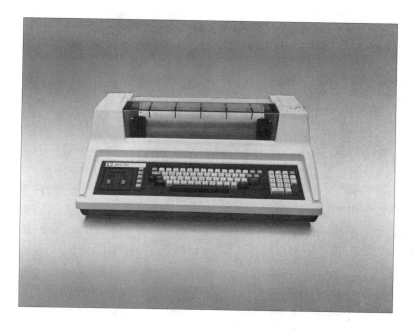

**FIGURE 2.2**
*A TI 820 KSR teleprinter.*

Manufacturers incorporated the microprocessor into modern teleprinters during the 1970s to reduce design, development, and production costs while providing a variety of applications that can be implemented by either the vendor or the user. The microprocessor delays the time when a particular teleprinter design will become obsolete because future applications can be accommodated by reprogramming the microprocessor to perform other jobs. From the user's point of view, microprocessor technology also offers the major advantage of lower cost because the manufacturer's savings from using microprocessors are passed on to the customer.

Compared to total terminal sales, few new teleprinter units are sold outside of the traditional record services markets (Telex and private teleprinter network). Even most of these are specialized. An example is the portable printing terminal that is often used by a traveling businessperson whose needs are satisfied by a small, lightweight (3 to 8 pounds), hand-carried terminal.

## Portable Terminals

The rapid decrease in the price and size of portable computers means that they now can be used for applications that previously were reserved for portable terminals. Not only can portable personal computers communicate with large corporate computers, but these portables also enable the traveling businessperson to compose memoranda and letters and to analyze business decisions with spreadsheet programs. Although portable terminals communicating with corporate computers could perform such functions, the personal computer can complete these tasks in a local mode of operation, which eliminates many long-distance communication sessions. In addition, through the development of PC Card fax/data modems, it is now extremely convenient for people working at home or traveling to use their portable computers to send electronic mail messages, surf the Internet, or communicate with the corporate mainframe.

The first type of portable computer was more appropriately referred to as transportable, due to its weight, which ranged from 20 to 30 pounds. Fortunately for the executive who travels, as well as for students and employees who work at home, advances in the development of integrated circuits and disk drives brought about three new types of personal computers in the late 1980s and early 1990s: laptops, notebooks, and palmtops, the latter also often referred to as personal digital assistants.

- Laptops are so named because they could literally be placed on a person's lap, normally weigh less than 12 pounds, and generally can fit into an attaché case.
- Notebooks are so named because they are similar in size to an 8 1/2-by-11-inch notepad, easily fit into an attaché case and usually weigh less than four pounds.
- Palmtops are so named because they can be lifted by closing one's hand around the device and usually weigh less than 2 pounds.

All three types of portable computers can perform most, if not all, computing functions associated with conventional personal computers while providing a high level of portability.

The chief drawbacks of portable computers include a compressed keyboard, in which multiple keystrokes might be required to generate some of the key functions for normal keyboards, and poor to fair screen readability. Although considerable advances in screen technology have occurred over the past decade, many portable computer screens must still be viewed from a certain angle to be readable. This viewing requirement is based on the reflection of light from the screen or the angle by which light is generated by a back-lighted screen.

During the late 1990s, active matrix or TFT video displays were introduced, which enhanced the readability of portable computer displays. However, most of these still require the screen to be viewed directly and result in a loss of clarity when viewed at an angle. Another problem associated with portable computers is their battery life, which means that many devices are restricted to an operating life of under four hours before recharging is necessary. Although this may be sufficient for many airline flights, it can cause problems for people flying coast to coast or internationally.

Figure 2.3 illustrates the interface of a Hewlett-Packard HP95XL palmtop computer to a U.S. Robotics (now part of 3COM Corporation) Worldport fax/data modem. The HP95XL was one of the first palmtop computers to be sold. It included a copy of Lotus Development Corporation's popular 1-2-3 electronic spreadsheet program built into read-only memory (ROM). The Worldport fax/data modem enables an HP95XL user to transmit and receive text and fax messages. By examining the size of the HP95XL, the modem, and the hands of the person holding both devices, you will note that the HP95XL and the Worldport modems both can easily fit into the palm of one's hand. Hence, both the computer and the modem are referred to as palmtop devices.

**FIGURE 2.3**

*An HP95XL palmtop computer connected to a U.S. Robotics Worldport palmtop fax/data modem. (Courtesy of U.S. Robotics.)*

In the early 1990s, a new type of computer became available that has the potential to revolutionize the method by which we transmit and receive information. This device is commonly referred to as the personal digital assistant, or PDA. PDAs can be considered to represent a palmtop computer and are commonly marketed with integrated cellular communications capability to include data and fax modems designed to transmit and receive information via a cellular telephone connection. With this capability, the PDA enables a user to bypass the necessity of connecting his device to a telephone to communicate. This can be a major benefit for travelers because connecting a portable computer to a telephone-line jack can be difficult or impossible in many hotels, motels, and airports.

Moving into the new millennium, the 3Com Palm III connected organizer, which is shown in Figure 2.4, was by far the most popular of all connected organizers being marketed during the late 1990s, with more than a million sold prior to its second anniversary. Through the use of 3Com's HotSync technology, a 3Com Palm III connected organizer can be used to exchange information with a PC or even a corporate server. With a cellular modem, this device is used by the investment community to obtain real-time access to stock quotes regardless of their location, while other people use it to send and receive e-mail, track expenses, and even submit expense reports while they are traveling. During 2000, Palm was spun off from 3COM as a separate company and is now Palm, Inc.

The Palm III organizer uses an open architecture proprietary operating system, while several competitive products, such as the Phillips NINO and Everex Freestyle, are based upon a slimmed-down version of Microsoft's Windows operating system referred to as Windows CE. In competition with Palm, Microsoft revised its PDA operating system several times. The latest version is referred to as Windows for Pocket PC. Companies including Compaq Computer and Hewlett-Packard now offer Pocket PC PDAs that include slimmed-down versions of Microsoft's Word word processor and Excel spreadsheet programs, referred to as Pocket Word and Pocket Excel. Both hardware products using Windows for Pocket PC and the Palm OS now support wireless e-mail, while the addition of certain types of application software makes it possible to surf the Web using a PDA. This places wireless-enabled PDAs in competition with the PDA phone previously shown in Figure 1.16 and similar cellular telephones for the consumer dollar. Both certain cellphones and PDAs are equipped to support the Wireless Application Protocol (WAP), which enables these small-screen display terminals to access specialized Web sites similar to a browser on a PC accessing a Web server.

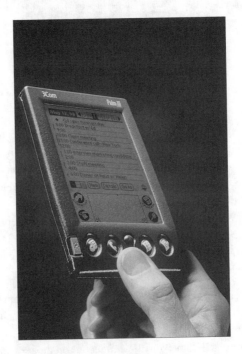

**FIGURE 2.4**

*The Palm Pilot III connected organizer can be used to send and receive e-mail while traveling, as well as to access a conventional PC or the corporate server. (Courtesy of Palm Computing, a 3Com company.)*

# Teleprinters Versus CRT Terminals

The drawbacks to teleprinters involve speed, formatting, and reliability. Teleprinters are far slower in operation than CRT terminals; even their highest print speed doesn't compare to the 300 or 1,200 characters per second on the CRT. Because teleprinters are designed primarily for message communications, they do not provide sophisticated capabilities for data editing or formatting. It is quite difficult to create a form on a teleprinter, and, of course, such attributes as blinking, highlighting, and similar enhancements that are available on a CRT terminal are impossible on a teleprinter. Although teleprinters are quite reliable, they nevertheless are electromechanical devices that are subject to wear and misalignment. CRT terminals, on the other hand, generally have higher reliability because of far fewer parts, most of which do not move.

# Serial Printers

Teleprinter terminals use serial (or character) printers, so named because they print one character at a time. Such printers can be classified into two categories: impact printers, which mechanically strike the paper to produce a printed image, and nonimpact printers, which produce an image by some other means. Impact printers are further divided into two subcategories: those that produce a fully formed character, in which the character is created by impact from a single piece of type, and dot-matrix printers, in which the character image on the paper is formed by a matrix of dots. Nonimpact teleprinters form characters by the dot-matrix method only, using an electrothermal, an ink-jet, or a laser-printing method.

## Impact Printers

All of the mechanisms used by impact printers share the same advantages of fully formed characters in almost any style and shape, and all have the capability to make "carbon" copies. They also share the same disadvantages of low speed and mechanical complexity. No matter how the character is mounted or engraved on the type element, it must be positioned in front of the platen and then struck against an inked ribbon and paper to produce an image. This process limits the speed of the printer to a maximum of 120cps (but it's usually much slower), and it creates a large amount of noise in the process.

Impact printing mechanisms include

- Replaceable type-ball elements, as used on the IBM electric typewriters.
- The daisywheel, a flat disk with petal-like projections for the character elements.
- Elements shaped like cups with finger-like projections.
- Moving-type belts with the characters engraved on the belt.

- A rotating cylinder containing the characters.
- A type block with characters embedded in the block.

The aforementioned speed limitation was an incentive for printer manufacturers to seek a different approach that would extend the upper limit of printing speed for serial impact printers. Their search led to the development of the dot-matrix printer. Dot-matrix printers are a compromise (and often a successful one) between decreased character quality and substantially higher print speeds of 180cps or more. The printed image is formed from a rectangular matrix of dots, which was initially nine dots high by seven dots wide. Printing is performed by moving a print head containing a column of nine pins across the paper and selectively actuating the pins at seven successive intervals to form each character. Developments in dot-matrix printer technology increased the number of pins that could be placed on the print head, resulting in the availability of 18- and 24-pin print-head printers. Dot-matrix printers with these high-density print heads print characters whose pin dots overlap to produce a nearly solid character format. This type of printing, which provides the appearance of an impact printer output, is referred to as near-letter quality. Although dot-matrix printers contain comparatively few moving parts, they are subject to much wear and heat within the print head as a result of the succession of pin movements required to create each character.

Dot-matrix teleprinters are typically less expensive than similarly featured fully formed character teleprinters. With the improved print quality that's now available with high-resolution dot-matrix printing, most teleprinter users are satisfied with dot-matrix printers. In addition, by selectively firing pins on the dot-matrix print head, different typefaces and graphics can be supported, which is beyond the capability of fully formed character teleprinters.

Another development that improved speed in teleprinters was the bidirectional print head with logic-seeking control. The print head can print while moving in either direction (left to right or right to left). The logic-seeking control circuitry determines the shortest horizontal distance to move the print head to print the next line. Thus, on full pages of text, one line is printed left to right, the next is printed right to left, and so forth. This feature, available on both fully formed character printers and dot-matrix printers, eliminates the time required for a full carriage return to the left side for every line.

## Nonimpact Printers

The nonimpact types of teleprinters employ various electronic, optical, and chemical techniques to produce printed images. Some of the printing techniques have been developed from xerography and facsimile communications techniques. Others were specifically developed for use in high-speed printing applications in which print speeds of more than 2,000 lines (that's lines, not characters) per minute are not uncommon. Still others were designed to meet a specific goal, such as quiet operation.

The electrothermal printing technique is one nonimpact method. The print head applies heat through the matrix pins to chemically coated paper. The heat causes a chemical reaction, which produces a matrix of colored dots that form the character. It is quiet and efficient but requires special paper, to which some people object.

The inkjet technique uses a stream of electrically charged ink droplets sprayed onto ordinary paper to produce the characters, as shown in Figure 2.5. Dot placement is accomplished by electrostatic deflection plates that control the direction of the charged ink droplets, in much the same manner as electron beam position is controlled within a cathode ray tube. Because electronics control the switching between reservoirs of different colored ink, instant color changes can be made as the printer operates. Inkjet printers were originally very expensive, but prices have decreased substantially in the past few years.

Laser printers create images of entire pages by "recording" on a rotating drum with a laser beam and imparting these images to paper. The laser beam focuses on a minute spot that continually scans along the length of the light-sensitive coated drum. Turning the scanning beam off and on creates the pattern that is transferred to paper. The spot (or dot) resolution is as high as $2400 \times 2400$ per square inch.

Reliability of nonimpact printers is high compared to that of impact printers because they have fewer mechanical parts. Their incapability to produce more than one copy at a time (no carbon copies) might sometimes be a disadvantage, but their rapid, quiet, and reliable operation is certainly an advantage. Due to the rapid increase in the use of nonimpact printers, economies of scale of production resulted in steep declines in their cost, providing another advantage to their utilization.

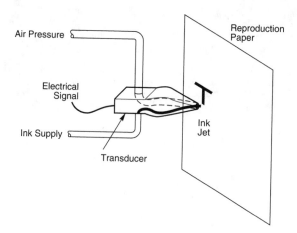

**FIGURE 2.5**
*The basic inkjet printing technique.*

# CRT Terminals

The cathode ray tube (CRT) terminal, also called a video display terminal (VDT), is a common interface between people and computers. The CRT terminal was originally developed as an alternative to teleprinter terminals. Its introduction in 1965 revolutionized the data communications environment, in which the teleprinter had been the only interface device. The advent of the integrated circuit, which combined many logic functions performed by wiring on a single chip of silicon, followed by large-scale integration, brought prices of CRTs down, although they were still out of reach of the ordinary individual. Then came the microprocessor, which replaced much of the integrated circuit logic and drove prices still lower. The result was high-quality, high-performance, and relatively low-cost CRT terminals that even the hobbyist can afford. A CRT terminal designed for businesses is shown in Figure 2.6.

**FIGURE 2.6**
*A TI 931 CRT terminal.*

# ASCII Terminals

In the computer industry, the term ASCII display terminal usually refers to a CRT terminal that operates without a separate controller, uses the ASCII code, and transmits and receives asynchronous data. This term originated with CRT terminals (the glass Teletype) designed to replace Teletype ASR 33/35 teleprinter terminals. ASCII terminals are still described as being TTY- or Teletype-compatible. ASCII terminals are available in a wide range of types, from low-end dumb units that do little more than emulate a teleprinter (or that emulate another CRT terminal, such as the ADM-3, which emulates a teleprinter) up to 132-column split-screen editing terminals with several pages of electronic memory storage.

CRT terminals have three capabilities in common:

- A keyboard that can generate a full alphanumeric character code set
- A CRT monitor that can display the characters of that code set
- The capability to send and receive data via communications lines to a remote host computer

CRT terminals fall into one of three categories: dumb, smart, and user-programmable. Of course, there is some overlap between categories, but the following list defines them in detail:

- Dumb terminals are Teletype-compatible; they offer a limited number of functions—perhaps none beyond keyboarding and display. They are of the lowest cost, but often the difference in price between them and the smart terminals is small compared to the difference in performance and features. This description of the capabilities of teleprinters also applies to the capability of the dumb CRT terminals, except for print speed. These terminals essentially consist of a CRT, video (display), memory, and interface electronics. Few truly dumb terminals are still manufactured; virtually all CRT terminals currently manufactured are microprocessor-controlled, making them smart terminals by definition. The microprocessor chips cost only a few dollars, which is less than the cost of the logic they replace.

- Smart terminals offer extended functions, such as editing and formatted data entry. The user might be able to tailor the terminal to fit a specific application such as data entry through limited programming (for example, format creation, parameter definition, or input checking).

- User-programmable (or intelligent) terminals feature software support. The manufacturer provides an operating system (an assembler, a compiler, or an interpretive programming language), subroutines (I/O utilities and one or more protocol emulators), and one or two application programs (such as data entry and text editing). The user-programmable terminal provides some form of program storage and more memory for text.

## Microprocessors

The microprocessor programs (firmware) reside in read-only memory (ROM) or programmable ROM (PROM). ROM-resident programs control those features that are "permanent," whereas PROM-resident programs are typically produced in smaller quantities and implement customized or modifiable features. Either type can be replaced by a different type with a different program by removal of the old chip and insertion of a new one, although this feature is more talked about than actually used. In addition to controlling basic terminal functions, the microprocessor can provide protocol emulation, define the character code sets to be generated by the keyboard, implement special features, set control parameters, and so forth. Moreover, the microprocessor delays obsolescence because future needs can be implemented via reprogramming.

In addition to the capability to simply display alphabetic and numeric characters, microprocessor control provides the capability for highlighting characters by means of underscoring, using reverse video, blinking, displaying differing levels of brightness, and using combinations of these attributes. One of the most impressive capabilities of these terminals is the capability to display a predefined form and let the operator "fill in the blanks" while checking the entries as they are made.

Many CRT terminals can display double-sized characters, and most have a graphics character set for creating forms and formats. Some also support business graphics—for example, bar, column, and pie charts to graphically show sales, income, expense, inventory levels, and so forth. Interactive or engineering graphics, on the other hand, is a highly specialized area usually requiring a completely different high-resolution graphics terminal.

## User-Programmable Terminals and Personal Computers

Taken separately, the words programmable and terminal are precisely definable. But when combined to describe one class of equipment, their meanings become vague and difficult to define with precision. In 1979, a popular periodical defined a user-programmable terminal as a terminal that permits local file updating and accommodates user-written applications programs. At that time, this definition stirred up quite a bit of controversy because such a terminal would have to provide for the following features in addition to the basic terminal functions:

- The availability of, and the support and documentation for, at least one general-purpose programming language for development of programs by customer personnel
- Entry of programs via the terminal keyboard
- The capability to access and retrieve programs stored in the host computer memory and the capability to execute (use) those programs at the terminal

Much of the value of user-programmable terminals is in their offline processing capability, which is provided by the previously listed items. All user-programming terminals have built-in main memory that the user can employ to store and execute programs, but the capacity varies from as little as 1 kilobyte (usually written as 1K or 1KB), which accommodates only a very small program, to as much as 512K, which accommodates a large program and much data. Most, although not all, user-programmable terminals also provide for local mass storage using floppy, hard, or cartridge disks, or cassette or cartridge magnetic tape.

With disks, tapes, memory, an operating system, and a programming language, the user-programmable terminal sounds a lot like a personal computer, doesn't it? This is the revolution in the terminal market. Dumb terminals and low-end smart terminals are rapidly being squeezed aside by personal computers, which relegate terminals to specialized tasks. Most office workers now have personal computers on their desks, which can be used as standalone units, used as a computer connected to a local area network for client/server computing (where the PC represents the client computer), or placed online to the large host computer. Files can be up- and downloaded and processed wherever it makes the most sense to do so. All of this is possible because of data communications and the microprocessor!

## Terminal Emulation Programs

When a personal computer operates a communications program that enables the computer to duplicate the attributes of a terminal, the software is known as a terminal emulator program. Such programs permit a personal computer to communicate with mainframe application programs developed to work with predefined types of terminals.

Depending on the terminal emulation software marketed for the personal computer, you might be able to replace several types of terminals with one computer. For an example, consider the organization that has both Hewlett-Packard (HP) and IBM mainframe computers. With HP 2645 and IBM 3270 terminal emulation software, one can use a personal computer to emulate common Hewlett-Packard and IBM terminal devices, and thereby get full-screen access to two different computer systems designed to operate with two specific types of terminals.

# Non-ASCII Terminals

This section describes CRT terminals that do not fit the ASCII label, together with some specialized terminals that use other displays. Of these, the most important type is the batch or cluster type.

## Distinguishing Between Interactive and Batch Terminals

Communications between terminal devices, including personal computers and other computers, tend to fall into two basic categories: interactive and batch. These are distinguished by the types of functions to be performed by the computer. Interactive communications support conversational inquiry/response, interactive data entry, and other such applications. Batch communications, on the other hand, support either remote job entry or remote batch data communications. In remote job entry (RJE), the terminal device acts as a remote console for the central computer, enabling local users to load and execute application programs. In remote batch data communications, the terminal acts as a remote input/output device for an application program being performed in the host.

The reasons for these distinctions are efficiency and accuracy. An interactive terminal designed to communicate in asynchronous character-by-character mode is not very efficient for transmitting large blocks of data as required in the batch mode, nor is the error checking (if present) adequate to ensure correct transmission. On the other hand, it would be wasteful to tie up a complete remote batch terminal just to enable one user to use the keyboard to ask questions about particular data stored in the host computer with the answers sent back by the computer.

Although batch terminals were commonly used to access a remote computer during the 1960s and 1970s, the personal computer also affected the use of this type of terminal device. The widespread use of personal computers during the 1980s resulted in the development of hardware and software that enables many types of personal computers to function as remote job entry type terminals.

## Clustered Terminals

When a remote location generates a large amount of data via key entry, the use of a clustered system might be indicated. This is typical in large-scale data-processing installations in which it is common practice to control many peripheral units, such as CRT terminals, at one location with a single control unit. Data entered through the keyboard devices is stored in a buffer for transmission. Then the output of many operators is transmitted in one block to the main computer at much higher speeds than those used by teleprinters and ASCII CRT terminals. In addition to the key entry devices, storage, and the controller, the cluster might include printers and mass storage. This type of architecture is fundamental to modern data processing. A widely used example is the IBM 3270 series.

## IBM 3270 Series

The IBM 3270 is not a terminal, per se, but it is a designation for a family of devices designed for use in clusters. The 3270 series has had a strong impact on the synchronous terminal market since its introduction in 1971. The first generation, which was discontinued in 1982, included the 3271/3272 control units, 3275 display station, 3277 display, and 3284/3286/3288 printers. In 1977, the product line was expanded and updated with the 3274 control unit, 3276 control/display, 3278 display, and 3287/3289 printers. In 1979, color displays and printers were added. In 1983, IBM made some long-awaited changes and enhancements to the 3270 product line. Added were the 3178 display station, a new 3274 control unit, the 3290 information panel (a gas plasma display), and the 3299 terminal multiplexer.

In 1986, a few years after the introduction of the new 3274, IBM announced its 3174 control unit. In some respects, the device is similar to a personal computer because it can be customized through the addition of special adapter cards. Three of the key functions that can be added to a 3174 control unit are asynchronous ASCII terminal support, in which the control unit performs protocol conversion and Ethernet and token-ring interfaces. The latter two interfaces enable devices on an Ethernet or token-ring LAN to access a mainframe via the 3174, which then functions as a gateway.

The 3299 multiplexer is normally used to reduce the amount of cable required to connect terminals to a control unit when the distance between the location of the terminals and the control unit exceeds a few hundred feet. Up to eight terminals can be connected to a 3299, and only one cable is required to connect the 3299 to a control unit.

Newer terminals in the 3270 series include the 3179 color display station, the 3279G color graphics display station, the 3180 and 3191 monochrome display stations, and the 3192 and 3194 color display stations. The latter two are most notable for their design, which minimizes the desk space required compared to earlier terminals in the 3270 series.

In the area of personal computer connectivity to the 3270 series, IBM has introduced many products. The more significant products include a new control unit, as well as adapter cards that are installed into a system-expansion slot of a personal computer. The adapter card permits direct connection of the personal computer to a control unit, which enables the PC to function as a 3270 terminal. With this configuration, personal computer users can also transfer files and do local processing, both of which are beyond the capability of conventional 3270 terminals. As previously mentioned, the 3174 control unit features an optional Ethernet or token-ring gateway. This feature enables one member of the IBM PC series to be cabled to the 3174 as a gateway device on an Ethernet or token-ring local area network. Other personal computers are then connected to the gateway personal computer, enabling many personal computers to access the network via one personal computer.

In providing the PC interface, IBM found itself in an interesting quandary. The 3270 line was quite profitable over the years; now it faced competition from personal computers, especially those manufactured by IBM! As personal computing became the rule rather than the exception in most major corporations, the terminal industry found itself facing the biggest change since the introduction of the CRT.

The many other firms that offer 3270-compatible products must likewise compete with personal computers. To remain competitive, these companies have traditionally offered some combination of lower prices, improved performance, and shorter delivery times to penetrate the IBM "plug-compatible" market. In addition to the 3270-compatible vendors, some ASCII terminal manufacturers have invaded the 3270 market through protocol conversion. On a 3270 network, synchronous terminals can be replaced with asynchronous terminals coupled with "black boxes" that convert the asynchronous data to synchronous form with the proper headers, check bits, and so forth. These devices allow an ASCII terminal to support the functional characteristics of the 3270 terminal. The advantage of this strategy is that ASCII terminals are considerably less expensive than their 3270 counterparts.

The capability to support LAN connectivity considerably expanded the functionality of the 3174 control unit and extended the use of IBM's proprietary 3270 networking technology to include the support of standardized client/server networks. This, in turn, has enabled many organizations to continue to use their 3270 networks well into the new millennium.

Figure 2.7 illustrates in schematic format communications in a modern 3270 network, in which a 3174 control unit provides connectivity to a mainframe from computers connected to a LAN, as well as for individual terminals directly connected to the control unit. In many organizations, the 3270 terminals shown cabled directly to the 3174 control unit were replaced by personal computers with emulation boards during the late 1980s and early 1990s. The 3745 communications processor represents a specialized minicomputer designed to perform communications processing, offloading those functions from the mainframe computer so that its processing can be focused on executing application programs.

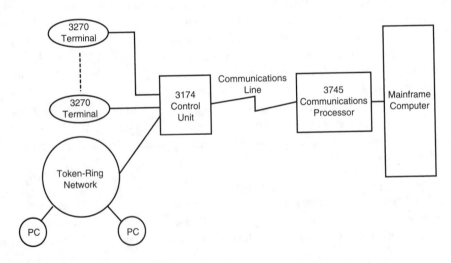

**FIGURE 2.7**

*Communications connectivity in a modern 3270 network.*

## Specialized Terminals

Most terminals manufactured today employ a keyboard and a CRT. The popularity of this combination stems from its flexibility, high character capacity, and relatively low cost. Specialized needs, however, led to the development of a broad range of other terminals, which include optical bar-code readers, voice-response units, portable terminals, and the ordinary tone-dialing telephone. In addition, such things as supermarket cash registers, portable communicating terminals for inventory management, and a host of other types of equipment now employ data communications. By the DTE/DCE definition, all of these are terminals.

## IBM's Support of TCP/IP

One interesting result of the explosion in the use of the Internet is the support of the TCP/IP protocol suite by IBM communications processors. This support allows any PC with a TCP/IP protocol stack, such as Windows 95 and Windows 98 systems, to use a 3270 terminal emulation program to directly access the mainframe via a LAN located on the same network as the mainframe or on a distant network. Due to the increased popularity of Windows-based PCs and the declining cost of terminal emulation software, it is probably safe to say that the days of the 3270 terminal are numbered.

# Parts of a Terminal

Now that you know the various types of terminals, you're ready to learn about the components of a typical CRT terminal. Note that the discussion is also applicable to the personal computer because that device represents an intelligent terminal. But first, you're going to read about one of the current buzzwords in the terminal business: ergonomics.

## Ergonomics

ANSI standards define ergonomics as "a multidisciplinary activity dealing with the interactions between man and his total working environment, plus such traditional environmental aspects as atmosphere, heat, light, and sound, as well as the tools and equipment of the workplace."

Terminal manufacturers have become increasingly aware of the need to consider ergonomics in the designs of their equipment. The trend toward making CRT terminals more "operator-friendly" began in Europe, and most people agree that European manufacturers still lead in this area. Such developments in terminals, such as sloped keyboards and green or amber displays, have come about because of ergonomic considerations.

## Keyboards

Most display terminals now have keyboards that are detached or detachable. Most of these are connected to the terminals console or, in the case of a personal computer, to the PC's system unit via a coiled cable. This type of cable is usually 3 to 6 feet long, which enables the operator to place the keyboard in a comfortable position while using the terminal. A recent development is the "light-link" or cordless keyboard, in which an infrared transmitter/receiver replaces the cable to allow even more freedom of movement.

Another design factor is the slope and thickness of the keyboard. Most keyboards today are either sloped or stepped, with the angle being 5[dg] to 15[dg]. Some terminals have sculptured key caps rather than flat key caps, which speeds data entry and improves operator comfort.

Audible keyboard feedback might be provided by a beep or key click from a speaker, and tactile feedback might be provided by a unique "feel" when the stroke is registered. Like many other ergonomic considerations, the previous features are not, in themselves, the most important criteria for choosing one terminal over another; what they do indicate is the manufacturer's commitment to providing equipment that is up-to-date and easy to use.

## Keyboard Layout

The layout of the keyboard is a primary concern of ergonomics. The de facto standard typewriter key layout is that of the IBM Selectric typewriter illustrated in Figure 2.8. A keyboard that has this arrangement of the alphabetic keys is called a QWERTY (pronounced "kwer-ty") keyboard because those are the first six letters of the top row of alphabetic keys. The QWERTY keyboard is far from the best layout. In fact, the QWERTY keyboard layout was designed for early mechanical typewriters to arrange the key hammers to reduce key hangups. This arrangement also slowed the typist so that he could not key faster than the early typewriters could operate! In the 1890s, more than a hundred different typewriter keyboards existed because almost every company that made a typewriter used a different keyboard. These keyboard types included the Crandall (ZPRCHMI), the American (CJPFUBL), the Hall (KBFG-NIA), and the Morris (XVGWSLZ).

Various attempts have been made to improve keyboard layout. Some had the letters of frequently used words close together. One proposed by Dr. August Dvorak put the five vowels under one hand and the five most common consonants under the other hand. There were circular keyboards, semicircular keyboards, keyboards with six rows, and keyboards with one long row. The idea of a Shift key didn't come along until 1875; before that, upper- and lowercase letters were on different keys.

Despite numerous attempts to improve keyboard layouts, the QWERTY keyboard remains the industry standard. In fact, a comparison of the IBM Selectric typewriter keyboard, a product introduced in the 1950s (illustrated in Figure 2.8), with the keyboard of the IBM PC Convertible, a product introduced in the 1980s (illustrated in Figure 2.9), indicates the high degree of similarity between keyboard layouts. The basic QWERTY keyboard structure remains the same some 30 years later, with keyboard changes related to the incorporation of computer operation–related keys on the PC Convertible keyboard. Those keys include the Alt, Ctrl, cursor position, function, Print Screen, and other specialized keys. As we enter the new millennium, the primary difference between personal computer keyboards relates to the position of the function keys (across the top of the keyboard or located in two columns on the left), the inclusion or absence of a numeric keypad, and the placement of cursor-positioning keys.

**FIGURE 2.8**
*The IBM Selectric typewriter keyboard layout.*

**FIGURE 2.9**
*The IBM PC Convertible portable computer keyboard layout. (Courtesy of IBM Corporation.)*

## Programmable Keyboards

You might be thinking that the operator has no choice but to adapt to the key positions because the keyboard is built in and the key arrangement is fixed. Ten years ago that was true, but now it's not always true. Alternative keyboard arrangements (including the Dvorak) are available from some manufacturers, either as standard equipment or as add-on devices for several terminals and computers. More important, many keyboards are programmable. The processor in the terminal considers each key depression simply as a contact closure in a matrix of contacts. The matrix location represented by that row and column is used by the processor to look up the character in the corresponding location in a table in memory. Thus, the keyboard layout can be changed by simply reprogramming the table; that is, the C key could be defined in the table so that a ? is printed rather than a C. The process of changing the assignments of keys on a personal computer is more formally referred to as keyboard remapping. This process facilitates the use of a personal computer as a specialized terminal device, such as a 3270 type terminal, which can have 20 or more additional keys beyond those on a PC keyboard. With the mapping of pairs of keys such as Shift+function keys to generate predefined codes, the 101 keys on a PC keyboard can be assigned values that correspond to 120 or more keys on a 3270 terminal keyboard.

## Numeric Keypads

Most terminals have some form of numeric keypad with the numerals 0 through 9 grouped like those on a 10-key adding machine to provide faster entry of numeric data. Other keys such as +, −, and . also might be included. The numeric keypad might be entirely separate from the main keyboard, or it might be implemented through an alternative definition of alphabetic keys (usually the "IOP" and "KL;" and "M,." groups). Using the main keyboard's number keys to enter numbers requires the use of both hands. Thus, number entry is faster with a numeric keypad because all the numerals are under the fingers of the right hand.

## Special Keys

In addition to the alphabetic and numeric keys, terminal keyboards offer various special keys that are unique to computer input. Unfortunately, there is no standard arrangement of these keys. These keys might include the following:

- The Ctrl (Control) key, which allows input of some or all of the ASCII control characters
- The Tab key (usually programmable)
- The Esc key
- The arrow keys that control cursor movement
- The programmable F (function) keys

Those users who think that the more keys, the merrier, should be very merry indeed because many terminals now have more than 100 keys. However, the keys are not always laid out in the most useful way. For example, the cursor arrow keys might be in a row instead of in a diamond pattern in which their direction can be felt. These additional keys might be packed closely around the regular keyboard or arranged in logical groups and slightly separated from the main keyboard. When keys have unusual or unexpected placement, the operator is likely to press them by mistake. The result can be devastating.

## Alternate Input Devices

Alternatives to keyboard input, which can make entry of specialized data easier, include light pens, touch-sensitive screens, graphics tablets, a mouse (a cursor-positioning device), and even speech input. Proponents of all of these devices (and more) suggest that they will eventually replace the keyboard for most input. Don't bet on it. Buy the most comfortable, best designed, easiest-to-use keyboard you can find; it and the display are your window into the computer. The other devices can be quite useful (especially the mouse), but most input will probably be through the keyboard for a long time to come.

# Display Considerations

There has been more discussion about CRT displays, including personal computer monitors, than about any other part of the terminal or PC. Some researchers have noted eyestrain, headaches, dizziness, back pains, nausea, and nervous symptoms in workers whose jobs require them to operate CRT terminals for long periods. Eyestrain and fatigue are considerations that designers must deal with when designing a CRT display screen. Most CRTs are etched or contain a bonded faceplate to reduce glare; tilt and swivel adjustments are also popular for the same reason. The swivel and tilt features also enable the operator to place the screen at the most comfortable viewing angle. The phosphor color and character size are important, too. White, green, or amber phosphors are generally used in the United States, with green probably being the most popular. The development of people-friendly terminal features is referred to collectively as ergonomics.

Most display terminals use the dot-matrix technique to form characters. The more dots that are contained in the character cell, the better defined the character will appear onscreen. For years, $5 \times 7$–dot characters were standard, but today, $7 \times 7$–, $7 \times 9$–, and $9 \times 11$–dot characters are more common. Some manufacturers use high screen-refresh rates and noninterlaced scanning to reduce image flicker and improve legibility. The size of the characters generated depends on the size of the screen and the display format used. Characters are larger on 15-inch screens than on 12-inch screens; likewise, characters are larger in an 80-character-per-line format than in a 132-character-per-line format. Display enhancements such as double-height and double-width characters can make characters larger, but these are intended for highlighting important data, not for routine use.

Most CRT terminals display 24 text lines with 80 characters each. Many also provide a 25th line, which is used for labels, status, or other terminal- or program-related information. The status line sometimes is displayed in reverse video.

## Memory-Mapped Displays

Most ASCII terminals use a technique called memory-mapped video. An advantage of the memory-mapped technique is that the microcomputer can write to and read from the video memory in the same way as ordinary memory because a portion of the ordinary memory is used for the video memory. The difference is that whatever characters are stored in video memory are displayed on the CRT when addressed by the microprocessor.

An 8-bit microprocessor uses 2 bytes (16 bits) for a memory address; thus, it can directly address $2^{16}$, or 65,536, memory locations. If each memory location can hold one character (which is the usual arrangement), and if the display size is 80 characters by 24 lines, then 1,920 character locations are needed in video memory. If the program memory is restricted to addresses below 63,615, memory locations from 63,615 through 65,535 could be used for video memory to store an array of characters for the display.

Assume that the upper-left corner of the CRT display receives the character from the first location (63,615) in video memory, the next horizontal position on the CRT receives the character from the second location (63,616), and so forth. Thus, if the first video memory location contains J, the second O, the third H, and the fourth N, the upper-left corner of the CRT displays JOHN.

Memory-mapped displays are fast and inexpensive. Because the character set is translated into dots within the dot-matrix using a table-lookup technique, it is also possible to redefine the character set by changing the table entries (if the table is user-accessible). Line insertion and deletion, scrolling, and other effects are easily accomplished by moving data around in video memory or, even simpler, by changing starting addresses. The principal disadvantage of memory-mapped video of the type described is that it takes up space in the memory used to store programs and data. This usually is not a problem for terminals, but, for computers, video memory is now usually separate. Also, computer video memory now is often bit-mapped rather than character-mapped, as discussed in the preceding paragraphs. With bit-mapping, each dot on the screen has a separate memory location. This feature allows high-resolution graphics displays, but it requires much more video memory.

## Other Types of Displays

Although the CRT is the dominant display device today, there are other devices for displaying information. These include solid-state devices such as light-emitting diodes, liquid crystal displays, and plasma (gas discharge) matrices such as those used in the IBM 3290. These alternative types of displays provide extremely sharp images, but the dominance of the CRT remains unchallenged for now due to lower cost.

2

# PC Terminals

The growth in the use of personal computers resulted in its adoption as a standard terminal device by many organizations. Some organizations, including several airlines, purchased tens of thousands of IBM PC and compatible personal computers for use with their online reservation systems during the 1980s. Other organizations use personal computers for both terminal emulation and local processing functions and have PCs coexisting with conventional terminals. Still other organizations connect personal computers to a local area network through the installation of an appropriate adapter card and the cabling of the adapter card to a network cable. This type of connection makes the personal computer function as a workstation terminal device on the LAN. Regardless of the application or utilization, the processing capability of the personal computer can be used with appropriate hardware and software to provide terminal capabilities not available through the use of conventional terminals.

Figure 2.10 shows an IBM PS/2 Model 30 computer with keyboard and graphics monitor. This computer is similar to other members of the PS/2 family, in that it contains a built-in serial port. The connector for this port, which is located at the rear of the computer, can be cabled to a modem. When appropriate communications software is loaded into the computer, it can then function as an asynchronous terminal.

**FIGURE 2.10**

*The IBM Personal System/2 Model 30 computer.*

# PC Adapter Cards

By inserting different types of adapter cards into expansion slots within the system unit of a personal computer, you can alter the functionality and capability of the computer. For example, the addition of an internal fax/data modem enables the computer user to transmit and receive both text and fax messages.

For synchronous transmission, IBM and third-party vendors manufacture various adapter cards that can be installed in system expansion slots in the system unit of that computer. Some adapter cards enable the personal computer to be attached directly to IBM 3174 or 3274 control units. When terminal emulation software is loaded, the computer functions as a 3278- or 3279-type terminal, providing the user with full-screen access to mainframe computer applications. Other hardware adapter cards can be used to provide the personal computer with batch terminal emulation capability to enable it to emulate various IBM and non-IBM remote job-entry devices.

Although the type of adapter card inserted into the expansion slot of a personal computer governs its functionality and capability, note also that most PCs can support the installation and operation of multiple types of adapter cards. In fact, many modern operating environments, such as Microsoft Windows, UNIX, Linux, and IBM's OS/2, enable you to switch easily between application programs that use different adapter cards. For example, you could first send a message to another user on the LAN through the use of an electronic mail program that communicates with the network by using a LAN adapter card. You then could switch to the use of a communications program that transmits data to a distant bulletin board through an internal modem card. Perhaps the most important thing to note concerning the use of communications adapter cards is that their use turns the personal computer into a multipurpose terminal. That is, with appropriate hardware and software, the PC can function as a LAN workstation, emulate a specific type of vendor terminal, function as a remote batch terminal, or perform other communications-related activities.

## LAN Adapter Cards

Perhaps the most popular type of communications adapter card used in a business environment is a LAN adapter card. Figure 2.11 depicts four members of the 3Com Fast EtherLink family of LAN adapter cards. Each of the LAN adapters shown in Figure 2.11 can operate at either 10 or 100Mbps and includes an autonegotiation capability that lets the adapter sense the speed of the network and adjust to that speed without human intervention. The major difference between members of the 3Com Fast Ethernet family shown in Figure 2.11 concerns the PC bus structure that they are manufactured to support. One adapter is designed for use in the Industry Standard Architecture (ISA) 16-bit bus, another supports the 32-bit Extended Industry Standard Architecture (EISA) bus, and others support the more modern Personal Computer Interface (PCI) bus, which offers the highest data-transfer rate between a LAN and a PC. The use of a

PCI LAN adapter is now considered essential for network servers that must sustain high data-transfer rates.

**FIGURE 2.11**
*The 3Com Fast Etherlink family of LAN adapter cards can be used to connect to either a 10 or 100Mbps Ethernet LAN.*

# The Need for Speed

As computer applications became more graphic-intensive, the 100Mbps data-transfer capability of Fast Ethernet became a bottleneck on certain LANs, such as those operated by large organizations with hundreds to thousands of employees. The need for speed resulted in the development of Gigabit Ethernet, which provides a data-transfer capability of 1Gbps, or 10 times that of Fast Ethernet's 100Mbps.

Because the migration of the operating rate of a LAN can represent a process that occurs over a period of time, not all devices may be upgraded at the same time. In a LAN switching environment, it is common practice to first upgrade servers to Gigabit Ethernet as they commonly represent the most heavily accessed device on a network. However, even servers may not be upgraded all at once. To provide LAN administrators with a degree of flexibility, some LAN adapter card vendors manufacture Ethernet cards that support 10, 100, and 1000Mbps operating rates. One such card is the Hewlett-Packard 1000Base-T LAN adapter shown in Figure 2.12. Note that the light-emitting diodes (LEDs) illuminate to indicate the operating rate of the LAN adapter.

**FIGURE 2.12**

*The Hewlett-Packard 1000Base-T LAN adapter card can operate at 10Mbps, 100Mbps or 1Gbps. (Used by permission of Hewlett-Packard Company, Palo Alto, CA © 2001.)*

## Modem Cards

By the mid-1990s, the use of laptops, notebooks, palmtops, and PDAs provided tens of millions of people the ability to exchange electronic mail, access the corporate mainframe, check the price of stocks or bonds, determine the availability of a product, compose memoranda, and perform different types of computer operations regardless of their location. Although the miniaturization of computer hardware was important in providing this capability, equally important were advances in modem technology that reduced the size of the modem to that of a credit card.

Figure 2.13 shows the Courier PC Card from U.S. Robotics, which provides an operating rate of 28,800bps for data transfer, as well as a fax transmission and reception capability. This modem is designed as a Type II PC Card, which can be inserted into a PC Card slot built into most modern portable personal computers. Although a data rate of 28,800bps was state-of-the-art just a few years ago, by the year 2000, a V.90 modem permitted data transfer to occur at 33.600bps upstream and 44,400bps downstream. Here the term upstream denotes a data transfer in the direction from a PC to a network, while the term downstream indicates a data transfer flowing from a network toward a PC. In 2001, a V.92 modem became available that enabled data transfer in each direction at 4400bps under certain conditions. In Chapter 5, "Synchronous Modems, Digital Transmission, and Service Units," we will examine the operation and utilization of analog modems.

The combination of portable computers with modem PC cards and cellular telephones give people on the go unlimited means of communication. Advances in computer and communications technology has truly revolutionized the manner in which many people live and work. For many people, the ability to communicate on the go enables them to have a virtual office without walls; for other people, such as students, it provides the convenience of being able to work at their own pace without having to get up early on the weekend to gain access to the university computer.

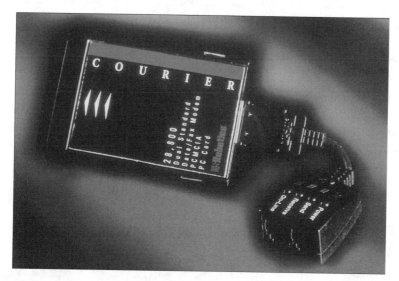

**FIGURE 2.13**
*The U.S. Robotics Courier PC Card modem. (Courtesy of U.S. Robotics.)*

## Advantages of a PC as a Terminal

The use of a personal computer as a terminal enables hardware and software manufacturers to take advantage of the processing capability of the computer to provide additional capabilities. For example, by using a portion of the memory of the computer for temporary printer data storage, the personal computer can be programmed to accept a mixed data stream of video and printer destination data. This enables the personal computer operator to maintain interactive transmission with a mainframe computer while a print job is routed to the PC, stored in memory, and dumped from memory to the printer.

Additional advantages in using personal computers as terminals include the expandability and upgradeability of PCs. For example, additional memory can easily be added to most personal computers. Concerning upgradeability, many personal computers get their display capability from the use of display adapters in a system expansion slot in the computer's system board. When a new video standard gains acceptance, the existing video display adapters in most personal computers can be removed, and new adapters that support the new standard can be installed. If video support was acquired from the use of a chip set installed on the system board, the installation of a video display adapter normally overrides the chip set, enabling the personal computer to support the new video standard.

## The Ubiquitous Terminal

Rapid advances in the development of personal computer hardware and software, coupled with the evolution of communications technology, caused the PC to become a ubiquitous terminal. In actuality, there is no standard PC because the personal computer includes desktop systems, laptops, notebooks, palmtops, and PDAs. Each of these is based on the use of a microprocessor and software that enables the computer to perform different types of processing, including the capability to communicate with other computers.

As you can see in Figure 2.14, a Windows 2000 screen display on a notebook computer could also represent the display on other types of computers. Windows 2000 includes support for multitasking operations, which enables users of this operating system to perform several tasks at one time.

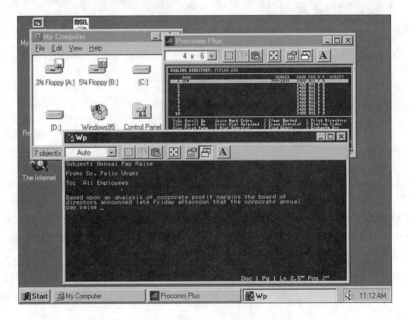

FIGURE 2.14

*The Windows 2000 desktop after three tasks were initiated.*

In Figure 2.14, three tasks are being performed, and each is represented by an open window. In the largest window, which is labeled Microsoft Word and represents a foreground operation, a word-processing program is being used to type an article. In the background window in the upper-left corner of the display, Microsoft's Excel spreadsheet program is operating. The window in the lower-left corner of the display provides the user with the ability to use the command prompt to access information. By simply clicking on a window or a window label at the bottom of the screen, the user can switch between windows. Although a user can operate in only one window at a time, the user can invoke an operation in one window, such as a file transfer, and then switch to a second window and continue writing a memorandum. Several versions of Windows from Microsoft Corporation, including Windows 95, 98, Millennium Edition (Me), and 2000, as well as and SUN Microsystems Solaris version of UNIX, represent two multitasking operating systems that enable computer users to enhance their productivity by eliminating the need to wait for one activity to terminate before performing another activity.

# Data Transmission

Terminals communicate with other devices (such as other terminals, computers, and peripheral devices) through data transmission. Data can be transmitted by two methods: serial transmission and parallel transmission.

## Serial and Parallel Transmission

Data is commonly transferred between computers and terminals by changes in the current or voltage on a wire or channel. Such transfers are called parallel if a group of bits moves over several lines at the same time, or serial if the bits move one by one over a single line. Figure 2.15 illustrates parallel and serial data transmission.

In parallel transmission, each bit of a character travels on its own wire. A signal, called the strobe or clock, on an additional wire indicates to the receiver when all the bits are present on their respective wires so that the values can be sampled. Computers and other digital systems that are located near one another (within a few feet) normally use parallel transmission because it is much faster. As the distance between equipment increases, not only do the multiple wires become more costly, but the difficulty of transmitting and receiving pulse signals on long wires increases.

Serial transmission is used for transmission over long distances. The conversion from parallel to serial and vice versa is accomplished with shift registers. Transmission of serial data is called synchronous if the exact sending or receiving time of each bit is determined before it is transmitted or received. It is called asynchronous if the timing of the bits in a character is not determined by the timing of a previous character.

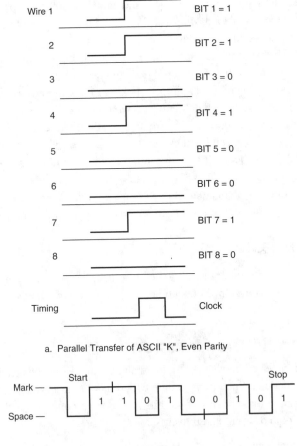

a.  Parallel Transfer of ASCII "K", Even Parity

b.  Serial Transfer of ASCII "K", Even Parity

**FIGURE 2.15**

*Parallel and serial data transfer.*

## Timing

Bit timing is critical to the accurate transmission and reception of data. One of the fundamental problems of data communications involves clock rates. Although both the sender and the receiver use the same nominal clock rate, the receiver must somehow determine a more exact clock for decoding the data. Figure 2.16 shows a series of bits transmitted serially over a line. In Figure 2.16a, the receiver retimes its clock on the negative-going edge of the transition (change) from 1 to 0 of the start bit and then uses its new timing to find the middle of the start bit. Notice in Figure 2.16b that although the receiver clock is slightly fast, it doesn't cause an error because the sample strobe still occurs within each bit time.

Figure 2.16c shows a different situation. Here, the receive clock is so much slower than the transmit clock that the sample strobe does not sample bit 4 at all; thus, an error occurs in the output. The communications system must somehow ensure that the receive clock is timed so that errors do not occur. Although bit timing is very important, it alone isn't enough to complete the communications process.

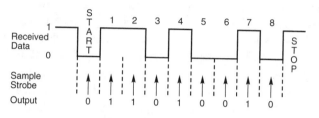

a. Ideal Sampling at Midpoint of Each Bit

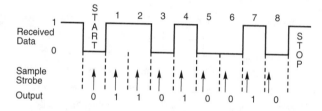

b. Sampling When Received Clock Is Slightly Fast

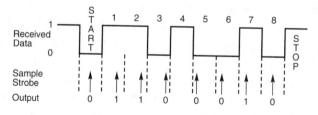

c. Sampling When Received Clock Is Too Slow

**FIGURE 2.16**

*Clocking asynchronous data.*

## Framing

Framing is the next step in timing after bit timing. The framing method used in asynchronous transmission defines a character by using start and stop bits to separate it from other characters. In the example of Figure 2.16, it could be called character timing because the start and stop bits frame one character for the receiver. This is the framing used in asynchronous data transmission, which is discussed in association with teleprinter operation in the next section. Synchronous data communications systems use different methods of framing, which are discussed in Chapter 5.

## Asynchronous Transmission

Asynchronous communications systems evolved before electronic systems. Therefore, electromechanical systems had to be used. The problem in those systems was the synchronization of the operation of two electromechanical devices (motors), one at each end of the line, whose speeds could not be easily adjusted. The timing and framing problem was solved by resuming each character using the edge of the start bit, which was required to be the first bit on the line. Nevertheless, if the difference in motor speeds was too great, the bit timing would drift with each successive bit until the sampling of the last received data bit in the character could be incorrect. Thus, 5 bits became the standard for the low-speed teleprinter code because the chance of error increased significantly if more bits were used.

Imagine an operator keying a teleprinter keyboard to produce characters for transmission. The framed character generated by each key depression begins with a start bit and ends with 1 or 1 stop bits. The stop condition is a mark or positive voltage on the line (negative voltage with double-current signaling). The positive voltage remains on the line until the next character starts because the line idle condition is internally defined as current flow or mark rather than no current or space. When a space (start bit) is detected, the receiving device starts, and it will be in synchronization with the transmitting device.

### Electromechanical Method

Electromechanical transmission uses current pulses to select the character to be printed through the synchronized receiver contacts. Figure 2.17 illustrates the operation of an electromechanical start-stop teleprinter machine. The sending device and the receiving device both have an armature, A, which rotates at a constant speed when a clutch connects it to an electric motor in the machine. Contacts on the armature connect an outer ring of contacts, B, to the transmission line. In the diagram, the armature is in its stop position. Current from the battery in the sender flows through the contact labeled STOP, through the armature, and through the line to the receiver. This current causes the receive relay to remain energized, keeping the clutch disengaged, the armature stationary, and the teleprinter in the idle condition.

Now suppose that an operator at the sending device presses the H key on the keyboard. In accordance with the 5-bit code shown back in Figure 1.4, data contacts 3 and 5 close to encode the H, and the start contact at the sending machine closes. This action energizes the start magnet to engage the clutch to turn the armature of the sending device counterclockwise. The armature connects the contacts on the outer ring to the line in sequence: start, 1, 2, 3, 4, 5, stop. Notice that the start contact and data contacts 1, 2, and 4 do not conduct current.

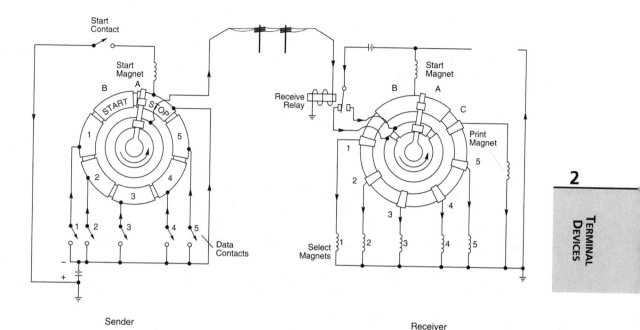

**FIGURE 2.17**

*Electromechanical start-stop coding and decoding.*

As soon as the armature of the sender travels to its start contact, the current through the line and the receive relay ceases. The receive relay is de-energized, and current flows through the other set of relay contacts and through the start magnet of the receiver. This action engages the clutch, and the receiver armature begins turning counterclockwise at approximately the same speed as the sender armature. When the sender armature is over data contact 3, current flows through the line and the receive relay. The receive relay is energized, and as the armature of the receiver passes over data contact 3 on the outer ring, current flows through select magnet 3.

Select magnet 5 is operated similarly. The operation of these two magnets causes the letter H to be selected on the type mechanism of the receiver. When the sender armature reaches its stop contact, the receiver armature passes over contact C, current flows to the print magnet, and the letter H is printed. Both armatures then come to rest in the position shown in the illustration, unless the sender is ready to transmit another character immediately.

Note that the start and stop elements have those exact functions; that is, they start and stop the armature rotation. As you can visualize, if there were much variation in the rotational speeds of the sending and receiving armatures, the armatures would not be in synchronization, and the character would be decoded incorrectly. As discussed previously, this is one reason why the Baudot code was limited to five symbols.

With start-stop transmission, a new character can begin at any time after the stop bits of the preceding character have been received. The time between one character and the next is indeterminate, but within a character, the timing is precisely defined. For that reason, it might be better to call this technique self-synchronized or internally synchronized, rather than asynchronous, meaning "not synchronized." (The lack of a continuous synchronous agreement between the transmitter and the receiver—specifically, the lack of a clocking signal within or accompanying the data channel—is the reason for the name "asynchronous.")

### Electronic Receiving Circuit

The electromechanical arrangements of the early teleprinters were replaced with electronic circuits. Because these can be synchronized within closer tolerances, an 8-bit code can be used. An electronic circuit for receiving asynchronous serial data in an 8-bit code is shown in Figure 2.18. It utilizes a clock that runs at 16 times the symbol rate of the incoming data. This rapid rate is used to detect the 1 to 0 transition (when the start bit begins) as soon as possible after it occurs. The circuit that detects the 1 to 0 transition enables a spike-detection circuit. Eight "ticks" of the 16X clock (one-half a bit time) are counted, and then the line is checked to see whether it is still in the 0 state. If it is not, it is assumed that the initial 1 to 0 transition was due to noise on the line, the spike-detection circuit is reset, and no further action is taken.

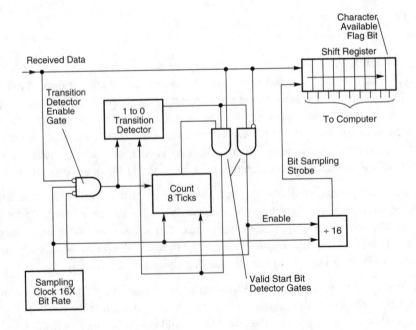

**FIGURE 2.18**

*An asynchronous receiver.*

If the line is still at 0, a valid start signal has arrived. A counter is enabled that divides the 16X clock by 16 to produce a sampling clock that ticks once per bit time for the shift register. This tick occurs roughly at the center of the bit being sampled. The off-center error can be made smaller by sampling at 32 times the bit rate, and can be even further reduced by sampling at 64 times the bit rate. However, when higher sampling rates are used, the counter in the spike-detection circuit and the counter in the bit-sampler circuit must count proportionately higher.

The bit-sampler circuit strobes the shift register eight times to sample the state of the line to get the 8 bits into the serial-to-parallel shift register. Then a signal, called a flag, is sent to the computer or controller with which it is associated to announce that a character has been received. The computer then signals the shift register to transfer the 8 bits in parallel into the processing circuits.

A problem with using only a shift register (called a single-buffered interface) is that when characters are arriving continuously, the computer has only the duration of the stop bit to read the received character before the next character begins entering the register. A simple improvement is to provide a holding register into which the received character can be parallel transferred as soon as the eighth bit has been sampled. A character-available flag is sent to the computer when the parallel transfer occurs, and the receiving register becomes available for the next character. This arrangement, called a double-buffered interface, is shown in Figure 2.19. In either case, the arrival of a character that cannot be handled because the preceding character has not been read is called data overflow. If overflow occurs, most receiver circuits overwrite the old character with the new one (the old one is lost) and place an error signal on a separate lead to the computer.

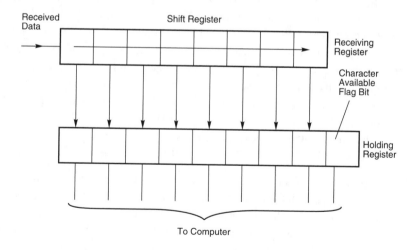

**FIGURE 2.19**

*A double-buffered interface.*

## Stop Bits and Timing Errors

With a double-buffered interface, the stop bit arrival time is no longer the only time available to the computer for reading the character, so there is time for circuitry to check the stop bit (sometimes called the ninth bit) to confirm that it is a 1. If it is not a 1, one of the following conditions exists: The communications channel path is broken, the receiver timing is confused, or the transmitting station is sending a special signal. The existence of one of these conditions typically provides an error signal on a lead in the asynchronous receiver.

Such an error occurs when the receiver has lost track of which zeros in the transmission are the start bits and which are just zeros in the data. If, for some reason, the receiver treats a data bit as a start bit, it assembles the next 8 bits as a character. Because these 8 bits are really parts of two characters (the end of one and the beginning of another), the ninth bit to arrive will not be the stop bit, but rather a data bit from the second character. If it is a 0, the error-checking circuit detects an error. Because framing is the process of deciding which groups of 8 bits constitute characters, and because this error is due to a failure in that process, it is called a framing error.

Failure in the framing process generally can be avoided. The idle line condition is a mark condition, and any amount of idle time more than a character time corrects this condition. Even if characters are sent continuously, the receiver eventually becomes realigned to the correct start elements, no matter which 0 bit is chosen as the start bit. Of course, the characters received while the framing is not in alignment are decoded incorrectly.

## The UART

The electronic circuitry previously described has been reduced through the use of very large-scale integrated circuitry onto a communications chip referred to as a UART (Universal Asynchronous Receiver Transmitter). A UART in its transmit mode converts the bits received in parallel, which represent a character within a computer, into a serial data stream and then transfers each bit onto the serial interface at an appropriate time. In addition, the UART frames the character to include the addition of start and stop bits and optionally adds a parity bit before transmitting the bits in a serial sequence. When in its receive mode, the UART samples the line for incoming bits; forms a stream of bits into a character after removing the start, stop, and parity bits; and transfers the received character to the computer. The use of a parity bit for error detection is covered in Chapter 8, "Protocols and Error Control."

Through the use of UARTs, which are no bigger than a thumbnail, it became possible to provide every type of personal computer, ranging in size from a desktop to a personal digital assistant, with a serial port. The UART normally is included on the motherboard of modern computers and is connected to the physical connector that represents the interface to the serial port. Although most readers are probably familiar with 9- and 25-pin connectors labeled "serial port" on many computers, a UART inside the computer performs the actual work in which parallel data inside the computer is converted into a serial bit sequence transmitted through the connector.

When the IBM PC was introduced in 1981, the computer's serial communications capability was obtained via the installation of a serial adapter card that included a National Semiconductor 8250 UART. That UART, which was used in motherboards of other computers during the 1980s and early 1990s, did not include an internal buffer. This limited its data-transfer capability to 19,200bps before data loss might occur. Today, most computers, as well as modems fabricated on adapter cards, use the more capable 16550 UART.

The UART contains a built-in 16-byte buffer that enables higher-speed data transfers before data loss might occur. The 16550 can support data transfers up to 115,200bps, which makes it suitable for transferring data to modern modems employing data compression and obtaining an average compression ratio of 4:1. Because many personal computers manufactured through the mid-1990s include the 8250 UART, that chip should be replaced if you want to effectively use high-speed modems with those computers. Fortunately, the more capable 16550 UART will fit into the socket used by the 8250, which can be easily removed if it is not soldered into the motherboard. As an alternative, the use of a modern modem fabricated on an adapter card for insertion into a computer will include a 16550 UART that supports the high-speed data transfer required to effectively use the modem.

## Other Types of Transmission

Asynchronous transmission is the most common in data communications simply because there are more terminals and small-computer applications in which it is used. Large systems and networks usually use methods other than asynchronous. This is because of the large overhead penalty of 20 percent associated with start-stop codes; that is, 2 (the start and stop bits) out of the 10 bits transmitted are for control rather than for information. This is not a problem in many other types of interactive applications, in which more time is spent looking at the screen than transferring a file of 500,000 characters (4 million bits) at 28,800 or 56,000bps.

A second problem in such large transfers is error checking. A file-transfer user originally had to check the input and output for errors by looking at the screen and rekeying or asking for retransmission of portions that contained errors. Such a procedure is clearly impractical for long file transfers that occur at fast rates and many times without an operator present. Although transmission protocols have been developed to provide error-free asynchronous transmission, the use of this type of communications is oriented for relatively short transmission requirements. Applications requiring large-volume, high-speed data transfers necessitate a different method of data transfer. This method is called synchronous transmission.

In synchronous transmission, start and stop bits are not used. Characters are sent in groups, called blocks, and special synchronization characters are placed at the beginning of the block and within it to ensure that enough 0-to-1 or 1-to-0 transitions occur for the receiver clock to remain accurate. Error checking is performed automatically on the entire block. If any errors occur, the entire block is retransmitted. This technique also carries an overhead penalty (nothing is free), but the overhead is far less than the 20 percent for blocks of more than a few dozen characters. Figure 2.20 compares asynchronous and synchronous transmission of a sequence of characters.

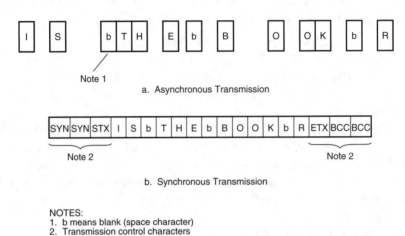

**FIGURE 2.20**

*A comparison of asynchronous and synchronous data transmission.*

In addition to the asynchronous and synchronous transmission methods of achieving receiver timing, a third method called isochronous transmission is now used in a few computer networks. It involves timing that is controlled by the network rather than the DCE or DTE, as is true for synchronous and asynchronous transmission. Chapter 5 covers synchronous and isochronous data transmission in detail.

# What You Have Learned

- Compared to CRT terminals, teleprinters are much slower at printing, have limited formatting capability, don't have enhancements such as blinking and highlighting, and are less reliable in operation.
- Teleprinters as well as modern terminal devices can be categorized as representing two-state binary communications systems.

- A serial or character printer prints one character at a time. The printer can be either an impact or a nonimpact printer. An impact printer can produce fully formed characters or characters formed by a dot matrix. A nonimpact printer usually uses a thermal, optical (laser), or inkjet method.

- CRT terminals can be classified as dumb, smart, and user-programmable. A dumb terminal is essentially the same as a teleprinter, except for printing speed. A smart terminal has capabilities such as editing, formatting, highlighting, and blinking. A user-programmable terminal has a built-in programming language and the capability to store and execute programs.

- As applied to terminals, ergonomics has to do with the color, character size, and nonglare surface of the display, and with the shape, position, and layout of the keys. It also is concerned with the physical position of both the display and the keyboard with respect to the operator.

- The communications functionality and capability of a personal computer is altered through the addition of different types of adapter cards and the use of appropriate software.

- In serial transmission, the bits are transmitted one at a time over a single wire. In parallel transmission, each bit of a group moves over its own wire, and all bits of the group move at the same time.

- Both bit timing and framing are necessary to maintain synchronization for proper decoding in data communications. Bit timing usually is accomplished by clocking the bits. Framing usually is accomplished by inserting special bits or characters in the data stream just for that purpose.

- In asynchronous transmission, each character is sent by itself and is framed by a start bit and a stop bit. This is the transmission method used by teleprinters and ASCII terminals.

- The UART receives data from a parallel format within a computer, frames the data by the addition of start and stop bits and an optional parity bit, and transmits the data 1 bit at a time serially.

- In synchronous transmission, many characters are sent together in groups called blocks. Each block is framed by special synchronization characters.

# Quiz for Chapter 2

1. Teleprinters

    A. Are only for printing at remote locations, not for input.

    B. Offer both high-speed operation and various formatting controls.

    C. Have printers for output and might have keyboards for input.

2. Impact printers

    A. Strike a ribbon against the paper to produce character images.

    B. Include inkjet and thermal devices.

    C. Are rapidly becoming obsolete.

3. Glass Teletypes

    A. Are among the most recent developments in CRT terminals.

    B. Were so named because they had the same interface as teleprinters.

    C. Are teleprinters designed to interface with fiber-optic transmission systems.

4. Electromechanical teleprinters

    A. Use a complex mechanical buffer to match speed between transmitting and receiving machines.

    B. Use start and stop codes to synchronize sending and receiving equipment.

    C. Are rarely used today.

5. ASCII terminals are generally defined as

    A. Terminals using synchronous transmission in EBCDIC.

    B. Terminals using synchronous transmission in ASCII.

    C. Terminals using asynchronous transmission in ASCII.

    D. Terminals having an American (dollar-sign) keyboard.

6. Which of the following is a drawback associated with laptop and notebook computers?

    A. Pop-out keyboard.

    B. Screen viewing angle.

    C. Portability.

    D. Weight.

7. "3270" terminals refer to

    A. Asynchronous terminals made by IBM.

    B. All terminals that are painted blue.

    C. Synchronous terminals that interface with an IBM-type cluster controller.

8. The use of IBM's proprietary 3270 networking technology was extended by

    A. The standards committee.

    B. The use of mainframes.

    C. The addition of LAN connectivity.

    D. Graphics terminals.

9. A multipurpose terminal refers to

    A. A terminal with a serial port.

    B. A computer with both serial and parallel ports.

    C. A terminal with a UART.

    D. A computer to which communications functionality is added through the addition of hardware and software.

10. Which of the following describes the difference between timing and framing?

    A. Timing is concerned with the individual bits, whereas framing is concerned with the boundaries between characters.

    B. Timing refers to serial transmission, whereas framing refers to parallel transmission.

    C. Timing is concerned primarily with asynchronous systems, whereas framing is concerned with synchronous systems.

11. Escape codes are so called because

    A. In effect, they provide a means to temporarily "escape" from the standard meanings of the character set.

    B. They initiate operation of the escapement mechanism in teleprinters.

    C. They cause the cursor to escape from the boundaries of the CRT screen and roam around in memory.

12. The QWERTY keyboard

    A. Is still considered to be the layout allowing the greatest typing speed.

    B. Is the most popular keyboard but not necessarily the best.

    C. Is a keyboard layout that is rarely used.

13. Memory-mapped displays

    A. Are associated with electromechanical teleprinters.

    B. Have the advantage that they do not take up memory space.

    C. Allow direct addressing of display locations by the processor.

14. The major differences between personal computer keyboards are

    A. In the use of QWERTY versus other key layouts.

    B. In the use of the Shift key.

    C. In the position of function keys and the inclusion or omission of a numeric keypad.

    D. In the placement of the numeric keys on the keyboard.

15. Serial printers

    A. Are used to transmit grain prices.

    B. Are faster than CRT terminals and offer more flexibility.

    C. Print one character at a time.

    D. Usually use serial interfaces.

16. Nonimpact printers

    A. Are normally quieter than impact printers.

    B. Generate carbon copies easily.

    C. Produce fully formed characters.

17. CRT terminals

    A. Are the most widely used hard-copy terminals.

    B. Offer high-speed display and formatting flexibility.

    C. Do not normally use microprocessors.

18. User-programmable terminals

    A. Are replacing personal and professional computers.

    B. Offer more flexibility at lower cost.

    C. Are being replaced by personal and professional computers.

19. A multitasking operating system enables

    A. Several windows to be displayed.

    B. Communications between computers.

    C. The use of the UART.

    D. Several tasks to be performed at the same time.

20. Ergonomics

    A. Involves the interface between people and machines, such as terminals.

    B. Is the application of ergo-economics to communications.

    C. Utilizes three-level ergo-coding for transmission over certain channels.

21. Serial and parallel transmission

    A. Differ in how many bits are transferred per character.

    B. Are used in synchronous and asynchronous systems, respectively.

    C. Differ in whether the bits are on separate wires or all on one wire.

22. Memory-mapped displays

    A. Are used for high-resolution graphics, such as maps.

    B. Use ordinary memory to store the display data in character form.

    C. Store the display data as individual bits.

23. Asynchronous transmission

    A. Is less efficient but simpler than synchronous transmission.

    B. Is much faster than synchronous transmission.

    C. Is another name for isochronous transmission.

24. Single-buffering

    A. Is more efficient than double-buffering.

    B. Is less efficient than no buffering.

    C. Provides very little time for unloading the incoming character from the register.

25. Most terminal keyboards

    A. Provide numerous additional specialized keys.

    B. Are strictly typewriter style, with few extra keys.

    C. Use the Dvorak layout.

# Messages and Transmission Channels

## IN THIS CHAPTER

Messages represent information useful to people, but the sender and receiver might or might not be human. The medium must be suitable to convey the type of message. In this chapter, you will examine in more detail the types of messages and the media that carry them. Concerning the latter, you will also examine impairments that affect the data-transfer capability of different media and why certain types of media have a higher data-transfer capacity than other types of media.

Useful communication requires four elements, as shown in Figure 3.1:

1. A message (information) to be communicated

2. A sender of the message

3. A medium or channel over which the message can be sent

4. A receiver

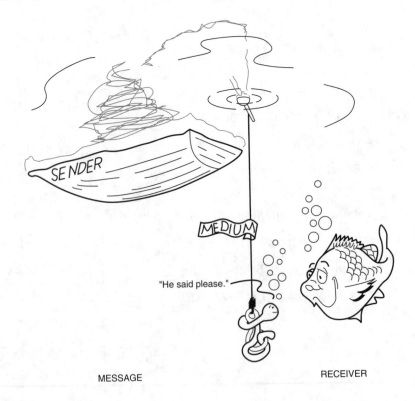

MESSAGE                                                    RECEIVER

**FIGURE 3.1**

*The elements of communication.*

# Information as a Quantity

Information can be defined as "a numerical quantity that measures the uncertainty in the outcome of an experiment to be performed." This definition has an application in the sending of messages. For example, suppose you have a machine that can send only two symbols: A1 and A2. You can then say that the "experiment" is the accurate recognition of the two symbols (A1 and A2) being sent from one machine to another. As far as the receiving machine is concerned, it is just as likely to receive one symbol as the other. So, you can say that the "numerical quantity" in this experiment is a unit of information that allows a selection between two equally likely choices. This quantity, or unit of information, is usually called a bit (a contraction of the terms "binary digit"), and it has two possible values, 0 and 1. If these two values are used to represent A1 and A2, A1 could be represented by the bit value 0, and A2 could be represented by the bit value 1. The number of bits per symbol is 1, but you still need a way of selecting which symbol (bit) you want to use. A machine that needs only two symbols needs only a 1-bit select code (0 and 1).

A machine that uses only two symbols is not of much use for communication, but suppose the machine could use 128 symbols (like the standard ASCII character set). Then the number of equally likely choices to be handled would be 128, and the number of bits (information) required to represent each of those 128 symbols would be seven (refer to Table 1.1 in Chapter 1, "An Overview of Data Communications"). You can see, then, that if the knowledge (or intelligence) to be communicated can be represented by a set of equally likely symbols, the amount of information required per symbol to communicate that knowledge is necessarily dependent on the total number of bits of information.

The standard ASCII character set is particularly useful for selecting the information to be communicated because it can select 1 of 128 ASCII symbols with only one 8-bit byte, a common bit grouping in computers (the eighth bit is not used in this case). The extended ASCII character set that uses all 8 bits per byte supports 256 symbols, doubling the number of ASCII symbols.

## Information Content of Symbols

In many information systems, not every symbol is equally likely to be used in a given communication. The English language is a good example. In a message written in English, the letter *e* is 12 times more likely to occur than the letter *s*. This uneven distribution is also characteristic of particular groups of letters and of words. This means that each of the 128 symbols in ASCII (or 256 symbols in extended ASCII) is not likely to occur an equal number of times in any given communication. For example, notice that the uses of the letters *e* and *g* and the letter combinations *th* and *er* are unequal in this paragraph.

In 1949, Claude Shannon published a book entitled *The Mathematical Theory of Communication*. In this book, he discussed the uncertainty or amount of disorder of a system, which he called entropy. Entropy can also be considered as a measure of randomness, and, as you will shortly note, it has a significant role in communications, both for verification of the accurate arrival of messages and as a mechanism for reducing the physical size of messages while retaining their meaning.

The entropy of a set of equally likely symbols (such as the digits 0–9 in a table of random numbers) is the logarithm to the base 2 of the number of symbols in the set. The entropy of the English alphabet, which contains 26 letters and a space, is then $\log_2(27) = 4.76$ bits per symbol. Because of the uneven use of letters in the English language, however, its entropy was estimated by Shannon as 1.3 bits per symbol.

Because the probability of occurrence of each character in the English alphabet differs, entropy of the alphabet is calculated as follows:

$$H = -(P_1\log_2 P_1 + P_2\log_2 P_2 + \ldots + P_i\log_2 P_i + \ldots + P_{26}\log_2 P_{26})$$

Here, $P_i$ is the probability of occurrence of the *i*th character in the English alphabet. Note that the symbol H is used by mathematicians to represent entropy. The preceding calculation can be simplified as follows for any code or language:

$$H = \sum_{i=1}^{n} P_i{}^1\log^2 P^1$$

Here, *n* represents *n* possible distinct characters or symbols in a language or code.

When entropy was computed for the English language, Shannon discovered that the language is about 70 percent redundant and that it should be possible to reconstruct English text accurately if every other letter is lost or changed due to noise or distortion. Obviously, redundancy is desirable to raise the chances of receiving a good message when the medium is noisy. (The words *noise* and *noisy* in this book refer to electrical noise—that is, an electrical signal that is not supposed to be present.)

## Using Redundancy in Communications

So, you wonder, what does all this have to do with the real world of data communications? Quite a bit, because almost every scheme in current use for sending data uses redundancy in an attempt to verify that the data has been received exactly as sent (that is, no errors have been introduced by the sending mechanism, the transmission medium, or the receiver). The redundant information might consist simply of a retransmission of the entire original message.

Although it's simple to implement, retransmission is not efficient. Special techniques are therefore used to generate redundant information that is related to the message in a way that is known to both the sender and the receiver. The sender generates the redundant information during transmission and sends it with the message. The receiver regenerates and checks the redundant information when the message is received. This scheme is represented in Figure 3.2. Verification usually occurs at the end of each link in the chain making up the transmission path. The details of this process and various methods in current use are described in Chapter 10, "WAN Architectures and Packet Networks."

## Using Redundancy for Data Compression

A second area where entropy plays a considerable role is as a foundation for data compression. Because the entropy of an alphabet indicates the average number of bits per symbol, this information provides software and hardware developers with a goal for implementing various data-compression schemes.

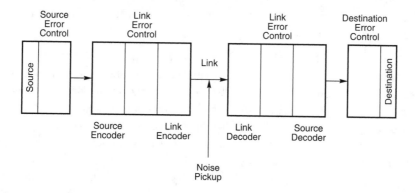

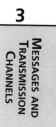

3

MESSAGES AND
TRANSMISSION
CHANNELS

FIGURE 3.2

*Error-checking points.*

For example, if the uneven use (different probabilities) of the letters in the English alphabet results in an entropy of 1.3 bits per symbol, why use an 8-bit byte to transmit each character? This tells software and hardware designers that by compressing data and temporarily removing redundancies via the use of one or more algorithms prior to transmission, larger quantities of data can be transmitted per unit time. Recognizing the value of entropy, almost all modems today include a built-in data-compression mechanism.

96

# Bounded Medium

The physical channels (the media) that carry data are of two types: bounded and unbounded. In a bounded medium, the signals are confined to the medium and do not leave it (except for smaller leakage amounts). A pair of wires, coaxial cable, waveguide, and optical-fiber cable are examples of bounded media.

## Wire Pairs

The simplest type of a bounded medium is a pair of wires providing go and return paths for electrical signals. Early telegraph systems used the Earth itself rather than a wire for one of the paths, as shown in Figure 3.3a. Repeaters were inserted along the line to reduce the effects of noise and attenuation (loss of signal strength). This scheme did not work well, however, because the Earth is not always a good conductor, and the path was susceptible to large noise currents induced by lightning. Losses were reduced by using two wires, as shown in Figure 3.3b, but because the line was still unbalanced to ground, it was subject to noise from almost every noise-producing device. Finally, the balanced two-wire line, shown in Figure 3.3c, was used to greatly reduce noise pickup.

The most common type of bounded medium consists of wire pairs twisted together and made into cables of from 4 to 3,000 pairs. Because a wire acts as an antenna, several techniques are used to reduce electromagnetic interference (EMI). Most wires are shielded, and some wires are also twisted at 90° angles every so often. The twists additionally suppress EMI. The size of the wire used varies from 16 AWG (American Wire Gauge) with a wire diameter of 0.05082 inch to 26 AWG with a diameter of 0.01594 inch. AWG wire sizes are inversely proportional to the diameter of the wire. That is, the lower the AWG is, the thicker the wire is, whereas a higher AWG indicates a thinner wire. In modern cables, each wire is insulated with a polyethylene or polyvinyl chloride (PVC) jacket; however, a large quantity of older cable is still in use in which the insulation for each wire is paper.

Table 3.1 provides a representative comparison of the characteristics of AWG cables from gauge number 10 through 26 in even increments. Note that, as you might expect, the resistance in ohms per kilometer increases. This is because the cable diameter is inversely proportional to the gauge number. Hence, the wire becomes smaller, which makes it more difficult for electrons to flow, and it can be viewed similar to the effect of different diameters of hoses on the flow of water.

Open-wire lines have a low attenuation of voice frequencies due to the large size of the wire and the relatively large distance between the two wires when mounted on the crossarm of a utility pole. A typical value of attenuation for 104-mil (0.104 inch) diameter open wire lines is 0.07 decibel (dB) per mile, whereas 19-gauge (0.03589-inch diameter) twisted-wire pairs in a multipair cable have a voice frequency attenuation of about 1dB per mile.

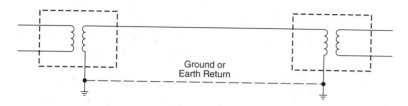

a. Single-Wire Unbalanced to Ground

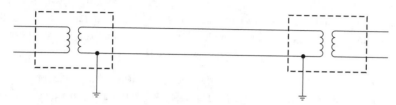

b. Two-Wire Unbalanced to Ground

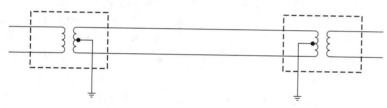

c. Two-Wire Balanced to Ground

**FIGURE 3.3**

*Types of transmission circuits.*

3

MESSAGES AND
TRANSMISSION
CHANNELS

**TABLE 3.1** Representative American Wire Gauge (AWG) Characteristics

| AWG | Diameter (inches) | Diameter (millimeters) | Ohms/Gauge Number km |
|-----|-------------------|------------------------|----------------------|
| 10 | 0.101 | 2.588 | 3.3 |
| 12 | 0.080 | 2.053 | 5.2 |
| 14 | 0.064 | 1.628 | 8.3 |
| 16 | 0.050 | 1.291 | 13.2 |
| 18 | 0.040 | 1.024 | 20.9 |
| 20 | 0.031 | 0.811 | 33.3 |
| 22 | 0.025 | 0.643 | 53.0 |
| 24 | 0.022 | 0.573 | 84.2 |
| 26 | 0.016 | 0.404 | 133.9 |

The attenuation of twisted-wire pairs rises rapidly with increasing frequency, and the amount of crosstalk between adjacent pairs also increases with frequency. The maximum usable frequency for wire pairs in cables is around 1MHz without special treatment.

## The Effect of Inductance

A concept that might not be obvious about paired wire circuits is that the addition of inductance in the line can help reduce attenuation at voice frequencies. The line impedance (AC resistance) is increased so that a given amount of power can be transmitted with less current but at a higher voltage. The result is a reduction in the series losses and an increase in the shunt losses. Because the series losses are usually more severe, there is a net reduction in attenuation until the inductance rises to the point where series and shunt losses are equal.

Adding inductance to wire pairs is called loading, and a circuit to which inductance has been added is called a loaded line or loaded circuit. The effect of loading is illustrated in Figure 3.4. The typical frequency-versus-attenuation performance is shown for a nonloaded 19-gauge cable pair and a 19-gauge cable pair loaded with 88 millihenrys of inductance every 6000 feet. (The standard notation for this is 19H-88 loaded pair.) Figure 3.4 shows that the attenuation of the loaded circuit is less than that of the unloaded one and that it changes very little with increasing frequency, up to a certain point above 3KHz. This point is called the cutoff point or cutoff frequency.

Loading was introduced around 1900 on long-distance open-wire lines to reduce losses due to attenuation because there were no amplifiers for the signals.

## Electronic Amplifiers

When the use of the DeForest triode as an amplifier began in 1914, it was no longer necessary to load long-distance circuits because the losses in the line could be compensated for by amplification. However, loading is still used on longer local loops (from the telephone office to the customer) because it is cheaper than adding active components for amplification. The presence of loading on local circuits has a considerable effect on their capability to carry high-frequency data signals, which causes problems for some new types of telephone service.

In 1883, Thomas Edison discovered the rectifying properties of the thermionic vacuum tube. A thermionic vacuum tube is one in which a stream of electrons is emitted by an incandescent substance. Edison's device was a two-element tube (called a diode) consisting of a cathode (the incandescent substance) and an anode.

The principle of thermionic vacuum tubes lay unused, however, until 1904. At that time, Sir John Ambrose Fleming, an English physicist and engineer, adapted the diode for use as a demodulator (detector) of radiotelegraph signals for the Marconi Wireless Telegraph Co. In 1906, Lee DeForest introduced a third element, called a control grid, to the diode and created the triode. By 1912, the triode and its associated circuits were developed for use as an amplifier.

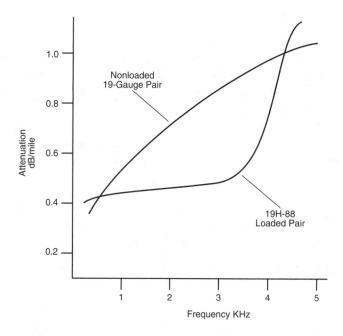

**FIGURE 3.4**

*Effect of inductance loading.*

## Twisted-Pair Wire

A special type of wire pair that deserves a degree of elaboration is twisted-pair wire. This type of wiring represents the vast majority of cabling used in the local loop from a telephone company central office to a subscriber, as well as in local area networks.

There are two general types of twisted-pair cable, shielded (STP) and unshielded (UTP). The former is a type of cable with a thin foil of lead wrapped around each pair to provide a degree of immunity to electromagnetic interference (EMI). When LANs were initially developed, STP cabling was primarily used; however, a large degree of twists in cable have the effect of canceling out electromagnetic interference. Because UTP is considerably less expensive than STP cabling, today the vast majority of LAN cabling is unshielded twisted-pair cabling. In comparison, because twisted-pair wire used for voice dates to the 18th century, telephone wire is unshielded.

In any communications system that will include twisted-pair cabling, the bit error rate depends upon the ability of a receiver to distinguish a signal from noise. The ratio of signal strength to noise is the well-known signal-to-noise ratio (S/N). In a twisted-pair cabling system, the S/N ratio is highly dependent upon near-end crosstalk (NEXT) and the attenuation of the cable.

## NEXT

Near-end crosstalk represents the electromagnetic coupling between a transmit pair and a receive pair. That is, as data is transmitted on one wire pair, a small portion of the transmitted signal flows onto the receive pair, interfering with the received signal. Because the transmit signal is strongest at its source, a majority of crosstalk will occur where a LAN adapter is connected to a cable via a modular jack, but it will decrease in intensity as the signal traverses the cable. This explains the term "near-end" in NEXT. In a voice environment, NEXT can adversely affect a conversation. This is because frayed wiring at the base of a handset will allow a portion of a conversation to "bleed" over to the wiring connected to the receiver in a handset.

Figure 3.5 illustrates how NEXT is generated. NEXT is defined mathematically as follows:

$$NEXT = 20 \log_{10} \frac{\text{Transmit voltage}}{\text{Coupled voltage}}$$

Here, the coupled voltage is the voltage flowing on the receive pair when a transmit signal is placed on the transmit pair.

### Attenuation

Attenuation on a twisted-pair cable is the same as on any medium: It represents the loss of signal power as a signal flows from transmitter to receiver.

Attenuation on twisted-pair is measured in decibels, as follows:

$$\text{Attenuation} = 20 \log_{10} \frac{\text{Transmit voltage}}{\text{Receive voltage}}$$

# Coaxial Cable

To make telephone service economical, more than one conversation had to be put on a channel. This problem drove the evolution of coaxial cables. Indeed, the invention of the telephone arose out of Alexander Bell's experiments on a "harmonic telegraph," an attempt to put more than one telegraph signal on a channel. Putting more conversations or more data on a single channel requires a larger bandwidth (capability to carry more frequencies), which, as a practical matter, means higher frequencies. Because the practical frequency limit for wire pairs is around 1MHz, some other method had to be developed.

Some significant and interesting effects occur in the vicinity of a wire carrying an alternating current signal. One of these effects is that both an electric field and a magnetic field are created around the conductor. The magnetic field can induce the signal that it is carrying into adjacent conductors. (In communications, the induced and unwanted signal is called crosstalk.) However, if one conductor of the pair is the ground side of the circuit and is made to surround the other conductor, both the radiated electric field and the magnetic field can be confined within the tube formed by the outer conductor, as illustrated in Figure 3.6.

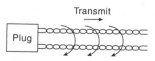

## FIGURE 3.5

*Signal coupled from transmit pair to receive pair.*

This medium is called a coaxial cable because the two conductors have a common axis. At frequencies higher than about 100KHz, the self-shielding works well; at lower frequencies, however, the "skin depth" of the current is comparable to the thickness of the outer conductor, and the shielding becomes ineffective. The resistive loss of coaxial cable increases in proportion to the square root of the frequency, making coaxial cable generally usable at frequencies of up to 2000MHz, although some types can be used up to 10000MHz.

## Waveguide

If the frequency of transmission is high enough, the electric and magnetic components of a signal can travel through free space, requiring no solid conductor. However, to avoid interference and losses due to signal spreading and to be able to route the signal as desired, it is sometimes useful to confine these waves to another bounded medium called a waveguide.

Waveguides are commonly used at frequencies from 2000MHz up to 110000MHz to connect microwave transmitters and receivers to their antennas. Waveguides are pressurized with dry air or nitrogen to drive out moisture from inside the waveguide because moisture attenuates the microwaves. Older waveguides were constructed with a rectangular cross section, but common practice today is to make the guides circular, as shown in Figure 3.7. Waveguides remain in use as a conductor of high-power, high-frequency signals, but optical-fiber cables are being used primarily in newer systems.

## Fiber-Optic Systems

The capacity of a transmission system is a direct function of the highest frequency that it can carry. Progress in transmission technology has therefore been measured by the bandwidth of the media available to carry signals. Recent developments in the use of glass fibers to carry binary signals have shown these systems to be extremely well suited to high-data-rate applications.

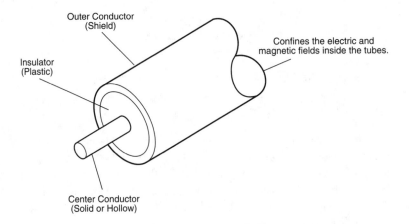

**FIGURE 3.6**

*Structure of coaxial cable.*

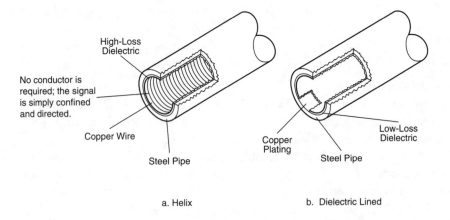

**FIGURE 3.7**

*Circular waveguides.*

Fiber-optic systems are attractive for several reasons:

- The low transmission loss, as compared with wire pairs or coaxial cable, allows much greater separation between repeaters. A fiber-optic system with no repeaters has been demonstrated that transmits 40 gigabits per second (Gbps) over a span of 75 miles with an error rate several times lower than that of high-quality coaxial cable systems.

- Because the optical fibers carry light rays, the frequency of operation is that of light. The transmission wavelength used for current single-mode fibers is 1.2 micrometers, equivalent to a frequency of around 800 terahertz (800 trillion hertz). Such frequencies allow data transmission rates of 20000Mbps at distances up to approximately 100km.

- Optical-fiber cables do not radiate energy, do not conduct electricity, and are noninductive. They are essentially free from crosstalk and the effects of lightning-induced interference, and they present no security problem from an inductively coupled "wire tap."

- Because optical-fiber cables transport light energy, they can be routed through most hazardous areas, such as oil refineries, grain elevators, and similar locations where the use of cables carrying electricity either is barred or represents a potential danger.

- Optical-fiber cables are smaller, lighter, and cheaper than metallic cables of the same capacity. It is economically feasible to provide several unused fibers in a cable for spares and for future growth.

A cross-section of a typical optical-fiber cable is shown in Figure 3.8.

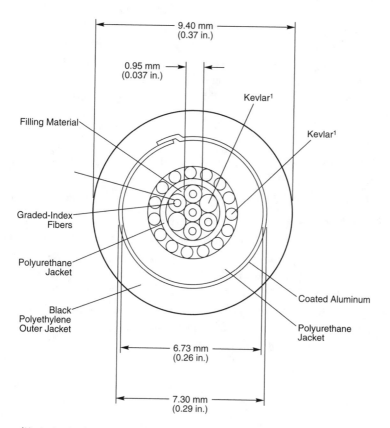

[1]Kevlar is a trademark of E.I. Du Pont de Nemours and Co.

**FIGURE 3.8**

*A typical optical five-fiber cable for direct burial.*

One of the earliest fiber-optic systems to be placed into commercial service was the AT&T FT3 lightwave system, which carried up to 80,000 two-way voice conversations at the same time. The cable for this system was one-half inch in diameter and contained 144 fibers. Each fiber pair operated at 90Mbps for a total data rate of about 6000Mbps. The system provided one spare fiber for every operating one, and switchover to a spare was automatic upon loss of signal in a fiber. A more detailed discussion of fiber-optic systems is given in Chapter 7, "Fiber-Optic and Satellite Communications."

## Building Cabling Standards

Although American Wire Gauge numbering governs the thickness of a conductor, other properties govern the capability of twisted pair to transport information. Recognizing the requirement to standardize cabling used within buildings for the transportation of voice, as well as for data on local area networks, the Electronic Industries Association (EIA) and the Telecommunications Industry Association (TIA) jointly developed a standard that specifies various building cabling parameters. Formally referred to as the EIA/TIA-568 standard, this standard specifies cabling parameters ranging from backbone cabling used to connect a building's telecommunications closets to an equipment room, to horizontal cabling used to cable individual users to an equipment closet. This standard defines the performance characteristics of both backbone and horizontal cables, as well as different types of connectors used with different types of cable.

### Backbone Cabling

Four types of media are recognized by the EIA/TIA-568 standard for backbone cabling. Table 3.2 summarizes the backbone media cabling options to include the maximum cabling distance support by each type of media.

Backbone cabling is commonly used to connect network devices known as hubs to form the backbone of a local area network. That connection can occur between hubs located on different floors or hubs located on the same floor. Thus, backbone cabling can consist of vertical and horizontal cabling. In comparison, restrictive horizontal cabling provides the connection from individual workstations to the ports on a hub. Because most hubs are located in a telecommunications or wiring closet, the EIA/TIA-568 standard for horizontal cabling governs the cabling from a telecommunications closet to a user's work area. Figure 3.9 illustrates the relationship between backbone and horizontal cabling, as well as their uses for connecting hubs and workstations.

**TABLE 3.2**  EIA/TIA-568 Backbone Cabling Media Options

| Media Type | Maximum Cabling Distance |
| --- | --- |
| 100-ohm unshielded twisted-pair (UTP) | 800 meters (2624 feet) |
| 150-ohm shielded twisted-pair (STP) | 700 meters (2296 feet) |
| 50-ohm thick coaxial cable | 500 meters (1640 feet) |
| 62.5/125mm multimode optical fiber | 2000 meters (6560 feet) |

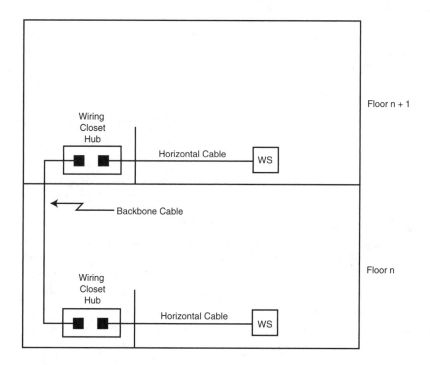

**FIGURE 3.9**
*Building cable relationship.*

## Horizontal Cabling

Under the EIA/TIA-568 standard, horizontal cable connects equipment in a telecommunications or wiring closet to a user's work area. The media options supported for horizontal cabling are the same as those specified for backbone cabling, with the exception of coaxial cable, for which 50-ohm thin cable is specified. However, the cabling distance for each type of cable is restricted to 90 meters in length from equipment in the telecommunications or wiring closet to a telecommunications outlet located in a user's work area. This cabling distance permits the use of a patch cord or drop cable up to 10 meters in length to connect a workstation to the outlet. The resulting total length of horizontal cabling is restricted to a maximum of 100 meters.

This 100-meter horizontal cabling restriction is associated with many LAN technologies that are based on the use of unshielded twisted-pair (UTP) cabling. Recognizing that different types of LANs use different signaling rates, the EIA/TIA-568 standard classified UTP cable into five categories. Table 3.3 outlines those categories and their suitability for different types of voice and data applications.

**TABLE 3.3**   EIA/TIA-568 UTP Cable Categories

| Cable Category | Description |
|---|---|
| Category 1 | Voice or low-speed data up to 56Kbps; not useful for LANs |
| Category 2 | Data rates up to 1Mbps |
| Category 3 | Transmission up to 16MHz |
| Category 4 | Transmission up to 20MHz |
| Category 5 | Transmission up to 100MHz |

When examining the entries in Table 3.3, note that UTP Categories 3, 4, and 5 support transmission with respect to indicated signaling rates. This means that the capability of those categories of UTP to support different types of LAN transmission depends on the signaling method used by different LANs. Category 3 cable is typically used for Ethernet and 4Mbps token-ring LANs. Category 4 is normally used for 16Mbps token-ring LANs, and Category 5 cable supports both versions of Ethernet to include 10Mbps and 100Mbps operations and the emerging ATM to the desktop at a 155Mbps operating rate. (Chapter 11, "Local Area Networks" contains a detailed discussion of LANs.)

The frequency or signaling rate supported by each cable category enables the cable to limit NEXT and attenuation. Table 3.4 summarizes the limits for Categories 3, 4, and 5 cable for attenuation and NEXT over frequency in dB.

When examining the entries in Table 3.4, note that because Category 3 cable supports signaling rates only up to 16MHz, there are no entries in the attenuation and NEXT columns for that type of cable beyond that frequency. Similarly, Category 4 cable supports transmission up to a 20MHz signaling rate, which explains the absence of entries for attenuation and NEXT beyond a 20MHz frequency.

**TABLE 3.4**  Categories 3, 4, and 5 Attenuation and NEXT Limits

| Frequency | Category 3 | | Category 4 | | Category 5 | |
|---|---|---|---|---|---|---|
| | NEXT | Attenuation | NEXT | Attenuation | NEXT | Attenuation (MHz) |
| 1.0 | 4.2 | 39.1 | 2.6 | 53.3 | 2.5 | 60.3 |
| 4.0 | 7.3 | 29.3 | 4.8 | 43.3 | 4.5 | 50.6 |
| 8.0 | 10.2 | 24.3 | 6.7 | 38.2 | 6.3 | 45.6 |
| 10.0 | 11.5 | 22.7 | 7.5 | 36.6 | 7.0 | 44.0 |
| 16.0 | 14.9 | 19.3 | 9.9 | 33.1 | 9.2 | 40.6 |
| 20.0 | — | — | 11.0 | 31.4 | 10.3 | 39.0 |
| 25.0 | — | — | — | — | 11.4 | 37.4 |
| 31.2 | — | — | — | — | 12.8 | 35.7 |
| 62.5 | — | — | — | — | 18.5 | 30.6 |
| 100.0 | — | — | — | — | 24.0 | 27.1 |

The literal need for speed resulting from the development of Gigabit Ethernet operating at 1000Mbps provided a driving force for the development of several new categories of cable. In May 2000, the TIA published a new standard titled "Transmission Performance specifications for 4-Pair 100 W Cabling—Addendum 5." This standard defines an enhancement to Category 5 and is commonly referred to as Category 5e or Enhanced Category 5 cable.

Category 5e cable has different limits for NEXT and attenuation than Category 5 cable. For example, at 10MH, Enhanced Category 5 cable limits NEXT to 6.3dB, while at 100MHz, the limit is 21.60dB. In comparison, in Table 3.4, Category 5 cable permits NEXT of 7.0dB at 10MHz and 24.0dB at 100MHz. Concerning attenuation, Category 5 cable permits a higher limit than Category 5 cable. At 10MHz, 47.30dB is permitted, while at 100MHz, 30.0dB is permitted. Whereas Category 5 cable is suitable for voice and data applications up to 155Mbps, Category 5e is suitable for supporting applications up to 250Mbps. In a Gigabit Ethernet environment, four pairs of Category 5e cable are used to support a 1Gbps operating rate.

Two additional evolving cable standards that warrant attention are Category 6 and Category 7. Category 6, like its predecessors, represents a standard for unshielded twisted-pair cable. In comparison, efforts at developing a Category 7 standard are focused upon shielded twisted-pair (STP) cable.

Under Category 6, crosstalk and attenuation are specified at a signal rate up to 200MHz. Under Category 7, a signal rate of 600MHz will be defined in a draft standard; one vendor using a

**3**

MESSAGES AND
TRANSMISSION
CHANNELS

special connector currently supports signaling via STP up to 1GHz. For the vast majority of businesses, Category 6 cable, which supports 200MHz signaling, should be more than adequate for most applications when the standard is finalized and cable is fabricated based upon the resulting specification.

Table 3.5 provides a comparison of the major characteristics of Category 5e, 6, and 7 cable standards. In examining the entries in Table 3.5, note that the term *PS* in PS NEXT represents power sum, a mathematical addition of noise from multiple sources of disturbance. When applied to NEXT, it represents the sum of the individual NEXT effects upon each wire pair by the other three pairs, and it is a critical parameter in full-duplex Gigabit Ethernet operations. Also note that although parameters remain to be defined (TBD) for Category 7 cable, the specifications will extend to 600MHz when defined.

**TABLE 3.5**    Comparing Evolving Cable Standards

|  | Category 5e | Category 6 | Category 7 |
|---|---|---|---|
| Number of pairs | 4 | 4 | 4 |
| Shielded | No | No | Yes |
| Connector | RJ-45 | RJ-45 | New |
| Attenuation (dB) | | | |
| 10MHz | 47.30 | 56.60 | TBD |
| 100MHz | 30.00 | 39.90 | TBD |
| 200MHz | — | 34.80 | TBD |
| 600MHz | — | — | TBD |
| NEXT (dB) | | | |
| 10MHz | 6.30 | 6.40 | TBD |
| 100MHz | 21.60 | 21.60 | TBD |
| 200MHz | — | 31.80 | TBD |
| 600MHz | — | — | TBD |
| PS NEXT (dB) | | | |
| 10MHz | 44.00 | 54.00 | TBD |
| 100MHz | 27.00 | 37.10 | TBD |
| 200MHz | — | 31.90 | TBD |
| 600MHz | — | — | TBD |

# Unbounded Medium

The atmosphere, the ocean, and outer space are all examples of unbounded media, in which electromagnetic signals originated by the source radiate freely into the medium and spread throughout it. The unbounded media are used by various radio frequency transmitting schemes to carry messages. The main feature of unbounded media is that when the signal is radiated from the transmitter, it radiates equally in all directions (unless restricted) and continues forever onward. As it moves farther from the source, the energy is spread over a larger area, so the level continually gets weaker at greater distances. As the wave moves through the medium, it is affected by natural disturbances that can interfere with the signal.

## High-Frequency Radiotelephone

By convention, radio transmission in the frequency band between 3MHz and 30MHz is called high-frequency (HF) radio. Frequency bands within the HF spectrum are allocated by international treaty for specific services, such as mobile (aeronautical, maritime, and land), broadcasting, radio navigation, amateur radio, space communications, and radio astronomy. HF radio has properties of propagation that make it less reliable than some other frequencies. HF radio does, however, allow communications over great distances with small amounts of radiated power.

HF radio waves transmitted from antennas on the Earth follow two paths when they leave the antenna. The groundwave follows the Earth's surface, and the skywave bounces back and forth between the Earth's surface and various layers of the Earth's ionosphere. The groundwave is useful for communications up to about 400 miles, and it works particularly well over water. The skywave propagates signals for up to 4000 miles with a path reliability of about 90 percent. Data signals are carried on HF radio systems as continuous wave (CW) radio telegraphy at about 15 bits per second (bps), and frequency shift-keyed (FSK) single sideband signals are carried on HF at 75bps. Higher data-bit rates (up to 19200bps) are converted to standard 3KHz voice channel analog signals by modems, and these analog signals are transmitted on voice frequency (VF) carrier systems using HF radio.

## Microwave Radio

The tall towers with large horns or the dish antennas that you see while driving through the countryside are the repeater stations for line-of-sight (LOS) microwave radio systems (sometimes called radiolink systems). Such systems can carry large quantities of voice and data traffic for several reasons:

- They require no right-of-way acquisition between towers.
- They can carry very large quantities of information per radio system, due to their high operating frequency.
- They require the purchase or lease of only a small area of ground for installation of each tower.
- Because the wavelength of the transmitted signal is short, an antenna of reasonable size can focus the transmitted signal into a beam. This provides greater signal strength at the receiver without increasing transmitter power.

Radiolink systems are subject to transmission impairments that limit the distance between repeater points and cause other problems. The microwave signals are treated as described here:

- They are attenuated by solid objects (including the Earth). In addition, the higher frequencies are attenuated by rain, snow, and fog.
- They are reflected from flat conductive surfaces (such as water and metal structures).
- They are diffracted (split) around solid objects.
- They are refracted (bent) by the atmosphere so that the beam can travel beyond the line-of-sight distance and be picked up by an antenna that is not supposed to receive it.

In spite of these possible problems, radiolink systems are highly successful and, until the late 1980s, carried a substantial part of all telephone, data, and television traffic in the United States. Beginning in the early 1980s, most long-distance communications carriers installed tens of thousands of miles of optical fiber. Since the late 1980s, most long-distance transmission has been moved off microwave systems to fiber-optic transmission systems. The microwave range of radio frequencies is allocated for various purposes by international treaty. Some of the frequency assignments for the United States are shown in Table 3.6.

Most common carrier radiolink systems carry analog signals, principally frequency modulation (FM). A few systems, however, carry digital signals. Two examples in the United States are the AT&T 3A-RDS radio system, which operates in the 11GHz band, and the AT&T DR-18 radio system, which operates in the 18GHz band. The 3A-RDS system carries DS3 digital signals at 44.736Mbps, and the DR-18 system carries DS4 digital signals at 274.176Mbps. The DS3 and DS4 signals, which are made up of several lower-bit-rate signals, are discussed in more detail later in this chapter.

**TABLE 3.6**  Frequency Assignments for Microwave Radiolink Systems

| Service | Frequency, GHz |
|---|---|
| Military | 1.710–1.850 |
| Operational fixed | 1.850–1.990 |

**TABLE 3.6**    continued

| Service | Frequency, GHz |
| --- | --- |
| Studio transmitter link | 1.990–2.110 |
| Common carrier | 2.110–2.130 |
| Operational fixed | 2.130–2.150 |
| Common carrier | 2.160–2.180 |
| Operational fixed | 2.180–2.200 |
| Operational fixed (TV) | 2.500–2.690 |
| Common carrier and satellite (downlink) | 3.700–4.200 |
| Military | 4.400–4.990 |
| Military | 5.250–5.350 |
| Common carrier and satellite (uplink) | 5.925–6.425 |
| Operational fixed | 6.575–6.875 |
| Studio transmitter link | 6.875–7.125 |
| Common carrier and satellite (downlink) | 7.250–7.750 |
| Common carrier and satellite (uplink) | 7.900–8.400 |
| Common carrier | 10.7–11.7 |
| Operational fixed | 12.2–12.7 |
| CATV studio links | 12.7–12.95 |
| Studio transmitter link | 12.95–13.2 |
| Military | 14.4–15.25 |
| Common carrier | 17.7–19.3 |

Terrestrial radiolink systems are point-to-point; that is, the signal is transmitted in a beam from a source microwave antenna across the Earth's surface to the antenna at which it is aimed. The width of the beam transmitted by a microwave antenna varies between 1° and 5° as a function of the frequency of transmission and antenna size. As a result, the transmission is highly directional, which is desirable if the information is intended for only one destination (for example, a telephone conversation). For many applications, however, the information has multiple destinations (for example, TV broadcasts), which makes the satellite radiolink system more practical and desirable.

## Satellite Radiolink Systems

Figure 3.10 is a simple model of a satellite radiolink system. The satellite contains several receiver/amplifier/transmitter sections, called transponders, each of which operates at a slightly different frequency. Each of the 12 transponders on a satellite (12 on many of those placed in orbit during the 1980s, more on later orbited communications satellites) has a bandwidth of 36MHz. Individual transmitter sites, called uplink Earth stations, send narrow beams of microwave signals to the satellite. The satellite acts as a relay station. A transponder receives the signal from a single transmitter, amplifies it, and then retransmits it toward Earth on a different frequency. Note that the transmitting Earth station sends to only one transponder on a single satellite. The satellite, however, sends to all downlink receiving Earth stations in its area of coverage, called its footprint.

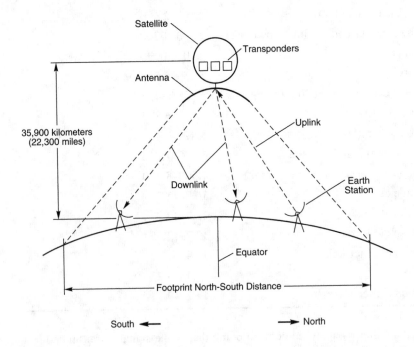

**FIGURE 3.10**
*Satellite radiolink system.*

Several types of signals are carried by satellite systems. For example, 6MHz bandwidth standard TV programs, multiplexed 64 kilobits per second (Kbps) telephone channels, and high-speed data all can be carried simultaneously. One privately operated system, the Satellite Business System, which was merged with Hughes Network Systems, is all digital, and each of the 10 transponders per satellite is capable of carrying 43Mbps of digital data.

## Commercial Satellites

Commercial communications satellites are launched into geostationary orbit at an altitude of 35,900 kilometers (22,300 miles) above the equator. This means that the geostationary satellite is orbiting the Earth at a constant speed and in the same direction as the Earth's rotation about its axis. The orbiting speed is such that it causes the satellite to have a fixed location with respect to the Earth. The Earth station antennas, therefore, can be fixed in position and do not have to track a moving target in the sky. The angle of view for a geostationary satellite is almost 120° wide. In principle, three such satellites equally spaced around the equator could cover the Earth from 60° north latitude to 60° south latitude. In practice, the coverage angle is restricted to less than 110° because the Earth station's antenna must be elevated above the local horizon by more than 5°.

## LEOS Satellites

A relatively new type of satellite system referred to as a low Earth orbit satellite (LEOS) began service during the mid-1990s and can be expected to gain in popularity over the next few years. Placing a satellite into a low Earth orbit substantially reduces the amount of power required by a transmitter on Earth to bounce a signal off the satellite. Similarly, the satellite does not need to produce as strong a signal as required by a geostationary satellite to reach a receiver. Alternately, with the same amount of signal power as that used by a geostationary satellite, a LEOS signal can be received by a substantially smaller receiver. This makes a LEOS system ideal for supporting two-way paging, international cellular communications, and similar applications.

Because a low Earth orbit satellite's footprint may encompass an area on Earth for a few hours or less instead of permanently as by a geostationary satellite, the system operator must launch a large number of satellites to provide constant coverage to a fixed geographical area.

One example of an LEOS system is the Iridium system of 66 planned satellites that supports cellular communications on a worldwide basis. Iridium employs a system of relaying a call from one satellite to another until the call reaches a satellite that serves an Earth station that covers the destination of the call. This design strategy resulted in a considerable level of complexity that drove up the cost of call routing. In addition, Iridium phones are rather bulky and require a line-of-sight to a satellite. Although the basic intention of the service was laudable, it never obtained more than a small fraction of potential subscribers and was saved from extinction only by a contract with the U.S. Department of Defense.

## Cellular Radio Systems

Americans have demonstrated an insatiable desire to communicate with each other anywhere, at any time. It seems that no location is too private, too noisy, or too busy to exclude the installation of a telephone or a data terminal. Because Americans spend a lot of time in their cars, mobile telephones and data terminals are in great demand. Each telephone conversation requires a separate radio channel, and because only a limited number of such channels were available in the past, the demand for mobile telephone channels far outstripped the radio frequencies available to provide them. However, in 1982, a system allowing the reuse of channels within a metropolitan area, called the cellular radio system, began trial operation in Chicago. This system provided many more mobile telephone channels. It rapidly gained acceptance throughout the United States in the late 1980s.

Figure 3.11 shows a diagram of a simple cellular system. A metropolitan area is divided into several cells, each of which is served by a low-powered transmitter and an associated receiver. The radio channels are suitable for data transmission up to 14.4Kbps as well as voice transmission. The number of radio channels assigned to each cell is sufficient for the predicted number of users in that cell at any one time. When a caller makes a call, his mobile unit automatically seizes a free channel in his current cell. When the caller moves out of the cell, the cell controller automatically switches control of the call from the cell being left to the one being entered. Even a different radio channel can be used, but the caller doesn't have to do anything and is never aware of anything happening. The call is linked from the cell controller to a central switching system. The central switching system can link the caller via radio to another mobile user or can access the public telephone network for connection to any fixed telephone.

In Chapter 15, "Wireless Transmission," the operation of different types of cellular radio systems to include analog mobile phone service (AMPS), time-division multiple access (TDMA), and code-division multiple access (CDMA) are explained in detail.

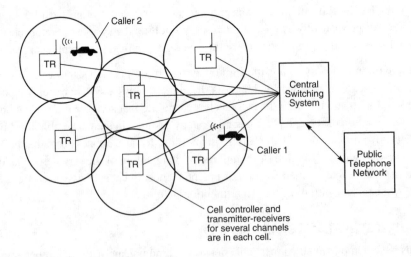

**FIGURE 3.11**

*Each cell contains a cell controller and transmitter-receivers for several channels.*

# Effects of Bandwidth on a Transmission Channel

All transmission channels of any practical interest are of limited frequency bandwidth. The limitations arise from the physical properties of the channel or from deliberate limitations on the bandwidth to prevent interference from other sources. For primarily economic reasons, most data communications systems seek to maximize the amount of data that can be sent on a channel.

## Handling Capacity of a Channel

Claude Shannon masterminded a formula to prove the maximum capacity of an ideal channel whose only impairments are finite bandwidth and noise randomly distributed over that finite bandwidth. That formula is shown here:

```
C = W x Log₂[1 + (P/N)] bits per second
```

In this formula, P is the power in watts of the signal through the channel, N is the power in watts of the noise out of the channel, and W is the bandwidth of the channel in hertz.

Neglecting all other impairments, some typical values for a voice-grade analog circuit used for data are W = 3000 hertz, P = 0.0001 watts (–10 dBm), and N = 0.0000004 watts (–34 dBm). According to Shannon's Law, the value of C is as shown here:

```
3000 x Log₂(1 + 250) = about 24,000 bits per second
```

Shannon's value of C is normally not achievable because there are numerous impairments in every real channel besides those taken into account in Shannon's Law. Also, there are no ideal modems. However, Shannon's Law provides an upper theoretical limit to a binary channel. It is important to note that, due to the nature of the function $Log_2$, the value of C in the formula can be increased more readily by increasing W than by increasing (P/N).

Readers familiar with the latest generation of modems might question how they achieve an operating rate of 33.6Kbps in the upstream direction when, according to Shannon's Law, the operating rate should be limited to approximately 24000bps. The answer to this question involves the actual bandwidth used by such modems. Figure 3.12 illustrates the amplitude-frequency response curve for a voice-grade telephone channel. At a 0db level, the bandwidth is very close to 3000Hz; however, at lower levels, the bandwidth slightly increases, enabling a higher operating rate to be achieved.

## Intersymbol Interference

One of the factors that tends to reduce the achievable capacity of a channel below the value of C in the formula is a problem called intersymbol (or interbit) interference. If a rectangular pulse like that shown in Figure 3.13 is input to a band-limited channel, the bandwidth limitation of the channel rounds the "corners" of the pulse, as shown in the output waveform, and causes an undesired signal to appear. The "tail" or overshoot part of the new signal interferes with previous and subsequent pulses, adding uncertainty to the signal; that is, the signal might be incorrectly interpreted at the destination.

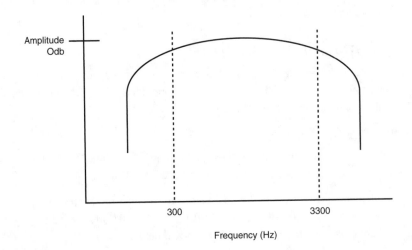

**FIGURE 3.12**
*The voice-grade channel amplitude-frequency response curve.*

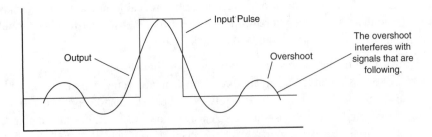

**FIGURE 3.13**
*A pulse response through a band-limited channel.*

Harry Nyquist analyzed the problem of intersymbol interference and developed an ideal rounded pulse shape for which that impairment is minimized. Nyquist also did much theoretical research dealing with sampling of analog signals for representation in binary form. Nyquist's Sampling Theorem (also known as Shannon's Sampling Theorem) says that if an analog signal is sampled 2f times per second, the samples can be used to perfectly reconstruct the original signal over a spectrum of hertz. For example, if a signal is sampled at the rate of 8,000 times per second, those samples can be used to reconstruct the original signal with perfect accuracy over the range of 0–4000 hertz.

# Bandwidth Requirements for Signals

The ratio at which information can be transmitted depends on the bandwidth of the transmission media.

## Analog Signals

Transmission rates for data communications seem to follow a corollary of Parkinson's Law—that is, data rates increase to fill the bandwidth available. A good example is the introduction of low-cost modems operating at 14400 and 28800bps for personal computers, which are 48 and 96 times faster than the rate of 300bps that was used for a long time. Large-scale integrated circuits made possible the remarkable increases in performance and decreases in price of these modems.

The 300bps full-duplex modem signals use two bands of frequencies, each occupying about 300Hz. Thus, the total 600Hz used out of the 3000Hz available bandwidth is inefficient. The 1200bps modems also are full-duplex and use most of the available bandwidth. Therefore, four times as much information can be sent in the same channel in a given time period. Modern modems operating at or above 9600bps use a sophisticated echo-canceling technique that enables both transmit and receive signals to flow on a common wire pair. Through sophisticated signal-processing techniques, modems can even carry up to 33600bps using an analog signal over a voice channel. A relatively new type of modem that permits only one analog-to-digital conversion is capable of supporting an operating rate of 56000bps. However, the use of this modem at that operating rate requires one end of the link to be directly connected to the communications carrier's digital network. In addition, the 56Kbps data rate is unidirectional, with the maximum modem rate being 33600bps in the opposite direction. This new modem is referred to as a V.90 modem. A more recent modem referred to as a V.92 modem permits data transmission up to approximately 44000bps in the uplink direction. Both V.90 and V.92 modems are discussed in Chapter 5, "Synchronous Modems, Digital Transmission, and Service Units."

## Digital Signals

Transmission of signals in binary form can require considerably more bandwidth than an equivalent analog signal. For example, the transmission of 24 analog voice channels requires about 96KHz (24 × 4KHz). Transmission of these same 24 voice channels in digital form using the standard T1 time division multiplexing format requires about 776KHz, or about eight times as much bandwidth (776/96). The advantages gained by sending the signals as binary data, however, more than offset the requirement for greater bandwidth. The primary advantage of digital signaling is the ability to regenerate pulses, which means that new pulses can replace ones with distortion. This results in a lower error rate than an analog signal because the latter uses amplifiers, which increase the signal as well as any prior distortion to the signal. (For a discussion of the trade-offs and advantages, refer to *Understanding Telephone Electronics,* by Stephen J. Bigelow.)

# Carrier Systems

In general, carrier systems are mechanisms that provide a means to send signals from more than one source over a single physical channel. The bandwidth available to carry signals in a particular medium can be allocated in two ways: by frequency or by time intervals.

## Using Frequency

The frequency spectrum represented by the available bandwidth of a channel can be divided into smaller bandwidth portions, with each of several signal sources assigned to each portion. This is the principle of frequency-division multiplexing (FDM). FDM is still used in some simple data communications systems, and, at one time, it formed the foundation for the long-haul part of the public telephone network. Since the 1980s, communications carriers have invested tens of billions of dollars in converting their infrastructure to digital technology, resulting in the replacement of essentially all carrier FDM systems by time-division multiplexing (TDM) systems. Chapter 6, "Multiplexing Techniques," covers multiplexing technology, including the operation of FDM and TDM systems. One common example of a frequency-division multiplexing system is a standard low-speed (300bps) modem, which divides the spectrum available in a voice channel into two portions—one for transmitting and one for receiving. (This concept of frequency division is discussed in more detail in Chapter 6.)

The electronic mechanisms that implemented FDM are called analog carrier systems. The carrier in an analog carrier system is a signal generated by the system, and the carrier is modulated by the signal containing the information to be transmitted. Table 3.7 shows the standard analog carrier systems in use in the public telephone network. As previously noted, however, most communications carriers have replaced their analog-based FDM equipment with digital-based TDM equipment.

## Using Time

The second method of dividing the capacity of a transmission channel among several separate signal sources is to allocate a very short period on the channel in a repeating pattern to each signal. This technique is called time-division multiplexing. It is well suited to binary signals consisting of pulses representing a 1 or a 0. These pulses can be made of very short duration and still convey the desired information; therefore, many of them can be squeezed into the time available on a digital carrier channel.

**TABLE 3.7**  Analog Carrier Systems

| Multiplex Level | No. of Voice Circuits | Frequency Band, KHz |
|-----------------|----------------------|---------------------|
| Voice channel   | 1                    | 0–4                 |
| Group           | 12                   | 60–108              |
| Supergroup      | 60                   | 312–552             |
| Mastergroup     | 600                  | 564–3084            |
| Jumbogroup      | 3,600                | 564–17,548          |

The original signal can be an analog wave that is converted to binary form for transmission (as in the case of speech signals in the telephone network), or the original signal can already be in binary form (as in the case of a business machine). The electronic systems that perform this TDM process are called digital carrier systems. As with the analog carrier systems, there is a standard hierarchy of digital carrier systems in the public telephone network, as shown in Table 3.8. Refer to Chapter 6 for specific information concerning time-division multiplexing and the operation and utilization of a T1 multiplexer that can be used with a DS1 digital carrier system.

The digital signals listed in Table 3.8 reference the type of signal that a particular digital line transports to include applicable framing. For example, a T1 line transports a DS1 digital signal. In Table 3.8, note that the lowest operating-rate digital signal is indicated as DS1, which consists of 24 voice circuits whose aggregate operating rate is 1.544Mbps. Although the DS1 digital signal is indeed the lowest operating-rate signal in the digital carrier hierarchy, it is not the lowest operating-rate digital transmission facility available for use. To understand why this is the case, you must have additional information about the DS1 signal.

## Using Pulse Code Modulation

In North America, the DS1 is commonly referred to as a T1 line or circuit. That circuit was developed to relieve cable congestion in metropolitan areas by providing a transport mechanism for 24 digitized voice conversations to be simultaneously carried over one cable. To do so, each voice conversation is digitized using a technique called pulse code modulation (PCM). Under PCM, an analog voice conversation is digitized at 64Kbps. To provide information that enables one conversation to be distinguished from another and switched into and out of a group of conversations, framing bits must be added to the T1 data flow. Those framing bits operate at 8000bps and carry control information, error-detection information, and a limited data-link capability. This capability, for example, enables two private branch exchanges (PBXs) to communicate with one another while transporting 24 voice conversations on a T1 circuit interconnecting the PBXs. The 24 channels, each operating at 64Kbps, result in an operating rate of 1.536Mbps. When the 8Kbps framing information is added to the T1 line, its operating rate becomes 1.544Mbps.

Each voice channel in a DS1 digital signal, referred to as a DS0 or digital signal level zero channel, represents the lowest operating rate digital circuit marketed by communications carriers for direct connection to a channel on their T1 lines. Communications carriers also offer low-speed digital services operating at data rates from 2.4Kbps up to 56Kbps, using time-division multiplexers to group multiple low-speed digital circuits onto a 64Kbps circuit. The 64Kbps circuit, in turn, is connected to a channel on a carrier's T1 line, which represents the basic backbone infrastructure used for transporting voice, data, and video across North America.

In the telephone company infrastructure, four DS1 signals are combined by a device referred to as an M12 multiplexer to generate a DS2 signal operating at 6.312Mbps that transports 96 DS0 voice channels. At the next stage in the telephone company hierarchy, either 28 DS1 signals can be combined by a M13 multiplexer or 7 DS2 signals can be combined by an M23 multiplexer to generate a DS3 signal operating at 274.176Mbps. The resulting DS3 signal is the signal transported by a T3 circuit. Six DS3 signals can be multiplexed by an M34 device to generate a DS4 signal. However, unlike T1 and T3 circuits that are commercially available, DS2 and DS4 signals are only internally used by communications carriers, which explains the absence of commercially available T2 and T4 circuits.

**TABLE 3.8** Digital Carrier Systems

| Digital Signal No. | No. of Voice Circuits | Bit Rate, Mbps |
|---|---|---|
| DS1 | 24 | 1.544 |
| DS2 | 96 | 6.312 |
| DS3 | 672 | 44.736 |
| DS4 | 4,032 | 274.176 |

## Dataphone Digital Service

The T1 circuit was originally limited to use by communications carriers to relieve the cable congestion in metropolitan areas. Because of the successful use of this transmission facility, AT&T and other communications carriers tariffed its use for commercial organizations and government agencies during the mid-1980s. Slower-speed digital transmission services, such as AT&T's Dataphone Digital Service (DDS), actually preceded the public offering of T1 service because DDS was introduced during the mid-1970s.

DDS is a leased-line digital transmission service with operating rates of 2.4, 4.8, 9.6, 19.2, and 56Kbps. A switched 56Kbps offering is also available in certain cities.

The economics associated with the T1 tariff caused the monthly cost of a T1 line to be four to eight times that of one 56Kbps DDS circuit. Because a T1 line has more than 24 times the capacity of a 56Kbps DDS circuit, most organizations that required the use of multiple 56Kbps DDS lines between common geographical locations soon replaced those circuits with T1 lines. In addition to the economics associated with the use of T1 lines, their additional data-transport capacity enabled organizations to merge voice, data, and video applications onto a common circuit. In fact, by the early 1990s, the T1 circuit formed the backbone for most corporate and government networks. By the late 1990s the T1 line was the primary mechanism by which tens of thousands of businesses, academic institutions, and government agencies connected LANs to the Internet. Because Web servers are connected to LANs, the T1 circuit also became the primary access line used to connect Web servers to the Internet.

## Fractional T1 Service

The difference between the maximum data rate supported by DDS and the operating rate of a T1 circuit left many organizations unsatisfied with respect to the traffic-handling capacity of communications carrier circuits. Recognizing the requirements of those organizations for the use of a fraction of a T1 line's operating rate, communications carriers introduced fractional T1 (FT1) service in the early 1990s. Today, most communications carriers offer FT1 service in operating rates from 64Kbps to 768Kbps in increments of 64Kbps. Although an organization contracts for a specific FT1 operating rate, the carrier normally installs a T1 line from the serving office to the customer's premises. The customer either installs equipment or gets equipment from the communications carrier, which places the customer's data into a group of DS0s that represents the contracted FT1 service.

Figure 3.14 illustrates an example of the digital multiplexing hierarchy used to transport FT1- and T1-based communications between cities. At the serving carrier office, data in the form of individual or groups of DS-Os from subscribers is removed (dropped) from some T1 lines and placed (inserted) onto other T1 lines. In this way, most (if not all) of the 24 DS-O slots on certain T1 lines are used. Next, groups of T1 lines are multiplexed onto a T3 or T4 line for the routing of voice and data that represents 672 or 4,032 voice-grade circuits routed between long-distance communications carrier offices.

To illustrate the economics associated with the use of FT1, Table 3.9 lists AT&T's monthly interoffice channel charges based upon a 350-mile circuit in effect in 1998 for that carrier's series of digital service offerings that provide data rates from 56Kbps to 155Mbps. The 155Mbps rate is not included in the table because it is currently priced on an individual customer basis (ICB). Also note that since 1994, AT&T converted its digital leased line pricing from a monthly charge per mile to a city-pair pricing structure. This helps explain why in many older books and articles, you will commonly see references to the monthly charge per mile for digital circuits operating at different data rates.

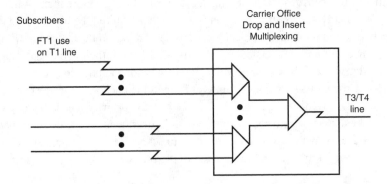

**FIGURE 3.14**

*The digital multiplexing hierarchy.*

Table 3.10 provides a monthly cost comparison between 56/64Kbps leased lines and T1 leased lines for five city pairs. If you compare the monthly cost of a 56/64Kbps leased line to a T1 line operating at 1.544Mbps, you will note that an increase in cost of approximately a factor of 7 to 8 results in an increase in data transmission capacity by a factor of 24.

**TABLE 3.9** AT&T Accunet Spectrum of Digital Services Interoffice Channel Charges

| *Channel Operating Rate* | *Monthly Charge Per Mile* |
| --- | --- |
| 56/64Kbps | $475 |
| 128Kbps | $854 |
| 256Kbps | $1,636 |
| 512Kbps | $2,956 |
| 768Kbps | $3,992 |
| 1.544Mbps | $5,462 |
| 4.6Mbps | $17,323 |
| 7.7Mbps | $27,553 |
| 45Mbps | $52,181 |

**TABLE 3.10**   AT&T 56/64Kbps/T1 Private Line Monthly Pricing Based on Representative City Pair Costs

| City Pair | Air Miles | 56/64Kbps | T1 |
|---|---|---|---|
| Atlanta–Chicago | 584 | $1,094.33 | $8,422.69 |
| New York–San Diego | 2,415 | $1,620.67 | $16,390.78 |
| New York–Atlanta | 745 | $1,130.51 | $9,147.20 |
| New York–Seattle | 2,406 | $1,655.39 | $16,861.96 |
| Atlanta–Erie | 621 | $1,202.36 | $8,154.99 |

The interoffice channel charges listed in Table 3.9 and city pair pricing listed in Table 3.10 are presented for illustrative purposes. AT&T and other communications carriers offer a range of discount plans based upon multiyear contracts that can considerably reduce monthly fees for organizations that are willing to make a commitment to maintain a level of service.

# What You Have Learned

- Information is a numerical quantity that measures the randomness of a system.
- Symbols such as letters have an information content. Not every symbol is equally likely to occur.
- The redundancy of a system measures how likely symbols are to be repeated.
- Data communications systems use redundancy to detect and correct errors in transmission.
- Entropy of a character set or alphabet serves as a goal for developing data-compression algorithms.
- Signals can travel through guided and unguided transmission media.
- Adding inductance to pairs of wires is called loading. Loading is used to reduce high-frequency attenuation over the wire pair.
- The EIA/TIA-568 standard specifies cabling parameters used to connect equipment in wiring closets to workstations.
- The most common type of twisted-pair cable used with LANs is currently Category 5 cable, while Category 5e is used to support Gigabit Ethernet.
- The bit error rate of a communications medium primarily depends upon the ability of a receiver to distinguish a signal from noise.
- Low-orbit satellites support low-power transmitters and are ideal for two-way paging and international cellular communications.

3

MESSAGES AND
TRANSMISSION
CHANNELS

- Fiber-optic transmission systems send data signals as light rays. These systems have much higher bandwidth and have immunity from most external interference.

- Transmission rates over channels are limited by the bandwidth of the channel, the signal-to-noise ratio, and the amount of intersymbol interference in the transmitted waveform.

- The use of different types of digital transmission systems is based on bandwidth availability and economics.

# Quiz for Chapter 3

1. The amount of uncertainty in a system of symbols is also called what?

    A. Bandwidth

    B. Loss

    C. Entropy

    D. Quantum

2. The twists in twisted-wire pairs

    A. Reduce electromagnetic interference.

    B. Occur at a 30° angle.

    C. Eliminate loading.

    D. Were removed due to cost.

3. Redundancy measures

    A. The transmission rate of a system.

    B. How likely symbols are to be repeated.

    C. The time between failure.

    D. The system cost.

4. If the entropy of an alphabet is 4 bits per character, you could theoretically develop a compression scheme that, on the average, will do which of the following?

    A. Compress two 8-bit characters into one.

    B. Remove 2 bits per character.

    C. Compress an 8-bit character into two 4-bit characters.

    D. Remove two characters per bit.

5. Which of the following statements is true according to the American Wire Gauge (AWG) method of defining the diameter of cable?

    A. The greater the wire gauge is, the larger the diameter of the cable is.

    B. The lower the wire gauge is, the smaller the cable's diameter is.

C. The greater the wire gauge is, the smaller the cable's diameter is.

D. The wire gauge is proportional to the resistance on a cable.

6. Near-end crosstalk (NEXT) has a maximum value

   A. At the receiver.

   B. At the transmitter.

   C. At the destination jack.

   D. At the 33rd twist in a cable.

7. Which of the following is an example of a bounded medium?

   A. Coaxial cable

   B. Waveguide

   C. Fiber-optic cable

   D. All of the above

8. Loading refers to the addition of what?

   A. Resistors

   B. Capacitors

   C. Bullets

   D. Inductance

9. Coaxial cable has conductors with

   A. The same diameter.

   B. A common axis.

   C. Equal resistance.

   D. None of the above.

10. Fiber-optic cable is suitable for

    A. Routing through conduits.

    B. Use in most hazardous areas.

    C. Pulling connectors.

    D. Mobile video applications.

11. Fiber-optic cables operate at frequencies near what?

    A. 20MHz

    B. 200MHz

    C. 2GHz

    D. 800THz

12. The EIA/TIA-568 standard

    A. Specifies building design parameters.

    B. Specifies cabling parameters.

    C. Defines the method for interconnecting buildings.

    D. Was developed by the Electrical Integration Association.

13. What is the maximum horizontal cabling distance from equipment in a wiring closet to a workstation under the EIA/TIA-568 standard?

    A. 100 feet

    B. 90 meters

    C. 100 meters

    D. 90 feet

14. Currently, most organizations that install LANs use which type of cable?

    A. Category 7 cable

    B. Category 2 cable

    C. Category 1 cable

    D. Category 5 cable

15. What type of copper cable is used in a Gigabit Ethernet environment?

    A. Category 5 cable

    B. Category 5e cable

    C. Category 2 cable

    D. Category 1 cable

16. What does PS NEXT represent?

    A. The sum of individual NEXT effects upon each wire pair by the other three wire pairs in a four-wire bundle.

    B. The sum of NEXT for the odd wire pairs in a wire pair bundle.

    C. The sum of NEXT for the even wire pairs in a wire pair bundle.

    D. Paul Smith, the inventor of NEXT.

17. HF radio waves follow how many basic paths upon leaving the transmitter?

    A. Two

    B. Four

    C. One

    D. Many

18. A low Earth orbit satellite

    A. Enables low-power transmitters to access the satellite.

    B. Is stationary over an area.

    C. Supports the globe.

    D. Is designed to support portable television operations.

19. The area of coverage of a satellite radio beam is called its

    A. Beamwidth.

    B. Circular polarization.

    C. Footprint.

    D. Identity.

20. In a mobile cellular radio system, the movement of a caller between cells

    A. Requires the caller to request a new cell from a base station.

    B. Is handled transparently by the cellular system.

    C. Results in the cell controller searching for the next subscriber.

    D. Generates a radio beam to Dr. Spock.

21. Transmission of binary signals requires

    A. Less bandwidth than analog.

    B. More bandwidth than analog.

    C. The same bandwidth as analog.

    D. A license from the FAA.

22. The standard first-level digital multiplex system in the United States operates at what speed?

    A. 2.048Mbps

    B. 44.736Mbps

    C. 1.544Mbps

    D. 9600bps

23. How many DS1 signals are transported on a DS3 signal?

    A. 24

    B. 672

    C. 14

    D. 28

**3**

MESSAGES AND
TRANSMISSION
CHANNELS

24. How many DS2 signals are multiplexed to form a DS3?

    A. 24

    B. 28

    C. 7

    D. 14

25. The use of Dataphone Digital Services

    A. Can be expected to increase.

    B. Provides a higher operating rate than FT1 service.

    C. Can be expected to be replaced by FT1 service due to the lower cost of that service.

    D. Provides a higher operating rate than T1.

# Asynchronous Modems and Interfaces

## IN THIS CHAPTER

Having laid the groundwork by describing the form of the data (codes), the source of the data to be transmitted (terminals), and the transmission media, you're ready to see how the data is transmitted. This chapter explains how modems work in terms of frequency, bandwidth, and modulation, and it describes the data terminal equipment/data communications equipment (DTE/DCE) interface. Due to the role of the microprocessor in adding intelligence to modems, this chapter also covers smart modem features. Features described and discussed in this chapter include command sets, error detection and correction, data compression, and the Microcom MNP protocol.

# Why Data Can't Be Transmitted Directly

Although it might not have been obvious at the time, the reasons modems are necessary were discussed in Chapter 3, "Messages and Transmission Channels." Remember that the switched telephone network uses various transmission methods from wire pairs to microwave, but only in the local area (primarily within the area served by a central office) does an actual metallic path (wire) exist from one telephone to another. This means that you cannot transmit data in its original form as a series of pulses much farther than from your telephone to the central office (CO). Actually, if loading coils are used in the local loop, you can't even transmit the data that far. As Chapter 3 discussed, the bandwidth (the passband) of the telephone channel beyond the CO after it has been filtered and amplified is approximately 300–3400Hz, as shown in Figure 4.1. Because direct current (0Hz) is below 300Hz, it is not within the passband. Thus, data in its original pulsed DC or "baseband" form cannot be transmitted over this channel.

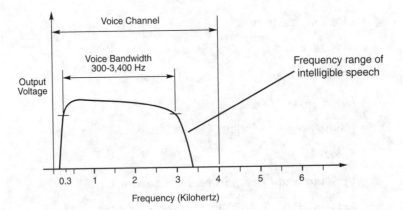

## FIGURE 4.1

*The telephone channel bandwidth.*

# Solving the Problem with Modems

Because you are interested in transmitting data beyond the CO using the existing telephone network, you need to change the data pulses to another form that can be transmitted over the telephone channel. Because the telephone network is designed and optimized for transmission of analog signals in the voiceband, why not make the data look like these analog signals for transmission? This is exactly the function of a modem. The ones and zeros of the data stream from the DTE are converted to tones (or analog waveforms resembling tones) with frequencies in the range of 300 to 3400Hz. Thus, the modem is nothing more than a rather complex interface device.

At the transmitting end, incoming pulses from the DTE are converted to tones and transmitted over the telephone channel; at the receiving end, the tones are converted back to pulses, which are passed to the DTE. In other words, the transmitting modem modulates an analog signal, called a carrier, with the data and uses the analog signal to carry to the other end of the telephone circuit (more about modulation in the next section). The receiving modem demodulates the analog signal to restore the data to its original pulse form and passes it to the receiving DTE. In fact, the name "modem" is a contraction of the words modulator-demodulator. One important fact to remember is this: A modem does not operate on the content of the data; it merely changes the form for transmission. The data-compression capability of modern smart modems is discussed later in this chapter. In actuality, software in the form of instructions burned into read-only memory (ROM) and referred to as "firmware" controls a microprocessor in the modem that operates on data before its modulation. Although many articles and books note that modems operate on data, technically it is the microprocessor in the modem that does so. The modem's internal circuitry merely changes the form of the data for transmission.

Later in this book when you examine a new modem technology referred to as a Digital Subscriber Line (DSL), you will note that this type of modem uses up to approximately 1MHz of frequency spectrum on the wire pair to the central office. However, the first 4KHz of frequency is left as is, permitting voice or conventionally modulated data to continue to use that well-established segment of frequency. The remaining upper portion of the frequency spectrum is demodulated at the central office and enters a digital network, bypassing the switched telephone network. This technique does not require any modification to the basic design of the public switched telephone network, but it permits data rates of up to 8–10Mbps to be achieved on the twisted-pair wiring used to connect hundreds of millions of homes and businesses to the telephone network. DSL modems operate at a much broader range of frequencies to obtain the capability to transmit and receive at a much higher data rate than modems that operate in the telephone channel. Thus, DSL modems are commonly referred to as broadband modems.

**4**

ASYNCHRONOUS
MODEMS AND
INTERFACES

## Telephone Channel Restrictions on Modems

In addition to the bandwidth limits, a restriction of the telephone channel that affects modem design is inherent in any analog transmission facility; that is, the transmission is best at frequencies near the center of the passband and poorest at frequencies toward the upper and lower limits of the passband. High-speed modems use almost all the voiceband for one channel. Therefore, most high-speed modems in North America use a carrier frequency of 1700–1800Hz because these frequencies are very near the middle of the voiceband. Low-speed modems, because of their narrower bandwidth requirements, can use more than one carrier frequency within the voiceband and still operate in the "good" portion of the band.

Still another restriction of the telephone channel is that certain frequencies cannot be used. The telephone network uses the transmission channel for passing information and control signals between the switching offices. This process, called in-band or in-channel interoffice signaling, uses tones at frequencies within the voiceband. A modem cannot use these same frequencies because the network might interpret them as control tones, with disastrous results to the call.

## Modem Interfaces

A modem has an interface to the telephone network and an interface to the DTE. The one to the telephone network is simpler because that interface consists of only two wires, referred to as tip and ring. The terms tip and ring can be traced to the manner by which a connection to a switchboard occurred. As an operator patched a call, the connector on the end of the cord known as the tip and the ring around the end formed an electrical connection. Today, the two wires on a local loop referred to as tip and ring also form an electrical connection. As long as the modem adheres to the voltage, current, power, and frequency rules of the telephone company, the telephone channel is really just a pipe to move analog tones from one place to another.

The interface wiring between the modem and the DTE is more complex and is governed by standards discussed later in this chapter. This interface also requires that certain procedures (called a protocol) be observed in establishing communications between the two ends. First, the DTE and the modem at the transmitting end must establish communication with one another. The DTE indicates to the modem that it wants to transmit, and this modem signals to the modem at the other end of the circuit to see whether it is ready to receive. Because, in general, modems do not store data, the receiving modem must contact its DTE to see whether it is ready to receive. (This communication between the equipment often is referred to as handshaking. Another version of handshaking references a negotiation process between modems, in which they inform one another of the data rates and features that they support in an attempt to decide upon the use of a common set of parameters.) After the transmitting modem knows that the receiving modem and DTE are listening on the line, it notifies the transmitting DTE, which then begins passing data to the transmitting modem for modulation and transmission. On the receiving end, the receiving modem demodulates the incoming signal and passes the received data to the receiving DTE.

In half-duplex transmission (only one direction at a time), when the transmitter is finished and wants a reply from the other end, the channel must be "turned around." To do this, much of the handshaking must be done again to establish transmission in the opposite direction, and this turnaround handshaking must occur each time the direction is changed. In full-duplex transmission (both directions simultaneously), the transmission uses two different carrier frequencies. Thus, the handshaking is necessary only for the initial setup.

# Analog Modulation

Modulation is the process of using some medium to carry information between two points. For example, you could send Morse code by turning a flashlight on and off to modulate the light beam. Reflection on this process reveals that you would be changing some property of the carrier to represent the data—in this instance, that property is the intensity of the beam. (You might more easily understand this if you imagine using a bright light for a mark and a dim light for a space. In this case, you would be modulating the brightness or amplitude of the light beam to send data.)

## Sine Waves

A sine wave that might be used as a carrier in a modem is illustrated in Figure 4.2. Sine waves not only are mathematical functions, but they also are fundamental phenomena of the physical universe. Sine waves are generated by devices such as electromechanical generators and electronic oscillators.

A man named Fourier discovered that any series of pulses, sounds, voltages, or similar waves can be broken down into a series of sine waves of varying frequencies and amplitudes. This means that human speech, in the air or on a telephone wire, can be analyzed in terms of the sine waves it contains. That is not to say that the human larynx creates speech by combining sound waves at different frequencies; it simply means that Fourier analysis is a fundamental and useful tool for analyzing the characteristics of any transmission channel or device, whether it be a modem or the speakers of a high-fidelity sound system.

As illustrated in Figure 4.2a, a sine wave can be defined by its frequency and amplitude. Frequency is measured in cycles per second, with the unit of measurement termed the Hertz (Hz). That is, one cycle per second equals 1Hz. Amplitude can be measured in units of volts peak to peak, volts peak, and volts root mean square (rms), as indicated in the figure.

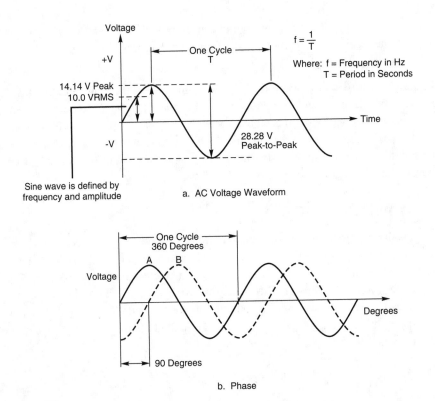

**FIGURE 4.2**

*The sine wave fundamentals.*

Another parameter of a sine wave is the phase of the wave, but it has meaning only in reference to another wave of the same frequency. Two different sine waves having the same frequency can be compared by the amount by which one leads or lags the other. Because one complete cycle of a sine wave occurs in 360°, you can consider the difference between the two waves in terms of degrees, as indicated in Figure 4.2b. The amplitudes of the two waves compared do not have to be the same, but the frequencies must be exactly the same.

Because the frequency, amplitude, and phase completely characterize a sine wave, these are the only parameters of the carrier sine wave that can be changed to modulate the carrier for transmitting information from one modem to another. All modems, therefore, use amplitude, frequency, or phase modulation, or some combination of these parameters.

Figure 4.3 illustrates the three modulation methods. Notice that the same sequence of ones and zeros of the data stream affect the carrier in different ways. After modulation, the pulses are represented by an AC signal having frequencies within the voiceband. Thus, the information can be transmitted over telephone channels. Actually, simple amplitude modulation is not used for data communications because it is very susceptible to electrical noise interference, which can cause errors in the received data. Low-speed modems use frequency modulation, higher-speed modems use phase modulation, and the very highest-speed modems for voiceband transmission use a combination of phase and amplitude modulation.

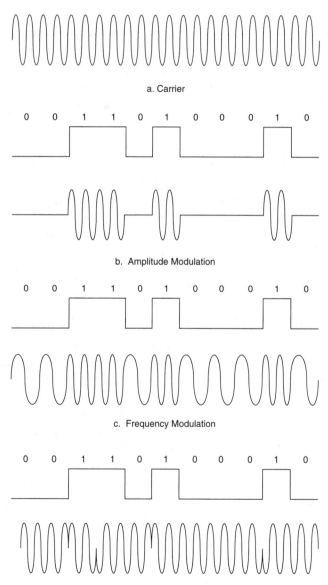

a. Carrier

b. Amplitude Modulation

c. Frequency Modulation

d. Phase Modulation

**FIGURE 4.3**

*The types of analog modulation.*

## Low-Speed Modem Frequency Modulation Methods

With this background, you're ready to look at how a standard 0–300–baud low-speed modem works. Figure 4.4 shows the voiceband divided into two subbands for transmission in both directions simultaneously. Recall that such two-way transmission is called full-duplex, meaning that the same bandwidth is available in both directions at the same time.

For some people, the process of transmitting data over one channel in two directions at the same time might be hard to visualize. One could think of it as being similar to two people talking on the same local call simultaneously. Both people can talk and hear at the same time—although they might have trouble understanding one another—because the entire bandwidth of the channel is available to both parties in both directions. However, the modems completely separate the data into the two bands shown, one for each direction, so that each can understand the other.

The separation is accomplished when one modem is set to originate mode and the other is set to answer mode by a switch on each modem or through the issuance of commands to each modem from attached DTEs. The terms originate and answer come from the use of low-speed modems in dial-up computer applications in which a user calls a computer. The calling modem is usually in originate mode, and the called modem is in answer mode (makes sense, doesn't it?). This way, the marking tone of the answer modem (the high-pitched "whistle" heard when it answers) also disables any echo suppressors (which interfere with data transmission) that might be in the circuit.

## Frequency-Shift Keying

In Figure 4.4, notice that the originate modem transmits zeros (spaces) at 1070Hz and ones (marks) at 1270Hz. The answer modem also transmits spaces and marks, but at 2025 and 2225Hz, respectively. This type of modulation is called frequency-shift keying (FSK). (The term keying refers to turning a transmitter on and off.) The appropriate mark or space frequency is simply turned on and off by the transmitting modem as it wants to send a 1 or 0. If you listen on a telephone line that is carrying low-speed FSK modem transmissions, you might hear a warbling sound as the frequencies shift back and forth.

If the originating modem transmits zeros at 1070Hz and ones at 1270Hz, at what frequency does it receive zeros and ones? For compatibility with the answer modem that transmits zeros and ones at 2025 and 2225Hz, the originating modem receives zeros and ones at those frequencies. Similarly, the answer modem receives zeros and ones at 1070Hz and 1270Hz to maintain transmission compatibility with the originating modem.

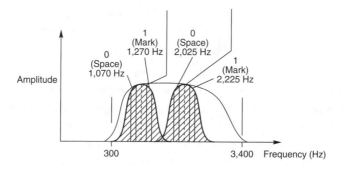

## FIGURE 4.4

*Frequencies used for 300-baud full-duplex transmission.*

The FSK modem just described is more commonly known as a Bell System 113-type device. Because each bit is converted into a distinct tone by a Bell system 113-type modem, the bit rate of this device is equal to its baud or signaling rate. As you will learn later in this chapter and in the next chapter, modem designers developed several techniques, such as dibit, tribit, and quadbit encoding, to pack more information into each signaling change. Such techniques permit modems to support higher data-transfer rates without much higher signaling rates (which could result in intersymbol interference if the energy in one signal were to adversely effect a succeeding signal). Originally, the Bell System supplied all modems that could be attached to the switched telephone network. By the time other vendors were permitted to sell modems for use on the switched network, the Bell System's monopoly had created a large base of telephone company devices, which encouraged vendors to manufacture modems compatible with Bell System products.

FSK is a straightforward and economical modulation method that works well over telephone channels, so the logical question is this: "Why not use it for higher-speed modems?" The answer is "between the lines" (no pun intended) of Figure 4.4. Higher data rates require more bandwidth. Thus, if you wanted to transmit at higher speeds, the mark and space frequencies for each subband would have to be farther apart, and the two subbands would have to be separated further to provide enough bandwidth. Soon you would be outside of the telephone channel. In other words, you would require more bandwidth than is available. Therefore, higher-speed modems use some form of phase modulation because phase modulation requires the least bandwidth of the three analog modulation methods.

# V.21 Standard

In Europe, the Consultative Committee for International Telephone and Telegraph (CCITT), now known as the International Telecommunications Union–Telecommunications

Standardization section (ITU-T), developed a series of standards that govern the operation of modems. This series is commonly referred to as the "V-series" because the letter prefix "V" is used to denote modem-related standards.

One such standard that governs the operation of an FSK modem is known as V.21. The V.21 standard uses different originate and answer frequencies for marks and spaces in comparison with the Bell System 113-type device because of a requirement to avoid control frequencies used on European telephone networks. The V.21 modem uses 980Hz for a mark and 1180Hz for a space in its originate mode, and it receives a mark and space at 1650 and 1850Hz, respectively. Due to the differences in operating frequencies, a Bell System 113 and a V.21 modem are incompatible.

## Bell System 212A and V.22 Modems

Until the mid-1980s, the Bell System 212A modem was the most popular upgrade for Bell System 113-type modem users. The 212A modem can be considered two modems in one because it employs FSK modulation using the Bell System 113 frequency assignments at 300bps. At its higher 1200bps rate, however, it uses dibit phase-shift keyed (DPSK) modulation. Under DPSK modulation, 2 bits at a time are encoded into one phase shift or signal change. Thus, the modem's signal rate (commonly known as its baud rate) is 600, or one-half of its 1200bps data rate. The phase shift encoding of the 212A-type modem is illustrated in Table 4.1.

**TABLE 4.1**   The 212A-Type Modem Phase Shift

| Dibit | Phase Shift (Degrees) |
| --- | --- |
| 00 | 90 |
| 01 | 0 |
| 10 | 180 |
| 11 | 270 |

When a 212A modem operates at 1200bps, it can transmit data either asynchronously or synchronously. One key advantage to using 212A-type modems is that when they're connected to a computer, they can receive transmissions from terminal devices operating at either 300 or 1200bps.

The V.22 standard is similar to the 212A at 1200bps. However, at the 212A's lower data rate, the two modems are incompatible. The V.22 modem's second data rate is 600bps, compared with the 212A's lower data rate of 300bps. A second major difference between the lower speeds of the two modems is in the method of modulation used. The 212A uses FSK modulation at 300bps, whereas the V.22 uses two-phase PSK at 600bps. Fortunately, the V.22 modem is used primarily in Europe, and the 212A-type modem is used primarily in North America. This also explains why an American businessman traveling in Europe with a transportable computer during the mid-1980s could not establish a communications session when he attempted to connect to a dial-in modem on the continent. A European businessman had the same problem when visiting North America.

## V.22bis

The V.22bis (bis meaning "second version" in Latin) received widespread acceptance throughout the United States and Europe during the late 1980s. It represents the first modem that can be used for worldwide communications. The V.22bis recommendation governs modems designed for asynchronous data transmission at 2400bps over the switched telephone network, with a V.22 fallback method of operation. When the V.22bis modem operates in its fallback mode, incompatibility problems can arise because of the different methods used to manufacture this modem.

In the United States, most, if not all, V.22bis modems follow the Bell System 212A specifications for fallback operations: DPSK at 1200bps and FSK at 300bps. In Europe, most V.22bis modems follow the V.22 specifications for fallback operations, which include two-phase PSK at 600bps. Thus, at their lowest fallback rate, V.22bis modems manufactured for use in North America are incompatible with those manufactured for use in Europe. Although it's important to consider modem operating rates, you should also consider their features because many products can be differentiated by examining their support of different features.

# Modem Features

Most modern modems include 30 to 100 or more built-in features. Although some of those features might represent proprietary technology, most of them represent the incorporation of de facto or de jure standards, such as the support of several types of modulation schemes. Two of the most common features now incorporated into modems designed for use on the switched telephone network are data compression and error detection and correction.

## Data Compression and the V.42bis Standard

Two of the most common features now incorporated into modems designed for use on the switched telephone network are data compression (including the LZW logarithm and V.42bis) and error detection and correction. Modems incorporating compression really operate at variable data rates because throughput depends on the susceptibility of the data to the compression algorithms in the modem. As an example of how a modem can compress data, consider the sequence ACCOUNTbbbbbbb AMOUNT, in which b indicates a blank or space character. This sequence could represent the column headings of a report; it's similar to most accounting reports that contain columns of data separated from the next column by spaces. If the modem uses a special character denoted as Sc to show space compression, the sequence is transmitted as ACCOUNT Sc7 AMOUNT between modems. At the receiving modem, the character Sc indicates the occurrence of space compression, and the number 7 indicates the number of space characters compressed. This information enables the receiving modem to decompress the data into its original form.

To prevent the natural occurrence in the data stream of a character indicating space compression (and thus falsely affecting the modem at the opposite end of the data link), the originating modem is programmed to stuff an extra space-compression-indicating character into the transmission sequence. Thus, if the data stream into the modem is XYZScABC, the modem transmits the sequence XYZScScABC. At the receiving modem, the occurrence of the first Sc character causes the modem to examine the next character. When the receiving modem finds a second Sc character following the first, it disregards the second Sc character, restoring the data stream to its original form and preventing a false decompression of the data.

Until 1990, most compression modems used a mixture of compression algorithms. Although the actual throughput is variable, the net effect of compression is roughly double the data-transfer rate of the device. In 1990, the ITU-T (formerly known as the CCITT) promulgated its V.42bis recommendation. V.42bis defines a modified Lempel-Ziv compression algorithm for use in modems. This data compression technique was adopted by more than 20 modem vendors by the beginning of 1991 and is now incorporated into most intelligent modems because it represents a standardized compression method and provides a more efficient method for compressing data than competitive algorithms do.

Although the v.42bis data compression standard is now used in more than 50 million dial-up modems, a new compression specification referred to as V.44 was developed and is expected to eventually replace the earlier ITU standard. V.44 represents a data-compression method originally developed for the satellite industry as a mechanism to maximize available bandwidth. V.44 uses a variation of the Lempel-Ziv compression algorithm referred to as Lempel-Ziv-Jeff-Heath (LZJH).

Two competitive data-compression methods are MNP Class 5 and Class 7. Microcom Corporation, now owned by Compaq Computer Corporation, licensed MNP Class 5 compression to more than 50 modem vendors during the 1980s. Later, Microcom licensed its enhanced data compression incorporated into MNP Class 7 to other modem manufacturers. Because of the large base of MNP-compatible modems that were manufactured before the development of the V.42bis compression standard, most modem manufacturers incorporate support for both

MNP and V.42bis. This dual compression support offers modern modems compression compatibility with older modems that support only MNP compression as well as with newer modems that support both MNP and V.42bis or only V.42bis compression. The MNP modem protocol is discussed later in this chapter.

## The LZW Algorithm

V.42bis compression is based on the theoretical work of Professors Abraham Lempel and Jacob Ziv at the Technion in Haifa, Israel, and the effort of Englishman Terry Welch, whose modifications to Lempel and Ziv's string compression algorithm resulted in the LZW algorithm. The LZW algorithm, which has its mnemonics in honor of the two Israeli professors and the Englishman, forms the heart of the V.42bis compression standard. In this section, you will turn your attention to the LZW algorithm and examine how it operates.

Under the LZW algorithm, the character set is initially selected as 256 individual dictionary entries whose codes range from 0 to 255. Then the algorithm operates on one character at a time in the input string to be compressed according to the following two-step method:

1. If the character is in the dictionary, get the next character.

2. If the character is not in the dictionary, output the last known string's encoding and add the new string to the table.

Under the LZW algorithm, characters to be compressed are read and used to form progressively larger strings until a string is formed that is not in the dictionary. When this situation occurs, the last known string's encoding is output, and the new string is added to the dictionary. The LZW algorithm uses a numeric code as a token to indicate the position of a string in the dictionary's string table. If you call the string previously read the prefix of the output string, and you call the last byte read the suffix, then the algorithm can be defined in the following way:

```
prefix + suffix = new string
```

After a new string is formed, the suffix becomes the prefix, as in this example:

```
prefix = suffix
```

As an example of LZW encoding, assume that the input string of data flowing into a modem is ababc. Initially, each character in the character set that forms the dictionary is assigned a numeric code value equivalent to its character code. Thus, in ASCII, an *a* would have the code value 97, a *b* would have the code value 98, and so on.

Under the LZW algorithm, the first operation assumes that the prefix has a value of the null string, which we will indicate by the symbol f. Thus, the first operation results in the addition of the null string to *a*, which forms the new string a. Because *a* is in the dictionary, the algorithm does not output anything. However, because the suffix becomes the prefix, a now becomes the prefix for the next operation. This is indicated at the top of Table 4.2.

Now consider that the second character in the input string is b. Processing that character according to the LZW algorithm results in the addition of the prefix (a) and the suffix (b) to form a new string (ab). Because the new string (ab) is not in the dictionary, rule 2 is followed. That is, the last known string's encoding, which is 97, is output for the character a, and the new string (ab) is added to the dictionary. Because codes 0–255 were previously used to represent the individual characters in an 8-bit character set, the next available code, 256, is used to represent the string ab. Note that this requires an increase in the number of bits used to form a token, and the initial token size must be negotiated between modems during the V.42bis negotiation process.

Returning to the input string to be compressed, b, which was the suffix when generating the string ab, becomes the prefix for the next operation. This is indicated in line 3 of Table 4.2.

Because the next character in the string to be encoded is a, it functions as the suffix in creating the new string ba. Because that string is not presently in the dictionary, the last known string (b) is output using its ASCII code value of 98. Next, the string ba is added to the dictionary, using the next available code, which is 257. Because a was the suffix in creating the string ab, it now becomes the prefix for the next string operation, as illustrated in line 4 in Table 4.2. The fourth character in the input string (b) is now processed as the suffix to form a new string. This results in the new string ab, which was previously added to the string table. Because it is already in the string table, no output is generated, and the string ab becomes the prefix for creating the next string.

The creation of the next string is shown in line 5 in Table 4.2. Here, the previously created string ab, which was in the string table, becomes the prefix for generating the next string, and the last character in the input data string (c) becomes the suffix in forming the next string. The resulting string (ab) is not in the dictionary. Thus, the last known string, ab, has its code value output. Because ab was previously assigned the value 256, that value is output, and the suffix (c) becomes the prefix for the creation of the next string. Because c was the last character in the input string, its code value of 99 is output.

**TABLE 4.2** LZW Encoding of the String ababc

| Prefix | Suffix | New String | Output |
|--------|--------|------------|--------|
| f | a | a | — |
| a | b | ab | 97 |
| b | a | ba | 98 |
| a | b | ab | — |
| ab | c | abc | 256 |
| c | f | c | 99 |

## Compression Parameters

In addition to specifying the use of LZW string compression, the V.42bis standard defines several compression-related parameters, such as the size of the dictionary and how the dictionary is emptied or flushed. Although some parameters are negotiated during the initial modem call setup process, other parameters, such as flushing the dictionary, can occur at any time during the transmission session.

The emerging V.44 data compression algorithm uses a variation of LZW referred to as LZJH. During a series of tests performed by a modem manufacturer, the V.44 algorithm operating on a series of test files provided compression ratios between 12 and 230 percent beyond compression ratios obtained using the V.42bis algorithm, with an average improvement of approximately 25 percent. This is equivalent to boosting the data-transfer capability of a modem by a quarter. When added to a new dial-up modem standard referred to as V.92 (described in Chapter 5, "Synchronous Modems, Digital Transmission, and Service Units"), dial-up modems can obtain a data throughput approaching 300Kbps, making them competitive with Digital Subscriber Line (DSL) and cable modems for many applications.

> **NOTE**
>
> For further information covering data-compression techniques and applications, refer to the book *Data and Image Compression, 4th Edition,* by Gilbert Held. Published by John Wiley & Sons in 1996, this book explains 15 compression algorithms and contains BASIC and C++ language programs that can be used to compress and decompress data.

## Bit Errors on Compressed Data

Although data compression can enhance throughput, if one or more bits are received in error, their impact can be very severe upon the reconstruction of the original data. Therefore, error detection and correction go hand-in-hand with data compression.

To illustrate the effect of bit errors on compressed data, assume that the data sequence AAAAAAAA occurred. Assume that the modem is programmed to replace a string of more than three repeated characters by a special compression-indicating character followed by the number of characters that were compressed and the character that was compressed. Further assume that the special compression-indicating character is represented by the bit sequence 11111111, and the character *A* is represented by the bit sequence 01000001.

Figure 4.5 illustrates the potential effect of a bit error on a compressed sequence of bits. In Figure 4.5a, the original repeated character sequence of eight *A*s is shown. In Figure 4.5b, that sequence is compressed into the character sequence Sc8A, in which Sc is the previously discussed compression-indicating character. Figure 4.5c indicates the compressed binary sequence. That sequence of 24 bits, in effect, represents 40 bits because the three-compressed-character sequence represents eight noncompressed characters.

In Figure 4.5d, it was assumed that a bit error occurred that changed the next-to-last bit in the 24-bit sequence. The effect of that bit error is to change the binary value of the third character in the compressed character sequence from decimal 65 to decimal 67. This causes the character to be changed from an *A* to a *C*, as indicated in Figure 4.5e, which shows the decompressed results in a string of eight *C*'s replacing the original noncompressed sequence of eight, as shown in Figure 4.5f.

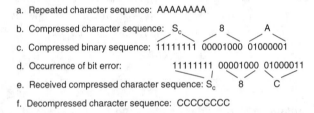

```
a.  Repeated character sequence:  AAAAAAAA
b.  Compressed character sequence:  S_c        8        A
c.  Compressed binary sequence:  11111111 00001000 01000001
d.  Occurrence of bit error:          11111111 00001000 01000011
e.  Received compressed character sequence: S_c    8      C
f.  Decompressed character sequence:  CCCCCCCC
```

**FIGURE 4.5**

*The potential effect of a bit error on compressed data.*

If the bit error occurred in the repeat character indicator position, the number of characters decompressed would be in error. If the bit error corrupted the compression-indicating character, the receiving modem would not recognize that compression had occurred. In this situation, the compression-indicating character would be received as some other character, and the modem's decompression algorithm would not know that it was supposed to operate on the following two characters. Thus, the original string of eight *A*'s would be received as the three-character sequence X8A, in which X would represent the character resulting from a bit error corrupting the compression-indicating character.

As indicated by the preceding examples, the effect of a bit error on compressed data can be significantly more pronounced than the effect of a bit error on noncompressed data. This is the rationale for the inclusion of an error-detection-and-correction feature being built into every modem that has the capability to perform data compression.

Although a modem's error-detection-and correction feature can be set to operate on noncompressed data, it is automatically placed into operation whenever the modem is set to perform compression. This ensures the integrity of compressed data.

# Error Detection and Correction

In an error-detection-and-correction mode of operation, the originating modem first groups data to be transmitted into blocks of characters. A mathematical algorithm is performed on each block, and one or more check characters are appended to each block. For example, the modem might treat each data block as one long binary number and divide that number by a fixed polynomial, resulting in a quotient and remainder, in which the remainder is used as a check character. The modem then transmits each block to include its check character or characters. The receiving modem performs a similar operation on each received data block. That is, the receiving modem might treat the block as one long binary number and divide that number by the same fixed polynomial used to generate the checksum.

When the division process is complete, the receiving modem would use the remainder as a locally generated checksum and compare that checksum to the checksum appended to the received data block. If the two checksums match, the data is assumed to be received without error, and the receiving modem transmits an acknowledgment to the transmitting modem. The acknowledgment informs the transmitting modem that it can discard the previously transmitted block because it was received without error. If the two checksums do not match, the receiving modem assumes that one or more bit errors occurred that altered the composition of the data block. The receiving modem discards the block and transmits a negative acknowledgment to the transmitting modem, which serves as a request for that modem to retransmit the preceding block. Thus, error correction is performed by retransmission.

Because modems performing error detection and correction must store a previously transmitted block until a receiving modem indicates that it was accepted, modems with this feature must have buffer storage. The actual amount of storage required is based on the method used to perform error detection and correction. Until the late 1990s, the most popular method of error detection and correction used by modems was MNP Class 4. With the development of V.42bis data compression, the ITU-T promulgated the V.42 error-detection-and correction standard, which now represents the favored method of error detection and correction.

The V.42 error-detection-and correction standard actually defines two methods of error detection and correction: LAPB and MNP Class 4. LAPB (Link Access Procedure Balanced) represents the error-detection-and-correction method used by the Higher-Level Data Link Control (HDLC) protocol used at the network layer. LAPB is the primary method of modem error detection and correction specified by the V.42 standard; MNP Class 4 represents a secondary or alternative method. Due to the large base of MNP-compatible modems, many V.42-compatible modem users typically set the modem's error-detection-and correction mode to MNP Class 4. Later in this chapter, you'll learn how to enable and disable such modem features as data compression and error detection and correction.

**4**

ASYNCHRONOUS
MODEMS AND
INTERFACES

# The MNP Protocol

Among the first modems to offer an error-detection-and-correction feature were products man-ufactured by Microcom, Inc., which was acquired by Compaq Computer Corporation. This company created a revolution in modem technology by developing a modem protocol known as MNP, an acronym for Microcom Networking Protocol.

MNP is a communications protocol built into MNP-compatible modems that supports interac-tive and file-transfer applications. In developing MNP, Microcom recognized that the first implementation of the protocol would not necessarily be the last and, therefore, structured it to accommodate changes in its implementation. To accomplish this, the major functions of the protocol are divided into classes. When an MNP modem communicates with another MNP modem, the two devices negotiate to operate at the highest mutually supported class of MNP service.

Table 4.3 summarizes the features associated with available MNP classes. Until 1990, Microcom licensed MNP only through Class 5 to other modem manufacturers. In that year, Microcom began to offer full MNP licenses. Thus, an MNP-compatible modem, although com-patible with all other MNP modems, might be compatible with only a subset of available MNP classes unless a third-party vendor got a full license and incorporated all MNP classes into the product.

In Table 4.3, note the inclusion of such terms as V.29 and V.32. Both reference ITU-T modula-tion standards, of which V.29 was originally developed as a half-duplex 9600bps modulation technique for use on leased lines. Microcom, as well as other vendors, modified that technol-ogy to work on the PSTN. In addition, using the intelligence of a microprocessor to monitor the direction of transmission, it became possible to quickly turn off the transmitter of one modem and turn on its receiver, enabling the half-duplex transmission mode to resemble full-duplex transmission. In comparison, a V.32 modem uses echo-cancellation technology to enable transmission and reception of data to occur simultaneously on the PSTN, and it pro-vides an inherent full-duplex transmission capability. Both V.29 and V.32 modulation are described in Chapter 5.

**TABLE 4.3**    MNP Classes

| Class | Description of Functions Performed |
| --- | --- |
| Class 1 | Uses asynchronous byte-oriented half-duplex transmission that provides an efficiency of approximately 70%. A 2400bps modem using MNP Class 1 gets a throughput of 1690bps. |
| Class 2 | Uses asynchronous byte-oriented full-duplex data transmission that provides an efficiency of approximately 84%. A 2400bps modem using MNP Class 2 gets a throughput of approximately 2000bps. |

**TABLE 4.3** continued

| Class | Description of Functions Performed |
| --- | --- |
| Class 3 | Strips start and stop bits from asynchronous data, enabling synchronous bit-oriented full-duplex transmission between modems. This provides an efficiency of about 108%, enabling a 2400bps modem to get a throughput of approximately 2600bps. |
| Class 4 | Adds adaptive packet assembly in which packet sizes are dynamically adjusted based on the number of retransmission requests. Also adds data phase optimization, which provides a mechanism for reducing protocol overhead. The efficiency of Class 4 is approximately 120%, enabling a 2400bps modem to get a throughput of 2900bps. |
| Class 5 | Adds data compression to Class 4 service, which provides an average compression ratio of 1.6:1, meaning that every 16 characters are compressed into 10 characters for transmission. This increases the protocol efficiency of Class 5 to approximately 200%, enabling a 2400bps modem to get a throughput of about 4800bps. |
| Class 6 | Adds universal link negotiation and statistical duplexing to Class 5. Universal link negotiation enables MNP modems to begin operation at a common low-speed modulation method and negotiate the use of an alternative higher-speed modulation method. At the end of a successful link negotiation for Class 6 operation, the two modems operate at 9600bps using V.29 technology. Statistical duplexing results in the monitoring of user traffic patterns to enable the dynamic allocation of V.29 half-duplex transmission to resemble full-duplex transmission. Under Class 6 9600bps operations, MNP provides an average throughput approaching 19,200bps. |
| Class 7 | Adds an enhanced data-compression capability to MNP based on a Huffman statistical encoding technique. Under Class 7, a compression ratio between 2.0 and 3.0 is achievable, which increases throughput from two to three times the modem's operating rate. |
| Class 8 | Is no longer marketed. |
| Class 9 | Adds support of V.32 modulation to Class 7, providing a throughput up to three times the 9600bps full-duplex operating rate of a V.32 modem. |
| Class 10 | Adds adverse channel enhancement (ACE), which optimizes modem performance in environments with poor or varying line conditions, such as cellular communications, rural telephone service, and some international connections. |

**4**

ASYNCHRONOUS
MODEMS AND
INTERFACES

## V.42 Recommendation

Although MNP error detection and correction is included in more than 1 million modems manufactured by Microcom and by more than 100 third-party vendors (as previously discussed in this chapter), it is not the primary method of error detection and correction recommended for use in modems by the ITU-T. In 1990, the CCITT (now known as the ITU-T) promulgated its V.42 recommendation.

Unlike other V series recommendations that govern modern modulation techniques, the V.42 recommendation defines a protocol in which modems block data for transmission and generate and add a cyclic redundancy check (CRC) to each block for error detection. In recognition of the large installed base of MNP modems, MNP error detection and correction is supported as a secondary standard. That is, a V.42-compatible modem first attempts to communicate in its error-free mode using LAPB. If the distant modem does not support the V.42 protocol, the V.42 modem next attempts to communicate using MNP error control.

### Data Compression

Although the V.42 recommendation supports MNP error control, the V.42bis recommendation, which is a data-compression scheme that requires the use of the V.42 protocol, does not support a secondary method of compression. This theoretically means that for your V.42bis modem to operate in a compressed mode, it must communicate with another V.42bis-compatible modem. Because V.42bis and the newer V.44 standards are the only data-compression schemes used in modern modems, this also means that if you require MNP compatibility, you need to determine the level of support, if any, for MNP in the modem you plan to acquire. Fortunately, most V.42bis modems also include MNP support through Class 5, enabling you to communicate in both a data-compressed mode and an error-control mode with another MNP modem.

The key difference between V.42bis, V.44, and MNP Class 5 or Class 7 lies in their methods of data compression. V.42bis uses the previously described Lempel-Ziv-Welch (LZW) algorithm, which can operate on single characters as well as on strings, whereas V.44 uses a modification of LZW, known as LZJH, which also operates on characters and strings. In comparison, MNP compression primarily operates on single characters and is slightly less efficient. When using a V.42bis modem that incorporates V.34 modulation, the 28,800bps operating rate of the modem can achieve a throughput of up to 115,200bps when data is very susceptible to compression. V.44 incorporated into a V.92 modem can provide a data-transfer capability of approximately 300Kbps.

### Interface Versus Operating Rate

To effectively use data compression, you must set your modem's interface data rate to exceed its operating rate and, if supported by your serial port, to four times its operating rate. To understand this requirement, consider Figure 4.6, which illustrates the relationship between the interface speed and the operating rate of a modem.

If the interface speed equals the operating rate, data compression will not increase the throughput of the modem. To increase the modem's throughput, you must set the interface rate to at least twice the modem's operating rate. For example, if the modem operates at 28,800bps, you should set the interface rate to at least 57,600bps. This setting allows more bits in the form of characters to enter the modem per unit of time than can be transmitted. Then data compression can attempt to reduce the bits entering the modem so that they can be transmitted at the modem's operating rate, increasing the modem's throughput.

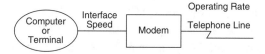

**FIGURE 4.6**

*The relationship between interface speed and modem operating rate.*

# Interface and Signaling Standards

Many "standards" and "recommended practices" are used to define data communications interfaces and signaling. In fact, the entire problem of data communications can be looked at as the task of passing information through a series of interfaces and transmission channels without loss of meaning.

The interface that is of the greatest interest is the one between the equipment that originates or receives the data (the data terminal equipment) and the equipment that handles the problem of transmitting the data from place to place (the data communications equipment). Computers are considered data terminal equipment (whether they look or act like a CRT or another terminal). Modems are considered data communications equipment (also called data circuit-terminating equipment or data sets) because their function is to communicate the data and not to consider, compute, or change the data in any way.

Terms such as *RS-232, V.24, RS-422, RS-423, RS-449, X.21, X.25,* and *current loop* are the designations of the various standards and recommendations designed to make the task of connecting computers, terminals, modems, and networks easier. As you'll see, manufacturers have, in many cases, used the standardized interfaces for functions that were never intended. This method helps by not increasing the number of interfaces, but it adds to the confusion of the user.

In terms of the present computer and communications world, the Electronic Industries Association (EIA) RS-232 is the standard interface. Therefore, the remainder of this chapter describes it and uses it as a way to explain interfaces in general. You'll examine some of the limitations of RS-232 and learn about some of the newer developments that eventually might replace RS-232.

# The RS-232 and V.24 Interface

The proper name of RS-232 is "Interface Between Data Terminal Equipment and Data Communication Equipment Employing Serial Binary Data Interchange." Currently, the most popular version of RS-232 is revision C, which is formally referred to as RS-232C. In the late 1980s, revision D was introduced, which was followed by revision E in the early 1990s. The latest version, RS-232E, will eventually supersede RS-232C and RS-232D. All three versions of the RS-232 standard have a core of common functions and operating features that will collectively be referred to as RS-232. This book designates an appropriate revision to describe specific functions associated with each version of RS-232. What is written here also applies to ITU-T Recommendation V.24, which is almost identical to RS-232, but the electrical signal characteristics are specified separately in ITU-T Recommendation V.28.

In addition to explanatory notes and a short glossary, the RS-232 standard covers the following four areas:

- The mechanical characteristics of the interface (which has some surprises)
- The electrical signals across the interface
- The function of each signal
- Subsets of signals for certain applications

## The Mechanical Interface

As with any standard, the purpose of RS-232 is primarily to function as a reference for designers of equipment; therefore, it is not a tutorial and not particularly easy reading. (Perhaps that explains why it seems that many people who write about RS-232 have never read it.) Almost anyone in the computer or communications field, including authors, will tell you that the DB-25 connector is defined in the standard. That is simply not true of RS-232C. It wasn't until reference D was introduced that the 25-pin interface connector was formally specified. Until RS-232D, all that the mechanical section covered was the assignment of signals to the connector pins (discussed in the next section), which piece of equipment has the female connector (the DCE), the recommended maximum cable length (50 feet), and the maximum cable capacitance (2500 picofarads).

Because the DB-25 connector became almost universally associated with RS-232C, its pin arrangement is shown in Figure 4.7. However, it was not defined in the standard until revision D, and many manufacturers use a different connector on most of their notebook computer equipment. That connector is referred to as a DB-9, which, as its nomenclature indicates, defines a nine-pin connector. This connector is also used on many desktop computers that combine serial and parallel ports onto a single adapter card. The DB-9 connector requires less mounting space on the rear of a computer and provides manufacturers with a mechanism for reducing the size of a computer while still providing a built-in serial port connection. A later portion of this chapter describes the RS-232 circuits carried within a DB-9 connector and their relationship to the circuits carried within a DB-25 connector. RS-232D additions and changes to RS-232C are indicated in parentheses in Figure 4.7.

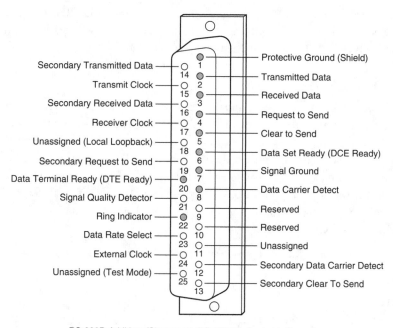

RS-232D Additions/Changes to RS-232C Indicated in Parentheses

**FIGURE 4.7**

*A typical RS-232 female (socket) connector.*

# Electrical and Functional Signals

Although it doesn't make much sense to say that one part of a standard is more important than another, the heart of RS-232 is certainly composed of the electrical and functional sections. The electrical portion covers the all-important voltage and current specifications for each pin, along with such features as the requirement that the equipment not be damaged if any two pins are shorted together (which is not to say that the equipment would still work, but it's not supposed to burn up). The functional portion, perhaps the most important of all, defines the sequencing of the signals and the action taken by the DTE and DCE in response.

Although the RS-232 standard defines the procedures for automatic answering by the modem and for reversing the transmission direction in half-duplex communications, it does not define automatic dialing. This is covered in EIA standard RS-366. As you will see later, almost all newer modems incorporate automatic dialing in ways that the authors of RS-232 and RS-366 did not imagine. In addition, the incorporation of microprocessors into modems resulted in the development of computer- or terminal-controlled commands, enabling an attached DTE to send commands to a modem. One of those commands is a dialing command that informs the modem of the number to dial and has essentially replaced the use of the RS-366 standard as well as many proprietary dialing methods. Later in this chapter, you will examine many smart modem commands to include a standardized dialing command.

## Subset of Signals

In Figure 4.8, the signals are numbered and named according to three standard systems, plus a fourth system that isn't a standard but that many people use. The first is by pin number, which is the way that people who deal regularly with the interface think of the signals: pin 2, pin 3, pin 5, and so forth. The second is the EIA designation: BA, BB, CB, and so forth. The third is the CCITT (now known as the ITU-T) designation: 103, 104, 106, and so on. The fourth is an abbreviation of the signal description: TD for "Transmitted Data," RD for "Received Data," CTS for "Clear to Send," and so forth. A given signal often has more than one of these abbreviations because they aren't standard.

The following sections take you on a pin-by-pin tour and look at the signals by category and function.

### Pins 1 and 7

If provided, pin 1 is connected to the chassis of the equipment and is intended to connect one end of the shield if shielded cable is used. Shielded cable can be used to minimize interference in high-noise environments. Never connect the shield at both ends of the cable. Pin 7 is the common reference for all signals, including data, timing, and control signals. Pin 7 must be connected at both ends for the DTE and DCE to work properly across the serial interface. Under RS-232D, pin 1's use is modified to provide shielding, and this conductor is referred to as "the shield."

| PIN NO. | EIA CKT. | CCITT CKT. | Signal Description | Common Abbrev. | From DCE | To DCE |
|---|---|---|---|---|---|---|
| 1 | AA | 101 | Protective Chassis Ground (Shield) | GND | | |
| 2 | BA | 103 | Transmitted Data | TD | | X |
| 3 | BB | 104 | Received Data | RD | X | |
| 4 | CA | 105 | Request to Send | RTS | | X |
| 5 | CB | 106 | Clear to Send | CTS | X | |
| 6 | CC | 107 | Data Set Ready (DCE Ready) | DSR | X | |
| 7 | AB | 102 | Signal Ground/Common Return | SG | X | X |
| 8 | CF | 109 | Received Line Signal Detector | DCD | X | |
| 9 | | | Reserved | | | |
| 10 | | | Reserved | | | |
| 11 | | | Unassigned | | | |
| 12 | SCF | 122 | Secondary Received Line Signal Detector | | X | |
| 13 | SCB | 121 | Secondary Clear to Send | | X | |
| 14 | SBA | 118 | Secondary Transmitted Data | | | X |
| 15 | DB | 114 | Transmitter Signal Element Timing (DCE) | | X | |
| 16 | SBB | 119 | Secondary Received Data | | X | |
| 17 | DD | 115 | Receiver Signal Element Timing | | X | |
| 18 | | | Unassigned (Local Loopback) | | | X |
| 19 | SCA | 120 | Secondary Request to Send | | | X |
| 20 | CD | 108/2 | Data Terminal Ready (DTE Ready) | DTR | | X |
| 21 | CG | 110 | Signal Quality Detector | SQ | X | |
| 22 | CE | 125 | Ring Indicator | RI | X | |
| 23 | CH | 111 | Data Signal Rate Selector (DTE) | | | X |
| 23 | CI | 112 | Data Signal Rate Selector (DCE) | | X | |
| 24 | DA | 113 | Transmitter Signal Element Timing (DTE) | | | X |
| 25 | | | Unassigned (Test Mode) | | X | |

RS-232D Additions/Changes to RS-232C Indicated in Parentheses

## FIGURE 4.8

*RS-232 pin designations.*

Pin 7 is the reference signal ground for all the other pins and thus is very important. The interface will not work without it because none of the signal circuits would be completed. One difficulty of RS-232 is the use of two separate grounding wires; grounding of distributed analog systems is often difficult, and having two ground paths doesn't help. To alleviate this difficulty, it is common to tie pins 1 and 7 together at one end of a cable.

## Pins 2 and 3: Transmitted Data (TD) and Received Data (RD)

At last you're getting down to the nitty-gritty. These are the pins that count; if it weren't for the data that passes through these pins, all the rest would be unnecessary. One important point to remember is that all signal names in the RS-232 standard are as viewed from the DTE. Thus, the DTE transmits on pin 2 and receives on pin 3, but the DCE transmits on pin 3 and receives on pin 2. If you imagine yourself as a computer (easier than imagining yourself as a modem), the names are easier to understand.

For people accustomed to more modern electronic interfaces, RS-232 signal levels might be a bit surprising because they are not TTL levels. In RS-232C, a positive voltage between 5 and 15 volts on pin 2 or 3 with respect to pin 7 represents a logic 0 level, and a negative voltage between –5 and –15 volts on either pin represents a logic 1. These are levels for data; the voltage polarities are reversed for logic 0 and 1 on the control lines. Under RS-232D and RS-232E, the ON and OFF voltage ranges were extended to +25 V and –25 V, respectively.

## Pins 4 and 5: Request to Send (RTS) and Clear to Send (CTS)

Terminals cannot transmit until Clear to Send (CTS) is received from the DCE. For private-line transmission, CTS is usually linked to Request to Send (RTS). In such cases, the DTE can use RTS to turn on the modem transmission carrier if the modem is so optioned. In this type of application, the relationship between RTS and CTS is usually a simple count-down timer that is optioned when the DCE is installed. The time delay will be set to such a value as to allow time for the carrier to turn on and become stable before CTS is returned to the DTE. If the DCE is optioned for constant carrier (without regard to RTS), the RTS/CTS delay is usually set to 0.

## Pins 6 and 20: Data Set Ready (DSR) and Data Terminal Ready (DTR)

Data Set Ready (DSR)—that is, Modem Ready—indicates that the modem is powered on and is not in test mode. In dial-data applications, Data Terminal Ready (DTR) creates the equivalent of an off-hook condition. When the modem is in autoanswer mode, DTR can be asserted in response to the ring indicator to tell the modem to answer the incoming call. Under RS-232D, the signal on pin 6 was renamed DCE Ready, and the signal on pin 20 was renamed DTE Ready.

## Pin 8: Received Line Signal Detector (DCD or CD)

The Received Line Signal Detector signal is usually called Data Carrier Detect (DCD) or Carrier Detect (CD). The term "CD" should be avoided, however, because it can be confused with the EIA designation of CD for pin 20. The modem asserts DCD whenever it receives a signal on the telephone line that meets its internal criteria for amount of energy at the carrier frequency. Many DTEs require this signal before they will transmit or accept data. For this reason, in applications in which no modem is present, pin 8 usually is tied to pin 20, which, in most cases, is asserted whenever the DTE is turned on.

## Pin 22: Ring Indicator (RI)

The Ring Indicator (RI) signal is the means by which the DCE tells the DTE that the phone is ringing. Virtually all modems that are designed to be directly connected (via an FCC-approved modular plug) to the telephone network are equipped for autoanswering. This means that the modem can recognize the standard ringing voltage, indicate the ringing to the DTE, and answer (take the line off-hook) when told to do so by the DTE. Pin 22 is asserted by the DCE in time with the cadence of the ringing signal on the line. Thus, when the ringing voltage is present, RI is true (on); between rings, RI is not true (off). The DTE tells the modem to answer the phone by asserting pin 20, DTR.

The 10 pins and signals in the foregoing descriptions are by far the most often used of those defined in RS-232 and V.24. It is very unlikely that equipment or cables for the small-computer market will be equipped with any other proper RS-232 signals, although sometimes (unfortunately) other pins are used in nonstandard ways that can cause problems when equipment is interconnected.

## Pins 15, 17, 21, and 24

Synchronous modems use the signals on pins 15, 17, 21, and 24. Because the transmitting modem must send something (a 1 or 0) at each bit time, the modem controls the timing of the bits from the DTE. Similarly, the receiving modem must output a bit and associated timing when received. Pin 15 (Transmitter Signal Element Timing–DCE source) and pin 17 (Receiver Signal Element Timing–DCE source) are used for these purposes. In instances in which the transmitter timing comes from a source other than the transmitting modem (such as another modem in a multiplexing situation), pin 24 (Transmitter Signal Element Timing–DTE source) is used. Pin 21 (Signal Quality Detector) indicates that the received carrier meets some predetermined criterion for quality.

## Pin 23: Data Signal Rate Selector

Pin 23 looks for two pins in the chart of Figure 4.8, but actually it is either Data Signaling Rate Selector (DTE source) or Data Signaling Rate Selector (DCE source). Some modems, called dual-rate or "gearshift" modems, allow switching between two transmission speeds. Sometimes the speed is selected automatically by the modem during the training (initializing) sequence, and sometimes it is selected by the transmitting DTE. The signal on pin 23 controls whether the modem uses the high or low speed. Usually the modem at the calling end sets the speed for the connection and informs its DTE. The calling modem signals the speed to the answering modem, which informs the called DTE by asserting Data Signaling Rate Selector (DCE source).

## Secondary Channels: Pins 12, 13, 14, 16, and 19

Some modems are equipped with both primary and secondary channels. The five secondary signals—Secondary Transmitted Data, Secondary Received Data, Secondary Request to Send, Secondary Clear to Send, and Secondary Received Line Signal Detector—allow control of the secondary channel in the same way as described for the primary channel. In these modems, the primary transmission channel usually has the higher data rate, and the secondary channel transmits in the reverse direction with a much lower data rate (for example, 75bps).

# Examples of RS-232 Connections

Now that you understand the functions of the various signals, take a look at some examples of RS-232 interfaces. You'll begin with a simple example in which the interface is used in the proper way. Then, in the "Nonstandard Use of the RS-232 Standard" section, you'll learn how the interface is used in ways for which it was not intended.

## Computer to Modem Interface

When you call from your home computer to another computer over telephone lines, you are using the universal seven-part data circuit that was defined in Chapter 1, "An Overview of Data Communications," and shown in Figure 1.17. Your computer is connected to a modem through an RS-232 interface, and the modem is connected to the telephone network. At the far end, whether it is a local or long-distance call, the other computer is similarly connected to a modem through an RS-232 interface. Figure 4.9a shows the absolute minimum RS-232 interface for the "normal" DTE-DCE connection.

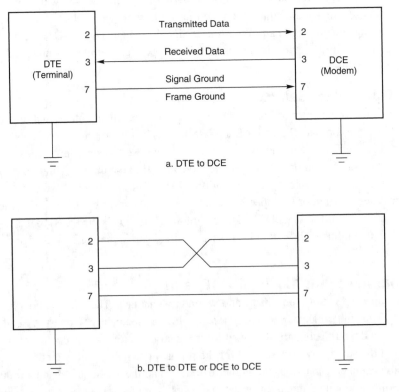

## FIGURE 4.9

*The minimum RS-232 interface.*

## Computer to Video Display Terminal Interface

The video display terminal (VDT) uses the simplest possible interface, as Figure 4.9 shows. If both the computer and the VDT are set up as DTE, pins 2 and 3 must be interchanged at the VDT end of the cable, as Figure 4.9b shows. Otherwise, each would expect to transmit data on the same wire.

This interchange usually is done at one of the cable connectors. However, an adapter with the wiring interchange done between its back-to-back connectors can be inserted between one end of a standard cable and the equipment. This adapter, often called a modem eliminator or null modem, enables the standard cable wiring to be left as is. These adapters are available in any combination of connector gender—that is, male to male, male to female, or female to female.

## Computer to Serial Printer Interface

The label on the box for your new printer says, "Serial interface connects directly to the RS-232 port of your computer." When you open the box, you see a connector on the back of the printer that looks just like the RS-232 connector on your modem. (The manufacturer also charges you quite a bit extra for the absolutely essential printer cable, but that's another story.) So, it appears that the RS-232 interface on your computer does double duty: It can connect to a modem or to a printer.

But the RS-232 was never intended to connect peripheral devices (such as printers) to DTEs (such as computers). It's not that it won't work; the problem comes in the confusion of identities. The computer is almost always (when you're talking about RS-232, it pays to say "almost always") internally wired as a DTE, and modems are always wired as DCEs (yes, always, because the role of the modem is defined precisely in the standard). But what about the poor printer? Is it DTE or DCE, fish or fowl? Does it use the same signals (and pins) that the modem uses, or are some different? Can you get by without buying that expensive special printer cable? Can you use your modem cable, which, after all, looks just like the printer cable and even has the same connectors? Now that you have an appreciation for some of the issues associated in cabling DTEs and DCEs, turn your attention to asynchronous modem control via the RS-232 standard.

# Asynchronous Modem Control

The major problem with the four-conductor interface shown in Figure 4.9a is the lack of control circuits routed between the modem and the terminal. For example, after you establish a connection to a distant modem, you likely would want a method to alert you to the fact that your communications connection with the distant modem was broken. This would require your terminal to monitor pin 8, which provides a carrier detect signal. As previously noted, intelligent modems include built-in buffer memory to hold data blocks until a distant modem acknowledges the correct receipt of the block. Because buffer memory is finite, the modem must have a method of informing the terminal device to suspend transmission to the modem until its buffer is emptied to the point at which the modem can again receive data. This process, known as flow control, can be implemented in several ways to include a toggling of the Clear to Send signal by the modem. The following section describes flow control in detail.

## Flow Control

Imagine that you decide to write your own software (called a printer driver) to pass data through the RS-232 port to the printer. You've bought the manufacturer's cable, and you've checked things such as bit rate, parity, number of stop bits, and character code. Suppose that the printer is set up for ASCII 7-bit characters, odd parity, and 1 stop bit. The printer manual says it can operate at 9600 bits per second, and because you will assume that's the fastest your computer can output serial data, you'll use that speed. Now you send a page of text to the printer using your driver program. What happens? After the first line or two, you see that more characters are missing than were printed. It looks as though they never made it to the printer! There doesn't seem to be any rhyme or reason to it, but every time you try to print using your program, data is lost. Why?

Let's compare data rates. Asynchronous ASCII uses 7 bits for the character code, 1 for the parity bit, 1 for the stop bit, and 1 for the start bit, for a total of 10 bits per character. Because the computer is transmitting 9600 bits per second to the printer, the character rate must be 960 characters per second.

Digging out the printer manual one more time, you see that the printer's maximum rate is 80 characters per second. That means you are sending 12 times as much data as the printer can accept. No wonder the data is getting lost. The printer buffer fills up, and then data is lost until buffer space becomes available again. What you need is a simple handshake mechanism to stop the computer from sending data when the buffer fills up and to turn it on again when the buffer empties. This is called flow control, and RS-232 is bound to have it, right? Wrong! RS-232 was designed for communicating between computers over telephone channels; the assumption is that any flow-control mechanism needed is built into the software at either end. As you'll see next, various schemes have been used for flow control with varying degrees of success.

Most modems support at least two methods of flow control, referred to as XON/XOFF and CTS/RTS. With the XON/XOFF method of flow control, the modem transmits an XOFF character to your computer to disable transmission and an XON character to enable transmission to resume. Because your computer might require a capability to regulate data from the modem if you are printing received data or performing another mechanical-related operation, you can also use XON and XOFF from your computer to the modem to enable and disable transmission from the modem to your computer.

The CTS/RTS method of flow control references the use of the Clear to Send (CTS) and Request to Send (RTS) control signals at the interface between the computer and the modem. When the modem regulates flow control, it drops the CTS signal to inform the computer to stop transmission and raises the CTS signal to inform the computer to resume transmission. When the computer regulates the flow of data from the modem, it toggles the RTS signal lead.

When setting flow control, you must ensure that your computer and modem are set to use the same method. Concerning which method to select, if you expect to transfer files that might contain control characters, including an XOFF, you should use the CTS/RTS method of flow control. Otherwise, the reception of an XOFF would inadvertently turn off your computer's capability to transmit data.

## Control Circuits

In addition to a missing flow control, Figure 4.9a is missing a Ring Indicator (RI) circuit on pin 22. Its omission precludes the automatic-answering operations.

For a terminal to inform an attached modem that it is operational and ready to receive data, it must include the Data Terminal Ready signal on pin 20. Similarly, for the modem to provide an indication to the terminal that it is powered on, the modem must include the Data Set Ready circuit on pin 6. Last but not least, for the terminal device to inform the modem that it has data to transmit, that device must include the Request to Send circuit on pin 4.

The preceding control circuits make up a core set of 10 circuits that are required for an asynchronous intelligent modem. It is common practice to strap frame ground to signal ground, which reduces the number of RS-232 circuits required for asynchronous intelligent modem operations to 9 and explains why computer manufacturers incorporated DB-9 connectors as the interface to serial ports on many desktop computers and almost all laptop and notebook computers.

Table 4.3 compares the DB-9 and DB-25 pins with respect to the DB-9 connector. Based on the entries in Table 4.3, it becomes obvious that a special type of cable is required to connect the serial port of a computer with a DB-9 connector to the DB-25P (P for plug) connector that will be plugged into the DB-25S (S for socket) connector built into almost all modems. That cable must cross pin 1 at the DB-9 connector to pin 8 at the DB-25 connector end of the cable. Similarly, pin 2 at the DB-9 connector end of the cable must be crossed to pin 3 at the DB-25 connector end of the cable, and so on.

**TABLE 4.3**   DB-9–to–DB-25 Pin Correspondence

| DB-9 | Conductor Circuit | DB-25 |
|------|-------------------|-------|
| 1 | Carrier Detect | 8 |
| 2 | Receive Data | 3 |
| 3 | Transmitted Data | 2 |
| 4 | Data Terminal Ready | 20 |
| 5 | Signal Ground | 7 |
| 6 | Data Set Ready | 6 |
| 7 | Request to Send | 4 |
| 8 | Clear to Send | 5 |
| 9 | Ring Indicator | 22 |

# Nonstandard Use of the RS-232 Standard

Earlier in the chapter, you learned about the potential identity problems associated with different devices. The RS-232 and other standards are intended to define the interface between DTEs and DCEs for communications over networks, usually telephone facilities. They don't address the idea of using the interface as a general serial input/output port. The wiring and control of a peripheral device in the same room, such as a printer (or another computer), is simply not considered in the standard. This means that the manufacturers are presented with a useful solution to the interfacing problem but have few guidelines (and no hard-and-fast rules) on how to apply it. The result is a certain amount of confusion in the marketplace. The purpose of this section is to help clarify what happens across the interface to aid in solving the problem, if necessary.

## Printers and DTE Standard

One source of the confusion is that printers and similar peripherals simply don't do the same things that modems do, and they therefore don't need the same control signals. The printer doesn't need to send and receive some of the signals that the modem needs, and it needs some signals that the modem doesn't.

One question is whether pin 2 or pin 3 of the RS-232 connector will be used for data transfer. In the sense of the standard, both the computer and the printer are DTE, and when a DTE is connected directly to another DTE, most of the signals defined in RS-232 are unnecessary. Although the manufacturer's special printer cable looks like an RS-232 cable, some of the pins aren't connected at all, and some of the pin connections are interchanged or jumpered together to adapt the interface on both ends. So, the printer manufacturer's claim that its product is "RS-232–compatible" really means that the equipment accepts and generates only a small fraction of the RS-232 signals and (probably) doesn't violate any other parts of the standard.

## Nonstandard Flow Control

From the previous discussion about RTS and CTS (pins 4 and 5), it would seem that these signals could be used for flow control. Although they often are used in this way, they shouldn't be—for many reasons. The problem is that the DCE is not allowed to drop Clear to Send until the DTE drops Request to Send. RTS and CTS are indeed handshake lines; the problem is that they indicate something besides that the DCE is ready to accept data.

The RTS and CTS signals are intended to allow the terminal to request control of the communications link from the modem. The terminal assumes that it will keep the link as long as it needs it, and the DCE cannot arbitrarily drop Clear to Send whenever it wants to do so. This means that CTS cannot properly be used by the DCE as a flow-control indicator; the DCE (or equipment such as a printer posing as DCE) can't raise and lower Clear to Send to tell the DTE to pause or restart transmission. Put another way, the DTE and the communications link—not the DTE and the DCE—are doing the handshaking. The handshake is for the purpose of establishing message transmission, not character-by-character or line-by-line acknowledgment for a printer.

Suppose that you decide to use RTS and CTS for flow control anyway (as some manufacturers who should know better have done). If the printer drops Clear to Send in the middle of a character transmission, what does that mean? If the transmitter stops immediately in the middle of the character, that character is sure to be garbled because timing is important in serial communications. If the transmitter waits until the character is transmitted and then stops, there might be no room in the printer's buffer for the last character. Because this possibility is not considered in the standard, the success of RTS-CTS as a flow-control mechanism cannot be predicted without studying the manuals for both of the devices involved. Even taking that action is no guarantee of success, but the odds are better.

Some manufacturers avoid the conflict by using the Data Terminal Ready or Data Set Ready (DTR or DSR) pins, depending on whether their printer thinks it is DTE or DCE. For example, if pin 6 (DSR) is used to provide flow control, the printer turns off pin 6 when it can accept no more data and turns it on again when its buffer is nearly empty. Still, there is no assurance that the device on the other end of the cable will recognize the signal or interpret it correctly because these lines were not intended to be used for flow control.

Another method for flow control is for the printer to send special characters for pause and return over the data line (pin 3, RD) to the computer. The software driver recognizes the special characters and controls the terminal output according to the character received. ASCII codes DC1 and DC3 (device controls 1 and 3) are often used, but they usually are called XON and XOFF. On the standard keyboard, these characters correspond to Ctrl+Q (resume) and Ctrl+S (pause). The printer logic transmits Ctrl+S when its buffer is approximately 80% full, and Ctrl+Q when the buffer is less than 20 % full.

Some printer manufacturers use both the DSR line and the RD line (XON/XOFF). However, problems might occur with either method. In instances in which the printer is connected to a modem (perhaps a short-haul modem on another floor of the building), there is no connection between the DSR circuits at the opposite ends (nor between RTS/CTS), so use of other pins is impossible. XON/XOFF should work fine in this instance, provided that the software recognizes it, and provided that the printer logic anticipates buffer overflow in time. Problems also can occur if several terminals are multiplexed together because the reverse characters are stored for a short time in the multiplexer.

Of course, these problems occur because RS-232 was never intended for flow control or for DTE-to-DTE connections. Do not be surprised when individually arranged flow-control methods don't always work; they simply are not part of the standard. In spite of the preceding, most intelligent modem manufacturers support the use of RTS and CTS control signals as a mechanism for enabling flow control from the DTE to the modem and the modem to the DTE. Fortunately, most of those modems also support XON/XOFF flow control and might also support other characters that can be used as flow-control mechanisms.

## Limitations of RS-232

It would seem that the lack of a flow-control mechanism is the major drawback of RS-232, but actually that isn't the case. Flow control is handled much better through software than through hardware, and that is the direction in which new systems are moving. Small-computer peripherals just haven't made it there yet. RS-232 does have some limitations that restrict its use, however. After you learn about these limitations, you'll look at some standards that don't have these limitations and that offer other advantages as well.

### Distance Limitations

The principal problem with RS-232 is its distance limitation of 50 feet. With all but the highest data rates, much longer cable runs can be successful, but they never seem quite long enough, and there's always a risk of losing data. The distance restriction is not a serious disadvantage when the modem is close to the computer or terminal and the long-haul transmission to a remote computer takes place over telephone lines. In local applications, however, RS-232 cables often are used to connect terminals directly to computers because it is convenient to use the same terminal and computer interface whether or not a modem connection is used. (Also, the RS-232 connector is probably the only one provided.) For these connections, the 50-foot limit becomes restrictive.

An RS-232 transmitter generates a voltage between 5 and 25 V for one of the two possible signal states (space), and a voltage between –5 and –25 V for the opposite state (mark). Unfortunately, these voltage levels are not the same as those inside the computer and terminal, which use standard TTL and MOS logic. This means that an additional power supply (usually ±12 volts) is required for the RS-232 levels. As Figure 4.10 shows, an RS-232 receiver circuit recognizes voltages above 3 V as spaces and voltages below –3 V as marks. When a signal changes from one condition to the other, the specification limits the amount of time in the undefined region to 5 percent of a bit period. This requirement determines the maximum amount of stray capacitance allowable in the cable because capacitance limits the rise time (or transition time) of the signal. RS-232 specifies that the capacitance must not exceed 2500 picofarads (pF). Because the cables generally used for RS-232 have a capacitance of 40 to 50 picofarads per foot, RS-232 limits cables to 50 feet (2500/50 = 50).

## Speed Limitations

A second limitation is the maximum transmission speed of 20,000bps, although this is not usually a disadvantage in applications between computers and terminals. The data rate between a computer and a terminal is usually less than or equal to 19,200bps, at best. When a PC is cabled to a modern high-speed modem that can operate at up to 56Kbps without performing data compression, the transfer of data to the modem via an RS-232 cable violates the standard's maximum transmission rate. This violation becomes possible by use of a cable considerably shorter than the 50-foot cable limit specified by the RS-232 standard; most modem manufacturers recommend a maximum cabling distance of 12 feet or less.

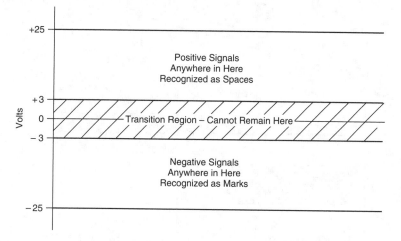

**4**

**FIGURE 4.10**

*RS-232 data signal levels at the receiver.*

When a high-speed modem is placed in its compressed mode of operation, you usually want to transfer data to the modem from two to four times its operating rate to effectively use its compression capability. This means that you would set the serial port of your PC to 67.2Kbps or 134.4Kbps if you were using a modem operating at 33.6Kbps. Unfortunately, at data rates above 115.2Kbps, the UART built into PC serial ports can lose data during sustained data-transfer operations. To overcome this problem, some modem vendors require the use of an "enhanced" serial port in the PC.

## Ground Limitations

The third disadvantage of RS-232, as discussed previously, is its grounding method. The problem is not so much with the protective (chassis) ground as with the control and data signals; all are referenced against the same signal ground wire (pin 7). This method, called unbalanced transmission, works satisfactorily most of the time. If, however, there is a difference in ground potential between the two ends of the cable (quite likely for long runs), the transition region between a space and a mark is narrowed. When this situation occurs, the possibility exists that a signal will be misinterpreted, as Figure 4.11 shows. Just as the various parts of the standard work together (speeds within the standard usually work fine over cables that are also within the standard), the various restrictions interact. If you try to drive cables that are too long at speeds that are too high, all these problems tend to bite you at once.

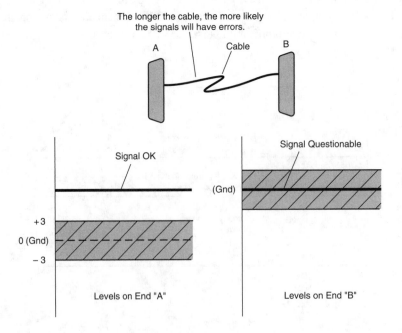

### FIGURE 4.11

*Problems because of differing ground potentials in RS-232.*

# Other Interfaces

Although RS-232 is the most commonly used interface, several additional interfaces are frequently used to connect data terminal equipment to data communications equipment. Those interfaces include the current loop, the RS series, ITU x.21, USB, and FireWire.

## An Old Standby: The Current Loop

RS-232, for all its faults, at least defines connector pins and signal levels. No such standards exist for teleprinters. The serial transmission format is defined, with start and stop bits, data bits, and parity bits, but the electrical interface varies with the manufacturer, and control signals are unknown. In teleprinters, the signal interface is called the current loop. Instead of using positive and negative voltages to represent logic ones and zeros, the current loop uses presence or absence of current. Presence can be either 20 or 60 milliamperes, depending on the teleprinter model and manufacturer. No standard connector or standard pinouts exist for current-loop operation.

The idea of the current loop is to switch a current on and off. The active side of the transmission line generates the current, and the passive side switches or detects it. Because either the receiver or the transmitter can be active, there are four possibilities: active receiver, active transmitter, passive receiver, and passive transmitter. Because of the convenience of locating the power supply at just one end of the link (usually at the computer), all four of these signals are found in a single computer-to-terminal connection.

Despite the lack of standards, designers of serial devices for computers like to include current-loop interface capability. It's a useful interface because teleprinters are still a cost-effective solution as a combination printer and terminal, and many devices other than teleprinters use it. Where RS-232 is limited to a 50-foot cable, a current loop can be up to 1500 feet long and can handle data rates of up to 9600bps without a special power supply. Unfortunately, the current-loop interface is completely incompatible with RS-232 and requires either hardware that has both interfaces built in or interface boxes. The interface boxes can be built to adapt to any of the four possible interfaces. For example, if two microcomputers that are to be connected both contain the active interface, an active-to-active converter is required to directly connect them. Similarly, to connect a passive terminal directly to another passive terminal, a passive-to-passive converter is required. Fortunately, the converters can be easily constructed using an optoisolator. The active-to-active converter does not even need a power supply, although the passive-to-passive converter must have one to generate the current.

# The RS Series

Useful as the current loop might be in some cases, most of the world is not moving away from RS-232 back to teleprinters. Instead, the movement is toward three types of interfaces. Two are similar to RS-232, but with some of the warts removed; the other is quite different, with hardware functions replaced by software. You'll examine the ones more like RS-232 first.

In the early 1970s, the EIA introduced the RS-422A, RS-423A, and RS-449 standards to overcome the defects of RS-232 and to incorporate and improve on the advantages of the current-loop interface. A major change was to separate the electrical, mechanical, and functional specifications of RS-232 into separate documents. RS-422A and RS-423A cover only electrical specifications; RS-449 covers control functions.

## RS-422A

To allow transmission at high data rates, RS-422A uses two separate wires for each signal. This technique, called balanced transmission, doubles the number of wires in the cable but enables very high data rates and minimizes the problem of varying ground potential. Because ground is not used as a voltage reference, RS-422A grounding requirements are much less critical than those of RS-232, and the use of the signal ground wire is optional with RS-422A.

Another major difference between RS-422A and RS-232 is the transition region between mark and space states. With the elimination of the ground potential problem, the transition region can be much narrower. In RS-422A, the difference between the voltages on the two wires determines whether a mark or a space is sent. This difference is only 0.4 V in RS-422A, whereas it is 6 V (3 V and ±3 V) in RS-232. If the difference signal between the two wires is positive and more than 0.2 V, the receiver reads a mark; if it is negative and more than ±0.2 V, the receiver reads a space. These voltage values allow suitable transmitters and receivers to be implemented with the ±5 V power supply commonly available in computers.

## RS-423A

RS-423A transmits at lower speeds and uses one wire as a common return path for all signals in a given direction (unbalanced transmission like RS-232, but with two return wires). The RS-423A standard operates in both RS-232 and RS-422A environments. It provides users of existing RS-232 interfaced equipment with a way to move to the new RS-422A regime, including a defined RS-232 to RS-422A adapter connector.

Because of the much smaller transition region, RS-422A transmitters do not drive RS-232 receivers correctly. RS-423A equipment, on the other hand, interfaces with RS-232 signals. Each direction of transmission uses a common return path that is connected to ground only at the transmitter end. The receiver determines whether a mark or a space is present by examining whether the signal wire is negative or positive with respect to the common return. Because this return path does not connect to the ground in the receiver, the problem of ground currents does not arise.

In an RS-423A transmitter, the voltage difference between the signal line and the common return must be at least 4 V, positive for a space and negative for a mark. This gives an 8 V transition region, which is compatible with RS-232 receiver circuitry but which presents the same power supply problem that occurs with RS-232. Because the RS-423A receiver must properly respond to the same 0.4 V transition region as an RS-422A receiver, an RS-422A transmitter can be used with RS-423A receivers.

## RS-449

RS-449 is the intended successor to the functional portion of RS-232, including the mechanical specification of the plugs and sockets. Apart from its improved speed and distance specifications, RS-449 offers some minor functional enhancements over RS-232 in automatic modem testing and provision for a standby channel, but it still does not incorporate outward dialing. The acceptance of RS-449 in the marketplace seems questionable at this time.

Figure 4.12 shows the RS-449 signals with the corresponding RS-232 and V.24 signals. Notice the similarity between the new and old standards. The major differences are in the grounding arrangements (Send Common and Receive Common) and testing facilities. Apart from these, only a few miscellaneous signals have been added. All signals use the RS-423A transmission standard except those that can optionally use the RS-422A for higher speed links. (Two wires are specified for each of these.) The signals are divided between a 37-pin and a 9-pin connector, and the ground and common signals are handled separately for each cable. Many applications will not need the smaller cable because it contains only signals relevant to the secondary channel.

One of the major problems that prevented more than a token acceptance of the RS-449 standard is its use of two connectors, each of which differs in size and conductor connection from the RS-232 connector used with tens of millions of DTEs and DCEs. Recognizing that RS-449 would probably not fulfill its intended role, the EIA announced the RS-530 standard in the late 1980s as the successor to RS-449. Both RS-442 and RS-423 standards will continue to exist, and both are referenced by the RS-530 standard.

## RS-530

RS-530 is similar to RS-449 in that it provides equipment with the capability to transmit data above the RS-232 limit of 20Kbps. Like RS-232, RS-530 uses the nearly universal 25-pin D-shaped interface connector.

4

ASYNCHRONOUS
MODEMS AND
INTERFACES

UNDERSTANDING DATA COMMUNICATIONS

| RS-449 | | RS-232* | | CCITT Recommendation V.24 | |
|---|---|---|---|---|---|
| SG | Signal Ground | AB | Signal Ground (Shield) | 102 | Signal Ground |
| SC | Send Common | | | 102a | DTE Common |
| RC | Receive Common | | | 102b | DCE Common |
| IS | Terminal in Service | | | | |
| IC | Incoming Call | CE | Ring Indicator | 125 | Calling Indicator |
| TR | Terminal Ready | DC | Data Terminal Ready (DTE Ready) | 108/2 | Data Terminal Ready |
| DM | Data Mode | CC | Data Set Ready (DCE Ready) | 07 | Data Set Ready |
| SD | Send Data | BA | Transmitted Data | 103 | Transmitted Data |
| RD | Receive Data | BB | Received Data | 104 | Received Data |
| TT | Terminal Timing | DA | Transmitter Signal Element Timing (DTE Source) | 113 | Transmitter Signal Element Timing (DTE Source) |
| ST | Send Timing | DB | Transmitter Signal Element Timing (DCE Source) | 114 | Transmitter Signal Element Timing (DCE Source) |
| RT | Receive Timing | DD | Receive Signal Element Timing | 115 | Receiver Signal Element Timing (DCE Source) |
| RS | Request to Send | CA | Request to Send | 105 | Request to Send |
| CS | Clear to Send | CB | Clear to Send | 106 | Ready for Sending |
| RR | Receiver Ready | CF | Received Line Signal Detector | 109 | Data Channel Received Line Signal Detector |
| SQ | Signal Quality | CG | Signal Quality Detector | 110 | Data Signal Quality Detector |
| NS | New Signal | | | | |
| SF | Select Frequency | | | 126 | Select Transmit Frequency |
| SR | Signaling Rate Selector | CH | Data Signaling Rate Selector (DTE Source) | 111 | Data Signaling Rate Selector (DTE Source) |
| SI | Signaling Rate Indicator | CI | Data Signaling Rate Selector (DCE Source) | 112 | Data Signaling Rate Selector (DCE Source) |
| SSD | Secondary Send Data | SBA | Secondary Transmitted Data | 118 | Transmitted Backward Channel Data |
| SRD | Secondary Receive Data | SBB | Secondary Received Data | 119 | Received Backward Channel Data |
| SRS | Secondary Request to Send | SCA | Secondary Request to Send | 120 | Transmit Backward Channel Line Signal |
| SCS | Secondary Clear to Send | SCB | Secondary Clear to Send | 121 | Backward Channel Ready |
| SRR | Secondary Receiver Ready | SCF | Secondary Received Line Signal Detector | 122 | Backward Channel Received Line Signal Detector |
| LL | Local Loopback | (LL) | (Local Loopback) | 141 | Local Loopback |
| RL | Remote Loopback | | | 140 | Remote Loopback |
| TM | Test Mode | (TM) | (Test Mode) | 142 | Test Indicator |
| SS | Select Standby | | | 116 | Select Standby |
| SB | Standby Indicator | | | 117 | Standby Indicator |

*RS-232D Additions/Changes to RS-232C Indicated in Parentheses

FIGURE 4.12

*Comparing RS-449 with RS-232 signals.*

The RS-530 standard is capable of transmitting data above 20Kbps due to the use of balanced signals in place of several RS-232 secondary signals and the Ring Indicator signal. This balanced signaling technique is accomplished by using two wires with opposite polarities for each signal to minimize distortion.

Table 4.4 summarizes the RS-530 interchange circuits based on their pin assignments. Although no equipment conforming to this new standard was marketed at the time this book revision was prepared, its elimination of the Ring Indicator signal suggests that its use will be reserved for non-PSTN applications.

**TABLE 4.4**    RS-530 Interchange Circuits

| Pin Number | Circuit | Description |
|---|---|---|
| 1 | | Shield |
| 2 | BA | Transmitted data |
| 3 | BB | Received data |
| 4 | CA | Request to send |
| 5 | CB | Clear to send |
| 6 | CC | DCE ready |
| 7 | AB | Signal ground |
| 8 | CF | Received line signal detector |
| 9 | DD | Received signal element timing (DCE source) |
| 10 | CF | Received line signal detector |
| 11 | DA | Transmit signal element timing (DTE source) |
| 12 | DB | Transmit signal element timing (DCE source) |
| 13 | CB | Clear to send |
| 14 | BA | Transmitted data |
| 15 | DB | Transmitter signal element timing (DCE source) |
| 16 | BB | Received data |
| 17 | DD | Receiver signal element timing (DCE source) |
| 18 | LL | Local loopback |
| 19 | CA | Request to send |
| 20 | CD | DTE ready |
| 21 | RL | Remote loopback |
| 22 | CC | DCE ready |
| 23 | DC | DTE ready |
| 24 | DA | Transmit signal element timing (DTE source) |
| 25 | TM | Test mode |

## RS-366

None of the RS standards discussed provides for automatic dialing of calls by a computer. RS-232 and RS-449 provide specifications for answering calls, but not for dialing. A different standard, RS-366, covers automatic calling units. The reason is that until the late 1980s, equipment for placing calls under computer control was expensive because the actions required in making a telephone call can be quite complicated. The dialing equipment must be capable of determining whether the line is free, taking the phone off-hook (in effect), waiting for and recognizing a dial tone, dialing the number, and understanding and responding to the various call progress tones (such as the busy signal) that the telephone system provides to indicate the status of a call.

The principal use of RS-366 automatic-dialing equipment in data communications is for dial backup for private-line data circuits and for automatic dialing of remote terminals to allow them to transmit data. For example, a company's central computer could be programmed to automatically dial the computer in each branch office each evening and to cause (via software) the day's transactions to be transmitted to the main office.

The growth in availability of low-cost intelligent modems that respond to commands generated by DTEs has considerably reduced the use of RS-366–based automatic-dialing equipment. Although RS-366 is still used to control the operation of synchronous modems, the use of RS-366 is expected to further decline because many modem manufacturers now are incorporating a synchronous dial control capability into their products.

# ITU X.21

The ITU has charted a course different from the RS-standards, a course that was predicated on the eventual availability of direct digital connection to a digital telephone network. Then all data transmission would be synchronous, and the communications equipment would provide bit and byte timing signals. The ITU X.21 recommendation, introduced in 1976, includes the protocol for placing and receiving calls and for sending and receiving data using full-duplex synchronous transmission. Byte-timing signals are an option, but one that nearly all digital telephone exchanges will almost certainly provide. In sharp contrast to RS-232, RS-449, and RS-530, X.21 uses only six signals. The electrical specifications are contained in recommendations X.26 (corresponding to EIA RS-422A) and X.27 (corresponding to EIA RS-423A).

The maximum line speed under X.21 is 64,000bps, the data rate now used to encode voice in digital form in the telephone network. In Europe, British Telecom offers X.21 customer data rate access to its Kilostream digital service at 2.4, 4.8, 9.6, 48, and 64Kbps. Customer data rates up to 9.6Kbps are converted to a line rate of 12.8Kbps, whereas data rates of 48 and 64Kbps both use a line rate of 64Kbps for transmitting through the Kilostream network.

The circuits used in X.21 are given in Table 4.5. The first two circuits listed provide the voltage reference and ground connections. The computer sends data to the modem on the transmit line, and the modem returns data on the receive line. The control and indication circuits provide control channels in two directions. The signal element timing line carries the bit timing, and the byte timing line carries the byte timing. Although the control and indication lines are control lines, most of the controlling information uses the transmit and receive lines. The computer changes the state of control when it wants to place a call, just as you lift the handset when you want to dial. To end the call, the computer changes control back to the idle state. Similarly, the modem changes the state of indication when the remote telephone is answered and changes it back if it shuts down. All the dialing information travels on the transmit line in coded form, and all the information about tones comes back on the receive line.

The major advantage of X.21 over RS-232, RS-449, and RS-530 is that the X.21 signals are encoded in serial digital form. For example, when a dial tone is received, a continuous sequence of ASCII "+" characters is sent to the computer on the receive wire. In effect, this is a digital dial tone. The computer dials the number by transmitting it as a series of ASCII characters on the transmit line, 1 bit at a time. After dialing the call, the computer receives call progress signals from the modem on the receive wire. These signals indicate such things as number busy, access disallowed, and network congestion.

By using serial digital coding instead of dedicated wires for special functions, X.21 establishes a basis for providing special services in computer communication. A short-code-dialing or repeat-last-call facility would be extremely useful, for example, to reconnect a call every time you complete a line of typing at the terminal. (Some European nations are trying this approach to networking right now.) If the line could be disconnected while you were typing, long-distance calls would be much cheaper. Of course, this would also depend on the tariff policies of the telecommunication carriers. Using X.21 could allow many of the advantages of telecommunications by the packet-switching technique without the associated complexity.

Although X.21 is defined as the "lowest" (or "physical") level of the international X.25 packet-switching protocol, it was far ahead of its time because direct digital connection to public telephone networks was not readily available when the standard was developed. For this reason, ITU offers the X.21bis recommendation as an interim measure to connect existing computer equipment to packet-communication services. X.21bis is virtually identical to ITU V.24 and RS-232. (Packet switching and ITU protocols are discussed more in Chapter 10, "Architectures and Packet Networks.")

**4**

ASYNCHRONOUS
MODEMS AND
INTERFACES

UNDERSTANDING DATA COMMUNICATIONS

**TABLE 4.5**  ITU X.21 Signals

| Interchange | Name | To DCE | From DCE Circuit |
|---|---|---|---|
| G | Signal Ground or Common Return | * | |
| Ga | DTE Common Return | X | |
| T | Transmit | X | |
| R | Receive | | X |
| C | Control | X | |
| I | Indication | | X |
| S | Signal Element Timing | X | |
| B | Byte Timing | | X |

*See Recommendation X.24.

# USB and FireWire Interfaces

Two relatively new PC interfaces can be expected to significantly gain in popularity over the next few years. Those new interfaces are the Universal Serial Bus (USB) and FireWire, the latter of which got its name from the IEEE 1394 specification.

Both USB and FireWire represent interfaces that permit PC users to daisy-chain multiple peripherals via external cables to their computers. USB Version 10 supports up to 127 devices and provides a data transfer capability up to 12Mbps. In April 2000, the USB Implementers Forum (USB-IF) released Version 2.0 of the USB specification, which replaces the previous version. That previous specification defined two speeds. Low-end devices, such as mouse devices and keyboards, could operate in a low-speed mode of 1.5Mbps. Higher-end devices, such as printers and scanners, could operate at 12Mbps. USB 2.0 now adds a higher-speed mode with a data transfer rate of 480Mbps that makes it suitable for use with videoconferencing cameras and high-capacity disk and tape storage systems. In comparison, FireWire supports up to 63 daisy-chained devices at data rates of 100, 200, and 400Mbps under its initial specification as the IEEE 1394a High-Performance Serial Bus. A newer version of FireWire, known as 1394b, extends the data-transfer rate to 1.6Gbps.

Both USB and FireWire are Plug and Play interfaces that enable users to dynamically add and remove devices. This modification is performed without powering down the computer, adding or removing adapter cards, or changing switch settings or jumpers. Eventually USB or FireWire, and perhaps both, will replace all the different types of serial and parallel port connectors in computers with one standardized plug and port combination.

Most PCs manufactured since 1997 include one or two USB ports on the back of the computer that look similar to rectangular plugs. Until Windows 98 was released with drivers to support

USB operations, it was relatively difficult to use this interface. However, since the introduction of Windows 98 (which contains USB drivers), hardware manufacturers have introduced devices ranging from keyboards and modems to printers and scanners with USB interfaces. In 2000, Compaq, IBM, and other PC vendors introduced "legacy-free" PCs that did away with parallel and serial ports. Such PCs commonly contain four or more USB ports and considerably simplify cabling.

A comparison of USB and FireWire indicates that they are complementary to one another and, until 2001, were not competitive. USB was originally designed to support low- to medium-speed peripherals and was only recently extended to support a data-transfer capability of 480Mbps. In comparison, FireWire, which currently has a top speed of 1.6Gbps, is ideal for connecting high-speed devices that require large data transfers, such as disk drivers and tape units.

FireWire actually dates to 1986 when Apple Computer developed the technology and provided its name. In 1990, Apple offered its specification to the IEEE Microcomputer Standards Committee, which adopted it as the IEEE 1394 specification in 1995 and clarified aspects of the specification in 2000 as the 1394a standard. Perhaps because it was the first high-speed bus, the 1394 was used in many consumers' digital-video equipment. In fact, the Sony PlayStation 2 as well as many digital camcorders have a 1394 port. When you view an advertisement from an iLink interface, you are viewing another term for the FireWire bus.

FireWire uses a relatively simple but rugged cable similar to that shown in Figure 4.13. Cabling consists of three twisted pairs, two for data and one for power and ground. If you are familiar with such video games as Sega, PlayStation, or Nintendo, you are also familiar with the FireWire connector, which is based on those used in video game players. Thus, these connectors are easy to attach, lock firmly in place, and are rugged to withstand frequent connecting and disconnecting. The actual cable length depends upon the gauge of the conductors. AWG 28 cable permits data to be transported 4.5 meters, whereas 24 AWG cable permits data to be carried for 14 meters.

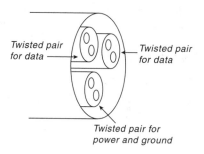

**FIGURE 4.13**

*The FireWire (IEEE 1394) cable.*

One key difference between USB and FireWire concerns their connectivity. USB devices are connected in a tiered-star arrangement, as illustrated in the top of Figure 4.14. Under this arrangement, each computer USB port functions as a root hub to which USB devices can be directly connected. Because a legacy-free PC might have only four USB ports, when you need to add more devices you would cable one or more external hubs to root hubs. You would then cable USB peripherals to the external hubs to form a tiered-star network configuration. In comparison, FireWire devices can be connected to one another in a peer-to-peer arrangement, as illustrated in the lower portion of Figure 4.14.

a.  USB devices are connected in a tiered-star arrangement

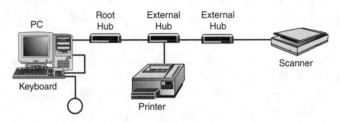

b.  FireWire devices can be connected in a peer-to-peer arrangement

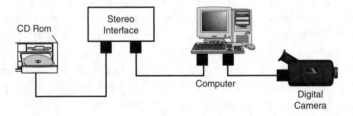

**FIGURE 4.14**

*Comparing USB and FireWire connections.*

# Asynchronous Modem Operations

Now that you have an appreciation for different computer interfaces, let's return to your examination of asynchronous modems. In doing so, turn your attention to the signals they use for dial and private line operations.

# Asynchronous Autoanswer Modem

Asynchronous modems are usually used with personal computers. The signals needed for these modems are Protective Ground, Signal Ground, Transmitted Data, Received Data, Request to Send, Clear to Send, Data Terminal Ready, Ring Indicator, Received Line Signal Detector, and possibly Data Set Ready. Pin 20 (DTR) indicates that the computer is ready to receive calls, and pin 22 (RI) indicates that the modem is receiving the telephone ringing signal, going high and low as the ringing current goes off and on. (This is how a modem can count how many rings to wait before answering.) If the computer leaves pin 20 (DTR) on all the time, the modem answers incoming calls without delay. If DTR is off, the computer turns it on in response to receiving an RI signal to tell the modem to answer the call. At the completion of the call, the computer turns off pin 20 (DTR) to cause the modem to disconnect the line (go on hook).

The following sequence of events is one possible set that can happen when a computer receives a call from another computer via a low-speed asynchronous modem and manual modem operations are employed. When the modem detects ringing, it turns on pin 22 (RI), the DTE responds by asserting pin 20 (DTR), and the modem goes off-hook to answer the phone. The answering DTE asserts pin 4 (RTS), which commands the modem to turn on its transmitter. After the RTS-CTS delay, the modem responds by asserting CTS. At the other end of the line, the computer operator hears the carrier signal and either pushes the data button or puts the telephone handset into the acoustic coupler. Now the calling modem's transmitter turns on, producing its own carrier tone. When the modem at the receiving computer hears this carrier, it turns on pin 8 (DCD). Upon receiving this signal, the receiving computer begins transmitting data to tell the sending computer to log on, and so forth. Some operating systems wait for the caller to transmit a special character to begin the logon process.

At the end of the session, the caller logs off, causing the receiving computer to terminate the call. It turns off pin 4 (RTS), which causes the receiving modem to turn off its carrier signal. The receiving computer then drops pin 20 (DTR), causing the modem to go on hook to "hang up" the telephone line. At the calling end, pin 8 (DCD) goes off, the operator replaces the handset, and the action is complete.

When modems with an automatic-answering capability are used, the previously described operations occur automatically and without operator intervention. If you can envision a typical data center or even a modern bulletin board system, you can get an appreciation for the use of automatic-answering modems. Without this capability, one or more operators would be required to be on duty to place receiving modems into their data mode in response to incoming calls generating ringing signals. In fact, data centers during the late 1950s and early 1960s relied on the use of operators to place modems into their data mode in response to incoming calls. Fortunately for operators whose level of job satisfaction in those days was probably equivalent to watching paint dry, the development of automatic-answering modems enabled computers to be programmed to answer incoming calls automatically. This formed the basis for the emergence of unattended bulletin board systems, which began to appear during the late 1970s and early 1980s, as well as access to the Internet, America Online, CompuServe, and Prodigy.

## The Full-Duplex Asynchronous Private Line Modem

The full-duplex asynchronous modem could be used on private lines as well as on the switched network. It is called a private line modem because it is not equipped for automatic answer. The signals used are Protective Ground, Signal Ground, Transmitted Data, Received Data, Received Line Signal Detector (pin 8), and Data Set Ready (pin 6). Pin 8 (DCD) says, in effect, "I hear something like a modem talking to me." In other words, it recognizes that another modem is trying to make contact on the line. Pin 6 (DSR) usually is not used in asynchronous modems, but it could indicate that the modem is ready and not in voice or test mode.

## The Half-Duplex Asynchronous Private Line Modem

A second common method of modem operation is half-duplex. In this mode of operation, modems can transmit and receive; however, they can perform only one operation at a time. The signals used in the half-duplex asynchronous modem are Protective Ground, Signal Ground, Transmitted Data, Received Data, Request to Send, Clear to Send, Received Line Signal Detector, and possibly Data Set Ready. Pins 4 and 5 (RTS and CTS) control the transmission direction in the half-duplex operation. The computer asserts pin 4 (RTS) when it wants to transmit. The modem responds by turning on pin 5 (CTS) to indicate that it is ready to receive characters to be transmitted. There is a built-in delay (typically 200 milliseconds) between the Request to Send and the Clear to Send response because the modem must generate the carrier waveform and allow it to stabilize. When transmission is completed in that direction, the computer drops pin 4 (RTS), causing the modem to turn off the transmitter and to drop CTS. The process of determining who transmits when, and how to tell when the other end is finished, is the responsibility of the software protocol, which is outside the modem and the RS-232 interface.

## Smart Modems

The so-called smart or "intelligent" modem combines a standard modem and a microprocessor to provide both data communications and automatic dialing in one unit. (One of the first intelligent modems to be marketed was the Smartmodem 1200 made by Hayes Microcomputer Products, Inc., which is now part of Zoom Technologies.) A smart modem accepts commands in ASCII form over the same RS-232 interface used for data transmission and can respond over the same interface with either status codes or sentences. For example, the computer operator would turn on the modem, load the terminal software, and then type a code such as AT DT1-800-555-1212. This code tells the modem to take the phone line off-hook, wait for a dial tone, and then tone dial (using DTMF tones) the number 1-800-555-1212. The modem will attempt to do this. If the number is busy, the modem's response, "number busy," appears on the computer's screen. Modems of this type usually can redial the last number entered, and many of these modems can be programmed to automatically keep trying a number at preset intervals if they encounter a busy signal. Some modems can store a list of frequently called numbers (such as the preceding one) that the user can select by entering only a two- or three-digit code.

The smart modem contradicts the earlier statement that modems don't look at the data that passes through them because it does examine some of the information coming over the RS-232 interface for its commands. Smart modems have essentially replaced the use of nonintelligent or "dumb" modems for use on the switched telephone network, and most software products support these modems. Virtually all the numerous newly developed communications software products support the basic Hayes modem command set, which has become a de facto standard. Thus, if you are considering the purchase of a smart modem, it would be wise to consider one that is compatible with the Hayes commands.

## Command Types

The Hayes command set consists of a basic set of commands, command extensions, proprietary commands, and register commands.

- Basic commands represent a core set of modem commands applicable for placing a modem off-hook and dialing a number, answering incoming calls, echoing characters to the attached DTE, and performing similar functions. Basic commands are almost universally supported by almost all Hayes and other modern manufacturer modems; however, certain modems within a product line may not support every basic command or every possible setting for each command. Basic commands are identified by the letters *A* through *Z* followed by an optional variable that identifies a feature within a command that supports two or more options. For example, the M command turns the modem's speaker on or off, and M0 is used to turn off the speaker.

- Extended commands represent an extension of basic commands that enable additional functions to be supported. The ampersand (&) is used as a prefix to the letters *A* through *Z* to identify extended commands. As with basic commands, most modem manufacturers support extended commands in the same manner.

- Proprietary commands are usually identified by either a percent sign (%) or a backslash (\) prefix. These commands vary widely among modem manufacturers.

- Register commands represent a specific physical location in the modem's memory area. Intelligent or smart modems include a small amount of onboard memory. Values associated with different memory locations are used to define certain modem functions. Because the value of each register can be set, modem registers are referred to as S registers. The use of the first 13 S registers (0–12) is fairly standardized; however, the use of other registers can significantly vary both between modem vendors and within a vendor's product line.

## Hayes Command Set

Commands in the Hayes command set are initiated by the transmission of an attention code to the modem, followed by an appropriate command or set of commands. The attention code is the character sequence AT, which must be input by the user or sent to the modem by a software program in all uppercase or all lowercase letters. The requirement to prefix all command lines with the code AT has led many modem manufacturers to denote their modems as Hayes AT–compatible or simply AT-compatible.

A Hayes Smartmodem can hold up to 40 characters in its command buffer, permitting a sequence of commands to be transmitted to the modem on one command line. This 40-character limit does not include the attention code, nor does it include spaces placed in a command line to make it more readable. Table 4.6 lists the major commands in the basic Hayes command set.

**TABLE 4.6**   Major Commands of the Basic Hayes Command Set

| Command | Description |
| --- | --- |
| A | Answer call |
| A/ | Repeat last command |
| B | Select the method of modem modulation |
| C | Turn modem's carrier on or off |
| D | Dial a telephone number |
| E | Enable or inhibit echo of characters to the screen |
| F | Switch between half- and full-duplex modem operations |
| H | Hang up telephone (on-hook) or pick up telephone (off-hook) |
| I | Request identification code or request checksum |
| L | Select the speaker volume |
| M | Turn speaker off or on |
| N | Negotiate handshake options |

**TABLE 4.6**   continued

| Command | Description |
|---------|-------------|
| O | Place modem online |
| P | Pulse dial |
| Q | Request modem to send or inhibit sending of result code |
| R | Change modem mode to "originate-only" |
| S | Set modem register values |
| T | Touch-tone dial |
| V | Send result codes as digits or words |
| W | Select negotiation progress message |
| X | Use basic or extended result code set |
| Z | Reset the modem |

# Hayes Communication in Practice

Although communications software that supports the basic Hayes command set operates with this modem, such software might not be capable of supporting many of the advanced features incorporated into modems manufactured by other vendors. In fact, communications software that supports only the basic Hayes command set might not be sufficient to use most of the advanced features incorporated into modem products developed over the past 10 years. Those features, such as error detection and correction, data compression, fax/data mode selection, and operating rates above 2400bps, are usually enabled through the use of extended command codes or settings in predefined modem S registers. This explains why it is no trivial exercise to develop a communications program that supports the features of a large number of modems developed by different vendors. The section "Extended Command Sets," later in this chapter, examines a few of the extended commands used to enable different features built into several popular modems.

This is the basic format required to transmit commands to a Hayes-compatible modem:

```
AT Command[Parameter(s)]Command[Parameter(s)]..Return
```

Each command line includes the prefix AT, followed by the appropriate command and the command's parameters. The command parameters are usually the digits 0 or 1, which serve to define a specific command state. As an example, C1 is the command that tells the modem to turn on its carrier signal, and C0 is the command that causes the modem to turn off its carrier signal. Up to 40 characters can be entered into a command line, and each command line must be terminated by a carriage-return character.

To illustrate the use of the Hayes command set, suppose that you want to automatically dial information for New York City. The number is 212-555-1212. First, you tell the modem to go off-hook, which is similar to picking up a telephone handset. Then you tell the modem the type of telephone system you are using (pulse or touch-tone) and the telephone number to dial. If you have a terminal or personal computer connected to a Hayes-compatible modem, you would send the following commands to the modem:

```
AT H1
AT DT9,1,212-555-1212
```

In the first command, the 1 parameter used with the H command places the modem off-hook. In the second command, DT tells the modem to dial a telephone number using touch-tone (T) dialing. The digits 9 and 1 are included in the telephone number because it is assumed that you had to dial 9 to gain access to an outside line through your company's switchboard and 1 for long distance. The commas between the outside line (9), long-distance access number (1), and area code (212) cause the modem to pause for 2 seconds before dialing the area code. Usually, 2 seconds is long enough for you to hear the outside line and long-distance dial tones before the modem dials the next number.

Because a smart modem automatically goes off-hook when dialing a number, the first command line is not required and is normally used for receiving calls. In the second command line, the type of dialing does not have to be specified if a previous call was made because the modem automatically uses the last type specified. Although users with only pulse dialing availability must specify P in the dialing command when using a Hayes Smartmodem, other vendors offer modems that can determine automatically what type of dialing facility the modem is connected to and then use the appropriate dialing method without requiring the user to specify the type of calling.

## Extended Command Sets

As previously mentioned, the ampersand (&) character is used as a prefix to a letter to identify an extended command. The extended command set became necessary because there are only 26 letters in the English alphabet, and within a few years of the development of the first series of smart modems, all those characters were used. Table 4.7 lists a portion of the extended Hayes modem command set. Although Hayes Microcomputer Products was very consistent in its use of ampersand commands, as you will learn later in this chapter, the use of those commands can vary considerably by modem manufacturer. More than 100 modem manufacturers use & commands differently. With an average of 50 ampersand commands per modem, it would require a table of 5,000 lines to list the most popular settings, and that is beyond the scope of this book. Readers can refer to specific modem manuals to obtain a listing of applicable commands for the modem they are using.

**TABLE 4.7**   Representative Extended Hayes Modem Commands

| Command | Description |
|---------|-------------|
| &B | Control automatic retraining |
| &C | Carrier Detect signal |
| &D | Data Terminal Ready signal |
| &F | Factory default control |
| &G | Guard tone control |
| &K | Flow control |
| &L | Select dial-up mode |
| &M | Select error control mode |
| &P | Select pulse dialing make/break ratio |
| &Q | Select data compression and error control mode |
| &S | Data Set Ready signal |
| &T | Perform modem test |
| &U | Control Trellis Coding for V.32 modem |
| &W | Store modem configuration |
| &Y | Set configuration at power-on |
| &Z | Store phone number |

## Modem Registers

In addition to the support of the command set, the degree of compatibility between Hayes Smartmodems and non-Hayes modems is governed by the number, use, and programmability of registers in the modem. Although many modern modems can include 100 or more registers, most devices support the use of the first 13 S registers supported by all Hayes modems.

Table 4.8 lists the functions of the first 13 registers built into Hayes Smartmodems to include the default value of each register and the range of settings permitted. To read the value of register *n*, you would issue the following command:

ATSn?

To set the value of register *n* to x, you would use the following command format:

AT Sn = x

4

ASYNCHRONOUS
MODEMS AND
INTERFACES

UNDERSTANDING DATA COMMUNICATIONS

**TABLE 4.8** S Register Control Parameters

| Register | Function | Default Value | Range |
|---|---|---|---|
| S0 | Ring to answer on | * | 0–255 |
| S1 | Count number of rings | 0 | 0–255 |
| S2 | Escape code character | ASCII 43 | ASCII 0–127 |
| S3 | Carriage-return character | ASCII 13 | ASCII 0–127 |
| S4 | Line-feed character | ASCII 10 | ASCII 0–127 |
| S5 | Backspace character | ASCII 8 | ASCII 0–127 |
| S6 | Dial tone wait time in seconds | 2 | 2–255 |
| S7 | Carrier wait time in seconds | 30 | 1–255 |
| S8 | Pause time caused by comma in seconds | 2 | 0–255 |
| S9 | Carrier detect response time in tenths of a second | 6 | 1–255 |
| S10 | Time delay between loss of carrier and hang up in tenths of a second | 7 | 1–255 |
| S11 | Touch-tone duration and spacing time in milliseconds | 70 | 50–255 |
| S12 | Escape sequence guard time in units of 1/20 seconds | 50 | 0–255 |

To illustrate the use of an S register setting, assume that you want to read the value in the S6 register. To do so, you would send the following command to the modem:

ATS6?

The modem's response to the preceding command would be a value between 2 and 255, indicating the amount of time in seconds that the modem will wait for a dial tone. Suppose that your modem is located behind a PBX that requires 3 to 4 seconds from noting a line going off-hook to issuing a dial tone. You would send the following command to your modem to set it to wait 4 seconds for a dial tone:

AT S6 = 4

# Viewing and Changing Modem Settings

The previous section examined several commands that, when transmitted to a Hayes-compatible modem, result in the occurrence of predefined conditions. What was missing from the previous discussion was information on how to transmit modem commands. Rather than have readers stare at their PCs and modems while scratching behind their ears, let's examine the "not-so-obvious" method to use to obtain the capability to configure a modem.

The key to unlocking your modem so that your PC can issue commands is to have your modem recognize AT commands. To do so, you must use a communications program that supports a direct connection. One such program is HyperTerminal, which is bundled in all versions of Windows.

When using HyperTerminal, you must configure the program for a direct connection using the communications port (com port) either cabled to the modem (external modem) or supported by an internal modem. Figure 4.15 illustrates how you would use the HyperTerminal Phone Number dialog box to set the connection to the applicable com port.

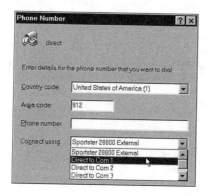

**FIGURE 4.15**

*Viewing and setting modem configuration parameters requires a direct connection to the modem.*

Once you establish a direct connection, you can view and modify modem settings. An example of the issuance of modem commands via a direct connection under HyperTerminal is shown in Figure 4.16. Because this author was using a U.S. Robotics Sportster 33600 modem, he used its manual to determine the command to issue to display current modem settings. That command is the I4 command and was sent to the modem by typing the sequence **at i4** followed by a carriage return. In examining the display of modem settings, it was noted that the S7 register was set to a value of 60 seconds. That setting was changed to a value of 90 seconds in the lower-left portion of Figure 4.16. One important fact to note is that the S7 register setting of 90 seconds is temporary and would be lost if power to the modem was turned off. Making the setting permanent requires the current configuration to be stored in the modem. Now that you have an appreciation of how to view and change modem settings, let's turn our attention to extended modem commands.

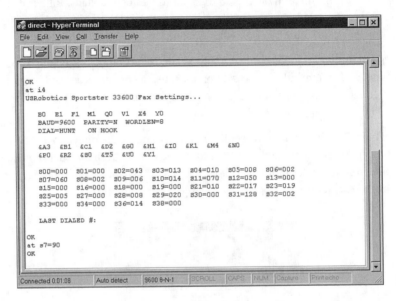

**FIGURE 4.16**

*Through the use of a direct connection, HyperTerminal provides the capability to view and modify modem settings.*

## Extended Command Set Variances

Although the basic Hayes command set was sufficient for supporting most intelligent-modem operations during the early 1980s, by the late 1980s, many modem vendors were introducing advanced features that were not supported by the basic Hayes command set. Although Hayes Microcomputer Products introduced a series of extended commands to govern the operation of advanced features incorporated into its product line, other vendors did not wait for Hayes and introduced features into their modems that were controlled by extended commands that they developed. The result of this action was the development of a series of extended command sets whose operations are applicable to only one or a few modems. To illustrate this fact, Table 4.9 lists the first 11 extended commands supported by two popular fax/data modems capable of transmitting at rates up to 14,400bps (the Practical Peripherals 14400 FXMT and the U.S. Robotics Sportster 14400 FAX). As you learned during your examination of the extended Hayes command set earlier in this chapter, because extended commands are prefixed with the ampersand, another term used to reference those commands is ampersand commands.

**TABLE 4.9**   Comparing Extended Command Operations

| Extended Practical Peripherals | Modem Function 14400 FXMT | Modem Function U.S. Robotics Sportster 14400 FAX |
|---|---|---|
| &A | Connect when autoanswering | ARQ results code |
| &B | V.32 automatic retrain | Data rate terminal to modem |
| &C | DSD signal operation | DCD signal operation |
| &D | DTE signal operation | DTE signal operation |
| &F | Undefined | Load factory settings |
| &G | Guard tone operation | Guard tone operation |
| &H | Undefined | Transmit data flow control |
| &I | Undefined control | Received data software flow |
| &K | Flow control | Data compression |
| &L | Dial/leased line mode | Undefined |
| &M | Synchronous mode selection | Error control |

In Table 4.9, note that the general modem function controlled by the extended command is listed for each modem. In many cases, several extended commands are based on a numeric value following the sequence ampersand letter. For example, &B0 would disable V.32 automatic retraining on a Practical Peripherals 14400 FXMT modem, whereas &B1 would enable that feature.

If you compare the functions controlled by each extended command listed in Table 4.9, you will note that software developed to control one modem cannot issue the same extended commands to control features on the other modem. This limitation explains why it is important to verify that a communications program that you intend to purchase supports a particular modem that you have or that you anticipate purchasing. Otherwise, you might have to either manually enter appropriate commands to take advantage of many of the features built into the modem or forego using those features.

## Extended Commands

Although it is quite common for modem vendors to assign different functions to the same extended command, many vendors use some extended commands in a similar manner. The series of &T commands used for modem testing represents the most common extended command that is almost universally used in a similar manner by different vendors.

Table 4.10 summarizes the functional assignment to the series of &T commands commonly used by most vendors.

## Modem Self Testing

Most modems designed for use on the switched telephone network support a self-test and three loopback tests. The self-test, designed to verify the operation of the modem's internal circuitry, uses a pattern generator to produce a known sequence of data that is used by the transmitter.

**TABLE 4.10**    The &T Extended Command Assignments

| Command | Function |
| --- | --- |
| &T0 | Terminate test in progress |
| &T1 | Initiate local analog loopback |
| &T2 | Initiate local digital loopback |
| &T6 | Initiate remote digital loopback |
| &T7 | Initiate local digital loopback with self-test |
| &T8 | Initiate local analog loopback with self-test |

Figure 4.17 illustrates the operation of a basic modem self-test. After a self-test is initiated, the modem's transmitter is tied to its receiver, breaking any previous connection to a communications line. Data modulated by the transmitter is demodulated by the receiver and passed to a pattern comparator, which includes a section of ROM that contains the same data sequence generated by the pattern generator. Thus, the pattern comparator enables the demodulated data to be compared to the sequence generated when the self-test is initiated. If the received data does not match the contents of the pattern comparator, the modem's circuitry causes a status indicator, typically labeled ER for error, to illuminate. This action informs you that the modem is defective and should be returned to the manufacturer.

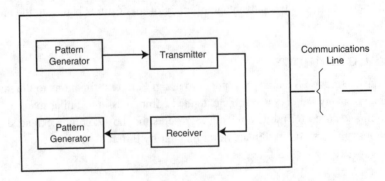

**FIGURE 4.17**
*A modem self-test.*

# Loopback Tests

Modems may be capable of performing four types of loopback tests, in which the position of each loopback indicates respect to a modem pair illustrated in Figure 4.18. Although most leased-line modems can perform all four loopbacks, a modem used on the switched network cannot perform a remote analog loopback.

- The local analog loopback test (2) ties the local modem's modulator to its demodulator. This tests both the analog and the digital circuits of the local modem.

- The local digital loopback test (1) is employed to test the operation of an attached DTE and the cable connecting the DTE to the modem. To perform this test, the local modem ties its transmitter and receiver circuits together, in effect bypassing its modulator and demodulator. Thus, input data received on pin 2 is routed to pin 3, which is the receive data conductor.

- The remote analog loopback test (3) results in a remote modem bridging the transmit and receive wire pairs of a leased line. This enables you to use test equipment at the local site to test both the local modem and the quality of the line. Because modems designed for use on the switched network operate on a two-wire system, this loopback test is not included in switched network modems.

- The remote digital loopback test (4) connects the remote modem's demodulator to its transmitter. This causes received data to be demodulated and passed to its transmitter for remodulation back to the local modem. Thus, this test checks the circuitry of the local and remote modems, as well as the line connection between the modems.

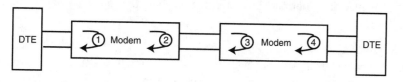

Legend:

① Local digital loopback
② Local analog loopback
③ Remote analog loopback
④ Remote digital loopback

**FIGURE 4.18**

*Modem loopbacks.*

# Fax Modems

Although in the preceding section you compared the use of several extended commands between fax modems manufactured by two vendors, you did not actually discuss what a fax modem represents. This section gives you an overview of the operation of this type of communications product.

In general, a fax modem is a modem that includes the capability to transfer fax image data over analog telephone circuits. To do so, the fax modem must support several fax standards. Two of the key standards governing fax transmission are the ITU-T T.4 and T.30 standards.

## The ITU-T T.4 Standard

The T.4 standard defines how fax data is formatted. This standard states that each scan line in a document consists of 1,728 dots and that scanning occurs left to right, line by line, until the right corner at the bottom of the page is reached. The T.4 standard also defines the vertical resolution of a document. The standard vertical resolution is 1,143 lines per page, and an optional fine resolution of 2,287 lines per page is defined. Concerning the higher resolution, most fax machines have a button labeled Fine or High Resolution that, when pressed, places the fax machine into its fine resolution mode.

## The ITU-T T.30 Standard

The second major standard governing the operation of fax modems is the T.30 standard. This standard governs the manner by which fax data is transmitted to include the initial call setup between two fax machines, during which information about the capability of each machine is exchanged.

Although the T.4 and T.30 standards govern the manner by which fax data is formatted and transmitted, they were developed for standalone fax machines. Thus, another standard was required to govern the interaction between a computer used to store or receive images and a fax modem used to transmit and receive images. That standard represents another extension to the AT command set in the form of fax modem commands.

## Fax Modem Commands

Currently, three commonly used sets of commands govern the operation of fax modems. Each set, which is more formally referred to as a fax modem service class, is based on certain properties originally developed by Hayes Microcomputer Products AT command set.

Class 1 represents a core set of six commands that was approved by the American National Standards Institute (ANSI), the Telecommunications Industry Association (TIA), and the Electronics Industry Association (EIA) as the ANSI/TIA/EIA-578 standard in 1990. A Class 1 fax modem requires the computer to perform most of the work involved in transmitting and receiving data according to the T.30 protocol. A key advantage of a Class 1 fax modem is that the fax protocol is implemented in software. This means that new extensions to the fax protocol can be implemented without having to upgrade or replace the modem. A disadvantage of the use of a Class 1 fax modem is its sensitivity to timing. If you are using a multitasking operating system with several processes active, it may be difficult to satisfy the timing constraints necessary to keep the fax connection alive.

A Class 2 proposal, which consisted of more than 50 commands and moved T.30 support into the fax modem, reached the ballot stage but was never approved. During the time the Class 2 standard was developed, many vendors manufactured and continue to manufacture modems that support the unapproved Class 2 draft standard. The primary advantage of a Class 2 fax modem is the fact that all time-critical aspects of fax communications are the responsibility of the modem. This allows faxing to occur under a multitasking operating system without worry over whether the operating system will interfere with the timing constraints necessary to keep the fax connection alive.

A third fax modem command standard is Class 2.0, which was approved as the EIA-572 standard. Although the Class 2.0 standard was based on the unapproved Class 2 draft, there are significant differences in the structure of commands that make the two incompatible. Although Class 2.0 is the officially approved standard, the unapproved Class 2 draft represents a more widely adopted fax command standard.

All fax modem commands begin with the prefix AT+F. The most basic fax modem command supported by each class is AT+FCLASS=?. That command is issued to the modem to determine what service class it supports. If the modem responds with 0,1,2, it supports data, Class 1 fax, and Class 2 fax. Most fax modems are sold with fax software that automatically issues appropriate fax commands based on the selection of menu entries displayed on the computer's screen. This insulates the computer user from having to know the function of individual fax commands; however, you might want to note a few fax commands in addition to the FCLASS command. Those commands, which are listed in Table 4.11 for Class 2– and Class 2.0–compatible fax modems, enable you to retrieve basic information about the modem that can be extremely valuable when you're attempting to configure software to work with a specific modem.

**4**

ASYNCHRONOUS
MODEMS AND
INTERFACES

**TABLE 4.12**   Basic Fax Commands for Retrieving Modem Information

| Description | Class 2 | Class 2.0 |
| --- | --- | --- |
| Service class | AT+FCLASS | AT+FCLASS |
| Manufacturer ID | AT+FMFR? | AT+FMI? |
| Modem ID | AT+FMDL? | AT+FMM? |
| Modem revision ID | AT+FREV? | AT+FMR? |

# What You Have Learned

- A modem (modulator-demodulator) changes data pulses to analog tones that the telephone channel will pass.
- Frequency-shift keying is the type of modulation used by most low-speed modems. Phase modulation or a combination of phase and amplitude modulation is used in high-speed modems.
- Data terminal equipment (DTE) is the equipment that originates or receives the data in digital form.
- Data communications equipment (DCE) is the equipment that converts the data from the DTE to the form required for the transmission channel. A modem is DCE.
- The signal levels, signal identification, and wiring between the DTE and the DCE are governed by standards.
- The RS-232 and CCITT V.24 standards for the DTE-DCE interface are the most commonly used in today's computer and communications world.
- The LZW algorithm forms the basis for compression performed by the V.42bis standard.
- RS-422A, RS-423A, and RS-449 are relatively new standards that overcome the defects of RS-232. The widespread adoption of RS-449, however, will probably be superseded by the RS-530 standard.
- Two new interfaces for personal computers that support daisy-chaining of devices to include modems to a PC are the Universal Serial Bus (USB) and FireWire.
- The types of commands that govern the operation of a modem include basic commands, extended commands, proprietary commands, and register commands.
- A communications program that is limited to supporting basic Hayes commands might not be capable of using the advanced features built into most modern modems.
- Without an appropriate method of flow control, a modem can lose data when its interface speed is set to a higher value than its operating rate.

• The capability to view and change modem settings requires the use of a communications program that supports a direct connection to the modem.

# Quiz for Chapter 4

1. What is flow control?

    A. What is done by people who open and close the floodgates on dams

    B. The process by which the modem matches the rate of the receiver

    C. The process of starting and stopping the terminal output to avoid loss of characters by the receiving device

2. What is buffering?

    A. The process of temporarily storing data to allow for small variations in device speeds

    B. A method of reducing the severity of communications headaches

    C. Storage of data within the transmitting modem until the receiver is ready to receive

3. Direct machine-to-machine transmission over long distances without modems is not practical because

    A. Copper wire does not transmit DC efficiently.

    B. No DC path exists that will handle data in pulse form.

    C. Data comes from the computer in the form of tones, not pulses.

4. What is modulation?

    A. The variance of some parameter of a carrier, such as its amplitude, to transmit information

    B. Utilization of a single transmission channel to carry multiple signals

    C. Transmission of pulses in DC form over a copper wire

5. RS-232, RS-449, RS-530, V.24, and X.21 are examples of what?

    A. Standards for various types of transmission channels

    B. Standards for interfaces between terminals and modems

    C. Standards for interfaces between modems and transmission facilities

    D. Standards for end-to-end performance of data communications systems

6. FireWire and USB represent

    A. Two new modems.

    B. Two high-speed interfaces.

    C. Two methods of flow control.

    D. Private line modems.

7. The actual transmission and reception of data on an RS-232 interface occurs

    A. On 25 conductors.

    B. On pins 2 and 3.

    C. On pins 4 and 5.

    D. On four conductors.

8. When a modem packs 2 bits into a signal change, its

    A. Bit rate equals its baud rate.

    B. Bit rate is half its baud rate.

    C. Bit rate is twice its baud rate.

    D. Bit rate is half its baud rate.

9. Which of the following is the most common method of data compression built into modems?

    A. V.42

    B. V.42bis

    C. MNP42

    D. MNP12

10. V.42 defines

    A. Compatibility with MNP Class 5 data compression.

    B. A method of data storage.

    C. Two methods of error detection and correction.

    D. Compatibility with MNP Class 7 enhanced data compression.

11. To provide compatibility with the error-detection-and-correction method used by an MNP modem, you would set a V.42 modem's error correction mode to which of the following settings?

    A. V.42bis

    B. V.42

    C. MNP Classless

    D. MNP Class 4

12. The cable connecting a DB-9 connector at one end to a DB-25 connector at the other end must cross-connect pin 8 at the DB-9 side to which pin at the DB-25 side?

    A. 4

    B. 22

    C. 5

    D. 2

13. A smart modem can

    A. Detect transmission errors and correct them automatically.

    B. Correctly answer multiple-choice quizzes.

    C. Accept commands from the terminal via the RS-232 interface.

14. What is RTS/CTS?

    A. The way the modem indicates ringing, and the way the terminal indicates that it is ready for the call to be answered

    B. The way the DTE indicates that it is ready to transmit data, and the way the DCE indicates that it is ready to accept data

    C. The pins that represent received transmissions and carrier transmissions

15. Pin 7, the signal ground

    A. Completes the circuit for control and data signals.

    B. Indicates a failure in the ground side of the transmission line.

    C. Completes the circuit for control signals but not data signals.

16. Pin 22, the ring indicator

    A. Must be present on all modems connected to the switched network.

    B. Is used on acoustic-coupled modems but not on direct-connect types.

    C. Is asserted when ringing voltage is present on the line.

17. Why do many cables have RS-232 connectors with some wires crossed or connected to one another?

    A. There are various RS-232 standards.

    B. Many computers and peripherals use RS-232 serial interfaces, but not as DTE-to-DCE.

    C. Asynchronous modems reverse the direction of transmitted and received data from the standard.

18. Extended command sets supported by modern modems

    A. Are standardized.

    B. Are prefixed with the letter *E*.

    C. Use different commands to control many advanced modem features.

    D. Can be counted on to provide a high-speed data-transfer capability without requiring flow control.

**4**

ASYNCHRONOUS
MODEMS AND
INTERFACES

19. What does a local digital loopback test?

    A. The local analog line

    B. The local digital line

    C. The operation of the local DTE and cable connecting the DTE to the modem

    D. The remote modem

20. Data rates above the 20,000bps limitation of the RS-232 standard become possible by

    A. Using the signal ground conductor.

    B. Extending the cable distance.

    C. Shortening the cable.

    D. Calling 911.

21. To set the S12 register to a value of 130, you would enter which of the following commands?

    A. AT130

    B. ATS12130

    C. ATS12=130

    D. AT130=S12

22. What do you need to view and change modem settings?

    A. A communications program that supports the modem command set

    B. A communications program that supports a direct connection to a modem via an applicable communications port

    C. A screwdriver to open the modem case

    D. A communications program that supports the register settings of the modem

23. Which is a primary application for the FireWire interface?

    A. Connecting PCs together

    B. Connecting PCs to modems

    C. Connecting PCs to scanners

    D. Connecting PCs to a video source

24. The T.4 standard defines

    A. The modem class.

    B. How fax data is formatted.

    C. How fax data is transmitted.

    D. The connection to a fax modem.

25. A response of 1 to the command AT+FCLASS=? would indicate that

    A. Your modem has a release date of 01/01/95.

    B. Your modem supports fax Class 1.

    C. Your modem supports fax Class 1.0.

    D. Your modem has a revision code of 1.0.

# Synchronous Modems, Digital Transmission, and Service Units

## IN THIS CHAPTER

In this chapter, you will be introduced to the signaling methods used by high-speed modems, the American and international standards that apply to synchronous data modems, and the concepts used in higher-speed (greater than 19,200 bits per second) wideband devices. Two relatively new types of high-speed modems are described in this chapter: Digital Subscriber Line (DSL) modems and cable modems. Because a high-speed interface is required to support data transfer between computers and high-speed modems, this chapter also covers the ITU V.35 interface. This will be followed by an examination of the techniques of direct transmission of binary signals without modems, called digital transmission. Because the transmission of binary signals over long distances without modems requires the use of devices known as service units, the operation and utilization of those devices will also be covered in this chapter.

# Synchronous Signaling and Standards

Synchronous signaling permits data to be transmitted without gaps between characters or timing discrepancies, enabling higher data-transfer rates to be achieved. To accomplish this, synchronous signaling requires a clocking source that enables bits to be transmitted and received at applicable times.

## A Search for Higher Data Rates

Like the Olympic athlete whose motto is "Alitus, cititus, fortitus," the aims of the data communications systems designer in the development of high-technology products are to pack more data per channel, deliver it at a faster speed, and deliver it at a lower cost. The transmission of a larger quantity of data through a channel of a given bandwidth with smaller and cheaper devices is a natural target. Because in many cases, the channel available is a standard voice-grade line and the cost of the channel dominates the cost of the system, a large amount of design effort has gone into the production of devices that will send the largest number of bits per unit time through standard (voice-grade) channels. One result has been synchronous signaling, which, as a side benefit, allows clocking or timing to be provided by the data.

## Sending the Clock with the Data

Binary signals sent over a channel represent the quantization of data in two dimensions: amplitude (voltage of the electrical wave) and time (the duration of each signaling element). As the number of signaling elements per unit time (the baud rate) increases, the duration of each element must decrease, as illustrated in Figure 5.1. If, as is the case with asynchronous modems, the time base for the transmitter and the receiver are independent, small differences between the two clocks become more likely to cause errors due to the sampling of the data at the wrong time. Synchronous modems overcome this problem by deriving the timing information from the received data.

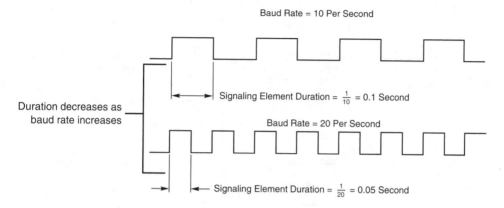

**FIGURE 5.1**

*Baud rate versus element duration.*

## More Bits per Baud

Recall that in Chapter 3, "Messages and Transmission Channels," it was stated that for a channel of given bandwidth, the maximum signaling rate is fixed by the channel bandwidth and the signal-to-noise ratio (Shannon's formula). Because voice-grade channels have a fixed bandwidth (about 3000Hz), they have a fixed maximum baud rate (about 2400 baud). The solution to this dilemma is to pack more than 1 bit into one signaling element—that is, to send 2 or more bits per baud.

## Typical Synchronous Components

The greater complexity and cost of synchronous modems over asynchronous units results from the circuitry necessary to derive the timing from the incoming data and pack more than 1 bit into one baud. Synchronous modems typically consist of four components: transmitter, receiver, terminal control, and power supply (see Figure 5.2). You will look at the first three of these items in some detail. Because the power supply simply operates equipment and does not regulate transmission other than enabling it to occur, you will not focus on that device.

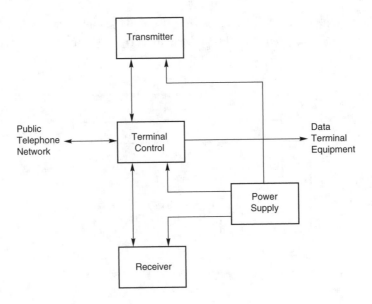

**FIGURE 5.2**

*A synchronous modem block diagram.*

# Transmitter

As you can see in Figure 5.3, the transmitter section of a synchronous modem typically consists of timing (clock) circuitry, scrambler, modulator, digital-to-analog converter, and equalizer circuits. As you progress through this chapter, we will examine the operation of those components.

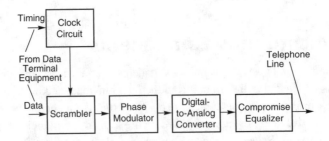

**FIGURE 5.3**

*A modem transmitter block diagram.*

## Timing Circuit

The timing circuit provides the basic clocking information for both the modem and the data terminal equipment (DTE) that is providing the data to be transmitted. Certain data circuit arrangements require that the clocking for the transmitted data be supplied by the DTE (which can be another modem). In these cases, an option is usually provided in the modem to phase-lock the internal clock to an external clock source, input through the DTE interface. A crystal oscillator to within about 0.05 percent of the nominal value usually controls the internal timing.

## Scrambler Operation

The function of a scrambler is to change the pattern of the data stream to ensure a sufficient amount of changes in the data. Because the receiver clock is derived from the received data, that data must contain enough changes from 0 to 1 (and vice versa) to ensure that the timing recovery circuit stays synchronized. In principle, the data stream provided by the associated terminal or business machine can consist of any arbitrary bit pattern. If the pattern contains long strings of the same value, the data will not provide the receiver with enough transitions for synchronization. The transmitter must prevent this condition by changing the input bit stream in a controlled way. The part of the transmitter circuitry that does this is called the scrambler.

Scramblers are usually implemented as feedback shift registers, which can be cascaded (connected in series), as shown in Figure 5.4. Input bit 1 is modified by adding the state of selected bits of the 7-bit register to the incoming bit. Input bits 2, 3, and so on are modified by the preceding bits, as indicated in the figure. Scramblers are designed to ensure that each possible value of phase angle is equally likely to occur, to provide the receiving demodulator with enough phase shifts to recover the clocking signal. Although sampling is necessary for the reasons cited previously, it increases the error rate because an error in one bit is likely (and in some cases is certain) to cause an error in subsequent bits. To counteract this problem, some modems encode the input to the scrambler into the Gray code so that the most likely error in demodulation (picking an adjacent phase state) will cause only a 1-bit error when decoded at the receiver. As Table 5.1 indicates, the Gray code causes only 1 bit to change states between any two successive binary numbers—tribit numbers, in this case.

**TABLE 5.1**   Binary and Gray Code Equivalence for 3-Bit Code

| Decimal | Binary | Gray Code |
| --- | --- | --- |
| 0 | 000 | 000 |
| 1 | 001 | 001 |
| 2 | 010 | 011 |

**TABLE 5.1** continued

| Decimal | Binary | Gray Code |
|---------|--------|-----------|
| 3 | 011 | 010 |
| 4 | 100 | 110 |
| 5 | 101 | 111 |
| 6 | 110 | 101 |
| 7 | 111 | 100 |

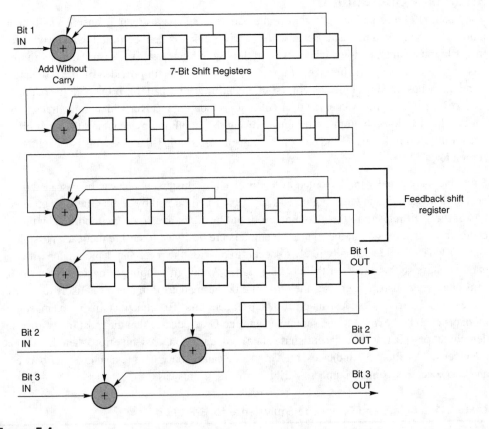

**FIGURE 5.4**

*A tribit scrambler.*

## Modulator Operation

The modulator section of the transmitter converts the bit patterns produced by the scrambling process into an analog signal representing the desired phase and amplitude of the carrier signal. The carrier frequency, baud rate, and number of bits represented by each baud is different for modems of different data rates. The modulator collects the correct number of bits and translates them into a number giving the amplitude of the electrical signal that is correct for the carrier frequency and phase of the carrier at that instant. Modulation techniques differ for modems of different speeds and from different manufacturers. Some of the more common ones are discussed later in this chapter.

## Digital-to-Analog Converter

The binary encoded signal from the modulator is fed to a digital-to-analog converter, which produces the actual analog voltage required. This, in turn, goes through a low-pass filter to remove frequencies outside of the voice baud and then through a circuit called an equalizer, which compensates for transmission impairments on the line.

## Compromise Equalizer

The transmission equalizer is called a compromise or statistical equalizer because it is set to compensate for the nominal or average characteristics of the transmission medium. The equalizer compensates for amplitude distortion in the medium and for a problem called group delay. Group delay compares the speed of one signal in the transmission medium to the speed of another signal traveling on a different frequency. Group delay usually is expressed in microseconds (uçs) at a given frequency. Nominal values of delay variation versus frequency for some commonly available voice-grade channels are given in Table 5.2.

# Receiver Equalizer Operation

The receiving equalizer must deal with actual errors in the received signal. The errors are measured and corrected by adjusting specific circuit parameters. As Figure 5.5 shows, the receiver section of a synchronous modem typically consists of an adaptive equalizer, clock (timing) recovery, a digital demodulator, a descrambler, and a DTE interface. Other common equalizer components include control logic that governs its operation, a local clock for synchronization, and an IF modulator that enables the demodulation of the received signal.

**TABLE 5.2**   Group Delay Variation Versus Frequency for Conditioned Transmission Lines

| Conditioning Applied to Voice-Grade Channel | Frequency Range (Hz) | Delay Variation (uçs) |
| --- | --- | --- |
| Basic (none) | 800–2600 | 1750 |
| C1 | 800–2600 | 1750 |
| C2 | 600–2600 | 1500 |
| C3 | 600–2600 | 260–300 |
| C4 | 800–2800 | 500 |
| C5 | 600–2600 | 300 |

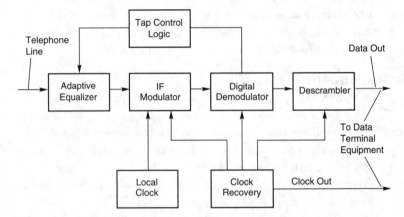

**FIGURE 5.5**
*A modem receiver block diagram.*

## Adaptive Equalizer

The equalizer section of the transmitter is relatively simple because it can compensate only for the average of expected errors on the output channel. The receiver equalizer, however, must compensate for the actual errors introduced in the transmission path. This is done via an adaptive equalizer, which measures errors observed in the received signal and adjusts some parameter of the circuit (usually the receiver clock frequency) to track slowly varying changes in the condition of the transmission line.

Delay distortion has the greatest effect on the transmission of an analog signal. As mentioned previously, analog signals of different frequencies travel at different rates through a transmission medium. Because each signaling element contains many frequencies, the signaling elements arrive at the receiver over a period of time rather than all at once. The frequencies that travel faster (leading frequencies) arrive earlier, and those traveling slower (lagging frequencies) arrive later. Leading frequencies travel faster and arriver earlier than lagging frequencies.

The leading and lagging frequencies not only fail to make their proper contribution to the proper signaling element, but they also cause interference with signaling elements behind and ahead of the proper element. The equalizer must get the parts of each element back together and cancel their effects on other elements.

The adaptive equalizer does this by use of a tapped delay line that stores the analog signal for a period. This time period includes the main signaling element to be corrected at the center and several times before and after the center, as shown in Figure 5.6. The taps in the delay line allow the analog voltage representing the signal to be picked off at specific time intervals before and after the element of interest. The time interval between taps is the reciprocal of the baud rate. The voltage from each tap is amplified by a variable-gain amplifier whose gain is controlled by an amount determined by the correction calculator circuit.

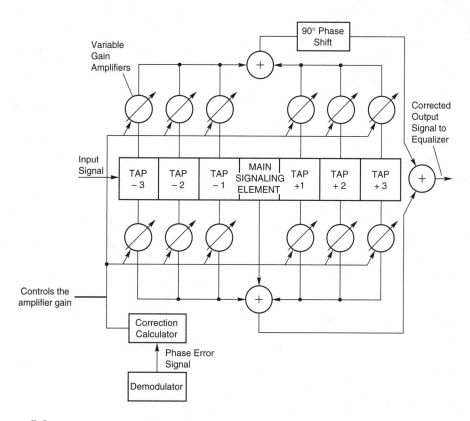

**FIGURE 5.6**

*An adaptive equalizer.*

In response to a phase error signal developed by the demodulator circuit, the correction calculator determines the amplitude and polarity of the signal needed from each tape amplifier. What makes the equalizer adaptive is that the error signal is continuously derived from the difference between the phase of the received signal and a nominal phase value determined by the demodulator.

## Time-Saving Techniques

All the delays caused by the changing line conditions result in a circuit that slowly adapts to changing line conditions. This can be a disadvantage for half-duplex operation or at start-up on a one-way link. To combat this, a start-up or training sequence of bits usually is sent first to allow the receiver to adapt more rapidly than it would on random data. This process is called training. The amount of time required for the modem to retrain after changing the direction of transmission must be less than the turnaround time or request-to-send, clear-to-send (RTS-CTS) delay. This delay effectively reduces the data-transmission rate on the circuit. For example, 4800bps modems have RTS-CTS delays in the 10 to 20 millisecond (ms) range (about 50 to 100 bit times).

The equalizer section of some modems attempts to minimize the amount of line time lost in turnaround by a dual-speed or "gearshift" technique. This technique causes the modem pair to start at a lower data rate (say, 2400bps), at which training is very fast, and to transmit data at that rate while the adaptive equalizer goes through its training cycle. The modems then "shift gears" to run at the full data rate, as shown in Figure 5.7. For short messages, the RTS-CTS delay is the controlling factor in throughput; for long messages, the transmission speed is dominant. Therefore, the speed-changing technique minimizes the delay while still providing the higher speed.

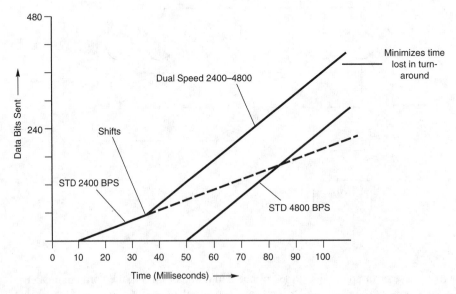

## FIGURE 5.7
*Dual-speed modem performance.*

## Automatic Equalization

The incorporation of microprocessors into modems enabled their processing capability to be used to control numerous functions, including automatic equalization. When a pair of modems performs automatic equalization, each modem periodically transmits a training signal to the modem located at the opposite end of the circuit. The receiving modem knows the expected composition of the training signal and automatically adjusts its equalization to enable the best reception of the signal. In fact, you can probably think of automatic equalization as being similar to fine-tuning on your television. After it's set, it operates without requiring operator intervention. Today, almost all synchronous modems include an automatic-equalization feature that compensates for both amplitude distortion and group delay.

To illustrate the operation of automatic equalization, consider Figure 5.8, which illustrates how a modem compensates for the amplitude distortion of a signal by a technique referred to as attenuation equalization. Because high frequencies attenuate more rapidly than low frequencies, the modem measures circuit attenuation similar to the inverted U-shaped curve over the pass band of the channel. The modem then sets its equalization circuitry to generate a level of attenuation inverse to that occurring from the circuit, as indicated by the upper U-shaped curve. The result of the attenuation equalization process is to produce a near-uniform or level amount of attenuation across the pass band of the circuit. In addition to simplifying procedures required for automatic equalization, the use of fast microprocessors has reduced the training time required for equalization. Because no data can be transmitted during the training process, decreasing training time results in an increase in modem throughput.

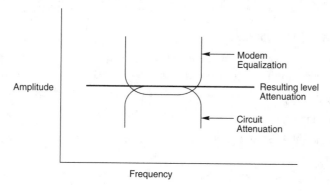

## FIGURE 5.8

*Attenuation equalization.*

SYNCHRONOUS
COMPONENTS

## Clock Recovery

Although modem equalization governs the capability of a signal to be understood, equally important for the correct interpretation of the signal is clock recovery. At the receiver, the incoming signal from the line is modulated or frequency-translated using an internal clock. The resulting intermediate frequency is processed to produce a clock signal at the rate at which the data is actually being received. This signal is applied as the reference to a phase-locked loop oscillator. The output of this oscillator is a stable signal locked to the incoming line frequency in both phase and frequency.

## Descrambler Operation

The descrambler section of the receiver performs an operation that is the inverse of the scrambler operation described in the section on the transmitter. If the data was Gray-coded by the transmitter before scrambling, it is converted back to straight binary and then applied to the DCE interface circuit.

## The DTE Interface

In addition to requiring equalization and clocking, an important characteristic of modems to consider is the DTE interface. The DTE interface for most modems conforms to one of two standards: the Electronic Industries Association (EIA) RS-232 or the International Telephone and Telegraph Consultative Committee (CCITT) Recommendation V.24. These standards were covered in Chapter 4, "Asynchronous Modems and Interfaces." A third standard that is used to interface high-speed analog modems and digital service units is the ITU V.35 standard. That standard is described later in this chapter in the section "The V.35 Interface."

# Terminal Control Section

The control section of synchronous modems must deal with two external interfaces: the telephone line at one end and the business machine at the other. If the modem is to be used on the public dial telephone network, it should be capable of performing the following tasks:

- Sensing the ringing signal
- Providing line supervision (connecting and disconnecting the modem and the telephone line)
- In some cases, providing a busy indication to the incoming line without tying up telephone central office equipment

## Interface Circuits

Most synchronous modems support the set of RS-232/ITU V.24 interface circuits shown in Table 5.3. The backward-channel circuits (ITU circuit numbers 118–122) are required only in modems that provide a reverse or backward channel for control information in the opposite direction to normal data flow. The Data Terminal Ready circuit (ITU circuit 108.2) is required only for modems used on the dial-up connections.

**TABLE 5.3**  Synchronous Modem RS-232/ITU V.24 DTE Interface Circuits

| EIA | Circuit Number CCITT | Designation |
|-----|----------------------|-------------|
| AA  | 101   | Equipment Ground |
| AB  | 102   | Signal Ground |
| BA  | 103   | Transmitted Data |
| BB  | 104   | Received Data |
| CA  | 105   | Request to Send |
| CB  | 106   | Clear to Send |
| CC  | 107   | Modem Ready (Data Set Ready) |
| CD  | 108.2 | Data Terminal Ready |
| CE  | 125   | Ring Indicator |
| CF  | 109   | Received Line Signal Detector (Carrier) |
| CG  | 110   | Signal Quality Detector |
| CH  | 111   | Data Signal Rate Detector (DTE Source) |
| CI  | 112   | Data Signal Rate Detector (DCE Source) |
| DA  | 113   | Transmitted Signal Element Timing (DTE Source) |
| DB  | 114   | Transmitted Signal Element Timing (DCE Source) |
| DD  | 115   | Received Signal Element Timing (DCE Source) |
| SBA | 118   | Secondary (Backward Channel) Transmitted Data |
| SBB | 119   | Secondary Received Data |
| SCA | 120   | Secondary Request to Send |
| SCB | 121   | Secondary Clear to Send |
| SCF | 122   | Secondary Received Line Signal Detected (Carrier) |

## Clear to Send

The Clear to Send signal is returned to the DTE in response to assertion of the Request to Send signal. It is delayed by the modem, however, by the amount of time necessary for the modem to "turn the line around"—that is, to send the required training pattern to the distant end.

**5**

**SYNCHRONOUS COMPONENTS**

## External Timing

Many standard 9600bps and higher-speed modems designed for leased-line operations contain internal time-division multiplexers, which allow more than one terminal to operate simultaneously over a single channel. In many cases, one or more channels are carried to terminals remote from the first modem, terminating the circuit as shown in Figure 5.9. In such cases, which apply only to full-duplex operation, the clock signal for all the modems in the path must be synchronized to only one of the modems. Systems that have terminals remote from the terminating modem on the main channel require that the remote modem be synchronized to the originating modem. The external clock input (EIA circuit DA) for the extension modem circuit is fed from the receive clock from the primary modem (EIA circuit DD), causing the clocks in all the modems to be slaved to the single modem at the originating end. Refer to Chapter 6, "Multiplexing Techniques," for information concerning the operation and utilization of time-division multiplexers.

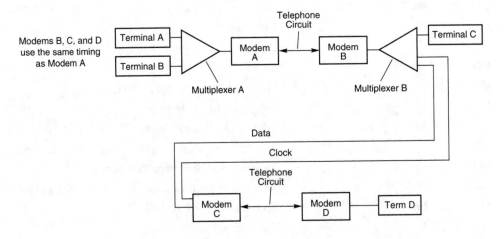

Modem C must be supplied an external clock from multiplexer B, which must use the received data clock from Modem B.

**FIGURE 5.9**

*A multiple-modem circuit requiring external clocking.*

# Standard and Evolving Modems

You'll now examine the implementation of some obsolete modems, as well as currently avail-able modems and evolving modems that are expected to be available by the time you read this book. The reason that you will spend a short period of time examining obsolete modems is that many of their functions and features were incorporated in some manner into more modern technology. In addition, many locations around the globe still use relatively obsolete modems that operate at 9600bps or less, and you need to have some knowledge of their operations and terminology to properly configure more modern modems that are downward-compatible with obsolete modems to work with those aged devices. The types of modems that will be examined include the following:

- 2400bps modems
- 4800bps modems
- 9600bps modems

After that, you'll switch to asymmetrical modems, which reached the marketplace in the late 1980s. They were considered to be potential successors to the V.22bis modem discussed in Chapter 4 due to the high price of V.32 modems. Unfortunately for asymmetrical modem man-ufacturers, the lack of standards governing the asymmetrical transmission technique, as well as a significant reduction in the cost of V.32 modems, inhibited the asymmetrical modem's wide-spread acceptance. Today, most people requiring high-speed data transmission on the PSTN use V.32, V.32bis, V.33, or V.34.

## 2400bps Modems

Two common 2400bps modems are the Western Electric 201 and the ITU V.26. These two types of modems illustrate the general properties of the 2400bps half-duplex two-wire and full-duplex four-wire (DPSK) because they have similar operating mechanisms.

### Western Electric 201

A good example of the basic synchronous modem is the Western Electric (WE) 201, dia-grammed in Figure 5.10. It operates at 1200 baud with a carrier frequency of 1800Hz. This modem uses a kind of phase-shift modulation called the differential phase-shift keying (DPSK) technique, and it encodes 2 bits (called a dibit) into one signaling element (2 bits per baud). Phase-shift keying encodes the binary values as changes of the phase of the carrier signal, as discussed in Chapter 4. *Differential phase shift* means that the reference point from which the phase angle is measured at any signaling interval is the phase angle of the immediately preced-ing interval. The WE 201 shifts the phase by multiples of 45°, according to Table 5.4.

5

UNDERSTANDING DATA COMMUNICATIONS

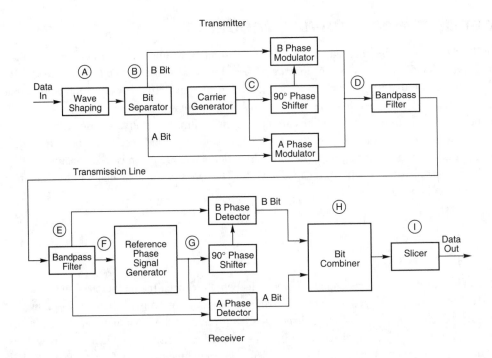

**FIGURE 5.10**

*WE 201 modem block diagram.*

The following list examines the interactions illustrated in Figure 5.10:

  A. At the transmitter input, pulses are generated according to the data input and then are fil-
     tered to shape them for modulation.

  B. Alternate bits in the stream become A bits, and the others become B bits.

  C. The two bit streams phase-modulate a sine wave carrier. The carrier for the B bit stream
     is phase-shifted by 90° with respect to the A carrier.

  D. The outputs of the modulators are combined, and the bandpass filter eliminates unwanted
     signals before transmission.

  E. At the receiver, another bandpass filter removes noise and another removes unwanted
     signals.

  F. The input signal is used to synchronize a sine-wave reference phase signal.

  G. The reference signal is applied directly to the A phase detector but is phase-shifted 90°
     before application to the B phase detector.

  H. The A and B bit streams from the detectors are combined into a single bit stream.

I. The slicer output consists of clean rectangular pulses that convey the same data as the transmitter input.

**TABLE 5.4**    WE 201 Phase Coding

| Dibit | Phase Change in Degrees |
| --- | --- |
| 00 | 45 |
| 10 | 135 |
| 11 | 225 |
| 01 | 315 |

With this technique, the signal is self-referenced: That is, no separate absolute phase information needs to be transmitted, and the most likely error (picking an adjacent phase value) causes only a 1-bit error. The WE 201 contains a local clock that is phase-locked to the detected phase of the incoming signal. Differences between the nominal phase values given in Table 5.4 and the detected phase of the incoming signal referenced to the phase of the local clock are used to measure the quality of the incoming line signal. Because the phase of the received signal changes for each signaling interval, there is always sufficient energy at the 1200-baud rate to recover the baud clock.

## ITU-T V.26

The ITU-T has published a recommendation for a standard 2400bps modem with the designation "Recommendation V.26: 2400 Bits per Second Modem Standardized for Use on Leased Telephone-Type Circuits." It specifies a full-duplex, 1200-baud DPSK modem with a modulation rate of up to 75 baud in each direction on an optional "backward channel." In Europe, V.26 modems are commonly built into television receivers to provide a transmission capability for accessing Videotex systems. When the modem is used in this manner, pressing buttons on a TV remote control transmits "page" selection numbers to a Videotex system. The Videotex system, in turn, transmits the requested "page," which is displayed on the TV set. Because a small quantity of data flows from the TV set to the Videotex system in the form of page number requests, the use of the V.26 modem is reversed. That is, the 75-baud "backward channel" is used to transmit page number requests while Videotex information flows on the primary channel to the TV set.

The V.26 recommendations are generally similar to the specifications for the WE 201 (largely because, by 1968, the WE 201 had become a de facto standard). One interesting difference is that the assignment of dibits to phase-change values is allowed alternative sets of values. Alternative A is given in Table 5.5, and alternative B is the same as that given in Table 5.4 for the WE 201. Use of alternative A leads to the problem of no phase change at all for long strings of 00 dibits. Thus, the energy content in the transmitted stream at the 1200 baud rate is greatly reduced, making baud clock recovery uncertain.

**TABLE 5.5**   V.26 Alternative A Phase Coding

| Dibit | Phase Change in Degrees |
|-------|-------------------------|
| 00    | 0                       |
| 01    | 90                      |
| 11    | 180                     |
| 10    | 270                     |

Recommendation V.26 specifies that the form of the synchronizing signal between two modems is to be continuous transmission of dibit 11 (giving continuous 180° phase shifts) during the RTS-CTS sequence. It also specifies incoming signal levels of –26 dBm or higher for the modem to assert the carrier detect (Circuit 109) and –31 dBm or lower for it to negate carrier detect. It is recommended that the modem be designed so that the operator cannot control the send level or receive sensitivity.

# 4800bps Modems

Modems representative of 4800bps devices include the ITU-T V.27 and Western Electric 208 modems.

## ITU-T V.27

The ITU-T Recommendation V.27 specifies a 4800bps modem for use on leased telephone-type circuits. This modem has the following features:

- Can operate in either half- or full-duplex
- Uses differential phase-shift keying with eight phases
- Provides an optional 75bps backward channel in both directions for supervisory signaling
- Has a manually adjustable equalizer

This recommendation was promulgated in 1972, and the state of the modem art has progressed far beyond the manually adjustable equalizer. However, the remainder of the recommendation is the basis for many current modems, particularly in the European market. The carrier frequency is 1800Hz, the modulation rate is 1600 baud, and the basic phase-shift interval is 45°. To signal at 4800bps with 1600 baud, each baud must represent 3 bits (tribits). Table 5.6 outlines the tribit to phase change amount for V.27.

**TABLE 5.6**  V.27 Phase Coding

| Tribit Value | Phase Change in Degrees |
|---|---|
| 001 | 0 |
| 000 | 45 |
| 010 | 90 |
| 011 | 135 |
| 111 | 180 |
| 110 | 225 |
| 100 | 270 |
| 101 | 315 |

The synchronization pattern for the V.27 modem is composed of continuous ones in tribits for at least 9ms to train the demodulator, plus continuous ones at the input to the transmit scrambler until the CTS lead (circuit 106) is asserted by the transmitting modem to synchronize the scramblers. The general operation of a scrambler was described earlier in the chapter, but the details of the V.27 scrambler follow.

The transmitter scrambler divides the message polynomial, of which the input data bits are the coefficients in descending order, by a generating polynomial, which for V.27 is equal to $1 + (X - 6) + (X - 7)$. This division is continuously performed as each bit enters the scrambler, and the result becomes the transmitted data pattern. The transmitted pattern is then searched continuously over 45 bits for repeating patterns of 1, 2, 3, 4, 6, 9, and 12 bits, which are eliminated. The result is sent as the scrambled data pattern. Figure 5.11 shows a feedback shift register that implements the polynomial division process.

## Western Electric 208

The WE 208 modem is another 4800bps modem that at one time was widely used in the United States. It had been supplied by AT&T and the Bell Operating Companies when they were part of the Bell System. It is a DPSK unit, using eight phase angles to represent eight different groups of 3 bits. The coding pattern (after Gray coding the binary input) for the WE 208 is given in Table 5.7.

**TABLE 5.7**  WE 208 Phase Coding

| Tribit Value | Relative Phase in Degrees |
|---|---|
| 001 | 22.5 |
| 000 | 67.5 |

**TABLE 5.7** continued

| Tribit Value | Relative Phase in Degrees |
|---|---|
| 010 | 112.5 |
| 011 | 157.5 |
| 111 | 202.5 |
| 110 | 247.5 |
| 100 | 292.5 |
| 101 | 337.5 |

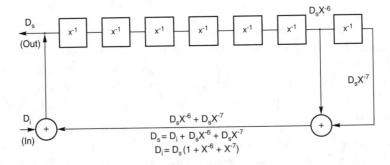

**FIGURE 5.11**
*ITU-T V.27 scrambler.*

The carrier frequency for the WE 208 is 1800Hz, and the baud rate is 1600 baud. The WE 208 is not equipped with an internal multiplexer because the 1600 baud rate of the modem is not a standard data rate for any other modem or business machine. The design of the WE 208 was covered in the previous section on typical synchronous modem components, including the scrambler implementation as four 7-bit feedback shift registers to randomize the first bit of each tribit.

The demodulator in the WE 208 multiplies the carrier frequency by eight and then measures the interval between the 1600 baud clock transition and the first positive value of the current carrier cycle. This measurement is done digitally, and successive values of the count are compared to determine the phase shift that occurred during the preceding signaling interval. The measured phase shift (with any errors that might be present due to line noise, demodulator errors, baud clock errors, and such) is rounded to the nearest permitted value (22.5°, 67.5°, and so forth), and the transmitted tribit sequence is extracted and decoded from Gray code to binary. An error feedback signal is developed as the difference between the actual phase of the signal, as demodulated, and the nominal value. This error signal is monitored, and it forces the modem to retrain if it becomes too large.

The WE 208 modem normally operates with a basic retraining time of 50ms, but it can be changed with internal strapping (jumper wires) to 150ms for operation on long circuits (more than 2000 miles). Even this delay probably is still too short for operation on satellite links because of the very long (about 650ms) round-trip propagation delay.

# 9600bps Modems

Two popular types of modems used to provide a data-transfer capability at 9600bps during the late 1970s and early 1980s were the Western Electric 209 and ITU-T V.29 modems. The Western Electric 209 had a near captive market in North America until the breakup of AT&T. The ITU-T V.29 modem represents an international standard that eventually dominated the market for 9600bps operations. In addition, the basic circuitry of the V.29 modem was used by several modem manufacturers during the late 1980s and early 1990s as a platform for developing several types of proprietary modems designed for use over the switched telephone network. To increase the data rate of a synchronous modem over 4800bps, it is necessary to either increase the baud rate or increase the number of bits per baud. Standard 9600bps modems do both.

## Modulation Types

Compared to a 4800bps modem, a 9600bps modem's baud rate is increased to 2400 bauds. In addition, the input data is taken 4 bits at a time (quadbits) for controlling the output of the modulator. Two modulation schemes are commonly used to read these extreme data rates: vestigial sideband modulation (VSB) and quaternary amplitude modulation (QAM).

Choosing between modems using one of these two modulation schemes is less a matter of performance than of economics. Some VSB modems require little or no line conditioning, whereas a few QAM unit manufacturers generally recommend at least C2 conditioned circuits. The VSB units are less complex internally, which usually allows a price advantage over QAM units.

### Vestigial Sideband Modulation

Because it is possible to transmit a double-sideband frequency-modulated (FM) signal (with a WE 202-type modem) at 1800bps, one would think that it should be possible to send at 3600bps using only one sideband because the entire bandwidth would be available for the one sideband. This is not possible, however, with an FM signal (the signal can't be recovered), but it is possible to use an amplitude-modulated (AM) single-sideband signal to transmit at 4800 baud. Four different carrier amplitudes are used to represent the four different values of bits taken two at a time; thus, each baud represents 2 bits, which gives an effective rate of 9600bps.

A VSB transmitter has a scrambler and Gray coder similar to those of 4800bps modems. The modulator, however, takes the bits two at a time to form a four-level signal, which modulates a

2853Hz carrier. The carrier and upper sideband are suppressed, and a 2853Hz pilot signal is added back to what remains, but 90° out of phase. A signal that is 90° out of phase is called a quadrature signal because "in quadrature" means at right angles to the original carrier. The quadrature signal does not interfere with the modulated single-sideband signal, but it is necessary for the receiver to recover the exact frequency and phase of the original carrier so that it can recover the data.

The receiver's local 2853Hz oscillator is locked to the phase and frequency of the pilot signal recovered from the received signal. This adjusted clock is used to demodulate the received single-sideband signal into the four-level 4800-baud baseband signal. The signal is processed by a 60-tap adaptive equalizer to remove intersymbol interference, and then it is put through a decision circuit to recover the dibits, which are then unscrambled.

Training a 60-tap equalizer is a lengthy process that reduces the cost-effectiveness of using 9600bps modems on half-duplex circuits. A four-segment training sequence must be sent to perform the following tasks:

- Set the automatic gain control circuits.
- Acquire the phase of the carrier tone.
- Set the equalizer tap coefficients.
- Synchronize the scrambler.

In the ITU-T Recommendation V.29 for a 9600bps modem, the total four-segment sequence takes about 250ms.

### Quadrature Amplitude Modulation

QAM modems use some combination of differential phase shifts and amplitudes totaling 16 states of encoded 4 bits per baud. This, combined with a baud rate of 2400, gives the desired 9600bps. The ITU-T Recommendation V.29 specifies eight phases, with two possible signal amplitudes at each phase change. The WE 209 modem uses 12 phases and 3 amplitudes, but some combinations of phase and amplitude are not allowed. Three common 9600bps constellation patterns are shown in Figure 5.12. The choice of the number of phases and level spacing represents the modem manufacturer's best guess at the type and severity of various transmission-line errors that the modem is likely to experience. It can be argued, however, that the V.29 recommendation resulted in a more optimal selection than the WE 209 due to the near-universal use of V.29 modems.

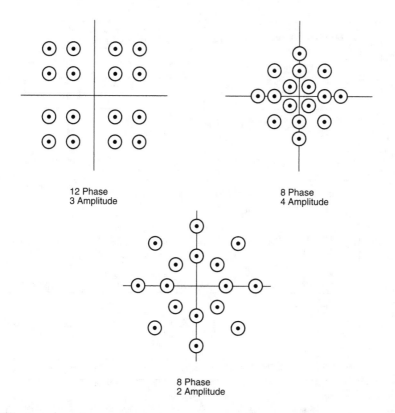

12 Phase
3 Amplitude

8 Phase
4 Amplitude

8 Phase
2 Amplitude

**FIGURE 5.12**

*Common 9600bps QAM modem constellation patterns.*

## ITU-T V.29

The carrier frequency for the ITU-T V.29 modem is 1700Hz, and it operates at 2400 baud. This modem is specified to operate at 9600bps with fallback rates of 7200 and 4800bps. It has an automatic adaptive equalizer and can optionally contain a multiplexer for carrying up to four separate data streams whose aggregate (combined) rate does not exceed 9600bps. The combined data stream to be transmitted is scrambled and then divided into sets of 4 bits (quadbits). The first bit (in time) of each quadbit determines the amplitude of the transmitted signal, as illustrated in Figure 5.13, and the remaining 3 bits determine the phase shift to be applied, as shown in Figure 5.14. The resulting "constellation pattern" resembles Figure 5.15.

5

SYNCHRONOUS
COMPONENTS

| Absolute Phase | Q1 | Relative Signal Element Amplitude |
|---|---|---|
| 0°, 90°, 180°, 270° | 0 | 3 |
|  | 1 | 5 |
| 45°, 135°, 225°, 315° | 0 | $\sqrt{2}$ |
|  | 1 | $3\sqrt{2}$ |

FIGURE 5.13

*Bit Q1 determines amplitude.*

| Q2 | Q3 | Q4 | Phase Change* |
|---|---|---|---|
| 0 | 0 | 1 | 0° |
| 0 | 0 | 0 | 45° |
| 0 | 1 | 0 | 90° |
| 0 | 1 | 1 | 135° |
| 1 | 1 | 1 | 180° |
| 1 | 1 | 0 | 225° |
| 1 | 0 | 0 | 270° |
| 1 | 0 | 1 | 315° |

FIGURE 5.14

*Bits Q2, Q3, and Q4 determine phase shift.*

## NOTE

The phase change is the actual online phase shift in the transition region from the center of one signaling element to the center of the following signaling element.

At the fallback rate of 7200bps, only 3 bits per baud are encoded, and there is no amplitude change. At the 4800bps fallback rate, 2 bits per baud are encoded, and they specify only four phase shifts.

Except for the WE 209-type modem, most 9.6Kbps modems manufactured throughout the world adhere to the V.29 standard. This makes a V.29 modem popular for use on international leased lines because the selection of the modem to be placed on either end of the line might be restricted to one or a few models due to some countries' government restrictions. Using V.29 ensures the modem's compatibility among different vendor products, which enables data transmission compatibility on international leased lines.

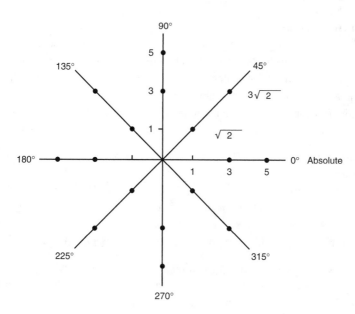

**FIGURE 5.15**
*Signal space diagram at 9600bps.*

Although the V.29 modulation method provides compatibility with respect to modulation, many modems employing this standard are not compatible. This lack of compatibility can be attributed to the fact that several vendors designed proprietary modems to provide a pseudo–full-duplex transmission capability over the two-wire public-switched telephone net-work. To accomplish this, modem designers added a microprocessor and memory to a V.29 data pump and developed several proprietary schemes to get a pseudo–full-duplex transmission capability. One scheme involves adding a slow-speed reverse channel to a V.29 data pump to provide transmission at 300bps in one direction and at 9600bps in the other direction. Each modem monitors the flow of data in both directions and changes the assignment of the primary and reverse channels to correspond to the quantity of data flow in each direction.

### Asymmetrical Transmissions

Although data can flow in both directions simultaneously, each direction operates at a different speed. Therefore, the modem is asymmetrical and provides users with the impression that it operates as a true full-duplex device. Asymmetrical transmission was incorporated by several modem manufacturers to support the communications requirements of personal computers. (The only ones currently popular are the U.S. Robotics HST and HST Dual series of modems.) Included in an asymmetrical modem is an asynchronous-to-synchronous converter, which enables the asynchronous data flow of personal computers to be used with a modified V.29 pump that operates synchronously.

### High-Speed Transmission

In the late 1980s, U.S. Robotics developed an asymmetrical 9600bps modem that was marketed as the HST, an acronym for "high-speed transmission." The company, among the first to recognize the growing popularity of bulletin board systems, provided bulletin board system operators with an attractive discount to enable them to purchase HST modems. This encouraged a large number of individual personal computer users to purchase HST modems to get a high-speed transmission file-transfer capability for accessing bulletin board systems.

Although reductions in the cost of V.32 modems significantly increased their popularity, a large base of HST modems was used with bulletin board systems. To provide compatibility with those modems, U.S. Robotics continues to manufacture HST modems as well as HST Dual modems (the latter is a term used to indicate that the modem supports two major modulation methods). Today, U.S. Robotics offers HST Dual modems that support most or all V-series recommendations from V.32 through V.90 and their proprietary HST modem operation.

The WE 209 represents a 9600bps modem marketed by AT&T that used a proprietary modulation scheme. Because the V.29 modem followed a standardized modulation method, the WE 209 represents a historical curiosity that will not be further discussed.

## ITU-T V.32 Standard

The V.32 standard is an ITU-T recommendation promulgated in the late 1980s whose modulation technique forms the foundation for a series of higher-speed modems used with personal computers. This standard is based on a modified quadrature amplitude modulation technique and is designed to permit full-duplex 9.6Kbps transmission over the switched telephone network. The key to the operation of a V.32 modem is a built-in echo-canceling technique that enables transmitted and received signals to occupy the same bandwidth.

When the V.32 modem connects to another V.32 modem, two high-speed channels in opposite directions are established, as illustrated in Figure 5.16. Each of these channels occupies roughly the same bandwidth as the other. Intelligence built into the receiver in each modem permits the modem to cancel the effects of its transmitted signal, which enables each device to distinguish its sending signal from the signal being received.

Early V.32 modems required sophisticated circuitry to carry out echo canceling. The circuitry made the cost of V.32 modems two to three times that of V.29 modems, which provide the same data transmission rate on leased lines, and this was one of the contributing factors for the development of asymmetrical modems. Because firms manufacturing semiconductors developed chip sets to implement echo canceling, the cost of V.32 modems significantly decreased in 1990. By 1991, the cost of V.32 modems had dropped to less than $1,000 per unit; by early 1996, their cost had fallen below $100 per unit, resulting in their widespread use in both home and office.

Although millions of V.32 modems are in use, by 1998 it was difficult to acquire this device because manufacturers were focusing production on the V.34 series and the V.90 modem. However, to provide backward compatibility, most newer modems are designed to work with other members of the V-series, including the V.32 modem as well as the V.22bis.

The V.32 modem uses a carrier frequency of 1800Hz and a modulation rate of 2400 baud. Under the V.32 standard, two methods of data coding are defined: nonredundant coding and Trellis coding.

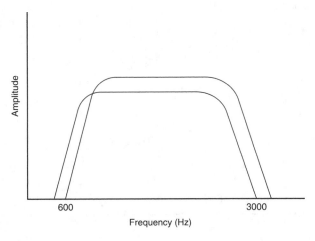

**FIGURE 5.16**
*ITU-T V.32 channel derivation.*

## Nonredundant Coding

Under nonredundant coding, the data stream generated by the DTE is first divided into groups of 4 consecutive data bits. The first 2 bits in time, which are designated Q1n and Q2n in each 4-bit sequence, are differentially encoded into Y1n and Y2n, according to Table 5.8. Bits Y1n, Y2n, Q3n, and Q4n are then mapped into the constellation pattern illustrated in Figure 5.17. This results in a 16-point signal constellation pattern when nonredundant coding is used at 9600bps.

**TABLE 5.8** V.32 Differential Quadrant Coding for 4800bps and for Nonredundant Coding at 9600bps

| Inputs Q1N | Q2N | Previous Y1n-1 | Outputs Y2n-1 | Phase Quadrant Change | Outputs Y1n | Y2n | Signal State for 4800bps |
|---|---|---|---|---|---|---|---|
| 0 | 0 | 0 | 0 | +90° | 0 | 1 | B |
| 0 | 0 | 0 | 1 | | 1 | 1 | C |
| 0 | 0 | 1 | 0 | | 0 | 0 | A |
| 0 | 0 | 1 | 1 | | 1 | 0 | D |
| 0 | 1 | 0 | 0 | 0° | 0 | 0 | A |
| 0 | 1 | 0 | 1 | | 0 | 1 | B |
| 0 | 1 | 1 | 0 | | 1 | 0 | D |
| 0 | 1 | 1 | 1 | | 1 | 1 | C |
| 1 | 0 | 0 | 0 | +180° | 1 | 1 | C |
| 1 | 0 | 0 | 1 | | 1 | 0 | D |
| 1 | 0 | 1 | 0 | | 0 | 1 | B |
| 1 | 0 | 1 | 1 | | 0 | 0 | A |
| 1 | 1 | 0 | 0 | +270° | 1 | 0 | D |
| 1 | 1 | 0 | 1 | | 0 | 0 | A |
| 1 | 1 | 1 | 0 | | 1 | 1 | C |
| 1 | 1 | 1 | 1 | | 0 | 1 | B |

## Trellis Coding

As with nonredundant coding, under Trellis coding, the data stream generated by the DTE is subdivided into groups of 4 consecutive data bits. The first 2 bits in time, Q1n and Q2n in each group, are first differentially encoded into the outputs Y1n and Y2n, according to Table 5.9.

**TABLE 5.9** V.32 Differential Encoding for Use with Trellis-Coded Alternative at 9600bps

| Inputs Q1N | Q2N | Previous Y1n-1 | Outputs Y2n-1 | Outputs Y1n | Y2n |
|---|---|---|---|---|---|
| 0 | 0 | 0 | 0 | 0 | 0 |
| 0 | 0 | 0 | 1 | 0 | 1 |
| 0 | 0 | 1 | 0 | 1 | 0 |
| 0 | 0 | 1 | 1 | 1 | 1 |

**TABLE 5.9**    continued

| Inputs Q1N | Q2N | Previous Y1n-1 | Outputs Y2n-1 | Outputs Y1n | Y2n |
|---|---|---|---|---|---|
| 0 | 1 | 0 | 0 | 0 | 1 |
| 0 | 1 | 0 | 1 | 0 | 0 |
| 0 | 1 | 1 | 0 | 1 | 1 |
| 0 | 1 | 1 | 1 | 1 | 0 |
| 1 | 0 | 0 | 0 | 1 | 0 |
| 1 | 0 | 0 | 1 | 1 | 1 |
| 1 | 0 | 1 | 0 | 0 | 1 |
| 1 | 0 | 1 | 1 | 0 | 0 |
| 1 | 1 | 0 | 0 | 1 | 1 |
| 1 | 1 | 0 | 1 | 1 | 0 |
| 1 | 1 | 1 | 0 | 0 | 0 |
| 1 | 1 | 1 | 1 | 0 | 1 |

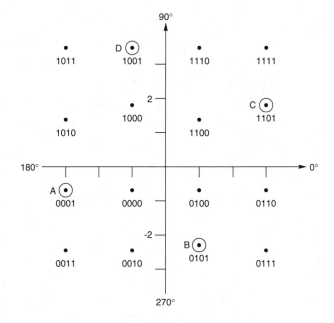

**FIGURE 5.17**

*16-point signal structure with nonredundant coding for 9600bps and subset A B C D of states used at 4800bps for training.*

The two differentially encoded bits, Y1n and Y2n, are then used as input to a convolutional encoder that generates a redundant bit, Y0n. That bit and the four information-carrying bits (Y1n, Y2n, Q3n, and Q4n) are then mapped into one of two sets of coordinates of the signal element to be transmitted. One set of coordinates is used with nonredundant coding, and the second set of coordinates is used with Trellis coding. Table 5.10 lists the two alternative V.32 signal-state mappings for 9600bps operations. When you plot each of the possible Trellis coding points listed in Table 5.10, you get a 32-point signal constellation. Figure 5.18 illustrates the 32-point signal constellation when Trellis coding is used by a V.32 modem, as well as the four states used at 4800bps and for modem training.

**TABLE 5.10**   Alternative Signal-State Mappings for 9600bps Operations

| (Y0) | Y1 | Y2 | Q3 | Q4 | Nonredundant Coding Re | Im | Trellis Coding Re | Im |
|------|----|----|----|----|------------------------|-----|--------------------|-----|
|  _Coded Inputs_ | | | | | _Nonredundant Coding_ | | _Trellis Coding_ | |
| 0 | 0 | 0 | 0 | 0 | −1 | −1 | −4 | 1 |
|   | 0 | 0 | 0 | 1 | −3 | −1 | 0 | −3 |
|   | 0 | 0 | 1 | 0 | −1 | −3 | 0 | 1 |
|   | 0 | 0 | 1 | 1 | −3 | −3 | 4 | 1 |
|   | 0 | 1 | 0 | 0 | 1 | −1 | 4 | −1 |
|   | 0 | 1 | 0 | 1 | 1 | −3 | 0 | 3 |
|   | 0 | 1 | 1 | 0 | 3 | −1 | 0 | −1 |
|   | 0 | 1 | 1 | 1 | 3 | −3 | −4 | −1 |
|   | 1 | 0 | 0 | 0 | −1 | 1 | −2 | 3 |
|   | 1 | 0 | 0 | 1 | −1 | 3 | −2 | −1 |
|   | 1 | 0 | 1 | 0 | −3 | 1 | 2 | 3 |
|   | 1 | 0 | 1 | 1 | −3 | 3 | 2 | −1 |
|   | 1 | 1 | 0 | 0 | 1 | 1 | 2 | −3 |
|   | 1 | 1 | 0 | 1 | 3 | 1 | 2 | 1 |
|   | 1 | 1 | 1 | 0 | 1 | 3 | −2 | −3 |
|   | 1 | 1 | 1 | 1 | 3 | 3 | −2 | 1 |

**TABLE 5.10**   continued

| (Y0) | Y1 | Y2 | Q3 | Q4 | Nonredundant Coding | | Trellis Coding | |
|---|---|---|---|---|---|---|---|---|
| | | | | | Re | Im | Re | Im |
| 1 | 0 | 0 | 0 | 0 | | -3 | -2 | |
| | 0 | 0 | 0 | 1 | | 1 | -2 | |
| | 0 | 0 | 1 | 0 | | -3 | 2 | |
| | 0 | 0 | 1 | 1 | | 1 | 2 | |
| | 0 | 1 | 0 | 0 | | 3 | 2 | |
| | 0 | 1 | 0 | 1 | | -1 | 2 | |
| | 0 | 1 | 1 | 0 | | 3 | -2 | |
| | 0 | 1 | 1 | 1 | | -1 | -2 | |
| | 1 | 0 | 0 | 0 | | 1 | 4 | |
| | 1 | 0 | 0 | 1 | | -3 | 0 | |
| | 1 | 0 | 1 | 0 | | 1 | 0 | |
| | 1 | 0 | 1 | 1 | | 1 | -4 | |
| | 1 | 1 | 0 | 0 | | -1 | -4 | |
| | 1 | 1 | 0 | 1 | | 3 | 0 | |
| | 1 | 1 | 1 | 0 | | -1 | 0 | |
| | 1 | 1 | 1 | 1 | | -1 | 4 | |

The extra bit generated by Trellis coding permits interdependencies between signal points to be noted, in effect permitting the receiving modem to recognize misplaced signal points in the signal constellation and to correct most errors. This means that a modem using Trellis coding has an error rate up to an order of magnitude less than another modem without this coding capability. Thus, almost all V.32 modems are operated using their Trellis coding capability rather than their nonredundant coding capability.

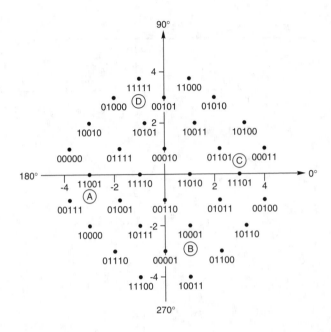

**FIGURE 5.18**

*32-point signal structure with Trellis coding for 9600bps (states A B C D used at 4800bps and for training).*

# ITU-T V.32bis Standard

Like the V.32 standard, V.32bis uses echo cancellation to get full-duplex transmission on the two-wire switched telephone network. It also uses Trellis coding to reduce the probability of errors occurring at the receiving modem due to the modem mistaking one constellation point for an adjacent point. The V.32bis standard was ratified by the ITU-T in February 1991. It provides a mechanism for achieving data rates up to 14,400bps over the switched telephone network.

## The Difference "bis" Makes

Key differences between the V.32bis and V.32 modems lie in the areas of modem operating rates, bit-encoding methods used, resulting signal-constellation patterns, fall-forward capability, and retraining time. Table 5.11 summarizes those differences, which are then examined in some detail.

Concerning modem operating rates, the V.32bis supports data transmission at 14,400bps and 12,000bps, which are beyond the capability of a V.32 modem. At 14,400bps, a V.32bis modem divides data into groups of 6 consecutive bits. Thus, the signal constellation pattern increases from 32 signal points for a V.32 modem operating at 14,400bps. At 12,000bps, the V.32bis modem divides data into groups of 5 consecutive bits, resulting in a 64-point constellation pattern.

## The Fallback Feature

The fallback feature listed in Table 5.11 refers to a modem's capability to automatically lower its operating rate if it encounters a predefined signal-to-noise (S/N) level that would result in an unacceptable error rate if transmission continued at the current operating rate. Although both V.32 and V.32bis modems support fallback, once a V.32 modem reverts to a lower operating rate, it cannot restore itself to the original rate if line quality improves. This omission was addressed by the V.32bis standard; it introduced a fall-forward capability, which allows that modem to monitor the quality of the line and return to a higher operating rate if line quality improves.

**TABLE 5.11** V.32 Versus V.32bis Features

| Feature | V.32 | V.32bis |
|---|---|---|
| Operating rates (bps) | 9600 | 14,400 |
| | 7200 (optional) | 9600 |
| | 4800 | 7200 |
| | | 4800 |
| Encoded bits/symbol and signal constellation points | | |
| 14,400bps | N/A | 6(+TCM)128 |
| 12,000bps | N/A | 5(+TCM)64 |
| 9600bps | 4(+TCM)32 | 4(+TCM)32 |
| Fallback | Yes | Yes |
| Fall-forward | No | Yes |
| Retrain time | 15 seconds | 10 seconds |

## Retraining Time

The last major difference between V.32 and V.32bis modems concerns their retraining capabilities. As indicated in Table 5.11, a V.32 modem has a 15-second retrain time. In comparison, a V.32bis modem reduces retraining to 10 seconds, which minimizes the effect of modem retraining upon actual data transmission.

**5**

## Compression Time

Most V.32bis modems support V.42 compression. This combination provides a potential throughput of 57.6Kbps because that compression technique typically provides an average compression ratio of 4:1. In comparison, a V.32 modem with V.42 compression enabled provides a maximum throughput of 38.4Kbps based on a compression ratio of 4:1.

# ITU-T V.33 Standard

Similar to the V.32bis modem, which actually followed the V.33, the V.33 modem operates at 14,400bps by packing 6 data bits into a baud and using a 2400 baud rate. The ITU-T V.33 modem standard was promulgated in 1988 and formed the basis for the V.32bis standard.

Developed to provide 14,400bps full-duplex operations on leased lines, the V.33 modem does not use echo cancellation. This is because the four-wire leased line provides two signal paths, which eliminates the necessity for that technique.

At that data rate, the V.33 modem adds a redundant bit, which results in the generation of a 128-point signal constellation pattern. Like the V.32bis modem, the V.33 has a secondary signaling rate of 12,000bps. However, the V.33 modem, unlike the V.32bis, has no additional downward compatibility because it was developed for use on leased lines.

## V.22bis Modem Support

Although the lowest operating rate shown in Table 5.11 is 4800bps for V.32 and V.32bis modems, it is important to note that most manufacturers add V.22bis modem support to such devices. This enables both V.32 and V.32bis to be downward-compatible with other modems at data rates to 2400bps. In addition, many manufacturers also add Bell System 212 compatibility to their products, providing downward compatibility to 1200bps.

One additional difference between the V.33 modem and its switched network V.32bis equivalent concerns a multiplexing option specified by the V.33 standard. Under the V.33 standard, a multiplexer option can be included that enables the combination of 2400, 4800, 7200, 9600, and 12,000bps data sources to produce a single aggregate bit stream at either 12,000 or 14,400bps for transmission. The multiplexer is a time-division multiplexer (discussed in Chapter 6) that enables multiple data sources to share the use of a leased line. Because it is very difficult to get people to agree to access the same switched telephone number at the same time, multiplexers are not incorporated into dial modems. In comparison, leased lines are used to permanently provide a connection between two fixed locations. Leased lines provide an opportunity for economic savings by sharing the use of the line among two or more users.

# ITU-T V.34 Standard

Previously referred to as V.fast, the V.34 standard represents several years of effort by modem manufacturers to develop a product that could support data rates up to 28.8Kbps using multidimensional Trellis codes and an advanced equalization technique known as precoding. Under the V.34 standard, which was completed by the latter part of 1994, three-dimensional Trellis coding is employed to provide a significantly greater level of performance in comparison to V.32 and V.32bis modems. This increase in performance results not only from the higher data-transfer rate of V.34 modems, but also from their lower error rate due to the use of three-dimensional Trellis coding. The lower error rate reduces the need for retransmission, which improves modem performance.

To achieve its top speed of 28,800bps, a V.34 modem operates at 3200 baud, packing 9 bits into each signal change. In addition to supporting a 3200 baud rate, the V.34 standard specifies two additional mandatory baud rates and three optional rates. The two additional mandatory baud rates are 2400 and 3000; baud rates of 2743, 2800, and 3429 represent optional signaling rates.

At a 3200 baud rate, the mapping of 9 bits into each symbol results in an operating rate of 3200 baud × 9 bits/baud, or 28,800bps. The 2743 and 2800 baud rates represent two optional signaling rates that can be most important when voice is digitized using Adaptive Differential Pulse Code Modulation (ADPCM).

## Adaptive Differential Pulse Code Modulation (ADPCM)

ADPCM is a voice-digitization technique that samples the line 8,000 times per second. But instead of encoding each sample into 8 bits (as under PCM), ADPCM uses a predictor at each end of the circuit to encode each voice sample into 4 bits. To do so, the predicted value of the sample is subtracted from the sample, enabling the difference to be transmitted as a 4-bit word. At the receiver, the value of the predictor is added to the received difference to generate or reconstruct the actual sample. The use of a 4-bit difference enables ADPCM to convey high-quality digitized voice at 32Kbps. This digitization technique is commonly used on private networks, on satellite channels by public carriers, and on terrestrial international circuits. Unfortunately, ADPCM's predictor is not good enough to support modem signaling rates above 3000 baud. Thus, the V.34 optional 2743Hz and 2800Hz rates can be used to support relatively high-speed communications over an ADPCM infrastructure.

## Shell Mapping

Although several V.34 signaling rates result in a data rate nine times the signaling rate, this is not always the case. Some V.34 signaling rates use a noninteger number of bits per symbol. When this occurs, a special technique referred to as a shell-mapping algorithm is used to generate the constellation points. Table 5.12 indicates the carrier frequency, bandwidth requirements, and maximum bit rate for a V.34 modem based upon its signaling rate. When the maximum bit rate is not an integral multiple of the signaling rate, a noninteger number of bits per symbol is used.

## Optional Features

In addition to several baud rate options and an enhanced Trellis coding capability, the V.34 standard includes several features that can significantly boost the capability of this modem over its V.32bis predecessor. Those features include an asymmetrical transmission capability, an auxiliary channel, and a nonlinear encoding and precoding capability. Unfortunately, although these features are mandatory for incorporation into the modem's transmitter section, they are optional with respect to their inclusion in the modem's receiver section. This means that the evaluation of V.34 modems must include determining the optional features supported in the modem's receiver.

**TABLE 5.12**  V.34 Carrier Frequency, Bandwidth, and Maximum Bit Rate Based on Signaling Rate

| Signaling Rate (Hz) | Carrier Frequency (Hz) | Bandwidth Requirements (Hz) | Maximum Bit Rate (bps) |
|---|---|---|---|
| 2400 | 1600 | 400–2800 | 21,600 |
| 2743 | 1646 | 274–3018 | 24,000 |
| 2800 | 1680 | 280–3080 | 24,000 |
| 3000 | 1800 | 300–3300 | 26,400 |
| 3200 | 1829 | 229–3429 | 28,800 |
| 3429 | 1959 | 244–3674 | 28,800 |

### Asymmetrical Transmission

The asymmetrical transmission capability of a V.34 modem enables the modem to send and receive at different data rates. This feature can be extremely useful if one modem user is located a relatively long distance from the telephone office serving the user. In such situations, the V.34 modem might be limited to an operating rate of 24.0 or 26.4Kbps. If the other modem user is located a relatively short distance from the telephone office serving her location, she might be able to obtain a 28.8Kbps operating rate. Without an asymmetrical transmission capability, transmission might be limited to 24.0 or 26.4Kbps in both directions. The inclusion of an asymmetrical transmission capability in both modems would allow each modem to support the highest operating rate obtainable in each direction, without having to have a common data rate in each direction.

The auxiliary channel option enables a V.34 modem to support a low-speed 200bps management channel in addition to a high-speed data-transfer capability. This optional channel would enable, for example, a network-management system to control a distant router or multiplexer without requiring an additional circuit. Because the auxiliary channel is an option for inclusion in the receiver section of a V.34 modem, it must be supported by both modems to obtain its functionality.

Figure 5.19 illustrates one possible use of a V.34 auxiliary channel. In this example, the V.34 modem is used on an analog leased line to connect a computer to a port on a multiplexer in a distant city. By connecting a port on a network-management console to the local V.34 modem's auxiliary channel, an operator at the local site can control the multiplexer at the remote site without using a second line.

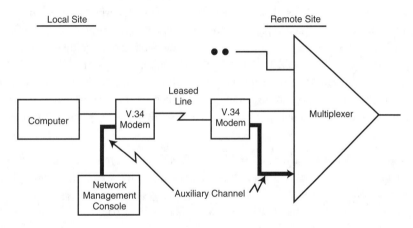

**FIGURE 5.19**
*Using an auxiliary channel.*

## Nonlinear Coding

The nonlinear coding capability of a V.34 modem increases its immunity to interference created by the pulse-code modulation of analog signals when they are converted into digital signals at a telephone company office. Through a nonlinear coding capability, constellation points are spaced unequally, so those points in the constellation pattern that are most susceptible to noise are spaced farther apart. Through nonlinear encoding, the error rate when a V.34 modem operates at 28,800bps can be reduced by as much as 50 percent.

## Precoding

The last major feature incorporated into V.34 modems is precoding, which represents a form of equalization. Through precoding, the amount of high-frequency noise on a channel is reduced, which decreases intersymbol interference.

## Problems with Compatibility

Until early 1996, it was expected that the ITU-T would issue a new standard for 33,600bps operations that many vendors referred to as V.34bis. Instead of issuing a new standard, however, the ITU-T completed the technical specification for a new version of V.34, which adds two new speed options. Those speed options include 33,600bps and 31,200bps, maintaining speed differences of 2400bps between the different V.34 operating rates and the new speed options.

To provide compatibility with previously developed modems, the V.34 modem is downward-compatible with V.32bis and V.32 modems. Because the V.32 modem provides compatibility with V.22bis and most modem vendors add V.23, V.21, and Bell System 212 compatibility, a V.34 modem can provide the capability to support seven distinct modulation methods.

One of the problems that V.34 users can expect to encounter concerns the capability to use the modem effectively when it is set to perform compression and is communicating with another V.34 modem. The reason is that when compression is enabled, the modem becomes capable of receiving data from an attached DTE at 115.2Kbps to support an operating rate of 28.8Kbps and a compression ratio of 4:1. Unfortunately, the UART built into the serial port of almost all previously manufactured non-Pentium computers is either 8250 or 16450. This nomenclature refers to part numbers of National Semiconductor chips, although the actual chips are available from many vendors.

The 8250 UART, which was used in all IBM PC, PC XT, and compatible computers, starts to lose characters at data rates beyond 19.2Kbps. The 16450, which was originally used with the PC AT and compatible computers as well as most 80386 systems, encounters lost data at operating rates above 57.6Kbps, limiting its use to V.32bis modems. To effectively support data-transfer rates at 115.2Kbps, the 16450 UART must be used. This means that you might have to replace an existing UART on an older computer to effectively use a V.34 modem. To prevent the need to replace a UART, several vendors market V.34 modems that can be cabled to the parallel port of a personal computer because that port can support a sustained data-transfer rate of more than 150Kbps. Because most communications programs are limited to supporting the use of serial ports, users might be restricted to employing a modem manufacturer–supplied program to use a V.34 modem connected to a parallel port.

# High-Speed Modems

To understand how V.90 technology, x2, and K56flex obtain the capability to receive data at up to 56Kbps, you must understand how analog modem connections occur and the effect of a direct digital connection at the distant end of the connection. Toward that end, turn your attention to how high-speed modems operate and how a direct digital connection affects their capability.

# ITU-T V.90 Standard

In the never-ending quest to obtain a higher transmission capability over the public-switched telephone network, modem designers recognized the conversion of the backbone infrastructure from analog to digital signaling and designed equipment to take advantage of the new infrastructure. To do this, two types of 56Kbps modems were developed in 1997, one from U.S. Robotics (now part of 3COM), whose modem technology and modem were referred to as x2. A second competitive product was developed by Rockwell Semiconductor Products and Lucent Technology. The technology and modem resulting from the joint efforts of Rockwell and Lucent are referred to as K56flex.

Although the technology behind each product's capability to theoretically operate at up to 56Kbps is the same, the manner by which the technology was implemented differs, resulting in incompatibility between the two products. This initially forced Internet service providers to operate two modem groups to support 56Kbps transmission to consumers who, without a standard to select, typically purchased one based upon cost, advertising hype, or another variable. Recognizing the need for a 56Kbps standard, the ITU V.90 specification was developed in February 1998 at a meeting in Geneva, Switzerland, enabling modem manufacturers to ship standard-based products and upgrades during the first quarter of 1998. The resulting recommendation is similar to x2 and K56flex in that it defines an asymmetrical transmission technology that allows V.90 modems to receive data at up to 56Kbps but restricts transmission to a maximum of 33.6Kbps.

# Modem Pair Operations

Until the development of x2, K56flex, and V.90 modems, such devices were designed to operate in pairs. That is, it was assumed that the originator and the receiver would be connected by analog local loops to a central office as illustrated in Figure 5.20. Based on this assumption, analog modems had to be installed at each end of the connection, which caused the need for two conversions when data was transmitted in each direction. For example, when data is transmitted from location A to location B, the local modem at location A performs a digital-to-analog conversion, and the remote modem at location B then performs an analog-to-digital conversion. Similarly, when data is transmitted from location B to location A, it is first converted from digital to analog form at location B and then converted from analog to digital by the modem at location B. This dual conversion takes place in spite of the fact that almost the entire long-distance infrastructure of communications carriers was converted to a digital infrastructure by the mid-1990s.

**UNDERSTANDING DATA COMMUNICATIONS**

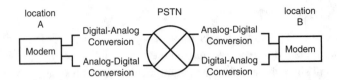

**FIGURE 5.20**

*Normal operation on analog modems requires two analog-to-digital conversions.*

## Modem Limitations

From a technical perspective, three factors limit the capability of analog modems to transmit at data rates up to but not beyond the 33.6Kbps operating rate of V.34 modems. Those factors are available bandwidth on a voice channel, the signal-to-noise ratio on the channel, and the amount of quantization noise encountered during analog-to-digital conversions.

As the sensitivity of modems increases, they become capable of receiving signals on the edges of the passband, which enables the modem to support a higher signaling rate. This was illustrated in Table 5.12. If you examine the entries in that table, you will note that the signaling rate is proportional to the bandwidth. However, because the maximum passband is fixed at less than 4KHz, the signaling rate of the modem is limited regardless of its receiver's level of sensitivity.

A second factor that limits the data-transmission capability of modems is the signal-to-noise ratio obtainable on a channel. Although the ratio is proportional to the modem's capability to transmit data per unit time, the S/N ratio obtainable by modems is limited. Under the best conditions, when a signal undergoes analog-to-digital conversion, the maximum signal-to-noise ratio is between 38 and 39dB. This limits a V.34 modem to 33.6Kbps.

A third factor that limits the data-transfer capability of conventional analog modems is quantization noise introduced by analog-to-digital converters at the central office where the modem's analog signal transmitted on the local loop is digitized for transmission over the communication carrier's backbone digital infrastructure. At each central office, both voice and analog modem data are sampled 8,000 times per second, and the height of each sample is encoded into an 8-bit byte. Because analog waveforms are continuous, each sample can have an infinite number of heights. In comparison, a binary number can have only one value and is referred to as a discrete number. Thus, when each analog sample is converted into a discrete binary number, the difference between the actual sample height and the encoded binary value represents quantization noise.

When the digital signal is reconverted into a modem analog signal at the distant central office, quantization noise limits the capability to reconstruct the original modem signal. Thus, quantization noise places a limit on the degree of signal changes that can flow end-to-end and limits the theoretical data transfer capacity of a voice channel to approximately 35Kbps. When you consider the maximum obtainable signal-to-noise ratio of 38dB to 39dB, the data-transfer rate of the V.34 modem is limited to 33.6Kbps.

## Overcoming the Speed Barrier

Recognizing that a service provider can directly connect its equipment to a communication carrier's digital infrastructure, modem designers realized that this method of connection eliminates one analog-to-digital conversion. Therefore, this type of connectivity would also reduce quantization noise because the analog and digital value differences per sample would then occur at only one point in the communications path. This type of communications path—in which one end of the connection terminates at a digital circuit—also slightly enhances the overall signal-to-noise ratio. When taken together, it becomes possible for a V.90 analog modem to receive data at 56Kbps, although transmission in the opposite direction must still flow through two analog-to-digital conversions and is limited to 33.6Kbps.

The effective use of a V.90 analog modem requires three things. First, one end of the connection must terminate in a digital circuit, such as a channelized T1 or ISDN circuit. Because it is common for information utilities and Internet service providers to directly connect their access controllers to a digital circuit analog, V.90 modems receive data at 56Kbps. A second requirement concerns V.90 support. V.90 must be supported at both ends of the connection, with an analog V.90 modem at the dial-up link and a V.90 digital modem at the other end of the link. The third restriction is that, as previously discussed, there can be only one analog-to-digital conversion.

Although a V.90 modem is commonly marketed as providing a 56Kbps operating rate, in reality its operating rate is lower, for two reasons. First, due to FCC regulations, transmission from the digital side is limited with respect to signal power, which reduces the maximum theoretical transmission to 53Kbps. Similarly, there is still one analog loop that data must flow over. Because the characteristics of local loops can significantly differ with respect to distance from a central office and line impairments, a typical V.90 will average between 40Kbps and 44Kbps, as opposed to the 56Kbps stamped on the fancy box it's packaged in.

## ITU-T V.92 Standard

Although broadband modems to include Digital Subscriber Line (DSL) devices and cable modems have received a considerable amount of press coverage and will be described later in this chapter, to paraphrase Mark Twain, "The demise of the voice-grade modem is premature!" Although the Nyquist Theorem and Shannon's Law place restrictions on the maximum signaling rate and data-transfer capability of voice-grade modems, modem designers were still able to squeeze additional performance from a redesign of their products. The resulting redesign,

5

SYNCHRONOUS
COMPONENTS

which was standardized during 2001 as the ITU-T V.92 Recommendation, builds upon the capabilities of the V.90 modem.

A V.92 modem has three new features. The first additional feature is referred to as Quick Connect (QC). QC provides a standard method to reduce the handshaking time between calling and answering modems. To accomplish this, the client modem originating calls saves the analog channel characteristics, such as echo canceller and equalizer settings learned from a previous call. Because most modems dialing an Internet service provider are at fixed locations and the local loop characteristics do not change, this permits a fast training to occur on subsequent calls. That is, the client modem examines the answer tone generated by the ISP modem to verify that the local loop conditions are similar to its saved parameters. If the parameters are equivalent to those previously learned, a fast connection is attempted. Otherwise, a regular V.90 handshake occurs. Through QC, a V.92 modem's connection time is reduced by approximately 10 seconds from the 20 to 25 seconds required for a V.90 connection.

A second feature added to V.92 modems is formerly referred to as Modem on Hold (MOH) and informally is known as Internet call waiting. Because a call-waiting signal can result in a line disconnect, many session terminations result from subscribers failing to disable call waiting before accessing the Internet. Under the Modem on Hold feature, a V.92 modem works in conjunction with call waiting provided by the local phone company. This feature enables a PC user to place the server-side modem on hold for up to 16 minutes when a call arrives without dropping the modem connection and having to redial and reestablish a connection.

A third feature added to V.92 modems is referred to as PCM upstream. In a V.90 modem, PCM modulations occur in only the downstream direction. Under V.92, PCM modulations occur in both upstream and downstream directions. PCM upstream operates in a network topology similar to that previously described for V.90 PCM downstream. That is, there can be only one analog loop in the client-to-server modem connection. Through the use of PCM upstream, it becomes possible for a V.92 modem to obtain a maximum upload data-transfer capability of 48Kbps, representing a 30 percent increase over the 33.6Kbps data rate of V.90 modems.

Although it is not a direct modem feature, the addition of V.44 data compression to V.92 modems enables data throughput up to approximately 300Kbps to be obtained. This provides consumers with a viable alternative to DSL and cable modems for Internet surfing without having to pay the typical $40 per month fee associated with broadband modem services.

Now that you have an appreciation for the technology associated with the latest ITU standardized modem, you will complete your examination of analog modems by focusing your attention on two types of broadband devices: Digital Subscriber Line (DSL) modems and cable modems.

# Digital Subscriber Line Modems

Because an overwhelming majority of access lines that connect business and residential subscribers to the telephone network will continue to use twisted-pair metallic cable for the foreseeable future, engineers looked for methods to enable higher-speed transmission over the local loop. As a result of engineering efforts, a family of technologies referred to as Digital Subscriber Lines (DSL) was developed. DSL technologies recognize the fact that although the passband of a voice channel is approximately 3000Hz, the actual range of frequencies supportable on a twisted-pair circuit from a subscriber to a serving central office is much higher, with some access lines supporting approximately 1MHz of usable bandwidth. Because the voice channel passband is constructed at the central office through the use of filters or loading coils, it becomes possible to use a wider range of frequencies on the access line to transport data and to remove the used frequencies before the voice portion of the access line flows into the telephone network. This technique, as you will soon learn, enables the voice portion of an access line to continue to be used to transport voice, while frequencies above the voice passband are modulated to transport data.

The major restrictions governing the data rate obtainable on an access line include the distance of the subscriber from the central office, the gauge of the wire and its condition, and the modulation method used by DSL modems.

Since early 1997, a range of DSL techniques have been developed, each of which typically falls into one of the six DSL categories listed in Table 5.13.

**TABLE 5.13**  Major DSL Categories

| Maximum Data Rate Category | Upstream | Downstream |
|---|---|---|
| Asymmetrical Digital Subscriber Line (ADSL) | 1Mbps | 8Mbps |
| High Bit Rate Digital Subscriber Line (HDSL) | 1.544/ 2.048Mbps | 1.544/ 2.048Mbps |
| G.Lite | 512Kbps | 1.4Mbps |
| Rate Adaptive Digital Subscriber Line (RDSL) | 784Kbps | 4Mbps |
| Symmetric Digital Subscriber Line (SDSL) | 2Mbps | 2Mbps |
| Very-high-bit-rate Digital Subscriber Line (VDSL) | 1.5Mbps | 52Mbps |

**5**

SYNCHRONOUS
COMPONENTS

The following list describes the different lines in more detail:

- Asymmetric Digital Subscriber Line (ADSL), as its name implies, allocates bandwidth asymmetrically in the frequency spectrum. This enables a greater data rate to be obtained downstream toward the user than on the return upstream channel.

- G.Lite represents a lower data rate version of Asymmetric Digital Subscriber Line (ADSL). Although it uses the same modulation scheme as ADSL, its lower operating rate theoretically avoids the necessity of installing a splitter at the customer premises. Unfortunately, other factors, including the age of copper wiring, usually require a splitter.

- High Bit Rate Digital Subscriber Line (HDSL) allocates the bandwidth symmetrically in both directions and functions as a replacement for T1 and E1 four-wire metallic circuits. Because HDSL permits subscribers to be located farther from a central office but doesn't require repeaters, telephone companies often employ it as a substitute for more expensive repeated local loops.

- Rate Adaptive Digital Subscriber Line (RDSL) adapts to the highest speed obtainable on a local loop or can be set to a fixed operating rate. RDSL represents the latest DSL permutation.

- Symmetric Digital Subscriber Line (SDSL) allocates bandwidth symmetrically, much like HDSL does. However, unlike HDSL (which operates on a four-pair circuit), SDSL is a single-pair implementation of DSL technology.

- Very-high-bit-rate Digital Subscriber Line (VDSL) provides the highest downstream data rate. However, this technology is limited with respect to transmission distance, which is typically less than a thousand feet.

Of the six DSL technologies, ADSL appears to have the highest probability of wide-scale deployment because it is ideal for Web surfing and other asymmetrical applications. In addition, because G.Lite more often than not requires the installation of a splitter at the customer premises, another advantage of this technology disappears, in the form of eliminating the cost of dispatching a phone company installer. Thus, most phone companies offering residential subscribers are primarily marketing ADSL service. Therefore, for the remainder of this section, you will focus your attention on ADSL operations.

## ADSL

ADSL is similar to other DSL technologies in that it requires the use of two modems on the local loop—one located on the subscriber's premises and the other located at the carrier's central office. Currently, several versions of ADSL modems are being marketed, with the major differences between products primarily in the method of modulation used and whether a customer must install filters at his location to prevent voice from being affected by the frequencies used for data transmission.

## ADSL Operation

The top portion of Figure 5.21 illustrates the basic operation of an ADSL local loop; the lower portion of the figure indicates the manner by which the frequency spectrum of the local loop is used. In the lower portion of Figure 5.21, note that an ADSL modem subdivides the local loop into three channels by frequency: a high-speed downstream channel that uses a majority of the bandwidth of the local loop, a medium-speed upstream channel, and a standard 4KHz voice telephone channel.

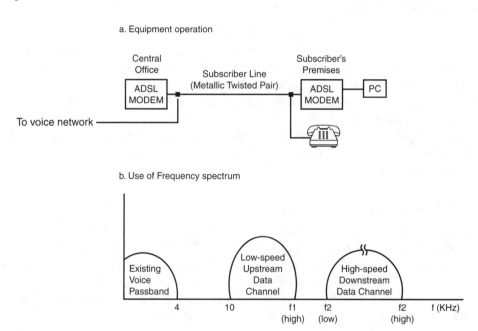

### FIGURE 5.21
*ADSL operation and frequency spectrum utilization.*

The 4KHz voice telephone channel is split off from the digital modems by filters, enabling subscribers to continue to obtain the use of the voice portion of the access line even if one or both of the ADSL modems fail. Until mid-1998, field trials of ADSL technology required the communications carrier to send technicians to the customer site to install a splitter at the junction box where the four-wire telephone twisted-pair enters the home or business. The splitter consists of a high-pass filter that isolates the frequencies carrying voice from the frequencies carrying data, permitting voice to flow into the home or business on the existing wire pair while data signals typically are branched onto a second wire pair routed to an ADSL modem in the home or business.

Although the splitter is relatively easy to install, a technician must visit, which significantly adds to the cost of the service. In an attempt to eliminate the need for a technician's visit, several ADSL modem vendors announced splitter-less modems with built-in high-pass filters, enabling telephones and answering machines to be directly plugged into modems via RJ-11 jacks after low-pass filters are connected between those devices and the ADSL modems. Because low-pass filters can easily be connected to telephones and answering machines, it is presumed that splitter-less ADSL modems can be installed by the subscriber, alleviating the need and expense of a technician.

The actual data rate obtainable over the subscriber line shown in Figure 5.21 depends upon the length of the subscriber line, its wire gauge, the presence or absence of bridged taps, and the level of interference on the line. Because attenuation is proportional to line length and frequency and is inversely proportional to the diameter of wire, the performance of ADSL can be noted with respect to wire gauge and subscriber line distance. Ignoring sections of unterminated twisted-pair cable connected in parallel across the cable under consideration (bridged taps), the results of a series of basic ADSL tests are summarized in Table 5.14. This table indicates the general operational capability of ADSL modems based upon the distance and wire gauge of the local loop.

## Central Office Equipment

Although Figure 5.21 illustrates a standalone ADSL modem located in a telephone company central office, from an economic perspective it is more efficient to use rack-mount modems. Because it is also more efficient to combine traffic from a group of modems, central offices use a device referred to as a Digital Subscriber Line Access Multiplexer (DSLAM). Most DSLAMs support many "flavors" of DSL, including ADSL, HDSL, G.Lite, and SDSL. This provides a communications carrier with the flexibility to mix and match different technology better suited to different customer requirements while obtaining the capability to aggregate transmission via a common DSLAM. Although most DSLAMs use the ATM protocol (described in Chapter 14, "Asynchronous Transfer Mode"), some DSLAMs transmit using the Internet Protocol (IP), which is described in Chapter 12, "Internet." Regardless of the protocol used, the primary function of the DSLAM is to aggregate data transmission from a large number of individual subscriber lines via a high-speed serial connection to the Internet.

## Signal Processing

Two competing technologies are used in ADSL modems: Discrete Multitone (DMT) modulation and Carrierless Amplitude Phase (CAP) modulation. DMT represents an ANSI standard, whereas CAP represents a proprietary technology developed by Paradyne Corporation. Both DMT and CAP permit the transmission of high-speed data using frequency-division multiplexing (FDM) to subdivide the local loop into independent channels by frequency. (This was illustrated in the lower portion of Figure 5.21.) FDM creates one channel for downstream transmission from the central office to the subscriber, a second channel for upstream transmission from the subscriber's premises to the central office, and a third channel for normal telephone operations. Both the upstream and the downstream channels can be optionally subdivided through the use of time-division multiplexing to enable two or more digital devices, such as a PC data session and a video conference call, to be simultaneously transmitted.

## Discrete Multitone Modulation

Figure 5.22 compares Discrete Multitone (DMT) and Carrierless Amplitude and Phase (CAP) modulation techniques.

**TABLE 5.14**  ADSL Performance

| Operating Rate Upstream/Downstream | Wire Gauge | Subscriber Line Distance |
|---|---|---|
| 64Kbps to 384Kbps/2.0Mbps | 24 AWG | 18,000 feet |
| 64Kbps to 384Kbps/2.0Mbps | 26 AWG | 15,000 feet |
| 64Kbps to 384Kbps/8.0Mbps | 24 AWG | 12,000 feet |
| 64Kbps to 384Kbps/8.0Mbps | 26 AWG | 9,000 feet |

a. Discrete multitone modulation

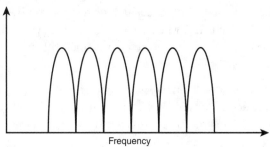

Frequency

b. Carrierless Amplitude and Phase

**FIGURE 5.22**

*Comparing popular ADSL modulation techniques.*

Under DMT, available bandwidth is split or subdivided into a large number of independent subchannels, as illustrated in the upper portion of Figure 5.22. Because the length of each access line from the central office to the subscriber's premises can differ, the level of attenuation (which is based upon the length of the line and on the wire gauge) can also be expected to differ. Recognizing that, an ADSL modem employing DMT technology at the central office will transmit tones to the remote modem to determine which subchannels are usable. The remote modem analyzes the received tones and responds to the central office modem at a relatively lower operating rate to minimize the probability that the returned signal analysis is misinterpreted. Based upon the returned signal analysis, the central office modem will select up to 256 4KHz-wide subchannels for downstream transmission. Through the use of a reverse process, the remote modem will use up to 32 4KHz-wide subchannels for upstream transmission.

Each upstream and downstream subchannel transmits data through the use of a quadrature amplitude modulation (QAM) process. This means that each of the subchannels shown in the top of Figure 5.22 has its own signal constellation pattern. This also causes data being transmitted in each direction to be subdivided for encoding on separate channels and summed after demodulation at the receiver. A key advantage of DMT is its capability to take advantage of the characteristics of twisted-pair wire at the local loop, which can considerably vary from one local loop to another.

## Carrierless Amplitude and Phase Modulation

Carrierless Amplitude and Phase (CAP) modulation represents a derivative of QAM that was developed by Paradyne. Unlike DMT, which subdivides the bandwidth of the wire into 4KHz segments, CAP uses the entire bandwidth in both upstream and downstream channels, as illustrated in the lower portion of Figure 5.22.

Under CAP, serial data is encoded by mapping a group of bits into a signal constellation point using both Trellis coding and a forward error-correction scheme. The latter self-corrects transmission errors against such impairments as crosstalk and line noise.

Figure 5.23 illustrates the CAP modulation process. After a group of bits is mapped to a predefined point in the modem signal constellation pattern, the in-phase and quadrature filters implement the actual positioning in the signal constellation. Because the amplitude and phase are adjusted without a constant carrier (as used by other modems), the technique is referred to as "carrierless."

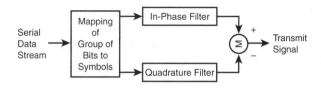

**FIGURE 5.23**

*Carrierless Amplitude and Phase modulation.*

One ADSL modem marketed by Paradyne employs a 256-point signal constellation pattern for downstream operations within the 120KHz to 1224KHz frequency band. The composite signaling rate is 960K baud, and 7 bits are packed into each signal change to provide an operating rate of 6.72Mbps. However, the use of a forward error-correction code reduces the actual capability of the modem to transport data to the subscriber to 6.312Mbps. In the upstream direction, a 16-point constellation pattern in the 35KHz to 72KHz frequency band provides a composite signaling rate of 24K baud across 16 subchannels. A 72Kbps upstream line rate is obtained by packing 3 bits per signal change, with 64Kbps available for data.

Figure 5.24 illustrates the SpeedStream ADSL modem manufactured by Efficient Networks. This ADSL modem provides Ethernet LAN connections for up to two computers. Another ADSL modem from Efficient Networks supports USB connectivity, while a third modem is manufactured as an internal adapter card designed for insertion into a PCI bus.

**FIGURE 5.24**

*The Efficient Networks SpeedStream ADSL modem supports up to two computers through the use of Ethernet interface RJ-45 jacks. (Photograph courtesy of Efficient Networks.)*

**5**

**SYNCHRONOUS COMPONENTS**

Because we previously noted that DMT and CAP are competing modulation technologies, it is interesting to note that SpeedStream supports both. A chip set from Alcatel MicroElectronics is used by Efficient Networks to support both modulation methods, which provides flexibility for marketing a common modem to telephone companies that may have selected one modulation technique over another.

Because the ADSL modem shown in Figure 5.24 supports two Ethernet connections, it requires a method to direct input from the serial communications line to each attached computer, as well as to direct transmission from each computer onto the serial connection. This capability is obtained through the use of transparent bridging software that operates in the modem and whose operation is described in Chapter 11, "Local Area Networks."

In examining the photograph of the SpeedStream modem shown in Figure 5.24, note that it can be placed in either a horizontal or a vertical position. Also note that, similar to other ADSL modems, this modem is designed to be "always on," providing an instant connection capability to the Internet. Although not shown in the figure, it should be noted that the modem uses an RJ-11 jack to interface the telephone line and an RJ-45 jack for interfacing a computer via an Ethernet connection.

As noted in this section, ADSL technology is well suited for supporting Internet access where the downloading of Web pages requires substantially more bandwidth than the uploading of Web addresses. Depending upon the evolution of video compression, ADSL may also provide competition to the cable TV industry for video-on-demand applications. However, the cable TV industry is not letting the potential challenge to its revenue stream have a free ride. Instead, the cable TV industry is in the process of modifying its network infrastructure to support telephone calls as well as the transmission of data, the latter of which is accomplished through the use of cable modems.

# Cable Modems

To obtain an appreciation for the operation and utilization of cable modems, you must review the manner in which the cable TV wiring infrastructure is presently constructed and how a new wiring topology is being implemented by many cable TV operators. Thus, before examining the operation and utilization of cable modems, you will first examine the current and evolving infrastructure used to transmit TV signals.

## The Cable TV Infrastructure

The original cable TV infrastructure was based upon the use of unidirectional amplifiers. Although this design strategy was sufficient for supporting television transmission through the 1980s, the capability to support video-on-demand, interactive TV, and, more recently, Web surfing, requires a bidirectional transmission capability. Thus, most cable TV operators need to upgrade their infrastructure to support bidirectional transmission to enable Web surfing and other applications if telephone over cable TV is to become a viable offering.

The cable TV wiring infrastructure resembles a tree, with signals transmitted from a head end (located at the beginning of the tree) onto branches for distribution to subscribers. Signals on each main branch, which might represent routes to residential areas within a city, are further subdivided via splitters onto additional branches as feeders to groups of homes. Signals on those feeders are then routed through smaller residential areas into junction boxes from which individual coaxial cables are routed into residences. After a signal flows through a few split-ters, it usually requires an amplifier to boost signal power because signal loss results from both cable distance and the effect of the splitting of the cable signal.

Figure 5.25 illustrates the previously described cable TV wiring infrastructure that was commonly installed from the 1950s through the early to mid-1990s. Note that each amplifier is shown as unidirectional, making two-way transmission over such cable TV systems impossible.

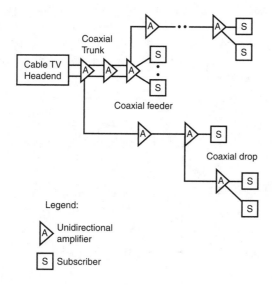

**FIGURE 5.25**

*Cable TV wiring infrastructure built during the 1950s and used through the mid-1990s.*

Traditional coaxial cable-based systems operate with approximately 330 to 540MHz of capac-ity, using 6MHz per TV channel. During the design of cable TV systems, downstream video signals were selected to begin at approximately 50MHz, the equivalent of Channel 2 for over-the-air broadcast TV signals.

This selection enabled subscribers to receive cable service with the same TV that they used to receive over-the-air broadcast TV signals, but without a new tuner. Because they were using 50MHz and higher frequencies for downstream transmission, the 5MHz to 42MHz portion of the frequency spectrum was reserved for future upstream transmission, such as supporting telephony, data services, and control channels used by interactive video set-top boxes.

## Evolution

A coaxial-based cabling infrastructure and unidirectional amplifiers could not accommodate the requirements of a large and growing subscriber base for additional TV channels, a high-speed data transmission capability, and even digitized telephone service. Thus, cable operators began to install trunks of fiber that were routed to residential areas, using the fiber to provide greater bandwidth to individual areas within geographical locations that would then be connected to the existing coaxial infrastructure.

As cable operators began to install these hybrid fiber/coax (HFC) systems during the mid-1990s, they also began to upgrade their cabling infrastructure through the use of bidirectional amplifiers to support two-way communications. In an HFC infrastructure, a star topology is typically used, with fiber routed from a cable TV head end to optical distribution nodes commonly located in residential subdivisions or a building complex. From optical distribution nodes, coax is then used to route data to individual subscribers. Figure 5.26 illustrates the emerging HFC cable TV wiring infrastructure.

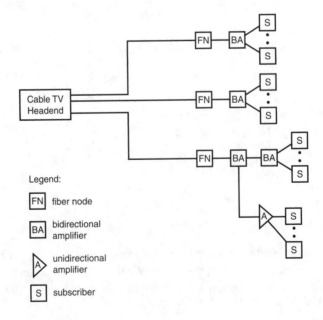

**FIGURE 5.26**

*Emerging hybrid/fiber coaxial (HFC) cable TV wiring infrastructure.*

Under the more modern HFC architecture, downstream bandwidth expanded to 750MHz or more, typically providing support for up to 110 channels, each occupying 6MHz of bandwidth. In comparison, older, pure coaxial-based cable TV is commonly limited to a maximum of 83 channels. In Figure 5.26, note that an HFC system can evolve from the use of unidirectional amplifiers to bidirectional amplifiers as portions of the network are upgraded. Thus, conversion to a two-way system can require several years or more of effort, and some locations within an area will obtain the capability to use cable modems months or years before others will.

## Cable Modem Operation

Because cable TV is currently an analog technology, modems are required to transmit data over the cable TV infrastructure. During the early to mid-1990s, a number of manufacturers, including LANCity (now owned by Bay Networks, which was acquired by Nortel Networks), Zenith Electronics, Scientific Atlanta, and other vendors, developed proprietary methods for transmitting data over cable TV. Because most cable TV systems were unidirectional, until recently most cable modems developed through the mid- to late 1990s included a built-in V.34 modem for upstream transmission via the telephone network.

Needless to say, because it is common practice to have a telephone plug mounted on one wall and the cable TV outlet on another wall or perhaps even in a different room, this type of modem was not well received. In addition, it tied up the subscriber's telephone while a user was surfing the Web.

## Cable Modem Standards

Although cable TV modems initially used different modulation techniques, the effort of two groups is resolving the standardization problem. One effort is represented by the IEEE's 802.14 Working Group whose title is "Standard Protocol for Cable-TV Based Broadband Communications." This Working Group was formed in May 1994 to develop standards for transmitting data over cable.

The original goal of the IEEE 802.14 Working Group was to submit a cable modem Media Access Control (MAC) and physical (PHY) connection standard to the IEEE by December 1995. Unfortunately, delivery of the standard slipped to late 1997, making cable operators so impatient that several industry leaders, including Comcast, Cox, TCI, and Time Warner, formed a limited partnership known as Multimedia Cable Network System Partners, Ltd. (MCNS). MCNS released its own Data Over Cable System Interface (DOCSI) for cable modem products to manufacturers in April 1997.

At the physical layer, both the IEEE 802.14 and MCNS specifications define the same modulation methods, in which two levels of modulation based upon 64 QAM and 256 QAM are

5

SYNCHRONOUS
COMPONENTS

defined to provide implementation flexibility. A signaling rate of 5MHz using a carrier frequency between 151MHz and 749MHz spaced 6MHz apart is used for downstream transmission and corresponds to current TV channel assignments.

Figure 5.27 illustrates the signal constellation pattern for 64 QAM modulation. Note that each quadrant has 16 signal points, resulting in a total of 64 points.

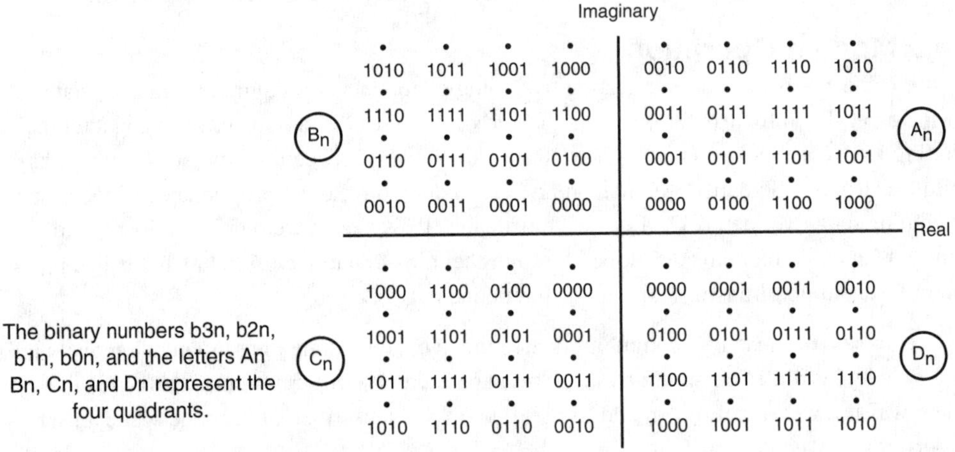

Imaginary

|       |       |       |       | |       |       |       |       |
|-------|-------|-------|-------| |-------|-------|-------|-------|
| 1010  | 1011  | 1001  | 1000  | | 0010  | 0110  | 1110  | 1010  |
| 1110  | 1111  | 1101  | 1100  | | 0011  | 0111  | 1111  | 1011  |
| 0110  | 0111  | 0101  | 0100  | | 0001  | 0101  | 1101  | 1001  |
| 0010  | 0011  | 0001  | 0000  | | 0000  | 0100  | 1100  | 1000  |

$B_n$ (left), $A_n$ (right)

Real

|       |       |       |       | |       |       |       |       |
|-------|-------|-------|-------| |-------|-------|-------|-------|
| 1000  | 1100  | 0100  | 0000  | | 0000  | 0001  | 0011  | 0010  |
| 1001  | 1101  | 0101  | 0001  | | 0100  | 0101  | 0111  | 0110  |
| 1011  | 1111  | 0111  | 0011  | | 1100  | 1101  | 1111  | 1110  |
| 1010  | 1110  | 0110  | 0010  | | 1000  | 1001  | 1011  | 1010  |

$C_n$ (left), $D_n$ (right)

The binary numbers b3n, b2n, b1n, b0n, and the letters An Bn, Cn, and Dn represent the four quadrants.

**FIGURE 5.27**

*The signal constellation pattern for 64 QAM modulation.*

Figure 5.28 illustrates the constellation pattern for one quadrant of 256 QAM modulation. As you might surmise, it has 64 points in each quadrant, creating a 256-point pattern.

When a 5MHz signaling rate is used with 64 QAM (which packs 6 bits per signal change), a data rate of 6 bits/symbol × 5MHz, or 30Mbps is obtained. In comparison, 256 QAM packs 8 bits per signal change, which provides a transmission rate of 8 bits/symbol × 5MHz, or 40Mbps. Because forward error correction is employed, the actual maximum data-transfer rate is limited to 35.504Mbps for 256 QAM and 27.378Mbps for 64 QAM.

The upstream modulation method is quadrature phase-shift keying (QPSK) modulation and 16 QAM. Under QPSK, the phase of the carrier signal varies based upon the binary value of the data to be transmitted. For example, a binary 1 might be transmitted by generating a 180° phase shift in the carrier, whereas a binary 0 could be represented by a 0° phase shift. The term *quadrature* comes from the carrier's capability to shift into one of four possible phases (0°,

90°, 180°, 270°) based on the dibit value of the data to be transmitted. Figure 5.29 shows the four-point QPSK constellation pattern. Under QPSK, a 10Mbps operating rate is obtained by using 5MHz of bandwidth in a 6MHz TV channel.

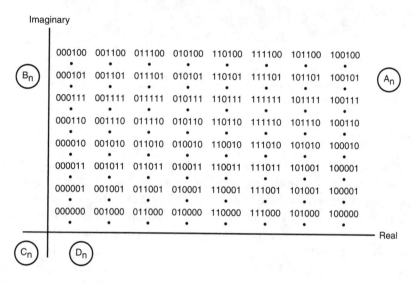

**FIGURE 5.28**

*The constellation pattern for 256 QAM modulation (one quadrant illustrated).*

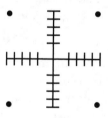

**FIGURE 5.29**

*Four-point QPSK signal constellation.*

Figure 5.30 shows the Zenith Electronics Corporation Home Works cable modem. This cable modem is marketed as a system to include a PC LAN adapter and a cable that connects the modem to the PC. The modem includes a "Super Tuner" developed to support 750MHz HFC systems.

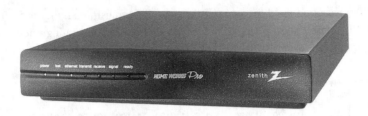

**FIGURE 5.30**

*The Zenith Electronics Corporation Home Works cable modem cabled to a LAN card in the system expansion slot of a PC. (Photograph courtesy of Zenith Electronics Corporation.)*

# Access Control

Although IEEE 802.14 and MCNS modulation standards are essentially the same, the rules used to govern the method by which a station accesses and receives data over the cable network differs between the two standards. Under the IEEE 802.14 standard, Asynchronous Transfer Mode (ATM) is specified as the transport protocol, whereas MCNS uses the Internet Protocol (IP). (Both ATM and IP are covered in later chapters in this book.) Both cable modem standards specify a 10Base-T Ethernet connection from the cable modem to the PC. The two are connected by a straight-through Cat 5 cable. The use of a 10Base-T LAN adapter card can be viewed as an interim connectivity measure because the availability of the Universal Serial Bus (USB) was limited to relatively new PCs. In addition, because each upstream and downstream channel is shared by many users, the Ethernet access protocol with its carrier sense multiple access/collision detect (CSMA/CD) is ideal for use on a shared-media environment.

## Network Configuration

Figure 5.31 illustrates the typical cable TV infrastructure from head end to subscriber that's required to support data transmission via the use of cable modems. By examining the infrastructure shown in Figure 5.31, you can see that the frequency converter is required to change the downstream frequency to an upstream frequency, and vice versa. This conversion is required to enable one user to communicate with another and is limited to the 6MHz channels used for data, ignoring other cable services. The configuration server supports the TCP/IP or ATM network formed over the cable TV infrastructure. The server is responsible for address-resolution services, and it manages addresses for subscriber computers connected to cable modems.

The router is responsible for taking data from the local cable TV network and packaging it for delivery to other networks beyond the local network. Similarly, the router is responsible for receiving data from other networks and placing it on the local cable TV network. The operation of Ethernet, ATM, and routers are described in detail in later chapters in this book.

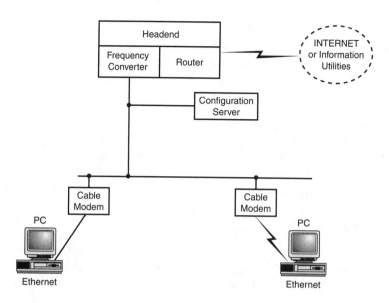

**FIGURE 5.31**

*A typical cable TV infrastructure supporting bidirectional communications from the head end to the subscriber.*

## Utilization

Although marketing hype holds the promise for a 36Mbps downstream transmission capability transferring graphics-intensive Web pages and large files in fractions of a second, it is important to note that using Ethernet results in a shared media. This means that if a 36Mbps channel is shared by 4,000 homes, and one fourth are downloading data, your delivery rate might become 36Mbps/1000 or 36Kbps (very similar to that of a V.34 modem). Thus, it is important to note how many subscribers will share the downstream channel and then estimate the effect from a reasonable percentage of those subscribers being active at the same time. Although cable modems certainly appear to offer a considerable throughput improvement over many other technologies, the actual improvement that subscribers experience will depend on how many subscribers share each channel and on their activity.

# Digital Transmission

In transmission systems that are not restricted by the bandwidth limitations of the voice-grade channel, it is advantageous to transmit the binary information from the source as binary data without converting it to analog form. The reasons for this were explained in Chapter 3. For end-user applications, the devices that connect between the business machine (DTE) and the

**5**

channel usually are called service units, digital modems, wireline modems, or channel interface units; most people and organizations now use the term *service unit*. Although data is transmitted end to end in digital form, the line coding used on digital transmission facilities differs from the digital coding used by computers and at the familiar RS-232 interface between DTEs and DCEs.

When digital transmission facilities were first made available for commercial use, two types of service units were required by customers who used this service: data service units (DSUs) and channel service units (CSUs). Because a discussion of the operation and utilization of DSUs and CSUs requires basic knowledge of digital line coding and code violations, you will cover those topics before focusing on the two types of service units used with digital transmission facilities. In addition, because high-speed DSUs and CSUs use the V.35 interface, you will also examine the characteristics of that interface in this section.

The most obvious difference between voiceband modems and direct digital transmission units is the increased bandwidth required by the latter. Recall from Chapter 3 that this increase is about a factor of eight. Thus, digital transmission is restricted to channels with bandwidths greater than the 3KHz voiceband.

## Line Coding

Several techniques can be used to code data. To help you understand the advantages and disadvantages of different methods, you'll examine the operation of several coding techniques.

### Unipolar Code

The waveform of binary signals normally used in computers and terminals is called unipolar—that is, the voltage representing the bits varies between 0 V and +5 V, as shown in Figure 5.32a. (The code shown is called NRZ, nonreturn to zero, because the voltage does not return to 0 between adjacent 1 bits.) This representation works well inside machines in which the transmission paths are short and well shielded, but it is unsuitable for long paths because of the presence of residual DC levels and the potential absence of enough signal transitions to allow reliable recovery of a clocking signal. Signal-conditioning devices (the previously mentioned channel interface units) are used to convert the unipolar waveform to one of several different patterns that meet the goals of no long-term DC residual in the signal and strong timing content. Several of these signal patterns are shown in Figure 5.32b through 5.32e.

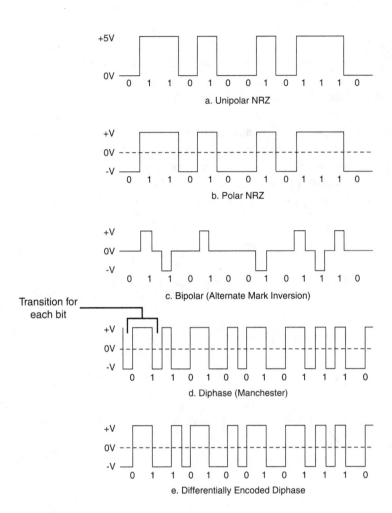

**FIGURE 5.32**

*Line coding of binary pulses.*

## Polar NRZ Code

The simplest pattern that eliminates some of the residual DC problem is called a polar NRZ line code. It is shown in Figure 5.32b. This coding merely shifts the signal reference level to the midpoint of the signal amplitude. This shift has the effect of reducing the power required to transmit the signal by one half compared with unipolar; its disadvantage, however, is that most of the energy in the signal is concentrated around zero frequency, as illustrated in Figure 5.33.

## Alternate Mark Inversion

A more satisfactory coding scheme is that used in the so-called T1 digital-transmission system. This scheme, called bipolar or alternate mark inversion (AMI), is illustrated in Figure 5.32c. This format has no residual DC component and has zero power in the spectrum at zero frequency, as Figure 5.33 shows. It achieves these goals by transmitting pulses with a 50 percent duty cycle (only half as wide as the pulse interval allows) and by inverting the polarity of alternate 1 bits that are transmitted. Note that the bipolar format is really a three-state signal (+V, 0 V, −V). This increase in the code space of the signal adds redundancy without increasing the bandwidth of the signal and makes performance monitoring easier. Ensuring that long strings of zero bits do not occur (with an accompanying lack of timing information) is left to the transmitting terminal or channel interface.

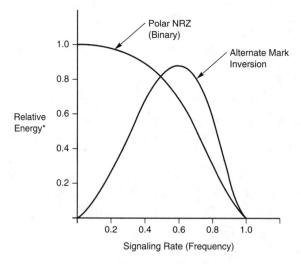

### FIGURE 5.33
*Energy distribution of encoded pulses.*

*With equally likely ones and zeros

Figure 5.34 shows the block diagram of a circuit to receive the bipolar signal and decode it into straight binary. Note that the AMI pulse format is rectified into polar pulses inside the receiver, where suppressing the DC component of the signal is no longer critical.

## Diphase Code

Another technique that has received considerable acceptance is called digital biphase, diphase, or Manchester coding. It is illustrated in Figure 5.32d. The diphase code provides strong timing information by supplying a transition for every bit, whether it is a 1 or a 0. If the diphase signal is encoded differently, as Figure 5.32e shows, it is even possible to determine the absolute phase of the signal because only a 0 has a transition at the beginning of an interval. It also eliminates the residual DC problem by providing both a positive and a negative polarity for every bit.

All these desirable characteristics are gained, however, at the expense of twice the bandwidth of a bipolar signal. Thus, diphase coding is not used by communications carriers, for whom bandwidth is a precious commodity. Instead, diphase coding has found considerable use providing digital signaling on several types of local area networks because the bandwidth of the LAN cable does not have to be used to support the communications requirements of different organizations. The diphase scheme is used on the Ethernet local area network originally developed by the Xerox Corporation, Digital Equipment Corporation, and Intel Corporation. A modified diphase coding technique, referred to as differential Manchester coding, is used on the token-ring local area network.

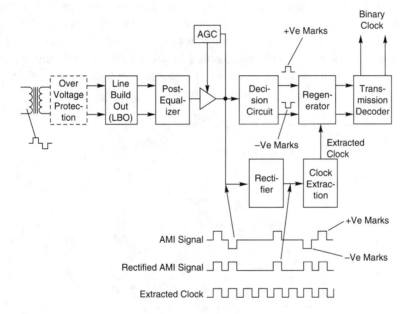

**FIGURE 5.34**
*Bipolar decoder.*

# Repeaters

Because it is not possible to separate noise from an analog signal after the two are mixed on a transmission path, both the noise and the desired signal are amplified in repeaters. The signal-to-noise ratio gets progressively worse as the path length increases.

This effect does not occur when digital signals are used, however, because a different kind of repeater, called a regenerative repeater, can be used (see Figure 5.35). This repeater doesn't just amplify the pulses; it regenerates them to restore the shape of the binary signal exactly as it

UNDERSTANDING DATA COMMUNICATIONS

was when it left the originating transmitter. This is a major advantage of the digital transmission technique because it is possible, in principle and, to a large extent, in practice, to reduce the error rate of the signal to as low a value as desired merely by putting the repeaters closer together.

The regenerative repeater, like the sending line terminal circuit, has some of the same functions as a modem. For example, it does certain electrical transformations on the input waveform to make it suitable for the transmission path. Both the sending and the receiving ends of these operations can be studied in Figure 5.35. On the input end, the line build-out (LBO) circuit matches the post-equalizer circuit with the length of the transmission cable on the input end. The post-equalizer circuit compensates for the frequency and phase nonlinearities of a standard length of input circuit, which is represented by the output of the LBO. An amplifier controlled by an automatic gain control (AGC) circuit amplifies the equalized input signal; then the stabilized and normalized input go to a clock-extraction circuit and a decision circuit/regenerator. The clock-extraction circuit, which is driven by the received data transitions, clocks the regenerator so that the original signal is regenerated exactly.

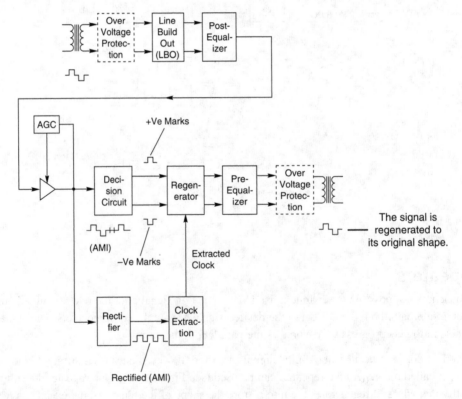

FIGURE 5.35

*Regenerative repeater.*

# Bipolar Violations

Bipolar transmission requires that each data pulse representing a logical 1 is transmitted with alternating polarity. A violation of this rule is defined as two successive pulses that have the same polarity and are separated by a zero level.

A bipolar violation indicates that a bit is missing or miscoded. Some bipolar violations are intentional and are included to replace a long string of zeros that could cause a loss of timing and receiver synchronization or to transmit control information. Figure 5.36 illustrates one example of a bipolar violation. The top of the figure shows the correct encoding to the bit sequence 01101010, using bipolar return-to-zero signaling. In the lower portion of Figure 5.36, the third 1 bit is encoded as a negative pulse. It represents a violation of the bipolar return-to-zero signaling technique, in which ones are alternately encoded as positive and negative voltages for defined periods.

On DDS low-speed transmission facilities, a maximum of five consecutive zeros is permitted. This means that a bipolar violation must be employed to maintain synchronization whenever a string of six or more zeros is encountered. Otherwise, repeaters on the line connecting the carrier office and the customer, as well as service units at the line interface, might not be capable of getting clocking as a result of an absence of ones from the signal. This could cause a loss of synchronization with the signal.

A. Bipolar Coding of Data

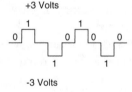

B. Bipolar Violation

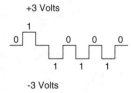

## FIGURE 5.36

*Two successive negative or positive pulses represent a bipolar violation of a bipolar return-to-zero signaling technique.*

5

SYNCHRONOUS
COMPONENTS

To ensure a minimum ones density at 2.4, 4.8, 9.6, and 19.2Kbps, any sequence of six consecutive zeros is encoded as 000X0V, in which the following are true:

0 denotes zero voltage transmitted (binary zero).

X denotes a zero or + or –A volts, with the polarity determined by conventional bipolar coding.

V denotes a + or –A volts, with the polarity in violation of bipolar rule.

Figure 5.37 illustrates the zero suppression sequence used to suppress a string of six consecutive zeros. For transmission at 56Kbps, any sequence of seven consecutive zeros is encoded as 0000X0V.

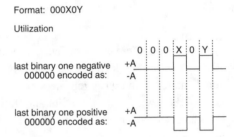

**FIGURE 5.37**

*DDS zero suppression sequence.*

In addition to providing a mechanism for suppressing a string of binary zeros, bipolar violations can be used to transmit network codes that affect the operation of digital circuit-terminating equipment, such as DSUs and CSUs. For example, when a DTE does not have data to transmit, the absence of a signal results in the loss of clocking by repeaters on the line between the customer and the carrier's office. In this situation, the DSU/CSU transmits a bipolar violation sequence that enables repeaters to maintain clocking but that is recognized as an idle sequence and, therefore, is ignored by equipment at the carrier's office. Another example of the use of an intentional bipolar violation would be in a sequence of bits that forms a loopback code. The loopback code would be recognized by the line-terminating equipment as a request to interconnect transmit and receive wire pairs on a four-wire circuit, enabling the circuit to be tested without human intervention.

For T1 circuits, AT&T publication G2411 sets the ones density requirement to be $n$ ones in each window of $8x\ (n + 1)$ bits, in which $n$ varies from 1 to 23. This means that a T1 carrier cannot have more than 15 consecutive zeros ($n = 1$) and that there must be approximately three ones in every 24 consecutive bits ($n = 2$ to 23). Several methods are used to provide this minimum ones density on T1 circuits, including binary 7 zero code suppression and binary 8 zero substitution (B8ZS). The latter, which represents the use of intentional bipolar violations, is discussed in Chapter 6.

# Service Units

Two distinct types of service units can be categorized by the type of transmission facility they are used with. Those two digital transmission facilities are AT&T's Dataphone Digital Service (DDS) and equivalent offerings by other carriers, and T1 transmission lines.

# Data Service Unit

Data service units are used at data rates from 2.4Kbps through 56Kbps for transmission on DDS. DSUs can also be used at 64Kbps to get access to a fractional T1 line operating at that data rate. In actuality, transmission on DDS and on a 64Kbps fractional T1 facility requires the use of a DSU and a channel service unit. The CSU, which is located between the DSU and the digital line, physically terminates the line while providing signal amplification and initiating remote loop-back operations in response to special codes received over the line. The DSU is located between the user's terminal equipment and the CSU. The DSU converts unipolar digital signals from terminal devices into a bipolar digital format for transmission over the digital network. In addition, the DSU provides timing recovery, control signaling, and synchronous sampling.

Before deregulation, the CSU was provided by the communications carrier, whereas the DSU could be obtained from the carrier or from third-party sources. This resulted in an end-user connection to the DDS network similar to that illustrated in the top portion of Figure 5.38, in which the CSU terminated the carrier's four-wire loop and the DSU was cabled to the CSU. In this configuration, the CSU terminates the carrier's circuit. In addition, a separate CSU was designed to perform signal regeneration, monitor incoming signals to detect bipolar violations, and perform remote loop-back testing.

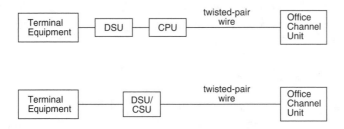

**FIGURE 5.38**

*Most manufacturers combine the functions of a DSU and a CSU into a single device for use on low-speed digital transmission facilities.*

Since deregulation, most communications vendors have manufactured combined DSU/CSU devices, integrating the functions of both devices into a common housing that is powered by a common power supply. The lower portion of Figure 5.38 illustrates the connection of end-user terminal equipment to DDS using a combined DSU/CSU unit.

Although a 56Kbps operational capability represented a high-speed data-transfer rate when DDS was first introduced, the data-transfer requirements of users continued to grow. Recognizing the need to provide a higher data-transfer capability while enabling economical 56 and 64Kbps leased digital lines to continue to be used (instead of more costly higher-speed lines), several vendors introduced compression-performing DSUs/CSUs. Such products use a similar algorithm to the Lempel Ziv Welch compression algorithm used in the V.42 standard, providing a 2:1 to 4:1 compression ratio. This means that a 64Kbps digital circuit can support a data-transfer rate between 128Kbps and 256Kbps when compression-performing DSU/CSUs are used.

## Channel Service Unit

Unlike transmission on DDS and equivalent carrier facilities in which the DSU originated as a separate device, these functions are built into most types of data terminal equipment (DTE) designed for operation on T1 lines. Thus, a CSU designed for 1.544Mbps operation was developed as a separate entity to both interface a T1 line and provide a mechanism for the built-in DSU of most DTEs to be connected to the digital transmission facility.

In addition to performing a line-termination function, a CSU used on a T1 facility provides signal amplification and initiates remote loopbacks similar to the functions performed by the CSU portion of a combined DSU/CSU used on DDS transmission facilities. Two additional functions performed by the CSUs connected to T1 transmission facilities include frame formatting and the computation of performance-measurement statistics. Frame formatting is the process of encoding every 193rd bit to provide synchronization framing and, in some instances, to generate and store performance-measurement data. Concerning the latter, industry standards require CSUs to both compute various performance statistics and store those statistics for transmission when predefined codes embedded in the T1 framing are received. Refer to Chapter 6 for specific information concerning frame-formatting and performance-measurement statistics associated with T1 lines.

## The V.35 Interface

The ITU promulgated the original version of the V.35 recommendation in 1968. At that time, the V.35 recommendation was viewed as an interface for wideband analog modems and DTEs at data rates between 48Kbps and 64Kbps. As the use of wideband analog modems declined, the V.35 interface gained acceptance for cabling DTEs to different types of service units developed to support emerging digital transmission facilities. The original V.35 recommendation was revised several times and currently supports data-transmission rates up to 6Mbps, making it a very popular high-speed interface. Today, most service units (as well as routers, remote bridges, and gateways) can be obtained with a V.35 interface.

The V.35 interface's capability to support high-speed transmission results from its signaling method. Similar to RS-422, the V.35 interface is a balanced interface for data and timing signals. A balanced interface is an interface in which each signal has its own return current path on its own wire and pin. This design technique can reduce or prevent interference and allows support for higher data rates than when individual signals are placed on individual wires and use a common return through one signal ground wire (as in the RS-232 interface). When multiple individual circuits share a common return, those circuits are commonly referred to as "single-ended" circuits. In comparison, when multiple individual circuits each have their own return paths, such circuits are referred to as "differential circuits."

The V.35 interface uses both single-ended and differential circuits. As previously mentioned, data and timing signals are carried on balanced circuits that are also known as differential circuits. Because control signals can operate more slowly, they are placed on single-ended circuits.

The V.35 interface uses a 34-pin rectangular connector specified in ISO 2593. Figure 5.39 shows the 34-pin V.35 connector with the recommendation circuit numbers shown above their appropriate pin positions. Common practice in V.35 cabling and connectors is to place male pin connectors on both cable ends and place female pin connectors on DTEs and DCEs.

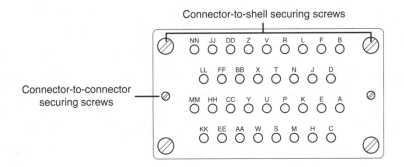

### FIGURE 5.39

*The V.35 connector and its signal connections.*

In concluding this chapter, we will turn our attention to the pins commonly used on the V.35 interface.

Table 5.15 indicates the assignment of 21 pins commonly used on the V.35 interface. Note that the V.35 pin pairs tied together by a brace indicate differential signaling circuits that use a common wire pair. For balanced signals, a binary 0 or space condition exists when the voltage on the A pin is greater or more positive than the voltage on the B pin. Similarly, a binary 1 or mark condition occurs when the voltage on the B pin is greater or more positive than that on the A pin. The actual voltage under the V.35 recommendation is 0.55 V, plus or minus 20 percent, resulting in an acceptable range from 0.44 V to 0.66 V. Also note that of the 34 pins in the V.35 connector, only 21 are assigned functions in common use. Occasionally manufacturers will assign functions to unused pins; therefore, you need to make sure that you obtain an appropriate V.35 cable if you do not own a fully populated V.35 cable.

**TABLE 5.15**  V.35 Pin Assignments

| Connector Pin | V.35 Designation | Function | Signal Direction |
|---|---|---|---|
| A | 101 | Protective (Frame) Ground | — |
| B | 102 | Signal Ground | — |
| C | 105 | Request to Send | DTE to DCE |
| D | 106 | Clear to Send | DCE to DTE |
| E | 107 | Data Set Ready | DCE to DTE |
| F | 109 | Receive Carrier Detect | DCE to DTE |
| H* | * | Data Terminal Ready | DTE to DCE |
| J* | 125 | Ring Indicator | DCE to DTE |
| L* | 141 | Local Loopback | DTE to DCE |
| S | 103 | Transmit Data A wire | DTE to DCE |
| P | 103 | Transmit Data B wire | DTE to DCE |
| R | 104 | Receive Data A wire | DCE to DTE |
| T | 104 | Receive Data B wire | DCE to DTE |
| Y | 114 | Transmitter Signaling Timing Element B wire | DCE to DTE |
| AA | 114 | Transmitter Signaling Timing Element B wire | DCE to DTE |
| V | 115 | Receiver Signaling Timing Element A wire | DCE to DTE |
| X | 115 | Receiver Signaling Timing Element B wire | DCE to DTE |
| U | 113 | Receiver Signaling Timing Element (Ext) A wire | DTE to DCE |
| W | 113 | Receiver Signaling Timing Element (Ext) B wire | DTE to DCE |

**TABLE 5.15**   continued

| Connector Pin | V.35 Designation | Function | Signal Direction |
|---|---|---|---|
| N* | 140 | Loopback/Maintenance Test | DTE to DCE |
| NN* | 142 | Test Indicator | DCE to DTE |

*Indicates pins specified in ISO 2593 whose use may depend upon vendor product implementation of the V.35 interface.

# What You Have Learned

- The bandwidth of a channel limits the modulation or baud rate of the channel.

- The data rate through a channel can be increased by sending more than 1 bit per baud.

- Synchronous modems modulate a carrier wave in phase, amplitude, or both to send more than 1 bit per baud.

- Synchronous modems send the clock signal along with the data. They are more expensive than asynchronous modems because of the additional circuitry necessary to recover the clock from the data.

- Usually, only phase modulation is used in 2400bps modems, but both phase and amplitude modulation are used in 4800 and 9600bps modems.

- The most important transmission impairment that synchronous modems must deal with is differential delay distortion. Such modems have adaptive equalizers to correct for this distortion.

- Accurate recovery of the signal in both synchronous modems and digital transmission of binary signals depends on a sufficient number of 1 bits being transmitted.

- Asymmetrical transmission involves the assignment of different transmission operating rates for each direction.

- The use of a high-speed modem with its data-compression facility enabled might require the replacement of your computer's UART to support the modem's effective data transfer capability.

- The introduction of V.92 modems supporting V.44 data compression provides a high-speed data-transfer capability that represents a viable alternative to the use of DSL and cable modems.

- A family of Digital Subscriber Line (DSL) products enables high-speed symmetrical and asymmetrical transmission over the local loop connecting subscribers to a telephone company central office.

5

SYNCHRONOUS
COMPONENTS

- For cable modems to provide a true bidirectional transmission capability, cable TV networks must be upgraded to support bidirectional transmission.

- Digital transmission uses regenerative repeaters rather than amplifiers to correct the line signal.

- Compression-performing DSU/CSUs support a data-transfer rate typically between 128Kbps and 256Kbps on a 64Kbps circuit.

- Intentional bipolar violations can be used to maintain synchronization and to transmit control information on digital circuits.

- A V.35 interface supports a data transfer rate up to 6Mbps.

# Quiz for Chapter 5

1. What is one principal difference between synchronous and asynchronous transmission?

   A. The bandwidth required is different.

   B. The pulse heights are different.

   C. The clocking is mixed with the data in asynchronous transmission.

   D. The clocking is derived from the data in synchronous transmission.

2. Why do synchronous modems cost more than asynchronous modems?

   A. They are larger.

   B. They must contain clock-recovery circuits.

   C. The production volume is larger.

   D. They must operate on a larger bandwidth.

3. Where is the scrambler located in a synchronous modem?

   A. Control section

   B. Receiver section

   C. Transmitter section

   D. Terminal section

4. In modems, binary codes are sometimes transformed into what?

   A. Hexadecimal

   B. Huffman codes

   C. Gray code

   D. Complementary codes

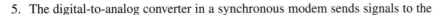

5. The digital-to-analog converter in a synchronous modem sends signals to the

    A. Modulator.

    B. Transmission line.

    C. Terminal.

    D. Equalizer.

6. What is the receive equalizer in a synchronous modem called?

    A. A compromise equalizer

    B. A statistical equalizer

    C. An adaptive equalizer

    D. An impairment equalizer

7. The receive equalizer reduces delay distortion using a

    A. Tapped delay line.

    B. Difference engine.

    C. Descrambler.

    D. "Gearshift."

8. A Western Electric 201 modem operates at which of the following carrier frequencies?

    A. 1000Hz

    B. 1200Hz

    C. 1800Hz

    D. 600 baud

9. What is the modulation rate of the CCITT V.26 modem?

    A. 1200Hz

    B. 1200 baud

    C. 1560 cps

    D. None of the above

10. What is the transmission signal coding method for a T1 carrier called?

    A. Binary

    B. NRZ

    C. Bipolar

    D. Manchester

**5**

11. If a modem packs 6 bits into each signal change and operates at 2400 baud, what is its operating rate?

    A. 2400bps

    B. 4800bps

    C. 9600bps

    D. 14,400bps

12. Using V.42bis compression with a V.32bis modem operating at 14,400bps can result in what maximum throughput?

    A. 14,400bps

    B. 19,200bps

    C. 38,400bps

    D. 57,600bps

13. Which of the following is a key difference between a V.32bis modem and a V.32 modem?

    A. A V.32bis modem supports fallback operations.

    B. A V.32bis modem supports fall-forward operations.

    C. A V.32 modem supports V.22bis operations.

    D. A V.32 modem is more expensive.

14. The 2743 and 2800 baud rates of a V.34 modem enable high-speed transmission over voice circuits digitized using which of the following?

    A. PCM

    B. ADPCM

    C. DPCM

    D. CMP

15. The V.90 modem provides near 56Kbps data-transmission capability

    A. In both directions.

    B. At night.

    C. Downstream.

    D. Only through two analog-to-digital conversions.

16. Which of the following features does not represent an addition occurring under the V.92 standard that is not supported by the V.90 standard?

    A. Quick Connect

    B. Echo cancellation

    C. Modem on Hold

    D. PCM upstream

17. Quantization noise

    A. Is loud.

    B. Represents the difference between the height of the analog sample and its encoded value.

    C. Occurs when data flows through a repeater.

    D. Is minimal at night when sunspot activity decreases.

18. Digital Subscriber Line technology is based on

    A. The use of the 4KHz voice channel.

    B. The use of subscribers.

    C. The 1MHz bandwidth on an access line or local loop.

    D. The weather.

19. An ADSL modem subdivides the local loop into how many channels by frequency?

    A. 1

    B. 2

    C. 3

    D. 4

20. ADSL performance is based upon which of the following?

    A. Wire gauge and subscriber line distance

    B. Upstream rate

    C. Downstream rate

    D. The number of loops in the local loop

21. Which two modulation techniques are used by ADSL modems?

    A. XDSL and DMT

    B. CAP and DMT

    C. CAP and XDLS

    D. DMT and WHAM

22. What device located in a telephone company central office aggregates data from individual subscriber lines?

    A. AWG

    B. CAP

   C. DMT

   D. DSLAM

23. Some first-generation cable modems obtained an upstream transmission capability

   A. Via the telephone.

   B. Using unidirectional amplifiers.

   C. Using teletype circuits.

   D. Via bandwidth sharing.

24. The 50MHz beginning frequency for cable TV downstream transmission is based on

   A. Where channel 14 begins.

   B. Where channel 26 begins.

   C. Where channel 2 begins.

   D. Where CNN begins.

25. HFC systems

   A. Decrease TV channel capacity.

   B. Increase TV channel capacity.

   C. Neither increase nor decrease TV channel capacity.

   D. Never get the Weather Channel.

26. Which of the following are two cable modem standards?

   A. IEEE 802.14 and MSNBC

   B. IEEE 802.02 and MCNS

   C. IEEE 802.14 and MCNS

   D. IEEE 802.12 and MCTV

27. Cable modems use what modulation scheme for downstream transmission?

   A. QPC

   B. QVC

   C. QAM

   D. QPX

28. Transport methods used to move data over the cable TV network include

   A. ATM and Ethernet.

   B. Ethernet and MCNS.

   C. IP and ATM.

   D. UDP and MCNS.

29. A bipolar violation

   A. Represents a 0 bit followed by a 1 bit.

   B. Occurs when two successive pulses have the same polarity and are separated by a 0 level.

   C. Occurs when two successive pulses have the same polarity and are separated by a 1 level.

   D. Represents a 1 bit followed by a 0 bit.

30. On a digital circuit, the absence of a transmitted signal

   A. Has no effect on equipment.

   B. Occurs when a DTE has no data to transmit.

   C. Is compensated for by the transmission of intentional bipolar violations to maintain equipment clocking.

   D. Occurs only after 9 p.m.

31. What is the maximum data rate supported by the V.34 interface?

   A. 10Mbps

   B. 60Mbps

   C. 6Kbps

   D. 6Mbps

# Multiplexing Techniques

## IN THIS CHAPTER

Until now, this book has primarily focused on communications between individual devices, such as a personal computer user transmitting information to a mainframe computer or an individual using a telephone to place a long-distance call. Whenever there is a requirement for the use of two or more transmission paths that are partially or completely routed in parallel, there also exists an opportunity to economize on transmission cost through multiplexing. Multiplexing provides a mechanism for sharing a common channel or circuit by two or more users. As such, its original development was based on economics.

This chapter will focus on the multiplexing techniques used by communications carriers and business organizations to share transmission facilities. After examining communications carrier multiplexing techniques, including frequency-division multiplexing (FDM) and time-division multiplexing (TDM), you will examine the applicability of those techniques to business organizations, as well as the use of statistical time-division multiplexers (STDM) by those organizations. To conclude this chapter, you will turn your attention to a relatively new category of multiplexer commonly referred to as a low-speed voice/data multiplexer. This device enables voice and data transmission requirements of small offices to be transported over a common communications circuit. Because an understanding of low-bandwidth voice-digitization methods is essential for obtaining an appreciation for the operation of low-speed voice/data multiplexers, you will also review several voice-digitization methods in the last section of this chapter.

# Sharing a Channel

Just as modulation can be explained with the idea of sending code with a flashlight, multiplexing has a simple analogy. Imagine that you have several letters to take to the post office. You could get into the car and take one letter, mail it, come back home and get the second letter, take it to the post office and mail it, come back to get the third... but that sounds silly, doesn't it? Why not take all the letters in the same trip because they're all going to the post office?

This is what multiplexing amounts to: using a resource (in this case, the car going to the post office) to carry more than one message at a time. In the systems you are concerned with, a leased line, a microwave system, a fiber cable, or another transmission medium represents a transmission facility (like the car), and a telephone call is the message (like the letter). The transmission facility is divided for sharing in one of two ways: by frequency or by time.

## Frequency-Division Multiplexing

The use of frequency-division multiplexing to carry more than one telephone conversation over a transmission channel is shown in Figure 6.1. In effect, the frequencies in each call are changed so that they can be placed side by side in a wideband channel and transmitted as a group. At the other end, the frequencies in each call are changed back to the original frequencies. FDM was the mainstay of telephone transmission for many years; it is more efficient than digital systems in terms of bandwidth. The problem is that noise is amplified along with the voice. This fact, and the great decrease in cost of digital electronics, has led to the widespread replacement of FDM systems with time-division multiplexing systems.

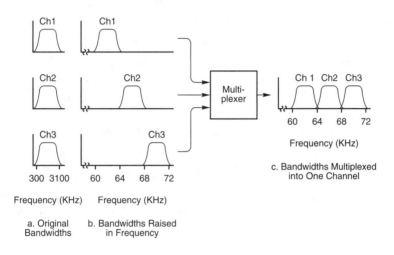

**FIGURE 6.1**

*Frequency-division multiplexing.*

A second and perhaps more important reason for the tremendous decrease in the use of FDM during the past three decades was the conversion of most long-distance communications carrier transmission facilities from analog to digital. This conversion resulted in voice conversations being digitized at a carrier central office and carried in digital format to another central office. At the distant central office, the digitized conversation was converted back into its analog form and was routed to the destination telephone connected to that central office. By 1990, Sprint had converted all of its long-distance circuits to digital, and AT&T and MCI had converted more than 90 percent of their long-distance transmission facilities. A few years later, all long-distance communications in the United States were being transported over digital circuits, and most European communications carriers were well along on similar conversion efforts.

If you are familiar with the works of Mark Twain, you may have come across a copy of a letter that he wrote in which he said that reports of his apparent demise were greatly exaggerated. If we fast-forward to the wonderful world of frequency-division multiplexing, its demise never occurred. Although its use as a multiplexing technique to directly combine multiple voice conversations onto one analog wideband circuit has indeed fallen by the wayside, a new technology has evolved that makes good use of FDM. This new technology is optical transmission, which uses frequency-division multiplexing to transmit multiple sources of light at different wavelengths onto a common fiber. If you remember high school physics, you probably memorized the name Roy G. Biv as a mechanism to remember the spectrum of colors when light flows through a prism. That name helped you remember that light consists of the primary colors red, orange, yellow, green, blue, indigo, and violet. Because each color occurs at a predefined frequency, it is possible to transmit certain colors at certain frequencies onto a common fiber.

Although this is a rather simple explanation of FDM in an optical environment, its intention is to make you recognize that the demise of FDM is greatly exaggerated. In Chapter 7, "Fiber-Optic and Satellite Communications," you will examine how frequency-division multiplexing in an optical environment is now called wavelength-division multiplexing (WDM). However, because frequency is the reciprocal of wavelength ($\lambda = 1/f$) and wavelength is the reciprocal of frequency ($f = 1/\lambda$), when different wavelengths are transmitted onto an optical fiber, transmission occurs at different frequencies. Thus, FDM lives on!

To get an appreciation for the method by which analog voice is converted into a digital format, you'll examine digital modulation and PCM voice digitization, which forms the basis for the use of TDMs by communications carriers.

## Digital Modulation

Sine waves are all you have to work with when transmitting over the analog telephone channel because pulses are not transmitted. Digital transmission systems will transmit pulses, and with them you can encode either analog or digital information by modulating pulses.

Figure 6.2 shows three ways to modulate a series of pulses to carry data:

- PAM—When the amplitude of the pulses is varied to represent analog information, the method is called pulse amplitude modulation. This method is very susceptible to electrical noise interference.

- PWM—In pulse width modulation, the information is represented by varying the width of the pulses. Both PWM and PAM are used in telephone switching equipment, such as a private branch exchange (PBX).

- PPM—Pulse position modulation varies the position of pulses within a group of pulses (called the frame) to represent information.

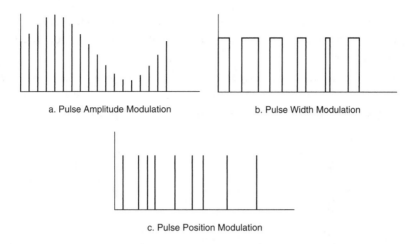

a. Pulse Amplitude Modulation          b. Pulse Width Modulation

c. Pulse Position Modulation

**FIGURE 6.2**

*Pulse modulation.*

## PCM

A process called pulse-code modulation (PCM) overcame the noise interference problem of PAM. Figure 6.3 shows the process of sampling an analog signal as in PAM, but the amplitudes of the samples are encoded into binary numbers represented by constant amplitude pulses that are transmitted. The conversion of a vast majority of telephone company infrastructure to digital transmission on trunks routed between central offices, in addition to the use of PCM to digitize voice, virtually ensures that almost all long-distance calls are transmitted in PCM format.

The PCM system used by communications carriers employs a three-step process: sampling, quantization, and coding.

1. The sampling process's analog signal is sampled 8,000 times per second. This sampling rate is based on the Nyquist theorem, which states that to faithfully reconstruct an analog signal, the number of sample points must equal twice the maximum frequency of the signal. Because each voice channel has a bandwidth of 4 kilohertz (KHz), the sampling rate becomes 8,000 samples per second. The resulting samples, which are illustrated in the top portion of Figure 6.3, represent an infinite number of voltages. This is because each sample height can have an infinite range of possible values.

2. Quantization reduces the PAM signal to a limited number of discrete amplitudes. As you learned in Chapter 5, "Synchronous Modems, Digital Transmission, and Service Units," when you examined the reason for limitations on the data-transfer capacity of analog

modems, one reason is quantization noise. Quantization noise represents the difference between the height of each PAM signal sample and the discrete value of the height that is encoded in binary.

3. Coding reduces the number of unique values of the PAM signal so that they can be coded through the use of an 8-bit byte. For simplicity, the lower portion of Figure 6.3 uses 4 bits to represent each PAM signal sample; in actuality, 8 bits are used.

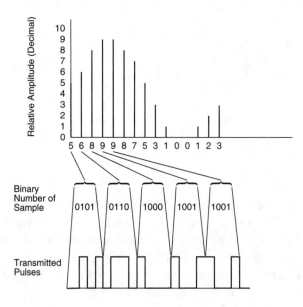

**FIGURE 6.3**

*Pulse-code modulation.*

One of the earliest uses of PCM systems was to relieve cable congestion in urban areas during the 1960s. At that time, communications carriers installed equipment called channel banks in their central offices. Each channel bank contained a codec, a time-division multiplexer, and a line driver. The codec (coder-decoder) accepts and samples 24 analog voice signals. It produces a series of PAM signals that are quantized and coded into 8-bit bytes. The TDM combines the digitized bit stream from each of the 24 inputs into 1 high-speed serial bit stream, and the line driver converts the electrical characteristics of the bit stream for transmission on the circuit linking channel banks. Figure 6.4 illustrates a channel bank system that was the forerunner of what is now commonly known as a T-carrier transmission system.

The repeater illustrated in Figure 6.4 actually represents a series of devices installed approximately 6,000 feet from one another on the span line. Each repeater examines the digital pulses transmitted on the span line connecting a pair of channel banks and regenerates each pulse. Because the repeater "throws away" the old pulse and generates a new pulse, it removes any previous distortion. In comparison, amplifiers used with analog transmission boost the strength of an analog signal, including increasing any previous distortion to the signal. This explains why, in general, digital transmission provides a higher level of signal quality and lower error rate than analog transmission does.

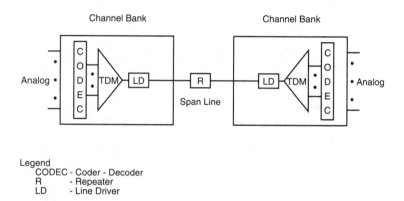

**FIGURE 6.4**

*Channel bank system.*

## Framing

To provide a method of synchronizing transmission, a framing format was developed for use with channel banks. Over the past 40 years, several framing formats were used to synchronize transmission between channel banks. Two of the most popular framing formats are D4 and ESF. Until the late 1980s, D4 was the most popular framing format. However, since then, the ESF framing format has achieved a wide degree of acceptance for use on T1 circuits and now represents the most popular framing format used on such circuits.

Under the D4 framing format, which is illustrated in Figure 6.5a, a frame bit is used to prefix each group of 24 8-bit bytes, where each byte represents a digitized voice sample for each of 24 voice channels. Thus, a D4 frame contains $1 + 24 \times 8$, or 193 bits. The framing bits of 12 frames are used to develop a framing pattern that enables a receiving channel bank to synchronize itself to the transmission of data from a channel bank at the opposite end of a span line.

The framing bits in a D4 superframe are alternately designated as terminal framing bits (Ft) or signal framing bits (Fs). The terminal framing bits consist of the odd framing bits, as illustrated in the lower portion of Figure 6.5. Under D4 framing, the Ft bits form an alternating pattern of ones and zeros, enabling one frame to be distinguished from another. Thus, the sequence of terminal framing bits is also referred to as a frame alignment signal.

The signal framing bits that represent the repeating pattern 001110 are the even frame bits. These bits are used to define multiframe boundaries and enable the extraction of signaling bits from frames. Signaling bits are used to carry such mechanical signaling information as on-hook, off-hook, dialed digits, and call progress information. The method used to provide signaling bits, called bit robbing, is beyond the scope of this book. If you want more on that subject, refer to my book *High Speed Digital Networking Second Edition,* published by John Wiley & Sons, Inc., of New York, for detailed information concerning digital transmission systems, including the bit-robbing process.

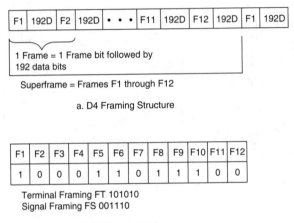

a. D4 Framing Structure

b. D4 Framing Pattern

## FIGURE 6.5

*The D4 framing structure pattern.*

A second framing format, known as extended superframe, or ESF, extends D4 framing to 24 consecutive frames. Unlike D4 framing, which contains a specific repeating pattern, ESF framing contains both fixed and variable patterns. Of the 24 frame bits in an extended superframe, only 6 are used for a framing pattern for synchronization. The remaining frame bits are used to transmit error performance and network-monitoring information.

Table 6.1 lists the use of the 24 bits in the ESF framing pattern. The entries for d in the two columns labeled "Bit Use" in the table denote bits that form a data link between channel banks or a pair of CSUs connected to a T1 circuit. This data link enables the communications carrier to activate and deactivate loopbacks, to request the transmission of performance data from distant CSUs, and to transport performance data to the requester. The d bits appear in the odd frame positions (1, 3, 5, … 21, 23) and represent a 4Kbps data link because they are used by 12 out of the 24 framing bits and the framing bits occur 8,000 times per second.

The entries prefixed with a "c" in the two columns labeled "Bit Use" are used to compute a cyclic redundancy check (CRC) over the 4,632 bits in the previous extended superframe. These 6 bits in frame positions 2, 6, 10, 14, 18, and 22 enable the receiver to compute its own CRC on received data and compare it to the transmitted CRC. This enables the receiver to detect the frame error rate and provides a measurement of the quality of the T1 circuit. In actuality, ESF-compliant CSUs perform the CRC computations. Because 6 framing bits are used to compute the CRC, this error-check link has an operating rate of 2000bps.

The third type of ESF frame bit is the framing pattern used for synchronization. As indicated in Table 6.1, the framing pattern appears in frame bits 4, 8, 12, 16, 20, and 24 and generates the bit pattern 001011. Using 6 out of the 24 framing bits, the framing pattern also consumes 2Kbps of the 8Kbps ESF link.

**TABLE 6.1** ESF Framing Bit Utilization

| Frame Number | Bit Use | Frame Number | Bit Use |
| --- | --- | --- | --- |
| 1 | d | 13 | d |
| 2 | c1 | 14 | c4 |
| 3 | d | 15 | d |
| 4 | 0 | 16 | 0 |
| 5 | d | 17 | d |
| 6 | c2 | 18 | c5 |
| 7 | d | 19 | d |
| 8 | 0 | 20 | 1 |
| 9 | d | 22 | C6 |
| 10 | c3 | 23 | d |
| 11 | d | 24 | 1 |
| 12 | 1 | | |

*Legend: d = data link   cx = CRC - 6 bit x*

## The T-Carrier

The span line illustrated in Figure 6.4 is now commonly referred to as a T-carrier. This circuit originally provided communications carriers with the capability to multiplex 24 voice conversations on 1 high-speed digital circuit.

Because each voice conversation is sampled 8,000 times per second and each sample is encoded into 8 bits, the digitization rate per channel is 8,000 samples per second × 8 bits per sample, or 64Kbps. The aggregate of 24 channels represents a data rate of 64Kbps × 24, or 1.536Mbps. Because the framing rate is 8,000 bits per second, the operating rate of the T-carrier is 1.536Mbps + 8Kbps, or 1.544Mbps.

Until the early 1980s, the use of T-carrier transmission facilities was limited to communications carriers. Since then, the use of the T-carrier has been made available to commercial organizations. In the digital transmission hierarchy of carrier facilities, the 1.544Mbps transmission rate represents the first level in the hierarchy and is commonly referred to as a "T1 transmission facility." As a result of the commercial availability of this transmission facility, a large number of independent companies began to manufacture T1 multiplexers. Through the use of this type of multiplexer, companies could integrate the transmission of voice, data, and video between locations, routing this mixture of data onto a common high-speed transmission line operating at 1.544Mbps.

Figure 6.6 illustrates one example of an organization's use of a T1 multiplexer that enables the integration of voice, data, and video transmission. In the example shown, the T1 multiplexer contains PCM cards that enable analog voice conversations routed from a private branch exchange to be digitized before being multiplexed. If a digital PBX was installed, data could be directly multiplexed without the use of PCM cards.

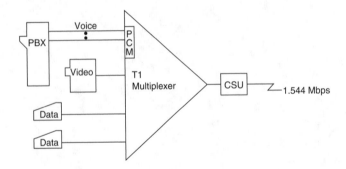

Legend:

PCM - Pulse Code Modulation cards that sample, quantize, and encode each
        analog voice signal into a 64 Kbps digital data stream.
CSU - Channel Service Unit

**FIGURE 6.6**
*A typical T1 multiplexer application.*

Digital data is manipulated within a T1 multiplexer in a unipolar NRZ format, as previously indicated in Figure 5.31a. Although this data representation format is commonly used by the computer systems, electronic equipment, and the interface from data terminal equipment (DTE) to data communications equipment (DCE), it is unsuitable for transmission on a T1 transmission facility.

When span lines were first routed between channel banks, communications carriers desired a method that would enable them to transmit both a digital signal and power on the same circuit, separating the signal from the power through the use of a transformer at each channel bank location. Getting this capability required a signaling method with no residual DC voltage, which would enable the use of transformers to separate the signal from the power carried on the line. The resulting line-coding method that provided this capability is the bipolar alternate mark inversion (AMI) coding format previously illustrated in Figure 5.31c.

Most T1 multiplexers convert unipolar RTZ signals into bipolar AMI signals for transmission. Before actual transmission on the T1 line, however, the digital signal must be framed according to the line code supported by the communications carrier—D4 or ESF. The framing function is but one of several operations performed by the channel service unit (CSU). Other functions performed by CSUs include storing performance data when an ESF framing format is used, recognizing and responding to network codes transmitted by the communications carrier and equipment connected to the T1 line, and transmitting a minimum number of binary ones, referred to as ones density.

## Ones Density

The requirement for a ones density level on T1 circuits resulted from the need of repeaters to maintain timing. If a long string of binary zeros was transmitted, the repeaters on a span line could conceivably lose timing. Thus, the CSU must be capable of ensuring that a binary 1 or mark pulse occurs every so often, which enables repeaters to get timing from the pulse.

Specifically, carrier requirements are such that the number of consecutive zeros must be less than 15, and each 8-bit byte must include at least one 1 bit. To support carrier ones density requirements, several techniques are used, including binary 7 (B7) zero code suppression and binary 8 zero substitution. Under B7 zero code suppression, a 1 bit is substituted in bit position 7 of an all-zero byte. Although this technique ensures that the carrier's ones density requirements are met, it also restricts data to 7 usable bits rather than 8. This means that each 64Kbps voice channel multiplexed on a T1 line is restricted to 64Kbps $\times$ 7 / 8, or 56Kbps, when used for data transmission.

To understand why bit position 7 was selected for substitution, consider a worst-case scenario, as illustrated in Figure 6.7. In this example, the 8-bit byte representing the 24th channel contains a mark in bit position 1 followed by the remainder of the byte's bit positions set to 0. If the framing bit following the 24th channel has a value of 0 and is followed by an all-zero byte, 16 bit positions would be between marks if bit position 8 had its value altered to 1. Normally, this would be more desirable because it represents the least significant position in a byte and would minimize its effect on a digitized voice signal. Selecting bit position 8, however, would then violate the carrier's ones density requirements, which resulted in the selection of bit position 7 for substitution.

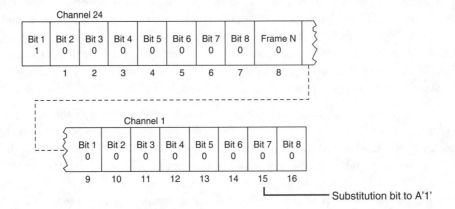

**FIGURE 6.7**

*A B7 zero code suppression worst-case scenario.*

Binary 8 zero substitution (B8ZS), developed by Bell Laboratories, represents a considerable improvement over B7 zero suppression because it enables data to be transmitted at 64Kbps on a voice channel. This capability, which maintains a minimum ones density without corrupting data, provides what is known as a clear channel. Under B8ZS coding, each byte of eight consecutive zeros is replaced by a code that includes an intentional bipolar violation. Figure 6.8 illustrates the B8ZS coding process.

The coding used in Figure 6.8 becomes more meaningful if you review how bipolar coding normally functions. That is, under bipolar coding, marks or binary ones are encoded using alternating polarities, and spaces are encoded as a zero voltage level. Thus, the encoded byte, when the pulse preceding an all-zeros byte was positive, commences with bit position 4 high, which represents a bipolar violation. This is illustrated at A in Figure 6.8. Next, bit positions 5 and 7 are both encoded as negative marks, which represents another bipolar violation. Because bits 4 and 8 are positive pulses and bits 5 and 7 are negative pulses, the encoded byte does not result in any DC voltage buildup, although it violates bipolar coding rules. At the receiving CSU, the encoded byte is recognized as defining the occurrence of an all-zeros byte, and the CSU then replaces the B8ZS code with eight binary zeros. Similarly, if the pulse preceding an all-zeros byte is negative, the all-zeros byte is encoded in the opposite manner, as illustrated at B in Figure 6.8.

## Intentional Bipolar Violations

The state of bit position 4 represents a bipolar violation with respect to the pulse preceding the all-zeros byte, whereas bit positions 5 and 7 represent a bipolar violation with respect to each bit position's polarity. Also note that there are equal numbers of positive and negative pulses to prevent DC voltage buildup.

The bipolar violations contained in the B8ZS coding represent intentional bipolar violations. Other examples of intentional bipolar violations are loopback codes that, when recognized by a CSU, bring about a loopback mode of operation. Intentional bipolar violations do not represent coding errors. In comparison, unintentional bipolar violations do represent coding errors resulting from line impairments whose measurement over a period of time provides an indication of the quality of a digital circuit.

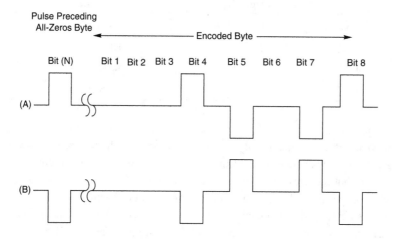

**FIGURE 6.8**

*B8ZS coding.*

## The Digital Transmission Hierarchy

Throughout the world, communications carriers constructed a hierarchy of digital-transmission facilities. In North America, the beginning of the hierarchy is based on the T1 circuit. The actual signal on a T1 circuit is referred to as a "DS1 signal," with "DS" representing a mnemonic for "digital signal" and 1 representing the term level 1. As communications carriers expanded their digital transmission hierarchy, they used various multiplexing schemes to combine multiple DS1 digital signals onto a higher signal. Table 6.2 indicates the relationship between the circuit type, the signal level, the number of DS1 signals transported, and the operating rate for a series of four digital circuits commonly used that form the North American digital transmission hierarchy.

If you examine the relationship between the number of DS1 signals included in higher-level signals in the digital hierarchy and the operating rate of the higher signals, you will note that they are not precise multiples of the 1.544Mbps DS1 operating rate. This is because intermediate multiplexers used in the infrastructure created by communications carriers perform what is referred to as "bit stuffing" to compensate for the differences in clocking between DS1 signals. That is, when the data rate of multiple DS1 signals differ slightly, higher-level multiplexing equipment compensates for clocking differences.

**TABLE 6.2**   North American Digital Transmission Hierarchy

| Circuit | Speed | Number of DS1 Signals | Operating Rate (Mbps) |
|---------|-------|-----------------------|-----------------------|
| T1      | DS1   | 1                     | 1.544                 |
| T1C     | DS1C  | 2                     | 3.152                 |
| T2      | DS2   | 4                     | 6.312                 |
| T3      | DS3   | 28                    | 44.736                |

Of the four circuits listed in Table 6.2, only T1 and T3 circuits are offered as commercial leased-line services. Both T1 and T3 circuits can be ordered as channelized or nonchannelized circuits. You should order channelized circuits if you are using them to interconnect PBXs or similar equipment that requires 24 predefined time slots per DS1 signal to transport 1 digitized PCM voice channel per time slot. A channelized digital circuit is subdivided into a series of 64Kbps time slots developed to transport PCM digitized voice conversations. In comparison, nonchannelized circuits provide users with the full bandwidth for use by T1 or T3 multiplexers to subdivide and provide much greater flexibility for transporting data or a mixture of voice and data.

## Time-Division Multiplexing

The T1 multiplexer that evolved from channel banks represents one of the earliest types of TDMs. Until T1 lines were made available for use by commercial organizations, most TDMs were manufactured for use with analog leased lines or low-speed Dataphone Digital Service (DDS) digital transmission facilities. When a TDM is used with analog leased lines, the aggregate data rate of the TDM is normally limited to 28.8Kbps, whereas its use with DDS limits its aggregate data rate to 56Kbps. The 28.8Kbps operating-rate limitation on analog leased lines is a constraint resulting from the operating rate of leased-line modems. In comparison, the 56Kbps DDS operating-rate limitation is a service offering constraint.

Most communications networks used by organizations include several TDM systems that are used primarily because of economics. When one circuit and a pair of multiplexers replace two or more data circuits, the savings that accrue from the elimination of data lines usually can pay for the required equipment in less than a year.

## A Cost Comparison

To understand the rationale for using multiplexers, consider an example in which eight terminals located in San Francisco must communicate with a mainframe computer located in Chicago. If each terminal requires five hours of computer access per day and the cost of one hour of communications on the switched telephone network is $9, conventional dialing by each terminal operator to Chicago costs the organization $360 per day. If a month has 22 business days, the monthly cost for accessing the Chicago computer would be slightly less than $8,000, exclusive of the cost of the modems or DSUs used on the leased line routed between the two locations.

When terminal devices at one location require access to a computer at a second location, multiplexing should be considered. Figure 6.9 illustrates a network configuration that could be used to satisfy the San Francisco-to-Chicago communications requirements of the organization.

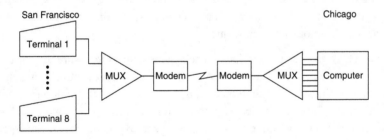

**FIGURE 6.9**

*Using multiplexers to reduce communications costs.*

Assuming that the cost of each multiplexer is $2,000 and the leased line costs $1,000 per month, during the first year, the multiplexing method would cost $16,000, exclusive of modems or DSUs. In the second year of operation, the cost of multiplexing would be reduced to $12,000, assuming that the equipment was purchased the first year. Thus, in this example, the two-year cost of multiplexing is $28,000. Because dialing without multiplexing would cost more than $190,000 during the two-year period, multiplexing results in substantial savings.

An additional cost-related reason for the use of multiplexers is the relative fixed cost associated with their use. Multiplexer systems are connected to one another by leased lines with rates that can increase slightly from year to year because of tariff changes. The cost of the multiplexer system is rather stable and predictable because the cost of the line is billed monthly based on the distance between locations and is not dependent on usage. In comparison, the cost of using the switched telephone network depends on many factors, including the duration of the call, the distance between calling and called parties, the day and time that the call was originated, and whether operator assistance was required. If only a few terminal users increase their connect time 15 minutes per day, the monthly cost of communications could substantially increase.

## Operation

A TDM, as its name implies, uses time as a reference for multiplexing data. To understand the operation of a TDM as well as the limitations associated with this technology, you'll examine how data from a few terminals or personal computers is multiplexed and demultiplexed. Figure 6.10 illustrates the multiplexing of data from three terminal devices at a remote location to a mainframe computer at another location. For simplicity of illustration, it was assumed that terminal 1 transmitted the character sequence BA, terminal 2 transmitted DC, and terminal 3 transmitted FE. The TDM at the remote location scans each port connected to a terminal for data, recognizing A, C, and E as input to ports 1, 2, and 3 of the multiplexer during the first scan. The TDM accepts data from each port and builds a multiplexing frame that represents the data from each port during the scan. Thus, frame 1 contains the character sequence ECA, and frame 2 contains FDB. In actuality, each TDM frame will also contain synchronization characters prefixing data, as well as data from one or more scans.

At the receiving TDM, the position of data in each frame is used to ensure the correct demultiplexing of data. As indicated in Figure 6.10, A is the first position of frame 1, which tells the TDM that that byte of information should be output onto port 1 of the multiplexer. Similarly, in frame 1, the characters C, which is located in the second position, and E, which is located in the third position, inform the multiplexer at the central site to output those characters onto ports 2 and 3, respectively. Next, the central site multiplexer examines the data in frame 2. Because B is in position 1, it is output onto port 1. Next, D and F, which are located in positions 2 and 3 of frame 2, are output onto ports 2 and 3. Thus, the TDM demultiplexing process depends on the position of data within each frame.

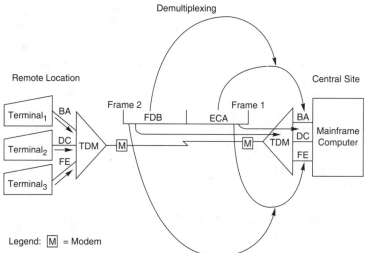

**FIGURE 6.10**

*Multiplexing and demultiplexing.*

To understand the limitation of the TDM process, consider the actual operation of terminal devices. Some terminal operators might be reading a manual, attempting to determine how to correct a programming error or how to respond to a message requesting a specific type of data entry. Other terminal operators might be diligently entering data or receiving information, while some operators might be on a coffee break or simply thinking about the response they should enter to an application program that they are accessing. Thus, at any instant, it is highly probable that there is no data-transmission activity from or destined to one or more terminal devices. Because a TDM demultiplexes by the position of data in each frame, the absence of activity could result in the misinterpretation of data. To prevent this problem from happening, a TDM inserts null characters in each frame anytime there is no activity when input from a port is sampled by the TDM scanning process.

At the receiving multiplexer, the null characters maintain the positioning within the frame required for correct demultiplexing. They are "stripped," however, by the receiving multiplexer and are not output to devices attached to the TDM.

Although the use of null characters ensures correct demultiplexing, it also indicates that the multiplexing process is not as efficient as it could be. For example, when several terminal users are on a break, are thinking, or are even entering data at a normal typing rate, most frames flowing between multiplexers contain a large percentage of null characters. Thus, for most periods, data transmission between TDMs is highly inefficient. Although a T1 multiplexer has the same inefficiency, its 1.544Mbps operating rate enables the transmission of up to hundreds of devices to be carried on one very high-speed line. In comparison, TDMs connected to analog or DDS circuits operating at much lower data rates are limited to supporting a much smaller population of devices. Thus, the inefficiency of TDMs is much more pronounced when used with analog or DDS transmission facilities. This inefficiency resulted in the development of a different type of multiplexer for use on those transmission facilities. This type of multiplexer, referred to as a statistical time-division multiplexer (STDM), provides a much higher level of line-utilization efficiency than TDMs and has essentially replaced the use of TDMs by many organizations.

# Statistical Time-Division Multiplexing

In comparison to TDMs, which use fixed frames with data positioned in each frame, STDMs use variable-length frames. To understand the operation of STDMs, you must understand how variable frames are created. This section covers one of several methods used to create variable positional information within a multiplexing frame.

## STDM Operation

To understand the operation of STDMs, assume that eight terminal devices are connected to a multiplexer, as illustrated in Figure 6.11a. Further assume that during one scan operation, terminals 1, 2, 3, and 6 were active and transmitted the characters X, Y, Z, and Q, respectively. If the STDM employs a bit-map character to denote the activity of each port during a scan, the multiplexer sets the bit position that corresponds to a port and a 1 if there is activity. Otherwise, a bit-map position setting of 0 indicates that no activity occurred on a port during the scan.

The frame construction example illustrated in Figure 6.11b indicates how the use of a bit map can reduce the size of a frame when some ports connected to the STDM are inactive. In this example, terminals 1, 2, 3, and 6 were active; hence, bit map positions 1, 2, 3, and 6 were set to ones. Therefore, the character from each terminal can be added after the bit map to form a variable-length frame, and null characters are not required because the bit map indicates the actual position of each character in the frame.

In general, an STDM can double to quadruple the number of asynchronous data sources serviced by a conventional TDM. This additional servicing capability is known as the multiplexer's service ratio. In addition to taking advantage of idle times, the STDM strips start, stop, and parity bits from each asynchronous character before transmission and "rebuilds" the character when it is demultiplexed. Some STDMs add data compression to a list of functions that they perform, further increasing their service ratio.

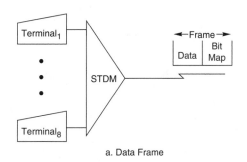

a. Data Frame

| Terminal | Terminal Activity | Frame | |
|---|---|---|---|
| 1 | X | 00100111 | Bit Map |
| 2 | Y | X | Frame |
| 3 | Z | Y | Data |
| 4 | No Activity | Z | |
| 5 | No Activity | Q | |
| 6 | Q | | |
| 7 | No Activity | | |
| 8 | No Activity | | |

b. Frame Construction

**FIGURE 6.11**

*STDM operation.*

## Service Ratio

To understand the concept of an STDM's service ratio, first consider Figure 6.12a, which illustrates the use of a conventional TDM connected to a modem operating at 9600bps. When a conventional TDM is used to multiplex data, the aggregate input data rate cannot exceed the output data rate. Hence, up to eight terminals operating at 1200bps could be serviced by the TDM, resulting in a total input of $8 \times 1200$, or 9600bps, which is equal to the line operating rate.

If the STDM's service ratio is 2, on the average it can service an aggregate input twice that of the line operating rate, or 19,200bps. The term "on the average" is used because, during a long period, some terminals are powered off and unused, some terminal operators are thinking about what to do next, and other terminal operators are entering data or receiving responses to their queries. Due to the previously explained STDM functions, over a prolonged period, the multiplexer can accept an input data rate of twice its output rate.

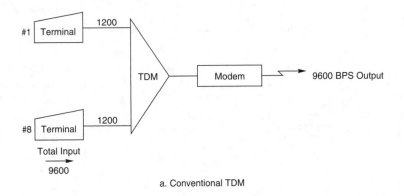

a. Conventional TDM

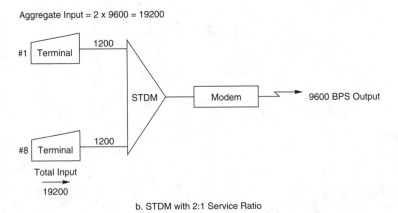

b. STDM with 2:1 Service Ratio

**FIGURE 6.12**

*STDM service ratio.*

Consider a worst-case scenario in which each terminal is a personal computer and every terminal operator attempts to transmit a large file at the same time. In this situation, the total input to the STDM reaches 19,200bps, and the multiplexer cannot take advantage of idle times because each terminal is transmitting a continuous sequence of data. Even after stripping start, stop, and parity bits, the aggregate input data rate exceeds the line operating rate. Although the STDM contains a buffer area, as each terminal continues to transmit data, the buffer area would eventually fill and overflow, resulting in a loss of data. To prevent the loss of data, the STDM initiates flow control to turn off one or more devices whenever its buffer reaches a certain level of occupancy. Then, as data from its buffer is transmitted onto the line and the level of buffer occupancy decreases to a certain level, the STDM turns off flow control, allowing devices connected to the multiplexer to resume transmission.

Because STDMs can service, on average, two to four times the aggregate data rate of the line-connecting multiplexers, they have been widely accepted by most organizations. By 1990, almost 80 percent of all TDMs incorporated a statistical multiplexing process. Convention TDMs are primarily used in cases where the delays caused by flow control cannot be tolerated. An example of this would be T1 multiplexers, where a delay in voice transmissions would be annoying.

Similar to the manner in which STDMs replaced TDMs, routers are replacing STDMs. Although some STDMs include a limited routing capability, they are difficult to use to form a complex network structure. In addition, routers commonly support LAN connections, while STDMs are primarily designed to support direct or dial-in terminal connections. Today the primary use of STDMs are for devices that add a low-speed voice-multiplexing capability and operate on point-to-point circuits linking branch offices to a regional office.

# Low-Speed Voice/Data Multiplexers

Combining the operational capability of TDM and statistical time-division multiplexers resulted in a new type of multiplexer for use by organizations requiring the transport of both voice and data. Known as a low-speed voice/data multiplexer, this device was developed for organizations that required the use of a few voice and data circuits between two locations. As such, this device fills a rapidly expanding market for organizations with small branch offices that require both voice and data communications capability to a regional office of company headquarters. Because the key to the operation of this multiplexer is its capability to digitize voice at data rates significantly below the PCM operating rate of 64Kbps, you will first focus on a few of the methods used by this class of communications equipment to digitize voice conversations through voice compression.

## Voice-Digitization Methods

Over the past 40 years, a large number of voice-digitization techniques have been developed. These techniques can be placed into three general categories: waveform coding, voice coding, and hybrid coding. This section discusses each category, as well as a few of the techniques that fall into each category of voice digitization.

### Waveform Coding

Waveform-coding methods involve the analog waveform only, converting each sample into a discrete value and coding the value. This type of voice-digitization method usually requires the most bandwidth to transport a digitized conversation but provides the highest quality of reconstructed voice. Waveform coding methods include PCM, ADPCM, and CVSD, and are usually referred to as *toll-quality reproduced speech*.

## Voice Coding

Voice coding, which is also referred to as *vocoding*, represents a technique in which the voice signal is analyzed and speech parameters are extracted to model small time periods of a voice conversation. Parameters modeled can include speech energy, inflection, tone, and the manner by which voiced and unvoiced sounds are produced.

Voice coding usually results in a very low voice-digitization rate; however, the quality of reproduced speech may appear metallic. One of the more popular voice-coding methods is linear predictive coding, which samples 20ms segments of speech and encodes the parameters necessary for speech reproduction into a 2400bps or 4800bps data stream.

During the 1970s and 1980s, voice-coding devices were commonly employed on international portions of private networks and enabled organizations to transport as many as four simultaneous conversations on a multiplexed analog circuit operating at 9600bps. Although vocoders were popularly used on international circuits, their high cost precluded their use on national circuits.

## Hybrid Coding

Recognizing the shortcomings of waveform and voice-coding techniques, engineers went back to the drawing board and combined the best features of each to produce a series of hybrid coding techniques. Hybrid coders first sample the voice waveform. Next, like vocoders, they analyze the sample. However, instead of immediately transmitting analyzed speech parameters, a hybrid coder uses those parameters to synthesize speech and compares the synthesized sample to the actual sample. By rapidly adjusting one or more speech parameters, they construct a better model. Hybrid codes combine the best features of waveform and voice coding to generate high-quality low-bit-rate digitized voice.

Currently more than 10 popular hybrid coding methods are in use. Perhaps the most popular one is General Systems for Mobile (GSM), which is used to digitize GSM cellular communications. A popular family of hybrid coders known as Coded Excited Linear Prediction (CELP) was recently standardized by the ITU. CELP supports digitized data rates from as low as approximately 5Kbps to 16Kbps. Members of the CELP family create a codebook of speech and periodically transmit the entry number in the codebook instead of several speech parameters, further reducing the data-transmission rate.

Although hybrid coders were considered more than a decade ago, it was the recent development of 200 million instructions per second and faster digital signal processor (DSP) chips that made their development practical. Today different members of the CELP family of hybrid coders are being incorporated into multiplexers, Frame Relay access devices (FRADs), and voice gateways to provide high-quality low-bit-rate digitized voice transmission over private networks, Frame Relay networks, and the Internet.

# Adaptive Differential Pulse-Code Modulation (ADPCM)

ADPCM is a voice-digitization and compression technique that reduces PCM 8-bit samples to 4-bit words, in which each 4-bit word represents 16 quantization levels. Those levels, which represent sample amplitudes under PCM, represent the difference between successive samples under ADPCM. They permit a digitization data rate of 32Kbps rather than the 64Kbps operating rate required by PCM.

The key to the operation of ADPCM is the fact that the amplitude of voice does not rapidly change when sampled 8,000 times per second. This enabled engineers to design adaptive predictor circuitry into ADPCM equipment that anticipates the value of the next sample based on the level of the previously sampled signal. A feedback loop used by the predictor minimizes the possibility of deviations between samples. Because this technique results in a very accurate prediction value, the difference between the predicted and the actual signal is relatively small, enabling it to be encoded through the use of 4 bits. If successive samples increase in their value difference, the adaptive predictor adapts to this change by increasing the range represented by the 4 bits. This adaptation process decreases the signal-to-noise ratio, however, and reduces the accuracy of the decoded signal. For normal voice conversations, ADPCM provides a voice quality that is most difficult to differentiate from a PCM digitized voice conversation.

The key difference between ADPCM and PCM lies in the area of modem transmission support. PCM can support modems operating at data rates up to 33.6Kbps. In comparison, due to the use of an adaptive predictor, ADPCM is limited to supporting modem rates up to 9.6Kbps. At higher operating rates, the modem signal changes too fast to be accurately predicted by ADPCM, resulting in an increase in transmission errors as the modem operating rate increases. Thus, ADPCM is primarily used in private networks that can restrict the use of voice channels to ADPCM digitized voice and other channels to data. In comparison, communications carriers normally cannot restrict the use of the switched telephone network to modems that operate at or below 9600Kbps, which explains why most carriers use PCM equipment to digitize voice communications for transportation over the switched telephone network.

Currently several ADPCM methods are relatively similar to that just described. Although many communications carriers use 32Kbps ADPCM on international circuits, other standardized versions of this voice-digitization technique support data rates of 40Kbps and 16Kbps. As you might surmise, a 40Kbps rate produces a better quality of reproduced voice than the 16Kbps operating rate does.

# Continuously Variable Slope Delta Modulation (CVSD)

Continuously Variable Slope Data (CVSD) modulation is a voice-digitization technique originally developed for military use. This digitization technique has gained acceptance in the commercial market as a mechanism for digitizing voice at a low data rate.

UNDERSTANDING DATA COMMUNICATIONS

The key to the operation of CVSD is the fact that the higher the rate is at which an analog signal is sampled, the smaller the resulting difference between sampled amplitudes will be. This means that at a high enough sampling rate, the difference between sampled amplitudes can be represented by a single bit. That bit represents the change in the slope of the analog voice conversation. The bit is set to 1 to represent an increase in the slope between two samples, or 0 to represent a decrease in the slope. Figure 6.13 illustrates the operation of CVSD.

CVSD commonly operates at 32KB and 16KB samples per second, resulting in digitization rates of 32Kbps and 16Kbps. At 16Kbps, CVSD is four times as efficient with respect to its data rate than PCM and twice as efficient as ADPCM. However, because it uses only a single bit to represent a change in slope, CVSD is not recommended for use by modems transmitting data.

Although CVSD is not to be used for transporting modulated data, its capability to represent a voice conversation at a low data rate resulted in the use of this technique as well as ADPCM as a mechanism to transport digitized voice by low-speed voice/data multiplexers.

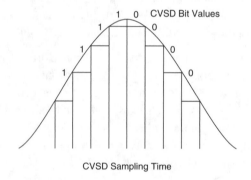

**FIGURE 6.13**

*Under CVSD, an increase in the slope of the sampled conversation is represented by a 1, and a decrease in the slope is represented by a 0.*

## Using a Voice/Data Multiplexer

As previously noted, a low-speed voice/data multiplexer can be considered a combination TDM and statistical time-division multiplexer. The TDM portion of the device is used exclusively for multiplexing two or more digitized voice conversations onto a fixed portion of the operating rate of the high-speed line that the multiplexer is connected to. Although the term *high-speed line* is used, the operating rate of the composite channel of the voice/data multiplexer is typically 56 or 64Kbps—relatively low in comparison to a T1 multiplexer. This explains why this voice/data multiplexer is commonly referred to as a low-speed voice/data multiplexer. For example, a low-speed voice/data multiplexer connected to a 64Kbps digital leased line might multiplex three voice conversations using CVSD onto 48Kbps of the 64Kbps leased line. The statistical time-division multiplexer would then contend with one or more data sources for the remaining 16Kbps operating rate of the leased line.

Figure 6.14 illustrates the bandwidth allocation of a 64Kbps digital leased line based on the previously mentioned scenario. In this example, each voice conversation is digitized and is always placed into a fixed slot of 16Kbps. In comparison, data sources contend for the remaining 16Kbps. This technique ensures that each voice-digitized signal is always carried by the multiplexer and eliminates potential delays from the statistical-multiplexing process that could cause havoc to a reconstructed voice conversation.

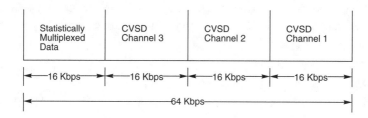

**FIGURE 6.14**

*Potential voice/data multiplexer bandwidth allocation.*

To illustrate the potential use of low-speed voice/data multiplexers in an organizational environment, assume that a branch office and a regional office each have a PBX. Also assume that branch office employees regularly converse with persons at a regional office and have between one and three simultaneous calls between offices during normal business hours. Also assume that 10 low-speed (2400bps) terminals in the regional office require access to a computer located in the regional office.

Figure 6.15 illustrates, as a network diagram schematic, the use of a pair of low-speed voice/data multiplexers between branch and regional offices to consolidate both voice and data communications requirements between the two locations onto one 64Kbps digital circuit. In this example, each PBX has three lines routed into a data/voice multiplexer installed at each office. Through the use of CVSD adapter cards installed in both multiplexers, each voice conversation will be digitized into a fixed 16Kbps time slot, as previously illustrated in Figure 6.14. The 10 2400bps terminals illustrated in the lower-left portion of Figure 6.15 would be statistically multiplexed into a fixed 16Kbps time slot, as previously illustrated in Figure 6.14. If all 10 terminals were transmitting files to the computer in the regional office, the aggregate terminal data rate of 24Kbps would exceed the capacity of the fixed 16Kbps time slot. If this situation or another situation occurs in which enough terminals become active that their aggregate transmission exceeds the fixed 16Kbps time slot, the multiplexer issues flow control to inhibit one or more data sources from transmitting.

Although flow control affects only the throughput of data, its use on voice traffic would result in random voice delays that would be entirely unacceptable for conducting a conversation. Thus, a voice/data multiplexer uses TDM for multiplexing voice conversations and STDM onto a fixed time slot for multiplexing data.

From an economic perspective, a voice/data multiplexer can pay for itself in as little time as one or two months. Of course, the actual payback period depends on the distance between locations, current and anticipated switched-telephone-network usage, the number of voice and data sources to be multiplexed, and the cost of voice/data multiplexers.

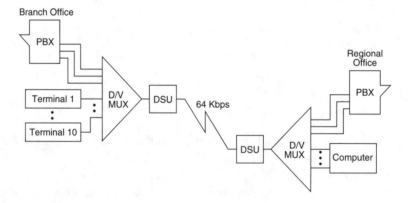

**FIGURE 6.15**

*Using low-speed voice/data multiplexers.*

# What You Have Learned

- Multiplexing is the process of sharing the use of a transmission facility by time or by frequency.
- The conversion of most long-distance communications carrier transmission facilities from analog to digital resulted in a large replacement of FDM by TDM systems.
- To faithfully reproduce an analog signal, it must be sampled at a rate equal to twice the bandwidth that it occupies.

- Repeaters regenerate digital pulses, removing any previous distortion. In comparison, amplifiers boost the strength of analog signals, including increasing any previous distortion.

- Framing is used to provide a method of synchronization between channel banks.

- D4 framing is restricted to providing synchronization data, whereas ESF framing enables the flow of performance-measurement information as well as synchronization data.

- The extended superframe framing format results in the transmission of data bits, error link bits, and a framing pattern in each series of 24 F bits.

- Bipolar transmission allows a digital signal and power to be carried on the same line and separated from one another by the use of transformers.

- A minimum number of binary ones, known as ones density, must occur on a digital transmission line to enable repeaters to get timing from data.

- Intentional bipolar violations, which occur when two successive marks have the same polarity, can be used to convey information or maintain a minimum ones density on a digital transmission facility.

- In the North American digital transmission hierarchy, the T1 and T3 circuits are the only ones commonly made available to customers.

- When no activity occurs on a TDM input port, the multiplexer inserts a null character into the frame it builds. This character maintains the correct positioning of data from all ports, enabling the demultiplexing by position of data within a frame.

- Similar to the manner by which statistical time-division multiplexers (STDMs) replaced the use of many applications that used TDMs, routers are now replacing the use of STDMs.

- Three general categories of voice digitization include waveform coding, voice coding, and hybrid coding.

- ADPCM and CVSD enable voice conversations to be digitized at data rates one-half to one-fourth that of PCM.

- A voice/data multiplexer uses time-division multiplexing to support multiple voice conversations and uses statistical time-division multiplexing to support multiple data sources.

# Quiz for Chapter 6

1. What is multiplexing?

   A. The process of increasing bandwidth on a channel

   B. A technique that enables more than one data source to share the use of a common line

   C. Mailing letters at the post office

   D. The capability to share frequency by time

2. Which of the following is one reason that frequency-division multiplexing has essentially been replaced by time-division multiplexing?

   A. There is more time than frequency.

   B. It is difficult to place channels side by side.

   C. Noise is amplified with voice when an FDM system is used.

   D. Most available frequencies have been used.

3. When the amplitude of pulses is varied to represent analog information, it is called what?

   A. PCM

   B. PWM

   C. PAM

   D. PPM

4. The PCM sampling rate is 8,000 samples per second because

   A. That represents the maximum rate that the technology supports.

   B. This rate allows unique values.

   C. This rate allows the faithful reconstruction of an analog signal.

   D. This rate is easily produced by a sampling chip.

5. In general, why does digital transmission provide a higher level of signal quality than analog transmission?

   A. Repeaters regenerate digital pulses and remove distortion, whereas amplifiers increase an analog signal, including any previous distortion to the signal.

   B. Digital signals are smaller than analog signals and cannot be easily distorted.

   C. Analog signals are continuous and are not easily distorted.

   D. Digital signals are easier to sample than analog signals.

6. The D4 framing pattern contains a sequence of

    A. 24 bits.

    B. 4 terminal and 8 framing bits.

    C. 8 terminal and 4 framing bits.

    D. 12 bits.

7. The ESF framing pattern operates at what rate?

    A. 6Kbps

    B. 8Kbps

    C. 10Kbps

    D. 12Kbps

8. How many of the 24 bits in the EFS framing pattern are used for the error link?

    A. 4

    B. 6

    C. 12

    D. 24

9. Bipolar signaling is used in place of unipolar signaling on T1 lines because

    A. Bipolar signaling produces twice as many marks as a unipolar signal.

    B. It allows transmission at polar locations.

    C. Bipolar signaling reduces residual DC voltage buildup, allowing a digital signal to be separated from power through the use of a transformer.

    D. It allows transformers to be spaced far from one another, which reduces the cost of transmission.

10. B7 zero code suppression is a technique that

    A. Allows data to flow on a digital line.

    B. Ensures that each byte has at least one mark bit.

    C. Is the latest clear channel encoding technique developed by Bell Laboratories.

    D. Provides a clear-channel transmission capability, allowing 64Kbps data transmission on a voice channel.

11. Intentional bipolar violations

    A. Represent coding errors caused by line impairments.

    B. Are used to convey information or maintain a minimum number of ones on a digital line.

    C. Result in successive marks having opposite polarities.

    D. Occur only in the laboratory.

12. How many DS1 signals are carried within a DS3 signal?

    A. 28

    B. 14

    C. 7

    D. 3

13. Demultiplexing by a time-division multiplexer occurs based on which of the following?

    A. The position of data within a frame

    B. The position of a frame within a group of frames

    C. The activity of a connected device

    D. The priority assigned to a connected device

14. Which of the following is the key to the operation of ADPCM?

    A. Fast sampling

    B. High amplitude

    C. Adaptive predictor

    D. Digitization

15. What is the maximum modem operating rate that can be transported by ADPCM?

    A. 300bps

    B. 1200bps

    C. 4800bps

    D. 9600bps

16. Which of the following usually produces high-bit-rate, high-quality reproduced voice?

    A. Waveform coding

    B. Voice doing

    C. Data coding

    D. Sample coding

17. Which of the following usually produces low-bit-rate, high-quality reproduced voice?

    A. Waveform coding

    B. Voice coding

    C. Data coding

    D. Sample coding

18. The higher the rate of an analog signal that is sampled,

    A. The smaller the difference will be between sampled amplitudes.

    B. The larger the difference will be between sampled amplitudes.

    C. The greater the noise level will be.

    D. The more bits will be required to represent the sample.

19. Common CVSD digitization rates are

    A. 8 and 64Kbps.

    B. 64 and 128Kbps.

    C. 4 and 8Kbps.

    D. 32 and 16Kbps.

20. A voice/data multiplexer will not provide flow control for which of the following?

    A. Voice

    B. Data

    C. Time slots

    D. Odd channels

# Fiber-Optic and Satellite Communications

## IN THIS CHAPTER

This chapter is about two communications technologies that provide the potential to revolution-ize the manner by which we communicate: fiber-optic and satellite communications. Although both technologies date to the 1960s, only within the past decade have they been extensively used for communications. This chapter details some of the history of the development of both forms of communications and explains why these techniques generate so much excitement in the communications world. First you will examine why fiber-optic systems work and will learn some of the terms used to describe their operation. Some current terrestrial and undersea fiber-optic systems will be described. Later you will look at the application of fiber optics to local area data networks. Finally, you will study some of the techniques and considerations in trans-mitting data via geostationary and low Earth orbit satellites.

## Introduction and Historical Perspective

Alexander Graham Bell was a very curious and inventive man. In 1880, four years after he invented the telephone, he patented an "apparatus for signaling and communicating, called Photophone." This device, illustrated in Figure 7.1, transmitted a voice signal over a distance of 2000 meters using a beam of sunlight as the carrier. As he spoke into the Photophone, the speaking trumpet vibrated the mirror, varying the light energy that reflected onto the photo-voltaic cell. The electric current produced by the cell varied in conjunction with the varying light energy.

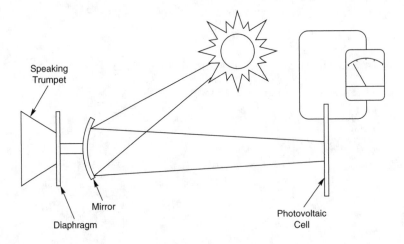

**FIGURE 7.1**

*The Photophone demonstrates basic principles of optical transmission.*

The Photophone demonstrated the basic principle of optical communications as it is practiced today. The two requirements for commercial success, however, were almost a hundred years

Fiber-Optic and Satellite Communications

CHAPTER 7

307

7

FIBER-OPTIC AND
SATELLITE
COMMUNICATIONS

away. These requirements were a powerful and reliable light source and a reliable and low-cost medium for transmission.

In 1960, the laser was recognized as the long-sought light source, and systems were tried using both the atmosphere and beam waveguides as the transmission media. The application of a glass fiber with a cladding was proposed in 1966, and by 1970, fibers with losses of only 20 decibels per kilometer (dB/km) were demonstrated. Since then, progress in the invention and application of fiber optics has been startling. Fibers with losses of less than 0.2dB/km have been demonstrated in the laboratory (in 1979) and by the new millennium were commonly employed by communications carriers, along with systems that can transmit at data rates at 10 billion bits per second (Gbps) over distances in excess of 100km without repeaters or amplifiers. Advances in fiber optics began to threaten to make satellite systems obsolete for some kinds of communications (point-to-point where large bandwidths are required, such as transoceanic telephone systems) only 15 years after the satellite systems were commercially employed as the communications systems of the future. Today modern optical fibers are capable of transporting information at data rates exceeding 40Gbps. In fact, applying the principle of frequency-division multiplexing to light in the form of wavelength-division multiplexing (WDM) enables a single fiber to transport up to 10 multi-Gbps transmissions while dense WDM (DWDM) systems now enable 64 or more multi-Gbps transmissions to flow over a common optical fiber as thick as a strand of hair! To put this in context with something that we might appreciate, this is equivalent to transporting the contents of the Library of Congress in perhaps a second!

Optical-fiber transmission has come of age as a major innovation in telecommunications. Such systems offer extremely high bandwidth, freedom from external interference, immunity from interception by external means, and cheap raw materials (silicon, the most abundant material on Earth).

# Fundamentals of Fiber-Optic Systems

Optical fibers guide light rays within the fiber material. They can do this because light rays bend or change direction when they pass from one medium to another. They bend because the speed of propagation of light in each medium is different. This phenomenon is called refraction. One common example of refraction occurs when you stand at the edge of a pool and look at an object at the bottom of the pool. Unless you are directly over the object, as shown in Figure 7.2a, it appears to be farther away than it really is, as indicated in Figure 7.2b. This effect occurs because the speed of the light rays from the object increases as the light rays pass from the water to the air. This causes them to bend, changing the angle at which you perceive the object. You can obtain an appreciation for the manner by which light flows by focusing upon Snell's Law.

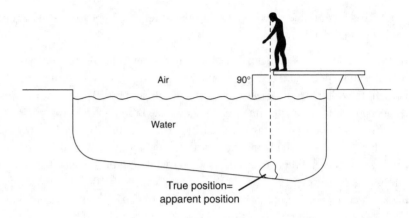

a. View from directly above

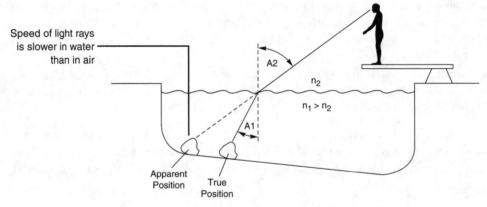

b. View from an angle

**FIGURE 7.2**

*Bending of light rays.*

# Snell's Law

How optical fibers work can be explained by Snell's Law, which states that the ratio of the sine of the angle of incidence to the sine of the angle of refraction is equal to the ratio of the propagation velocities of the wave in the two respective media. This is equal to a constant that is the ratio of the refractive index of the second medium to that of the first. Written as an equation, Snell's Law looks like this:

$$\frac{\sin A_1}{\sin A_2} = \frac{V_1}{V_2} = K = \frac{n_2}{n_1}$$

In this equation,

A₁ and A₂ are the angles of incidence and refraction, respectively.

V₁ and V₂ are the velocities of propagation of the wave in the two media.

n₁ and n₂ are the indices of refraction of the two media.

The parameters are demonstrated graphically in Figure 7.3. In each case, A₁ is the angle of incidence, and A₂ is the angle of refraction. The index of refraction of material ₁, n₁, is greater than the index of refraction of material ₂, n₂. This means that the velocity of propagation of light is greater in material ₂ than in material ₁.

Figure 7.3a demonstrates how a light ray passing from material ₁ to material ₂ is refracted in material ₂ when A₁ is less than the critical angle. Figure 7.3b demonstrates the condition that exists when A₁ is at the critical angle and the angle A₂ is at 90[dg]. The light ray is directed along the boundary between the two materials.

As shown in Figure 7.3c, any light rays that are incident at angles greater than A₁ of Figure 7.3b will be reflected back into material ₁ with angle A₂ equal to angle A₁. The condition in Figure 7.3c is the one of particular interest for optical fibers, and it is discussed further in later sections of this chapter.

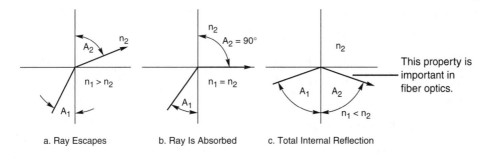

a. Ray Escapes      b. Ray Is Absorbed      c. Total Internal Reflection

**FIGURE 7.3**
*The index of refraction.*

## Fiber Composition

An optical fiber is a dielectric (nonconductor of electricity) waveguide made of glass or plastic. As shown in Figure 7.4, it consists of three distinct regions: a core, the cladding, and a sheath or jacket. The sheath or jacket protects the fiber but does not govern the transmission capability of the fiber.

**UNDERSTANDING DATA COMMUNICATIONS**

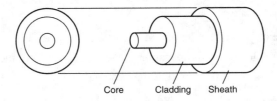

Core          Cladding      Sheath

## FIGURE 7.4
*Optical-fiber construction.*

The index of refraction of the assembly varies across the radius of the cable, and the core has a constant or smoothly varying index of refraction called nc. The cladding region has another constant index of refraction called n. The core possesses a high refractive index, whereas the cladding is constructed to have a lower refractive index. The result of the difference in the refractive indices keeps light flowing through the core after it gets into the core, even if the fiber is bent or tied into a knot. For a fiber designed to carry light in several modes of propagation at the same time (called a multimode fiber), the diameter of the core is several times the wavelength of the light to be carried. Wavelength is a measure of the distance between two cycles of the same wave measured in nanometers (nm), or billionths of a meter, and the cladding thickness will be greater than the radius of the core. Following are some typical values for a multimode fiber:

- An operating light wavelength of 0.8 micrometers($\mu$m)
- A core index of refraction nc of 1.5
- A cladding index of refraction n of 1.485 (=0.99 × nc)
- A core diameter of 50, 62.5, or 100$\mu$m
- A cladding thickness of 37.5$\mu$m

The clad fiber would have a diameter of 125$\mu$m, and light would propagate as shown in Figure 7.5.

A light source emits light at many angles relative to the center of the fiber. In Figure 7.5, light ray A enters the fiber perpendicular to the face of the core and parallel to the axis. Its angle of incidence $A_1$ is 0; therefore, it is not refracted, and it travels parallel to the axis. Light ray B enters the fiber core from air ($n_1 = {}_1$) at an angle of incidence of $A_{1B}$ and is refracted at an angle $A_{2B}$ because $n_2$ is greater than $n_1$. When light ray B strikes the boundary between the core and the cladding, its angle of incidence, $A_1'_B$, is greater than the critical angle. Therefore, the angle of refraction, $A_2'_B$, is equal to $A_1'_B$, and the light ray is refracted back into the core. The ray propagates in this zigzag fashion down the core until it reaches the other end.

If the angle of incidence, $A_{1C}$, is too large, as it is for light ray C, the light ray strikes the boundary between the core and the cladding with an angle of incidence, $A_1'_C$, less than the critical angle. The ray enters into the cladding and propagates into, or is absorbed into, the cladding and jacket (which is opaque to light).

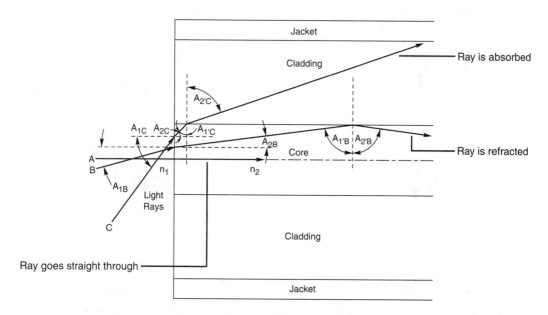

**FIGURE 7.5**

*Light ray paths in multimode fiber.*

## Modal Delay

For optical fibers in which the diameter of the core is many times the wavelength of the light transmitted, the light beam travels along the fiber by bouncing back and forth at the interface between the core and the cladding. Rays entering the fiber at differing angles are refracted varying numbers of times as they move from one end to the other and consequently do not arrive at the distant end with the same phase relationship as when they started. The differing angles of entry are called modes of propagation (or just modes), and a fiber carrying several modes is called a multimode fiber. Multimode propagation causes the rays leaving the fiber to interfere both constructively and destructively as they leave the end of the fiber. This effect is called modal delay spreading.

Because most optical communications systems transmit information in digital form consisting of pulses of light, the effect of modal delay spreading limits the capability of the fiber to transport recognizable pulses. This is because modal delay spreading broadens the pulses in the time domain, as illustrated in Figure 7.6. The effect of pulse spreading is to make it difficult or impossible for an optical receiver to differentiate one pulse from another after a given transmission distance. Thus, after a predefined transmission distance, a multimode fiber either causes a very high error rate or precludes the capability of the pulse to be recognized and terminates the capability of the cable to be used for communications.

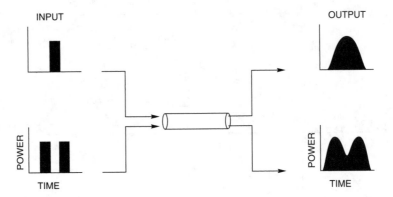

**FIGURE 7.6**

*Pulse spreading.*

If the diameter of the fiber core is only a few times the wavelength of the transmitted light (say, a factor of 3), only one ray or mode will be propagated, and no destructive interference between rays will occur. These fibers, called single-mode fibers, are the media that are used in most transmission systems. Figures 7.7a and 7.7b show the distribution of the index of refraction across, and typical diameters of, multimode and single-mode fibers. One of the principal differences between single-mode and multimode fibers is that most of the power in the multimode fiber travels in the core, whereas, in single-mode fibers, a large fraction of the power is propagated in the cladding near the core. At the point where the light wavelength becomes long enough to cause single-mode propagation, about 20 percent of the power is carried in the cladding, but if the light wavelength is doubled, more than 50 percent of the power travels in the cladding.

## Refractive Index

Fiber can also be classified by its type of refractive index. Figure 7.7 illustrates a few of the classifications, which are outlined here:

- Stepped index fiber—The fiber core has a uniform refractive index throughout with a sudden change of the refractive index at the core-cladding boundary.
- Graded index fiber—The fiber core has a refractive index that gradually decreases as the distance from the center of the fiber increases.

- Single-mode fiber—Also known as monomode, this has a uniform refractive index. This type of fiber permits only a single light ray to pass through the cable.

- Graded index multimode fiber—The index of refraction varies smoothly across the diameter of the core but remains constant in the cladding. This treatment reduces the intermodal dispersion by the fiber because rays traveling along a graded-index fiber have nearly equal delays.

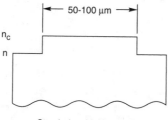

a. Step Index, Multimode Fiber

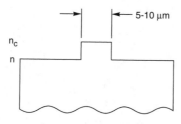

b. Step Index, Single-Mode Fiber

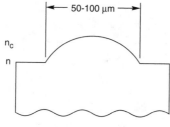

c. Graded Index, Multimode Fiber

**FIGURE 7.7**

*Refractive index profiles.*

Other refractive-index profiles have been devised to solve various problems, such as reduction of chromatic dispersion. Some of these profiles are shown in Figure 7.8; the step and graded profiles are repeated for comparison.

Figure 7.9 compares the flow of light through step-index, graded-index, and single-mode fiber. A step-index fiber typically has a core diameter between 100μm and 500μm. A graded-index fiber commonly has a core diameter of 50μm or 62.5μm, while single-mode fibers have core diameters between 8 and 10μm. Both stepped-index and graded-index fiber support multimode transmission.

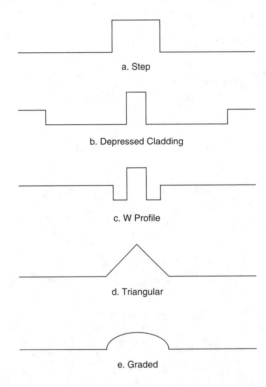

a. Step

b. Depressed Cladding

c. W Profile

d. Triangular

e. Graded

**FIGURE 7.8**
*Different refractive index profiles for optical fibers.*

# Bandwidth

The limitations on bandwidth in fiber-optic systems arise from two main sources: modal delay spreading and material dispersion. Modal delay spreading, which was previously described, is evident primarily in multimode fibers. Material dispersion arises from the variation in the velocity of light through the fiber with the wavelength of the light.

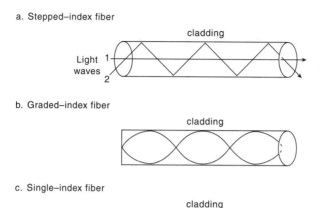

**FIGURE 7.9**

*Light flow through different refractive index fibers.*

If the light source, such as a light-emitting diode (LED), emits pulses of light at more than one wavelength, the different wavelengths travel at different velocities through the fiber. This causes spreading of the pulses. At a typical LED wavelength of 0.8μm, the delay variation is about 100 picoseconds (ps) per nanometer (nm) per kilometer. If the width of the spectrum emitted by the LED is 50nm, pulses from the source are spread by 5 nanoseconds (ns) per kilometer. This limits the modulation bandwidth product to about 50 to 100MHz/km. Fortunately, at certain wavelengths (near 1.3 and 1.5μm for some types of fibers), there is a null in the material dispersion curve, giving much better modulation bandwidth performance. Figure 7.10 shows the relationship of loss in doped silicon glass fibers versus light wavelength. Most development work was aimed at making fibers, light sources, and detectors that work well at the loss nulls at 1.3 and 1.5μm.

## Reading Cable Measurements

When examining fiber cable, you will commonly note a dual numeric specified for the fiber, such as 62.5/125. The first number references the core size, and the second number references the cladding diameter in microns. Three common multimode fiber cables in use are 62.5/125, 50/125, and 100/140.

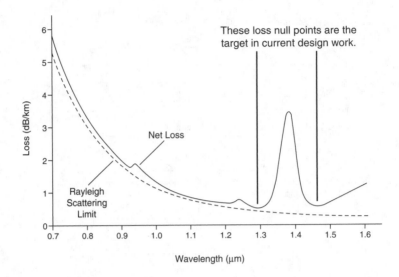

**FIGURE 7.10**

*The net spectral loss curve for a glass core.*

# Attenuation

The loss in signal power as the light travels down the fiber is called attenuation. Attenuation in the fibers is controlled mainly by four factors: radiation of the propagated light, called scattering; conversion of the light energy to heat, called absorption; connection losses at splices and joints in the fiber; and losses at bends in the fiber.

## Scattering Losses

Scattering occurs due to microscopic imperfections in the fiber, such as the inclusion of water in the glass. The effect of impurities in the transmission medium is evident when we look up at the sky and see a blue color. In fact, deep space has no color (appears as black), but due to the scattering of sunlight by the dust in the atmosphere, the sky appears bright blue.

There is a limit below which scattering cannot be reduced, no matter how perfectly the glass fiber is made, because of irregularities in the molecular structure of glass. This limit, called the Rayleigh scattering limit, has a strong wavelength dependence (1/l4). Thus, as the wavelength of the light source increases, the effect of Rayleigh scattering on optical loss is reduced. This effect is shown graphically in Figure 7.10. For light with a wavelength of 0.8µm, it is about 2.9dB/km. At a wavelength of 1.3µm, the value is about 0.3dB/km, and at 1.55µm wavelength, the limit is about 0.15dB/km. Commercially available glass fibers exhibit losses of about 3.5dB/km at 0.8µm, and 0.7 to 1.5dB/km at 1.3 and 1.5µm. There is less attenuation through 6

Fiber-Optic and Satellite Communications

CHAPTER 7

317

7

FIBER-OPTIC AND
SATELLITE
COMMUNICATIONS

meters (about 20 feet) of good quality optical-fiber glass than through an ordinary clean window pane.

## Absorption Losses

Absorption refers to the conversion of the power in the light beam to heat in some material or imperfection that is partially or completely opaque. This property is useful, as in the jacket of the fiber, to keep the light from escaping the cable, but it is a problem when it occurs as inclusions or imperfections in the fiber. Current fiber-optic systems are designed to minimize intrinsic absorption by transmitting at 0.8, 1.3, and 1.5μm, where there are reductions in the absorption curve for light.

## Connection Losses

Connection losses are inevitable. They represent a large source of loss in commercial fiber-optic systems. In addition to the installation connections, repair connections will be required because experience has shown that a typical line will be broken accidentally two or three times per kilometer over a 30-year period. The alignment of optical fibers required at each connection is a considerable mechanical feat. The full effect of the connection is not achieved unless the parts are aligned correctly. The ends of the fibers must be parallel within 1° or less, and the core must be concentric with the cladding to within 0.5μm. Production techniques have been developed to splice single-mode fibers whose total diameter is less than 10μm by using a mounting fixture and small electric heater.

The heater is usually an electric arc that softens two butted fiber ends and allows the fibers to be fused together. Due to the cost of an electric arc and the time required to let the heated ends cool, other methods to connect broken fibers, such as mechanical splices and couplers, are more commonly used. Mechanical splicing is based on the use of a mechanical clamp to permanently splice together two fibers. This task is accomplished with a portable workstation that is used to prepare each fiber end. That preparation includes stripping a thin layer of plastic coating from the fiber core before its splicing. The typical mechanical splice loss is approximately .15dB. In comparison, the use of a connector enables fibers to be glued to the device by a special epoxy after each fiber is stripped to its proper dimension. The connector provides a splice that joins the two fibers to enable light to pass from one fiber to the other. Although connector loss can range from .25 to 1.5dB, use of connectors is preferred for many labor-intensive applications because the process is relatively quick and can usually be accomplished in 30 minutes or less with a minimal amount of equipment.

## Bending Losses

Bending an optical fiber is akin to playing crack-the-whip with the light rays. As light travels around the bend, the light on the outside of the bend must travel faster to maintain a constant phase across the wave. As the radius of the bend is decreased, a point is reached at which part of the wave would have to travel faster than the local speed of light—an obvious impossibility. At that point, the light is lost from the waveguide. For commercial single-mode fiber-optic cables operating at 1.3 and 1.5μm, the bending occurring in fabrication (the cables are made with the fibers wound spirally around a center) and installation does not cause a noticeable increase in attenuation.

## Numerical Aperture and Acceptance Angle

The numerical aperture of the optical fiber is a measure of its light-gathering capability (much like the maximum f-stop of a camera lens). The numerical aperture is defined as the maximum angle of incidence of a ray that is totally reflected at the core/cladding interface. Mathematically, the numerical aperture, NA, is expressed in this way:

```
NA = _n² core - n² cladding
```

The optical power accepted by the fiber varies as the square of the numerical aperture, but unlike the camera lens f-stop, the numerical aperture does not depend on any physical dimension of the optical fiber.

The acceptance angle is the maximum angle that an entering light ray can have relative to the axis of the fiber and still propagate down the fiber. A large acceptance angle makes the end alignment less critical when fibers are being spliced and connected.

## Optical Windows

The minimal loss areas shown in Figure 7.10 at 1.3 and 1.5μm are referred to as optical windows. In actuality, each window represents a range of wavelengths where the loss per kilometer is minimal. This results in manufacturers favoring the development of lasers and photodetectors to operate within an optical window.

Until recently, most high-speed optical transmission products were manufactured for use in the 1530–1565nm window, referred to as the C-band. In 2000, work began on the manufacturer of optical fiber, lasers, and photodetectors in the 1565–1620nm range, referred to as the L-band. Today just about all optical transmission systems operate in one of three so-called optical windows—wavelengths around 1.3nm as well as the previously mentioned C- and L-band wavelengths.

## Fiber-Optic Subsystems and Components

Several components provide the foundation for the construction of fiber-optic systems and subsystems. Those components include fiber production, light sources, and light detectors.

# Fiber Production

Optical fibers are fabricated in several ways, depending on the vendor and the purpose of the system. The core and cladding regions of the fiber are doped to alter their refractive indices. This doping is carried out by heating vapors of various substances such as germanium, phosphorus, and fluorine, and depositing the particles of resulting oxidized vapor or "soot" on high-quality fused-silica glass mandrels, called preforms. The preforms are large-scale version of the core and cladding that are then heated to a taffy-like consistency and drawn down into the actual fiber. The core and cladding dimensions have essentially the same relationship in the final fiber as in the preform. Deposition of the dopants is done in one of three standard ways: outside, inside, and axial vapor deposition.

# Light Sources

Light sources for fiber-optic systems must convert electrical energy from the computer or terminal circuits feeding them to optical energy (photons) in a way that allows the light to be coupled effectively to the fiber. Two such sources currently in production are the surface light-emitting diode (LED) and the injection laser diode (ILD).

## Light-Emitting Diodes

A cross-section of a surface LED is shown in Figure 7.11. It emits light over a relatively broad spectrum, and it disperses the emitted light over a rather large angle. This causes the LED to couple much less power into a fiber with a given acceptance angle than does the ILD. Currently, LEDs are capable of coupling about 100 microwatts (mW) of power into a fiber with a numerical aperture of 0.2 or more and a coupling efficiency of about 2 percent. The principal advantages of LEDs are low cost and high reliability.

## Injection Laser Diodes

A cross-section of a typical ILD is shown in Figure 7.12. Because of its narrow spectrum of emission and its capability to couple output efficiently into the fiber lightguide, the ILD supplies power levels of 5 to 7 milliwatts (mW). At present, ILDs are considerably more expensive than LEDs, and their service life is generally less by a factor of about 10. Other disadvantages of laser diodes are that they must be supplied with automatic level control circuits, the laser power output must be controlled, and the device must be protected from power supply transients.

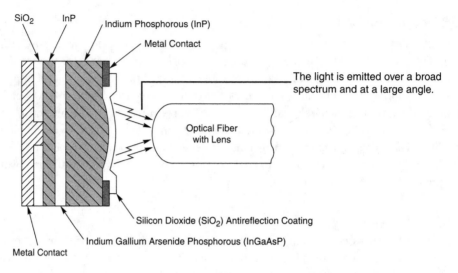

**FIGURE 7.11**

*Construction of a light-emitting diode of 1.3μm operation.*

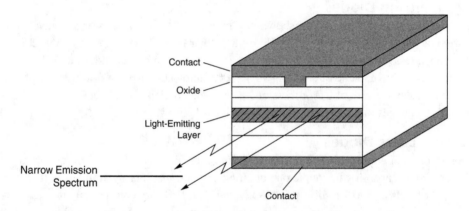

**FIGURE 7.12**

*Construction of an injection laser diode.*

# Light Detectors

At the receiving end of the optical communications system, the receiver must have very high sensitivity and low noise production. To meet these requirements, there is a choice of two types of devices to detect the light beam, amplify it, and convert it back into an electrical signal: the integrated p-i-n field-effect transistor (FET) assembly and the avalanche photodiode (APD). In the p-i-n FET device, a photodiode with unity gain (the p-i-n device) is coupled with a high-impedance front-end amplifier. This device combines operation at low voltage with low sensitivity to operating temperature, high reliability, and ease of manufacture.

The avalanche photodiode produces a gain of 100 or more; however, it also produces noise that might limit the receiver sensitivity. The APD devices require high-voltage bias that varies with temperature. Receivers using APDs are so sensitive that they require as few as 200 photons to be detected at the receiver per bit transmitted at data rates of 200 to 400Mbps.

# Transmission Systems

During the past decade, most carrier transmission systems have moved from the use of copper wire to optical fiber. In fact, by mid-1994, almost 100 percent of long-distance communications was carried over optical transmission systems.

An AT&T study in 1978 noted a striking advantage of installing a digital transmission system over comparable analog systems: a $900 savings per circuit termination when interconnecting multiple digital switching machines. The savings came from the difference in requirement for terminal multiplexing equipment. The AT&T FT3C lightwave system was devised to provide the most economical digital transmission system possible with the current state of the fiber-optic art. It used wavelength multiplexing techniques to send three 90Mbps signals over the same fiber, giving more than 240,000 digital channels at 64,000bps in a cable containing 144 optical fibers.

The FT3C system represents the first commercial implementation of wavelength-division multiplexing (WDM). Each of the three 9Mbps signals was generated through the use of LEDs, with the signals coupled onto a common multimode fiber to generate a composite transmission of 270Mbps.

The first application of the FT3C system was in the Northeast Corridor project by AT&T, between Boston and Washington, and in the North/South Lightwave Project on the West Coast of the United States by Pacific Telesis, between San Francisco and San Diego. Figure 7.13a is a map of the Northeast Corridor system, which contains 78,000 fiber-kilometers of lightwave circuits. Figure 7.13b is a map of the North/South Lightwave Project. The two systems were placed in service in 1983 and have been expanded considerably since then.

The significant advantages associated with the use of fiber-optic transmission systems resulted in tens of thousands of miles of fiber being installed during the 1980s. By early 1991, U.S. Sprint had converted 100 percent of its intercity transmission facilities from microwave to fiber. A few years later, AT&T and MCI Communications completed the conversion of their systems to fiber.

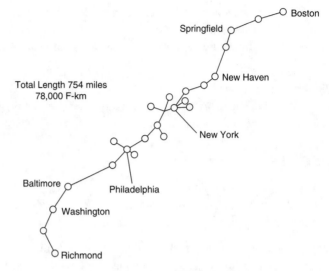

a. Fiber-Optic Network for Northeast Corridor

b. Pacific Telephone North/South Lightwave Project

**FIGURE 7.13**

*Fiber-optic networks.*

During the mid- to late 1990s, the growth in the use of the Internet and other data applications resulted in the use of traditional long-distance communications carriers such as AT&T, MCI, and Sprint being supplemented by a number of newly formed communications carriers such as IXC Communications, Quest Communications, and Level 3 Communications. The newly formed companies installed more than 50,000 route miles of fiber along gas, railroad, and electric utility right of ways to develop their own long-distance networks. In the face of competition, the traditional long-distance communications carriers spent billions of dollars upgrading their previously installed fiber-based infrastructure to compete with the newly formed carriers. Upgrading of existing fiber included new optical transmitter/receivers capable of supporting data rates as high as 10Gbps, as well as the use of wavelength-division multiplexing which permits up to eight separate optical channels, each transporting a 2.4Gbps data stream to provide a 19.2Gbps composite transmission capability over existing fiber links. These same fiber links may have been hard pressed to support a data rate of 300Mbps earlier in the decade.

## Wavelength-Division Multiplexing

A combination of the single-mode fiber (low dispersion by the transmission medium), narrow output spectrum (power concentration at a single frequency), and narrow dispersion angle (good power coupling) from ILDs makes possible the extreme bandwidth-distance characteristics given for systems at the beginning of this chapter. The narrow ILD emission spectrum also makes it possible to send several signals from different sources down the same fiber by a technique called wavelength-division multiplexing (WDM). The capability to multiplex several analog signals in the frequency domain has been described in detail in Chapter 6, "Multiplexing Techniques." As illustrated in Figure 7.14, wavelength multiplexing at optical frequencies is the equivalent of FDM at lower frequencies. Light at two or more discrete wavelengths is coupled into the fiber, and each wavelength carries a channel at whatever modulation rate is used by the transmission equipment driving the light source. Thus, the information capacity of each fiber is doubled or tripled.

As indicated earlier in the section "Transmission Systems," the first commercial use of wavelength-division multiplexing dates to 1983 when AT&T installed its FT3C lightwave system. The FT3C system was based upon the coupling of wavelengths from three LEDs, each operating at 90Mbps onto a multimode fiber to generate a composite operating rate of 270Mbps.

Since the development of the FT3C system, a considerable amount of effort occurred in the field of optical transmission systems. First, it became practical to manufacture single-mode fiber, which has essentially replaced the use of multimode fiber in the backbone networks used by communications carriers. Next, developments in laser technology resulted in the capability to design lower-power, longer-life devices that replaced the use of LEDs in long-distance optical systems. A third significant development occurred when the effect of doping a short portion of optical fiber with erbium resulted in the creation of erbium-doped fiber amplifiers (EDFA), which made it practical to transmit long distances without having to convert an optical signal back into an electrical signal and reconvert the electrical signal into another optical signal, an expensive technology referred to as an optical-electrical-optical (OEO) repeater. Together, the use of lasers with single-mode fiber and EDFAs permitted manufacturers to develop multiplexing systems that support the transmission of a large number of individual wavelengths over a common fiber. When more than eight wavelengths are transmitted over a common fiber, the transmission system is referred to as a dense WDM (DWDM) system.

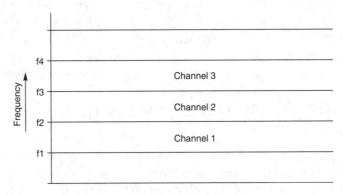

a. Frequency Division Multiplexing

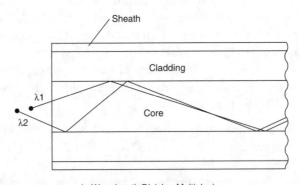

b. Wavelength Division Multiplexing

**FIGURE 7.14**
*Wavelength multiplexing.*

# Dense WDM Systems

As previously mentioned, a DWDM transmission system consists of more than eight individual wavelengths transported over a common optical fiber. The maximum number of individual wavelengths that can be transported has yet to be determined because every few months during

Fiber-Optic and Satellite Communications

**CHAPTER 7**

325

**7**

FIBER-OPTIC AND
SATELLITE
COMMUNICATIONS

2001, an optical manufacturer appeared to announce a system with a greater capacity. Today systems supporting 48 to 64 individual wavelengths are in commercial use, while systems with a capacity for supporting up to 1,024 individual wavelengths are being put through their paces in a laboratory environment.

Figure 7.15 illustrates the major components of a DWDM system. The dense wavelength-division multiplexer shown in the left portion of Figure 7.15 receives individual light sources at distinct wavelengths ($\lambda_1$, $\lambda_2$ through $\lambda_n$) coupling the light sources onto a common optical fiber. The number of individual wavelengths that can be supported depends upon the operating rate of each wavelength. As the operating rate increases, pulse dispersion increases. Because a multiplexer designer needs to place a minimum spacing between signals, referred to as a minimum channel spacing, higher operating rates result in an increase in the minimum separation between signals. This additional channel spacing is required because pulse dispersion increases at higher data rates and additional spacing prevents a pulse at one wavelength interfering with a pulse operating at another wavelength. Thus, as spacing increases between channels, the number of channels that can be supported decreases. Because optical systems are restricted to transmission within optical windows to obtain a low level of attenuation, this acts as a further constraint concerning the number of individual wavelengths that can be multiplexed.

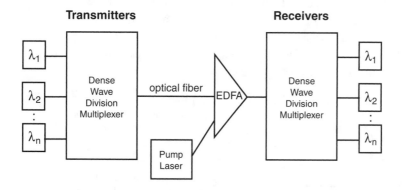

**Legend:**
EDFA   erbium doped fiber amplifier

**FIGURE 7.15**

*The major components of a dense wavelength-division multiplexing system include multiplexers, demultiplexers, single-mode fiber, and one or more optical amplifiers.*

The Erbium doped fiber amplifier represents a short length of silica-based optical fiber doped with erbium. The element erbium is excited by a laser and functions as an active amplifier. That is, the laser excites erbium electrons that, in turn, excite photons flowing through the fiber within a predefined range of wavelengths. EDFAs operate from approximately 1530 to

1560nm, which further limits the number of distinct wavelengths that can be multiplexed. However, a new type of optical amplifier referred to as a silica erbium fiber-based amplifier (DBFA) extends the optical amplifier bandwidth to wavelengths from 1528nm to 1610nm. The DBFA can actually be considered as a dual-bind amplifier. The first is in the range of the EDFA, while the second extends the range. Because the second band supports the L-band optical window, the use of the DBFA is expected to result in the capability of optical component manufacturers to place wavelengths in both the C- and L-bands onto a common optical fiber and use one amplifier to support the amplification of optical signals in both bands.

The pump laser shown in Figure 7.15 provides the excitation for the doped portion of optical fiber and obviously requires shelter and power. Currently, approximately every 100km a communications carrier constructs a building referred to as an optical hut where the EDFA and pump laser are installed. Thus, on a 3000km backbone, the carrier must construct 30 huts, which illustrates why communications carriers are extremely interested in the development of DWDM systems that use optical amplifiers to extend transmission distances before requiring the signals to be reamplified.

At the demultiplexer, the optical signal is broken out into its various individual wavelengths. To do so, the demultiplexer uses a series of mirrors that let all light other than a specific wavelength flow through the mirror. Thus, each mirror reflects a specific wavelength, enabling the multiplexed wavelengths to be broken out for distribution to their intended receivers. Figure 7.16 illustrates how a mirror-based DWD demultiplexer operates. In this example, only four wavelengths are shown being demultiplexed, for simplicity of illustration. However, in actuality, many systems support 64 wavelengths.

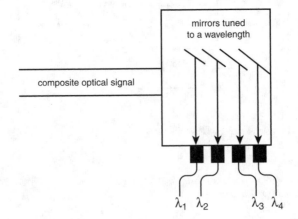

**FIGURE 7.16**

*Optical demultiplexing.*

Returning to Figure 7.15, it should be noted that a DWDM can be implemented in one of two ways—unidirectional or bidirectional. In a DWDM unidirectional system, all wavelengths travel in the same direction within the optical fiber. Thus, a unidirectional system requires a second fiber to be installed to support transmission in the opposite direction. In a DWDM bidirectional system the channels in the fiber are split into two separate bands, each supporting transmission in one direction. Although this eliminated the requirement for a second fiber, it reduces the overall system capacity and also results in each multiplexer having to perform both multiplexing and demultiplexing operations. Thus, the equipment required at each end is a bit more complex—no pun intended.

## Other DWDM Components

Two important components of a DWDM system are gaining attention due to the capabilities that they provide. Those components are an add/drop multiplexer (ADM) and an optical switch.

The add/drop multiplexer, as its name implies, permits the selective addition and removal of wavelengths from an optical fiber without having to convert the optical signal into an electrical signal. Figure 7.17 illustrates the use of a wavelength add/drop multiplexer. This type of device is suitable for use in areas on the route of a DWDM fiber as a large number of voice and data calls are first aggregated onto each wavelength and the wavelength can be added to a DWDM system. Similarly, a wavelength can be dropped at selective locations.

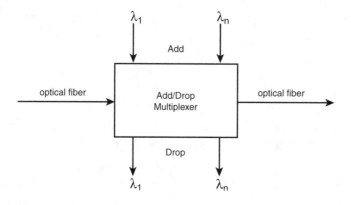

**FIGURE 7.17**

*Through the use of an add/drop multiplexer, wavelengths are selectively added and removed from a fiber transporting multiple signals.*

A second component that is in field trials and should shortly be in commercial service is the optical switch. Fabricated as an n input port by n output port device, the optical switch is designed to permit any wavelength on an input port to be routed to any output port. Currently several companies are testing optical switches based upon the use of miniature mirrors, bubbles in semiconductors, and the use of waveguides as a mechanism to switch wavelengths. In 2001, significant progress occurred in the development of an optical switch based upon miniature electromagnetic mirrors, referred to by the mnemonic MEMS. It is expected that optical switches will be commercially deployed during either late 2001 or early 2002, with MEMS being the leading candidate for use.

Figure 7.18 illustrates an example of an N by N optical switch. Note that the input to the switch can be in the form of individual wavelengths from a dense wavelength-division demulti-plexer or from direct input from other types of optical systems that generate wavelengths compatible with the optical switch. Similarly, the output from the optical switch can be directed onto individual ports of a DWDM or directly onto other optical transmission systems. By placing optical switches within communications centers, it becomes possible for a communications carrier to achieve a high degree of flexibility by routing wavelengths between DWDM systems. Because optical switching works on wavelengths, it eliminates the need to perform an optical-to-electrical conversion along with the expenses associated with equipment required to perform those conversions.

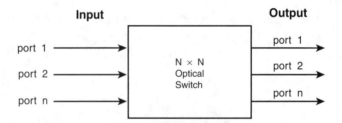

**FIGURE 7.18**

*An optical switch transfers individual wavelengths between input and output ports.*

## Synchronous Optical Network (SONET)

Advances in the use of fiber-optic transmission systems resulted in a requirement for standards to enable interoperability between interexchange carriers and telephone companies. In addition, a considerable growth in communications from companies and government agencies resulted in a requirement to define the interface of commercial communications equipment to an evolving optical network. The resulting standard, known as the Synchronous Optical Network (SONET) in North America and Synchronous Digital Hierarchy (SDH) in Europe, represents a transport vehicle capable of supporting data rates in the gigabit range, optical interfaces, network management, and diagnostic testing methods.

Until SONET standards were developed, there was a void in compatibility between fiber terminal equipment operating at rates above the DS3 transmission rate of 44.736Mbps. That operating rate is formed by a communications carrier using a device known as an M13 multiplexer to combine 28 DS1 channels into a DS3 signal. The resulting DS3 signal is asynchronous because each DS1 signal is independently timed. Although each DS1 signal includes 8000bps for framing, the resulting multiplexed DS3 signal includes three intermixed framing signals, which makes it almost impossible to locate an individual DS0 signal within the DS3 signal. Thus, to remove one PCM digitized voice signal in a carrier's DS3 transmission hierarchy, the carrier typically had to first demultiplex the DS3 signal, requiring additional equipment and adding to the cost of the carrier's infrastructure. Recognizing this problem, the developers of the SONET standard developed a frame structure that enables lower-speed channels within a higher-speed signal to be easily removed from or added to the signal. This process is known as drop (removal of the signal on a channel) and insert (addition of a signal on a channel).

## Frame Structure

As previously indicated, the basic SONET frame consists of 9 rows of bytes with 90 bytes per row, and 8,000 of these frames are transmitted each second. This arrangement results in a composite data rate of 51.84Mbps. Because 27 bytes of each 810-byte frame represent overhead, the payload of the basic SONET frame is limited to 50.112Mbps, of which 2.3Mbps represent overhead. That overhead includes positioning information that enables a single DS0 channel to be identified and data to be easily extracted or inserted into the channel position. These characteristics of SONET's frame structure are illustrated in Figure 7.19.

This also means that a DS3 signal representing 28 DS1 signals can be carried within the basic SONET frame, and each of the 672 DS0 channels within the 28 DS1 signals can have data easily removed (dropped) or added (inserted).

The basic SONET frame illustrated in Figure 7.19 that occurs 8,000 times per second is referred to as a Synchronous Transport Signal-Level 1, or STS-1. SONET is called synchronous because the frame is synchronized with respect to each input DS0 channel through the use of pointers in the 27 bytes of overhead per frame, which results in a synchronous multiplexing format. In addition to pointers, a significant portion of the overhead bytes in the STS-1 frame are reserved for management data, enabling network-management functions to include loopback, bit error rate testing, and collection and reporting of performance statistics to be carried within the SONET frame.

UNDERSTANDING DATA COMMUNICATIONS

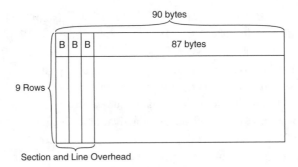

**FIGURE 7.19**

*The SONET frame structure.*

## The Optical Interface

One of the major elements included in the SONET standard is its set of defined optical interfaces. Until the development of SONET, each manufacturer designed its fiber terminal device to its own optical signal interface. This "do-it-yourself" approach prevented the interconnection of terminal devices from different vendors with a common fiber backbone. Under SONET, 256 OC (optical carrier) optical interfaces are defined, although the current standard explicitly calls for the use of 10 interfaces. Those interfaces, listed in Table 7.1, define the SONET digital signal hierarchy. Note that the OC-1 level represents an STS-1 signal, whereas higher levels represent multiplexed STS-1 signals.

Although SONET primarily represents a standard for optical interoperability among public network transmission providers, it also furnishes the capability for large organizations and government agencies to provide an STS-1 signal to the central office of a public network provider. This is accomplished using an optical multiplexer connected to a fiber routed from the customer premise to the carrier's central office. Figure 7.20 illustrates the use of an STS-1 signal to the public network. Note that because of the pointers imbedded into the SONET frame, the carrier can easily break out previously multiplexed signals originating at the customer's optical multiplexer without having to demultiplex and remultiplex the data stream, which would be required with a DS3 signal. Eventually, SONET should reduce the cost of transmission for large network users and increase network reliability as fiber is routed directly to the customer premises.

**TABLE 7.1**   The SONET Signal Hierarchy

| Level | Line Rate | DS3 Channels |
|-------|-----------|--------------|
| OC-1  | 51.84Mbps | 1            |
| OC-3  | 155.52Mbps | 3           |

**TABLE 7.1**    continued

| Level | Line Rate | DS3 Channels |
|---|---|---|
| OC-9 | 466.56Mbps | 9 |
| OC-12 | 622.08Mbps | 12 |
| OC-18 | 933.12Mbps | 18 |
| OC-24 | 1.244Gbps | 24 |
| OC-36 | 1.866Gbps | 36 |
| OC-48 | 2.488Gbps | 48 |
| OC-192 | 9.952Gbps | 192 |
| OC-768 | 39.808Gbps | 768 |

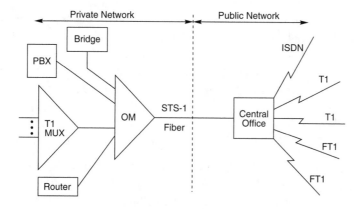

Legend OM optical multiplexer
PBX private branch exchange

**FIGURE 7.20**

*Using SONET to connect public and private networks.*

## SONET Structure

Over the past decade, SONET has been deployed on both a point-to-point and a ring structure topology. When deployed as a ring topology, SONET consists of two concentric rings formed by a series of point-to-point connections, with one ring used as a nearly instant backup facility for the in-use ring. If Joe Backhoe cuts a SONET fiber, the absence of light is near instantly detected at a point-to-point termination location, which then routes transmission onto the backup ring. Due to this near-instantaneous backup capability, SONET provides the highest level of availability of all types of communications systems.

# International Systems—The SL Underwater Cable

The advent of optical-fiber technology for undersea cables provides point-to-point channel capacity equal to satellite systems at reduced cost and without long transmission delays, unstable environmental interference, induced noise, and broadcast of potentially sensitive information to half the world.

Undersea cable systems have some understandably difficult environmental requirements. The environment includes pressures of 10,000 pounds per square inch (psi) at depths of 7300 meters, salt water, and the possibility of mechanical damage from anchors and earth movement in shallow waters. An important requirement for these systems is that the regenerator spacing be as wide as possible to cut down on the system failure probability and the power requirements because power must be fed from the ends of the cable.

A schematic of the SL Undersea Lightguide System is shown in Figure 7.21. It is composed of a high-voltage power supply, a supervisory terminal, a multiplexer with inputs for several types of information, the cable light source, the cable itself, and the repeaters. The cable is made of a central core and a surrounding support, as shown in Figure 7.22. The core has an outside diameter of 2.6μm and consists of 12 optical fibers wound helically around a central copper-clad steel wire called a kingwire, all embedded in an elastomeric substance and covered with a nylon sheath. This assembly is, in turn, covered with steel strands, a continuously welded copper tube, and an insulation of low-density polyethylene for electrical insulation and abrasion resistance. The outside diameter of the completed cable is 21μm (about 0.8 inches).

The fibers are single-mode optical lightguides operating at 1.312μm. The data rate on each fiber pair is 280Mbps, and repeaters are spaced every 35km. The total capacity of the system is more than 35,000 two-way voice channels. Inputs from binary data sources are multiplexed directly into the stream. Analog channels are first converted to binary by the adaptive delta modulation technique and are then processed by a type of digital circuit (Digital TASI) that interleaves inputs from a number of input speech channels onto a smaller number of output channels. The light sources for the systems are ILDs operating near 1.3μm with an average output power of 1mW (0dBm). Light detectors are indium-gallium-arsenide (InGaAs) p-i-n diode receivers followed by silicon bipolar transimpedance amplifiers. Three spare laser diodes, which can be switched in remotely if a failure occurs, are provided per circuit.

By the late 1980s, several fiber-optic undersea cables were laid across the Atlantic, linking New York to England, France, and Spain via light transmission. The successful operation of those systems resulted in communications carriers expanding their plans for fiber-optic undersea cables. During the early 1990s, several trans-Pacific and trans-Mediterranean fiber-optic cables were installed. By the mid-1990s, most voice, data, and video transmissions between the United States and Europe, Japan, and Australia were routed via fiber-optic cable between continents.

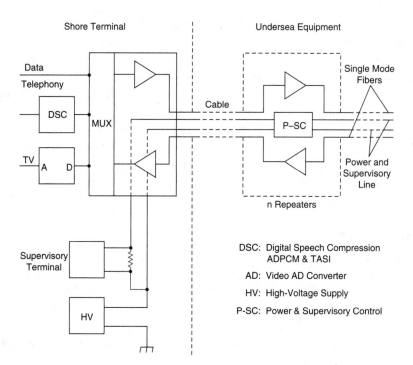

DSC: Digital Speech Compression
     ADPCM & TASI

AD: Video AD Converter

HV: High-Voltage Supply

P-SC: Power & Supervisory Control

**FIGURE 7.21**

*The SL Undersea Lightguide System.*

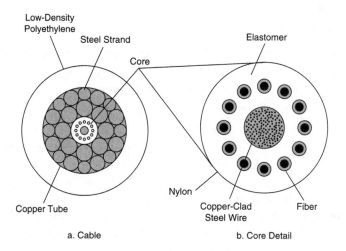

**FIGURE 7.22**

*Embedded fiber core cable.*

As the use of fiber-optic cable has increased, a corresponding decrease has resulted in the use of geostationary satellites for voice transmission between fixed locations. The primary reason for the wide acceptance of fiber-optic cable over geostationary satellites is the immunity of the fiber-optic cable to electromagnetic interference. An additional factor was the elimination of one-half second or longer delays associated with the use of geostationary satellites caused by the 50,000 plus miles the signal had to travel during transmission. Today, most geostationary satellites are used for television and data transmissions that are insensitive to transmission delays. However, a new series of low Earth-orbiting satellites during the late 1990s (described in the next section in this chapter) significantly enhance the use of satellites for voice communications. Those satellites support a new class of mobile communications referred to as Personal Communications Service (PCS), which is also described later in this chapter.

## LAN Applications

The use of fiber in local area networks has considerably expanded over the past decade. During the late 1980s, fiber was commonly used between electrical-optical repeaters as a mechanism to extend the length of LANs. Currently one LAN referred to as FDDI (Fiber Distributed Data Interface) represents an optical fiber-based local area network that supports data transmission at 100Mbps. FDDI can support transmission distances beyond 50 miles, which makes it suitable for creating campus-wide backbones. Another type of LAN referred to as Gigabit Ethernet requires the use of optical fiber on all connections beyond 100 meters due to the extreme difficulty in transmitting very narrow pulses over copper media and having them recognizable at a receiver. As organizations require higher data-transfer rates, the use of fiber can be expected to grow in local area network applications.

## Fiber to the Home

One of the most publicized terms in the field of communications is the so-called *digital highway*. First promoted by then Vice President Gore as a term to represent the interconnections of computer research centers via high-speed optical transmission, the term has been applied to all types of high-capacity communications to include fiber cables routed to the home.

By early 1994, several field tests of fiber to the home were being conducted in California and Florida. Each test was similar in that the large bandwidth capacity of an optical fiber enabled the simultaneous transmission of up to hundreds of television signals along with voice conversations and interactive data channels. Where each test differed was in the scope of interactivity offered to the home consumer and the capability of the consumer to request different functions interactively. Some tests enabled the consumer to order films to be displayed at a predefined time, a feature known as video-on-demand. Other tests primarily focused on providing consumers with online banking, grocery ordering, and catalog shopping. A new term used to define the provider of integrated voice, data, and video is *multimedia*, although the range of services offered by different multimedia vendors currently varies considerably from vendor to vendor.

Currently a competition between cable TV operators and telephone companies for the multimedia consumer dollar is being waged with competitive technology. Most telephone companies are gradually making available Digital Subscriber Line (DSL) technology to their customers. In comparison, cable TV operators are installing hybrid fiber coax cable combinations, upgrading their infrastructure to support bidirectional communications and offering cable modems to their subscribers.

## HFC and Cable Modems

In addition to conducting fiber-to-the-home trials, the cable TV industry has been busy upgrading a good portion of its infrastructure using a hybrid fiber coax (HFC) cable combination. Through the use of HFC between 500 and 3,000, cable TV subscribers can be supported by one fiber main trunk node being connected to coax feeder and drop cables. In addition, the large bandwidth of the fiber trunk cable enables the CATV operator to support transmission in the return direction from subscribers in a large service area via the fiber trunk. Thus, an HFC infrastructure provides the opportunity for cable TV operators to provide telephone service, Internet access, and other services that require economical bidirectional transmission.

Figure 7.23 illustrates in schematic form a hybrid fiber coax network. Note that each main trunk consists of a fiber cable, and feeder and drop cables routed to the subscriber continue the use of coax. This method of cabling enables the CATV operator to considerably increase the capacity of the system in an economical manner because the existing coaxial cable previously routed to subscribers remains in place.

In Figure 7.23, notice that to provide two-way services, CATV operators must upgrade their amplifiers to support bidirectional transmission. In addition, note that the cable TV head end represents the broadcast area where satellite video feeds are received and broadcast to subscribers. Although Figure 7.23 illustrates a hybrid fiber coax network bidirectional transmission necessary to support telephone service, note that interactive TV, Internet applications, and similar applications can be supported on conventional coaxial TV systems that were upgraded to support bidirectional transmission. The key difference between the two is that the use of fiber trunks significantly reduces the number of trunks that must be routed into neighborhoods, and it provides immunity to noise and other transmission impairments resulting from electrical disturbances.

Most cable modems have a receiver that's tunable to the 50–750MHz range in 6MHz increments, enabling the modem to use a full TV channel for data reception. Through the use of 64- or 256-point quadrature amplitude modulation (QAM) using a majority of the bandwidth of the TV channel, a data rate up to 36Mbps can be supported. In the return direction, cable modems operate in the 5–42MHz spectrum and support a 10Mbps upstream rate. See Chapter 5, "Synchronous Modems, Digital Transmission, and Service Units," for a detailed discussion of cable modem technology.

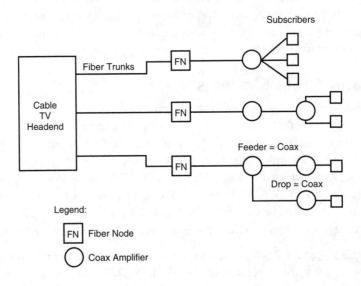

**FIGURE 7.23**
*A CATV hybrid fiber coax network.*

Today, the home multimedia effort is in its infancy, probably equivalent to where the personal computer industry was during the 1970s. Although it's difficult to predict the range of services that will be offered to consumers, one thing is certain: Regardless of the resulting suite of services offered to the consumer under the labels "video-on-demand," "multimedia," or another term, those services will be transported through the use of fiber-optic cable to the home, either directly or via the use of hybrid fiber coax systems.

# Satellite Transmission Systems

Satellite transmission systems provide users with the capability to bypass conventional communications carrier offices, as well as to broadcast information to multiple locations for a nominal cost.

# Basic Satellite Technology

Satellite communications systems are basically line-of-sight microwave systems with a single repeater. As stated in Chapter 3, "Messages and Transmission Channels," the satellite is said to be in geostationary orbit when the speed of the satellite is matched to the rotation of the Earth at the equator. Because of the great distance of the satellite from the Earth (about 22,300 miles) and antenna size limitations that limit focusing capability, the cone of coverage for a single satellite transmitter can be as large as the entire continental United States.

For those transmission services that originate at a single point and flow to many points in one direction, such as television and radio signals, the large area of coverage is ideal. The relatively long delay between the instant that a signal is sent and when it returns to Earth (about 240 milliseconds) has no undesirable effect when the signal is going only one way. However, for signals such as data communications sessions and telephone conversations, which go in both directions and are intended to be received at only one other point, the large area of coverage and the delay can cause problems.

Data and telephone conversations usually proceed as a series of messages in one direction that are answered or acknowledged by messages in the other direction. When the delay between the message being sent and the reply or acknowledgment is long, the transmission rate of information slows down. In the case of voice messages, long delays between utterance and reply make the speaker think that he has not been heard or understood. This leads to requests for repeating (the equivalent of negative acknowledgment in the data world) and increased frustration. There is also a serious privacy issue with communications that are intended for only one destination but are broadcast so that an entire continent can receive them. One of the factors causing the rush to all-digital transmission is the ease of encrypting information in digital form so that when the inevitable interception of broadcast signals occurs, the information intercepted is at least somewhat difficult to decipher.

A satellite transmission system consists of one or more Earth stations and a geostationary satellite that can be seen by the stations. Figure 7.24 illustrates the Americatel "teleport," consisting of three large-diameter satellite dishes located in Miami, Florida, that represent Earth stations. Americatel is a regional telecommunications carrier that provides voice, data, and facsimile services via a gateway and switching center in Miami to common carriers and private organizations throughout Central and South America. In Central and South America, many subscribers to Americatel use Very Small Aperture Terminals (VSATs) to communicate with North America, bypassing the necessity to use terrestrial lines. Through the use of VSAT facilities in remote areas, such as mining locations, users can receive a modern communications capability that was previously restricted to major metropolitan locations. To facilitate satellite communications, as well as to eliminate interference between transmission and reception, standards govern the use of satellite frequencies. Separate frequencies are assigned for sending to the satellite (the uplink) and receiving from the satellite (the downlink). The general frequency assignments for satellite systems are shown in Table 7.2.

**FIGURE 7.24**
*Americatel's U.S. teleport consists of three large-diameter satellite dishes. (Courtesy of Americatel Corporation.)*

Satellites are equipped with multiple repeater units called transponders. Many systems have 10 or 12 transponders, but a series of international satellites, called INTELSAT VI, has 46 transponders. Transponders are assigned different uses, but in the case of those used for voice or voice-equivalent data communications channels (nominal 4KHz bandwidth), the transponder capacity can be as large as 3,000 channels.

The INTELSAT VI satellite provides a total bandwidth, using frequency reuse techniques, of 3460MHz.

Transponders operate at different carrier frequencies. Currently seven frequency bands are used for most space communications applications. Table 7.3 lists the frequency range assignments for seven space frequency bands. Note that the C-band and Ku-band are currently used exclusively for broadcasting purposes, such as for providing HBO, Showtime, and other television broadcasts to wide areas of the world.

# Multiple Access Systems

Telephone switching systems and data multiplexers are designed based on the fact that not every telephone or terminal that can send information will do so at the same time, or, alternatively, that the telephone or terminal user does not need or want to pay for the entire capacity of a channel. These conditions are also true for the users of satellite systems. Several methods have been devised to allow sharing of the satellite and Earth station resources among several users so that it appears that the transmission channel is dedicated to each user.

**TABLE 7.2**   General Frequency Assignments for Satellite Systems

| Uplink Frequencies | Downlink Frequencies |
| --- | --- |
| 5.925–6.425GHz | 3.700–4.200GHz |
| 7.900–8.400GHz | 7.250–7.750GHz |
| 14.00–14.50GHz | 11.70–12.20GHz |
| 27.50–30.00GHz | 17.70–20.20GHz |

## Frequency Division Multiple Access

Frequency division multiple access (FDMA) is simply another example of the familiar data and voice transmission technique called frequency-division multiplexing (FDM). This technique is used to allocate small portions of a large bandwidth (500MHz for satellite transponders) to individual users. For instance, a telecommunications common carrier in a particular country—say, Brazil—might want 132 voice-grade channels for sending voice- and analog-coded data to various other countries. The bandwidth required on the current international satellite systems for this many channels is 10MHz. Because 1 transponder has a bandwidth of 500MHz, it could accommodate 50 users, each requiring 132 channels. The Brazilian user might be allocated the frequency band between 5990 and 6000MHz for the uplink to the satellite, and the corresponding downlink frequencies would be 3765 to 3775MHz. Other users might be assigned similar portions of the bandwidth in the same transponder. For example, a Portuguese user might be allocated the 6220–6230MHz uplink band and the 3995–4005MHz downlink band. A Canadian user might operate on the 5930–5940MHz uplink band and the 3705–3715MHz downlink band. Figure 7.25 illustrates how the three users each have one uplink, all into a single transponder, but all users can receive all three downlinks. This arrangement makes possible simultaneous two-way transmissions between any of the three sites using only a part of one satellite transponder.

**TABLE 7.3**   Space Communications Bands and their Frequency Range

| Band | Frequency Range |
|------|-----------------|
| L    | 1.0–2.0GHz      |
| S    | 2.01–4.0GHz     |
| C    | 4.01–8.0GHz     |
| X    | 8.01–12.0GHz    |
| Ku   | 12.01–18.0GHz   |
| K    | 18.01–27.0GHz   |
| Ka   | 27.01–40.0GHz   |

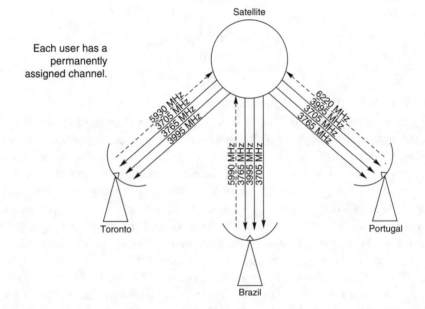

**FIGURE 7.25**
*Multiuser satellite system.*

## Time Division Multiple Access

Time division multiple access (TDMA) is the equivalent of FDMA, but in the time domain rather than the frequency domain. TDMA works just like time-division multiplexing (TDM) for land-based data and voice transmissions, with each satellite transponder having a data rate capacity of between 10 and 100Mbps. While a station is sending on the uplink, the entire data rate capacity of the transponder is available, but then it must stop sending for a short time to allow another station access to the transponder. The information flows to the satellite in frames, with each frame containing one burst of information from each Earth station allowed access to the single transponder. A typical format for a frame is shown in Figure 7.26. The sum of the durations of the individual bursts does not quite equal the frame time, to give some guard time between bursts.

Timing for keeping the station bursts apart is a major problem, and it is complicated by two facts. First, the satellites are not perfectly stationary in orbit (each appears to travel in a small figure-eight pattern). Second, the times of travel of the signal between different Earth stations and the same satellite are different because of different slant range distances. TDMA techniques allow the satellite transmitter to be operated at higher power levels than FDMA. This method is permissible because only one carrier at a time occupies the transponder, reducing the amount of intermodulation distortion that's generated.

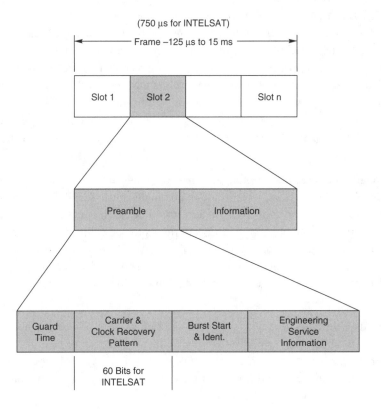

**FIGURE 7.26**

*TDMA transmission frames.*

## Demand Assignment Multiple Access

Using the demand assignment multiple access (DAMA) technique, each satellite transponder is used much like a telephone switch; that is, a subchannel is assigned only when traffic is available to be carried on it. This is in contrast to the FDMA and TDMA techniques described previously, in which channels are assigned to users permanently, even if there is no traffic demand. DAMA is a variant of FDMA in that a part or all of the transponder is divided into individual channels that can be accessed by all DAMA terminals on the ground that are serviced by the DAMA transponder. A central computer system, or a system of distributed and cooperating computers, on the ground keeps track of who gets which channel when. DAMA is particularly useful for loading transponders efficiently when each of several ground sites needs only a few channels.

## Personal Communication Services

During the 1970s and 1980s, satellite communications were often thought of as the data communications technology of the future. In fact, many authors wrote about the use of satellite technology eventually replacing the use of most terrestrial communications. This conversion did not, however, occur primarily due to the delays associated with transmitting a signal more than 25,000 miles into the atmosphere and then having that signal retransmitted back to Earth. The delay time associated with the use of satellites significantly affects their use for data transfer when data blocks have to be periodically acknowledged. Due to the minimal effect on voice conversations, the use of satellites has taken on a new role as a mechanism for personal communication services.

The key difference between the evolving personal communications satellite-based systems and existing cellular telephones is in their method of communication. A cellular telephone user communicates with a cell site connected via terrestrial lines to the public switched telephone network. In comparison, although initial PCS offerings provide cellular-like voice services using different frequencies to transmit to cell stations, ground users can also subscribe to a low Earth orbit satellite-based communications service. Such subscriptions enable ground users to make cellular calls or receive pages through low Earth orbiting satellites from just about every area on Earth.

Several companies developed satellite systems consisting of 12 to 60 or more nongeostationary low and middle Earth-orbiting satellites to provide either continental or near-global communications coverage. Such systems were developed to support a new type of wireless telephone service that transmits in the L- and Ka-band frequency spectrums and supports high-quality voice service as well as facsimile and paging signal transmission.

One of the first satellite-based personal communications services is the Iridium system from Iridium, Inc. This firm represents a consortium of telecommunication operators and industrial companies originally sponsored by Motorola, Inc., which still has a minority interest in this venture. The actual concept behind Iridium dates to 1985 when Karen Bertiaer, the wife of a Motorola executive, could not place a cellular call to the United States when vacationing in the Caribbean. She convinced her husband of the need for a global mobile wireless system. Initially, Iridium planned to launch 77 low Earth orbit satellites, but later the plan was scaled back to 66. Although the name of the consortium was based upon the 77th element, it fortunately was not changed. Otherwise, we might refer to the consortium as Dysprosium for the 66th element, which translates to difficulty of access! The first Iridium satellite flight bus was delivered by Lockheed Martin to Motorola Satcom facilities in October 1995. By 1997, Iridium had placed 47 satellites into orbit and by 1998, the constellation of 66 satellites circling the Earth was completed.

The Iridium satellite network consists of 66 satellites in six orbital planes approximately 480 miles above the Earth. Communications to Iridium satellites are via special Iridium mobile telephones and via conventional telephone systems through the use of satellite Earth station gateways that convert terrestrial signals to the Ka-band for transmission to an Iridium satellite. Although Iridium achieved a significant amount of publicity, its subscriber base never materialized to more than a small fraction of company expectations. Iridium declared bankruptcy and had planed to adjust the orbits of their satellites to burn up in the Earth's atmosphere. Fortunately, the U.S. Department of Defense came to the rescue with a contract to use Iridium, which resulted in a reorganized company continuing its operations. In addition to Iridium, other major communications firms provide competitive satellite-based personal communications services. One such competitive service is provided by ORBCOMM, a partnership owned by Orbital Sciences corporation, Teleglobe, Inc., of Canada, and Technology Resources Industries of Malaysia.

Low Earth orbit satellites are ideally suited for two-way cellular and paging operations. This is because the low orbit of those satellites requires less power to reach those satellites. Anyone who has seen an old Tom Clancy made-for-TV movie in which an intelligence agent opens a suitcase and constructs a small Earth station to bounce a signal off a satellite can now recognize that the person was accessing a geostationary satellite. In comparison, in the movie *Air Force One*, Harrison Ford was able to use a small handheld cellular phone because he was accessing a low Earth orbit satellite. Unfortunately, the size of cell phones required to access low Earth orbit satellites both resemble the size and weight of a brick while costing several thousand dollars. Due to this, Iridium and other low Earth orbit satellite operators never achieved a significant subscriber base, and most satellite operators experienced significant financial difficulties.

# What You Have Learned

- Light traveling in an optical fiber obeys Snell's Law.

- Light can travel in a multimode optical fiber along several paths or in a single-mode fiber along only one path.

- The index of refraction of the glass making up an optical fiber varies across the diameter of the fiber, with the highest index in the middle of the fiber.

- Fiber-optic system bandwidth is limited by modal delay spreading and material dispersion.

- Fiber-optic system transmission distance is limited by scattering, absorption, losses at connections, and losses at bends in the cable.

- Fibers with varying indices of refraction across the fiber are made by heating a preform that has been doped with metal salts such as germanium and phosphorus and drawing it down to a small diameter.

- When a dual numeric is specified for a fiber, the first number denotes the core diameter, and the second references the cladding diameter.

- Transmitters for fiber-optic systems are light-emitting diodes or semiconductor injection lasers.

- Receivers in fiber-optic systems are avalanche photodiodes or integrated p-i-n field-effect transistors.

- An optical window represents a band of wavelengths where attenuation per kilometer is minimal.

- The use of an erbium-doped fiber amplifier enables an optical signal to be amplified without having the optical signal converted into an electrical signal.

- The number of channels supported by a dense wavelength-division multiplexing system depends upon the data rate of individual wavelengths as well as the wavelengths used for multiplexing.

- SONET provides a set of standards that enables the interoperability between fiber-optic transmission systems of interexchange carriers and telephone companies.

- The use of fiber in local area networks is gaining in popularity.

- New services to the home consumer under such terms as video-on-demand and multimedia can be expected to be based on the use of fiber to the home.

- Satellite transmissions have four uplink bands and four downlink bands.

- TDMA techniques allow the satellite transmitter to be operated at higher power levels than FDMA.

- Low Earth orbit satellites are ideally suited for supporting cellular communications because they are closer to the Earth and require less power to access.

# Quiz for Chapter 7

1. What are the requirements for a successful transmission system using light?

   A. A powerful, reliable light source

   B. Strong glass

   C. A reliable, low-cost transmission medium

   D. Powerful amplifiers

2. The core of an optical fiber has

   A. A lower index of refraction than air.

   B. A lower index of refraction than the cladding.

   C. A higher index of refraction than the cladding.

   D. None of the above.

3. For single-mode fibers, the core diameter is about

   A. 10 times the fiber radius.

   B. 3 times the wavelength of the light carried in the fiber.

   C. 15μm.

   D. 10 times the wavelength of the light carried in the fiber.

4. Over a period of 30 years, how often is a kilometer of fiber-optic cable likely to be broken?

   A. Not at all

   B. Once

   C. 10 times

   D. 2 or 3 times

5. What is a fiber whose core has a uniform refractive index called?

   A. Stepped-index fiber

   B. Graded-index fiber

   C. Uniform-index fiber

   D. Nonuniform-index fiber

6. A 62.5/125 fiber has a

   A. 62.5 micron diameter cladding.

   B. 125 micron diameter cladding.

   C. 62.5 micron diameter core.

   D. 125 micron diameter core.

7. Deposition of dopants on fiber preforms is done by

   A. Outside vapor deposition.

   B. Axial vapor deposition.

   C. Inside vapor deposition.

   D. All of the above.

8. A light-emitting diode can couple how much power into an optical fiber?

   A. 10W

   B. 10 milliwatts

   C. 100 microwatts

   D. 1 picowatt

9. Avalanche photodiode receivers can detect bits of transmitted data by receiving which of the following?

   A. 1 photon

   B. 10 photons

   C. 100 photons

   D. 200 photons

10. Which of the following represents one unsolved problem with satellite systems?

   A. Coverage

   B. Privacy

   C. Bandwidth

   D. Access

11. The AT&T FT3C fiber-optic transmission system is designed to use how many light wavelengths?

    A. 1

    B. 2

    C. 3

    D. 10

12. Which device excites the erbium electrons in an erbium-doped fiber amplifier?

    A. Pump laser

    B. WDM

    C. DWDM

    D. Silica

13. Two constraints that govern the number of channels on a dense wavelength-division multiplexing system include

    A. Silica and erbium.

    B. Fiber-doping level and excitation.

    C. Channel spacing and wavelength data rate.

    D. Sum of C-band and L-band wavelengths.

14. The SL Undersea Lightguide system can carry how many two-way voice channels?

    A. 10,000

    B. 100,000

    C. 35,000

    D. 760

15. When the index of refraction is greater in material 1 than it is in material 2, the velocity of propagation in material 1 compared to material 2 is what?

    A. Equal or greater

    B. Greater

    C. Lesser

    D. Equal

16. The different angles of entry of light into an optical fiber in which the diameter of the core is many times the wavelength of the light transmitted are called what?

    A. Emitters

    B. Modes

    C. Sensors

    D. Refractors

17. In single-mode fibers, a large fraction of the power is propagated in the

    A. Sheath.

    B. Core.

    C. Cladding.

    D. Air.

18. The loss in signal power as light travels down a fiber is called what?

    A. Propagation

    B. Scattering

    C. Absorption

    D. Attenuation

19. What is the coupling efficiency of an LED light source to an optical fiber with a numerical aperture of 0.2 or more?

    A. 60 percent

    B. 10 percent

    C. 2 percent

    D. 0.1 percent

20. How many fibers does the FT3C lightwave system contain?

    A. 12

    B. 144

    C. 128

    D. 64

21. A key advantage of SONET is its capability to enable

    A. Data to be carried at high operating rates.

    B. The interoperability of optical transmission between interexchange carriers and telephone companies.

    C. Routing of data to the home.

    D. Interconnection of private networks.

22. How many bytes of overhead exist in a SONET frame?

    A. 90

    B. 9

    C. 27

    D. 87

23. How many OC-1 signals are there within a SONET OC-3 signal?

    A. 3

    B. 6

    C. 9

    D. 12

24. A geostationary satellite used for communications systems

    A. Is stationary in the sky.

    B. Rotates with the Earth.

    C. Is positioned over the equator.

    D. Remains stationary relative to the Earth's surface.

    E. A and C.

    F. B, C, and D.

25. Multiple repeaters in communications satellites are known as what?

    A. Transponders

    B. Detectors

    C. Modulators

    D. Stations

26. In the current frequency assignments, how many frequency bands are there for the uplink frequencies?

    A. 16

    B. 8

    C. 4

    D. 2

27. How much bandwidth is required to send 132 voice-grade channels by FDM on an international satellite system?

    A. 500MHz

    B. 10MHz

    C. 1320MHz

    D. 50MHz

28. What is Iridium?

    A. A geostationary series of 77 satellites

    B. A low Earth orbit series of 77 satellites

    C. A geostationary series of 66 satellites

    D. A low Earth orbit series of 66 satellites

29. Which of the following is a primary advantage of low Earth orbit satellites for two-way communications?

    A. Ground locations

    B. Power to access

    C. Weather

    D. Immunity to solar flares

30. A major problem concerning the use of low Earth orbit satellites for personal communications is

    A. The distance to the satellite.

    B. The satellite area of coverage.

    C. The size of the satellite.

    D. The cost and size of the handset.

# Protocols and Error Control

## IN THIS CHAPTER

This chapter is about the rules that data communications systems use when communicating with one another, the ways in which systems discover that an error has been made in transmission, and some methods used to correct those errors. Because many data-transmission schemes are in use (for example, asynchronous and synchronous, and half- and full-duplex), many sets of rules, called protocols, and many error-detection and correction schemes have been devised. The most common of these techniques are explained in this chapter.

# Protocols Versus Interfaces

Protocols are agreements between persons or processes (usually nowadays, the processors are computer programs) about which of them can do what to whom and when. A protocol is different from an interface. An *interface* is a set of rules, often embodied in pieces of hardware, that controls the interaction of two different machines or processes, such as a computer and a modem. A *protocol*, on the other hand, is a set of rules defining the interactions between two machines or processes that are alike or that have similar functions. The difference is illustrated in Figure 8.1. House A and house B look alike but are occupied by a curious set of people. The British engineer on the top floor of house A needs to communicate with another engineer, also British, on the top floor of B. The only telephone, however, is guarded by a Swedish businessman on the bottom floor of each house. The engineer speaks no Swedish, and the businessman speaks no English.

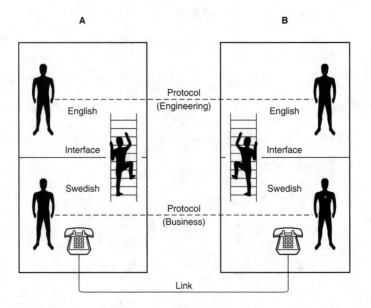

## FIGURE 8.1
*Protocols and interfaces.*

The two engineers, like most people who talk on the telephone, have a routine for communication that they've worked out over many years. The one answering says, "Hullo." The one calling says, "Hullo, this is Reggie." Then the first says, "Oh, hullo, Reggie. How are you, old boy?" This is called a preamble. The men then begin discussing Wimbledon, the weather, and even some business. At the end of most sentences, the one being questioned makes a reply, even if it is only a sound rather than a word or sentence. If one party does not hear some sort of reply from the other at fairly short intervals, he might say, "I say, are you still there?" If he still receives no reply, he might terminate the conversation and begin the whole process over. If one party does not understand the other, he says, "What?" and the second party repeats the last sentence. When the conversation is over, the person terminating the call says, "Well, good-bye for now." The called party replies, "Good-bye," and both hang up. The Swedish businessman has a similar technique for conversing with his counterpart. All of these conventional conversational actions make up a protocol. As we will see in the remainder of this chapter, protocols developed for communication between processes in computers have all the same mechanisms as those used between humans—for exactly the same reasons.

Although these two engineers can communicate reliably with one another because they have a communications protocol, they still have the problem of having no direct access to the communications channel, which is jealously guarded by the large Swedish businessman. The solution is an interface. The engineers engage a person who stands midway up the stairs and who speaks both engineering English and business Swedish. The engineer in house A speaks in English to the person halfway up the stairs, who relays the conversation in Swedish to the businessman, who relays it over the telephone to his Swedish counterpart in house B, who relays it in Swedish to another person on the stairs, who finally conveys the messages in English to the called party.

This seems like a clumsy and inefficient procedure, and in many respects it is. But it is the same procedure used in millions of data communications systems to enable an application program communicating in one set of symbols (perhaps ASCII) and at one rate of symbol production to communicate through a teleprocessing monitor using another set of symbols (perhaps EBCDIC) at a vastly different rate to a line interface program dealing with yet a third set of symbols (bits). The story of standard interfaces was told in Chapter 4, "Asynchronous Modems and Interfaces." The story in this chapter is about protocols.

# Elements of a Protocol

The basic elements of a communications protocol are a set of symbols called a character set, a set of rules for the sequence and timing of messages constructed from the character set, and procedures for determining when an error has occurred in the transmission and how to correct the error. The character set consists of a subset that is meaningful to people (usually called printing characters) and another subset that conveys control information (usually called control characters).

There is a correspondence between each character and a group of symbols on the transmission channel. For instance, the character A might correspond to the binary code 1000001, which has a decimal value of 65. Several standard codes with equivalent sets of ones and zeros (bits), such as ASCII (discussed in previous chapters), have been defined over the years. The set of rules to be followed by the sender and receiver gives the meaning, permissible sequences, and time relationships of the control characters and messages formed from the symbols. The error-detection and correction procedure allows for the detection of and orderly recovery from errors caused by factors outside the control of the terminal at either end.

# Teletypewriter and XMODEM Protocols

The simplest protocols in general use are those associated with the transmission of start-stop or asynchronous data that were originally developed for communications between teleprinter machines. For a long period after the development of the teleprinter, the machines were electromechanically controlled, and protocols had to be appropriate to a very simple mechanical controller in each machine. One of the first teletypewriter (TTY) protocols used a character set containing 58 symbols: 50 printing characters, a space, and 7 control characters. This character set, which was originally referred to as CCITT (now known as the ITU-T) Alphabet No. 2, is shown in Figure 8.2. The symbols were encoded into a 5-bit binary code as shown (the octal representation is shown only for readers familiar with octal).

The printing characters are the uppercase letters, the numbers, and 14 punctuation marks. Three control characters allow for carriage return (CR), line feed (LF), and ringing the terminal bell (BELL) to announce a message. Also provided are a NULL (or blank) character (which is not the same as a space) and a WRU character. WRU, which stands for "Who Are You," causes a mechanical device in the teleprinter to send a character sequence identifying that particular terminal. The other two control characters are the FIGS character, which causes the machine to print numbers and punctuation, and the LTRS character, which causes the machine to print the uppercase alphabet. As mentioned in Chapter 1, "An Overview of Data Communications," this character set and associated binary code is commonly referred to as the Baudot code, after Emile Baudot, who invented the first code with symbols of a fixed length.

The protocol for operation of a message system using the Baudot code goes something like this (the procedure varies somewhat according to the operator of the system):

1. A communications channel is connected between the two machines. This might be a temporary dialed connection or a permanent private line.

2. The sending machine sends a WRU, to verify that the receiving machine is the proper one for the message to be sent.

3. The sending machine sends a "Here is...," which is normally the same sequence of characters that is sent when it receives a WRU, to identify the sender.

4. The sending machine sends a preamble or message header that identifies the name and address of the intended message recipient, the date and time entry of the message into the system, the date and time of transmission, and the message sequence number assigned by the sender. In some systems, the sender uses two sequence numbers: one to count the number of messages sent by the sender that day, and the other to count the number of messages sent to the receiver's terminal that day.

5. At the end of the message, the sending machine sends another "Here is..." and another WRU. The second WRU is to determine whether the receiving machine is still connected to the line. If the message is being sent manually, the operator of the sending machine sometimes sends several BELL characters to alert a person at the receiving end that a message is ready for delivery.

| Binary | Octal | LTRS | FIGS |
|--------|-------|------|------|
| 0 0 0 0 0 | 00 | BLANK | BLANK |
| 0 0 0 0 1 | 01 | E | 3 |
| 0 0 0 1 0 | 02 | LF | LF |
| 0 0 0 1 1 | 03 | A | – |
| 0 0 1 0 0 | 04 | Space | Space |
| 0 0 1 0 1 | 05 | S | ' |
| 0 0 1 1 0 | 06 | I | 8 |
| 0 0 1 1 1 | 07 | U | 7 |
| 0 1 0 0 0 | 10 | CR | CR |
| 0 1 0 0 1 | 11 | D | WRU |
| 0 1 0 1 0 | 12 | R | 4 |
| 0 1 0 1 1 | 13 | J | BELL |
| 0 1 1 0 0 | 14 | N | , |
| 0 1 1 0 1 | 15 | F | ; |
| 0 1 1 1 0 | 16 | C | : |
| 0 1 1 1 1 | 17 | K | ( |
| 1 0 0 0 0 | 20 | T | 5 |
| 1 0 0 0 1 | 21 | Z | + |
| 1 0 0 1 0 | 22 | L | ) |
| 1 0 0 1 1 | 23 | W | 2 |
| 1 0 1 0 0 | 24 | H | |
| 1 0 1 0 1 | 25 | Y | 6 |
| 1 0 1 1 0 | 26 | P | 0 |
| 1 0 1 1 1 | 27 | Q | 1 |
| 1 1 0 0 0 | 30 | O | 9 |
| 1 1 0 0 1 | 31 | B | ? |
| 1 1 0 1 0 | 32 | G | |
| 1 1 0 1 1 | 33 | FIGS | FIGS |
| 1 1 1 0 0 | 34 | M | . |
| 1 1 1 0 1 | 35 | X | / |
| 1 1 1 1 0 | 36 | V | = |
| 1 1 1 1 1 | 37 | LTRS | LTRS |

**FIGURE 8.2**
*CCITT Alphabet No. 2.*

This protocol was developed over many years of sending messages manually between individual terminals operated by people. You will note that it has all the elements described in the opening paragraphs: a previously defined set of symbols and corresponding codes suitable for electronic transmission, a preamble, a message, and even a rudimentary error-detection procedure (the invocation of the WRU at the beginning and end of the session).

The simple teletypewriter protocol described does not work very well in the presence of even fairly low error rates on the path between the machines. Individual characters can be mutilated in such a way to cause the receiving machine to begin printing gibberish, and the transmitter will never know. The WRU check at the end of a message ensures only that the receiving machine received the WRU correctly and that the circuit is still good in the backward direction. The WRU check says nothing about whether the message got through. To provide better assurance of correct transmission, two more techniques are sometimes used for simple protocols: character parity and echoplex.

# Parity

This is the Communicator's Creed: "Now abideth faith, hope, and parity, but the greatest of these is parity."

The addition by the transmitter of another bit to the bits that encode a symbol for the purpose of error detection is called parity. When parity is employed, the parity bit is always transmitted, and it is usually set to the value that will cause the coded symbol to have an even number of 1 bits; thus, the scheme is called even parity. The parity bit is recomputed by the receiver. If the newly computed value gives the correct parity, all is well. If not, some indication is given to the receiving terminal, usually by substituting a special error character for the one received.

## Methods of Parity Checking

Two methods of parity checking are employed by asynchronous communications systems, even parity and odd parity checking. Three additional types of parity checking include mark parity, space parity, and no parity, with the latter indicating that the parity bit is not used for error detection. Under even parity, the parity bit is set when necessary to provide an even number of set bits in a character to include the parity bit. Similarly, under odd parity, the parity bit is set when necessary to provide an odd number of set bits in a character to include the parity bit. Under mark parity, the parity bit is always set to a binary 1; under space parity, the parity bit is always set to a binary 0.

For an example of parity checking, consider the ASCII character $M$, which has a bit composition of 1001101. Because the character has four 1 bits, a 1 bit is added if odd parity checking is used, whereas a 0 bit is used if even parity checking is employed. Figure 8.3 illustrates the formation of the parity bit for odd and even parity checking for the ASCII character $M$.

The parity scheme detects single-bit errors in the transmitted symbols, but it might not detect multiple bit errors. The capability of the scheme to detect multiple bit errors is dependent on the location in the character where the bit errors occur and the composition of bit settings in the character. For example, assume that noise on the transmission line causes the values of the first 2 bits of the ASCII character $M$ to be inverted, resulting in the bit composition of the character becoming 0101101. In this situation, the number of set bits remains the same, which precludes parity being used to detect the transmission error. Now assume that transmission noise adversely affects the second through fourth bits, changing the composition of the character $M$ to 110101. Note that 5 bits are now set, which enables parity to detect the error. Thus, parity might or might not be capable of detecting multiple bit errors. Error correction can occur by the receiver sending a message back that requests retransmission.

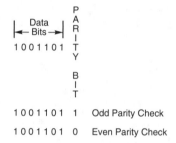

**FIGURE 8.3**

*Parity bit formation for the ASCII character M.*

## Checksums

In the preceding discussion on parity, the bit required to make the number of 1 bits in an individual character was added to the end of the character and sent along with it. This scheme is sometimes called vertical redundancy checking (VRC), or vertical parity, because if you hold a punched paper tape with its length in the horizontal, each character would appear as a vertical column of holes across the tape. It is possible, and is common in some systems, to include a horizontal check character that performs the parity function for each row of holes in the tape.

Figure 8.4 shows a set of characters represented as holes punched in a tape, with the vertical or character parity bit at the top of each character, and the horizontal or block parity character at the right. The block parity character is usually called a checksum because it is formed by performing a binary addition without carrying each successive character. It also is sometimes referred to as a longitudinal redundancy check (LRC) character. It is sent as an extra character at the end of each message block. A system that uses both vertical parity and a checksum usually can detect all single-bit errors in a single character and some multiple-bit errors within a single character. In fact, this method of error detection is one of the three types supported by the BiSync protocol described later in this chapter.

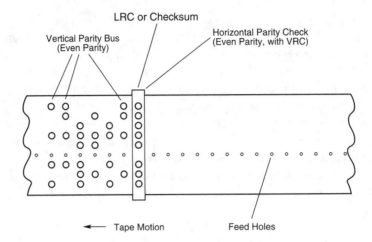

**FIGURE 8.4**

*Vertical and horizontal parity.*

# Echoplex

Echoplex is perhaps not properly classed as an element of protocols, but it is discussed here anyway. It is a technique in which the receiver sends back (or echoes) each character as the characters are received. The sender can then see by the copy printed locally whether the characters are making the round trip without being mutilated. When an echoed character is received in error by the original sender, it is not possible to tell whether the data was received correctly at the destination and scrambled on the return path, or whether it was erroneous when it was received at the original destination. But at least some error indication is immediately available to the sender.

# XMODEM Protocol

The XMODEM protocol was devised by Ward Christensen as a simple error-checking scheme suitable for file-transfer operations between microcomputers. It requires that one terminal or computer be set up (by an operator or a computer program) as the sender, and that the other be set up as the receiver. After the protocol is started, the transmitter waits for the receiver to send a Negative Acknowledge (NAK) character. The receiver, meanwhile, is set to send NAKs every 10 seconds. When the transmitter detects the first NAK, it begins sending messages as blocks of 128 data characters, surrounded by some protocol control characters. The beginning of each block is signaled by a Start of Header (SOH) character. This is followed by a block number character in ASCII, followed by the same block number with each bit inverted. The bit inversion, known as the ones complement, results in the block number being followed by the ones complement of the block number. A 128-character piece of the file is sent, followed by a checksum that is the remainder of the sum of all the 128 bytes in the message divided by 255. Mathematically, the XMODEM checksum can be represented as follows:

$$\text{CHECKSUM} = R \left[ \frac{\sum_{1}^{128} \text{ASCII Value of Character}}{255} \right]$$

in which R is the remainder of the division process.

Figure 8.5 shows the XMODEM protocol block format.

The receiver checks each part of the received block for the following things:

- Was the first character an SOH?
- Was the block number exactly one more than the previous block received?
- Are the block number and the ones complement of the block number the complement of each other?
- Were exactly 128 characters of data received?
- Was the locally computed checksum identical to the last character received in the block?

If the receiver is satisfied, it sends an Acknowledge (ACK) back to the transmitter, and the transmitter sends the next block. If not, a NAK is sent, and the transmitter resends the block with the error. This process is continued, block by block, until the entire file is sent and verified. At the end of the data, the transmitter sends an End of Text (EOT) character. The receiver replies with an ACK, and the session is terminated.

| Start of Header | Block Number | 1s Complement of Block Number | 128 Data Characters | Checksum |
|---|---|---|---|---|

**FIGURE 8.5**
*The XMODEM protocol block format.*

## Drawbacks of XMODEM Protocol

Several points can be made here about the XMODEM protocol. First, it is easy to implement with a small computer, but it does require a computer at each end. Second, it requires manual setup for each file to be transferred. Third, the error-detection technique (ordinary sum of the data characters) is unsophisticated and incapable of detecting reliably the most common type of transmission error, which is a noise burst that can last on the order of 10 milliseconds (the duration of about 12 bits at 1200bps). Fourth, it is a half-duplex protocol—that is, information is sent, and then the sender waits for a reply before sending the next message. Because operation of the XMODEM protocol generally assumes a full-duplex line, it is inefficient in use of the transmission facility.

You can visualize the key problem associated with a half-duplex protocol, such as XMODEM, by examining data flow via a time chart. Figure 8.6 illustrates the transmission of two blocks of data via the XMODEM protocol in the form of a time chart. Note that once transmission commences, block *n*+1 cannot be sent until block *n* is acknowledged. In this half-duplex procedure, the transmitting station waits between blocks for an acknowledgement, which reduces transmission throughput.

In spite of the previously mentioned limitations, the XMODEM protocol and several derivatives are supported by most asynchronous communications programs designed for operation on personal computers. The rationale for the widespread support of those protocols is related to the initial placement of the XMODEM protocol into the public domain. This action enabled software developers to use the protocol without cost. In addition, it provided communications compatibility between programs developed by different vendors, which was extremely important in the 1970s when many software developers preferred to introduce proprietary protocols that worked only when two computer systems used the same software program.

Most of the asynchronous communications programs developed during the early 1980s eventually included XMODEM support. In the late 1980s, several derivatives of the XMODEM protocol gained acceptance due to the increased level of functionality that they provided. Some versions of the XMODEM protocol added CRC error checking, a process described later in this chapter. Other versions provided a full-duplex transmission capability with CRC error detection, further increasing the efficiency of the protocol. Today, almost all communications programs designed for use on personal computers support XMODEM and several of its derivatives.

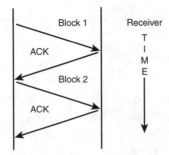

**FIGURE 8.6**

*Under the XMODEM half-duplex protocol, the originator cannot transmit block* n+1 *until block* n *is acknowledged.*

## XMODEM Derivatives

If you use an external modem and transfer a file under the XMODEM protocol, you can visually observe two deficiencies of the protocol: its small block size and the half-duplex method of transmission. If you are receiving a file, you will note that your modem's Receive Data (RD) indicator light illuminates for a short time, after which your modem's Send Data (SD) light momentarily illuminates as a flash. This process of RD being on for a second and SD flashing on and off continues until the file transfer is completed or until it aborts if 10 retransmissions occur due to a poor-quality line.

In observing the illumination of SD and RD, note that one always follows the other because transmission is half-duplex. Thus, after receiving a block of data, your computer stops receiving data and then transmits an ACK or a NAK. By turning off the modem's receiver and turning on its transmitter, the computer creates a small delay. This delay is further increased because the distant computer has to wait for an ACK or a NAK response to the previously transmitted block before it can resume transmission. In comparison, file-transfer protocols that support full-duplex transmission enable the simultaneous transmission and reception of data, which increases the effective throughput of the file-transfer operation.

When XMODEM was developed during the 1970s, a data block the size of 128 bytes was probably a reasonable size with respect to line quality because increasing the block size would result in more characters being retransmitted when an error was detected. Beginning in the late 1970s, hundreds of thousands of miles of fiber-optic cable were installed by communications carriers. Because fiber-optic cable is immune to electromagnetic interference, the probability of transmission errors occurring has substantially decreased. This, in turn, made the 128-byte block size used by the XMODEM protocol inefficient for modern communications.

In a laboratory where transmission conditions are ideal, you could probably transmit an entire file in one large block. Unfortunately, in the real world, you can always expect a certain level of transmission errors that vary primarily based upon the transmission facility used. If you transmit an entire file within a single block and a transmission error occurs, the entire block will have to be retransmitted. At the opposite end of the spectrum, the use of very small transmission blocks results in very short retransmissions when a transmission error occurs. However, because there is a fixed number of overhead characters per block, the use of very small transmission blocks is very inefficient. Figure 8.7 provides a general indication of the relationship between block size and data throughput on a transmission facility. Recognizing that the block size used by the XMODEM protocol resulted in its throughput close to the left of center of Figure 8.7, some derivatives of the protocol expanded the block size by a factor of approximately 8.

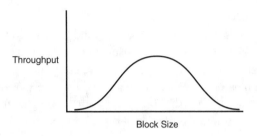

Throughput

Block Size

**FIGURE 8.7**

*Block size versus data throughput.*

By examining the relationship between throughput and block size shown in Figure 8.7, you will note that an optimum block size maximizes throughput. Unfortunately, the characteristics of communications lines vary considerably, which makes it impossible to have one optimum block setting. Recognizing this situation, some protocols adaptively adjust their block size based upon the level of transmission errors encountered on a circuit. One such protocol is the Microcom Networking Protocol (MNP), which was developed for use in modems and was previously discussed in this book.

Although the XMODEM protocol is still very popular, you might want to consider using such derivatives as XMODEM/CRC, YMODEM, and ZMODEM (among others), which provide enhanced file-transfer capabilities.

The selection of an appropriate file-transfer protocol first depends on what protocols are supported by your computer and the computer you want to communicate with. Although this limitation might narrow your choice, you might still be faced with choosing from a half dozen or more commonly supported protocols. Possible choices are outlined in Table 8.1 and are explained in greater detail shortly.

**TABLE 8.1**   File-Transfer Protocol Comparison

| Protocol | Support Batch | Block Size | Error Detection | Transmission Mode | Data Characters |
|---|---|---|---|---|---|
| ASCII | No | — | None | — | 7 |
| XMODEM | No | 128 | CS | H | 8 |
| XMODEM/CRC | No | 128 | CRC | H | 8 |
| XMODEM-1K | No | 128/1024 | CRC | H | 8 |
| XMODEM-G | No | 128/1024 | None | H | 8 |

**TABLE 8.1**    continued

| Protocol | Support Batch | Block Size | Error Detection | Transmission Mode | Data Characters |
|----------|---------------|------------|-----------------|-------------------|-----------------|
| YMODEM   | Yes | 128/1024 | CRC | H | 8 |
| YMODEM-G | Yes | 128/1024 | None | H | 8 |
| WXMODEM  | No | 128 | CRC | F | 8 |
| ZMODEM   | Yes | 128/1024 | CRC | F | 8 |
| KERMIT   | Yes | 1024 max | CRC/CS | H/F | 8 |

*Note: CS = Checksum, H = Half-duplex, F = Full-duplex*

## XMODEM/CRC

This protocol is the same as the previously described XMODEM protocol, with the exception that the checksum is replaced by a polynomial-generated CRC whose formation is described later in this chapter. Because the use of a CRC provides a higher level of error detection than the use of a checksum, this protocol reduces the probability of an undetected error in comparison with the XMODEM protocol.

## XMODEM-1K

XMODEM-1K is essentially an XMODEM/CRC protocol that uses 1024-byte (1KB) data blocks. For most transmissions, this protocol reduces transmission time in comparison to XMODEM or XMODEM/CRC. The transmission time is reduced because the large block size reduces both the number of line turnarounds and the number of times that the transmitting device must wait for a response before sending the next block or retransmitting the previously sent block. Thus, the XMODEM-1K protocol can be considered a mechanism for obtaining enhanced throughput.

## XMODEM-G

The XMODEM-G protocol is a variation of XMODEM-1K that was developed in recognition of error-detection and correction capabilities being incorporated into many types of modems. The transmission of a file using error detection and correction via modems that have an error-detection and correction feature would be inefficient and would introduce additional delays that would adversely affect the efficiency of the file-transfer process.

XMODEM-G is the same as XMODEM-1K, except that it lacks an error-detection and correction capability. This makes XMODEM-G a "streaming" protocol in which 1KB blocks are sent one after another. Although the protocol computes a CRC similar to XMODEM-1K, it is ignored by the protocol. Because this protocol does not provide any error-detection capability, it should be used only with modems that have that capability enabled. Otherwise, the transfer of a file occurs without error protection.

## YMODEM

Unlike XMODEM and its variations that are limited to transferring a single file, YMODEM supports the transmission of multiple files. Because the protocol enables you to batch a group of files for transmission, many software programs refer to YMODEM as YMODEM BATCH. To provide a multiple file-transmission capability, YMODEM uses a header block that carries the filename of each file being transferred, its date of creation or last modification, and the file length.

Figure 8.8 illustrates the basic YMODEM block format. Although this block format is similar to XMODEM's, it has some distinct differences. First, YMODEM replaces the SOH character used by XMODEM with the Start of Text (STX) character. That character informs the receiver that the block contains 1,024 data characters. YMODEM can switch to a 128-data-character block by replacing the STX character with the SOH character. It automatically does so under certain conditions, such as concluding the transfer of a file when the use of one or more 128-data-character blocks is more efficient than the use of one 1,024-data-character block.

| STX | Block Number | 1s Complement of Block Number | 1024 Data Characters | CRC High Byte | CRC Low Byte |
| --- | --- | --- | --- | --- | --- |

**FIGURE 8.8**

*YMODEM block format.*

A second difference between the XMODEM and YMODEM block formats concerns the block number field. Unlike XMODEM, which commences block numbering at 1, YMODEM supports a block number 0, a special block used to transport the filename, its date of creation or last modification, and its length. In addition to the previously discussed capability to transport 1,024 data characters per block, another difference between the YMODEM and XMODEM block formats concerns the error detection data contained in the block. As indicated in Figure 8.8, YMODEM contains 2 bytes of CRC data, so this file-transfer protocol has the capability to transport a 16-bit polynomial in place of XMODEM's 8-bit checksum.

Like XMODEM-1K, YMODEM uses 1024-byte (1KB) data blocks and is a half-duplex protocol. Some implementations of YMODEM enable you to specify filenames using global, or wildcard characters, such as the asterisk (*) and the question mark (?), within the filename and filename extension. For example, specifying test*.doc would select all files with the prefix "test" that have the extension "doc" for downloading. Other implementations of YMODEM require you to enter each filename to be batched for transmission. Regardless of the method of specifying filenames, using YMODEM enables you to eliminate the delays between the end of one file transfer and the time it takes you to specify the name of the next file to be transferred. Before you use YMODEM, however, it is a good idea to check your available disk storage against the storage requirements of the files that you want to transfer. Otherwise, you could initiate the transfer of several files and go to the coffee machine, only to return and find that the file-transfer operation was only partially completed. Unfortunately, YMODEM does not tell you that it aborted due to a lack of storage capacity, and you must take a directory listing to determine that there is no available storage and that the lack of storage caused the file transfer to abort.

### YMODEM-G

YMODEM-G can be considered a batch-transfer version of XMODEM-G. That is, YMODEM-G transmits data from one file after another file in 1024-byte (1KB) data blocks without providing error detection or correction. Like XMODEM-G, YMODEM-G should be used only with error-correcting modems.

### WXMODEM

The WXMODEM protocol is a full-duplex "sliding window" protocol that allows the transmission of up to four XMODEM 128-byte data blocks before requiring an acknowledgment. This protocol uses a CRC for error checking. It was developed for use on packet-switching networks in which the flow of data in small packets that require acknowledgments could adversely affect throughput. By transmitting multiple data blocks before requiring an acknowledgment from the receiving device, it increases transmission efficiency. Unfortunately, WXMODEM does not support multiple file transfers.

The use of a sliding window has been incorporated into several protocols, including the Transmission Control Protocol (TCP) of the TCP/IP protocol suite used on the Internet. Through the use of a sliding window transmission, throughput can be considerably enhanced, especially when it's used over modern wide area networks where data primarily flows over a fiber-optic infrastructure.

### The ZMODEM Protocol

The ZMODEM protocol is a full-duplex protocol that supports both 128 and 1,024 data-block transfers. Unlike the file-transfer protocols previously discussed, ZMODEM varies the block size based on the quality of the line determined by the number of retransmission requests received. That is, on a poor-quality line with a large number of retransmission requests, ZMO-

DEM uses a 128-byte data block because the small block size requires fewer characters to be retransmitted when an error occurs. Conversely, on a good-quality line with a small number of retransmission requests, ZMODEM uses a 1024-byte data block size. Although additional characters will be retransmitted when ZMODEM is using a 1024-byte data block and an error is detected, the low error rate results in a higher level of throughput because most 1,024-byte data blocks are received correctly.

In addition to varying the block size to correspond to the line error rate, ZMODEM enables an interrupted file transfer to be restarted from the point of failure. In contrast, the other protocols require you to restart the file-transfer process from the beginning. Two additional features of ZMODEM are its support of multiple file transfers and its support of conventional and extended CRC error checking. Extended CRC checking results in the generation of a 4-byte CRC using 32 bits and reduces the probability of an undetected error to less than one in many millions of characters. Although many people prefer to use ZMODEM as their first choice because of its full-duplex transmission mode, in actuality, a streaming protocol provides an equivalent to slightly better level of throughput.

Similar to YMODEM, ZMODEM transfers the filename of the file transmitted, as well as the file length and creation date, at the beginning of the transmission. Given this information, a communications program can be developed to provide a status report of the progress of a file-transfer operation or a series of file transfers.

Figure 8.9 illustrates the File Progress dialog box generated by the ProcommPlus for Windows communications program for a ZMODEM file transfer. Note that at the time the file-transfer screen was captured, 40960 bytes had been received. By using the file length of 145263 bytes and keeping track of the transfer rate in bytes per second (916), the communications program can provide a real-time display of the time remaining for the file transfer. As indicated in Figure 8.9, at the time the screen was displayed, 1 minute and 53 seconds remained before the file transfer operation would be complete. Also note that the file progress bar at the top of the display indicates that 28% of the file transfer was complete when the screen was captured.

If you transfer multiple files using ProcommPlus for Windows, the program uses ZMODEM information sent at the beginning of the transmission about each of the files to provide batch progress information. Thus, if multiple files were being transferred rather than a single file, the batch progress bar would indicate the percentage of the batch transfer complete, and the batch remaining display field would indicate the time remaining for the batch transfer.

## The KERMIT Protocol

The KERMIT protocol, developed at Columbia University, was named after Kermit the Frog, one of Jim Henson's popular Muppets. This protocol differs from the XMODEM series of file-transfer protocols primarily due to the characteristics of the operating system used on some mini- and mainframe computers. The XMODEM series and its derivatives were developed for 8-data-bit transfers. Some computer operating systems are limited to 7-bit characters, however, and might not be capable of working with ASCII control characters (ASCII 0–31) and the delete character (ASCII 127). To provide a file-transfer mechanism for such computers, KER-MIT was developed.

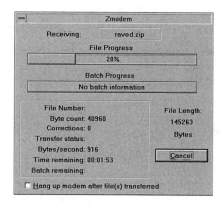

**FIGURE 8.9**

*ProcommPlus for Windows ZMODEM File Progress dialog box.*

KERMIT was originally developed as a half-duplex protocol. It uses 7 or 8 data bits per character. The protocol is designed to convert the eighth bit by stripping it and prefixing the resulting character with another character. Doing so enables operating systems that cannot support 8-bit data characters or certain ASCII control characters to support file transfers in which those characters are disguised.

Since KERMIT was originally developed, many enhancements have been added to the protocol. This protocol now supports multiple file transfers, can operate in a full-duplex sliding window mode, and supports variable block sizes up to 1024 characters per block. Although this protocol is a necessity for accessing computers that cannot handle 8-bit characters or ASCII control characters, it should not be used otherwise. This is because the prefixing of characters significantly adds to the overhead of the protocol and makes the protocol approximately 10 to 20 percent less efficient than the XMODEM protocol, which is the least efficient of all protocols in that series.

## Protocol Selection

Each of the protocols examined in this section becomes the preferred method of error control for a specialized situation. Your particular networking situation is something to consider when choosing a protocol. Table 8.2 is a list of some of the possible circumstances that you may encounter and the recommended protocol for that situation.

8

PROTOCOLS AND
ERROR CONTROL

## ASCII and E-mail Considerations

Because the ASCII protocol has no error-detection capability, you might wonder why you should consider using it. The answer to this question is that, originally, most electronic mail systems required ASCII input. Thus, if you composed a message offline using a word processor, you would save the file in its ASCII format and then transmit the file using the ASCII protocol when you were online to the electronic mail system.

An exception to the preceding statements concerns the attachment of one or more files to electronic messages. Today you can attach binary files to many, if not most, electronic messages. Although gateways between many electronic mail systems are still limited to supporting 7-bit characters, most e-mail systems use one or more coding systems to convert 8-bit binary characters to multiple 7-bit characters. Some popular coding methods include UUencode/UUdecode, XXencode/Xxdecode, and MIME.

**TABLE 8.2**   Protocol Recommendations

| Situation | Choices | Recommendation |
|---|---|---|
| Common error-detection scheme | XMODEM-G for single file; YMODEM-G for multiple files | Both are "streaming" protocols that do not implement error detection. Effective use is dependent on enabling error detection in your modem to match the distant modem's method of error detection. |
| Poor-quality transmission | ZMODEM | Excels in its capability to restart a transmission at its previous point of failure, alleviating the necessity to retransmit the entire file when a transmission session breaks. |
| Limited to XMODEM, XMODEM/CRC, and XMODEM-1K | | XMODEM-1K uses 1024-byte data blocks as well as a CRC for error detection and provides a higher throughput than XMODEM/CRC. XMODEM/CRC and XMODEM both use 128-byte data blocks, but the use of the CRC by the XMODEM/CRC protocol provides a higher probability of data integrity than is possible from the use of a checksum in the XMODEM protocol. |

**TABLE 8.2**    Continued

| Situation | Choices | Recommendation |
|---|---|---|
| Multiple files to transfer | YMODEM; YMODEM-G | Use YMODEM-G only if your modem can communicate with the distant modem using a modem error- correction protocol. Otherwise, use the YMODEM protocol because it includes an error-detection capability based on the use of a CRC. |
| Communicating with computer systems whose operating system cannot support the extended ASCII code and ASCII control characters | KERMIT | KERMIT strips the eighth bit and prefixes the resulting character with another character, but the conversion degrades throughput. Use KERMIT only when absolutely necessary for access to a computer that requires its use. |
| Packet-switched network | ZMODEM; WXMODEM | ZMODEM uses a larger data block than WXMODEM. If it is available, use ZMODEM before WXMODEM. |

# Convolutional Coding—Cyclic Redundancy Checks

Several schemes have been devised to detect errors in binary communications systems using feedback or convolutional coding. These coding methods all append information computed at the transmitter to the end of each message, enabling the receiver to determine whether a transmission error has occurred. The added information is mathematically related to the messages and is therefore redundant. The receiver recomputes the value and compares the recomputed number with the number received. If the two are the same, all is well. If not, the receiver notifies the transmitter that an error has occurred, and the message is resent. These methods go by the name of cyclic redundancy checking (CRC), and the values appended to the messages are called CRCs or block check characters (BCCs). A CRC is calculated by dividing the entire numeric binary value of the block of data by a constant, called a generator polynomial. The quotient is discarded, and the remainder is appended to the block and transmitted along with the data.

CRCs can be computed in hardware using multiple section feedback shift registers with Exclusive-OR (XOR) logic elements between sections and at the end. A typical arrangement is shown in Figure 8.10. This register implements the ITU/ISO High-Level Data Link Control (HDLC) CRC, which is known as the ITU-T-CRC. The circles with a plus sign (+) in the middle represent XOR logic elements. For B = 0 or B = 1, these are the two rules for XOR:

```
B XOR 1 = 0

B XOR 0 = B
```

The shift register is initialized to all ones at the beginning of the CRC calculation for a message. As each bit of the transmitted characters is applied to the transmission facility, it is also applied at point A of Figure 8.10, and then the entire register is shifted right 1 bit. As the bits are transmitted and shifted, each 1 bit that appears at A also affects the state of the other XOR elements, and that effect is propagated throughout the register for several bit times after the bit initially appears. Thus, any bit continues to have an effect on the transmitted data for a considerable time after that bit is sent. When the last data bit has been sent, the bits in the CRC shift register are complemented and transmitted.

At the receiver, the identical process is performed, and when the end of the message including the CRC is detected, the CRC is tested for the unique value 0001110100001111. If this value is found, all is well, and the CRC register is reset to all ones for the next message. If the special value is not found, the program is notified that a transmission error has occurred, and a negative acknowledgment is returned to the sender.

The CRC process has the advantage that the current state of the shift register is the result of considerable past history. It is therefore unlikely that a burst of errors, such as normally occurs in serial data transmission, will produce a calculated CRC at the receiver that is the same as that which was originally sent. In fact, the 16-bit CRC calculation procedures, CRC-16 and ITU-CRC, detect all error bursts of 16 bits or less in length. They also detect more than 99.9% of error bursts of greater than 16 bits. Another advantage of CRC is that it does not require the addition of another bit per character sent, as do the VRC and LRC schemes. It does, however, require one or two (two for CRC-16 and ITU-CRC) extra characters to be sent at the end of each transmitted block.

CRC algorithms were initially implemented in hardware, and integrated circuits were developed to do the entire process for more than one method (for example, CRC-12, CRC-16, and ITU-CRC). It is also possible to perform the calculations in software, for which table lookup techniques provide reasonable performance.

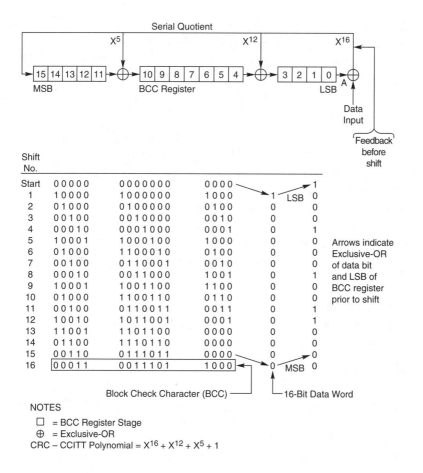

**FIGURE 8.10**

*Shift register implementation of ITU-T-CRC.*

# Half-Duplex Protocols

A half-duplex protocol is also commonly referred to as a stop-and-wait protocol. This is because transmission in one direction must stop for transmission to occur in the opposite direction. In this section, you will examine the network topology, operating characteristics, and actual operation of the once very popular half-duplex protocols.

## Link Protocols

The basic notion in link protocols is that of the data link. A data link is an arrangement of modems or other interface equipment and communications circuits connecting two or more terminals so that they can communicate. Probably the most widely used link protocol through the mid-1980s was represented by the Binary Synchronous Communications procedures defined by IBM (usually abbreviated as BiSync or BSC). These procedures allow for operation on a data link in one direction at one time. BiSync can be operated on full-duplex circuits, but information still flows in only one direction at a time, so, in many cases, the advantage of the full-duplex circuit is minimized.

For the purpose of discussing protocols, the physical form of the link is important. The procedures for connecting and disconnecting the link might be different depending on whether the link is permanently connected or is a dial-up, and also depending on the delay between when a data bit is sent and when it is received. The latter factor is of particular concern on satellite links due to the large difference in round-trip propagation delay between satellite links and terrestrial links. Regardless of the physical form of the link, however, the data is sent over it as a serial stream of symbols encoded as bits, and the control procedures between the ends of the link are affected using the transmission and recognition of the line-control characters or control codes.

## Point-to-Point Links

A point-to-point link is one that connects only two stations at a time, as Figure 8.11a shows. Point-to-point links can be established on dedicated or dial-up circuits, and they can be half-duplex or full-duplex.

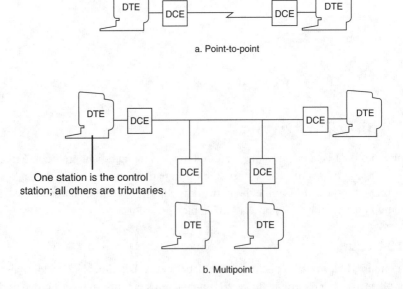

a. Point-to-point

One station is the control station; all others are tributaries.

b. Multipoint

**FIGURE 8.11**

*Point-to-point and multipoint links.*

## Multipoint Links

Multipoint links connect more than two stations at a time, as Figure 8.11b shows. Because communications equipment at intermediary points can be considered to be connected as a drop from the common line, this type of topology is also commonly referred to as a multidrop link or circuit. Obviously, some control procedure must be in place to designate which stations can use the link at any one time. For this purpose, one station on the multidrop lines is designated as the control or master station, and all other stations are designated as tributaries or slaves. The control station is the traffic director, designating which stations are to use the link by a polling and selection process. At any instant, transmission on a multipoint link will be between only two stations, and all other stations on the link are in a passive receive mode.

## Transmission Codes—Character Sets

BiSync is defined by IBM to accommodate three character sets and their associated binary codes. Each set consists of a set of graphics (letters, numbers, and punctuation), a set of terminal-control and format-control codes (BELL, Form Feed, WRU, and so forth), and a set of data-link control codes (Start of Text, End of Transmission, and so on). The three sets are the Six-Bit Transcode (SBT), Extended Binary Coded Decimal Interchange Code (EBCDIC), and United States of America Standard Code for Information Interchange (USASCII, or more commonly, just ASCII).

The codes differ in number of bits per symbol encoded (6 for SBT, 7 for ASCII, and 8 for EBCDIC) and in number of characters in the character set (64 for SBT, 128 for ASCII, and 144 for EBCDIC). The sets also have significantly different properties, such as the sorting order between letters and numbers.

## Link Control Codes

Link control is affected by the proper recognition of control characters and the appropriate actions. The control codes used in BiSync are listed here:

- End of Transmission Block (ETB)—Identifies the end of a block started with an SOH or STX. A BCC is sent immediately following an ETB. Receipt of an ETB requires a status reply (ACK0, ACK1, NAK, WACK, or RVI).

- End of Text (ETX)—Terminates a block of data started by an STX or SOH that was transmitted as an entity. A BCC is sent immediately following an ETX. ETX also requires a status reply.

- End of Transmission (EOT)—Indicates the end-of-message transmission by this station; the message might have contained one or more blocks. Upon receipt of an EOT, all receiving stations become reset. The EOT is also used as a response to a poll when the polled station has nothing to send, and as an abort signal when the sender cannot continue transmission.

- Enquiry (ENQ)—Requests a repeat transmission of a response to a message block if the original response is garbled or is not received. ENQ can also indicate the end of a polling or selection sequence, and it is used to bid for the line when the line is a point-to-point connection.

- Affirmative Acknowledgment (ACK0 or ACK1)—Indicates correct receipt of the previous block and that the receiver is ready to accept the next block. ACK0 and ACK1 are used alternately, and receipt of the wrong one is an indication of an error in the protocol. ACK0 is the correct response to a station selection (on a multipoint circuit) or a line bid (on a point-to-point circuit).

- Wait-Before-Transmit Affirmative Acknowledgment (WACK)—Indicates a temporary not-ready-to-receive condition to the sending station and affirmative acknowledgment of the previously received data block. The normal response to WACK by the sending station is ENQ, but EOT and DLE EOT are also valid. If ENQ is received after sending WACK, the sending station continues to send WACK until it is ready to continue sending data.

- Negative Acknowledgment (NAK)—Indicates that the previously received block was received in error and that the receiver is ready to receive another block. NAK is also used as a station-not-ready reply to a station selection or line bid.

- Data Link Escape (DLE)—Indicates to the receiver that the character following the DLE is to be interpreted as a control character.

- Reverse Interrupt (RVI)—Indicates a request by a receiving station that the current transmission be terminated so that a high-priority message can be sent (such as a shutdown notice). RVI is also an affirmative acknowledgment to the previous block received. In a multipoint circuit, RVI sent from the control station means that the control station wants to select a different station. When a sending station receives an RVI, it responds by sending all data that would prevent it from becoming a receiving station.

- Temporary Text Delay (TTD)—Indicates that the sending station is not ready to send immediately but wants to keep the line. The receiving terminal reply to TTD is NAK. TTD normally is sent after 2 seconds if the sender cannot transmit the next block; this control code holds off the normal 3-second abort timer at the receiving terminal. The response to TTD is NAK, and TTD can be repeated several times. TTD also is used as a forward abort, by sending EOT in response to the NAK reply.

- Switched Line Disconnect (DLE EOT)—Indicates to a receiver that the transmitter is going to hang up on a switched line connection.

## Code Sequences

By looking at the ASCII and EBCDIC code charts, you can see that no code is assigned to several of the control characters mentioned in the preceding listing. Such control codes are represented by two-character sequences of the characters that are defined in the charts. Table 8.3 gives the correspondence between these control characters and sequences of standard characters.

## Polling and Selection

The active participants on a BiSync link are managed by a control station that issues either a Poll or a Select message addressed to the desired tributary. The Poll is an invitation to send from the control to the tributary. This allows the tributary to send any messages desired to the control station. The Select is a request-to-receive notice from the control station, telling the tributary that the control station has something to send to it. The control station thus controls which station has the link and the direction of transmission.

**TABLE 8.3**   Character Sequences for BiSync Control Characters

| BiSync Data Link Character | Character Sequences for Various Code Sets | | |
|---|---|---|---|
| | ASCII | EBCDIC | SBT |
| ACK 0 | DLE 0 | DLE 70 | DLE – |
| ACK 1 | DLE 1 | DLE / | DLE T |
| WACK | DLE ; | DLE , | DLE W |
| RVI | DLE | DLE @ | DLE 2 |
| TTD | STX ENQ | STX ENQ | STX ENQ |

Stations on the data link are assigned unique addresses that can consist of one to seven characters. The first character defines the station, and succeeding characters define some part of the station, such as a printer, as required. Some BiSync implementations repeat the station address for reliability purposes.

## Error Checking

BiSync uses three types of error detection: VRC/LRC, CRC-12, and CRC-16. Table 8.4 shows under what conditions each is used. Transparency mode is described later in this section. The VRC is an odd-parity check performed on each character transmitted, including the LRC character at the end of the block. Each bit in the LRC character provides odd parity for the corresponding bit position of all characters sent in the block. Figure 8.12 illustrates the formation of the VRC and LRC for an eight-character data block. Note that the LRC is formed in the same manner as the VRC; however, the LRC covers all characters in the data block, whereas the VRC covers individual characters.

In BiSync, the LRC character is called the Block Check Character (BCC). It is sent as the next character following an ETB, ITB, or ETX character. The BCC sent with the data is compared at the receiver with the one accumulated by the receiver; if the two are equal, all is well. The BCC calculation is restarted by the first STX or SOH character received after the direction of transmission is reversed (called a line turnaround). All characters except SYN characters received from that point until the next line turnaround are included in the calculation. If the message is sent in blocks with no line turnaround, each block is followed by an ITB and then the BCC. The BCC calculation is then restarted with the next STX or SOH character received.

The cyclic redundancy check codes are used for error checking in the same fashion as the LRC code. If the transmission code set is SBT, the CRC-12 method is used because each transmitted character is only 6 bits. For EBCDIC, the CRC-16 scheme is always used. For the ASCII code set, IBM has specified that the VRC/LRC scheme be used in the nontransparency (standard) mode and that CRC-16 be used in transparency mode. Transparency mode is described in detail later in the chapter.

## Messages and Blocks

Messages consist of one or more blocks of text, called the body of the message, surrounded by synchronization, header, and error-control characters. The beginning of each block is identified by the STX control character, and all blocks except the last in a message are ended by either an ETB or an ITB character. The last block of the message is ended by an ETX character.

**TABLE 8.4**  Type of BiSync Redundancy Check

| Code Set | No Transparency | Transparency Installed and Operating | Transparency Installed but Not Operating |
|----------|-----------------|--------------------------------------|------------------------------------------|
| EBCDIC   | CRC-16          | CRC-16                               | CRC-16                                   |
| ASCII    | VRC/LRC         | CRC-16                               | VRC/CRC-16                               |
| SBT      | CRC-12          | CRC-12                               | CRC-12                                   |

| Character | ←—— Data Bits ——→ | Character Parity Bit (VRC) |
|---|---|---|
| 1 | 1 0 1 0 1 1 0 1 | 0 |
| 2 | 0 1 1 0 1 0 1 0 | 1 |
| 3 | 0 1 1 1 0 1 0 1 | 0 |
| 4 | 1 0 1 0 0 1 0 1 | 1 |
| 5 | 1 0 0 1 0 0 1 0 | 0 |
| 6 | 0 1 0 0 1 0 0 1 | 0 |
| 7 | 1 0 0 1 0 0 1 0 | 0 |
| 8 | 0 1 1 0 1 0 0 1 | 1 |
| Block Parity Character (LRC) | 1 1 0 0 1 0 0 1 | 0 |

**FIGURE 8.12**

*VRC/LRC parity check.*

# Message Formats

Information is carried in BiSync as messages. Each message can have several parts: a synchronization sequence, a header, some text, and a block check sequence. Each part is identified by one or more control characters. In the case of messages used only for control, some parts such as the header, the text, or the BCC might be missing.

## Synchronization

Unless the transmitter and the receiver agree on the exact (to the bit) starting point of a message, they cannot communicate. Achieving this synchronization requires three steps:

1. The modems or other data communications devices at both ends of the circuit must acquire bit synchronization. The methods for doing this were discussed in Chapter 5, "Synchronous Modems, Digital Transmission, and Service Units."

2. The link interface equipment in the DTE must acquire character synchronization. This is done by searching the bit stream for a specific pattern of bits called a Synchronization Character (SYN). In ASCII, the bit pattern for SYN is 0010110. To help prevent recognition of a false SYN, most systems including BiSync require transmission and detection of two successive SYNs before they proceed with the next step in the synchronization process. The two SYN characters taken as a control set are called a Sync Sequence and are shown in most diagrams as a 0. To ensure that the first and last characters of a transmission are correctly sent, some BiSync stations add a PAD character before the first SYN and after every BCC, EOT, and ACK. This stratagem was devised primarily to overcome hardware limitations in some early hard-wired BiSync terminals.

3. The program operating the protocol must acquire message synchronization. In other words, the program must be capable of finding the beginning of each message or control character sequence. It does so by performing a program search of the characters received after the sync sequence for a control character that is defined to begin a block of data or control sequence. Such characters are SOH, STX, ACK0/1, NAK, WACK, RVI, and EOT.

## Heading

A heading is a sequence of characters beginning with the SOH character that is used for message type identification, message numbering, priority specification, and routing. Receipt of the SOH initiates accumulation of the BCC (but the SOH is not included in the BCC). The heading can be of fixed or variable length, and it is ended by an STX.

## Text

The text part of the message contains the information to be sent between application programs. The text begins with an STX and ends with ETX. Text can be broken into blocks for better error control. Each block begins with an STX and ends with an ETB, except for the last block, which ends with an ETX. The normal end of a transmission is signaled by an EOT following the ETX. Control characters are not allowed within the body of a text block. If a control character is detected, the receiving station terminates reception and looks for a BCC as the next two characters.

## Timeouts

Timeouts must be provided by the communications program or terminal to prevent indefinite delays caused by data errors or missing line-turnaround signals. Four functions are specified in BiSync for timeouts: transmit, receive, disconnect, and continue.

Transmit timeout is normally set for 1 second. It defines the rate of insertion of synchronous idle (SYN SYN or DLE SYN) sequences in the data to help maintain bit and character synchronization.

Receive timeout is normally set for 3 seconds. It carries out a few actions including these:

- It limits the time that a transmitting station will wait for a reply.
- It signals a receiving station to check the line for synchronous idle characters, which indicate that transmission is continuing. The receive timeout is reset each time a sync sequence is received.
- It sets a limit on the time that a tributary station in a multipoint circuit can remain in control mode. The timer is reset each time that an end signal such as an ENQ or ACK is received, as long as the station stays in control mode.

Disconnect timeout causes a station on a switched network to disconnect from the circuit after 20 seconds of inactivity.

Continue timeout causes a transmitting station sending a TTD to send another if it is still incapable of sending text. A receiving station must transmit a WACK if it becomes temporarily incapable of receiving within a 2-second interval.

## Transparent-Text Mode

It is often necessary in communicating between machines to send data that does not represent characters but that instead represents some purely arbitrary quantity or object. An example is the binary representation of a computer program. In such a case, it is likely that some of the data will have the same bit pattern as a BiSync control character. Transparent-text mode, sometimes called transparency, allows such data to be sent without being misinterpreted by the communications program. The basic technique in transparency is to precede each true control character with the DLE character, as Figure 8.13a shows. If a DLE bit pattern appears in the text of the message, it also is preceded by a DLE. Thus, a bit pattern is interpreted as a control character only if it is preceded by a DLE. The resulting message, after processing by the link interface program to remove the DLE, is shown in Figure 8.13b. Note that for any DLE DLE sequence in the text, the first DLE is suppressed, and the second is sent along as part of the data.

**8**

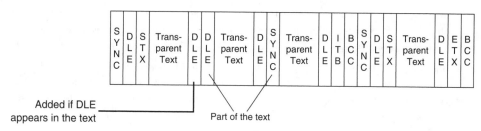

a. Block as Transmitted

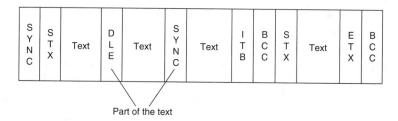

b. Block After Stripping Transparency Control Characters

**FIGURE 8.13**

*BiSync transparency mode.*

# Full-Duplex Protocols

The Binary Synchronous Communications procedures were devised at a time when most data communications circuits were operated at 2400bps and were two-wire half-duplex circuits connecting remote job-entry card reader/printer terminals to mainframes. As online applications using remote CRT terminals became more cost-effective, and as four-wire private line circuits became available, the demand for a communications protocol that could handle full-duplex operations arose. These were the requirements for such a protocol:

- Messages must flow in both directions simultaneously.
- It must be possible to have more than one message in the channel at one time. (BiSync allows only one.)
- Transparency must be designed in, not tacked on as an afterthought.
- The protocol must allow switched-network, half-duplex, and multipoint operation, as well as full-duplex point-to-point operation.
- The error-detection and correction scheme must be powerful and must prohibit the problem of aliasing.

The last condition is a particularly difficult one. Aliasing occurs when a message fragment caused by a transmission error is interpreted as a good message at the receiver (that is, when a bad or broken message "looks like" a good message). This can be a serious problem, especially in critical applications such as those that handle funds transfer and military command and control. Much design effort in the international standards organizations and in private companies was devoted to the development of protocols that prevented the aliasing problem. This led to the development of three widely used schemes. Two of them were alike in principle and operation and in the fact that they require special hardware, but they were promulgated by different organizations. The third, developed at Digital Equipment Corporation, uses a different technique but can operate with standard character-oriented line-interface equipment.

## High-Level Data Link Control Procedures

The critical issue in preventing aliasing lies in determining where a legal message block begins and ends, and exactly what part of the information taken in by the receiver is to be included in the CRC. As a result of work done at IBM by J. Ray Kersey and others in the early 1970s, a protocol was proposed and later adopted as an international standard by the International Standards Organization in 1979. It is called the High-level Data Link Control (HDLC) procedures. Although HDLC dates to the 1970s, it is used in modified form as the transport vehicle for Integrated Services Digital Network (ISDN), the data link-layer protocol for X.25 packet switching and as the data link protocol for modem-to-modem communications. In its use for

ISDN it is referred to as link access protocol-D (LAP-D), while its use for X.25 packet switching and modem-to-modem communications are referred to as LAP-B and LAP-M, respectively.

In HDLC, the message synchronization indicator (called a flag) was originally generated by a hardware circuit, and other hardware circuits were used to prevent any data being transmitted from having the same pattern as the flag. The flag then becomes a kind of out-of-band framing signal, much like the break signal in the teletypewriter protocol. Today, HDLC operations can be performed via software due to the enhanced processing capabilities of modern microprocessors.

Because the data being transmitted is examined bit by bit to screen out possible aliases of the flag, HDLC and other similar protocols, such as IBM's Synchronous Data Link Control (SDLC), are referred to as bit-oriented protocols, or BOPs. Unlike BiSync and DDCMP (which will be described later), the text part of messages sent using the HDLC protocol can, in principle, be any arbitrary number of bits long, and HDLC is defined to allow this. In practice, as with BiSync and DDCMP, most implementations of BOPs restrict the text (and, in fact, all of the message, including the flag) to be an integral multiple of the number of bits in a character (almost always eight).

## Frames, Flags, and Fields

In HDLC, all information is carried by frames that can be of three types: information frames (I-frames), supervisory control sequences (S-frames), or unnumbered command/responses (U-frames). Figure 8.14 shows one information frame as a rectangular block divided into its six fields: a beginning Flag (F) field, an Address (A) field, a Control (C) field, an Information (I) field, a Frame Check Sequence (FCS) field, and a Final Flag (F) field. S-frames and U-frames have the same fields, except that the I field is left out.

I-frames perform information transfer and independently carry message acknowledgments and Poll or Final bits. S-frames perform link supervisory control, such as message acknowledgments, retransmit requests, and requests for temporary holds on I-frame transmissions (like a WACK in BiSync). U-frames provide a flexible format for additional link-control data by omitting the frame sequence numbers and thus providing a place for an additional 32 command and 32 response functions. The functions of the fields in the HDLC frame are detailed here:

- Flag field—Every frame begins and ends with a flag, which is the bit pattern 01111110. The same flag can end one frame and begin the next. Every station connected to a link must continuously search the received data for the flag.

- Address field—In command frames, the address identifies the destination station for the command. In response frames, the address identifies the station sending the response.

- Control field—The control field carries commands and responses, according to Figure 8.15.

- Information field—The information field can contain any sequence of bits, which, in principle, need not be related to a particular character set or data structure. In practice, the Information field is almost always an integral multiple of one character in length, which is usually 8 bits.

- Frame Check Sequence field—The FCS (or CRC) for HDLC is the ITU-CRC, as previously discussed.

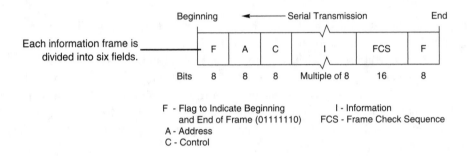

**FIGURE 8.14**

*HDLC format.*

To ensure that the flag is unique, the transmitting hardware must monitor the bit stream continually between the beginning and ending flags for the presence of strings of five 1 bits in a row. If such a string occurs, a 0 bit is inserted (called bit stuffing) by the hardware after the fifth 1 bit so that the string will not look like a flag. The added 0 bit is removed at the receiver. This procedure makes any appearance of strings of 1 bits greater than five in number a flag, an error on the transmission line, or a deliberately sent fill pattern between frames of all 1 bits. One method of aborting transmission of a frame is to begin transmitting continuous ones.

Specification in the protocol of a unique, hardware-generated flag pattern and the length of the Address, Control, and FCS fields provides complete transparency for the Information field. The hardware prevents any bit pattern sent by the applications program from having more than five continuous ones, and the hardware-added zeros are stripped from the data stream as it passes through the receiver. Also, the position of the FCS is defined by the receipt of the ending flag so that the residual pattern in the CRC register can be immediately compared with the fixed value (0001110100001111).

The order of bit transmission is defined for addresses, commands, responses, and sequence numbers to be low-order bit first, but the order of bit transmission for the information field is not specified. The FCS is transmitted beginning with the coefficient of the highest order term (x15). An invalid frame is defined as one that is not properly bounded by flags or that is shorter than 32 bits between flags. Invalid frames are ignored (in contrast with frames that have a bad FCS, which require a NAK).

## HDLC Semantics

The preceding discussion dealt with what is called the syntax of HDLC. The syntax is the definition of the bit patterns and order of sending bits that will make correctly formed messages— that is, those that are legal in the protocol. For you to understand what happens when HDLC is used, however, it is necessary to define the semantic content of messages, or the meanings that should be assigned to correctly formed messages.

The normal sequence of messages in HDLC consists of the transfer of one or more frames containing I-fields from a data source (the transmitting station) to a data sink (the receiving station). The receipt is acknowledged by the sink by sending a frame in the backward direction. The source must retain all transmitted messages until they are explicitly acknowledged by the sink. The value of N(R) indicates that the station transmitting the N(R) has correctly received all I-frames numbered up to N(R) – 1. I-frames and S-frames (see Figure 8.15) are numbered from 0 to 7 (for unextended control fields). An independent numbering sequence is carried for each data source/data sink combination. The response from a sink can acknowledge several (but not more than seven) received messages at one time and can be included in an I-frame being sent from the sink to the source.

A data link consists of two or more communicating stations, so, for control purposes, it is necessary to designate one station as the primary station with responsibility for managing data flow and link error-recovery procedures. Primary stations send command frames. Other stations on the link are called secondary stations, and they communicate using response frames. Primary stations can send to secondaries using the Select bit in the control field of an I-frame, or a primary can allow a secondary to send by sending a Poll bit.

Secondary stations can operate in one of two modes: Normal Response Mode (NRM) or Asynchronous Response Mode (ARM). In NRM, the secondary can send only in response to a specific request or permission by the primary station. The secondary station explicitly indicates the last frame to be sent by setting the final bit in the control field. In ARM, the secondary can independently initiate transmission without receiving an explicit permission or Poll from the primary.

If you want to learn more about HDLC, refer to International Standards ISO 3309-1979 (E), ISO 4335-1979 (E), and ISO 6256-1981 for the complete definition of the HDLC protocol. There is a data-link control procedure standard promulgated by the American National Standards Institute (ANSI) in the United States called Advanced Data Communications Control Procedures (ADCCP), which is functionally equivalent to HDLC.

| HDLC Frame Format | Bits in Control Field | | | | | | | |
|---|---|---|---|---|---|---|---|---|
| | 1 | 2 | 3 | 4 | 5 | 6 | 7 | 8 |
| I-frame (Information transfer commands/ responses) | 0 | | N(S)[1] | | P/F[2] | | N(R)[3] | |
| S-frame (Supervisory commands/responses) | 1 | 0 | S[4] | | P/F | | N(R) | |
| U-frame (Unnumbered commands/responses) | 1 | 1 | M[5] | | P/F | | M | |

Notes:
[1]N(S) is the transmitting station send sequence number, bit 2 is the low order bit.
[2]P/F is the Poll bit for primary station transmissions, and the final bit for secondary station transmissions.
[3]N(R) is the transmitting station receive sequence number. Bit 6 is the low-order bit.
[4]S are supervisory function bits.
[5]M are modifier function bits.

**FIGURE 8.15**
*Control field contents.*

# Synchronous Data Link Control

The standard full-duplex synchronous data link control protocol used by IBM in products conforming to its System Network Architecture is called Synchronous Data Link Control (SDLC). It is functionally equivalent to HDLC, but with these exceptions:

- SDLC information fields must be an integral multiple of 8 bits long.
- SDLC contains additional commands and responses not defined in the ISO Elements of Procedure (for example, a TEST command and response). Figure 8.16 shows the frame structure of SDLC (which is the same as HDLC), along with the common modes, commands, and responses. A close examination of this illustration will help you understand the SDLC format and the differences between HDLC and SDLC.

# Digital Data Communications Message Protocol

At about the same time that SDLC was being developed at IBM, George Friend, Steven Russell, and Stuart Wecker were given the task of developing a synchronous protocol at Digital Equipment Corporation, now a part of Compaq Computer Corporation. The requirements were similar to those given before full-duplex protocols, but with one important additional item: The protocol must run on existing data communications hardware, and preferably on asynchronous as well as synchronous links. The result was the Digital Data Communications Message Protocol, or DDCMP.

DDCMP is a character-oriented protocol rather than a bit-oriented protocol like SDLC. Therefore, DDCMP requires no special bit stuffing and destuffing hardware, and it can be used with various types of line interfaces, including asynchronous units. The method of specifying the length of a message to look for the BCC at the right time is inclusion of a 14-bit count field in the header. This is a count of the number of characters in the information field of the message. Because error-free transmission depends on the count field being detected correctly, the header of DDCMP messages is a constant length and has its own BCC, which is checked before setting up to receive the information part of the message. The format of DDCMP messages is shown in Figure 8.17. A detailed study of this figure reveals the bit pattern of the various fields in the frame for different types of messages.

DDCMP has two principal advantages and some disadvantages. One advantage is that it is usable without special hardware on asynchronous, synchronous, or even parallel data channels. Another advantage is that the sequence number field allows for up to 255 messages to be outstanding on the channel at one time, a requirement when operating full-duplex channels over satellite links. On the other hand, it does not support a go-back-N or selective reject mode of operation, and it is, in principle, more vulnerable to the aliasing problem than are bit-oriented protocols. It also has been mistakenly criticized for inefficiency because of the inclusion of a BCC after the header on the equivalent of I-frames. In fact, for messages of average length, DDCMP is somewhat more efficient than bit-stuffing protocols because of the extra bits added by the hardware in the bit-oriented schemes. In practice, aliasing has not caused noticeable problems with DDCMP.

**8**

**PROTOCOLS AND ERROR CONTROL**

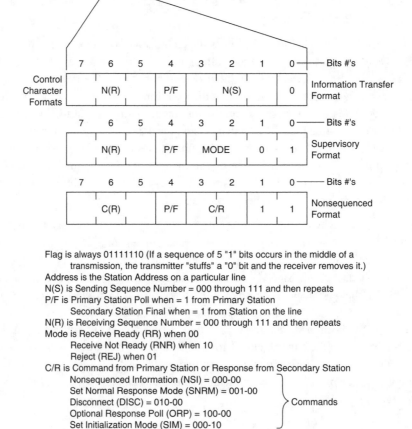

Flag is always 01111110 (If a sequence of 5 "1" bits occurs in the middle of a
    transmission, the transmitter "stuffs" a "0" bit and the receiver removes it.)
Address is the Station Address on a particular line
N(S) is Sending Sequence Number = 000 through 111 and then repeats
P/F is Primary Station Poll when = 1 from Primary Station
    Secondary Station Final when = 1 from Station on the line
N(R) is Receiving Sequence Number = 000 through 111 and then repeats
Mode is Receive Ready (RR) when 00
    Receive Not Ready (RNR) when 10
    Reject (REJ) when 01
C/R is Command from Primary Station or Response from Secondary Station
    Nonsequenced Information (NSI) = 000-00 ⎫
    Set Normal Response Mode (SNRM) = 001-00 ⎬
    Disconnect (DISC) = 010-00 ⎬ Commands
    Optional Response Poll (ORP) = 100-00 ⎬
    Set Initialization Mode (SIM) = 000-10 ⎭

    Nonsequenced Information (UI) = 000-00 ⎫
    Nonsequenced Acknowledgment (UA) = 110-00 ⎬
    Request for Initialization (RIM) = 000-10 ⎬ Responses
    Command Reject (FRMR) = 001-10 ⎬
    Request Online (DM) = 000-11 ⎭
Info is Information = Variable Length for Information Transfer
    Prohibited for Supervisory Format
    Variable Length for Nonsequenced Format with NSI
    Fixed Format with CMDR
CRC = Cyclic Redundancy Check Remainder

**FIGURE 8.16**

*SDLC format.*

Data Messages          1000001   Character Count   QS   Resp #   Message#    Address
Acknowledgment         0000101   00000001000000    QS   Resp #   00000000    Address
Negative Acknowledge   0000101   00000010Reason    QS   Resp #   00000000    Address

    Reason
        BCC Header Error          000001
        BCC Data Error            000010
        Rep Response              000011
        Buffer Unavailable        001000
        Receiver Overrun          001001
        Message Too Long          010000
        Header Format Error       010001

Reply Message          00000101   000000011000000   QS   00000000   LstMess#    Address
Start Message          00000101   00000110000000    11   00000000   00000000    Address
Start Acknowledgment   00000101   00000111000000    11   00000000   00000000    Address
Maintenance Message    10010000   Character Count   11   00000000   00000000    Address

Notes

1. Only the Data Message and the Maintenance Message have character counts, so only these messages have the information and CRC2 fields shown in the message format diagram above.

2. "Resp #" refers to Response Number. This is the number of the last message received correctly. When used in a negative acknowledge message, it is assumed that the next higher numbered message was not received, was received with errors, or was unaccepted for some other reason. See "Reasons."

3. "Message#" is the sequentially assigned number of this message. Numbers are assigned by the transmitting station modulo 256; i.e., message 000 follows 255.

4. "LstMess#" is the number of the last message transmitted by the station.

5. "Address" is the address of the tributary station in multipoint systems and is used in messages both to and from the tributary. In point-to-point operation, a station sends the address "1" but ignores the address field on reception.

6. "Q" and "S" refer to the quick sync flag bit and the select bit.

**FIGURE 8.17**

*DDCMP message format in detail.*

8

PROTOCOLS AND
ERROR CONTROL

# What You Have Learned

- Protocols are rules for communications between processes that are alike. Interfaces are rules for communications between processes that are different.

- Data communications protocols are made up of symbols to be communicated, a code set translating those symbols to binary code, and rules for the correct sequencing of the symbols.

- Parity is a method of adding redundancy to coded symbols to help detect errors in transmission.

- XMODEM is a simple protocol used in asynchronous transmission between microcomputers.

- YMODEM permits multiple files to be transferred between computers.

- ZMODEM supports the resumption of a file transfer at its point of interruption, as well as the dynamic adjustment of the size of data blocks based on the error rate on the line.

- A cyclic redundancy check is a number calculated from the data transmitted by the sender and recalculated by the receiver that allows the data to be checked for errors in transmission.

- The most widely used code sets in the United States are ASCII and EBCDIC.

- Protocols must be suitable for use on dial-up and private line connections and for point-to-point and multipoint network arrangements.

- The most widely used protocols in the United States are TTY, XMODEM, BiSync, SDLC, and DDCMP.

# Quiz for Chapter 8

1. Communications protocols always have which of the following?

    A. A set of symbols

    B. A start of header

    C. A special flag symbol

    D. BCC

2. The Baudot code uses how many bits per symbol?

    A. 9

    B. 7

    C. 5

    D. 8

3. When transmitting odd-parity coded symbols, the number of bits that are zeros in each symbol is

   A. Odd.

   B. Even.

   C. Unknown.

   D. None of the above.

4. Suppose that you're transmitting the 7-bit character whose decimal value is 65 using 8-bit odd parity. What is the binary value of the character?

   A. 10000010

   B. 10000000

   C. 11000001

   D. 10000011

5. Under mark parity, each parity bit is

   A. Alternated between 0 and 1.

   B. Always set to 0.

   C. Always set to 1.

   D. Not used.

6. In the XMODEM protocol, the sender waits for what character from the receiver before beginning transmission?

   A. WACK

   B. ACK

   C. RVI

   D. NAK

7. If each character in an XMODEM block has an ASCII value of 50, what is the value of the checksum that's added to the block?

   A. 50

   B. 23

   C. 41

   D. 25

8. Throughput using a half-duplex protocol

   A. Exceeds that of a full-duplex protocol.

   B. Is less than that of a full-duplex protocol.

   C. Equals throughput on a full-duplex protocol.

   D. Is faster than all other types of protocols.

9. The varying characteristics of transmission lines

    A. Enable a fixed block size to be optimum for use on all circuits.

    B. Enable a long block size to be optimum on noisy circuits.

    C. Enable a variable block size to be optimum for use on all circuits.

    D. Enable a short block size to be optimum on non-noisy circuits.

10. Under the YMODEM protocol, block 0 is used to transport which of the following?

    A. Error-recovery information

    B. Two checksums

    C. Information about the file to be transferred

    D. A 1024-byte data character block

11. The second YMODEM block used to transport an 1100-byte file would use a data field of how many characters?

    A. 1,024

    B. 100

    C. 128

    D. 64

12. A streaming protocol

    A. Provides error detection.

    B. Does not provide error detection.

    C. Uses 64-byte blocks.

    D. Requires a manual setup.

13. Which of these protocols is a sliding window protocol?

    A. XMODEM

    B. YMODEM

    C. YMODEM-G

    D. WXMODEM

14. Which of these protocols adjusts its block size based on the line error rate?

    A. XMODEM

    B. YMODEM

    C. ZMODEM

    D. WXMODEM

15. Which of the following is not a valid rule for XOR?

    A. 0 XOR 0 = 0

    B. 1 XOR 1 = 1

    C. 1 XOR 0 = 1

    D. B XOR B = 0

16. Which of the following BiSync control codes is not defined in the EBCDIC character set?

    A. STX

    B. ACK0

    C. ENQ

    D. TTD

17. How many messages can be outstanding (unacknowledged) on a BiSync link?

    A. 1

    B. 2

    C. 4

    D. 8

18. Which code set is used in BiSync when VRC/LRC is being used but not in transparency mode?

    A. EBCDIC

    B. ASCII

    C. SBT

    D. Fieldata

19. Which of the following is the escape character that identifies control characters in BiSync transparency mode?

    A. ESC

    B. SYN

    C. DLE

    D. RVI

20. One primary difference between DDCMP and SDLC is

    A. DDCMP does not have a transparent mode.

    B. SDLC does not use a CRC.

    C. DDCMP has a message header.

    D. DDCMP does not require special hardware to find the beginning of a message.

# PC Communications Software

## IN THIS CHAPTER

In this chapter, you will turn your attention to software that enables personal computers to communicate via the switched telephone network.

This chapter covers some important communications software features that enable you to control the operation of a modem, emulate a specific type of terminal, transfer binary and ASCII files, and perform other communications functions. Because the best way to become acquainted with personal computer communications software is through the use of representative programs, this chapter shows the use of several popular programs.

First you will examine the use of dial-up networking built into several versions of Microsoft's Windows operating system, as well as the use of the HyperTerminal program included with Microsoft's Windows 95, Windows 98, Windows Millennium Edition (Me), Windows NT 4.0, and Windows 2000 operating systems. Then you will shift your attention to two third-party communications programs, ProcommPlus and ProcommPlus for Windows. Through a series of personal computer screen images, readers are walked through the use of each program to establish a communications session, change dialing directory entries, and perform a file transfer operation.

# Communications Program Features

You can gain an appreciation for the features built into many personal computer communications programs by learning about their general operation and utilization. First and foremost, the program must be written to operate on the PC platform that you use.

## Operating System and Operating Environment Support

Until the late 1980s, there was essentially one operating system for each type of personal computer, which simplified the selection of a communications program. The IBM PC and compatible line of products were based on the Disk Operating System (DOS), whereas Apple became primarily a Macintosh vendor. The Macintosh operating system was later significantly revised with the introduction of System 7. In the IBM PC and compatible computer world, DOS was supplemented by several versions of the Microsoft Windows operating systems. This means that you now must consider whether the communications program was written to work under a specific operating environment as well as a specific operating system.

Although various versions of Windows (including 95, 98, Me, NT, Windows 2000, and Windows XP) provide facilities to operate DOS programs, when run in that mode, the program will not support such operating environment features as the cutting and pasting of information between applications and the familiar graphical user interface (GUI) of the previously mentioned operating systems.

# Modem Support

After you select a communications program that satisfies your operating environment and computer platform requirements, you must also consider an important hardware device: the modem you plan to use. Although most modems support the Hayes Microcomputer Products modem command set, that support primarily references a core set of commands that govern the operation of basic modem functions. As you learned in Chapter 4, "Asynchronous Modems and Interfaces," when such features as data compression, flow control, and error detection and correction were added to intelligent modems, vendors incorporated the control of those features in different ways. Some vendors used AT commands, and others used different S register settings to control new features. As a result, most vendors used proprietary methods to control the operation of modem features beyond the basic modem control functions supported by the standard Hayes modem command set.

Whereas a few years ago the support of the standard Hayes command set was sufficient to operate most modems, today a communications program might include the support of a dozen to 50 or more modems. As an alternative to supporting the command sets used by a large number of modems, some programs enable users to configure the program to operate with any intelligent modem. In doing so, such programs provide users with a menu of modem functions and enable the entry of the appropriate AT command or S register setting for each function. Although this requires users to spend a considerable amount of time looking through a modem manual to locate the command or register setting for each function and then manually entering the function, it also allows the program to support any modem.

Now that you've read about the relationship of software to the computer platform and modem, turn your attention to the interface between the two devices and the communications program features that you might want to consider to control the transfer of data between the devices.

# Controlling the Interface

Communications software must provide control over the movement of data between a computer and a modem. To help you understand the control features you should consider when examining communications software, this section outlines the flow of data between the two devices and how that flow must be controlled if such modem features as data compression and error detection and correction are enabled.

Figure 9.1 illustrates in schematic diagram format the relationship of the flow of data between a computer and a modem. Note that the computer's data-transfer rate does not necessarily have to equal the modem's operating rate. In fact, when you use a compression-performing modem, you will normally use the communications program to set the computer's serial port to a data rate two to four times or more over the operating rate of the modem. For correct operation during data compression, the data rate into the modem must exceed the modem's operating rate. For example, if a modem has an average compression ratio of 4:1 and an operating rate of 9600bps, the computer's serial port should be set to transfer data to the modem at four times the modem's operating rate, or 38400bps. However, because the compression ratio varies based on the compressibility of data, what happens when the modem cannot compress data or compresses data at a lower compression ratio?

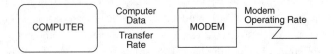

**FIGURE 9.1**

*Data flow between a computer and a modem.*

If data is flowing into the modem at 38,400bps but the modem compresses data at a rate less than a 4:1 compression ratio, its output is less than its input. This means that within a very short period, the modem's limited buffer storage will overflow, and data will be lost. Obviously, modem users do not want this to happen; this can be prevented by enabling flow control.

## Flow Control

Flow control can be defined as the orderly regulation of the transfer of data. You can turn on or enable modem flow control via an appropriate command or S register setting. When flow control is turned on, the modem signals the attached computer whenever its buffer fills to a predefined level. That signal tells the computer to suspend transmission. When the modem's buffer is emptied to a certain level, it sends another signal to the computer, which disables flow control.

Three types of flow control are supported by most modems: inband signaling, outband signaling, and ENQ/ACK. Inband signaling references the transmission of XON and XOFF control characters. Outband signaling references the modem raising and lowering the Clear to Send (CTS) signal on the RS-232 interface. ENQ/ACK references a signaling method similar to XON and XOFF that's used primarily by Hewlett-Packard terminal devices. Thus, the communications software that turns your computer into a terminal must support one or more modem flow-control techniques to prevent the loss of data when the modem operates in its compressed mode. In addition, flow control becomes a necessity when a modem performs error detection and correction and when transmission errors occur.

This is because the modem must retain blocks of data in memory until they are positively acknowledged. If line errors occur, the modem's buffer rapidly fills as additional data is transferred from the computer to the modem and the modem cannot purge previously transmitted data from memory. Again, the modem will transmit a flow-control signal to the computer that the communications program operating on the computer must recognize.

## Operating Rates

The computer data-transfer rates supported by most communications programs range from 300 to 115200bps. Typically, a 115200bps rate is set when a modem operates at 28800bps or higher and has its compression feature enabled. Other high-speed computer data-transfer rates supported by some communications programs include 57600bps and 76800bps, which are normally used to support compression-performing modems operating at 14400 and 19200bps, respectively.

Before setting the computer data-transfer operating rate, you should ensure that the modem's serial port is set to autobaud detect, or you should set it to the computer data transfer rate that you want to use. Otherwise, the modem will not be capable of recognizing the data being transferred to it from the computer due to an interface data rate mismatch.

You set both the modem serial port and the modem operating rate via command codes or S register settings. Both settings are independent of the capability of the communications program because they are dependent on the operating capability built into the modem. Thus, the method by which the communications program enables you to set those operating rates should not be evaluated because the actual settings depend on the modem used.

## Dialing Directory

One of the more important features of many communications programs is the dialing directory. The basic function of the dialing directory is to enable a user to enter telephone numbers to be dialed as well as to provide a description of each number. Most communications programs expand the functionality of the dialing directory by building into the directory the capability of the user to assign, view, and modify different communications settings. Some of the more common communications settings that are changed through the use of a dialing directory include the following:

- Operating rate of the computer's serial port
- Parity
- Number of data bits and stop bits per character
- File-transfer protocol to be used as a default for file transfers

- Type of terminal that the communications software emulates
- Whether a script file is associated with the dialing directory

Of those previously mentioned settings, the ones that most persons will want to evaluate are the range of serial port operating rates supported, the types of file-transfer protocols and terminal emulations included with the program, and the inclusion of a script programming language, as well as the commands supported by the programming language and its ease of use.

The supported file-transfer protocols govern your capability to upload and download files from bulletin board systems, other personal computers, and information utilities. Although almost all communications programs support a core set of file-transfer protocols, some programs include WXMODEM, ZMODEM, and other protocols that were developed to satisfy one or more communications requirements lacking in other protocols. For example, ZMODEM uses a 32-bit CRC, which reduces the probability of an undetected error to an order of magnitude below that of other file-transfer protocols, and WXMODEM facilitates the transfer of files through packet networks.

The types of terminal emulations supported by the communications program govern its capability to communicate with different types of computer systems. This can be extremely important when the program is accessing mainframes and minicomputers designed to support certain types of full-screen terminal devices. Those computers transmit special control codes to perform such functions as clearing the screen, moving the cursor to a specific location, displaying different colors, establishing protected fields, and highlighting information. Without the correct terminal emulator, your personal computer will more than likely fail to correctly display information received from a distant computer. In addition, certain keystrokes from your computer will probably be received incorrectly at the mainframe or minicomputer if you do not use a correct terminal emulator. This problem occurs because terminal emulators use different key combinations to represent certain control keys, such as IBM program function (PF) keys that are not included on conventional personal computer keyboards.

With a script programming language, you can automate communications functions, such as logging onto an electronic mail system, checking for new mail, and downloading messages from your mailbox. Some communications programs include a script-learning capability. This feature enables you to perform the required operation once while the program constructs the appropriate script language commands that duplicate the functions manually performed. Thereafter, you can invoke the script to automatically perform the series of manual operations you previously conducted.

The following list shows the communications program features that you might want to consider. This list can be used to evaluate the suitability of two or more programs that you are considering purchasing or as a means of comparing the functionality of a program against your communications requirements.

- Operating system compatibility

- Operating environment compatibility

- Modem support

- Flow-control support

- Serial port operating rates supported

- Number of dialing directory entries allowed

- File-transfer protocols supported

- Terminal emulations supported

- Script programming language support

Now that you have an appreciation for the main features incorporated into many communications programs, let's turn to the use of several programs. In doing so, we will commence our use of communications programs with two similar and highly related modules bundled into several versions of Microsoft's Windows operating system. Those modules are the operating system's Dial-Up Networking facility and its HyperTerminal communications program.

# Dial-Up Networking

Although Dial-Up Networking permits you to gain access to shared information on another computer, its primary function is to enable users to configure a modem and to gain access to an Internet service provider whose computer acts as a server. For interactive communications with bulletin boards, mainframes, and minicomputers, you should use the HyperTerminal program bundled with just about all modern versions of Windows to include Windows 95, Windows 98, Windows ME, Windows NT, Windows 2000, and Windows XP or another third-party program designed to run under the computer operating system that you are using.

Dial-Up Networking is currently included in all versions of Windows after Windows 3.11. For several versions of Windows, access to Dial-Up Networking is the same.

That is, you first double-click on the My Computer icon. In the dialog box that opens, if you are using Windows 95, 98, or Me you double-click on the Dial-Up Networking icon. In other versions of Windows, such as Windows 2000, you will note a link labeled Network and Dial-Up connections in the My Computer display. Clicking on that link will display a similar dialog box labeled Network and Dial-Up Connections. However, unlike other versions of Windows, Windows 2000 includes a Network Connection wizard, which facilitates the configuration of your computer to support your networking needs.

Recognizing the old adage that "the proof of the pudding is in the eating," examine how you could use Dial-Up Networking to create a connection to an Internet service provider. In doing

9

PC
COMMUNICATIONS
SOFTWARE

so let's use Windows Me. When applicable, we note some of the differences between that version of Windows and earlier versions of the operating system.

Figure 9.2 illustrates the selection of the icon labeled Make a New Connection from the Dial-Up Networking screen that results in the display of a new dialog box with that name. Note that you can enter a name for the computer that you want to access or accept the default of My Connection. Although you could click on the button labeled Next and accept hidden defaults for the modem shown selected in Figure 9.2, click on the button labeled Configure to examine the options available for configuring a dial-up connection.

**FIGURE 9.2**

*The Make a New Connection dialog box provides a mechanism to configure a selected modem.*

The tab labeled General (shown in Figure 9.3) enables you to set the communications port that will be used to communicate with the modem, its speaker volume, and its maximum speed. Note that the latter references the interface to the modem, not the modem's operating rate.

Although the highest operating rate of the modem in use is 56000bps, the maximum speed was set to 115,200bps to take advantage of the data-compression capability of the modem. Thus, data will be transferred at 115200bps from the computer to the modem, where it is compressed and transmitted to its destination at a line operating rate of 56000bps. In actuality a 56Kbps modem operates asymmetrically, with a maximum downward rate higher than the maximum upload rate. In addition, its highest data-transfer rate is less than 56Kbps due to Federal Communications Commission power regulations.

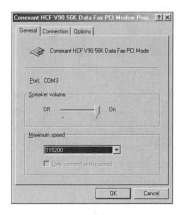

**FIGURE 9.3**

Figure 9.4 shows the Connection tab, which governs the connection to the previously selected modem. With the options on this tab, you can set both connection and call preferences to include the number of data bits per character, the parity, and the number of stop bits per character. By clicking on the Port Settings button, you can reset a first-in, first-out (FIFO) UART buffer for default use or to tune performance. Clicking the Advanced button takes you to a dialog box in which you can specify whether to use modem error control, data compression, modulation, and either hardware or software flow control. In most cases, when a Windows user selects a modem, Dial-Up Networking automatically uses default values that are sufficient enough that the user does not have to alter the program's settings on the General tab or the Connection tab.

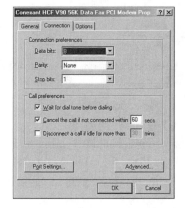

**FIGURE 9.4**

*The Connection tab enables you to set both connection and call preferences.*

**9**

**PC COMMUNICATIONS SOFTWARE**

The third tab in the External Properties dialog box is the Options tab. Its options allow you to control when the terminal window is displayed with respect to dialing activity, to select manual dialing instead of the default automatic dialing, and to specify a waiting period if you plan to use a credit card for billing your call.

When you complete the entries in the External Properties dialog box, the program prompts you to enter the area code and telephone number of the computer that you want to call. Figure 9.5 shows this screen, completed using a telephone number that provides a connection to an access carrier that, in turn, supports dial access to several Internet service providers in mid-Georgia by CompuServe. After you enter the relevant telephone number, Dial-Up Networking informs you that you successfully created a new connection and displays the name of the connection. However, that message is a bit misleading because if you need to access an Internet service provider, you must return to your newly created connection icon to perform some additional tailoring.

Figure 9.3 illustrates the Modem Properties dialog box that is displayed after clicking on the button labeled Configure, located in the lower-right portion of Figure 9.2. This dialog box has three tabs, labeled General, Connection, and Options.

## Tailoring Dial-Up Networking for Internet Access

After you create the icon for your new connection, you can tailor its use in several ways. Double-clicking on the icon permits you to specify a username and password for automating logons. By right-clicking the icon and selecting Properties, you can tailor dialing properties for the connection.

When you double-click the My Connection icon, a Connect To dialog box appears. Note that you can enter your username and password into this dialog box, as well as perform the following tasks:

- Specify prefix codes to access local and long-distance numbers if your computer's telephone line is located behind a PBX.
- In cities with multiple area codes, specify which area codes require a "1" for long distance and which require only the area code.
- Use a so-called 1010 bypass communications carrier to avoid using your default long-distance company or to charge the call to your calling card.
- Disable call waiting and specify the type of dialing used by the telephone system at your location.
- Force long distance for telephone numbers that are in the same area code but are not local calls.

Right-clicking on an icon in the Dial-Up Networking folder displays a pop-up menu. That menu includes a Properties entry, which enables you to tailor or configure your computer's dial-up connection for access to a specific type of server.

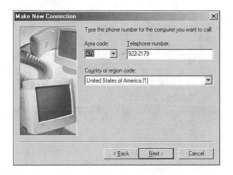

**FIGURE 9.5**

*Entering the telephone number of the computer to be contacted.*

Under Windows 95 and Windows 98, you would select Properties to access a Properties dialog box associated with the icon that you chose. That dialog box has four tabs: General, Server Types, Scripting, and Multilink. The General tab identifies and allows you to change the telephone number to be dialed, along with the modem to be used for dialing. The Scripting tab enables you to select a previously created script file and associate its use with the connection process. On the Multilink tab, you can choose to use multiple modems to increase the bandwidth of your connection. You can also choose additional devices to be used simultaneously for the connection. Your ISP must provide support for this feature for you to use it. The last tab, which is of key interest to many Windows users, is the Server Types tab. This tab permits you to specify the communications protocol to be used to access a specific type of server. Supported protocols include the Point-to-Point Protocol (PPP), the Serial Line Interface Protocol (SLIP) for supporting UNIX connectivity, a special version of PPP for accessing the CompuServe network, and other protocols.

Under Windows Me, the number of tabs were increased to six, as shown in the left portion of Figure 9.6. Clicking on the TCP/IP Settings button displays the TCP/IP Settings dialog box, which is shown in the right portion of Figure 9.6.

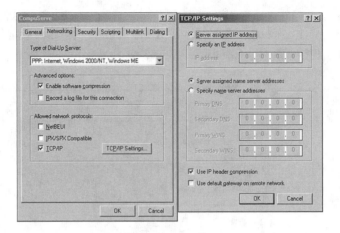

**FIGURE 9.6**

*Right-clicking on a Dial-Up Networking icon and selecting Properties enables you to tailor the program to provide communications support for Internet access.*

Under Windows 98, support was added for CSLIP (UNIX connection with IP header compression), NRN (NetWare Connect version 1.0 and 1.1), and SLIP for UNIX and Windows for Workgroups and Windows NT 3.1.

Using the options in this dialog box, you can specify a particular IP address for your computer and a series of IP addresses for the server and its network facilities, or you can choose to use server-assigned addresses. With more than 2,000 Internet service providers, there are bound to be differences between service providers with respect to the manner by which they support addressing and the addresses that they use. Therefore, you should consult your ISP to find out which method it uses and then complete the settings shown in this dialog box accordingly. (In Chapter 12, "The Internet," you will examine IP addressing and the use of such dial-up protocols as PPP and SLIP to gain access to the Internet.)

Once you appropriately configure Dial-Up Networking, you can use it to access a server. When you attempt to access a server, Windows normally displays a series of prompts informing you of the status of the pending connections, such as dialing, verifying username and password, and establishing a connection. At this point, you could invoke a browser and begin surfing the Web; however, your ISP will probably provide you with a script that creates the appropriate dial-up connection icon, which invokes the browser automatically and hides the status messages.

Even if your ISP has automated the dial-up process, you should find the preceding discussion of Dial-Up Networking useful because it indicates where to go and what to do to change configurations. For example, you might need to access Dial-Up Networking to connect via a different phone number to establish a connection with a modem that's connected to a mainframe. When the connection is established, you could invoke a terminal emulator program to obtain full-screen access to the mainframe and to use certain key combinations, such as substitutes for program function keys PF13 through PF24, which are not found on PC keyboards.

Now that you have an appreciation for the use of Dial-Up Networking, let's turn to the use of a communications program bundled in all versions of Windows after Windows 3.11: HyperTerminal.

## HyperTerminal

HyperTerminal is accessible via the Start menu from Programs, Accessories. This program was developed by Hilgraeve of Monroe, Michigan, for Microsoft and was first included in Windows 95.

HyperTerminal comes preconfigured for accessing several information utilities and electronic mail systems. This preconfiguration resulted in an applicable icon and phone number associated with the data configured for an icon. Later versions of HyperTerminal included in Windows Me and Windows 2000 do not include any preconfigured icons; however, the program retains the same icons that you can use to create your own preconfigured connections and its use is relatively simple.

When you select an applicable icon, a dialog box labeled Connect To is displayed. Figure 9.7 illustrates the HyperTerminal Connect To dialog box after the MCI icon was selected from a series of program icons and the toll-free number for accessing MCI Mail was entered. When you click on the button labeled OK, you will have a preconfigured icon that you can then use to connect to MCI Mail.

**FIGURE 9.7**

*Older versions of HyperTerminal include several preconfigured icons for accessing popular electronic mail systems, while more recent versions of the program require users to create all configured icons.*

9

PC
COMMUNICATIONS
SOFTWARE

After you create a preconfigured icon, double-clicking on the icon results in the display of a dialog box labeled Connect. For the previously created MCI icon, the left portion of Figure 9.8 shows the Connect dialog box. If you click on the button labeled Dial, the program directly dials the number previously entered. However, before doing so, click on the button labeled Dialing properties to obtain an appreciation of some of the additional options supported by the program. The right portion of Figure 9.8 illustrates the Dialing Properties dialog box. In examining the entries in that box, note that instead of specifying the prefix to access long distance or make a local call from behind a PBX in a phone number string, you need to specify the prefix in the Dialing Properties box. Otherwise, the program will tell you that an improper phone number was entered. Also note that through the Dialing Properties box, you can select the type of dialing used, disable call waiting, and even specify the use of a calling card.

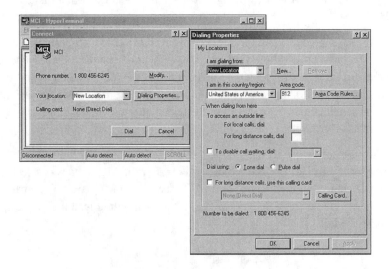

**FIGURE 9.8**

*Before using HyperTerminal to initiate a connection, its Dialing Properties box facilitates defining the manner by which local and long distance service occurs, disabling call waiting and even the use of a calling card.*

Returning to Figure 9.8, click on the button labeled Dial in the Connect box to initiate a call to this author's MCI Mail account. Figure 9.9 illustrates the connection process for a typical day at the office, with 54 messages awaiting action.

Although you may not be an AT&T or MCI Mail subscriber, the preconfigured information functions as a learning tool that may be valuable to you if you need to create other configurations. By examining the configuration and properties associated with one or more preconfigured accounts, you might notice certain configuration characteristics that you'll want to duplicate. The old adage that "innovation is the son of experimentation" holds true when applied to communications software.

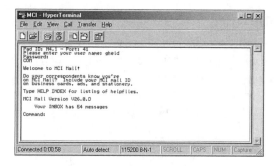

**FIGURE 9.9**
*Using HyperTerminal to access an MCI Mail account.*

In this examination of HyperTerminal, you will briefly look at its protocol support capability for file-transfer operations. From the program's Transfer menu, you can send and receive files based upon the use of several popular protocols. Figure 9.10 shows the program's Send File dialog box with its Protocol list pulled down. The protocols displayed are not the only ones available; scrolling up shows one additional file-transfer protocol supported by the program: the 1KXMODEM protocol.

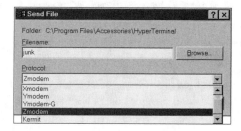

**FIGURE 9.10**
*HyperTerminal supports several versions of the XMODEM file-transfer protocol as well as Kermit.*

Although HyperTerminal is not as feature-rich as other communications programs, it is bundled with all modern versions of Windows. If you need an elementary communications program and do not need multiple terminal emulators or the capability to initiate online chatting and other functions, HyperTerminal may suffice for your purposes. However, you might need features not available within HyperTerminal and might therefore decide that the purchase of a standalone third-party communications program warrants consideration. For those readers who will consider third-party programs, this chapter concludes by focusing on two versions of the popular Procomm program. Each version of that program contains numerous features that are available only through the purchase of a standalone communications program.

9

PC
COMMUNICATIONS
SOFTWARE

## Using ProcommPlus

ProcommPlus is a comprehensive communications program that is easy to use when you understand a few Alt key combinations. After you install the program on your computer and invoke its operation, the program displays its name onscreen as it loads and then displays a screen in which only the top and bottom lines display information. This initial program screen is shown in Figure 9.11. Although the top line is self-explanatory, the bottom line warrants an explanation for persons not familiar with this program.

**FIGURE 9.11**

*The initial ProcommPlus program screen, with status information on the bottom line of the display.*

The bottom line on the ProcommPlus display can be considered as a status line that indicates the state of key program functions and provides users with a prompt concerning the use of the program. That prompt is the message "Alt-Z FOR HELP," which indicates the key combination that you can press for assistance. Other information displayed on the status line in Figure 9.11 includes the following:

- The current terminal emulation (ANSI)
- The transmission mode (FDX)
- The operating rate
- The parity
- Data and stop bit settings (1200 E71)
- Whether the program's log facility was enabled or disabled (LOG CLOSED)
- Whether each line of information displayed will be printed (PRINT OFF)
- The status of communications (OFF-LINE)

Later in this chapter, when you use the program to establish a communications session, you will see how several entries on the status line automatically change.

## ProcommPlus Command Menu

To see the ProcommPlus help facility, press the Alt+Z key combination. The program's command menu appears, as shown in Figure 9.12. Because this menu is easy to invoke, it provides a quick way for you to look up the keystrokes required to perform different communications functions without using the program's manual. In Figure 9.12, note that most program functions are invoked by pressing two keys. As you examine the use of the program, you will learn how communications functions are easily invoked by pressing multikey combinations.

The first key combination listed in Figure 9.12 is Alt+D, which invokes the dialing directory. That key combination is listed first in the command menu because the dialing directory enables users to set communications parameters and establish communications sessions using previously specified communications parameter settings.

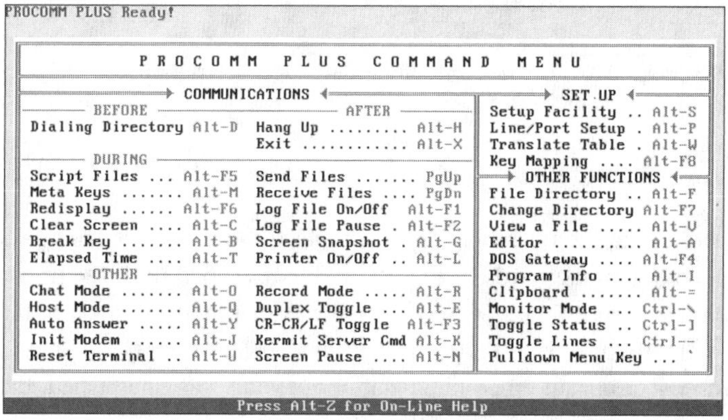

## FIGURE 9.12

*The ProcommPlus command menu indicates the key and key combinations required to invoke different program functions.*

## Dialing Directory

Figure 9.13 shows the ProcommPlus dialing directory with directory information for all entries except the first, which is the default entry that enables you to dial the bulletin board system of the program developer. If you were to compare ProcommPlus or another standalone communications program to HyperTerminal, you would note that a dialing directory facilitates program operation instead of requiring you to specify a separate configuration for each location to be called. With a dialing directory, you can enter individual telephone numbers and configuration information for each number in one common database instead of having to work with a number of separate files.

In the ProcommPlus dialing directory (shown in Figure 9.13), you move the highlight bar over an entry in the dialing directory and press Enter, and the program transmits the telephone number stored in the entry to the modem for automatic dialing. By placing the highlight bar over the first entry and pressing Enter, for example, you can communicate with the program developer.

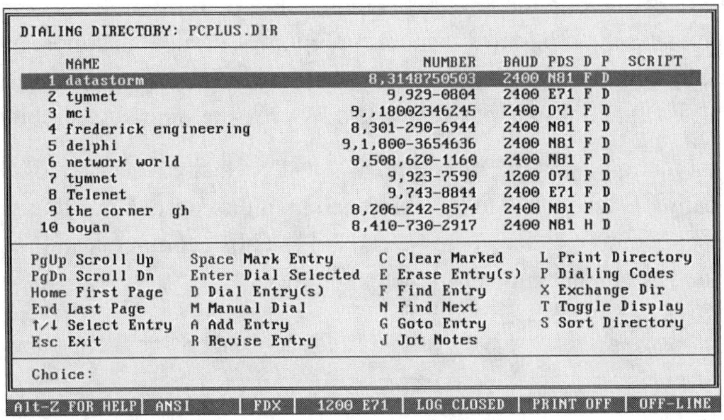

```
┌──────────────────────────────────────────────────────────────────────────┐
│ DIALING DIRECTORY: PCPLUS.DIR                                              │
│                                                                            │
│       NAME                       NUMBER     BAUD PDS D P    SCRIPT         │
│    1 datastorm               8,3148750503   2400 N81 F D                   │
│    2 tymnet                     9,929-0804  2400 E71 F D                   │
│    3 mci                    9,,18002346245  2400 D71 F D                   │
│    4 frederick engineering   8,301-290-6944 2400 N81 F D                   │
│    5 delphi                 9,1,800-3654636 2400 N81 F D                   │
│    6 network world          8,508,620-1160  2400 N81 F D                   │
│    7 tymnet                     9,923-7590  1200 D71 F D                   │
│    8 Telenet                    9,743-8844  2400 E71 F D                   │
│    9 the corner  gh         8,206-242-8574  2400 N81 F D                   │
│   10 boyan                  8,410-730-2917  2400 N81 H D                   │
│                                                                            │
│  PgUp Scroll Up      Space Mark Entry     C Clear Marked   L Print Directory│
│  PgDn Scroll Dn      Enter Dial Selected  E Erase Entry(s) P Dialing Codes │
│  Home First Page     D Dial Entry(s)      F Find Entry     X Exchange Dir  │
│  End Last Page       M Manual Dial        N Find Next      T Toggle Display│
│  ↑/↓ Select Entry    A Add Entry          G Goto Entry     S Sort Directory│
│  Esc Exit            R Revise Entry        J Jot Notes                     │
│                                                                            │
│  Choice:                                                                   │
│                                                                            │
├──────────────────────────────────────────────────────────────────────────┤
│ Alt-Z FOR HELP| ANSI    |  FDX  | 1200 E71 | LOG CLOSED | PRINT OFF | OFF-LINE│
└──────────────────────────────────────────────────────────────────────────┘
```

**FIGURE 9.13**

*The ProcommPlus dialing directory screen.*

Figure 9.14 illustrates the establishment of a communications session using ProcommPlus. Note that certain entries in the status line changed to correspond to the settings in the dialing directory entry you selected. Thus, 2400 N81 indicates that the serial port of the computer is transmitting data at 2400bps using 8 data bits per character, no parity bit, and 1 stop bit per character. Also note that because a communications session was established, the extreme right of the status line now contains the entry ON-LINE.

In the event that one or more dialing directory entries do not satisfy your communications requirements, you can use the dialing directory screen to change various communications settings. From the dialing directory screen, you can press the R key to revise the selected entry. Figure 9.15 shows the Revise Entry 1 window, which lists the communications-related features, functions, and settings that you can revise. As you move the highlight bar down the second column in that window, other windows are displayed. When the highlight bar is positioned over the protocol entry, the program displays a window listing the supported file-transfer protocols. You can move the highlight bar over a file-transfer protocol and press Enter to assign a new protocol to the selected entry in the dialing directory.

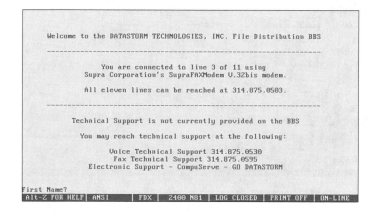

**FIGURE 9.14**

*Establishing a communications session.*

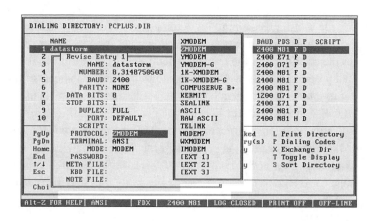

**FIGURE 9.15**

*Using the dialing directory to change the file-transfer protocol assigned to a directory entry.*

Figure 9.16 illustrates how you can use ProcommPlus to select or change a file-transfer protocol when you are online. Press the Page Down key, and the Download Protocols window appears. Here, you can change a previously established default protocol or press the Enter key to retain the default file-transfer protocol. If you compare file-transfer protocols supported by ProcommPlus or another third-party communications program to protocols supported by HyperTerminal, you will note another considerable difference between the two programs. To see that difference, compare Figure 9.10 to Figure 9.16.

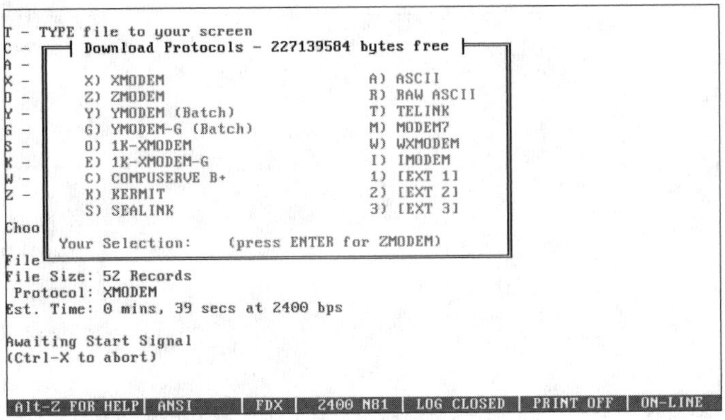

```
T - TYPE file to your screen
C - ┌─┤ Download Protocols - 227139584 bytes free ├─
A -
X -     X) XMODEM                    A) ASCII
D -     Z) ZMODEM                    R) RAW ASCII
Y -     Y) YMODEM (Batch)            T) TELINK
G -     G) YMODEM-G (Batch)          M) MODEM7
S -     O) 1K-XMODEM                 W) WXMODEM
X -     E) 1K-XMODEM-G               I) IMODEM
W -     C) COMPUSERVE B+             1) [EXT 1]
Z -     K) KERMIT                    2) [EXT 2]
        S) SEALINK                   3) [EXT 3]
Choo
File│   Your Selection:   (press ENTER for ZMODEM)
File
File Size: 52 Records
 Protocol: XMODEM
Est. Time: 0 mins, 39 secs at 2400 bps

Awaiting Start Signal
(Ctrl-X to abort)


  Alt-Z FOR HELP│ ANSI    │  FDX  │ 2400 N81 │ LOG CLOSED │ PRINT OFF │ ON-LINE
```

## FIGURE 9.16

*You can change the download file-transfer protocol while online by pressing the Page Down key and selecting the desired protocol.*

After you initiate a file transfer, ProcommPlus automatically provides you with a visual indication of the status of the transfer by displaying a window indicating the progress of the transfer. Figure 9.17 shows the progress of a file transfer when the ZMODEM protocol is used. The window in the right portion of Figure 9.17, which shows information about the file transfer, varies with respect to information content based on the file-transfer protocol used. Some protocols, such as XMODEM, do not transfer information concerning the file size or its date of creation or last modification. For those protocols, ProcommPlus cannot compute the percentage of the file transmitted, nor can it display the progress of the file transfer visually as a horizontal bar like that shown in the lower portion of Figure 9.17. In the file-transfer window, note that one entry is Average CPS. By transferring the same file using different file transfer protocols, you can determine which protocol provides you with higher throughput based on a specific communications environment.

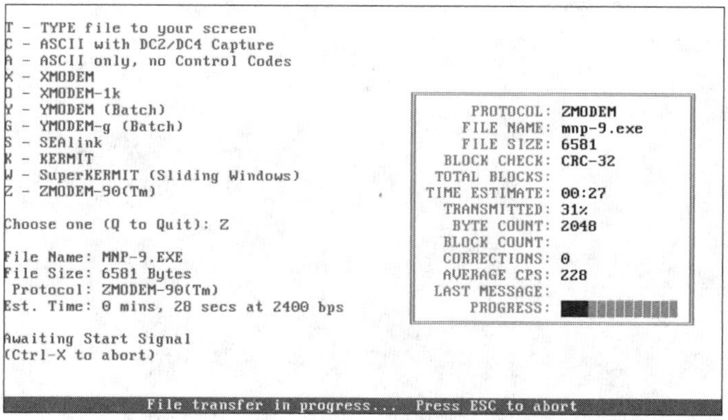

```
T - TYPE file to your screen
C - ASCII with DC2/DC4 Capture
A - ASCII only, no Control Codes
X - XMODEM
D - XMODEM-1k
Y - YMODEM (Batch)
G - YMODEM-g (Batch)
S - SEAlink
K - KERMIT
W - SuperKERMIT (Sliding Windows)
Z - ZMODEM-90(Tm)

Choose one (Q to Quit): Z

File Name: MNP-9.EXE
File Size: 6581 Bytes
 Protocol: ZMODEM-90(Tm)
Est. Time: 0 mins, 28 secs at 2400 bps

Awaiting Start Signal
(Ctrl-X to abort)

              PROTOCOL: ZMODEM
             FILE NAME: mnp-9.exe
             FILE SIZE: 6581
           BLOCK CHECK: CRC-32
          TOTAL BLOCKS:
         TIME ESTIMATE: 00:27
           TRANSMITTED: 31%
            BYTE COUNT: 2048
           BLOCK COUNT:
           CORRECTIONS: 0
           AVERAGE CPS: 228
          LAST MESSAGE:
              PROGRESS: ████▐▌▌▌▌▌▌▌

      File transfer in progress... Press ESC to abort
```

**FIGURE 9.17**

*The ProcommPlus file-transfer window indicates the status of a file transfer using the ZMODEM protocol.*

# Using ProcommPlus for Windows

The previously described communications program was a DOS program. Its developer followed it up with the ProcommPlus for Windows program, which could run under several GUI environments to include the original Microsoft Windows, its updated Windows 95 operating system, and Windows NT.

## Viewing the Main Program Screen

The adage "you be the judge" is applicable when comparing many DOS and Windows programs. Figure 9.18 shows the ProcommPlus for Windows main screen. The cursor is shown positioned over the second icon from the left, which resembles a book with the label Dialing Directory.

If you compare Figure 9.11 with Figure 9.18, you will note a considerable difference between the main program screens used by the DOS and Windows versions of ProcommPlus. When working with the DOS version of ProcommPlus, you had to either remember command key combination sequences or press Alt+Z to get a command menu. In contrast, in the Windows version, you can simply click an icon to perform most of the operations that once required the use of a command key or multikey sequence.

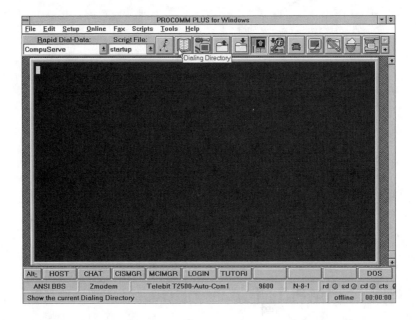

**FIGURE 9.18**

*The main screen of ProcommPlus for Windows.*

Because no standards define the functions associated with different icons, it can be a bit confusing if you switch between two Windows-based programs that incorporate a series of icons, or if you infrequently use a program containing a series of icons. To facilitate the recognition of the meanings associated with different icons, ProcommPlus for Windows uses two methods to display the meanings associated with icons. First, when you move the cursor over an icon, a short label that defines its function is displayed. For example, the label associated with the dialing directory icon is shown slightly below and to the right of the icon when the cursor is placed on the icon. The second method involves the display of text information on the program screen's status line. If you look in the lower-left corner of Figure 9.18, you will note the text message Show the Current Dialing Directory. When you position the cursor over an icon, the program provides an extended description of the function of that icon on the icon on the screen's status line.

## Window-Oriented Dialing Directory

Because the cursor in Figure 9.18 is placed on the dialing directory, click that icon. Doing so displays the program's dialing directory, which is shown in Figure 9.19. Compare that dialing directory to the DOS version's dialing directory that you saw in Figure 9.13.

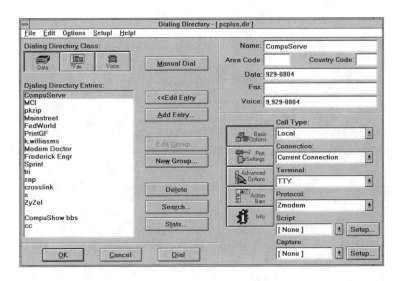

**FIGURE 9.19**

*The ProcommPlus for Windows dialing directory.*

When comparing the DOS and Windows programs' dialing directories, note that the Windows version has numerous buttons. Those buttons initiate predefined operations that perform functions associated with one or more key sequences. In addition to eliminating the necessity of knowing and entering key sequences, many times a point-and-click operation can be considerably faster to perform, enhancing user productivity.

## Multiple Choices

Another advantage associated with many GUI-based communications programs is the fact that they normally support multiple methods for accomplishing the same task. Typically, many commands selected from a menu can also be invoked by an icon selection. This enables users to employ whichever method they are most comfortable with, further enhancing user productivity.

Figure 9.20 shows the ProcommPlus for Windows Online menu. Notice the first two entries in the menu: Send File and Receive File. You can also initiate those functions by clicking the folder icons with the upward (Send) and downward (Receive) pointing arrows. In addition, you can initiate other functions, such as Clear Screen, by selecting a menu entry, by clicking an icon, or (as a leftover from the DOS version) by entering a multikey combination. Specifically, to clear the screen, you could enter Alt+C, you could select that function from the Online menu, or you could click the fourth icon from the right. As an old politician would say, a GUI interface gives you a choice, not an echo!

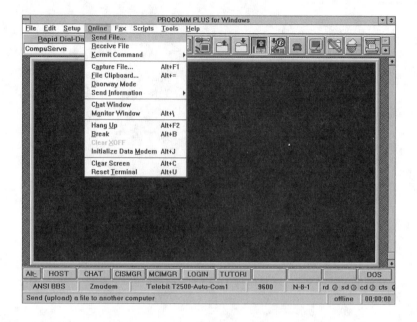

**FIGURE 9.20**

*The ProcommPlus for Windows Online menu.*

## ProcommPlus for Windows Operation

To see how ProcommPlus for Windows works, access CompuServe and download a file from that information utility. If you have previously set up the program's dialing directory to include an entry for CompuServe, you can select that entry either from the program's dialing directory or from the program's Rapid Dial-Data drop-down menu (previously shown in the upper-left corner of Figure 9.18). When you select the CompuServe entry, the program displays the Dialing Using dialog box, which indicates the modem that's being used to dial the selected entry. Figure 9.21 shows the dialog box, which displays information about the call in progress and enables you to cancel the call.

When you're connected to CompuServe and are located in the appropriate library, you can initiate a file-transfer operation. The beginning of this file-transfer operation is shown in Figure 9.22.

Examine the left portion of the background of Figure 9.22, and you will note a series of numbers from 1 to 7 followed by the names of seven file-transfer protocols supported by CompuServe. Although CompuServe supports XMODEM and YMODEM, it does not support ZMODEM, which was the default file-transfer protocol previously set for use. To change the program's file-transfer protocol, click the button labeled ZMODEM. This displayed a pop-up menu of protocols supported by the program. From that pop-up menu, select CIS-B+, a file-transfer protocol developed by CompuServe that is commonly used with file transfers to or from that information utility. Thus, the dialog box labeled CIS-B+, shown in Figure 9.22, indicates that the CompuServe B+ file transfer protocol is being used to transfer the files THM-PLS.EXE.

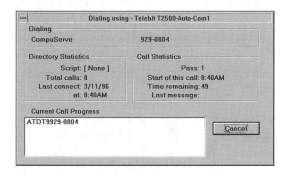

**FIGURE 9.21**

*Dialing CompuServe.*

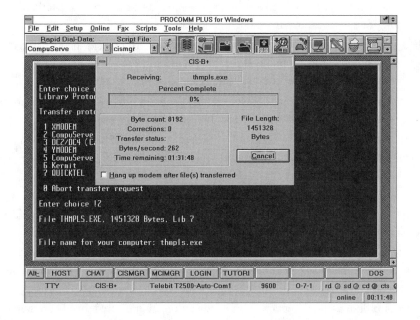

**FIGURE 9.22**

*Initiating a file-transfer operation using ProcommPlus for Windows.*

As you learned by studying a series of program screen displays shown in this section, a GUI-based application program can significantly enhance user productivity. Programs supporting point-and-click operations, enabling users to select from several methods to perform the same function, and providing a mechanism for viewing the functions associated with icons make it easier for persons to use a computer. By eliminating the necessity to remember and enter commands and use multikey sequences to invoke predefined functions, a GUI-based application program has made the PC easier to use. This, in turn, has increased the number of persons using PCs from the technically literate to encompass the occasional user as well as students starting with grade school.

# What You Have Learned

- Both the support of a specific operating system and the operating environment govern the capability of a communications program to operate on a specific computer platform with a graphical user interface.

- Support of the Hayes modem command set normally references the operation of basic modem functions. For the control of advanced modem functions, the communications program must support the modem that you want to use.

- For a modem to operate effectively when compressing data, the computer's serial port operating rate must exceed the modem's operating rate.

- Flow control is the orderly regulation of data transfer. To prevent the loss of data between a computer and a modem, the communications program must be configured to support the method of flow control used by the modem.

- The Microsoft Windows Dial-Up Networking program provides a standardized method for selecting a modem and accessing an Internet service provider.

- The Microsoft Windows HyperTerminal program provides a basic set of communications functions for accessing a bulletin board or certain types of computers via a limited set of terminal emulation capabilities.

- The dialing directories of most communications programs provide both a facility for selecting and dialing different telephone numbers and the capability to assign specific communications parameter settings to each entry.

- The terminal emulations supported by a communications program govern its capability to be used to communicate as a full-screen terminal device with minicomputers and mainframe computers.

- A script programming language permits the automation of predefined communications functions.

- The capability of a program to display different information concerning the status of a file transfer depends on the protocol used to transfer the file.

- The use of a graphical user interface–based application program can enhance user productivity.

# Quiz for Chapter 9

1. Hayes Microcomputer Products modem command set compatibility refers to

    A. The control of basic modem functions.

    B. The control of advanced modem functions.

    C. Flow control.

    D. Data compression.

2. XON/XOFF is

    A. Seldom used.

    B. Always enabled.

    C. A method of flow control.

    D. A data-compression function.

3. To effectively use a compression-performing modem, you must do what?

    A. Set the serial port rate equal to the modem operating rate.

    B. Set the serial port rate higher than the modem operating rate.

    C. Set the serial port rate lower than the modem operating rate.

    D. Set the serial port rate to automatic speed detect.

4. A compression-performing modem operating at 14400bps that has a 4:1 average compression ratio requires which computer serial port operating rate to operate effectively?

    A. 14400bps

    B. 28800bps

    C. 55400bps

    D. 57600bps

5. Which of the following is an example of outband signaling?

    A. XON/XOFF

    B. ENQ/ACK

    C. RS-232

    D. CTS

**9**

PC COMMUNICATIONS SOFTWARE

6. The basic function of a dialing directory is to

    A. Store address information.

    B. Enable a user to enter telephone numbers to be dialed.

    C. Store communications parameters.

    D. Enable flow control.

7. Which of the following file-transfer protocols uses a 32-bit cyclic redundancy check (CRC)?

    A. YMODEM

    B. XMODEM

    C. XYMODEM

    D. ZMODEM

8. Dial-Up Networking

    A. Is a full-featured communications program for accessing mainframes.

    B. Supports 12 terminal emulations.

    C. Provides a communications connection to an Internet service provider.

    D. Enables file transfers between mainframes using 14 different file-transfer protocols.

9. The term *maximum speed* as used by Dial-Up Networking refers to what?

    A. The interface rate to the modem

    B. The modem signaling rate

    C. The modem modulation rate

    D. The modem compression scheme

10. HyperTerminal

    A. Supports the Point-to-Point Protocol for Internet access.

    B. Enables access to bulletin boards.

    C. Supports 12 file-transfer protocols.

    D. Costs $29.95.

11. In ProcommPlus, where is information concerning communications parameter settings displayed?

    A. Main menu

    B. Status line

    C. Protocol window

    D. Log facility

12. In ProcommPlus, which key or key combination do you press to invoke the line hang-up function?

   A. Alt+X

   B. Page Down

   C. Alt+Q

   D. Alt+H

13. Information concerning the progress of a line transfer displayed by ProcommPlus varies based on which of the following?

   A. The file-transfer protocol used

   B. The average CPS

   C. The date that the file was created

   D. The size of the file

14. You can initiate a file transfer using ProcommPlus for Windows by

   A. Clicking the icon with an arrow flowing into a folder.

   B. Selecting the Receive File entry from the Online menu.

   C. Clicking on the Rapid Dial entry.

   D. Either clicking the icon with an arrow flowing into a folder or selecting the Receive File entry from the Online menu.

# WAN Architectures and Packet Networks

## IN THIS CHAPTER

This chapter deals with several wide area data networking architecture concepts—that is, the way wide area data networks are arranged or structured. These include the concept of architectural levels or layers. To provide a frame of reference for describing the operation of packet networks, the International Standards Organization (ISO) Open Systems Interconnect (OSI) Reference Model will be described at the beginning of this chapter. Following that, you will examine protocol layering associated with packet networks and then turn your attention to the operation of two popular packet networks: the ITU X.25 packet switching network and its eventual successor, Frame Relay.

# The Open Systems Interconnect Reference Model

In 1983, the International Organization for Standardization (ISO) culminated six years of intensive effort to develop and publish a guideline—a reference model—for describing data communications architectures. The resulting document, International Standard #7498, has been redrafted by the ITU using its own terminology, and the redraft has been designated ITU-T X.200. The generic name for both documents is the Open Systems Interconnect Reference Model (OSI/RM)—usually called simply OSI.

OSI is not a protocol, nor does it contain protocols. What OSI does is define a consistent language and boundaries for establishing protocols so that systems that abide by its rules should be "open" to one another—that is, capable of communicating.

Decades of frustration caused by incompatibility between competitive or geographically distinct communications systems created such an appetite for the establishment of cooperative systems that there is a virtual stampede toward global standardization of data communications architectures. Many standard committees in several organizations are now engaged in the development of protocols for the various layers in the numerous systems to which OSI will apply.

## OSI Layers

OSI defines a complete architecture consisting of seven layers. There is no specific reason why it is seven rather than six or eight; the functions that must be performed just happened to fall into roughly seven groupings. The lowest three layers (physical, data link, and network) correspond closely to the physical, link, and packet levels of X.25. A second packet network known as Frame Relay corresponds closely to the lowest two layers of the OSI reference model. As you will note later in this chapter, a streamlining of functions to enable Frame Relay to operate at Layer 2 significantly enhances the throughput obtainable over that packet network in comparison to the transmission of data over an X.25 packet network.

Protocols have been and are being developed for other kinds of systems, such as facsimile, integrated voice/data networks, and videotex. Even if the protocols were never written, however, OSI has had a tremendous impact in standardizing the way we view communications.

Here are the official names of the seven layers, from top to bottom:

7. Application

6. Presentation

5. Session

4. Transport

3. Network

2. Data link

1. Physical

As data is generated by an application, an appropriate header is added, and as data flows down the protocol stack, lower layers add additional headers. Data with a sequence of headers then flows on the communications path to the destination, where the recipient removes previously appended headers as data flows back up a new protocol stack to the destination application. Figure 10.1 shows how the seven levels relate for a system whose lower three layers correspond to X.25. (In this case, NH, which represents the network layer, is the packet header.) When you examine Frame Relay, you will notice that eliminating Layer 3 operations significantly enhances throughput over that packet network.

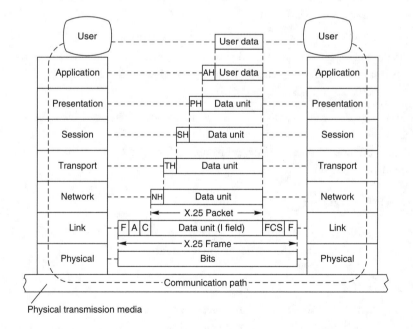

**FIGURE 10.1**

*The seven embedded layers of OSI.*

## An Analogy

Whenever people communicate, whether by computer or verbally, they invoke protocols at all seven levels of OSI. Without going into the laborious details and vocabulary of the OSI standard, this list illustrates the OSI categorizations of the seven levels from bottom to top for a typical telephone call.

- Physical layer concerns—These are the actual sounds being uttered into the mouthpiece and heard from the receiver.

- Data link layer concerns—Talk when you're supposed to, and listen when you're supposed to. Ask for a repeat if you don't understand something. Tell the other party to slow down if he or she is talking too fast.

- Network layer concerns—Dial the number and listen for call-progress signals. Redial if you get a busy signal or if you're cut off. Disconnect when the conversation is completed.

- Transport layer concerns—What is the most cost-effective way to handle this call (or these calls) that's consistent with priorities? What long-distance carriers should be used?

- Session layer concerns—Can this situation be handled in one call or several? Will other people need to be brought in at different times? Who will control the discussion in a multiparty conversation? Who will re-establish the call if it's cut off?

- Presentation layer concerns—Are you speaking the same language and dialect?

- Application layer concerns—Are you talking to the right person? Who is paying for this call? Is this the best time to talk, or should you call back later? Does the other party have a pencil and paper to take notes?

Anyone who has used a telephone in everyday business situations can relate to all seven levels of the reference model just described. By examining X.25 and Frame Relay and their relationship to the OSI reference model, you should be able to identify the analogies to the physical, data link, and network layer protocols.

# Protocol Layering

A protocol is a set of rules governing a time sequence of events that take place between peer entities—that is, between equipment or layers on the same level.

## Physical Layer

Chapter 4, "Asynchronous Modems and Interfaces," covered the mechanical, physical, electrical, logical, and functional relationships between the various wires and signals in a serial interface and how the bits of data are passed through them between data terminal equipment (DTE) and data circuit-terminating equipment (DCE). You learned, for example, that bits passing through the transmit data wire from a source DTE should eventually pass through a receive data wire to a sink DTE. These are called physical layer or Level 1 protocols, and they represent the lowest layer of the OSI reference model.

Level 1 protocols deal with the physical layer of data communication, or the passing of the bits through the wires to and from DTEs. At the physical layer the manner by which bits are coded for transmission, the order that they flow onto the medium, and the connector to the medium are specified. In comparison, link protocols cover a higher level of architecture; they are concerned with all aspects of maintaining order within the link.

## The Data Link Layer

Chapter 8, "Protocols and Error Control," discussed means by which various fields, such as address, text, and error checking, can be present within the same bit stream. Several specific data-link protocols were discussed. Those techniques are used to define (without any possibility of confusion) the boundaries of the fields within a bit stream, send information to a specific terminal on a multipoint link, check for and correct transmission errors, and generally maintain order within the line.

Architecturally speaking, data-link protocols are at a higher level (a more "intelligent" level) than physical protocols, yet all the information used in the data-link protocol is actually contained in the bit stream transmitted through the serial interface. Conceptually, we speak of data-link protocol fields as embedded (contained within) or layered within the physical protocol bits.

Data-link protocols are primarily concerned with the delivery of data between two points or network connections. The data link layer specifies the fields within a frame and the manner by which error detection and correction is accomplished. With respect to the OSI reference model, the data link layer represents the second layer in the model.

## The Network Layer

At the third layer in the OSI reference model is the network layer. Protocols at this layer can be used to route data from link to link through a network containing intelligent nodes. These nodes can be routers or packet switches. The method by which this routing and associated administration takes place is called the network-layer protocol. The network-layer protocol information, called the packet header, is embedded in the information field of a link-level frame. A Layer 3 packet switch uses part of this information to route the data to the next link, and so on. The packet header, together with the user data, is called a packet on an X.25 network.

**10**

ARCHITECTURES
AND PACKET
NETWORKS

# Packet Networks

A packet network is a special kind of data network containing intelligent switching nodes. Packet networks have the following general characteristics:

- Before transmission, each data message is segmented into short blocks of specified maximum length, and each block is provided with a header containing addressing and possibly sequencing information. Each packet becomes the information field of a transmission at the link protocol level, which usually contains error-control capabilities.

- The packets are passed very quickly from node to node, arriving at their final destination in a fraction of a second.

- The node computers do not archive (store) the data. Messages are "forgotten" by the sending node as soon as the next node checks for an error (if required) and acknowledges receipt.

The terms *DTE* and *DCE* have been discussed previously. In packet networks, an additional term is introduced: the *Data Switching Exchange (DSE)*. A DSE is a network node joining three or more links. Figure 10.2 shows the relationship between DTEs, DCEs, and DSEs in a packet network. The point where the serial interface cable connects to the DCE is sometimes referred to as the *network gateway*.

Unlike in Level 1 switching, in which a specific link is dedicated to a particular message or group of messages, data packets are forwarded between DSEs in such a way that packets from many sources and to many sinks can pass through the same internode link at different moments during the same short period. Because packets from many sources can flow over a common link between DSEs, it becomes possible for the costs of those links to be shared by many users. This represents one of the primary benefits of a packet network, the capability to use transmission facilities that an organization might otherwise find cost prohibitive. As we will shortly note, other economic advantages are associated with the use of packet networks in comparison to the use of other methods for transmitting data.

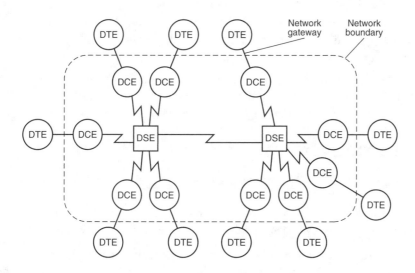

**FIGURE 10.2**

*A two-node packet network.*

# Advantages of Packet Switching

Depending on the situation, packet switching can offer several possible advantages over other data communications techniques:

- For data applications in which the amount of traffic between terminals cannot justify a dedicated circuit, packet switching might be more economical than transmission over private lines.

- For applications in which data communication sessions are shorter than a minimum chargeable time unit for a telephone call, packet switching might be more economical than dialed data.

- Because destination address information is inherently a part of the packet, a large number of messages can be sent to many different destinations as fast as the source DTE can turn them out. Depending on the type of packet service being used, there might not be any connection time delay before transmission of packets containing actual data.

- Because of the intelligence built into the network (that is, computers at each node), dynamic routing of data is possible. Each packet travels over the route established by the network as the best available path for that packet at that time. This characteristic can be used to maximize efficiency and minimize congestion.

- Built-in intelligence also facilitates a "graceful degradation" property of the packet network because, whenever there is a failure of a link or node, packets can be automatically rerouted around the defective portion of the network.

- Because of the intelligence within the network, a rich array of basic communications services is possible. Examples include error detection and correction, message delivery verification, group addressing, reverse billing, message sequence checking, and diagnostics.

# X.25 Packet Systems

The ITU X.25 standard for packet switching systems is one of the most significant networking architectures affecting data communications for the present and the foreseeable future. The X.25 standard is actually only a part of a much larger collection of ITU recommendations on public data networks. To fully understand the subject, one must study the entire "X" series.

The X.25 standard itself describes the physical, link, and network protocols in the interface between the DTE and the DCE at the gateway to a packet switching network. At first glance, the concept of describing a packet network in terms of gateway parameters might seem peculiar, but from the user's point of view, it's all that's needed. In voice telephone network terms, if you were to collect all the standards relating to the physical, electrical, logical, and functional properties of local loops and their signals into one document, you would have the telephone network equivalent of X.25. As shown in Figure 10.3, X.25 relates a data terminal to the gateway of a packet network in precisely the same way that local loop signaling standards relate a telephone to the central office of a telephone network.

If you had never seen a telephone or placed a telephone call, your knowing all there is to know about a local loop and its signaling wouldn't teach you much about the design of the telephone or of the network—but you would know how to use them. Similarly, the X.25 standard describes neither the data terminal nor the packet data network, but it reveals a great deal about what the terminal and the network must be capable of doing. It is for this reason that the X.25 standard has taken on so much importance.

As already mentioned, the X.25 standard specifies three separate protocol layers at the serial interface gateway. The physical-layer characteristics of X.21 (or X.21bis) are specified as the physical-layer protocol (*bis* is the Swiss/French equivalent of "alternate form"). X.21 uses a 15-pin synchronous interface, which has not enjoyed enthusiastic acceptance in the United States because of the popularity of RS-232 and V.35, which existed before X.21. In recognition of this fact, the ITU has endorsed X.21bis as a suitable alternative. X.21bis specifies V.24/V.28 (essentially the equivalent of RS-232), X.26/IS-4902 (essentially the equivalent of RS-449), and V.35 at their appropriate respective bit rates. Because U.S. vendors generally provide RS-232 or V.35, no change is required.

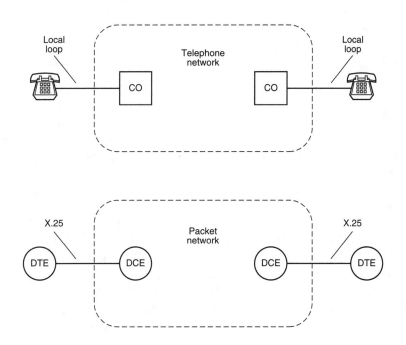

**FIGURE 10.3**

*An analogy between X.25 and the total specifications for a local loop.*

## Data Link Layer

At the data link layer, the protocol specified is a subset of HDLC, referred to in X.25 terminology as LAPB (Link Access Procedure Balanced). (An older version of X.25 used a link protocol called LAP, which has been essentially phased out.) LAPB provides for two-way simultaneous communication between the DTE and the DCE at the network gateway. LAPB frame structure is identical to that of SDLC, which was explained in Chapter 8. The delimiter (flag), abort, idle channel, transparency (zero insertion), frame sequencing, flow-control, and error-control mechanisms are identical to those of SDLC. The differences between the LAPB procedures and the SDLC procedures are mainly in the areas of line control and addressing; these topics are covered in the LAPB section later in this chapter.

## Network Layer

The network layer of X.25 is referred to in the standard as the packet layer. All X.25 packets are transmitted as information fields in LAPB information command frames. A packet contains at least a header of three or more octets. (An octet is a group of 8 bits.) Most packets also contain user data, but some packets are only for control, status indication, or diagnostics. (The preceding terms will be explained in later text and illustrations.) The maximum amount of user data that can be included in a data packet is determined by the network vendor but is usually 128 octets.

# Capabilities of X.25

The X.25 standard, together with its references, specifies two essential services that must be offered by carriers to be in full compliance with the standard. These services are Virtual Call service and Permanent Virtual Circuit service.

## Virtual Call Service

In Virtual Call Service (VC), a virtual "connection" normally must be established between a logical channel from the calling DTE and a logical channel to the called DTE before any data packets can be sent. Establishing a virtual connection is the functional equivalent of placing a telephone call before beginning a telephone conversation. The virtual connection is established and disestablished by use of special packets that have unique bit streams but usually contain no data. After the connection has been established, the two DTEs can carry on a two-way dialog until a "clear request packet" (disconnect) is sent.

The VC connection is referred to as virtual because a fixed physical path through the network does not exist. The intelligence in the network simply relays a specified logical channel number at one DTE to that at the other DTE.

A given DTE can have many logical channel numbers active in the same X.25 interface at the same time. (That statement was important. Read it again.) After a virtual connection has been established—say, between logical channel 319 on one DTE and 14 on another DTE—the actual data packet headers need refer only to logical channel numbers. The intelligent network keeps up with their conversational relationship—that is, a data packet from logical channel 319 at the one DTE will appear on logical channel 14 at the other, and the network performs the conversion. Further details on this subject are given in the following sections.

## Permanent Virtual Circuit Service

Permanent Virtual Circuit (PVC) service is the functional equivalent of a private-line service. As in VC, no end-to-end physical pathway exists; the intelligent network relates the respective logical channels of the two DTEs involved. No special packets are sent by the DTE to establish or disestablish connections. A PVC is established by requesting it in writing from the carrier providing the packet network service, and it remains in effect until disestablished by written request. Terminals between the ends of the connection for which a PVC has been established send only data packets on the carrier-assigned logical channels as required. Because a DTE can have many logical channels active at the same time within the X.25 interface, some can be assigned as PVCs, and others can be used for setting up VCs as required—all in the same X.25 interface!

For both VC and PVC, the network is obligated to deliver packets in the order submitted, even if the physical path changes due to circuit loading, failure, or whatever. Cost-wise, the relationship between VC and PVC is similar to that between long-distance telephone and private-line services. Other standard packet-network features, such as error control and diagnostics, are equivalent for VC and PVC.

### Facilities

In ITU-T terminology, a facility is an optional feature offered with a service, sometimes at extra cost. X.25 specifies a rich array of facilities for VC and PVC services. In any case, the final choice of services and facilities is up to the customer.

Examples of facilities for VC service are fast select, incoming calls barred, outgoing calls barred, closed user group, and reverse billing. Fast select gives the user the capability to send and receive data to and from a number of different remote stations very quickly and efficiently without actually establishing regular virtual connections. Such a capability has many potential uses for distribution of electronic mail, polling of inventories, and so on.

## LAPB Procedures

Space does not allow for a complete discussion of the link-layer protocol of X.25; the following information, however, provides general knowledge of the LAPB procedures. A thorough treatment is included in the X.25 standard, and examples of operation are included in ISO 4335 Addendum 2.

LAPB provides for two-way simultaneous transmission on a point-to-point link between a DTE and a DCE at the packet network gateway (see Figure 10.2). Because the link is point-to-point, only the address of the DTE or the address of the DCE can appear in the A (address) field of an LAPB frame. These addresses are shown in Figure 10.4. The A field refers to a link address, not to a network address. The network address of the destination terminal is embedded in the packet header (PH), which is part of the I field.

Both stations (the DTE and the DCE) can issue commands and responses to one another, as shown in Figure 10.4. Whether a frame is a command or a response depends on a combination of two factors:

- The direction in which it is moving. That is, whether it's on the transmit data wires from the DTE or the receive data wires toward the DTE.
- The value of A.

Because of the addressing scheme, there can be no uncertainty even if frames are moving in opposite directions at the same time between the DTE and the DCE.

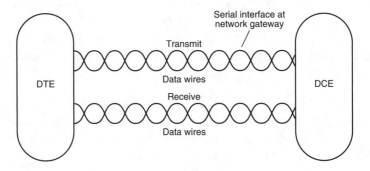

**FIGURE 10.4**

*Commands versus responses in LAPB.*

Table 10.1 and Table 10.2 show the legitimate commands and responses in the LAPB frame, along with their respective control octet values. Explanations of the abbreviations and terms are given in the following paragraphs.

During LAPB operation, most frames are commands. A response frame is compelled when a command frame is received containing P = 1; such a response contains F = 1. All other frames contain P = 0 or F = 0. Here the P/F bit represents a poll (P) or final (F) bit. A command includes a poll bit in bit position 5 (see Table 10.1), while a response includes a final bit (see Table 10.2) in bit position 5.

SABM/UA is a command/response pair used to initialize all counters and timers at the beginning of a session. Similarly, DISC/DM is a command/response pair used at the end of a session. FRMR is a response to any illegal command for which there is no indication of transmission errors according to the frame check sequence (FCS) field.

I commands are used to transmit packets—that is, in the I field. Packets are never sent as responses. N(S) is a 3-bit packet counter capable of counting from 0 through 7 (000 through 111 in binary). After seven packets have been sent, the counter simply rolls over to 000 again for the next value of N(S).

**TABLE 10.1** The LAPB Commands

| Command Name | Content of 876 | Control 5 | Octet 432 | Bit Number 1 |
|---|---|---|---|---|
| I (Information) | N(R) | P | N(S) | 0 |
| RR (Receiver Ready) | N(R) | P | 000 | 1 |
| RNR (Receiver Not Ready) | N(R) | P | 010 | 1 |
| REJ (Reject) | N(R) | P | 100 | 1 |
| SABM (Set Asynchronous Balanced Mode) | 001 | P | 111 | 1 |
| DISC (Disconnect) | 010 | P | 001 | 1 |

**TABLE 10.2** The LAPB Responses

| Response Name | Content of 876 | Control 5 | Octet 432 | Bit Number 1 |
|---|---|---|---|---|
| RR (Receiver Ready) | N(R) | F | 000 | 1 |
| RNR (Receiver Not Ready) | N(R) | F | 010 | 1 |
| REJ (Reject) | N(R) | F | 100 | 1 |
| UA (Unnumbered Acknowledgment) | 011 | F | 001 | 1 |
| DM (Disconnect Mode) | 000 | F | 111 | 1 |
| FRMR (Frame Rejected) | 100 | F | 011 | 1 |

Whereas N(S) counts packets sent from one end of the link, the value of N(R) indicates the next value of N(S) expected to be returned from the other end of the link. By updating the value of N(R), a station acknowledges correctly received packets in the same way that SDLC frames are acknowledged. For example, if a DTE sends an I command (a packet) for which N(S) = 5 and P = 1, and the DCE returns an RR response with N(R) = 6 and F = 1, the DTE knows that the packet was received correctly. If N(R) = 5 and F = 1, the packet was received incorrectly. No more than seven unacknowledged packets can be outstanding because an ambiguity would result.

RR is what a station sends when it needs to send something but has no packets to send. For example, a compelled response to an I command might be an RR with F = 1. This procedure is called checkpointing. Checkpointing is one of the techniques that LAPB makes available for error detection.

REJ is another way of requesting transmission of frames. RNR is used for flow control to indicate a busy condition. It prevents further transmissions until cleared by an RR.

## Packet-Level Procedures

The most interesting feature of X.25 is the network (packet) layer protocol. Remember that the packets are contained in the I command frames at the link (frame) level, and that each packet has a header of at least three octets. Most, but not all, packets contain user data; other packets are used for control, status indication, or diagnostics. Figure 10.5 illustrates the general layout of X.25 packet headers.

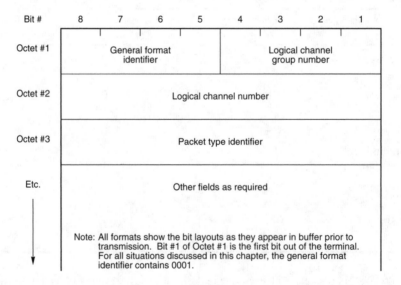

**FIGURE 10.5**

*The general layout of X.25 packet headers.*

## Data Packets

A packet that has 0 as the value of bit 1 in octet 3 of the header is a data packet. Data packet headers normally contain three octets. A standard X.25 data packet contains up to 128 octets of user data following the header. Figure 10.6 illustrates the layout of a typical data packet. This section is not intended to cover all possible ramifications and extensions of X.25. There is, for example, the provision for modulo 128 P(S) and P(R) counters, each of which requires 7 bits. A data packet header in such a system would require a minimum of four octets.

It was pointed out earlier that X.25 specifies two essential services: Virtual Call and Permanent Virtual Circuit. After a VC has been set up, the operation of data packets under VC service is identical to that under PVC. In the paragraphs that follow, operation under PVC is described first; then the additional concerns of VC, such as call setup, are described.

Theoretically, every X.25 gateway interface can support up to 16 logical channel groups, each containing up to 256 logical channels, for a grand total of 4,096 simultaneous logical channels per gateway. It is up to the company that establishes the networks to say how many it will actually support in each type of service—that is, PVC and VC.

Notice in Figure 10.6 that octet 3 of the data packet header contains two 3-bit fields, P(S) and P(R), and a 1-bit field, M. M is the "more data" mark. When M has a value of 1, additional data packets will follow that are to be considered as a unit; when it has a value of 0, no more packets will follow in this unit. P(S) and P(R) are data packet counters, each of which can vary from 000 through 111 (0–7). The counters roll over to 000 again after passing 111. (These are not the same as N(S) and N(R), discussed earlier.) Only data packets have a P(S) counter; there will be a P(S) in each data packet sent across the DTE-to-DCE interface at the network gateway (see Figure 10.2) and a P(S) in each data packet sent from DCE to DTE at the network gateway.

By definition, P(R) is the amount of the next expected value of P(S) from the other direction on that logical channel (this will be explained in a moment). The values of P(S) and P(R) relate to each other within a logical channel at the network level in exactly the same way that N(S) and N(R) relate to each other on a point-to-point link. The Ns are not related to the Ps, however, because the Ns refer to all packets sent in a link, and the Ps refer only to data packets sent in a particular logical channel within that link.

The use of P(S) and PP(R)is illustrated in Figure 10.7. A sequence of two-way simultaneous (full-duplex) transmissions of data packets within a logical channel across a DTE/DCE interface at a packet network gateway is shown. In this illustration, each rectangle represents a packet. The first number in the rectangle is the value of P(S), and the second is the value of P(R) in that packet's header.

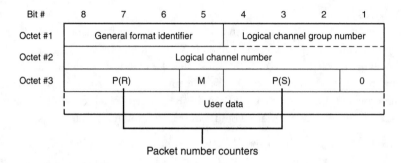

**FIGURE 10.6**

*A typical ITU-T X.25 data packet.*

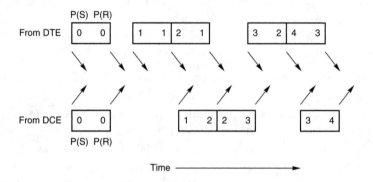

**FIGURE 10.7**

*The values of P(S) and P(R) for a sequence of data packets.*

Inspection of the sequence in Figure 10.7 confirms two facts already implied:

- The values of P(S) in a particular direction in a logical channel proceed in numerical order: 0, 1, 2, 3, and so forth.

- The value of P(R) sent in a packet is not updated to I until the entire packet whose value of P(S) is I – 1 has been completely received error-free. Such an update is an acknowledgment of all packets in that logical channel through P(S) = I – 1.

The dynamic establishment and disestablishment of a VC using special packets is very similar to that of placing and terminating a telephone call on the public telephone network, as indicated in Table 10.3 and Table 10.4. As you can see in these tables, seven new packet names have been introduced. An event occurring on one side of the network is usually paired with a complementary event on the other side. For example, a Call Request packet from calling DTE to DCE at one interface results in an Incoming Call packet from the DCE to a called DTE at another interface. Table 10.5 shows the packet type identifiers (octet 3 of the header) for these pairs of packet types.

**TABLE 10.3**   Network Analogies for Call Establishment

| Telephone Network | X.25 Packet Network |
| --- | --- |
| Place call | Send "Call Request" packet |
| Hear telephone ring | Receive "Incoming Call" packet |
| Pick up handset of ringing phone | Send "Call Accepted" packet |
| Hear "Hello" | Receive "Call Connected" packet |
| Fail to answer ring | Send "Clear Request" packet* |
| No answer, busy, or fast busy | Receive "Clear Indication" packet |
| Hang up | Send "Clear Confirmation" packet* |

*Causes are shown in packet.

**TABLE 10.4**   Network Analogies After Call Is Established

| Telephone Network | X.25 Packet Network |
| --- | --- |
| Hang up to disconnect | Send "Clear Request" packet |
| Hear other person hang up | Receive "Clear Indication" packet* |
| Hang up after other person hangs up | Send "Clear Confirmation" packet |
| Call disconnected by network | Receive "Clear Indication" packet* |

*Causes are shown in packet.

Figure 10.8 shows a "normal" sequence of a VC setup, two-way simultaneous data transfer, and terminal-initiated disconnect. Note that the four packet type identifiers of Table 10.5 are simply passed through the network, but the network does not modify them.

Figure 10.9 shows what happens when a VC does not complete. If the VC is refused by the called DTE, the called DTE sends Clear Request. If the VC is refused by the network, the calling DTE receives Clear Indication.

**TABLE 10.5**  Packet Type Identifiers for Call Setup and Clearing

| DTE to DCE | DCE to DTE | Octet #3 |
| --- | --- | --- |
| Call Request | Incoming Call | 0 0 0 0 1 0 1 1 |
| Call Accepted | Call Connected | 0 0 0 0 1 1 1 1 |
| Clear Request | Clear Indication | 0 0 0 1 0 0 1 1 |
| DTE-Initiated–<br>Clear Confirmation | Network-Initiated–<br>Clear Confirmation | 0 0 0 1 0 1 1 1 |

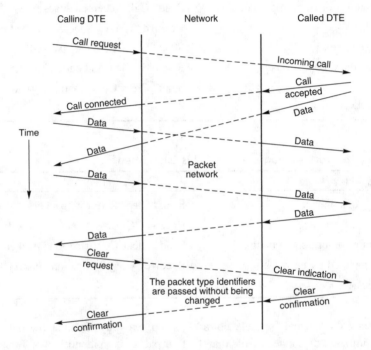

**FIGURE 10.8**

*A "normal" VC sequence.*

## Call Request/Incoming Call Packets

The headers of the Call Request/Incoming Call pair of packets are the most complex of the various header formats. They contain not only the basic three octets shown in Figure 10.5, but also destination addressing and facility selection information. In certain cases, they also contain user data.

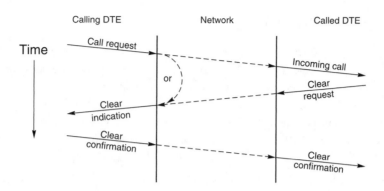

**FIGURE 10.9**
*VC not completed.*

The logical channel numbers (LCNs) and logical channel group numbers (LCGNs) for PVC service are assigned by the carrier from the ranges of numbers that the carrier decides to designate for PVC service. The numbers assigned to opposite ends of a given logical channel do not have to be the same. Different numbers could be assigned to the opposite ends of the channel, and the intelligent switches within the network would make the appropriate conversions as the packets pass back and forth.

In the case of VC service, the numerical values of logical channels at the opposite interfaces are never the same; the network always converts these numbers to and fro. The channel numbers used are assigned from a pool of numbers available at the time of call setup.

When placing a Call Request, a calling DTE selects the highest logical channel number that does not exceed a limit specified by the carrier and that is not already being used on another VC. The network then pairs the selected logical channel number with that VC from that calling DTE. At the destination end, the network selects the lowest logical channel number that is not less than a limit specified by the carrier and that is not already in use with that called DTE. The network then pairs that logical channel number with that VC to that called DTE. The two DTEs engaged in PVC or VC transactions never know (or care) which LCGN or LCN is being used by the other DTE/DCE interface.

## VC Destination Addressing

The DTE Address field in the Call Request/Incoming Call Packet format contains digits that are handled much like telephone numbers, with up to 14 digits on international VCs. The arrangement of these 14 digits is given in X.121. For domestic calls, fewer digits are required.

Many other details in X.25 cannot be covered here, and the list of facilities and diagnostic codes continues to grow. Refer to the standard for details.

# Value-Added Services

X.25 describes a highly flexible basic point-to-point service through a public network. To the user whose terminals operate in the X.25 packet mode, have a significant amount of traffic to send to many locations, and connect via a DTE/DCE serial interface to an X.25 network gateway, X.25 has few shortcomings. For the user who cannot meet all these criteria, X.25 does have limitations. Enhanced (value-added) service offerings, such as those provided by AT&T, Sprint (formerly GTE Telenet), BT Tymnet (formerly Tymnet), and others seek to address these and other matters:

- Broadcast services (sending the same data at the same time to many receivers).
- Dial access. (Because the DTE/DCE interface is intended as a two-way simultaneously synchronous gateway, packet-mode access normally cannot be provided via the public telephone network.)
- Conversion to lower-speed start-stop transmission for low-volume terminals.
- Code and protocol-conversion services.

The ITU has provided guidance with regard to the third item, as will be shown later.

# The X Series of Recommended Standards

As stated earlier, X.25 is part of the "X" series of recommended standards for public data networks being made public by the ITU-T. The X series is classified into two categories: X.1 through X.39 (which deal with services, facilities, terminals, and interfaces), and X.40 through X.200 (which deal with network architecture, transmission, signaling, switching, maintenance, and administrative arrangements). From a packet network user viewpoint, the most important X standards are given in the following list with their titles and brief descriptions:

- X.1—International User Classes of Service in Public Data Networks. Assigns numerical class designation to different terminal speeds and types.
- X.2—International User Services and Facilities in Public Data Networks. Specifies essential and additional services and facilities.
- X.3—Packet Assembly/Disassembly Facility (PAD) in a Public Data Network. Describes the packet assembler/disassembler that normally is used at a network gateway to allow connection of a start-stop terminal to a packet network.
- X.20bis—Use on Public Data Networks of DTE Designed for Interfacing to Asynchronous Duplex V-Series Modems. Allows use of V.24/V.28 (essentially the same as EIA RS-232).

- X.21bis—Use on Public Data Networks of DTE Designated for Interfacing to Synchronous V-Series Modems. Allows use of V.24/V.28 (essentially the same as EIA RS-232) or V.35.

- X.25—Interface Between DTE and DCE for Terminals Operating in the Packet Mode on Public Data Networks. Defines the architecture of three levels of protocols existing in the serial interface cable between a packet-mode terminal and a gateway to a packet network.

- X.28—DTE/DCE Interface for a Start-Stop Mode DTE Accessing the PAD in a Public Data Network Situated in the Same Country. Defines the architecture of protocols existing in a serial interface cable between a start-stop terminal and an X.3 PAD.

- X.29—Procedures for the Exchange of Control Information and User Data Between a PAD and a Packet Mode DTE or Another PAD. Defines the architecture of protocols behind the X.3 PAD, either between two PADs or between a PAD and a packet-mode terminal on the other side of the network.

- X.75—Terminal and Transit Call Control Procedures and Data Transfer System on International Circuits Between Packet-Switched Data Networks. Defines the architecture of protocols between two public packet networks.

- X.121—International Numbering Plan for Public Data Networks. Defines a numbering plan including code assignments for each nation.

## Interrelationships Between X Standards

Figure 10.10 shows the interrelationships among many of these X standards. In summary, X.25 specifies the relationship between a packet-mode DTE and a packet network. X.28 specifies the relationship between a start-stop (asynchronous) DTE and an X.3 PAD that must reside between a nonpacket DTE and a packet network. X.29 specifies additional relationships above those in X.25 that a packet-mode DTE must satisfy when communicating with a nonpacket mode DTE through a packet network and PAD. X.29 also covers the relationships between two PADs when two non–packet-mode DTEs are communicating through a packet network.

The PAD represents a key device that enables non–packet-aware terminals to communicate via a packet network. The PAD can be located within a packet network with terminal devices first communicating remotely to the PAD to access the packet network, or the PAD can be located onsite at an organization. Concerning the latter, this enables the terminals to be directly connected to the PAD, with the PAD supporting multiple connections into the packet network. Originally the PAD supported only start-stop (asynchronous) operations; however, during the past decade, several vendors developed conversion devices that enabled IBM BCS and SNA traffic to be converted for the transmission over an X.25 network.

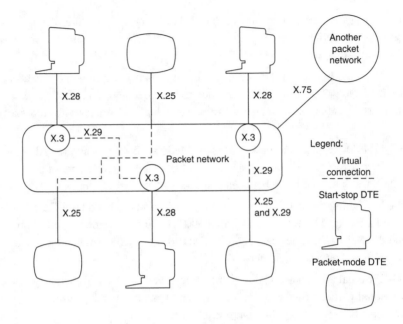

**FIGURE 10.10**

*Relationships between some X interface standards.*

Although the next section in this chapter is focused on the more modern Frame Relay network, it should be noted that X.25 packet networks continue to transport a considerable amount of traffic. In fact, when you visit a department store, shop at a discount store, or purchase gasoline or groceries and use a charge card, your transaction will more than likely flow over an X.25 network to the data center of the credit card company.

## Frame Relay

Although X.25-based packet networks have gained widespread acceptance, their data handling capability in an era of increasing use of fiber-optic cable represents a severe limitation. The growth in the installation of fiber-optic cable for the transmission of voice, data, and video between communications carrier central offices has reduced the potential of transmission errors to fewer than 1 in $10^9$ bits from the rate of 1 in $10^5$ typically encountered on analog transmission facilities. However, the use of X.25 packet networks results in the flow of packets through numerous data switching exchanges, and each DSE performs error checking and sometimes performs flow-control procedures, both of which introduce delays that adversely affect the throughput of data.

Although X.25 error-checking procedures were necessary when packet networks were established using analog leased lines to interconnect DSEs, for many communications applications in which data flows over fiber-optic cable, the use of a series of error-checking procedures is both unnecessary and detrimental to developing high-speed transmission that effectively uses available bandwidth. Because of this limitation to X.25, a form of fast packet switching referred to as *Frame Relay* was developed.

Frame Relay can be considered a logical progression of X.25 packet switching. Under Frame Relay, most error-checking and flow-control functions performed in an X.25 network are eliminated. As a result, Frame Relay transmission occurs at data rates up to the approximate 45Mbps rate of a T3 circuit, which are significantly higher than those obtainable using X.25 packet networks.

The key differences between Frame Relay and X.25 are in the areas of protocol operation, error control, congestion, data dropping, and flow control. As previously noted in this chapter, Frame Relay represents a streamlined Layer 2 packet switching protocol. Through streamlining, each Frame Relay node simply forwards frames and does not perform error checking as performed by an X.25 packet network. In addition, when too much data flows toward a network switch, the switch can drop frames during periods of congestion. In comparison, an X.25 switch will implement flow control downstream to other switches to control the flow of data to the switch beginning to experience congestion.

Another key difference between Frame Relay and an X.25 network concerns latency or the delay associated with the flow of frames through each network. Because Frame Relay switches simply "read" the destination address and forward a frame, latency is minimized. In comparison, each X.25 node error checks each packet that introduces a short delay. Furthermore, any flow control implemented on the path of a packet further delays the flow of data through the network.

By eliminating flow control and minimizing network latency, it became possible for Frame Relay to transport digitized voice as well as data and fax information. In fact, commencing during the late 1990s and continuing to the present, one of the most rapidly growing fields of data communications was the use of Frame Relay networks to transport digitized voice calls between branch offices of a company. When the cost of equipment necessary to digitize voice is amortized over a three-year period, it often becomes possible to transport voice at a cost as low as a penny a minute, low enough to make the Sprint dime lady blush! Table 10.6 provides a general comparison of X.25 and Frame Relay features.

## Frame Relay Components

The connection of a computer or data terminal to a Frame Relay network involves the installation of various hardware components, as well as knowledge of features unique to this data-transport mechanism. From a physical perspective, the connection from a customer premise to a Frame Relay service provider is quite similar to the connection used for other types of services provided by communications vendors.

Figure 10.11 illustrates a typical connection from customer premises to a Frame Relay service provider's nearest serving office. Note that communications equipment located at the customer premises can be any type of Frame Relay-compliant device, such as a front-end processor, multiplexer, or router. The router illustrated in Figure 10.11 is assumed to provide each workstation on the LAN with access to the Frame Relay network. Similar to a PAD used by an X.25 network, a Frame Relay access device (FRAD) can be used to convert transmissions from different types of terminal devices that are not Frame Relay–compliant into frames suitable for transmission into a Frame Relay network. The key difference between a FRAD and a router is the fact that the router is a more comprehensive device that also performs FRAD functions. In comparison, FRADs are designed to support a specific application, such as the concentration of a number of low-speed data and digitized voice data sources into a Frame Relay network.

**TABLE 10.6**   X.25 Versus Frame Relay

| Feature | X.25 | Frame Relay |
|---|---|---|
| OSI layer operation | 3 | 2 |
| Node error checking | Yes | No |
| Node flow control | Yes | Frames dropped when congestion occurs |
| Line access rate | Up to 56/64Kbps | Up to 45Mbps |
| Latency | High | Low |
| Capability to transport voice | No | Yes |

The CSU/DSU converts unipolar digital signaling into a bipolar format for transmission on the local digital access line, as described in Chapter 5, "Synchronous Modems, Digital Transmission, and Service Units." Although there is no reason why an analog local access line cannot be used to provide access to a Frame Relay service, present service provider policy is to commence the access rate to a Frame Relay service at 56Kbps via a digital leased line. The local access line is routed to the serving telephone company office, where it is connected to the Frame Relay service provider's point of presence (POP), assuming that the service provider is a long-distance carrier. Recently, several local carriers announced Frame Relay service offerings, which enable organizations that require the transmission of data within only a limited geographic area to have their Frame Relay service requirements performed by a local carrier if that the carrier is cost-competitive. Regardless of the Frame Relay service provider, the local access line can transport (in effect) multiplexed data representing two or more destinations that are routed as virtual circuits by the Frame Relay service provider.

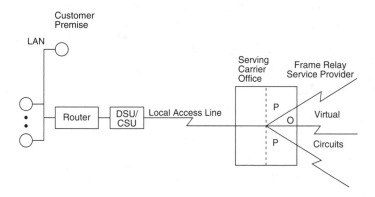

**FIGURE 10.11**

*Frame Relay components.*

Similar to an X.25 packet network, a Frame Relay service enables organizations to route data to many locations via the use of a single leased line. To better understand this concept, consider the four-site Frame Relay network shown in the top portion of Figure 10.12. In this example, an organization with four geographically distributed LAN locations installed four Frame Relay access lines, each of which connects one location to a Frame Relay access provider. Here, as requirements for transmission between locations occur, the mesh structured network of the service provider is used to get virtual circuits between each location. Note that only four routers, with one port per router, are required to get the capability to transmit between any location. In comparison, the use of leased lines to establish an organizational Frame Relay service would require 6 leased lines and 12 router ports, as indicated in the lower portion of Figure 10.12.

## Frame Format and Data Flow

To gain an understanding of data flow on a Frame Relay network, you must first examine the composition of the Frame Relay frame. Figure 10.13 illustrates the composition of the Frame Relay frame to include the subfields in the 2-byte frame header.

The two Flag fields consist of the bit sequence 01111110 and function in the same manner as an HDLC flag. That is, they serve as frame delimiters, and in any sequence of 6 set bits in data, a 0 bit will be inserted to prevent data from being misinterpreted as a flag.

The Header field consists of a series of subfields that define the initial destination of the frame (whether or not the frame can be dropped by the network), congestion indicators, and other information. Patience is a virtue, and if you have a bit of it, note that you will explore the use of each subfield in detail later.

The Information field contains data to be transmitted. That data can represent NetWare's IPX protocol, TCP/IP, or even IBM's SNA. The maximum length of the Information field is 8,192 bytes; however, most public Frame Relay networks support a lower maximum length value.

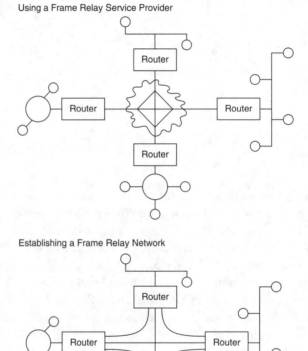

**FIGURE 10.12**

*Comparing the use of a Frame Relay service to that of a Frame Relay network.*

The Frame Check Sequence (FCS) field provides an error-detection capability. However, instead of being used as a mechanism to request a previous node to retransmit data, the FCS is used at the destination. At the destination, a local FCS is computed and compared to the transmitted FCS. If the two do not match (which indicates an error occurred), it is up to the higher layers in the protocol stack at the destination to request a retransmission. Thus, Frame Relay removes a large portion of the responsibility for error detection and correction from the network and assigns the responsibility to end stations, such as Frame Relay–compliant routers and Frame Relay Access Devices (FRADs).

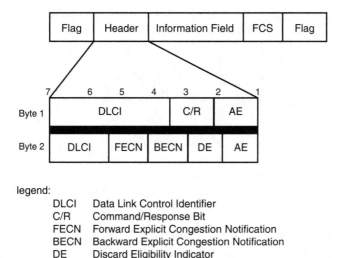

**FIGURE 10.13**
*The composition of the Frame Relay frame.*

The Data Link Control Identifier (DLCI) in Frame Relay is similar to the logical channel number used by X.25. That is, the DLCI specifies a permanent virtual path through the Frame Relay network. In actuality, the DLCI has local significance because it defines a virtual path from equipment connected to the network to the first Frame Relay switch in the network. The Frame Relay network operator configures routing at each switch by associating a switch port with a DLCI. An example of a possible DLCI association is shown in Figure 10.14. In this example, a DLCI value of 37 is shown on the route from the FRAD located in New York to port 1 on switch 1 at the entrance to the Frame Relay network in New York. Tables in switch 1 would be configured so that frames entering port 1 with a DLCI of 37 are switched to port 4 and exit in this example with a DLCI of 52. At switch 2, its tables are configured so that frames entering port 1 with a DLCI of 52 are switched out on port 3 after their DLCI is changed to 105. Eventually frames that originated in New York with a DLCI of 37 reach the FRAD in Chicago with a DLCI of 81.

Although only one PVC is shown in Figure 10.14, the connection between New York and Chicago—or, for that matter, between any two locations connected via a Frame Relay network—can support multiple PVCs over a common route. However, each PVC would have a different set of DLCIs.

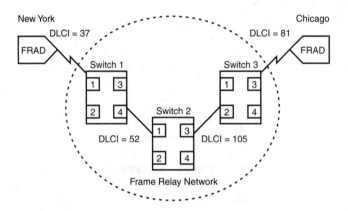

**FIGURE 10.14**

*DLCI associations form a private virtual circuit (PVC).*

The use of multiple PVCs enables different types of traffic to be transported between the same or different locations and routed at their destination based upon the DLCI value in each frame. For example, the FRAD in New York could use one PVC to support LAN-to-LAN transmission from New York to Chicago, and a second PVC could be used to support the communications requirements of an IBM System Network Architecture (SNA) control unit that needs to access an IBM mainframe located in Dallas.

The Command/Response (C/R) bit in the Frame Relay header is used by devices that employ a polling protocol to facilitate data transfer through the relay network.

The Address Extension (AE) bit indicates whether an additional byte is in the header field. When set to a value of 0, it indicates that another header byte follows; when set to a value of 1, it indicates that the byte that it is in is the last byte in the Header field. Because some Frame Relay networks support the use of extended DLCIs, the AE bits can be set to 0 to allow up to 4 bytes in the frame header. A 3-byte header extends the DLCI to 17 bits, whereas a 4-byte header extends the DLCI to 24 bits.

# Congestion Control

Three bits in the Frame Relay header are related to network congestion. Those bits are the Discard Eligibility (DE) bit, the Forward Explicit Congestion Notification (FECN) bit, and the Backward Explicit Congestion Notification (BECN) bit.

The DE bit is automatically set by the Frame Relay network whenever the data rate into the network exceeds what is referred to as *Committed Information Rate (CIR)*. Thus, before discussing the use of the DE bit, as well as the FECN and BECN bits, an examination of data transfer into a Frame Relay network is warranted.

Transmission into a Frame Relay network occurs over an access line that provides a fixed data rate, such as 56/64Kbps or 1.544Mbps. That access line is connected to a switch port that defines the highest possible speed that data can flow into the network and represents the maximum operating rate of any virtual circuit originating from the access line. Because a public Frame Relay network will transport traffic from many organizations, at times, the service provider's facilities may not be available to transport the full data rate flowing into the Frame Relay network.

For a fee, many Frame Relay service providers will guarantee a minimum end-to-end transmission rate for each permanent virtual circuit between your premises and a distant location. That minimum rate is the Committed Information Rate (CIR). The higher the CIR is, the higher the level of performance is, albeit at a higher cost.

Many Frame Relay service providers make available CIRs that vary in increments of 16Kbps or 64Kbps. For example, if your organization installed a 256Kbps fractional T1 access line to a Frame Relay service provider's switch, you might be able to select a CIR of 0, 64Kbps, 128Kbps, 192Kbps, or 256Kbps. A 0 CIR means that any frame entering the Frame Relay network can be discarded during periods of congestion. Similarly, a CIR of 64Kbps means that frames flowing into the network at a rate greater than 64Kbps can be discarded.

To indicate which frames can be discarded, the network sets the DE bit position in the frame. This signals switches experiencing congestion to drop such frames first in an attempt to relieve congestion. Because end stations are responsible for ensuring the correct arrival of data, after a short period of time, the receiving station will generate a request to the transmitting station for the dropped frame. Note that, as previously discussed, the end stations and not the network are responsible for recovering dropped frames.

Although it may appear risky to have a 0 CIR, most Frame Relay service providers guarantee the delivery of 99.9 percent of frames with their DE bit set. Thus, unless you have time-dependent applications that cannot tolerate delays associated with retransmission (such as transporting digitized voice), the use of a low or even a 0 CIR can provide a useful mechanism for reducing the cost of communications.

Because the CIR can never exceed the line access rate, it is possible for users to burst above the CIR. The term used to reference transmission above the CIR is the excess burst (Be) rate. Because the CIR, the Be, and other rates must be expressed as a measurement per unit of time, another measurement to note when discussing Frame Relay performance is the time interval (Tc) for measuring a burst of traffic.

**10**

The relationship between the CIR and Tc can be expressed as follows:

$$CIR = \frac{Bc}{Tc}$$

Here, Bc represents the committed burst into a Frame Relay network. That is, Bc represents the maximum transfer rate into a Frame Relay network before the DE bit in frames is set. For almost all Frame Relay networks, Tc is set to 1 second, resulting in the CIR equalizing the committed burst size (Bc).

Figure 10.15 illustrates over time the potential relationship between the line access rate, Be, Bc, and CIR. Note that the sum of Bc and Be equals the line access rate when Tc is 1 second. Also note that frames flowing above the CIR rate have their DE bits set.

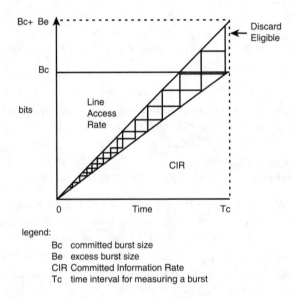

legend:

Bc   committed burst size
Be   excess burst size
CIR  Committed Information Rate
Tc   time interval for measuring a burst

**FIGURE 10.15**
*Relationship between Frame Relay transmission metrics.*

Now that you know how frames are marked as being eligible for discard, you can probe further and obtain an understanding of how the use of FECN and BECN bits throttle back data flow into a Frame Relay network, many times alleviating congestion before it becomes necessary to drop frames.

As a switch begins to experience congestion, it will set the FECN and BECN bits in frames flowing through the switch. For frames flowing from a subscriber toward the network, the FECN bit will be set to 1 once a predefined threshold is reached. For frames flowing in the opposite direction (from the network toward the subscriber), the BECN bit in each frame will be set. Figure 10.16 illustrates the setting of the FECN and BECN bits by switch 1, which is assumed to be experiencing congestion.

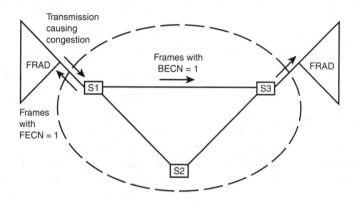

**FIGURE 10.16**

*As a switch experiences congestion, it sets the FECN bit in frames flowing toward the transmitting station and the BECN bit in frames flowing toward the receiver.*

Frames with the FECN bit set are flowing to the transmission device and can directly influence them by informing the station to throttle back its transmission into the network. Frames transmitted in the opposite direction that have their BECN bit set can only indirectly influence congestion. This is because they flow to the receiver, which can then recognize the BECN as a signal to delay acknowledgements to the transmitting device. Thus, the BECN bit setting can indirectly relieve congestion.

## Recent Developments

In the area of Frame Relay networking, three developments can be expected to have a considerable bearing upon the use of this packet network. Those developments include service-level agreement (SLA) guarantees, priority transfer through the network, and voice-compliant FRADs.

SLA was first introduced by one Frame Relay service provider in 1997; by 1998, most carriers offered some type of SLA. Currently, SLAs can include guarantees concerning network uptime, frame delivery, network transit time, or frame latency, and, to alleviate user concerns when things go wrong, a maximum repair time. If the carrier does not provide the level of service specified in the SLA, a rebate—typically 10% of the subscriber's monthly cost—is returned to the customer.

Priority transfer results in the Frame Relay service provider using its network switches to establish different levels of service based upon predefined classes of traffic. For example, a service provider might offer three levels of service across its network, each of which has a guaranteed maximum end-to-end latency. A subscriber could elect to use the highest level of service to obtain the lowest end-to-end latency for digitized voice transmission, while file transfers might be assigned the lowest level of service. Because an extra fee is charged for prioritized traffic, it should be used to support traffic that requires a minimal latency.

The third development driving the use of Frame Relay is the introduction of voice-compliant FRADs. Such FRADs include an interface to a PBX, voice-digitization cards that support the digitization of voice using low-bit-rate encoding such as a Code Excited Linear Prediction (CELP) algorithm, which enables a voice conversation to be transported as an 8Kbps data stream. Because digitized voice cannot tolerate more than a quarter second of network delay, the introduction of priority transfer by several Frame Relay service providers has significantly enhanced the capability of those networks to transport digitized voice conversations.

## Networking Cost Comparison

A comparison of the costs associated with the use of a Frame Relay service can involve an investigation of the pricing structure of many elements. Most Frame Relay service providers charge a Frame Relay port fee based on the operating rate of the interface to the service, as well as a fee for the CIR subscribed for. Some service providers bill for each CIR for each permanent virtual circuit, whereas other service providers bill for a bandwidth allocation that represents the sum of the CIRs for all virtual circuits. Other charges that Frame Relay providers might bill for include a fixed charge per virtual circuit, a usage charge based on frames transmitted, and a distance charge based on the length of virtual circuits.

## What You Have Learned

- Open Systems Interconnect is a reference architectural model that is revolutionizing the way we view telecommunications.

- When protocols are layered, the higher-level layers are embedded inside fields of less intelligent layers.

- Packet switching involves fast store-and-forward computers at each network node.

- X.25 is an international standard packet-switching architecture specifying three layers of protocols at the network gateway.

- When properly used, X.25 networks provide a fast, reliable, accurate, flexible, and cost-effective data communications alternative.

- X.25 specifies two services: Virtual Call service is analogous to a telephone call; Permanent Virtual Circuit service is analogous to a private line.

- X.25 doesn't provide for dial access or for start-stop transmission, but enhanced services do.

- A single X.25 interface can handle many logical channels at the same time.

- X.25 is but a part of a larger group of ITU-T standards on public data networks.

- X.25/X.121 provides for an extremely large worldwide population of terminals.

- Frame relay is a form of fast packet switching in which error checking and flow control is minimized.

- The Committed Information Rate (CIR) represents a guaranteed transmission rate through a Frame Relay network.

- Transmission above the CIR results in the Frame Relay network setting the Discard Eligibility bit in each frame.

- When a switch in a Frame Relay network experiences congestion, it sets the FECN and BECN bits to notify the transmitting and receiving stations to throttle back on their transmission and transmission acknowledgements.

- The Data Link Control Indicator (DLCI) defines a virtual path created through a Frame Relay network.

# Quiz for Chapter 10

1. The OSI reference model is

    A. Worthless.

    B. A protocol.

    C. Not a protocol.

    D. None of the above.

2. Which of the following is Layer 1 of the OSI model?

    A. Link layer

    B. Physical layer

    C. Network layer

    D. Transport layer

3. The applications layer holds which position in the OSI model?

    A. Seventh layer

    B. Sixth layer

    C. Fifth layer

    D. Fourth layer

**10**

ARCHITECTURES
AND PACKET
NETWORKS

4. The electrical state of the control leads in a serial interface is a concern of which protocol?

    A. The physical-layer protocol

    B. The link-layer protocol

    C. The network-layer protocol

    D. None of the above

5. The X.25 standard specifies a

    A. Technique for dial access.

    B. Technique for start-stop data.

    C. Data bit rate.

    D. DTE/DCE interface.

6. The X.25 standard is

    A. Required for all packet-switching networks.

    B. A recommendation of the ITU-T.

    C. A complete description of a public data network.

    D. Used by all packet terminals.

7. The X.25 standard for packet networks is analogous to which of the following?

    A. PBX standards for a telephone network

    B. Handset standards for a telephone

    C. Local loop standards for a telephone network

    D. Switching standards for a telephone network

8. What does the value of the A field in an LAPB frame specify?

    A. The calling DTE for a virtual call

    B. The called DTE for a virtual call

    C. The data sink for a VC or PVC

    D.One of the two ends of a serial interface

9. A group of packets from a source through an X.25 packet system to a sink

    A. Arrives in the same order sent for VC, but not PVC.

    B. Arrives in the same order sent for PVC, but not VC.

    C. Arrives in the same order sent for both VC and PVC.

    D. None of the above.

10. Which of the following correctly represents the value of N(S) as related to the value of P(S)?

   A. N(S) – P(S) = number of outstanding packets.

   B. N(S) – P(S) = number of outstanding frames.

   C. N(S) – P(S) = number of active logical channels in a link.

   D. None of the above. They are not related.

11. A protocol is a set of rules governing a time sequence of events that must take place

   A. Between peers.

   B. Between nonpeers.

   C. Across an interface.

   D. None of the above.

12. The OSI reference model defines the functions for seven layers of protocols

   A. Including the user and communications medium.

   B. Not including the user or communications medium.

   C. Including the communications medium but not the user.

   D. Including the user but not the communications medium.

13. The X.25 standard covers how many OSI layers?

   A. 3

   B. 4

   C. 7

   D. None

14. Architecturally, link protocols are at a level

   A. Lower than physical protocols.

   B. Higher than physical protocols.

   C. The same as physical protocols.

   D. None of the above.

15. A data packet is a packet header together with

   A. A network layer.

   B. An administrative layer.

   C. User data.

   D. A packet switch.

16. A network node joining three or more links is called what?

    A. DSE

    B. DTE

    C. DCE

    D. DTE and DCE

17. The X.25 standard specifies how many separate protocol layers at the serial interface gateway?

    A. 8

    B. 2

    C. 4

    D. 3

18. The LAPB frame structure and the frame structure of SDLC are

    A. Opposite.

    B. Identical.

    C. Reversed.

    D. None of the above.

19. Establishing a virtual "connection" is functionally equivalent to which of the following?

    A. Placing a telephone call before a conversation

    B. Connecting a virtual memory

    C. Physically connecting a DTE and DCE

    D. None of the above

20. In X.25 network-layer protocol, the data packets normally contain which of the following?

    A. One octet of header plus data

    B. Two octets of header plus data

    C. Three octets of header plus data

    D. Four octets of header plus data

21. The Frame Relay Committed Information Rate represents

    A. The maximum data rate on the network.

    B. The steady state data rate on the network.

    C. The minimum data rate on the network.

    D. The interface data rate.

22. How many circuits are required for the interconnection of equipment at four locations via a Frame Relay network?

    A. 2

    B. 4

    C. 6

    D. 8

23. How many ports are required for the connection of equipment at four locations to each other?

    A. 3

    B. 6

    C. 9

    D. 12

24. Responsibility for error detection and correction in a Frame Relay transmission environment is the responsibility of which of the following?

    A. The network operator

    B. The network

    C. The network protocol stack

    D. The end stations

25. The Data Link Control Identifier

    A. Is always fixed in value.

    B. Has global significance.

    C. Can vary through a Frame Relay network.

    D. Always matches the entry value at the exit from the network.

26. Notification of the occurrence of congestion in a Frame Relay service occurs through the

    A. Committed Information Rate.

    B. Forward Error Congestion Notification.

    C. Backward Error Congestion Notification.

    D. Both B and C.

27. Frames that enter a Frame Relay network at a data rate above the Committed Information Rate

    A. Have the DE bit set.

    B. Have the BECN bit set.

    C. Have the FECN bit set.

    D. Have the XON bit set.

**10**

ARCHITECTURES
AND PACKET
NETWORKS

28. The excess burst (Be) rate

    A. Is half the CIR rate.

    B. Equals the CIR rate.

    C. Represents transmission above the CIR.

    D. Always equals the CIR.

29. The CIR

    A. Can never exceed the line access rate.

    B. Always exceeds the line access rate.

    C. Never equals the excess burst rate.

    D. Is always discarded.

30. The failure to maintain a service-level agreement results in which of the following?

    A. A priority transfer

    B. A rebate to the subscriber

    C. A rebate to the carrier

    D. A renegotiation of the agreement

# Local Area Networks

## IN THIS CHAPTER

This chapter begins by describing the characteristics of an ideal *local area network (LAN)* and the major obstacles that might prevent you from achieving the ideal. The most common types of existing LAN architectures—contention-access-based systems, token-passing systems, polled-access-based coaxial cable systems, and frequency-division broadband systems—are discussed through examples of existing LANs. LANs examined in this chapter include the different types of Ethernet networks initially defined by the Intel, Digital Equipment, and Xerox specification and later by a series of IEEE 802.3 standards, including Fast Ethernet and Gigabit Ethernet, as well as Datapoint's ARCnet and IBM's 4 and 16Mbps token-ring networks. After presenting basic information concerning the operation of the most common types of LANs, this chapter focuses on network devices used to expand local area networks. Networking devices covered include bridges, routers, gateways, and LAN switches.

# Overview of LANs

In its most basic form, a LAN is a data communications facility that provides high-speed switched connections between processors, peripherals, and terminals within a single building or campus. Historically, LANs have evolved from the data processing or office processing industry, in which economics suggest that relatively expensive storage devices and printers should be shared by multiple computers. Thus, LANs have evolved partly in response to the emergence of low-cost computing and its need for high-cost peripherals. Indeed, the first-generation of LANs were actually one form of distributed computer systems using proprietary high-speed data links between processing nodes and peripheral equipment. A second rationale for the growth in the use of LANs is related to modern organizations' need for distributed computing. A LAN allows computing power to be directly distributed to the desktop, yet it enables the desktop user to tap into other computer resources connected to the LAN. This distribution of computer power enables users to be more productive and, in many organizations, also allows conventional data centers to be eliminated or reduced in size, a process commonly referred to as *downsizing*.

As LANs evolved, applications for the use of their technology expanded. Today special types of local area networks are used to provide the infrastructure for *storage area networks (SANs)*, whereas an emerging 10Gbps version of Ethernet based on transmission over optical fiber is being considered as a transport facility to both bypass and supplement traditional telephone company offerings within metropolitan areas.

# LANs Versus Other Techniques

Figure 11.1 shows a perspective of a local area network as a digital communications facility. This illustration depicts the bandwidth versus distance capabilities of four data communications technologies: computer buses, voiceband data links, digital subscriber lines (DSL), and

LANs. The computer buses are internal to a computer mainframe. They achieve very high data transfers by using high clock rates (for example, a few hundred MHz) and parallel transmission (for example, 32 or 64 bits per clock cycle). Such systems are economical and practical only at distances up to a few meters. Voiceband data transmission uses readily available telephone wire pairs with modems. These systems are virtually unlimited in distance, but the standard analog telephone channel usually restricts voiceband data rates to approximately 33,600bps.

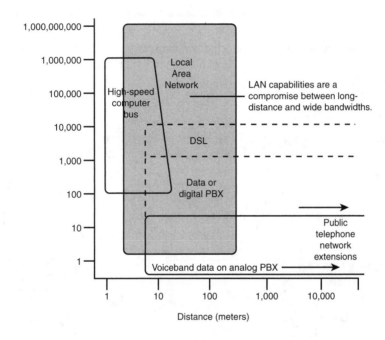

**FIGURE 11.1**

*Distance versus data rate comparison.*

As noted earlier in this book when we examined various flavors of digital subscriber line (DSL) technology, it is possible to use the full bandwidth of twisted pair at a data rate of approximately 1.5 Mbps at distances up to 18,000 feet from a subscriber to a telephone company central office.

As you can see in Figure 11.1, the capabilities of a typical LAN represent a compromise between long distances and wide bandwidths. Some computer architectures have moved in on the region occupied by LANs by moving away from high-speed parallel buses to more loosely coupled distributed systems. Thus, the LAN region is overlapped on the left edge by distributed computer systems. Similarly, digital subscriber lines and digital telephone systems are overlapping the LAN region on the bottom by providing moderate data rates as a low-cost addition to basic telephone service.

The distance versus data rate aspect of a local area network depicted in Figure 11.1 actually represents only one level of definition of a LAN. As the market and technology have grown, so has the recognition that a LAN should solve or alleviate more problems pertaining to data communications than merely the data transmission problem. The data communications manager or service organization responsible for a particular building or campus is typically concerned with various applications and associated types of equipment. If these different applications can be supported by one transmission facility, one type of hardware and software interface, and one set of maintenance procedures, total system's costs are reduced, and overall administration is greatly simplified. For example, Figure 11.2 illustrates a local area network serving several independent applications.

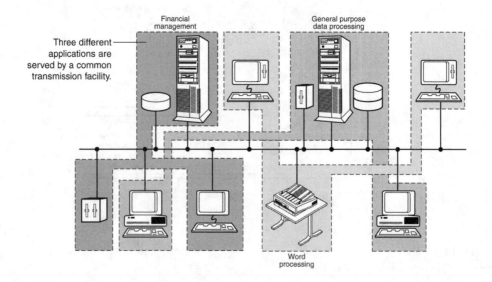

**FIGURE 11.2**

*Local area network supporting multiple independent applications.*

The next section presents the attributes of an ideal local area network, one that is supportive of all applications. In the sections that follow, present-day LANs are described and compared to the ideal as a means of contrasting one type of LAN with another.

# The Ideal LAN

11

The ideal LAN would be an information distribution system that is as easy to use as the conventional AC power distribution system in a building. Thus, adding a data terminal, processor, or peripheral to a local area network should require nothing more than plugging it into a conveniently located access port. When plugged in, it should communicate intelligently with any other device on the network. This ideal system is summarized by the features that make the AC power system so easy to use:

- One-time installation
- Widespread access
- Application independence
- Excess capacity
- Easy maintenance and administration

The features identified in this list have been developed over the years to minimize life-cycle costs for supplying AC power within a building. Although the costs of a typical installation can be reduced by wiring only to locations with immediate electrical needs, the costs of only small amounts of rewiring to supply additional locations later would more than offset the initial savings. To achieve a one-time installation, it is necessary to provide widespread access—that is, an electrical outlet virtually everywhere one might be needed. Furthermore, the capacity at every outlet is generally greater than the needs of the electrical appliances that connect to it. Adding wiring or rewiring becomes necessary only for particularly high-power consuming devices (for example, those needing 240 volts or dedicated, high-current circuits).

Recognizing the utility of the AC power distribution system in buildings, several companies introduced products over the past 20 years that attempted to use the electrical wiring within homes and offices as a built-in infrastructure for creating a local area network. Unfortunately, "data over power" transmission schemes have not been able to overcome such obstacles as transformers and have yet to obtain any degree of installation success in spite of their potential to use existing wiring.

## Major Obstacles to the Ideal LAN

If an information distribution system were available with all the desirable properties listed, you could move telephones, data terminals, printers, and storage devices as easily as you unplug and plug in a lamp. Moreover, the equipment could be supplied by various vendors. Although such an ideal system does not exist now, local area networks of several forms represent some of the first steps in the development of such a system. The major obstacles to overcome in the development of the ideal system are summarized in the following sections.

## No Single Standard

Because of the continually changing status of LANs and the competitive nature of the vendors, various local area network standards exist. As a result of different standards, many organizations must use special internetworking devices to include bridges, routers, and gateways. Interconnecting different types of LANs normally requires more complex and costly equipment, as well as increased equipment support requirements

## Diverse Requirements

The communications needs of a modern office building include voice, video, high-speed data, low-speed data, energy management, fire alarm, security, electronic mail, and so forth. These systems present transmission requirements that vary greatly in terms of data rates, acceptable delivery delays, reliability requirements, and error rate tolerance.

## Costly Transmission Media

Being able to deliver tens or even hundreds of megabits per second to one device and only a few thousand bits per second to another implies that the lower rate devices are burdened with a costly transmission media. The best economic solution must involve a hierarchical network design (one with stepped levels of capacity) that allows twisted-pair connections for low and medium data rate devices (a low step) feeding into a backbone high bandwidth transmission system (a higher step such as coaxial cable or optical fibers).

## Sophisticated Functional Requirements

Providing a network with the desired data rates and distances is only one item that must be considered in the data communications problem. Before one data device can communicate intelligently with another, numerous higher-level communications functions must be compatible. These include codes, formats, error control, addressing, routing, flow control, configuration management, and cost allocations.

# The ISO Model

A formal hierarchical identification of all data communications network functions has been established by the International Standards Organization (ISO) and referred to as the "ISO Model for Open Systems Interconnection" (OSI). This model, shown in Figure 11.3, identifies seven distinct levels of functional requirements pertaining to data communications networks. The lower three levels of this model were originally proposed by the ITU to encourage vendor commonality in interfacing to public packet-switching networks. This standard, designated as ITU recommendation X.25, is described in detail in Chapter 10, "WAN Architectures and Packet Networks," along with the ISO model.

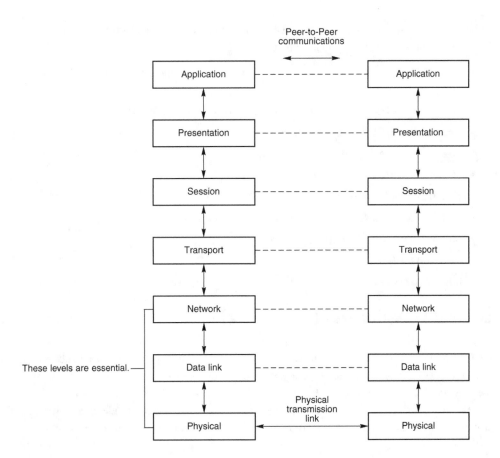

**FIGURE 11.3**

*The ISO Model for Open Systems Interconnection.*

Realization of the ideal LAN would require all levels of functions included in the OSI standard. However, not all levels of the OSI standard need to be implemented to provide effective communications in a LAN. If only the lower levels of the standard exist, a LAN can usefully support the multiple applications shown in Figure 11.2. In essence, the transmission media and lower-level interfaces are common so that data can be exchanged within virtual subnetworks—for example, the financial management group indicated in Figure 11.2.

## LAN Standards

Local area network standards (like other communications standards) are established by two groups: dominant manufacturers who attract plug-compatible competitors and official standards organizations. The leading official standards organization for LANs in the United States is the IEEE 802 Standards Committee. This committee has several working groups responsible for establishing these LAN standards including

- 802.1: Coordinates the interface between OSI levels 1 and 2 with the five higher-level layers
- 802.2: Logical data link standard similar to HDLC and ADCCP
- 802.3: CSMA/CDS standard similar to Ethernet
- 802.3ae: 10 Gigabit Ethernet
- 802.3: Fast Ethernet
- 802.3z: Gigabit Ethernet
- 802.4: Token-bus standard
- 802.5: Token-ring standard
- 802.9a: IsoENET
- 802.12: 100VG-AnyLAN

## Logical Link Control (IEEE 802.2)

To accommodate multiple LAN access methods, the IEEE 802 standards committee separated the OSI model's data link layer into two sublayers: a *logical link control (LLC)* sublayer and a *media access control (MAC)* sublayer, as shown in Figure 11.4. Under working group 802.2, the LLC control procedures have been defined to be basically the same as the ITU X.25 Link Access Procedure HDLC in a balanced mode (LAPB). The balanced mode is used for peer structured networks wherein any station can originate communications directly with any other station.

Two basic types of services are provided within 802.2 LLC. The type 1 service involves unacknowledged "connectionless" operation in which the source station sends a message to another station (or stations) without having established a logical connection for sequencing and acknowledging messages. This mode of operation is intended for transmission of messages that are not essential and for systems in which higher levels provide error recovery and sequencing functions (as in Ethernet).

The type 2 service is the more conventional balanced data communications service that establishes logical connections between two LLCs. Each LLC can send and receive both messages and responses. Each LLC also has the responsibility of ensuring complete and accurate deliveries of its outgoing messages.

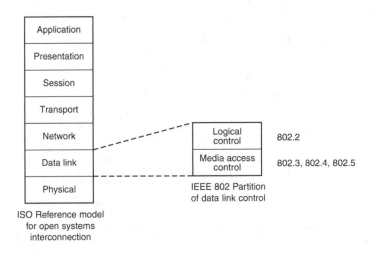

## FIGURE 11.4
*The relationship of the IEEE 802 partition to the ISO reference model.*

## Additional Sublayering

The development of new LAN technologies resulted in the realization that some local area networks would be developed to operate on different types of media, such as three metallic wire pairs in a four-pair group or one fiber-optic pair to transport data at 100Mbps. To support the use of different media, it became necessary to use different signaling rates and coding methods because, for example, it is easier to transmit using a higher signaling rate on fiber than on metallic cable due to the higher bandwidth of fiber.

To support different media under a common LAN standard, the IEEE subdivided the physical layer. That subdivision resulted in the creation of several sublayers to support different media used by relatively recently introduced high-speed LANs. Those sublayers include a physical coding sublayer (which defines the coding method used for transmission on different types of media) and a physical medium attachment sublayer (which maps messages from the physical coding sublayer onto the transmission media). A third sublayer, physical medium dependent, specifies the actual connector and its physical and electrical properties used to connect to the media. Figure 11.5 depicts the previously described subdivision of the physical layer. Note that two three-sublayer stacks are shown for illustrative purposes; however, it is possible for additional medium-independent interfaces to be developed by defining additional three-sublayer groups. Thus, the subdivision of the physical layer provides flexibility to tailor a LAN for operation on additional types of media at a later date.

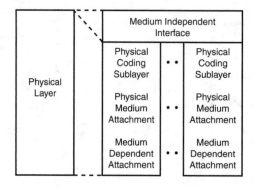

**FIGURE 11.5**

*The IEEE basic subdivision of the physical layer for high-speed LAN multimedia support.*

# CSMA/CD (IEEE 802.3)

The IEEE 802.3 standard defines the MAC sublayer for Carrier Sense Multiple Access/Collision Detection and a corresponding physical layer for connection to baseband and broadband coaxial cable and baseband operations over twisted-pair wiring. The standard is basically patterned after the Ethernet specification. As we will note later in this chapter when we examine Figure 11.6, broadband references the capability to transmit multiple signals on a common medium similar to cable TV. In comparison, baseband represents a term used to denote that only one signal flows on a medium.

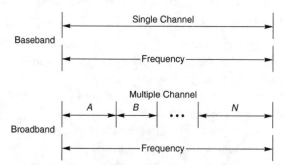

**FIGURE 11.6**

*Baseband versus broadband signaling.*

Variations in the physical layer allow signaling rates of 1, 5, 10, and 100Mbps, as well as 1Gbps. Possibly by the time you read this book a signaling rate of 10Gbps might become a reality. A multidrop coaxial cable segment is limited to 500 meters (with 100 stations) as opposed to 1500 meters in Ethernet, but as many as five coaxial segments are allowed in an IEEE 802.3 system. Later in this chapter, you will examine the original Ethernet and the IEEE 802.3 standards, including their network architecture and frame formats.

## Token-Passing Ring Access (IEEE 802.5)

The IEEE 802.5 standard defines a token-passing ring method in which access to a shared medium is controlled by the passing of a token. The token, which is a predefined sequence of bits, provides a receiving workstation on a token-ring LAN with the right to transmit a frame or a sequence of frames onto the ring.

When a workstation receives a free token, it builds a frame that includes the destination address of its transmission, its source address, and an information field, as well as a frame check sequence. The frame check sequence is used for frame verification in much the same way a CRC or BCC is used. As the frame circulates around the ring, each workstation examines the destination address. If the destination address matches the address of the workstation, the workstation receives data from the information field and sets a field in the frame to indicate the successful receipt of the frame. As the frame continues around the ring, it returns to the originator, which notes the successful transfer of information in the frame. The originator then generates a new token, which enables other workstations to gain access to the transmission medium. Although the use of token-ring provides predictability, it represents a more complex technology than Ethernet. This resulted in Token-Ring network adapter cards costing more than Ethernet network adapter cards. Although originally popular for use by large organizations to include financial institutions, the difference in adapter costs as well as the emphasis of vendors in developing Ethernet technology has reduced token-ring to approximately 15% of the LAN market.

## Ethernet (CSMA/CD)

Although Ethernet was not the first data communications network to technically qualify as a local area network, it is the most important because it represents the first major product offering with nonproprietary communications interfaces and protocols. Using an experimental design developed in a Xerox Corporation research laboratory, Digital Equipment, Xerox, and Intel (originally referred to as DIX) teamed up to define some commercial products based on jointly published communications standards. This action has invited other manufacturers to develop compatible products. The marketing strategy has been successful enough to establish the Ethernet interface as a standard even on systems utilizing transmission media different from the baseband coaxial cable originally specified for use in Ethernet.

The Ethernet architecture is based in concept on the Aloha satellite communications network developed at the University of Hawaii. The Aloha system allows multiple distributed devices to communicate with one another over a single radio channel using a satellite as a transponder. One station communicates with another by waiting until the radio channel is idle (determined by carrier sensing) and then sending a packet of data with a destination address, a source address, and redundant check bits to detect transmission errors. All idle stations continuously monitor incoming data and accept those packets with their address and valid checksums. Whenever a station receives a new packet, the receiving station returns an acknowledgment to the source. If an originating station does not receive an acknowledgment within a specified time interval, it retransmits the packet under the assumption that the previous packet was interfered with by noise or by a concurrent transmission from another station. (The latter situation is referred to as a *collision*.) Ethernet employs the same basic system concept, originally using coaxial cable for distribution throughout a building or campus.

## Ethernet's Physical Layer

The transmission media of Ethernet was originally restricted to the use of conventional thick coaxial cable using baseband transmission at 10Mbps. Other media now used for Ethernet transmission include thin coaxial cable, different types of twisted-pair wire, and different types of fiber-optic cable. Both types of coaxial cable media support the use of a bus technology, but the use of twisted-pair wire requires a star topology for an Ethernet LAN. Fiber is used both to extend individual Ethernet connections and as the primary method used to create a star-based Gigabit network topology.

Baseband transmission implies that data is transmitted without the use of a carrier and with only one channel defined in the system. In comparison, in broadband signaling, the bandwidth of the media is subdivided by frequency into multiple channels that can support the concurrent transmission of different types of signals, such as voice, data, and video. Figure 11.6 illustrates the operation of baseband and broadband signaling. Under the IEEE 802.3 set of LAN network standards, a broadband Ethernet referred to as 10BROAD-36 was standardized. Later in this chapter, you will compare Ethernet to the IEEE 802.3 series of standards.

In a 10Mbps Ethernet environment, when a station is transmitting, it uses the entire capacity of the system. Data is encoded using a Manchester code as shown in Figure 11.7. On 100Mbps and 1Gbps versions of Ethernet, different coding methods are used; those are described later in this chapter.

A Manchester code provides a strong timing component for clock recovery because a timing transition always occurs in the middle of every bit. In this type of coding, each bit period is divided into two complementary halves. A negative-to-positive voltage transition in the middle of the bit period designates a binary 1, and a positive-to-negative transition represents a binary

0. Another property of the Manchester code line is that it always maintains equal amounts of positive and negative voltages. This method prevents the build-up of a DC component, which simplifies the implementation of decision thresholds in the data detectors.

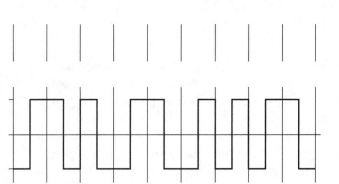

**FIGURE 11.7**

*Manchester line code.*

Although the data is not transmitted with a carrier per se, the continuous transitions of the Manchester code provide the equivalent of a carrier, so the channel can easily be monitored for activity (for example, by a carrier sense technique). Multiple access to a coaxial cable-based network is provided by passive taps, thereby allowing you to add or remove station connections (called *drops*) without disrupting traffic in the system.

Another requirement of the transmission link and its associated access electronics is that while transmitting, a transceiver must be capable of detecting the existence of another active transmitter. This is referred to as *collision detection*. Thus, the three basic steps for accessing an Ethernet line are denoted CSMA/CD (Carrier Sense, Multiple Access with Collision Detection).

The capability to detect collisions allows colliding stations to release the channel after using it for only a short period. A conventional Aloha system (one without collision detection), on the other hand, transmits entire messages without knowing whether a collision has occurred. Because an Ethernet station checks for carrier presence before transmitting, collisions occur only if two stations begin transmitting within a time interval equal to the propagation delay between the stations. By restricting the maximum distance between transceivers on a bus-based coaxial cable LAN to 2500 meters, you can limit the collision window to 23 microseconds (μS), including repeater delays.

When a station begins transmitting, it can be sure that no collision will occur if none is detected within a round-trip propagation of 46.4μS. Because one bit time is 0.1μS at 10Mbps, the collision detection decision is made within 464 bit times. The maximum length of a frame is 12,144 bits; thus, the collision detection feature detects a collision very early in the frame, saving significant transmission time that would be wasted if the entire frame were transmitted before detection.

Whenever a collision occurs, all colliding stations detect the condition and wait individually random amounts of time before retrying the transmission. The actual amount of time a station waits is governed by the use of a random exponential backoff algorithm. Thus, the stations do not wait for acknowledgment timeouts to trigger a retransmission. (Acknowledgments are unnecessary at this level of the protocol but might be used at a higher level to ensure that the message was received at the final destination.) The method of waiting random amounts of time before transmitting reduces the probability of repeated collisions. In heavy traffic conditions, the average delay before retransmission begins to increase after 10 unsuccessful attempts. After 16 collisions, no further attempts are made to transmit that message, and the station is notified of the error by the transceiver.

In preparation for transmitting a data frame, the physical layer must insert a 64-bit preamble so that all receivers on the network can synchronize with the data stream before the desired data frame begins. The preamble consists of alternating ones and zeros, ending in two ones that signify the start of a frame.

## Ethernet Physical Layer Interface

Standard Ethernet transceiver cable connectors are 15-pin D-shell connectors (MIL-C-24308 or equivalent). The transceiver has a male connector, and the station apparatus has a female connector. Thus, the interconnecting cable must have one connector of each type. These are the pin assignments:

| | | | |
|---|---|---|---|
| 1. | Shield | 9. | Collision Presence – |
| 2. | Collision Presence + | 10. | Transmit – |
| 3. | Transmit + | 11. | Reserved |
| 4. | Reserved | 12. | Receive – |
| 5. | Receive + | 13. | Power |
| 6. | Power return | 14. | Reserved |
| 7. | Reserved | 15. | Reserved |
| 8. | Reserved | | |

Figure 11.8 illustrates the relationship of the Ethernet hardware components required to connect a workstation to a bus-based coaxial cable. The interface board or adapter card is normally

installed in a system expansion slot within the system unit of a personal computer. That board or card is also known as a controller and is often referred to as an *Ethernet controller*.

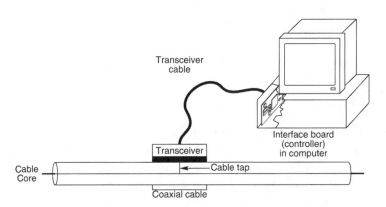

**FIGURE 11.8**

*The relationship of Ethernet hardware components.*

The Ethernet controller formats data from the computer into frames for transmission via the transceiver (transmitter/receiver) cable to the transceiver. The transceiver converts unipolar digital signals generated by the computer into Manchester encoded digital signals. In addition, the transceiver is responsible for detecting collisions by examining the voltage level on the cable. That is, a rise in the voltage level beyond its normal nominal height indicates the occurrence of a collision.

## Data Link Layer

The data link layer is primarily concerned with message packaging and link management. It is largely independent of the medium-dependent physical channel. The message packaging function includes the following:

- Framing—Identifying the beginning and end of a message
- Addressing—Specifying fields for source and destination addresses
- Error checking—Using redundant codes to detect channel errors

Figure 11.9 shows the format of an Ethernet frame. The preamble, which consists of the repeating sequence 101010… for 8 bytes or 64 bits, announces the occurrence of the frame. Generation and removal of the preamble are functions of the physical layer. Similarly, the end of a frame is provided by the removal of the carrier sense signal, as detected by the absence of a bit transition following the last bit of the frame check sequence. Notice that frame sizes must contain an integral number of bytes, ranging from 72 to 1526 bytes. (At 8 bits per byte, that's 572 to 12,208 bits.) The Type field is reserved to indicate which of several possible higher-level protocols might be in use.

| 8 Bytes | 6 Bytes | 6 Bytes | 2 Bytes | 46-1500 Bytes | 4 Bytes |
|---------|---------|---------|---------|---------------|---------|
| Preamble | Destination Address | Source Address | Type | Data | Frame Check Sequence |

**FIGURE 11.9**

*The Ethernet data link frame format.*

If you were to study the length of Ethernet frames, you would more than likely note differences concerning the minimum and maximum frame lengths. Some books and trade literature state that the minimum Ethernet frame length is 64 bytes, whereas other literature indicates 72 bytes. Similarly, some books and trade literature specify a maximum Ethernet frame length of 1518 bytes, whereas others indicate a maximum frame length of 1526 bytes.

The reason for the preceding differences can be traced to Ethernet and IEEE 802.3 standards and the manner by which each standard references frame length. Under the Ethernet standard, the frame length is measured from the Preamble field through the FCS field, resulting in minimum and maximum frame lengths of 72 and 1526 bytes, respectively. Under the IEEE 802.3 standard, the MAC layer is not concerned with synchronization bits added as the frame flows onto the media. Thus, the IEEE standard measures a frame length between 64 and 1518 bytes. However, when you add the synchronization bits, the physical frame length on the media must be between 72 and 1526 bytes—which is the same as Ethernet. As a popular radio announcer would say, "That's the rest of the story!"

## Ethernet Networking Configurations

In addition to the single cable system indicated in Figure 11.8, other Ethernet configurations are possible in which several multidrop segments (possibly one in each of several buildings) are interconnected with point-to-point cables and repeaters. Figure 11.10 shows a typical configuration of a multisegment system. The following specifications apply:

*Maximum Lengths*

1500 meters of multidrop cable

1000 additional meters of point-to-point cable between cable segments

300 additional meters in six transceiver cables

50 meters in a single transceiver cable

*Maximum Number of Stations*

1024

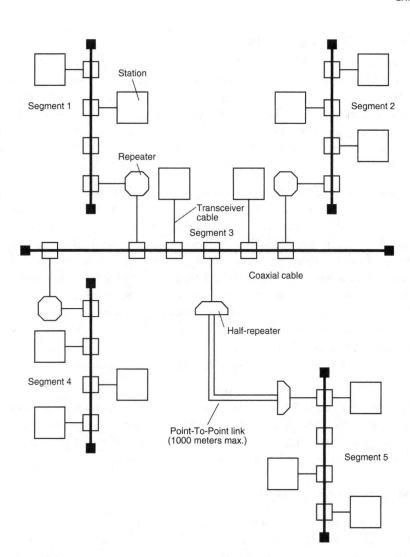

**FIGURE 11.10**

*A typical large-scale Ethernet configuration.*

## The 5-4-3 Topology Rule

The original coaxial-based version of Ethernet facilitated the use of a tree-structured network to interconnect various departments within an organization to a backbone cable. Under the CSMA/CD protocol, a signal transmitted onto the media must reach each part of the network within a certain period of time. Because each repeater (and later each shared hub that functions as a repeater) adds a small amount of delay to the propagation of a signal, a series of rules were developed concerning the permissible topology of an Ethernet network. As you will note shortly, there is a good reason for the rule to be known as the 5-4-3 rule.

Under the 5-4-3 rule, transmission between two nodes on an Ethernet network cannot traverse more than 5 segments connected by 4 repeaters, with a maximum of 3 populated segments allowed. Looking at the first part of the rule, there can be a maximum of 5 segments between any 2 nodes on an Ethernet network. That portion of the 5-4-3 rule results from the limit of 500 meters per Ethernet segment and a maximum of 2500 meters of cabling distance, resulting in a one-way collision window of 23 u[cd]S. The second part of the rule permits the connection between any 2 nodes via a maximum of 5 segments to occur through the use of 4 repeaters. The third portion of the rule refers to populated segments, which can have one or more nodes attached. Here the rule states that only a maximum of 3 segments can be populated if they are made of coaxial cable. Although the 5-4-3 rule is an important consideration, it is important to note that it does not apply to other LANs nor to Ethernet networks that use only fiber-optic cabling.

When examining Figure 11.10, you might be tempted to believe it violates the 5-4-3 rule. However, if you count the number of segments and repeaters between any two stations on the network, you will see that a maximum of three segments and two repeaters are traversed. Thus, there is no need for a non-populated segment.

## Other Ethernet Networks

In actuality, when referring to Ethernet, we reference a group of networks based on the CSMA/CD access protocol. The original Ethernet standard defined by Xerox, Digital Equipment, and Intel operated at 10Mbps over a bus-based 50 ohm thick coaxial cable. When Ethernet was standardized by the IEEE 802.3 committee, five additional "Ethernet" standards were promulgated that provided support for operating rates up to 10Mbps. Since then, several new high-speed "Ethernet" standards have been promulgated.

The IEEE 802.3µS Fast Ethernet standard actually references a series of three 100Mbps physical layer LAN specifications that use the CSMA/CD access protocol. Although some people refer to the IEEE 802.12 standard known as 100VG-AnyLAN as an Ethernet LAN, that standard actually represents a demand priority access scheme that can be used to support Ethernet or another type of local area network; however, such support is restricted to one type of LAN. The most recent version of Ethernet standardized by the IEEE, Gigabit Ethernet, actually represents a series of standards that support a 1Gbps transmission rate over several types of copper and fiber-optic cable. After giving you an appreciation for the operational characteristics of what is now considered low-speed Ethernet, this section will address Fast Ethernet and Gigabit Ethernet.

Table 11.1 compares the operational characteristics of each low-speed IEEE 802.3 network standard with the characteristics of the original Ethernet standard.

**TABLE 11.1** Ethernet and IEEE 802.3 Network Characteristics

| Operational Character- istics | Ethernet | 10BASE-5 | 10BASE-2 | 1BASE-5 | 10BASE-T | 10BROAD-36 |
|---|---|---|---|---|---|---|
| Operating rate (Mbps) | 10 | 10 | 10 | 1 | 10 | 10 |
| Access protocol | CSMA/CD | CSMA/CD | CSMA/CD | CSMA/CD | CSMA/CD | CSMA/CD |
| Type of signaling | baseband | baseband | baseband | baseband | baseband | broadband |
| Data encoding | Manchester | Manchester | Manchester | Manchester | Manchester | DPSK |
| Maximum segment length (meters) | 500 | 500 | 185 | 250 | 100 | 1800 |
| Stations/ segment | 100 | 100 | 30 | 12/hub | 12/hub | 100 |
| Media | 50 ohm coaxial (thick) | 50 ohm coaxial (thick) | 50 ohm coaxial (thin) | unshielded twisted pair | unshielded twisted pair | 75 ohm coaxial |
| Topology | bus | bus | bus | star | star | bus |

Under the IEEE 802.3 standard, changes occurred to the Ethernet frame illustrated in Figure 11.9. A few minor changes resulted in the incompatibility of equipment designed for use in computers based on the original Ethernet specification and the IEEE 802.3 frame format.

Figure 11.11 illustrates the IEEE 802.3 data link frame format. Compare that format to the Ethernet data link frame format illustrated in Figure 11.9, and you'll note that the Preamble field was reduced to 7 bytes, and a Start of Frame Delimiter field was added under the IEEE 802.3 frame format. The Start of Frame Delimiter field is actually a continuation of the preamble, with the sequence 10101011. However, the ending two bits are 11 rather than the 10 contained in the Ethernet Preamble field.

IEEE 802.3

| Preamble | Start of Frame Delimiter | Destination Address | Source Address | Length | Data | Frame Check Sequence |
|----------|--------------------------|---------------------|----------------|--------|------|----------------------|
| 7 bytes | 1 byte | 2/6 bytes | 2/6 bytes | 2 bytes | 46-1500 bytes | 4 bytes |

**FIGURE 11.11**

*The IEEE 802.3 data link frame format.*

Another difference between the two frame formats is the replacement of the Type field by a Length field in the IEEE 802.3 frame. Here the length field specifies the number of bytes that follow that field as data. Although this difference might appear trivial, it resulted in the necessity for a new Ethernet frame, as we will shortly note. Under the original Ethernet standard, different values placed in the Type field were used to identify the transmission of different protocols within the Ethernet frame. For example, a Hex value of 0800 identifies Internet Protocol (IP) data in the frame, whereas a Hex value of 8137 identifies NetWare IPX and SPX data carried within an Ethernet frame. Through the use of a Type field, it became possible to transport multiple protocols on an Ethernet LAN.

Under the IEEE 802.3 standard, the replacement of the Type field by a Length field appears to eliminate the potential for transporting multiprotocol traffic. Fortunately, a modification to the IEEE frame format referred to as *Ethernet Subnetwork Access Protocol (Ethernet-SNAP)* frame was standardized, enabling an IEEE 802.3 frame using a Length field to transport different protocols in different frames flowing on the same network.

Figure 11.12 illustrates the format of an Ethernet-SNAP frame. Note that the DSAP and SSAP fields, each one byte in length, represent mailbox facilities not used by the Ethernet-SNAP frame. The Control field contains one byte of information concerning the type and class of service being used to transport logical link control data. For an Ethernet-SNAP frame, the first three bytes are always set to a value of Hex AA-AA-03. The Organization Code field identifies the organization responsible for assigning the value used in the Ethernet Type field, and the value in the Ethernet Type field identifies the protocol transported in the frame. By using the Ethernet-SNAP frame, you can transport multiple protocols on an IEEE 802.3 network in a manner similar to the original Ethernet frame that included a Type field for this purpose.

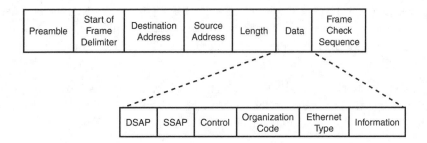

**FIGURE 11.12**

*The Ethernet-SNAP frame.*

# 10BASE-5 Ethernet

Although a 10BASE-5 network follows the same configuration rules as the original Ethernet network, certain changes in terminology cause some people confusion. To alleviate that potential confusion, Figure 11.13 illustrates the changes in terminology between the original Ethernet 50 ohm coaxial cable bus-based network and the IEEE 802.3 10BASE-5 bus-based network.

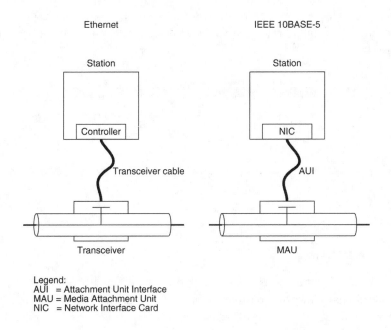

**FIGURE 11.13**

*Terminology changes between Ethernet and IEEE 10BASE-5.*

As indicated in Figure 11.13, the controller under 10BASE-5 is now a NIC (pronounced "nick"), or network interface card. The transceiver cable is now an AUI, or attachment unit interface, and the transceiver is called a MAU (pronounced to rhyme with "cow"), or media attachment unit.

Most 10BASE-5 NICs include both a DB-15 and a BNC connector. The DB-15 provides a connection to the AUI, whereas the BNC permits the use of the NIC on a 10BASE-2 network. Thus, the dual connectors permit the NIC to be used on two types of 802.3 standards.

## 10BASE-2 Ethernet

A 10BASE-2 network is based on the use of thin coaxial cable that provides a degree of cabling flexibility not obtainable with the thick coaxial cable used with a 10BASE-5 network. In addition, the thin coaxial cable is more economical. A 10BASE-2 workstation is connected to the thin coaxial cable by BNC connectors, which are also referred to as *barrel connectors*.

Figure 11.14 illustrates the cabling of stations to a 10BASE-2 network. This type of Ethernet network permits a maximum of 30 stations per cable segment. You can extend a 10BASE-2 network through the use of inter-repeater cable segments (IRCS), or you can combine 10BASE-2 and 10BASE-5 networks, although if you do that, you must make sure you do not violate any cabling rules. Refer to the book *Ethernet Networks, Fourth Edition*, written by Gilbert Held and published by John Wiley & Sons, for specific information concerning Ethernet IEEE 802.3 cabling restrictions and the interconnection of different types of IEEE 802.3 networks.

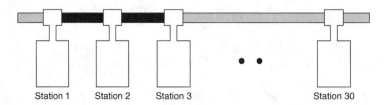

FIGURE 11.14
*Cabling a 10BASE-2 network.*

## 10BASE-T Ethernet

Another series of configurations is obtainable through the use of 10BASE-T, which is a more modern standard that allows the construction of 10Mbps Ethernet LANs over unshielded twisted-pair wire. Under the 10BASE-T standard, which is also referred to as the IEEE 802.3i standard, workstations are cabled, using twisted-pair wire, to a media attachment unit (MAU), more commonly called a hub. Each MAU or hub normally has a built-in attachment interface unit (AIU) that can be cabled to a coaxial transceiver attached to a coaxial cable. Thus, workstations can be configured in a star topology and cabled to a bus-structured backbone cable that serves to interconnect MAUs. Figure 11.15 illustrates a hybrid Ethernet media configuration in which personal computer workstations are cabled to MAUs via the use of twisted-pair wire. The MAUs in turn are connected to a coaxial cable that not only links MAUs, but also provides access to a mainframe computer.

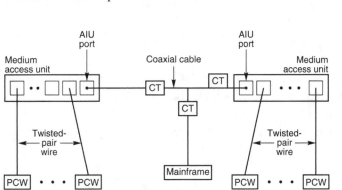

**FIGURE 11.15**

*A hybrid Ethernet media configuration.*

Each MAU functions as a repeater, accepting an incoming signal on one port and regenerating the signal onto all other ports. Because of this method of operation and because all connections to the hub share access to the media, MAUs are also called shared media hubs.

If you carefully think about the previously described operation of a shared media hub, its broadcast or regeneration of a signal received on one port onto all other ports is the key to its topology. That is, although workstations can be connected to a hub to physically resemble a star, data flow where one station transmits and all other stations hear logically resembles a bus. Thus, a shared media hub operates in a manner similar to a bus while providing the cabling flexibility associated with twisted-pair wiring.

## 10BROAD-36 Ethernet

The only broadband-based network standardized by the IEEE based on the CSMA/CD protocol is the 10BROAD-36 standard. Unlike low-speed Ethernet networks that transmit data using Manchester encoded signals, a 10BROAD-36 network requires the use of radio frequency (RF) modems. RF modems use one channel for transmission and a separate channel for reception of data.

A 10BROAD-36 network is constructed with 75 ohm coaxial cable that's similar to the cable used in modern cable TV systems. The channels are typically 6MHz wide and follow the standards and technology developed by the cable TV industry. Because the useable bandwidth of a coaxial cable is 500 to 750MHz, as many as 80 to 120 or more separate channels can use a common cable.

Under the IEEE 802.3 broadband standard, either single or dual cables can be used to construct a broadband LAN. If a single cable is used, a frequency translator must be installed at the end of the cable to convert signals received on one channel to the frequency assigned to the other channel, retransmitting the signal at the new frequency. Because the frequency translator is installed at the end of the cable, it is often referred to as a *headend translator*.

Figure 11.16 illustrates the location of a headend frequency translator on a 10BROAD-36 tree-structured network. Because the frequency band used for a transmitted signal is below the frequency band used by the receiver, it is common to say the frequency translator up-converts a transmitted signal as it retransmits it at a higher frequency.

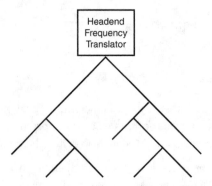

Headend
Frequency
Translator

**FIGURE 11.16**

*A tree-structured broadband network requires a frequency translator at the headend.*

The key advantage of a broadband-based system is its ability to support multiple transmissions. At one time it was expected that broadband networks supporting TV, videoconferencing, voice, and data over a common cable infrastructure would be very popular. However, the cost associated with the RF modems, as well as the constraints of coaxial cable and the greater appeal of twisted-pair, prevented broadband LANs from really reaching their anticipated potential.

# Fast Ethernet

As briefly noted earlier in this chapter, *Fast Ethernet* is a term used to reference a series of three 100Mbps physical LAN specifications described in the IEEE 802.3µS addendum to the

802.3 standard. Those specifications include 100BASE-T4, 100BASE-TX, and 100BASE-FX. Each specification maintains the use of the CSMA/CD access control protocol, and dual-functioning 10/100Mbps network adapter cards are available that allow an investment in 10Mbps technology today to be upgraded to a 100Mbps LAN tomorrow.

## Physical Layer Subdivision

Much as the data link layer was subdivided, under the IEEE 802.3u[cd]S specification, the physical layer was also subdivided. Here the subdivision of the physical layer was performed to facilitate the support of three types of media by the standard: unshielded twisted pair (UTP), shielded twisted pair (STP), and fiber optic.

Figure 11.17 illustrates the physical layer subdivision associated with Fast Ethernet. Because different coding schemes are required to support 100Mbps operations on different types of media, a physical coding sublayer was required to perform the necessary coding for each media. Under the physical coding layer is a physical media dependent (PMD) sublayer. The PMD sublayer transfers the physical coding onto the media by providing an appropriate interface to the media.

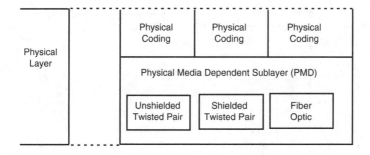

**Figure 11.17**
*The Fast Ethernet physical layer subdivision.*

## 100BASE-T4 Fast Ethernet

100BASE-T4 represents a 100Mbps CSMA/CD network that operates over four pairs of Category 3, 4, or 5 unshielded twisted-pair or shielded twisted-pair cable. Although 100BASE-T4 is similar to 10BASE-T in that it is a hub-based network, to ensure proper collision detection, the span of the network was reduced to 250 meters, with a maximum of 100 meters permitted between a workstation and a hub port.

Obtaining a 100Mbps operating rate required three changes at the physical layer. First, three pairs of wires are used for transmission (the fourth is used for collision detection), which provides a three-fold increase over 100BASE-T. Next, 8B6T coding, in which 8 input bits are transformed into a unique code group of 6 ternary symbols, is used to replace Manchester coding, boosting throughput to 265 times that of 10BASE-T. The third change was an increase in clock signaling speed from the 10BASE-T 20MHz to 25MHz, boosting throughput to 1.25 times that of 10BASE-T. When all three changes are considered, 100BASE-T can operate at 10 times 10BASE-T, or 100Mbps.

Figure 11.18 shows a typical 100BASE-T4 network structure, including cabling constraints and a breakout of pin assignments. Note that the connectors used for 100BASE-T4 are RJ-45, which simplifies connecting cable to workstations and hub ports to the insertion of a jack into a plug receptacle.

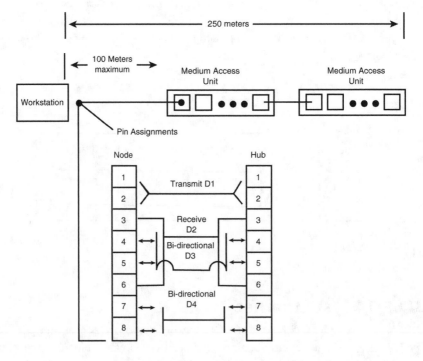

**FIGURE 11.18**

*A typical 100BASE-T4 network structure.*

## 100BASE-TX Fast Ethernet

100BASE-TX represents a second type of 100Mbps Fast Ethernet. This standard is based on the use of two pairs of Category 5 unshielded twisted-pair cable. One pair of wires is used for collision detection and reception of data.

The use of two wire pairs rather than the four used by 100BASE-T4 required a change to both the clock rate and the coding method used. 100BASE-TX uses a 125MHz frequency and a 4B5B coding stream in which every 4 data bits are mapped into a 5-bit code. Because this coding method requires only 16 symbols to represent data, the remaining symbols are available for control use. Because of the higher line frequency used by 100BASE-TX, it can be implemented only through the use of Category 5 UTP. In comparison, the 25MHz clock rate of 100BASE-T4 permits the use of four pairs of Category 3, 4, and 5 UTP or STP cable. Similar to 100BASE-T4, however, a 100BASE-TX network is limited to a maximum network diameter of 250 meters, and the maximum cable run is 100 meters from a hub port to a network station.

## 100BASE-FX Fast Ethernet

The third wiring scheme supported by Fast Ethernet is two-strand 62.5/125 micron multimode fiber media. This media is used by the 100BASE-FX version of Fast Ethernet, and the coding scheme is identical to that of 100BASE-TX.

The two strands of multimode fiber-optic cable support transmission and reception of data on individual strands, and signal crossover is performed by the network adapter. Transmission occurs using a light wavelength of 1350 nanometers (nm), and the 100BASE-FX standard supports segments up to 412 meters in length.

Three types of connectors are supported by the 100BASE-FX standard: SC, MIC, and ST.

- The SC connector is designed for ease of use and can be gently pushed into place.
- The MIC (Media Interface Connector) represents a standard connector used in FDDI LANs. MIC connectors are keyed to facilitate interconnection, ensuring that cabling is properly connected.
- The ST connector incorporates a spring-loaded, bayonet-type connection mechanism with a key on its inner sleeve and an outer bayonet ring. To make a connection using an ST connector, you would first line up the key on the inner sleeve of an ST connector plug with a slot on an ST connector receptacle, and then push the connector in, and lock it in place by twisting the outer bayonet ring.

## Repeaters

Following a departed politician who can be remembered by his campaign slogan "A choice is not an echo," Fast Ethernet provides you with a choice of repeaters. The Fast Ethernet standard defines two types of repeaters, referred to as Class I and Class II. A Class I repeater operates by first translating signals on an incoming port into a digital format before retranslating them to the appropriate line signal for transmission onto an outgoing port. Although this increases the time delay associated with the repeater, it permits the repeater to regenerate signals flowing between segments that use different signaling techniques, such as a 100BASE-TX segment and a 100BASE-T4 segment. Because a Class I repeater has a relatively large delay time, only one can be used in a given collision domain when a maximum cable length is used.

The second type of repeater supported by Fast Ethernet is a Class II repeater. A Class II repeater can only be used to connect segments using the same signaling method, such as a 100BASE-TX and a 100BASE-FX segment. Because a Class II repeater has a much lower timing delay, up to two Class II repeaters can be installed in a collision domain when a maximum amount of cable is used.

# Gigabit Ethernet

Gigabit Ethernet represents the latest version of Ethernet to be standardized by the IEEE. Operating at 1Gbps, Gigabit Ethernet represents a transmission capacity 10 times that of Fast Ethernet and 100 times that of the original Ethernet standard. To place this advance in perspective, an automobile capable of obtaining 12 miles per gallon in the late 1970s or early 1980s should be capable of driving from New York to Florida on one gallon of gas today!

The evolution of Gigabit Ethernet dates to March 1996, when the IEEE 802.3 committee approved a Project Authorization Request (PAR) to develop a 1Gbps Ethernet standard. The PAR resulted in the IEEE 802.3z Gigabit Ethernet Standardization project, whose efforts ended in a preliminary or draft standard covering transmission over fiber-optic and short-haul copper media in July, 1997. At that time, a special committee was formed (802.3ab) to develop a standard for transmission over twisted-pair copper, which was standardized in 1999.

## Media Support

Gigabit Ethernet supports transmission over three types of fiber-optic cable (9, 50, and 62.5 micron diameter), short-haul copper twin-axial shielded twisted-pair cable, and four pairs of Category 5 unshielded twisted-pair (UTP) cable. Transmission over each media category is designated by the use of a specific Gigabit Ethernet standard nomenclature of the form 1000BASE-X. Table 11.2 summarizes the four general Gigabit Ethernet standards based on the type of media supported.

The suffix SX denotes the use of a shortwave laser operating at 850nm. In comparison, LX indicates the use of a longwave laser, which operates at 1300nm. The suffix CX designates transmission over copper twin-axial shielded media, whereas the suffix T continues to identify transmission over category 5 UTP.

In Table 11.2, note that the use of a 1300 nm laser supports transmission on both single mode and multimode fiber. In addition, two types of multimode fiber are specified for use for Gigabit Ethernet: 50 and 62.5 micron. This creates three distinct types of fiber cable that can be used with two types of lasers. Because the type of laser and type of media governs transmission distance, you must consider both to determine the ability to transmit at a 1Gbps data rate. Table 11.3 lists the transmission distance supported by different types of media used by Gigabit Ethernet.

## MAC Layer Operations

As you learned earlier in this chapter, the CSMA/CD protocol used by Ethernet results in a round-trip propagation delay time that governs the minimum length of a frame, useable over the maximum cable length. The original Ethernet design included a maximum cable length of 2.5km. To maintain frame scalability, Fast Ethernet reduced the maximum cable length between two nodes to approximately 250 meters, and its maximum cabling distance from a station to the hub was 100 meters. Without altering the size of the frame, Gigabit Ethernet would only be able to support a maximum transmission distance of approximately 25m between two nodes via copper—a distance that is too short to provide users with the cabling flexibility necessary to effectively use the technology.

**TABLE 11.2**   Gigabit Ethernet Media Support

| 1000BASE-X Standard | Media Support |
|---|---|
| 1000BASE-SX | 850nm laser transmitting on multimode fiber |
| 1000BASE-LX | 1300nm laser transmitting on single mode or multimode fiber |
| 1000BASE-CX | Copper twin-axial shielded twisted-pair |
| 1000BASE-T | 4 pairs of Category 5 UTP copper |

**TABLE 11.3**   Gigabit Ethernet Transmission Distances

| Media | Transmission Distance in Meters |
|---|---|
| Single mode fiber (9 micron) 1300nm laser (LX) | 3000 |
| Multimode fiber (62.5 micron) 850nm laser (SX) | 300 |

**TABLE 11.3** continued

| Media | Transmission Distance in Meters |
|---|---|
| 1300nm laser (LX) Multimode fiber (50 micron) | 550 |
| 850nm laser (SX) | 550 |
| 1300nm laser (LX) | 550 |
| Copper twin-axial STP (CX) | 25 |
| Category 5 UTP (T) | 100 |

To maintain compatibility with prior versions of Ethernet yet support a transmission distance of 100 meters, the Gigabit Ethernet standard extends the length of all frames shorter than 512 bytes. In doing so, it pads the extension to the frame with special symbols that cannot occur in the frame. As you might expect, this technique is referred to as a *carrier extension*. Another technique, referred to as *packet bursting*, is used to compensate for the effect of carrier extension on network performance. The next sections examine both techniques.

## Carrier Extension

Gigabit Ethernet frames that do not exceed 64 bytes in length (72 when you count the Preamble and Start of Frame Delimiter fields) are extended to 512 bytes by the addition of special symbols (see Figure 11.19). Note that the non-data extension symbols extend the frame for collision detection purposes. However, because they follow the Frame Check Sequence field, the FCS is only computed on the original, non-extended frame. Because extension symbols are removed by a receiver, the higher layers in the protocol stack are innocuous to the extension.

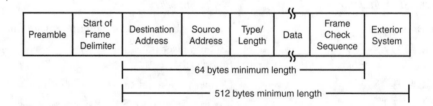

**FIGURE 11.19**
*Gigabit Ethernet carrier extension.*

To better understand the effect of carrier extension on network performance, assume that you are sitting at your terminal and receive the following message from an application: Enter 1 to continue, Q to Quit. Your one-character response will first cause 45 pad characters to be added to the Data field in the Ethernet frame. Assuming that transmission flows on a Gigabit Ethernet LAN, 448 carrier extension bytes are then added to provide a minimum 512 byte frame length. Thus, one data byte results in 511 overhead bytes transporting the data. This is obviously not very efficient and reaches a level of performance only marginally better than Fast Ethernet, when the actual amount of data to be transmitted is less than or equal to 512 bytes. Recognizing this problem, a second technique, packet bursting, was added to Gigabit Ethernet.

## Packet Bursting

With packet bursting, a station that has two or more packets to transmit sends the first packet using carrier extension if it is fewer than 512 bytes in length. If the first packet is transmitted without a collision, subsequent packets are then transmitted one after another until a burst timer, whose duration is 1500 bytes, expires. At that time, any packet being transmitted is transmitted to completion. Figure 11.20 illustrates packet bursting.

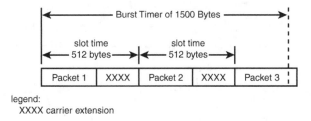

legend:
XXXX carrier extension

### FIGURE 11.20

*Gigabit Ethernet packet bursting.*

Both carrier extension and packet bursting are only applicable to shared media Gigabit Ethernet operations. If you are using Gigabit Ethernet to interconnect two LAN switches or for connecting workstations and servers directly to LAN switch ports, the connection is collision free. This means that there is no need to extend the length of a frame to ensure that collision detection occurs within a predefined period of time. Similarly, there is no need for packet bursting because there is no need to extend the length of Gigabit Ethernet frames.

## Bandwidth Utilization

The high bandwidth of Gigabit Ethernet makes it suitable for use as a backbone for interconnecting Ethernet and Fast Ethernet networks. An initial series of products incorporating Gigabit Ethernet technology included Gigabit switches with several 1Gbps ports and 100/1000bps switches that represent Fast Ethernet switches with one or more Gigabit Ethernet uplink ports.

Because many 100Mbps Fast Ethernet adapters can auto-sense 10 and 100Mbps operations, it becomes possible to construct a tier-structure network, permitting Ethernet support at 10100 and 1000Mbps. Figure 11.21 depicts a tiered-Ethernet network. In this example, it is assumed that an enterprise server used by all people in an organization is connected to the Gigabit backbone, and that departmental servers are connected to Fast Ethernet and conventional Ethernet switches and hubs. Later in this chapter, you will explore the operation of LAN switches. For the time being, note that a LAN switch provides the ability to support multiple simultaneous cross-connections through the device. Thus, a station connected to a switch could be cross-connected to a server connected to the switch, whereas another station is cross-connected to an uplink for connection to a server connected to a different switch.

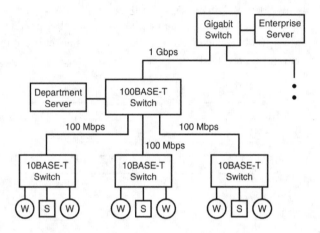

**FIGURE 11.21**

*A tiered Ethernet network structure.*

# 10 Gigabit Ethernet

10 Gigabit Ethernet represents an emerging Ethernet standard that might be a reality by the time this book is published. The standard is presently being defined by the IEEE 802.3ae Task Force. The goal of this emerging standard is to preserve the Ethernet frame format to include its minimum and maximum frame lengths, which provides backward compatibility with older versions of Ethernet. This emerging standard is limited to full duplex operations, which means carrier extension and packet bursting becomes unnecessary.

Two physical interfaces are being defined for 10Gbps Ethernet, both optical based. One interface is for LAN transmission, whereas the second is for attachment to a wide area network that provides compatibility with SONET at 10Gbps. Table 11.4 lists the physical layer specifications and transmission distances expected to be provided by 10Gbps Ethernet.

**TABLE 11.4**   10 Gigabit Ethernet Physical Layer Specifications

| Optical | Fiber | Fiber | Minimum |
|---------|-------|-------|---------|
| 850nm | Multimode | 50.0 | 65 |
| 1310nm | Multimode | 62.5 | 300 |
| 1310nm | Single mode | 9.0 | 10,000 |
| 1550nm | Single mode | 9.0 | 40,000 |

The motivating force behind 10Gbps Ethernet includes the migration of 56Kbps modem users to DSL and cable modems as well as the expansion of bandwidth intensive applications, such as multimedia and video on demand. Through the use of 10Gbps Ethernet, Internet service providers (ISPs) as well as firms providing Web hosting services will be better able to satisfy customer requirements. Thus, for the near future, 10Gbps Ethernet will not be used by the average company or college. Instead, it can be expected to be used in large data centers as well as in backbone switches at ISPs, with a connection to a SONET WAN facilitating long-haul communications.

# Token-Passing LANs

Because access to a CSMA network involves a certain amount of contention (competition) between stations trying to send messages at the same time, the behavior of the network must be analyzed and controlled statistically. Token-passing networks, on the other hand, provide a different access procedure. Access is determined by which station has the token; that is, only one station at a time, the one with the token, is given the opportunity to seize the channel. The token is passed from one idle station to another until a station with a pending message receives it. After the message is sent, the token is passed to the next station. In essence, a token-passing network is a distributed polling network.

Two basic topologies (configurations or arrangements) exist for token-passing networks: token-passing rings and token-passing buses. In a token-passing ring, like the one shown in Figure 11.22, the closed loop topology defines the logical topology (that is, the order in which the token is circulated). A token-passing bus, like the one shown in Figure 11.23, has more operational flexibility because the token-passing order is defined by tables in each station. If a station (for example, a printer) never originates communications, it will be a terminate-only station, and it need not be in the polling sequence. If a station needs a high priority, it can appear more than once in the polling sequence.

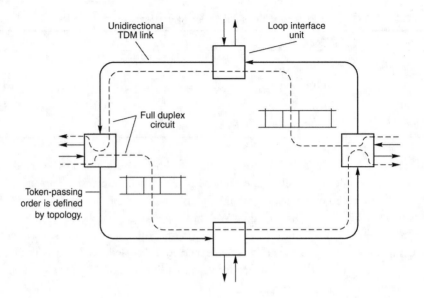

**FIGURE 11.22**

*A token-passing ring.*

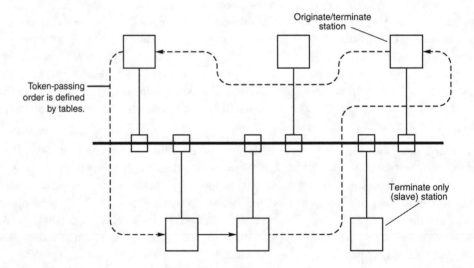

**FIGURE 11.23**

*A representative access sequence in a token-passing bus.*

Besides the operational differences between bus and ring topologies, the following major differences exist:

- A ring requires an active interface module in series with the transmission link. A bus uses a passive tap like a CSMA system.

- The point-to-point nature of a ring's transmission links implies that the signal quality is easily controlled. Multiple taps in a linear bus system, on the other hand, contribute to signal distortions.

- A ring has no inherent (built-in) distance limitation (as does the bus) because there is no delay dependence in its operation, and the access taps at each station serve as regenerative repeaters to the digital signals.

- A bus allocates the entire channel to an active device. The channel of a ring can be subdivided into time division multiplexed subchannels for time-continuous, lower-data-rate applications. Figure 11.24 shows a ring with time division multiplexed subchannels. Such a system, also known as a *loop*, typically requires a unique control node to define framing for the subchannels. Access to the TDM channels is distributed by passing tokens.

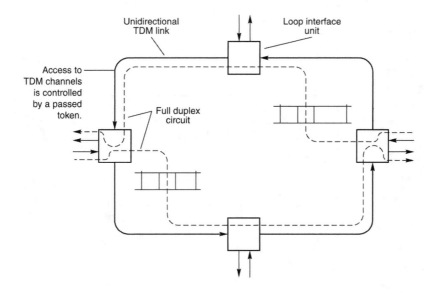

**FIGURE 11.24**

*A time division multiplex loop.*

- The ring topology is ideally suited to the particular capabilities of fiber-optic transmission. As discussed in Chapter 7, "Fiber-Optic and Satellite Communications," optical fibers provide very wide bandwidth and complete elimination of electrical interference, but they are presently practical only as point-to-point transmission links.

## ARCnet

The forerunner of token-passing networks in the United States is the Attached Resource Computer Network, ARCnet, developed by Datapoint Corporation. Initially, the network and protocol were kept proprietary, but the data-link protocol, interface specs, and even integrated circuits were made publicly available in 1982. Functionally, the ARCnet is a token-passing bus, but the physical topology, shown in Figure 11.25, is a hybrid bus/star. Instead of distributing taps along a linear bus as suggested in Figure 11.23, the ARCnet uses hubs with individual ports to connect Resource Interface Modules (RIMs) to the transmission media.

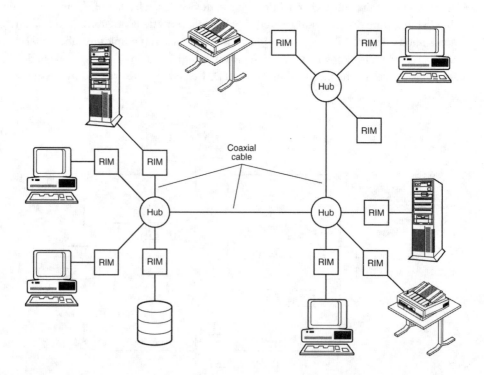

**FIGURE 11.25**

*The physical topology of the ARCnet.*

The hub-based architecture is an effective means of controlling the signal quality because the hub isolates each RIM port from the main coaxial cable. Unidirectional (one-way) amplifiers in the hubs provide zero insertion loss and suppress reflections because only one direction of transmission is enabled at a time. Amplifier switching is possible because a token-passing network transmits in only one direction at a time.

## The ARCnet Physical Layer

The ARCnet interconnects the hubs and RIMs with RG62 coaxial cable using baseband transmission at 2.5Mbps. Although 2.5Mbps is a relatively low data rate, ARCnet uses inexpensive coax and can be configured (laid out) with as much as four miles between stations. The cable length between a hub and a RIM is limited to 2000 feet, but a four-mile span can have up to a maximum of 10 hubs in a series path.

## ARCnet Link Protocol

The ARCnet employs five basic message formats, as shown in Figure 11.26. The first four formats are used for control messages; the fifth carries data between stations. All address fields consist of eight bits, which restricts the number of stations to 255 (address 0 is reserved as a broadcast address to all stations). As you can see in Figure 11.26, the destination address (DID) is duplicated with every message for error protection.

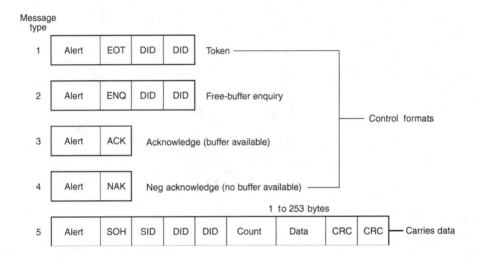

**FIGURE 11.26**

*Flow diagram of token-passing procedure in ARCnet.*

Figure 11.27 shows a logical flow diagram of the token-passing procedure implemented in every RIM. Upon receiving a token (message type 1) with the proper address, a RIM chooses one of two paths, depending on whether it has transmit data pending. If data is pending, the RIM sends a free-buffer request (message type 2) to the desired destination RIM asking whether it is ready to receive. The destination RIM responds with either an ACK (message type 3) if it has buffer space available or a NAK (message type 4) if it does not have buffer space available.

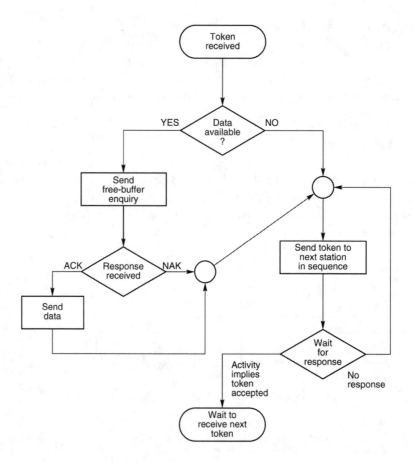

**FIGURE 11.27**

*Flow diagram of token-passing procedures in ARCnet.*

After a RIM has transmitted its data or determined that it cannot, it passes the token to the station with the next higher address. After sending the token, the RIM monitors the channel to see whether it is accepted. A message type 1, 2, or 5 indicates that the token has been accepted. No response on the channel within 74ms implies that the intended station is offline, and the token should be passed to the station with the next highest address.

## IBM Token-Ring Network

In the mid-1980s, IBM introduced its token-ring network based on the use of token passing. This token-ring network uses a logical ring topology that is physically wired as a star, with workstations connected to a wiring concentrator known as a multistation access unit (MAU, sometimes also known as MSAU). MAUs are cabled to one another to form a ring, resulting in a star-ring topology for the token-ring network.

Three types of transmission formats are supported on a token-ring network: token, abort, and frame. Figure 11.28 indicates the format of each type of frame.

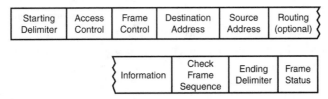

a. Token format

| Starting Delimiter | Access Control | Ending Delimiter |

| P | P | P | T | M | R | R | R |

b. Abort token format

| Starting Delimiter | Ending Delimiter |

c. Frame format

| Starting Delimiter | Access Control | Frame Control | Destination Address | Source Address | Routing (optional) |

| Information | Check Frame Sequence | Ending Delimiter | Frame Status |

**FIGURE 11.28**

*Token, abort, and frame formats.*

The token format illustrated at the top of Figure 11.28 provides the mechanism by which stations gain access to the network. If the token bit position is set to zero, the token is available. Depending on the setting of the reservation and priority bits in the access control field, a station can acquire the token. After it acquires the token, the station converts the token into a frame as indicated at the bottom of Figure 11.28. The destination and source address fields are each 48 bits in length and function in the same manner as equivalent Ethernet fields. A third transmission format, abort token, which is shown in the middle of Figure 11.28 is used to abort a previous transmission.

IBM's token-ring network was standardized by the IEEE as the 802.5 standard. The composition of the token ring-frame and the electronics required to control its operation are more sophisticated than Ethernet and create more costly network adapters and network equipment.

Although token-ring networks only captured approximately 10% of the market for local area networks, they provide a more deterministic level of transmission than Ethernet networks. This is because stations can reserve tokens. Such reservations are compared to the priority setting in the token, and a reservation process ensures that although high-priority transmissions are processed before most lower priority traffic, they do not monopolize the network.

Another key feature of token-ring networks is that the station with the highest network address is automatically selected as the active monitor. To ensure that tokens and frames do not endlessly wander the network, such as if a station was powered off just before a frame destined to its address arrived, the active monitor sets the M bit in each frame flowing on the network. If the frame returns to the active monitor with its M bit set, the active monitor knows it wasn't properly discarded. The active monitor then removes the token or frame and generates a new token with its M bit set to zero.

Figure 11.29 illustrates the wiring of workstations to each MAU. Each workstation uses one twisted-pair connection for *ring-in* and a second twisted pair for *ring-out*, and the data flows from station to station in one direction to represent a logical ring. In addition to functioning as a central wiring point, the MAU also controls access of each workstation to the LAN. This is accomplished through the use of relays in each MAU port, enabling the MAU to simply short the relay to bypass a workstation. To get access to the LAN, a workstation raises a 5-volt signal that causes the MAU to open the relay on the port and add the workstation to the ring. This technique enables all inactive stations on a ring to be automatically bypassed, which serves to maximize LAN performance.

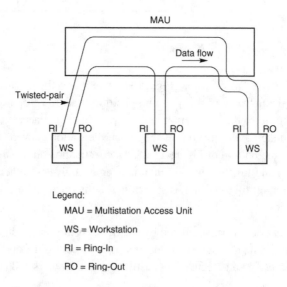

**FIGURE 11.29**

*Wiring workstations to a MAU.*

Although three workstations are shown connected to one MAU in Figure 11.29, in actuality, up to eight workstations can be connected. A token-ring network is expanded to support additional workstations through the use of additional MAUs, and the MAUs are interconnected to form a ring.

IBM and several third-party manufacturers produce token-ring adapter cards that can be installed in personal computers to allow PCs to be cabled to MAUs. The original IBM token-ring network operated at 4Mbps and supported a maximum of 72 device connections, which is the equivalent of interconnecting nine MAUs. This network, for which 4Mbps token-ring adapter cards are used in PCs, can use shielded or unshielded twisted-pair wiring. A second IBM token-ring network operates at 16Mbps and extends the support of devices to 250, but it requires the use of shielded cable. The 16Mbps network requires the use of 16Mbps token-ring adapter cards. Although IBM and third-party manufacturers market 4/16Mbps token-ring adapters that can operate at either data rate, all devices on a LAN must be set to operate at either 4 or 16Mbps. This means that users migrating from a 4Mbps token-ring network to a 16Mbps network must change all adapters for the LAN to operate at the higher rate.

## Network Expansion

As was previously mentioned, you can expand a token-ring network by adding one or more MAUs and connecting the ring-out (RO) port of one MAU to the ring-in (RI) port of another MAU. The original IBM MAU, known as the 8228, contained 10 ports, of which 8 provided connections to workstations because one was the ring-in port and another was the ring-out port used for network expansion. When an organization had many workstations to connect to a token-ring network, it would have to get a number of 8228s and cable the RI and RO ports of multiple devices together. In addition, one or more racks might be required to install the 8228s to facilitate cabling of workstations to ports on each 8228. Recognizing the problems associated with the cabling and rack mounting of individual 8228s, both IBM and third-party hardware vendors developed different types of products that essentially represent multiple 8228 MAUs. One such product is the IBM 8230 control access unit.

The *control access unit (CAU)* can be considered an expandable MAU. The basic unit consists of a control unit and one lobe attachment module, where the latter device provides the capability to cable individual workstations to the 8230. The 8230 can be expanded by adding one or more lobe attachment modules. Figure 11.30 illustrates the expansion of a token-ring network through the use of a MAU and CAU. Here it was assumed that many workstations were clustered in one portion of a floor in a building, and that eight workstations were clustered at another location on the same floor. Note that only two long-distance cables are required to connect the MAU and CAU. In comparison, if one CAU were used, you would need to install eight long-distance cables to connect the workstations located in the upper-right portion of Figure 11.30 to the CAU. Thus, the appropriate use of MAUs and CAUs can reduce cabling requirements, which can be an important consideration when conduits do not have room for any additional cables.

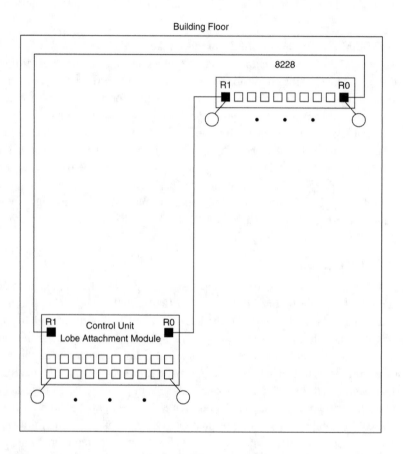

**FIGURE 11.30**
*Ring construction using a MAU and CAU.*

# Fiber Distributed Data Interface

*Fiber Distributed Data Interface (FDDI)* represents an evolving local area network technology that provides a 100Mbps operating rate over fiber cable. The FDDI standard was developed by the *American National Standards Institute (ANSI)* X3T9.5 Task Group because it was originally developed as a mechanism for connecting storage systems and loosely coupled microprocessors in a data center. Although FDDI was standardized as an I/O standard by ANSI rather than the IEEE 802 committee (which primarily focuses on LANs), the evolution of the standard during the 1980s resulted in the first widely implemented and multivendor LAN technology capable of supporting 100Mbps operations.

## Network Topology

FDDI is based on the use of two rings for backbone network transmission. One ring is known as the primary; the second is known as the secondary. The secondary ring provides a *self-healing* mechanism designed to negate the effect of a cable failure for the backbone ring. When a ring network failure occurs on an FDDI LAN, data flow on the secondary ring is initiated counter to the flow of data that occurred on the primary ring. Thus, many people refer to FDDI as a counter-rotating ring topology.

## Network Access

Similar to a token-ring, a rotating token is used on an FDDI network to provide stations with permission to transmit data. Three types of stations are supported by FDDI: a *single attached station (SAS)* and two types of *dual attached stations (DASs)*. Computers and other networking devices, such as bridges and routers, obtain access to an FDDI network via a connection to an SAS, which is then connected to a concentrator DAS.

Dual attached stations are used to form the backbone of an FDDI ring, as illustrated in Figure 11.31. This example shows the effect of a cable failure between a pair of dual attached stations. Each DAS contains two optical connection pairs known as A and B interfaces or ports. The A interface, or port, contains one primary ring input and the secondary ring input; the B interface, or port, contains the primary ring input. By using two optical transceivers, each DAS can transmit and receive data on each ring.

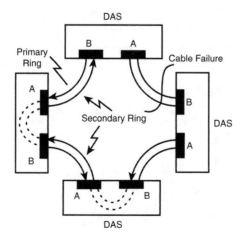

**FIGURE 11.31**
*Dual attached stations form the backbone of an FDDI network.*

By monitoring the light levels received, each dual attached station can recognize a cable failure. When a failure is noted, two adjacent dual attached stations wrap away from the detected cable failure, restoring connectivity by converting the dual ring into a single ring. After the failure condition is corrected, the restoration of an appropriate light level causes each DAS to remove the previously implemented wrap, which restores the network to its dual ring operation.

A second type of DAS functions as a concentrator, containing a series of extra ports as well as the previously described A and B interfaces. Those extra ports, known as M or master ports, are used to provide connectivity to single attached stations, a DAS, or another DAS concentrator. Thus, a DAS concentrator provides additional ports that extend the capability of accessing the primary ring to other stations.

Figure 11.32 illustrates the connection of several single attached stations to a multiple M port, dual-attached station. The M (master) port on the DAS concentrator and S (slave) port on the SAS reference the connector receptacles on each device and not their operations. FDDI was designed with different connectors on SAS and DAS concentrators to facilitate the correct connection of cable between S and M ports.

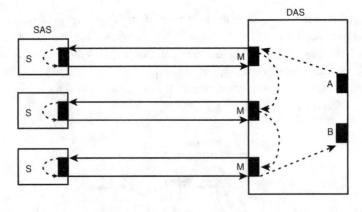

Legend

| | |
|---|---|
| A | Interface containing primary ring input and secondary ring output |
| B | Interface containing primary ring output and secondary ring input |
| M | Master port |
| S | Slave port |
| DAS | Dual attached station |
| SAS | Single attached station |

**FIGURE 11.32**

*FDDI SAS-DAS transmission.*

Note that the connection of an SAS's port to a DAS M port can resemble a star topology, even though the interconnection of DAS and DAS concentrators forms a ring. Also note that an SAS is connected to a DAS port via the cabling of a single cable sheath containing two fiber-optic cables—one for transmission and one for reception of data. This restricts the SAS-to-DAS connection to a single ring. Thus, the self-healing feature of an FDDI network is restricted to the backbone ring formed by interconnecting DASs.

A common use for FDDI networks during the mid to late 1990s was as a backbone for connecting lower speed LANs via bridges or routers to an FDDI network. Another popular use for FDDI was as a high-speed port on a switching hub to provide a 100Mbps connection from the switching hub to a file server. Because of the relatively high cost of optical components, work was proceeding on a copper-based version of FDDI. However, because of the advent of low-cost 100Mbps versions of Ethernet, CDDI technology might not result in a competitive, economically viable product.

# Internetworking Devices

Originally, local area networks resembled isolated islands, with transmission restricted to the physical media that formed the network. Recognizing the need to interconnect LANs, several manufacturers developed networking products. Those products include bridges, routers, gateways, and switches.

## Bridges

Bridges are devices that connect LANs at the ISO data link level. In a token-ring network, a local bridge can be used to connect two adjacent LANs into one LAN. One example of a local bridge is a personal computer containing two adapter cards, each of which is cabled to a port on an Ethernet hub or the MAU of a local token-ring network. Figure 11.33 shows how a local bridge is used to connect two token-ring networks.

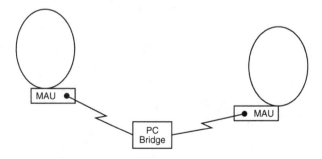

**FIGURE 11.33**

*Using a local bridge.*

Bridges used to connect two similar LANs are called *self-learning bridges*. Such devices learn the *media access control (MAC)* address associated with each port by reading the source address field of each frame. This enables the bridge to create a port-address table that lists MAC addresses known to each port. A transparent bridge performs three basic operations: flooding, filtering, and forwarding. If a bridge receives a frame with a destination address that is not in its port/address table, it transmits the frame onto all ports other than that from which the frame was received. This operation is referred to as *frame flooding*. If a bridge receives a frame and notes its destination is on the network connected to the port, there is no need to forward it through the bridge. Thus, the bridge *filters* the frame and stops it from flowing through the bridge. If the bridge receives a frame with a destination address that is listed in its port/address table, it *forwards* the frame onto the port associated with the address.

A second type of bridge is a remote bridge. This type of bridge is used to connect token-ring networks located at a distance from one another that require interconnection via the use of a communications carrier transmission facility. When remote bridging connects two LANs, a remote bridge must be installed on each LAN. In place of a second token-ring adapter, each remote bridge would contain a serial communications port, allowing the device to be connected to a modem or a DSU/CSU, which, in turn, would be connected to an analog or a digital transmission facility. Figure 11.34 illustrates the creation of a port-address table for a 3-port bridge connecting three Ethernet segments. For simplicity, in this example the bridge ports are numbered 1, 2, and 3, whereas the source addresses for workstations on the three segments are labeled with letters of the alphabet instead of 48-bit MAC addresses.

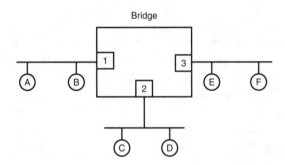

| Operation | Table Port | Creation Address |
|---|---|---|
| 1. A transmits to C | A | 1 |
| 2. C transmits to A | C | 2 |
| 3. B transmits to A | B | 1 |

**FIGURE 11.34**

*Creating a port-address table.*

In the first operation, the station whose source address is A transits a frame to destination address C. Assuming that the bridge was just powered on, the contents of its port-address table is empty. Thus, it does not know where station C is located. This means that the bridge transmits the frame onto all ports other than the port it was received on, representing a flooding operation. In addition the bridge notes the source address of the frame (A) and associates it with the port (1) it was received on. Thus, the first entry in the port address table shown in the lower right portion of Figure 11.34 reflects the identification of station C on port 1. Note that flooding the frame onto ports 2 and 3 results in the delivery of the frame to its intended recipient on port 2. Transmitting the frame onto port 3 results in the two stations on the LAN ignoring the frame; however, it places unnecessary traffic on the LAN connected to port 3 and represents a key problem associated with flooding and broadcasting.

Returning to Figure 11.34, the second operation results in C responding to the frame received from station A. Because the port associated with station A was previously learned, the bridge will forward the frame directly out of port 1. The bridge will also note the source address (C) of the frame was not previously learned and enter it and its associated port (2) in the port-address table.

For a third operation station, B transmits to station A. Because station A's location was previously learned, the bridge filters the frame at port 1. However, because the source address (B) was not learned, the bridge adds that address and its associated with port 1 to its port-address table.

A remote bridge is used to interconnect dissimilar types of LANs, such as an Ethernet and a token-ring network. Because the frames flowing on each LAN are dissimilar and require a translation process, the bridge used to connect dissimilar LANs is called a translating bridge. There are two types of self-learning and translating bridges—local and remote. A local bridge has two or more network adapter cards and is used to interconnect LANs in close proximity of one another. A remote bridge has at least one network adapter card and one serial port, with the latter used to provide communications to another remote bridge geographically separated from the first. The serial port can be connected to a modem or a DSU/CSU, which, in turn, would be connected to an analog or a digital transmission facility. The remote bridge examines addressing information in each frame, and on recognition of an address on the distant LAN, it routes the frame via the serial port of the device onto the communications carrier transmission facility linking the remote LANs. Figure 11.35 illustrates the use of a remote bridge to interconnect two LANs.

## Routers

Routers operate at the network layer of the OSI reference model and permit support of several functions that bridges are not capable of providing because they operate at the data link layer.

Two additional functions that routers can perform include dynamic path assignment and frame fragmentation.

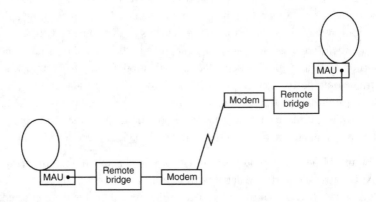

**FIGURE 11.35**

*Using remote bridges.*

The capability to dynamically assign different paths permits routers to use alternative paths in the event that a communications circuit becomes inoperative. In addition, this capability enables routers to perform a dynamic load balance of communications traffic when alternative routes are available between networks. This capability can reduce or eliminate the potential effect of congestion when too much traffic from one network destined to another exceeds the transmission capability of a single communications circuit.

Frame fragmentation permits routers to interconnect dissimilar LANs easily. For example, an Ethernet network has a maximum frame length of 1,526 bytes, a 4Mbps token-ring network has a maximum frame length of 4,500 data bytes, and a 16Mbps token-ring network has a maximum frame length of 18,000 data bytes. When connecting Ethernet and token-ring networks with bridges, you would have to set software configuration parameters on each workstation on the token-ring LAN to limit the maximum frame length to 1,500 data characters to enable interoperability between networks. In comparison, if routers are used, they can fragment frames exceeding 1,500 data characters that originate on the token-ring network into multiple frames for transmission on the Ethernet network. Because it's easier to configure one router than to configure numerous workstations connected via bridges, using routers can simplify network interoperability.

Routers must be configured in comparison to bridges that are self-learning devices. Another difference between bridges and routers concerns the manner by which workstations use their capabilities. In a bridge environment, a workstation operates transparently and the bridge learns its address. In a router environment, a workstation is configured with the address of the router. When the workstation has data to transmit, it compares the destination network to the network the station resides on. If they are different, this indicates that the destination is on a different network and the services of a router must be employed. Thus, the station sends the data to the router using the configured address. The router then forwards the data toward its destination.

A word or two concerning the terms router and gateway are in order to alleviate potential confusion. In the early days of LAN, internetworking a device that routed data between networks was called a gateway. Although that device was later named a router, one of its many functions as a gateway between networks was maintained. This explains why when you configure certain protocols, such as TCP/IP (which is discussed in detail in Chapter 12, "The Internet") the term *gateway* is used to reference the configuration of a workstation to access a router.

## Gateways

To provide an interconnection capability for accessing mainframe computers, IBM markets several products that can be equipped with token-ring adapters and function as gateway devices. Two examples of such products are the IBM 3174 control unit with token-ring adapter (TRA) and the IBM 3745 token-ring interface coupler (TIC). The 3174 control unit can be located locally or remotely from a mainframe computer and allows up to 32 terminal devices to share access to the mainframe over a common cable or transmission facility. When equipped with a TRA, the 3174 can serve as a local or remote LAN gateway for accessing an IBM mainframe.

Because the maximum data rate of a 3174 is 56Kbps, using a TRA on that device can result in degraded performance if too many LAN users attempt to access the mainframe simultaneously. To provide an increased level of gateway access, the IBM 3745 front-end processor (FEP) can be equipped with a TIC, which allows the FEP to be directly connected to a 4 or 16Mbps token-ring network. Figure 11.36 shows several methods by which the IBM 3174 control unit and the IBM 3745 front-end processor can provide token-ring network users access to an IBM mainframe computer.

## LAN Switches

A key problem associated with LANs is the fact that the bandwidth of the cable is shared among all workstations connected to the local area network. For example, in a 100-station 10BASE-T network, each workstation (on the average) obtains 10Mbps/100, or an average bandwidth of 100Kbps. With the development of multimedia applications that can incorporate audio, video, and still images with text, conventional LANs become severely taxed.

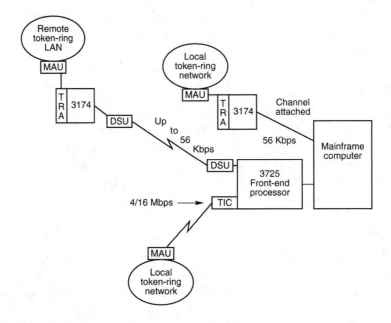

**FIGURE 11.36**

*Gateway access to an IBM mainframe.*

To illustrate the effect of images on the transmission capability of a LAN, consider the storage of a 3×5 color image versus a screen of text. If the image is scanned using a resolution of 300 dots per inch, each of the 15 square inches represents 90,000 dots, or *pixels*. If a color scan capable of representing 256 colors is used, each pixel must have 8 bits (28 = 256) associated with it to represent the color of the pixel. Thus, the 3×5 color image requires 1.35MB of storage. If a workstation obtains an average LAN bandwidth of 100Kbps, the transmission of the image can be expected to average 108 seconds. In comparison, an 80-row by 25-line screen consists of 2,000 characters or 16,000 bits. At an average LAN bandwidth of 100Kbps, the transmission of the screen of text can be expected to require .16 seconds.

The effect of multimedia applications was one of several factors governing the development of switching hubs. Other factors included the capability of switching hubs to enhance the operation of an existing network, as well as to provide an expansion capability to support traffic growth.

In Figure 11.37, you can see how a switching hub interconnects two Ethernet LAN segments. Note that by connecting two file servers to individual ports, you can enable up to two simultaneous connections between workstations and file servers, increasing the maximum bandwidth from 10Mbps on an Ethernet 10BASE-T LAN to 20Mbps via the use of the switch shown in Figure 11.35.

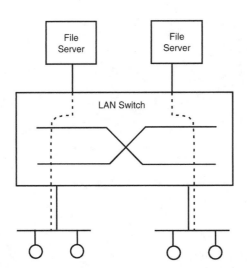

**FIGURE 11.37**

*The use of a LAN switch enables the network to support multiple simultaneous connections between networking devices.*

In general, an n port LAN switch is theoretically capable of providing an $(n/2) \times x$ data throughput, where x is the speed of each switch port. For example, a 64-port 10BASE-T LAN switch provides a data throughput capability of $(64/2) \times 10$Mbps, or 320Mbps. In actuality, LAN switches are rarely used for peer-to-peer transmission and primarily support client-server operations. This means that if there are four servers on the previously mentioned 64-port switch, the maximum practical data transfer would be 40Mbps even though the switch is capable of supporting 320Mbps data throughput.

To boost bandwidth even higher, many switches provide several high-speed ports, typically supporting a 100BASE-T4, FDDI, or Gigabit Ethernet connection. This enables access between the switch and highly used devices, such as file servers, to occur at 100Mbps or even 1Gbps, and it further enhances the throughput through a switch.

Figure 11.38 illustrates four 3Com Corporation SuperStack II Ethernet network switches. The first three switches (left to right, top to bottom) support 10/100Mbps Ethernet and Fast Ethernet connections as well as a Gigabit Ethernet connection. The fourth switch supports 12 Gigabit Ethernet connections and can be used as a backbone to interconnect the other switches via their Gigabit Ethernet ports.

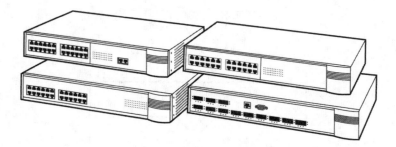

**FIGURE 11.38**

*Members of a 3Com Coporation family of Ethernet, Fast Ethernet, and Gigabit Ethernet switches. (Courtesy of 3Com Corporation.)*

## LAN Switch Operation

Internally, a switch functions as a bridge, keeping track of the source address of frames on each port and examining the destination address of frames as a mechanism for routing. The number of addresses per port a switch can store determines the capability of the switch to support individual stations or LAN segments that can contain multiple workstations. If the switch supports only one address per port, it functions as a port-switching device. If the switch supports multiple addresses per port, it functions as a segment-switching device.

In addition to the switching method, switches can be classified by their switching technique. Two switching techniques are *cut-through*, which is also known as *on-the-fly*, and *store-and-forward*. A cut-through switch immediately affects a cross-connection between source and destination port after it reads the destination address in a frame. This type of switch has a minimal delay or latency time. In comparison, a store-and-forward switch stores the entire frame in memory and performs an error check on the frame, discarding it if the CRC computation performed does not match the CRC in the frame.

Store-and-forward switching is required whenever a frame must be moved from a low-speed LAN to a high-speed LAN. Because it must store the entire frame, a small degree of latency is associated with this switching method.

A third switching technique that only works with similar speed LANs is referred to as hybrid switching. Under hybrid switching, a switch typically commences operation as a cut-through switch; however, it computes the CRC of frames on-the-fly and compares the computed CRC to the CRC in the frame. Although the switch can note errors, it cannot discard erroneous frames in a cut-through mode of operation. If the number of CRC mismatches reaches a predefined level, the switch then moves into a store-and-forward mode of operation, allowing it to discard erroneous frames. Once in a store-and-forward mode of operation, the switch continues to compute and compare the value of computed CRCs against the value of CRCs in each frame being switched. If the error rate decreases to a predefined value, the switch resumes cut-through operations.

One of the recent features added to switches is a virtual LAN creation method. Under the virtual LAN (vLAN) creation method, a grouping of switch ports, station addresses, network addresses of stations, or another criteria is used to form broadcast domains. The broadcast domain forms a logical grouping of switch ports, which restricts broadcasts to ports that form the virtual LAN.

Figure 11.39 depicts two vLANs on a 12-port switch. In this example, vLAN1 consists of ports 1, 2, 3, 4, 11, and 12, and vLAN2 consists of ports 5, 6, 7, 8, 9, and 10. This method of creating broadcast domains limits broadcasts generated by servers that advertise their services to a specific domain. Other advantages of vLANs include facilitating station adds, moves, and changes, as well as trouping personnel into communities of interest. Concerning the former, moving a station from a segment connected to port 6 to a segment connected to port 7 allows the station to retain its membership in vLAN2. Concerning the latter, vLAN1 could represent accounting personnel, and vLAN2 could represent marketing personnel. Thus, each group could use a common switch but would have its network activity segregated based upon a logical grouping of switch ports. For additional information concerning different types of virtual LANs, refer to the book *Virtual LANs*, published by John Wiley & Sons, Inc., and written by Gilbert Held.

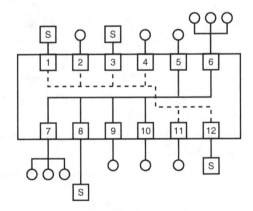

vLAN1 = ports 1, 2, 3, 4, 11, 12
vLAN2 = ports 5, 6, 7, 8, 9, 10

**FIGURE 11.39**

*VLANs restrict transmission to a broadcast domain logically created over a physical infrastructure.*

# What You Have Learned

- LANs provide high-speed switched connections between such data equipment as computers, storage devices, printers, word processors, and display terminals at distances up to a few thousand meters.

- The usefulness of a LAN is maximized if it provides higher level data communications support in addition to basic transmission and switching functions.

- Communications functions within a network should be partitioned in a hierarchical manner to isolate the implementation of major functional components.

- Myriad LAN architectures are possible, but the most prevalent include the following:

  Contention-access-based coaxial cable systems (for example, Ethernet)

  Token passing systems (for example, IBM token-ring network)

  Polled-access-based coaxial cable systems (for example, ARCnet)

  Frequency division broadband systems based on cable television technology and practice

- Some of the incompatibilities that traditionally arise in LAN equipment supplied by different vendors are being resolved by IEEE standards committee 802.

- The IEEE 802.3 standard is really a set of standards that defines several types of CSMA/CD LANs.

- The subdivision of the physical layer by the IEEE permits a common type of LAN to operate over different types of media.

- The Ethernet 5-4-3 rule allows transmission to occur between nodes over a maximum of 5 segments connected through the use of 4 repeaters, with a maximum of 3 populated segments.

- Ethernet is scalable from 10Mbps to 10Gbps using the same basic frame, and carrier extension technology used by Gigabit Ethernet enables a transmission distance of 100 meters to be supported over copper media.

- 10 Gigabit Ethernet includes the ability to provide a transmission distance up to 40Km as well as a connection to SONET.

- A virtual LAN represents a broadcast domain formed by a logical grouping of LAN switch ports.

# Quiz for Chapter 11

1. Which of the following transmission systems provides the highest data rate to an individual device?

    A. Voiceband modem

    B. Local area network

    C. Computer bus

    D. Digital PBX

2. Which of the following systems provides the longest digital transmission distances?

    A. Voiceband modem

    B. Local area network

    C. Computer bus

    D. Digital PBX

3. Which of the following options is a characteristic of a LAN?

    A. Parallel transmission

    B. Unlimited expansion

    C. Low-cost access for low-bandwidth channels

    D. Application-independent interfaces

4. The subdivision of the physical layer permits

    A. A common LAN technology to operate over different types of media.

    B. Low-cost access to higher network layers.

    C. Application-independent interfaces.

    D. None of the above.

5. Which of the following transmission media is not readily suitable to CSMA operation?

    A. Radio

    B. Optical fibers

    C. Coaxial cable

    D. Twisted pair

6. Which of the following functions is not provided as part of the basic Ethernet design?

    A. Access control

    B. Addressing

    C. Automatic retransmission of a message

    D. Multiple virtual networks

7.  Which of the following options is not a useful property of a Manchester line code for an Ethernet?

    A.  Continuous energy

    B.  Continuous clock transitions

    C.  No DC component

    D.  No signal change at a 1 to 0 transition

8.  Which of the following data communications functions is generally provided for in a LAN?

    A.  Data link control

    B.  Applications processing

    C.  Flow control

    D.  Routing

9.  What is the minimum length of an Ethernet frame?

    A.  64 bytes

    B.  72 bytes

    C.  1500 bytes

    D.  1526 bytes

10. Under the 5-4-3 rule, two nodes on an Ethernet network

    A.  Can be connected by 5 repeaters.

    B.  Must flow through 5 segments.

    C.  Can be connected via a maximum of 5 segments.

    D.  Are always directly connected to each other.

11. What is the function of the preamble in an Ethernet network?

    A.  Clock synchronization

    B.  Error checking

    C.  Collision avoidance

    D.  Broadcast

12. What is the difference between the Ethernet frame Preamble field and the IEEE 802.3 Preamble and Start of Frame Delimiter fields?

    A.  1 byte

    B.  1 bit

    C.  8 bits

    D.  16 bits

13. A 10BASE-2 network is limited to

    A. 20 bytes per data field.

    B. 30 stations per segment.

    C. 40 segments.

    D. 50 feet of cable.

14. An Ethernet-SNAP frame

    A. Permits two protocols to be carried in the same frame.

    B. Permits different protocols to be carried on the same network.

    C. Provides faster transmission.

    D. Cannot be bridged.

15. Each version of Fast Ethernet subdivides the physical layer to support

    A. Different operating rates.

    B. Different media.

    C. Different data.

    D. Different people.

16. An Ethernet hub

    A. Functions as a repeater.

    B. Connects to a digital PBX.

    C. Connects to a token-ring network.

    D. Functions as a gateway.

17. A single cable broadband LAN

    A. Requires a low-end converter.

    B. Uses a headend frequency converter.

    C. Commonly uses a bus design.

    D. Uses 50 ohm coaxial cable.

18. Which of the following represents a key difference between a 100BASE-T4 and a 100BASE-TX network?

    A. Operating rates

    B. Support of Ethernet frames

    C. Network span

    D. Use of cable pairs

19. Gigabit Ethernet operates over which of the following?

   A. Three types of copper cable

   B. Four types of fiber-optic cable

   C. Two types of fiber and two types of copper cable

   D. Two types of copper and three types of fiber-optic cable

20. Gigabit Ethernet carrier extension

   A. Is required to support a 100m transmission distance.

   B. Adds up to 512 carrier extension bytes to a frame.

   C. Requires the FCS to be recomputed.

   D. Is only used on fiber connections.

21. The 1000BASE-SX standard indicates

   A. 100Mbps transmission.

   B. Broadband transmission.

   C. The use of a shortwave laser.

   D. The use of an SX laser.

22. What type of network requires the use of carrier extension?

   A. Full-duplex Gigabit Ethernet

   B. Shared-media Gigabit Ethernet

   C. 10BASE-T

   D. 100BASE-T

23. 10 Gigabit Ethernet supports

   A. Auto-sensing with 10BASE-T.

   B. Two physical interfaces.

   C. One fixed transmission distance.

   D. Two types of lasers.

24. Which of the following is a key characteristic of an FDDI network?

   A. Self-healing capability

   B. 10Mbps operating rate

   C. Ring enable capability

   D. IEEE standardization

25. A common use for FDDI networks is for

    A. Extending fiber.

    B. Serving as a backbone for connecting lower speed LANs.

    C. Rotating rings.

    D. Transporting decision data.

26. Which of the following features is possible in a token-passing bus network?

    A. Unlimited number of stations

    B. Unlimited distances

    C. Multiple time division channels

    D. In-service expansion

27. Which of the following features is not possible in a token-passing loop network?

    A. Unlimited number of stations

    B. Unlimited distances

    C. Multiple time division channels

    D. In-service expansion

28. What is the function of the active monitor on a token-ring LAN?

    A. Check frame priority

    B. Check the frame reservation field

    C. Remove frames that have circulated the ring

    D. Remove frames whose priority value equals their reservation value

29. Which of the following options is not a characteristic of the hub architecture of ARCnet?

    A. Directionalized transmission

    B. RIM port isolation

    C. Zero insertion loss amplifiers

    D. Alternate routing

30. A bridge operates at which layer?

    A. The data link layer

    B. The application layer

    C. The network layer

    D. The segmentation layer

31. Flooding broadcasts a frame to all ports other than which of the following?

    A. Port one on a vLAN switch

    B. The port from which the frame was received

    C. The console port

    D. The general port

32. What is the function of a translating bridge?

    A. Connect similar remote LANs.

    B. Connect similar local LANs.

    C. Connect different types of LANs.

    D. Translate the network addresses into a layer 2 address.

33. What layer does a router operate at?

    A. The data link layer

    B. The application layer

    C. The network layer

    D. The segmentation layer

34. To use a router requires a workstation to be configured to recognize

    A. Remote networks.

    B. Bridge ports.

    C. Router ports.

    D. The router's address.

35. A major advantage associated with the use of a LAN switch is its capability to

    A. Convert frames.

    B. Support multiple simultaneous connections.

    C. Enable cut-through storage.

    D. Connect file servers.

# The Internet

## IN THIS CHAPTER

The Internet represents a network formed by the interconnection of subnetworks. In this chapter, you will examine its evolution, some of the protocols used to transport data, its addressing scheme, and a few of the applications that resulted in its progression from an academic-oriented facility to a network used by virtually everyone who has access to a computer. Because the use of the TCP/IP protocol suite is essential for transferring information on the Internet, this chapter focuses on portions of that protocol suite in its coverage of the Internet and Internet applications.

# Evolution of the Internet

During the 1960s, the United States Department of Defense sponsored research that resulted in the development of a communications network to interconnect research laboratories and data centers. Funded by the Defense Advanced Research Projects Agency (DARPA), this network was known as ARPANET. It represented one of the first layered communications networks, preceding the development of the seven-layer International Standards Organization (ISO) reference model by approximately a decade.

The work involved in establishing ARPANET resulted in the development of two specific protocols for the transmission of information: the Transmission Control Protocol (TCP) and the Internet Protocol (IP), commonly referred to collectively as TCP/IP. TCP represents a transport-layer protocol that provides end-to-end reliable transmission. To do so, TCP includes such functions as flow control, error control, and the exchange of status information. Status information includes determining that the destination is both operational and available to receive data, a process referred to as a connection-oriented process. In comparison, IP represents a connectionless-mode network-layer protocol designed to route messages between networks. To do so, IP includes the capability to segment or fragment and reassemble messages that must be routed between networks that support packet sizes other than the size supported by the source or destination network.

In addition to TCP, the Internet suite specifies an optional connectionless-mode Layer 4 transport protocol known as the User Datagram Protocol (UDP). UDP is commonly used for transaction-based applications, such as the transmission of network-management information when transmission efficiency is more important than reliability. Another emerging use for UDP is the transmission of digitized voice over the Internet. Because packets containing digitized voice cannot be delayed, there is no need to retransmit packets received in error. Instead, packets are dropped, and small intervals of noise replace the dropped packets at the receiver. This technique, which is referred to as Voice over IP (VoIP), does not require the use of a connection-oriented protocol, so UDP is more suitable than TCP for transmitting digitized voice. However, because it is important to ensure that the telephone number of the destination party flows error-free through an IP network, VoIP call setup occurs via the use of TCP. After a connection is established, UDP, which represents a layer 4 protocol in the TCP/IP protocol suite, is used to transmit packets containing digitized voice.

# Application Services

Various application services have been developed for transport by the TCP/IP protocol suite. The more well-known applications include the following:

- File Transfer Protocol (FTP), used to transfer single and multiple files between computers.
- Telnet, an interactive remote terminal access protocol that enables a terminal to be connected to a remote host as if it were directly connected to the computer.
- Simple Mail Transport Protocol (SMTP), which provides a standard method for exchanging electronic mail.
- Hypertext Transfer Protocol (HTTP), which enables the transportation of World Wide Web (WWW) pages from Web servers to browsers operating on client computers.
- Simple Network Management Protocol (SNMP), which supports the management of network devices.

Figure 12.1 illustrates the layering structure of the TCP/IP protocol suite to include a few of the application services included in the suite. Note that the subdivision of the transport layer in Figure 12.1 indicates which applications are transported by TCP and which are carried by UDP. Later in this chapter, you'll learn about several of the application services illustrated in Figure 12.1.

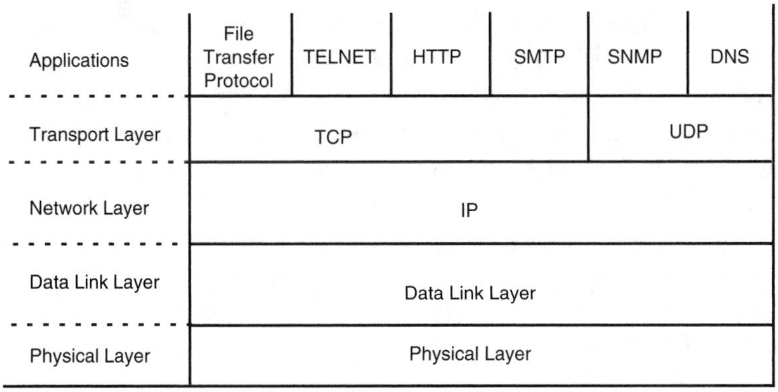

**FIGURE 12.1**
*A portion of the TCP/IP suite.*

One of the key reasons for the dramatic growth of the Internet can be traced to the development and structure of the TCP/IP protocol suite. Because TCP/IP was developed using taxpayer funds, its specifications were placed in the public domain, and they are available royalty-free for vendors to develop "protocol stacks" in software to implement TCP/IP's operational features. The growth of the Internet can also be attributed to the structure of TCP/IP, which makes it suitable for both LAN and WAN operations.

For example, on a LAN, TCP/IP can be transported within Ethernet, token-ring, FDDI, or another type of local area network frame. Because a considerable amount of effort was expended in developing LAN adapter cards to support the bus structures used in Macintosh, IBM PCs and compatible computers, Sun Microsystem workstations, and even IBM mainframes, the development of software-based protocol stacks to facilitate the transmission of TCP/IP on LANs provided the capability to interconnect tens of millions of LAN-based computers. This access is normally accomplished by commercial organizations, universities, and government agencies connecting their networks to the facilities of an Internet access provider.

In examining Figure 12.1, ICMP represents the Internet Control Message Protocol, which is often considered part of the Internet Protocol (IP) layer. In actuality, ICMP is communicated by the addition of an IP header to an ICMP message. ICMP messages are used to communicate error messages and status information. Two of the most commonly used ICMP messages are echo request and echo reply, which are used together to form a ping operation.

## Internet Access Providers

Through the late 1980s when the Internet was primarily used to communicate among colleges, universities, and government agencies, most Internet access providers represented nonprofit associations of schools located within a geographical area. As such, the Internet access provider typically constructed a high-speed backbone network that provided basic connectivity within the geographical area served and connected that backbone network to other backbone networks. The rapid growth in the use of the Internet by both individuals and businesses enabled many nonprofit associations to become commercialized, selling Internet access to both individuals and businesses. By the turn of the millennium, there were more than 2,000 Internet access providers in the United States, ranging in size from small providers with hundreds of subscribers to national providers with hundreds of thousands to millions of subscribers. Although all of those firms provide access to the Internet, a more popular term used to refer to such firms is *Internet service provider*, or ISP.

Most individuals use a dial-up protocol to access the facilities of an Internet access provider, whereas most businesses use leased lines to connect local area networks to the Internet. However, this relationship is gradually changing due to the growing availability of broadband communications, such as Digital Subscriber Lines (DSLs) and cable modems. As more persons that used modem dial-up access to the Internet migrate to different types of broadband access, cable TV operators and local telephone companies are emerging as significant ISPs as well.

Because a LAN can provide support for hundreds to thousands of workstations, it's likely that one or more workstation users require access to the Internet at any particular point in time. From an economic perspective, it is normally more economical to connect a LAN to the Internet via a leased line than to have individual users use the switched telephone network because the latter method is commonly billed on an hourly usage basis. Even when billed on a monthly basis for unlimited access, dial-up via the PSTN results in the use of a modem and business line for each employee, which on a cumulative basis can be quite expensive. In addition, a leased line provides immediate access from the Internet to any application residing on the LAN, such as a Web server, an FTP server, or an electronic mail system. Thus, a leased-line connection facilitates bidirectional access to and from the Internet. Figure 12.2 illustrates the two most common methods of Internet access.

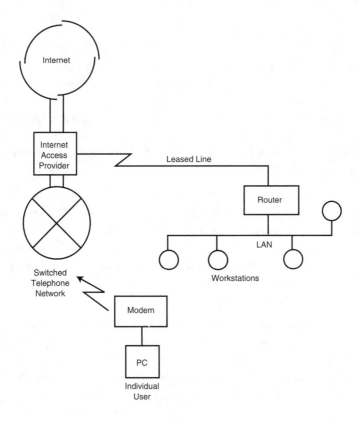

**FIGURE 12.2**

*Common business and individual Internet access methods.*

# IP Addressing

The routing of information on a TCP/IP network, including the Internet as well as other public and private networks, is based on IP addressing. The current version of the Internet Protocol, IPv4, uses addresses 32 bits long arranged in four octets or bytes. Such addresses are commonly expressed as four decimal numbers ranging from 0 to 255, separated by dots. Therefore, IP addresses are sometimes called dotted decimal addresses.

The value of each byte in an IP address depends upon the setting of bits in the byte. As a refresher for readers, the following indicates the decimal value of each bit position in a byte.

128     64      32      16      8       4       2       1

Thus, a byte with the bit composition of 11000001 would have the decimal value of 128 + 64 + 1, or 193. Similarly, a byte with the bit composition of 01100011 would have the decimal value of 64 + 32 + 2 + 1, or 99.

An IP address is divided into assigned network and host computer sections that combine to form a unique address. The network portion of the address until recently was assigned by the Internet Network Information Center (InterNIC), whereas network managers and administrators assign the host portion of the address to individual computer users. In October 1998, a broad coalition of the Internet's business, technical, academic, and user communities formed a nonprofit organization known as the Internet Corporation for Assigned Names and Numbers (ICANN). ICANN assumed responsibility for IP address space allocation, protocol parameter assignment, domain name system management, and other functions that literally make the Internet operate correctly.

To facilitate the assignment of addresses, the format of the 32-bit IP address was structured into five unique network classes, of which are typically allocated by ICANN to Internet access providers, who then distribute those addresses to organizations and individuals. IP address classes range from Class A through Class E. Figure 12.3 illustrates the structure of the first three IP classes into network and host subdivisions, whereas Class D and Class E addresses are used as is, with no subdivision. Class D addresses are reserved for multicast groups, and Class E addresses are reserved for future use.

When you examine the composition of the first three IP address classes shown in Figure 12.3, note that the leftmost bits of the address indicate its network class. Also note that the assignment of an IP address actually represents the assignment of the network portion of the address, which means that the manager or administrator of an organization's network that uses an assigned address class is responsible for assigning the host portion of the address.

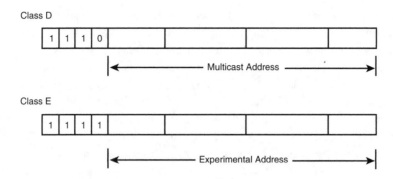

**FIGURE 12.3**
*IP address formats.*

A Class A address provides the largest range of addresses available for assignment to host computers. Thus, ICANN assigns Class A addresses to large organizations and countries that have national networks. Because a Class A address uses the first bit in the first octet or byte as the identifier for this class, a Class A network is restricted to having a network number between 1 and 127 for its first decimal number. Currently, all available Class A addresses have been distributed. The Class A 127 network is reserved for logical loopback of the TCP/IP protocol stack. All versions of TCP/IP use the IP address of 127.0.0.1 as the loopback address; however, some versions support other host numbers on the 127 network as a loopback.

A Class B address is evenly split, using 2 bytes for the network portion and 2 bytes for the host portion of the address. The availability of 2 bytes for host computer address assignments enables up to 65,636 hosts to be identified. Thus, Class B addresses are normally assigned to relatively large organizations with tens of thousands of employees. Although all Class B addresses were distributed years ago, occasionally, one is returned and made available for reuse.

A Class C address uses 3 bytes for the network portion and 1 byte for host identification. Thus, a Class C network address is restricted to supporting a maximum of 256 hosts. This means that either a Class C network address is assigned to small organizations, or multiple Class C addresses are assigned to organizations that require more than 256 distinct host addresses but are not large enough to justify a Class B address. In actuality, the maximum number of hosts for an address is $2^n - 2$, where $n$ represents the number of bits in the host portion of the address. The total is decreased by 2 because all zeros and all ones cannot be used in the host portion of an IP address. An address of all zeros represents "this network," and an address of all ones represents a broadcast address. Thus, a Class C address can support a maximum of $2^8 - 2$ or 254 hosts.

Two special address types are Class D and Class E addresses. Class D addresses are multicast addresses. Multicast represents a communications technique in which one conversation can flow to many users, but users interested in the conversation must join the multicast group specified in the address used in the transmission. This technique is popular for real-time audio and video distribution because only one flow of data is required through a network, significantly reducing bandwidth utilization. A Class E address is an experimental address, used for developing new communications techniques. Because Class D and Class E addresses are not commonly used, this chapter is primarily focused upon the use of Class A through Class C addresses, which are extensively used by academia, businesses, and government. Table 12.1 summarizes three key values for Class A, B, and C networks. Note that although the 127 network is normally considered as a Class A network, it is actually used for loopback purposes. Thus, it is not included in the table.

**TABLE 12.1** Class A, B, and C Network Numbers

| Class | First Byte Range | Network Bytes | Host Bytes |
|-------|------------------|---------------|------------|
| A | 1–126 | 1 | 3 |
| B | 128–191 | 2 | 2 |
| C | 192–223 | 3 | 1 |

# Subnetting

As the use of the Internet began to grow, it was recognized that the assignment of multiple Class A, B, or C addresses to organizations with multiple networks was inefficient. For example, suppose a business has two LANs in Chicago, one with 30 hosts and one with 40. If the business were assigned two Class C addresses, there would be a waste of $254 \times 2 - (30+40)$, or 438 Class C addresses. In addition to wasting increasingly scarce IP addresses, the use of multiple networks impacts routers that direct traffic across the Internet. Routers need to know where to forward data, with multiple networks requiring multiple entries in a router's routing table. As router routing tables increase in size, more time is required to search memory to locate a particular network. Thus, any method that cuts down upon the waste of IP addresses can provide an additional benefit of reducing the size of router routing tables.

One method for more economical assignment of IP addresses is to allow one address to be used to support multiple networks. Normally this would not be possible because a distinct IP address is required to identify each network. However, a technique known as subnetting permits an IP address to be subdivided, enabling it to support the addressing requirements of multiple networks.

Subnetting extends the network portion of an IP address and correspondingly decreases the host portion of the address. Figure 12.4 illustrates the relationship between a regular two-position IP address and a subnetted IP address.

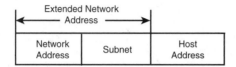

Subnetted Address

**FIGURE 12.4**

*Subnetting extends the network portion of an IP address.*

As you examine the construction of a subnetted IP address, it is important to note that subnetting is the responsibility of the network manager or LAN administrator. As far as the Internet is concerned, the organization has only one IP network address, and routers residing on the Internet are aware of that address only.

The best way to teach an appreciation of subnetting is by example. Therefore, assume that the Class C network address 192.37.12.0 was assigned to your organization. Suppose also that you want to use one common IP address to support multiple networks. From Figure 12.4, you would note that the extension of the network address into the host portion of the address enables you to define $2^n$ subnets, where $n$ represents the number of bits extended into the host position. If you use a single subnet bit, you can define two subnets and denote the relationship between the IP network address and each subnet as indicated in Figure 12.5.

In Figure 12.5, note that routers on the Internet have to be concerned with only one network address, even though that address is subnetted. This illustrates another reason for subnetting: to conserve entries in router tables. Because one bit position was removed from the host portion of the address to accommodate subnetting, the maximum number of hosts that can be placed on each subnet is $2^7 - 2$, or 126. As you will learn shortly, host addresses 1 through 127 can reside on subnet 0, and host addresses 128 through 254 can reside on subnet 1.

One question that you probably have by now is, "How does the router shown in Figure 12.5 route data to the appropriate subnet?" A second important question is, "How do stations on each subnet recognize data directed to each station?" The answer to both questions is, "Through the subnet mask." The next section discusses its composition and use.

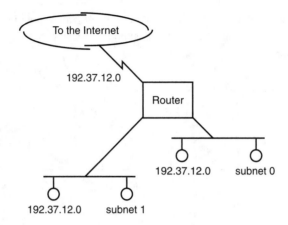

**FIGURE 12.5**

*When an IP address is subnetted, it still appears as a common network address to routers on the Internet.*

## Subnet Mask

The subnet mask is a 32-bit binary number consisting of a string of 1 bits that represents the network portion of an address. Normally, a Class A address would have a subnet mask of 255.0.0.0, and subnet masks of 255.255.0.0 and 255.255.255.0 would represent the default subnet masks of Class B and Class C addresses, respectively. By ANDing the subnet mask with an IP address, you can determine the network portion of an IP address. Although a subnet mask can be constructed with noncontinuous bits (1011000), most people who employ subnetting restrict the mask to contiguous bits because the results are easier to determine ahead of time.

IP routers and all stations on a LAN configured to support IP have an IP address and a subnet mask. Because you previously extended the network portion of the Class C IP address by one position, the subnet mask configured for the router and each station on the two LANs shown in Figure 12.5 becomes 255.255.255.128, where the last dotted-decimal digit (128) equates to a binary value of 10000000 and extends the network portion of the IP address by 1 bit.

To understand the use of a subnet mask, assume that a packet with the destination IP address of 192.37.12.39 arrives at the router. To which subnet does the router forward the packet? Because the first 2 bits in the first byte of the IP address (192) are set, the router knows the packet is a Class C address. This means that the first 24 bits in the 32-bit address represent the network address. However, the router also notes that the subnet mask is set to 255.255.255.128. That value indicates that the extended network address is in 25-bit positions; therefore, 25–24 indicates that the first bit position in the lost portion of the IP address represents the subnet. The router uses this information in examining the 8 bits of the address that normally make up the host address on the network. That is, a value of 39 equates to 00100111 binary, of which the first bit indicates that the subnet value is 0. The remaining bits have the value 39, which tells the router that the packet is internally addressed to host 39 on subnet 0. Figure 12.6 illustrates the use of the previously described IP address and subnet mask.

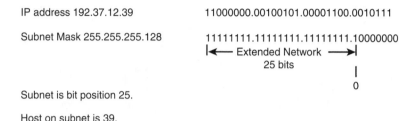

IP address 192.37.12.39      11000000.00100101.00001100.0010111

Subnet Mask 255.255.255.128      11111111.11111111.11111111.10000000
|◄──── Extended Network ────►|
25 bits

0

Subnet is bit position 25.

Host on subnet is 39.

**FIGURE 12.6**

*Using an IP address and subnet mask to determine the subnet and host address.*

If you examine the host portion of the IP address and the subnet mask, you will note that for subnet 0, the minimum and maximum host values are 0000001 and 1111111, resulting in a range of permissible host addresses from 1 to 127. For subnet 0, the addition of the prefix of 0 results in a dotted-decimal digit between 1 and 127 referencing a host on subnet 0. For subnet 1, the minimum and maximum host values are 0000000 and 1111110, or 0 to 126. Note that you can have a host address of all zeros because the subnet mask is 1, resulting in a beginning dotted-decimal digit of 128. When the subnet mask of 1 is added to the maximum host value of 1111110, you obtain a dotted-decimal value of 254. Thus, any host address between 128 and 254 is on subnet 1.

If you use a version of Microsoft Windows, you can set your computer's IP address and subnet mask through the Control Panel. When you open the Control Panel folder, you will find an icon labeled Network under versions of Windows earlier than Windows 2000. Under Windows 2000, the icon was relabeled Network and Dial-up Connections. Figure 12.7 illustrates the selection of that icon on a Windows 2000 computer. The left portion of that illustration shows the Local Area Connection Properties (named Network in earlier versions of Windows) dialog box with the Internet Protocol component selected. By clicking on the button labeled Properties, you can configure IP addressing information. This is indicated in the right portion of Figure 12.7, which shows the entry of an IP address and subnet mask.

## Domain Name Service

Although IP addresses consist of a sequence of dotted-decimal numbers, most readers are probably more familiar with names used to represent Internet addresses, such as www.whitehouse.gov, which represents the address of the World Wide Web server operated by the

White House. In this address, "www" represents the type of service residing on a server, "whitehouse" represents the name of the organization, and "gov" indicates that the organization is a government entity.

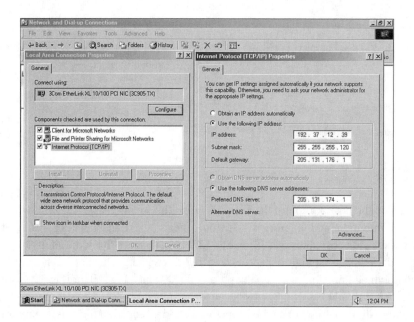

**FIGURE 12.7**

*Configuring the IP address and subnet mask using Windows 2000.*

To facilitate the use of names, each organization registers its name with ICANN. As part of the registration process, ICANN assigns the organization to one of six categories, referred to as domain names. Thus, in the registration process, a domain name consisting of the organization's name and its domain assignment is registered. In the preceding example, "whitehouse.gov" would represent the registered domain name. The top portion of Table 12.2 indicates the current category of domain name suffixes assigned by ICANN. One category of domain names not mentioned in the table is top-level geographical domains. Currently, there are approximately 240 such domains, ranging from Australia (au) to Israel (il) and the United Kingdom (uk).

In the top portion of Table 12.2, note that the domain name suffix indicates the type of organization. Thus, it is entirely possible for two organizations to use the same server hostname and have the same organization name, yet have separate identities: Each could represent a different type of organization if their registered names have different endings. The lower portion of Table 12.2 lists seven new top-level domains that were selected by the ICANN board at its meeting during November 2000 for negotiation of agreements concerning how they will operate and the manner in which organizations and individuals will be registered. It is expected that these new domains will become operational in early 2001.

**TABLE 12.2** Domain Names and the Type of Organization They Represent

| Domain Name Suffix | Type of Organization |
| --- | --- |
| *Currently Available* | |
| .com | Commercial organization |
| .edu | Educational organization |
| .gov | Government agency |
| .mil | Military organization |
| .net | Networking organization |
| .org | Not-for-profit organization |
| .int | International organization |
| *Pending Domain Name Suffixes* | |
| .aero | Air-transport industry |
| .biz | Business |
| .coop | Cooperatives |
| .info | Unrestricted use |
| .museum | Museums |
| .name | For registration by individuals |
| .pro | Accountants, lawyers, and physicians |

When an organization has a registered domain name, it can prefix that name to indicate specific hosts or applications residing on one host. For example, www.whitehouse.gov and ftp.whitehouse.gov, which could represent a World Wide Web (WWW) server and a File Transfer Protocol (FTP) server, could also represent two applications residing on a common computer. When you enter the IP address in an application as a name, a translation process occurs that converts the name into a 32-bit IP address. This translation process, which is invisible to a user, is facilitated by a TCP/IP application known as Domain Name Service (DNS).

DNS commonly operates on a separate server on a network and keeps track of the hostnames on the network. When a user on the network enters a name instead of an IP address when using a TCP/IP application, the name is transported to the DNS server. If the name resides on the network, the DNS server returns the IP address associated with the name. If the name does not represent a computer on the network, but a recent query using that name occurred, the IP address might be in the DNS server's cache memory. If so, it is returned to the requester. If the name is not in the DNS database or in cache memory, the server sends a request to a "higher" DNS server, usually located on another network. Explaining why this occurs requires a slight digression into the topic of DNS hierarchy.

## DNS Hierarchy

A top-level domain registers subdomains in its database in the form of the location of the name servers for those domains. Similarly, subdomains keep track of domains under them, in effect creating a naming hierarchy. Thus, if the name server on the current network does not have the name and associated IP address for the name in its database, it forwards the request to a higher-level DNS. This forwarding effort can be replicated several times and can traverse areas around the globe until the IP address is found and returned. It is important to note that DNS names play no role in the actual routing of IP packets. Instead, they simply provide the IP address associated with a domain name. It is the router used to connect networks that is responsible for the actual routing of packets. Because you can get a better feel for the flow of data on the Internet by examining IP, TCP, and UDP, turn your attention to those protocols.

## Datagrams

As was briefly discussed earlier in this chapter, IP is a network-layer protocol. IP provides for the transfer of a basic unit of information referred to as a datagram. In doing so, IP operates as an unreliable connectionless protocol. Although your first impression of those terms is negative, they are not as bad as they seem. First, although IP provides an unreliable transmission method, the term *unreliable* should be viewed in the context that delivery is not guaranteed. This means that queuing delays or other problems can cause data loss; however, higher layers, such as TCP, can provide error detection and correction and can retransmit IP datagrams. Second, the term *connectionless* refers to the fact that each datagram is treated independent of preceding and succeeding datagrams. This means that IP does not require that a connection be established between source and destination before it transfers the first datagram or succeeding datagrams.

Because datagrams can be routed through a network over different paths, some datagrams might arrive out of sequence from the order in which they were transmitted. In addition, as datagrams flow between networks, they encounter physical limitations imposed on the amount of data that can be transported based on the transport mechanism used to move data on the network. For example, the Information field in an Ethernet frame is limited to 1500 bytes. Thus, as a datagram flows between networks, it might have to be fragmented into two or more datagrams to be transported through different networks to its ultimate destination.

Figure 12.8 illustrates the routing of two datagrams from workstation A on a token-ring network to server B connected to an Ethernet LAN. Because the routing of datagrams is a connectionless service, no call setup is required, which enhances transmission efficiency. In comparison, when TCP is used, it provides a connection-oriented service regardless of the lower-layer delivery system (for example, IP).

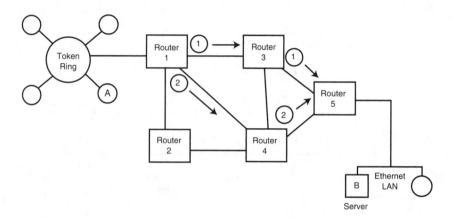

**FIGURE 12.8**

*Datagrams can be routed over different paths.*

TCP requires the establishment of a virtual circuit in which a temporary path is developed between source and destination. This path is fixed, and the flow of datagrams is restricted to the path established. When UDP is used in place of TCP, the flow of data at the transport layer continues to be connectionless and results in the transport of datagrams over available paths rather than a fixed path, resulting from the establishment of a virtual circuit.

Figure 12.9 illustrates the relationship of an IP datagram, a UDP datagram, and a TCP segment to a LAN frame. Note that the IP datagram flowing on a 4Mbps token-ring LAN can be up to 4500 bytes in length because that is the maximum length of a token-ring Information field. However, when that datagram flows onto an Ethernet LAN, whose maximum Information field length is 1500 bytes, the original datagram might have to be fragmented into thirds.

You can gain an appreciation for how datagram fragmentation is accomplished, as well as additional information about the flow of data, by examining the composition of the fields in the IP header.

## The Fields in the IP Header

Figure 12.10 shows the fields in the IP header. Note that the header contains a minimum of 20 bytes of control information, and Figure 12.10 illustrates the width of each field with respect to a 32-bit word.

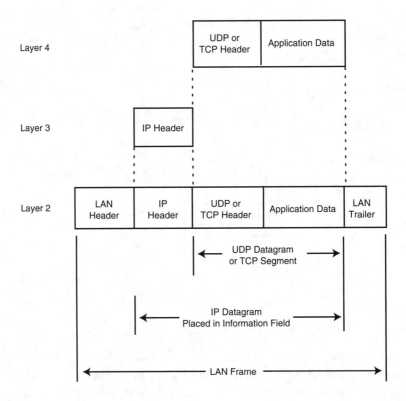

**FIGURE 12.9**

*Forming a LAN frame.*

The Vers field consists of 4 bits that identify the version of the IP protocol used to create the datagram. The current version of the IP protocol is 4.

The Hlen field also contains 4 bits. This field indicates the length of the header in 32-bit words. In comparison, the Total Length field indicates the total length of the datagram to include its header and higher-layer information. Because 16 bits are used for this field, an IP datagram can be up to $2^{16}$, or 65,535 octets in length.

The Service Type field defines how the datagram is handled. Three of the 8 bits in this field are used to denote the precedence or level of importance assigned by the sender. Thus, this field provides a priority mechanism for routing IP datagrams.

The Identification field enables each datagram or fragmented datagram to be identified. If a datagram was fragmented, the Fragment Offset field specifies the offset in the original datagram of the data being carried. In effect, this field indicates where the fragment belongs in the complete message. The actual value in this field is an integer that corresponds to a unit of 8 octets, providing an offset in 64-bit units.

The Flags field contains 2 bits that indicate how fragmentation occurs, along with a third bit that is currently unassigned. The setting of 1 bit can be viewed as a direct fragment-control mechanism because a value of 0 indicates that the datagram can be fragmented, whereas a value of 1 denotes that it can't be fragmented. The second bit is set to 0 to indicate that a fragment in a datagram is the last fragment, and it's set to a value of 1 to indicate that more fragments follow the current protocol.

The Time to Live (TTL) field specifies the maximum time, in milliseconds, that a datagram can live. Because an exact time is difficult to measure, many routers decrement this field by 1 as a datagram flows between networks and discard the datagram when the field value reaches 0. Essentially, this field represents a fail-safe mechanism because it prevents misaddressed datagrams from continuously wandering the Internet.

The Protocol field specifies the higher-level protocol used to create the message carried in the datagram. For example, a value of decimal 6 would indicate TCP, whereas a value of decimal 17 would indicate UDP. The source and destination address fields are both 32 bits in length. As previously discussed, each address represents both a network and a host computer on the network.

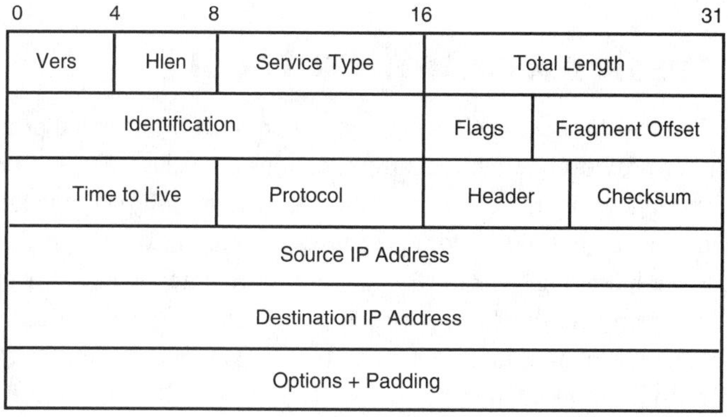

**FIGURE 12.10**
*The format of the IP header.*

## Address Resolution

The physical address associated with a LAN workstation is referred to as its hardware address. For an Ethernet network, that address is 48 bits or 6 bytes in length. In this chapter, I noted that

**12**

THE INTERNET

at the data link layer, IP uses a 32-bit logical address. One common problem associated with the routing of an IP datagram to a particular workstation on a network is the delivery of the datagram to its correct destination. The correct delivery of the datagram requires knowledge of the relationship between physical and logical addresses. This relationship is obtained by two protocols that map the physical and logical addresses to one another. One protocol, known as the Address Resolution Protocol (ARP), translates an IP address into a hardware address. The Reverse Address Resolution Protocol (RARP), as its name implies, performs a reverse mapping, converting a hardware address into an IP address.

To understand the use of ARP, assume that one computer user wants to send a datagram to another computer. Let's further assume that both computers are located on the same Ethernet network. The first computer broadcasts an ARP packet within an Ethernet frame to all devices on the LAN. That packet contains the destination IP address because it is known, and sets the hardware address field to zeros because its value is unknown. Although each device on the LAN reads the ARP packet as it is transmitted as a broadcast packet, only the device that recognizes its own logical address responds. When it does, it transmits an ARP reply, in which its physical address is inserted in the ARP address field that was previously set to 0. To reduce the necessity to constantly transmit ARP packets, the originator records received information in a table known as an ARP cache, allowing subsequent datagrams to be directed quickly to the appropriate address on the LAN. Thus, ARP and RARP provide a well-thought-out methodology for equating physical hardware addresses to IP's logical addresses.

# The Transmission Control Protocol

The *Transmission Control Protocol (TCP)* is a Layer 4 connection-oriented protocol. This protocol is responsible for providing reliable communications between hosts and processes on different hosts. Concerning the latter, TCP is structured to enable multiple application programs on a host to communicate concurrently with processes on other hosts, as well as for a host to demultiplex and service incoming TCP traffic among different applications or processes running on the host. To accomplish this task, a TCP header includes a destination port number for identifying the ultimate destination in a computer. To gain an appreciation for the functionality and capability of TCP, turn your attention to its header, which is illustrated in Figure 12.11.

Both the Source and Destination Port fields are 16 bits in length and are used to identify a user process or application. The Source Port field is optional; when it's not used, it is padded with zeros. The term *well-known port*, which is commonly used to denote an application-layer protocol or process, actually references the port address used within a TCP header. Because all ports whose value are less than 1024 are assigned applications, the term *well-known port* is also frequently used to reference a port value under 1024.

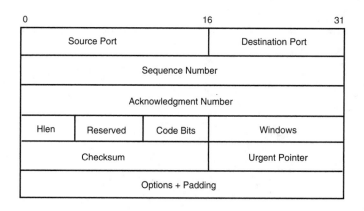

**FIGURE 12.11**

*The TCP header.*

Table 12.3 lists the well-known ports associated with eight popular TCP/IP application-layer protocols. In Table 12.3, note that some protocols, such as FTP, use two port addresses or logical connections. One address (21) is for commands and replies, and it functions as a control path. The second port address (20) is used for the actual file transfer.

**TABLE 12.3**  Popular TCP/IP Application-Layer Protocols

| Well-Known Protocol | Acronym | Description | Port |
|---|---|---|---|
| Domain Name Protocol | DOMAIN | Defines the DNS | 53 |
| File Transfer Protocol | FTP | Provides file transfer between computers | 20, 21 |
| Finger Protocol | FINGER | Provides information about a specified user | 79 |
| Hypertext Transmission Protocol | HTTP | Conveys information between a Web browser and a Web server | 80 |
| Post Office Protocol | POP | Enables PC users to access mail from a mail server | 110 |

**TABLE 12.3**   continued

| Well-Known Protocol | Acronym | Description | Port |
|---|---|---|---|
| Simple Mail Transfer Protocol | SMTP | Provides electronic mail transfer | 25 |
| Simple Network Management Protocol | SNMP | Provides the exchange of management information | 161, 162 |
| Telnet Protocol | Telnet | Provides remote terminal access to a host | 23 |

If you re-examine Figure 12.9 and compare it to Figures 12.10 and 12.11, you will note that the use of a TCP/IP application requires three addresses at both source and destination. A port address is required to identify the process or application and is contained within the TCP header. Within the IP header, an IP address is required to identify the network and host computer where the process or application resides. Finally, the delivery of information on a LAN requires the use of a hardware address, which is used within the LAN header shown in Figure 12.9 to deliver the IP datagram.

Returning to the examination of the TCP/IP header, the Sequence Number field identifies the position in the sender's byte stream of the data transported in the TCP segment. Thus, this field provides a means of maintaining the sequence of the data stream.

The Acknowledgment Number field identifies the number of the octet (Sequence Number) that the source expects to receive next. Thus, the Acknowledgment Number verifies the receipt of the previous $n - 1$ segment, when the Sequence Number is $n$. The Hlen field, which is 4 bits in length, denotes the length of the segment header in 32-bit multiples.

The Code Bits field contains 6 flag bits. Some of those bits, when set, indicate that a specific field in the header is significant and that the field value should be interpreted, whereas other bits are used to control the connection and data-transfer operation. Table 12.3 summarizes the use of the 6 code bits.

The 16-bit Window field indicates the number of bytes, beginning with the one in the Acknowledgment field that the originator of the segment can control. Because TCP represents a full-duplex communications path, each end of the path can use the Window field to control the quantity of data being sent to it. This enables the recipient to, in effect, have some say over its destiny. That is, if the recipient becomes overloaded with processing, or if some other situation renders it incapable of receiving large chunks of data, it can use the Window field to reduce the size of the chunks of data being sent to it.

The Checksum field provides reliability for the TCP header, the IP header, and data carried in the segment. Thus, this field provides the mechanism for detection of errors in the segment.

Skipping over certain options that are beyond the scope of this book, the Urgent Pointer field completes the header. This field enables the position of urgent data within a TCP segment to be identified, and a value in the field is interpreted only when the previously mentioned URG bit is set. When that bit position is set, the value in the Urgent Pointer field indicates the beginning of routine (nonurgent) data.

To illustrate the interrelated role of the Sequence, Acknowledgment, and Window fields, examine the transmission of data between two hosts via the use of a time chart that indicates some values for each field. This time chart is shown in Figure 12.12. At the top of Figure 12.12, assume that a Window size of eight segments is in use. Although TCP supports full-duplex transmission, for simplicity of illustration, this example uses a half-duplex model in the time chart.

Assuming that host A is downloading a program or performing a lengthy file transfer, the first series of segments will have sequence numbers 64–71. If no errors occur, host B returns an ACK value of 72 to indicate the next segment that it expects to receive. Suppose, however, that host B is running out of buffer space and, therefore, that it reduces the window size to 4. Thus, host A uses the Window field value in the TCP header sent to it and reduces the number of units of data that it will transmit to 4, using an initial SEQ field value of 72 and increasing that value by 1 to 75 as it transmits 4 units of data to host B. If all data is received error-free, host B then returns an ACK value of 76 to acknowledge receipt of sequence field numbers through 75.

Once again, host A transmits to host B, this time using sequence field values 76–79. Now assume that some type of transmission impairment occurs, sending the data into the proverbial "bit bucket" so that it is never received at host B. Because host B does not receive anything, it does not transmit anything back to host A. Although host A could wait forever, this would not be a good idea when data becomes lost. Instead, an internal timer clicks down to 0 while host A waits for a response. If a response does not appear before the timer expires, host A retransmits the segment, which is then acknowledged at the bottom of Figure 12.12.

The altering of the Window field values provides a "sliding window" that can be used to control the flow of information by adjusting the value of the Window field. In this process, two special field values, 0 and 1, further control the flow of information. A Window field value of 0 means that a host has shut down communications; a Window value of 1 requires an acknowledgment for each unit of data transmitted.

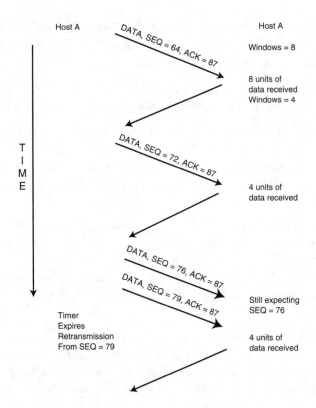

**FIGURE 12.12**
*A TCP transmission sequence.*

# The User Datagram Protocol

The *User Datagram Protocol (UDP)* represents a second transport-layer protocol supported by the TCP/IP protocol suite. UDP is a connectionless service, which means that the higher layers in the protocol suite are responsible for the reliable delivery of UDP transported data. As a connectionless service, UDP takes a best-effort approach to transmitting data and does not first require handshaking with the destination (which results in a delay when data is transmitted via TCP). Thus, UDP is better suited for certain applications to include the transmission of digitized voice, which is very delay-sensitive.

Figure 12.13 illustrates the composition of the UDP header; the Source and Destination port fields are each 16 bytes in length and identify the port number of the sending and receiving application process in a manner similar to their use in the TCP header. For example, a value of 161 in a port field is used by UDP to identify SNMP.

The Length field identifies the length of the UDP header packet in octets to include the header and user data. The checksum, which represents a ones complement arithmetic sum, is computed over the entire UDP packet and a pseudoheader, the latter including the source and destination IP addresses obtained from the IP packet header prefixed to the UDP header (see Figure 12.10). This checksum protects the key addressing fields of the UDP and IP headers, enabling routers to drop packets instead of forwarding them to the wrong destination if a transmission error should occur. If you compare the UDP header to the TCP header, it is easy to see that UDP represents a more simplified method of communication.

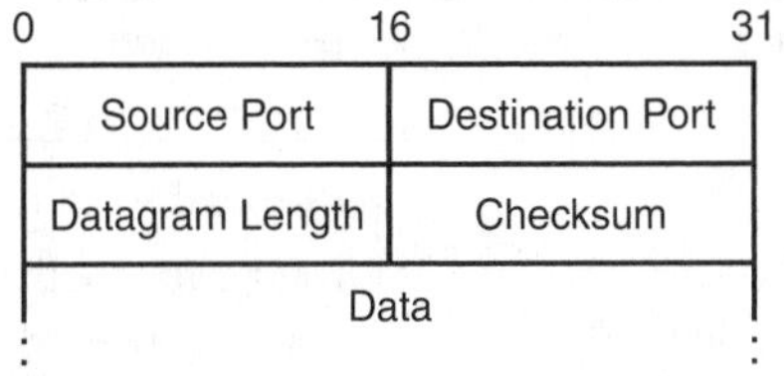

**FIGURE 12.13**
*The UDP header.*

# The Internet Control Message Protocol

The *Internet Control Message Protocol (ICMP)* can be considered to represent a mechanism by which special events are reported or for testing the operational state of devices. For example, a router may not be capable of locating the desired destination, or a datagram may be dropped due to the value in the IP header's Time to Live field being decremented to 0. The first situation would result in the router returning a "Destination Unreachable" message to the source address contained in the datagram that it cannot deliver. The second situation would result in the transmission of a "Time Exceeded" message to the source address in the datagram that was dropped.

Figure 12.14 illustrates the formation of an IP datagram transporting an ICMP message. The Type field identifies the type of ICMP message, while the Code field qualifies, when applicable, the type of message. The Checksum field, which is 2 bytes in length, provides integrity to the ICMP message. The Data field, which is variable in length, can provide additional information related to a message.

Table 12.4 lists seven of the more popular types of ICMP messages. Note that the Code field qualifies certain message types, while its value is set to 0 for other message types. For example, echo reply (message type 0) has a code value of 0. In comparison, Destination Unreachable (message type 3) can have one of the 15 code values that qualifies the reason for the destination being unreachable.

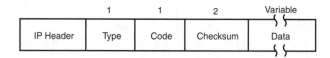

**FIGURE 12.14**

*The formation of an ICMP message byte.*

**TABLE 12.4**   Common ICMP Message Types

| Message<br>Type | Message<br>Type | Description<br>of Message |
|---|---|---|
| 0 | Echo Reply | Respond to echo request |
| 3 | Destination<br>Unreachable | Datagram could<br>not be delivered |
| 4 | Source Squelch | Choke datagrams |
| 8 | Echo Request | Ask an interface if it is operational |
| 11 | Time Exceeded | Time to Live field value became 0 |
| 12 | Parameter Problem | Bad IP header |
| 13 | Timestamp Request | Same as echo, but with timestamp |
| 14 | Timestamp Reply | Same as echo reply, but with timestamp |

ICMP provides the foundation for the pin application that uses an ICMP Echo Request to solicit an Echo Reply. This reply not only informs the originator that the destination is operational, but it also permits the round-trip delay between source and destination to be computed.

A second test application that uses ICMP is traceroute. Traceroute (implemented as tracert under Windows) traces the path from source to destination. To accomplish this, it commences operation transmitting a datagram with the Time to Live (TTL) field value set to 1. The first router in the path between source and destination decrements the TTL field value to 0, discards the datagram, and returns a time-exceeded ICMP message. The traceroute program learns the address of the first router by recording the source address of the datagram that transported the time-exceeded message. The traceroute program will then increment the value of the TTL field by 1 and transmit a second datagram to the destination that the second router in the path will send to the great bit bucket in the sky and return another time-exceeded message. This process is repeated until the destination is reached or a maximum number of tries is reached.

# Serial Communications Support

Although all Internet communications are serial, a special category of communications protocols were developed to transport TCP/IP over wide area network-transmission facilities. Probably because such facilities involve serial communications instead of host-to-printer parallel communications, the term *serial communications* is commonly used to reference these protocols. Two of the more popular serial communications protocols are the *Serial Line Internet Protocol (SLIP)* and the *Point-to-Point Protocol (PPP)*.

## The Serial Line Internet Protocol

SLIP is not actually an Internet standard, although it is described in an Internet Request for Comment (RFC) document. SLIP was included in several versions of the UNIX operating system and provides a transmission mechanism for conveying IP datagrams on a serial line. SLIP represents a relatively simple protocol in that it defines the use of only two characters, END (decimal 192) and ESC (decimal 219). When transmitting an IP datagram, SLIP replaces a data byte that has a value of 192 with the 2-byte sequence of ESC plus decimal 220, and any data byte with a value of 219 is replaced by the 2-byte sequence ESC plus decimal 221. Once a datagram transmission is complete, SLIP sends an END character.

One of the problems associated with the use of SLIP is that because it was never standardized, it lacks a maximum packet size. Thus, the use of SLIP requires compatible packet settings at both ends of the connection.

## The Point-to-Point Protocol

A second and more popular serial communications method is PPP. PPP represents a standardized protocol for transmission over asynchronous and synchronous dial-up and dedicated serial (point-to-point) lines, and it is based upon the High Level Data Link Control (HDLC) standard. As an Internet standard, PPP provides multivendor interoperability over all types of serial communications connections to include dial-up modem and ISDN transmission.

PPP was proposed as a standard in 1990 to replace SLIP, which had several deficiencies. Those deficiencies include the requirement to manually tear down links established through the use of SLIP, a lack of authentication, the incapability to transmit any protocol other than IP, and avoidance of error detection and correction (leaving it to higher layers in the protocol stacks to accomplish the latter).

Figure 12.15 illustrates the format of a Point-to-Point Protocol (PPP) frame, showing how the Information field is used to transport an IP datagram. RFC 1171, which defines PPP, also describes three key components of the protocol-HDLC encapsulation, a Link Control Protocol, and a family of independently defined protocols referred to as Network Control Protocols (NCPs) that can be used to encapsulate different network-layer protocols, such as TCP/IP, DECnet, and Novell's IPX/SXP.

The PPP frame transports information at the data link layer, using the bit sequence 01111110 as a flag delimiter byte at each end of the frame. The address field value is always set to hex FF (11111111) to indicate that all stations are to accept the frame. Because data is being transported on a point-to-point basis, this setting is not really required, but it is used as a default. The control field has a default value of hex 03 (00000011), which denotes an unnumbered frame. This means that PPP does not use the HDLC sequence numbering for reliable transmission as a default. The Protocol field contains a 2-byte value, which specifies the higher-layer protocol being transported, such as hex 0021 for the Internet Protocol (IP) and hex CO21 for the Link Control Protocol (LCP). The Information field carries the original frame, such as an IP datagram, and has a default maximum length of 1500 bytes. The Frame Check Sequence (FCS) field contains a checksum for error-detection purposes.

The Link Control Protocol (LCP) operates above the HDLC protocol and provides procedures for establishing, configuring, testing, and terminating the operation of a data-link connection. LCP performs authentication using either the Challenge-Handshake Authentication Protocol (CHAP) or the Password Authentication Protocol (PAP).

Above the LCP is the Network Control Protocol (NCP). In actuality, there is a series of NCPs, each independently defined in a separate RFC that describes the procedures for establishing, configuring, and terminating different network protocols, such as IP, IPX, and DECnet via PPP. Figure 12.15 shows the PPP stack. Note that the Network Control Protocol, as previously discussed, represents a family of protocols, with each NCP defined in a separate RFC that denotes the use of the protocol to transmit different network-layer protocols.

Now that you have a basic understanding of IP, TCP, UDP, and two serial protocols, you're ready to look at a few of the applications that use the TCP/IP suite.

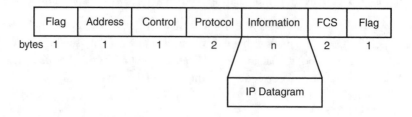

**FIGURE 12.15**

*The Point-to-Point Protocol stack.*

# The File Transfer Protocol

The *File Transfer Protocol (FTP)* was developed as a mechanism to facilitate the transfer of files between computers. As previously mentioned, FTP uses two well-known ports: port 21 for passing control information and port 20 for the actual data transfer.

FTP supports approximately 20 commands. Those commands enable a user to change directories (cd), obtain a directory list (`dir`), initiate a file transfer (`get`), and transfer a file (`put`). FTP permits multiple file transfers with the `mget` and `mput` commands when used with a filename containing one or more wildcard characters. For example, the command `mget *.gif` would transfer all files in the current directory that have the extension .gif.

One of the key advantages associated with the use of FTP is that various implementations exist that operate on a range of computers, from DOS PCs to IBM mainframes. This enables FTP to provide a mechanism for exchanging files between computers as long as both computers support FTP and can be reached via a TCP/IP connection. Concerning the TCP/IP connection, FTP relies on TCP at the transport layer to provide a reliable transmission path, ensuring the error-free arrival of data at its destination.

Table 12.5 lists 10 commonly used FTP commands. Because FTP was originally developed as a command-driven application, users had to remember command names and any associated parameter values to effectively use the application.

**TABLE 12.5** Common FTP Commands

| Command | Operation |
|---------|-----------|
| ASCII | Perform data transfer using ASCII format (default) |
| binary | Perform data transfer treating data as binary |
| bye | Terminate the FTP session with the remote server and exit the client FTP program |
| cd | Change the working directory on the remote server |
| delete | Delete a file on the remote server |
| dir | List the contents of the current directory on the remote server |
| get | Retrieve a specified file from the remote computer and store it on the local computer |
| mget | Retrieve multiple files from a remote computer and store them on the local computer |
| mput | Transfer multiple files from the local computer to the remote computer |
| put | Transfer a specified file from the local computer to the remote computer |

To facilitate the use of FTP, programs were developed that hide the necessity to know FTP commands through the use of a graphical user interface. Figure 12.16 shows the NetManage Chameleon.

This FTP client program can be used to establish a connection to a remote host. Note that the host address, which was entered as `ftp.mcom.com`, will be converted to a dotted decimal address by the domain name server on the network. Also note that the username was entered as anonymous. Many FTP servers are configured to accept public access. To facilitate such access, a user account named anonymous is established on the server.

Although many servers with an anonymous or a "guest" account do not require a user to enter a password, other servers might request that a user enter his email address. To provide a level of security and prevent the potential distribution of viruses, many organizations that operate anonymous FTP guest accounts restrict data transfer and prohibit public users from download- ing files onto the server.

Take a minute to examine the background of Figure 12.16. Notice that the screen is subdivided into three sections labeled Local, Transfer, and Remote. The Local section displays the direc- tory structure and the files in each directory on the local or client computer. The Transfer sec- tion includes a series of buttons that enable you to perform predefined operations by simply clicking a button. At the top of the Transfer section are two buttons associated with the method of file transfer; the button associated with Binary is shown selected. Thus, clicking either but- ton is the equivalent of entering an ASCII or a binary FTP command. The two columns of but- tons in the Transfer section are used to perform predefined operations on the local host (button arrow pointing left) or remote host (button arrow pointing right), and the capability to perform an operation is indicated by the highlighting of the button.

The screen shown in Figure 12.16 was printed during the process of establishing a connection to a remote computer. Thus, no operation in the Transfer section could be performed with respect to the remote computer, and none of the buttons in the right column of the Transfer section was highlighted.

However, after a connection to the remote host is established, all the buttons in the Transfer section are highlighted. This is illustrated in Figure 12.17, which shows the screen as it appeared after a connection was established to a Netscape Corporation FTP site and the beta 2.01 version of the well-known browser was selected. Note that by simply entering a filename in the local directory section of the screen and clicking the left-arrow button associated with Copy, you can initiate a file transfer from the remote to the local computer. No muss, no fuss, and no need to remember FTP commands, which is a key attribute associated with the use of different GUI TCP/IP–based application programs.

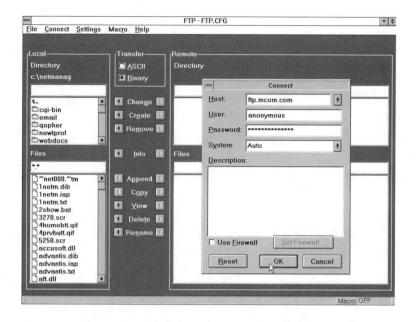

**FIGURE 12.16**

*Using the NetManage Chameleon FTP client program to initiate a connection to an FTP server.*

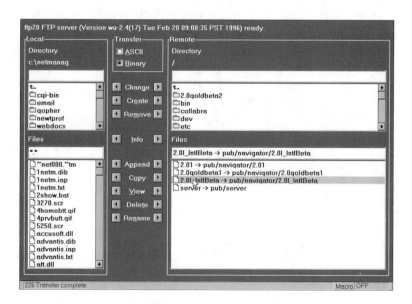

**FIGURE 12.17**

*Selecting a file on the remote FTP server.*

# Telnet

Telnet is an interactive remote access terminal protocol that was developed to enable users to access a remote computer as if they were directly connected to the computer. Similar to FTP, Telnet is based on a client/server model. Although Telnet was developed to provide terminal connectivity to hosts, the client does not have to be a physical terminal, such as one of the popular Digital Equipment Corporation's VT products. Instead, Telnet client programs have been developed that turn PCs, Macintoshes, and even various IBM, Sun, and HP workstations into interactive terminals.

As previously indicated in Table 12.3, Telnet uses a common TCP connection to transmit both data and control information, with the data flow on well-known port number 23. Similar to other TCP/IP applications, software developers over the past few years concentrated their development efforts on GUI-based applications to include Telnet.

Figure 12.18 shows the NetManage Chameleon Telnet Connection Dialog box that is displayed when you select the program's Connect, Connect menu option. Note that you must specify a host address, the type of terminal to emulate, and a port number when using the NetManage Telnet program. Concerning the port number, although 23 is the default port used for Telnet communications, some organizations select another port number. Often, a much higher port number is selected to "hide" the presence of a Telnet server from curious wanderers of the Internet.

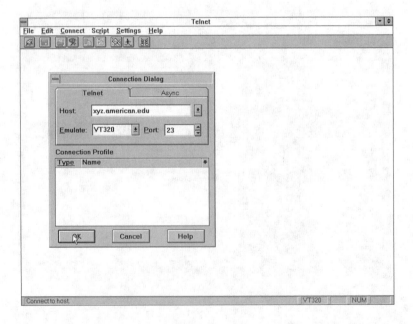

**FIGURE 12.18**

*Using the NetManage Telnet program to initiate a connection to a remote host computer.*

For readers that consider new software to be better than older products, Figure 12.19 shows the Telnet client implemented under Windows 2000. As you may note if you remember the good old days of DOS, Telnet represents a command-line version of the program. After you select Start, Run and enter the command `Telnet`, a window similar to Figure 12.19 is displayed, requiring you to enter the applicable command to open a connection to the desired host.

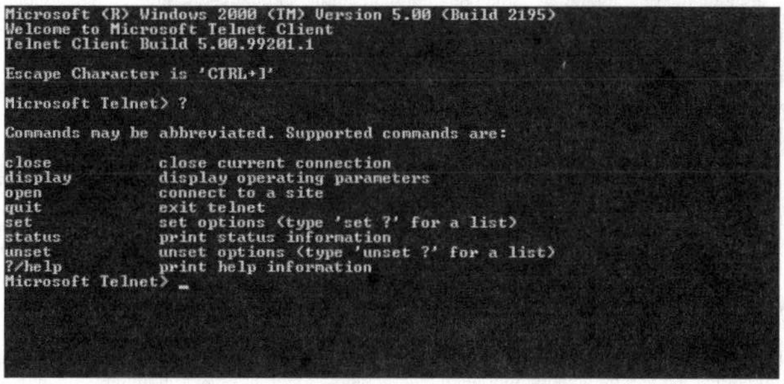

**FIGURE 12.19**
*Under Windows 2000 the Telnet client represents a command line program.*

## TN3270

In addition to Telnet, another popular remote terminal program is TN3270. This program was designed to work with the screen control codes used by IBM 3270–type terminals. It enables client computers using TN3270 to access IBM mainframes.

### The Hypertext Transfer Protocol

Perhaps the most popular Internet TCP/IP application is the *Hypertext Transfer Protocol (HTTP)*, which is used to convey information between a Web browser and a Web server. Here the term *browser* represents a software product that uses HTTP to transport information and supports the display of information encoded using the *Hypertext Markup Language (HTML)*.

## Navigating the Growing Web

The growth in the use of the Internet can be greatly attributed to the growth of the World Wide Web, the unstructured collection of Web servers containing text, graphics, and audio files whose contents can be viewed and heard through the use of a browser.

Figure 12.20 shows the popular Netscape browser displaying the Netscape Corporation (now a subsidiary of AOL) home page. The address of the page that's displayed is shown in the box to the right of the term Location, and it represents a file address encoded as a uniform resource locator (URL). URLs provide a mechanism to initiate an FTP or a TELNET session, as well as to access and view predefined files through the use of a browser.

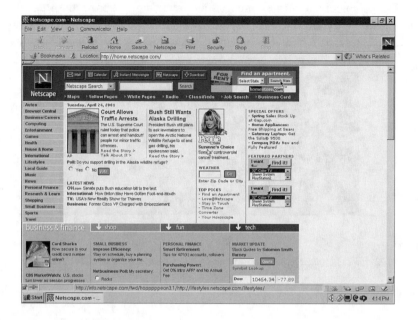

**FIGURE 12.20**

*The Netscape Corporation home page.*

In Web terminology, the file being viewed is referred to as a page. This particular page is the first page displayed when a browser accesses the top-level file on a Web server; thus, it is referred to as a home page.

Web pages can have embedded links to other pages, which are known as hyperlinks. Although the actual addresses of those links are hidden from view, the presence of a link is typically indicated by underlined text in the viewing area of the browser. In the example in Figure 12.20, note that the cursor, which is displayed as an arrow, is positioned over the highlighted text "Suzanne's choice." When you click on that hyperlink, the browser uses the address associated with the link to display a new page of information. You can see the URL associated with a hyperlink by moving the cursor over the link and viewing the browser's status bar at the bottom of the display. In the example shown in Figure 12.20, note that the following URL is associated with the previously mentioned hyperlink:

```
info.netscape.com/fwd/hoppppoon31/http://lifestyles.netscape.com/lifestyles/
```

The growth in the connection of Web servers to the Internet has been nothing short of phenomenal over the past few years. By late 2001, the number of servers connected to the Internet exceeded several hundred million, enabling persons to retrieve information about Olympic events, view the latest in automobile designs, and search for jobs, as well as order various products from online catalogs accessible through the use of a browser.

One of the key problems associated with the use of the World Wide Web is the effort involved in locating appropriate information. With more than several million Web servers, each of which has a distinct URL address, where does one search?

To facilitate the location of information, many companies have set up search sites. Those sites consist of large databases with search engine software that helps users locate information stored in the database. To construct the database, the search site typically uses "software robots" that search potential server addresses and index the contents of Web pages, page titles, or categories of information on Web pages. Figure 12.21 shows the Yahoo! search guide being used to locate information about Fast Ethernet.

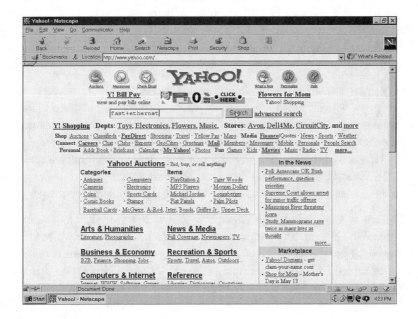

**FIGURE 12.21**

*Initiating a Yahoo! based search of the World Wide Web for information about Fast Ethernet.*

Although the retrieval of Web server–based information is normally free of cost, a token-based technology representing digital cash is being developed with which Web users could eventually have to pay for the information. Whether or not digital cash will be successfully implemented, and what its potential effect could be on the use of the Web, remain to be determined. In the interim, the use of the Web and the attachment of servers by businesses, government agencies, and educational institutions continues to grow very rapidly.

# Evolving Internet Applications

As the use of the Internet evolved, so did many applications designed for use on this literal mother of all networks. Two of the more prominent evolving applications that warrant discussion are voice transmitted over the Internet, which is referred to as VoIP because it uses the Internet Protocol as the network layer, and virtual private networks (VPNs).

# Voice over IP

Voice over IP, which is also referred to as Internet telephony, dates back to 1996, when software was developed that, in conjunction with a microphone, a sound card, and a pair of speakers, turned a personal computer into a digital telephone. The software digitizes voice spoken into the microphone at a low data rate using a hybrid coding technique. That technique combines the sampling of speech and the use of speech components, such as pitch, inflection, and speech energy, instead of the actual voice for encoding. By encoding the actual speech, it became possible to digitize voice at data rates as low as 4800bps.

Although early Internet telephone software required subscribers to first connect to a server to access another party, which limited talking to PC-to-PC communications, before long voice gateways were developed that connect the Internet to the public switched telephone network (PSTN). The use of gateways enabled PC users to originate calls from their computer that could literally be received by hundreds of millions of standard telephones connected to the PSTN. By 2001, several companies that operated online messenger services, such as MSN Messenger, Yahoo! Messenger, and AOL's ICQ, had added a "call" facility to their products.

Figure 12.22 illustrates the use of MSN Messenger to initiate a voice call to California from this author's home in Georgia. The left portion of Figure 12.22 shows the MSN Messenger Service dialog box. Note the icon labeled Call in the upper right area of the dialog box. Clicking on the Call icon results in the display of the MSN Messenger Phone dialog box shown in the right portion of Figure 12.22. At the time that this screen was captured, the 415 area code, which represents the San Francisco Bay Area, had been entered and was in the process of clicking on the digit 5. Because America Online (AOL), Yahoo!, and other companies have begun to offer no-cost voice calls within the United States, it is quite possible that the use of long-distance calling as we know it will significantly change. In fact, when this book was revised, AT&T was in the process of separating itself from its long-distance consumer business. After all, it is hard to compete with free long distance.

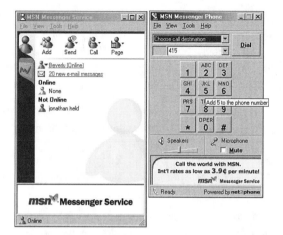

**FIGURE 12.22**

*Using the calling capability of MSN Messenger to initiate a call of the Internet.*

Although calling via MSN Messenger, Yahoo!, or another service is free, it does not presently provide the voice quality of calls made over the PSTN. The key reason for the lack of quality is the delays that packets containing digitized voice encounter as they are routed through the Internet. These delays, cumulatively referred to as latency, results in packets being displaced by time from one another. A second problem is the manner in which the Internet operates. When a router is congested, it may discard datagrams. Although dropping one datagram containing 20ms of digitized voice may not be noticed by the other party to a conversation, when a series of datagrams is dropped, the other party hears a gap of silence, making the conversation sound awkward. Although there is still work to be done to make Internet telephony into a quality product as the infrastructure of the Internet adds transmission capacity in the form of enhanced use of optical fiber, we can expect calling to become more popular. The demise of conventional long distance calling may be premature, but the handwriting is on the wall. For detailed information covering the transmission of Voice over IP, readers are referred to the book *Internetworking Voice and Data,* Third Edition, published by McGraw Hill in 2001, written by this author.

# Virtual Private Networking

A *virtual private network (VPN)* represents the routing of data through a mesh-structured network from one organizational location to another where the path taken between locations can vary. Although we normally associated a VPN with the Internet, VPNs can occur over any mesh-structured network to include a Frame Relay network and even the older X.25 packet network. The key attraction of a VPN over the Internet is one of economics.

Figure 12.23 compares the use of a private network consisting of two leased lines to intercon-nect three locations with the use of the Internet. Let's assume that each leased line operates at the T1 operating rate of 1.544Mbps. Although the monthly cost of a T1 line can vary by com-munications carrier and locations served, let's assume a cost of $4 per circuit mile per month. Let's also assume that T1 access to the Internet costs $1,000 per month.

For the first economic scenario, let's assume that locations B and C are 100 miles from loca-tion A, resulting in 200 circuit miles of T1 lines required to interconnect the three locations. Then the monthly cost of installing T1 lines to interconnect the three locations becomes $4 per mile/month × 200 miles, or $800 per month. In this situation, the cost of a private network is considerably less than the cost of using the Internet: The latter would cost $1,000 per month per location, or a total of $3,000 per month for the three locations to use the Internet to com-municate with one another. For a second economic scenario, let's assume that locations B and C are now each 1000 miles from location A. We would now require 2000 miles of T1 circuits at a cost of $4 per mile per month, for a total of $8,000 per month. However, the cost of Internet access would remain fixed at $3,000 per month, providing a potential savings of $5,000 per month.

Another advantage of VPNs is the fact that each location requires only one connection to the Internet. For the example shown in Figure 12.23, if the simple leased-line network uses routers, those routers would require four ports cumulatively to interconnect three locations. In compari-son, forming a VPN via the Internet requires only one port on each router at each location.

A third advantage associated with VPNs is the capability to take advantage of the structure of a mesh network. If one or more circuits linking routers or a router in the Internet becomes inop-erative, it is quite possible for your VPN traffic to be transparently rerouted. In comparison, to obtain a rerouting capability, your organization would have to construct a mesh-structured net-work that would add to its cost of operation.

Although cost, equipment configuration, and reliability are key advantages associated with the creation of a VPN, they are not problem-free. Three of the key problems associated with VPNs created over the Internet include throughput, reliability, and security.

When you use the Internet, your transmission competes with thousands to millions of other people for bandwidth. This means that when routers become saturated, they drop datagrams. Thus, your organization may not achieve a desired level of throughput and can be at the mercy of the transmission of other Internet users, as well as the state of the capacity of transmission lines and performance level of routers installed by different Internet service providers. Bandwidth constraints and reliability issues are important considerations, but for most organi-zations, a far more important consideration is security. When you connect an internal network to the Internet, it becomes a potential target for unscrupulous people that become aware of your presence on the Net. Some hackers simply take delight in breaking into Web servers and defacing the home page of an organization. Other hackers have broken into computer systems and accessed and manipulated databases that resulted in serious harm to organizations. Recognizing the potential threat to computational equipment when a network is connected to the Internet resulted in the development of a significant number of security-related products. Those products include authentication tokens that enable the verification of the identity of a remote person, virus scanners that check email, router access lists that are used to filter datagrams, and firewalls that provide organizations with the capability to develop a comprehensive security policy. That policy can include the encryption of datagrams flowing between organizational locations while other datagrams are passed in the clear. Chapter 16, "Network Security," discusses the role of hardware and software used for network security.

a. Using leased lines to interconnect three connections

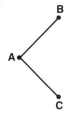

b. Using the Internet to form a VPN

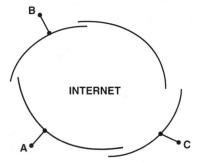

**FIGURE 12.23**
*VPN economics.*

# What You Have Learned

- TCP is a transport-layer protocol that provides end-to-end reliable transmission; IP is a connectionless-mode network-layer protocol designed to route messages between networks.

- Two key factors for the growth of the Internet are the fact that TCP/IP is in the public domain and its capability to be used on both LANs and WANs.

- Most individuals access the Internet via dial-up communications to an Internet access provider, whereas most businesses connect workstations on their LANs via the use of leased lines connecting their offices to an Internet access provider.

- An IP address is 32 bits long and can be expressed as four decimal numbers separated by dots, or by several names or mnemonics separated by dots.

- Subnetting and the subnet mask make it possible for one IP network address to be shared among two or more networks.

- The Domain Name Service is an application that is responsible for converting registered names used to represent Internet addresses into IP addresses.

- When an organization registers its name with the ICANN, it is assigned to one of six domains or a national domain.

- ICMP is used to communicate error messages and status information.

- The process of translating the logical IP address into a physical hardware address is referred to as address resolution; the reverse process is known as reverse address resolution.

- UDP is a connectionless transport-layer protocol that uses a best-effort approach to transmitting data without requiring handshaking between stations.

- TCP uses port numbers in its header to enable multiple application processes to be intermixed within a data stream.

- A TCP/IP application requires three addresses: a port address, an IP address, and a hardware address.

- The altering of TCP Window field value provides a "sliding window" that can be used to control the flow of information between source and destination.

- Popular Internet applications built on the use of TCP/IP include the File Transfer Protocol, Telnet, and the Hypertext Transfer Protocol (HTTP).

- The Point-to-Point Protocol (PPP) supports the transmission of different network-layer protocols to include IP over a serial communications link.

- A large number of graphical user interface–based TCP/IP applications have been developed to hide the complexities of command-based operations.

# Quiz for Chapter 12

1. What is ARPANET?

    A. Ralph Kramden's collection of networks

    B. A network funded by DARPA

    C. The transport-layer protocol

    D. A connectionless protocol network

2. Which of the following is a TCP/IP suite connectionless-mode Layer 4 transport protocol?

    A. TCP

    B. UDP

    C. IP

    D. SNMP

3. TCP/IP

    A. Is restricted to use on LANs.

    B. Operates only on IBM PCs.

    C. Is in the public domain.

    D. Was developed by Dr. Ethernet.

4. What authority is responsible for assigning the network portion of an IP address?

    A. NetCen

    B. Network Center

    C. Nicnet

    D. ICANN

5. Who is usually responsible for the assignment of the host portion of an IP address?

    A. The TCP/IP coordinator

    B. ICANN

    C. The local network manager or administrator

    D. The database administrator

6. The largest range of addresses available for assignment to a host computer is obtained by which of the following?

    A. A Class A address

    B. A Class B address

    C. A Class C address

    D. A Class D address

7. The network 198.78.41.0 is a

    A. Class A network.

    B. Class B network.

    C. Class C network.

    D. Class D network.

8. The subnet mask 255.255.255.192

    A. Extends the network portion to 16 bits.

    B. Extends the network portion to 26 bits.

    C. Extends the network portion to 36 bits.

    D. Has no effect on the network portion of an IP address.

9. The address `ftp.moscow.edu` more than likely is

    A. Located in Russia.

    B. An FTP server.

    C. A military organization.

    D. James Bond's mail drop.

10. The routing of datagrams

    A. Must follow a fixed path.

    B. Occurs on a virtual circuit.

    C. Can occur over different paths.

    D. Occurs exponentially.

11. The flow of datagrams is efficient due to

    A. Lack of a need for call setup procedures.

    B. Use of a virtual circuit.

    C. Exponential data flow.

    D. Use of IP.

12. On a LAN, where are IP datagrams transported?

    A. In the LAN header

    B. In the Application field

    C. In the Information field of the LAN frame

    D. After the TCP header

13. What is the maximum length of an IP datagram?

    A. 16 bits

    B. 32 bits

    C. 65,535 octets

    D. 32 octets

14. Which field in the IP header prevents datagrams from continuously wandering through the Internet?

    A. The Flags field

    B. The Protocol field

    C. The Time to Live field

    D. The Source Address field

15. The Address Resolution Protocol

    A. Translates a physical address into a hardware address.

    B. Translates an IP address into a logical address.

    C. Translates a hardware address into a physical address.

    D. Translates an IP address into a hardware address.

16. Which port is used by a Telnet communications session?

    A. 21

    B. 23

    C. 25

    D. 27

17. The receipt of an Acknowledgment Number field value of 27 indicates that

    A. The destination expects to receive 27 more segments.

    B. The destination expects to receive segment 27 next.

    C. The source expects to receive 27 more segments.

    D. Both the source and the destination expect to receive 27 more segments.

18. The TCP sliding window

    A. Can be used to control the flow of information.

    B. Always occurs when the field value is 0.

    C. Always occurs when the field value is 1.

    D. Occurs horizontally.

**12**

THE INTERNET

19. A key advantage of using a GUI-based TCP/IP application is that it

    A. Glues the application to an HP address.

    B. Hides the complexity of commands.

    C. Allows file transfers.

    D. Initiates server protection.

20. What is TN3270?

    A. A terminal emulator designed for asynchronous applications

    B. An FTP file-transfer method

    C. A terminal emulator developed in 1958

    D. A terminal emulator for accessing IBM mainframes

21. The ICMP message "Destination Unreachable" is generated by which device?

    A. Router

    B. Server

    C. Workstation

    D. LAN adapter

22. The program that you would use to determine the round-trip delay between a workstation and a destination address is

    A. Tracert.

    B. Traceroute.

    C. Ping.

    D. POP.

23. The decrement of the IP Time to Live field in a datagram to a value of 2 means

    A. It is discarded.

    B. The datagram can flow through two more routers.

    C. The datagram can flow through one more router.

    D. The datagram does not pass go and does not collect $200.

24. The first page displayed when a browser initially accesses a Web server's top-level file is known as

    A. The master page.

    B. The top page.

    C. The browser page.

    D. The home page.

25. What is a VPN?

    A. A Web browser

    B. A TCP/IP protocol

    C. A temporary path through a mesh-structured network

    D. A network-layer protocol

# ISDN

## IN THIS CHAPTER

ISDN, which is the acronym for Integrated Services Digital Network, augurs the potential for the development of a universal digital network that provides integrated voice and data on common telephone company facilities. In this chapter, we will examine the idea behind ISDN, its architecture, and some of the benefits that can be expected from its use.

# The Road to ISDN

The need to transmit human speech resulted in the development of a telephone system that was originally designed for the transmission of analog data. Although the telephone system satisfied the basic need to transmit human speech, its design required the conversion of digital signals produced by computers and terminals into an analog format for the transmission of digital data. This conversion was awkward and expensive because modems at both ends of a telephone channel were required to do the digital-to-analog and analog-to-digital conversions.

A rapid decrease in the cost of semiconductors and the evolution in digital signal processing resulted in the application of digital technology to the telephone network. In the 1960s, telephone companies began to replace the electromechanical switches located in their central offices with digital switches. By the early 1970s, several communications carriers were offering end-to-end transmission services. In these services, unipolar digital data from terminals and computers was converted first into a modified bipolar digital format. Then, through a series of digital repeaters in the network, the data was transmitted to its destination. At its destination, data was converted back to its original unipolar digital format. The unipolar-to-bipolar signal conversion enabled the telephone company to space repeaters farther apart, reducing the construction cost of the digital network. Figure 13.1 illustrates the use of amplifiers and repeaters on analog and digital circuits.

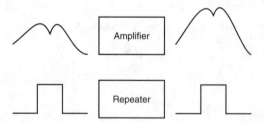

**FIGURE 13.1**
*Amplifiers versus repeaters.*

The amplifier used on analog circuits amplifies the entire signal, including any signal impairments such as noise. The digital repeater, also known as a *data regenerator*, regenerates a new digital pulse, eliminating any distortion to the pulse that occurs as it travels on a digital circuit.

Because analog amplifiers increase the size of an analog signal including any previous distortion, whereas digital repeaters regenerate a pure digital pulse and eliminate any previous distortion to the digital signal, the error rate on a digital network is significantly lower than that on an analog facility. In addition, the devices required to perform the unipolar-to-bipolar and bipolar-to-unipolar signal conversion are much less expensive than the modems required for signal conversion on analog facilities.

By the mid-1980s, most telephone companies had incorporated a large amount of digital technology into their plant facilities so that a significant portion of the lines connecting telephone company central offices transported speech in digital form, although speech continued to be carried in analog form from the subscriber to the central office via the local loop, also referred to as the subscriber line. At the central office, speech is digitized for transmission over the backbone network of the telephone system. Similarly, at the central office closest to the destination of the telephone conversation, the digitized speech is reconverted into its analog format and then transmitted to the receiver telephone.

The progression of telephone systems in the use of digital technology forms the basis for ISDN. Thus, ISDN can be viewed as an evolutionary progression in the conversion of the analog telephone system into an eventual all-digital network, enabling both voice and data to be transported end-to-end in a digital format.

Besides integrating voice and data, ISDN provides a level of communications capability above that obtainable with conventional analog technology. When voice and data are integrated, subscribers are able to talk on the telephone and use a computer or terminal at the same time over a regular telephone line. For business, this capability improves the productivity of office workers and reduces the cost of wiring buildings and offices because there should be no need to install separate wires to each desk for voice and data. Thus, ISDN offers subscribers a level of efficiency beyond that obtainable with conventional facilities.

For individual subscribers, ISDN can result in the offering of a series of new functions accessible to their homes over existing telephone wire. Electronic meter reading, slow scan video, Internet access for surfing the World Wide Web and transmitting and receiving electronic mail, and other applications are either offered or can be expected to be offered to individual subscribers and businesses.

# ISDN Architecture

Two methods of access to ISDN have been defined: Basic access and Primary access. ISDN Basic access deals with the connection and operation of individual telephone instruments and terminals to the digital network. Primary access governs the method by which many Basic access subscribers can be connected to the network over a common line facility.

# ISDN Basic Access

Basic access defines a multiple channel connection that is derived by the time division multiplexing of data on twisted-pair wiring. This multiple channel connection links an end-user terminal device directly to a telephone company office or to a local private automated branch exchange (PABX). Figure 13.2 shows the channel format of the ISDN Basic access method.

As you can see in Figure 13.2, Basic access consists of two bearer (B) channels and a data (D) channel. Thus, another term used to reference an ISDN Basic access line is a 2B+D line. The three channels are multiplexed by time onto a common twisted-pair wiring media. Each bearer channel can carry one digitized voice conversation or data stream at a transmission rate of 64Kbps. Digitized voice in ISDN is encoded by sampling voice signals 8,000 times per second and encoding each sample in 8 bits, which results in a 64Kbps data rate. The inclusion of two bearer channels enables Basic access to provide the subscriber with the ability to transmit data and conduct a voice conversation on one telephone line simultaneously or to be in conversation with one person and receive a second telephone call. In the latter case, assuming that the subscriber has an appropriate telephone instrument, he or she could put one person on hold and answer the second call—all on one line! With analog technology, two physical lines would be required to accomplish this.

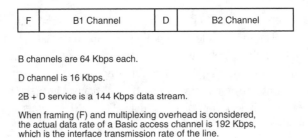

B channels are 64 Kbps each.

D channel is 16 Kbps.

2B + D service is a 144 Kbps data stream.

When framing (F) and multiplexing overhead is considered, the actual data rate of a Basic access channel is 192 Kbps, which is the interface transmission rate of the line.

**FIGURE 13.2**
*The ISDN Basic access channel format.*

In fact, a Basic access ISDN line can be used to connect up to eight different devices that can be independently accessed via one standard telephone circuit. Those devices could include separate telephones, fax machines, and computers. This expanded access is possible because the D channel is designed to control the B channels through the sharing of network signaling functions and for the transmission of packet switched data. However, only three devices can be accessed at a time because Basic access consists of three channels.

Figure 13.3 depicts the expanded capability ISDN Basic access offers over conventional telephone service. Figure 13.3a indicates how you might connect a telephone, fax machine, and computer modem to the public-switched telephone network via the installation of three separate telephone lines between your home or office and the telephone central office. Figure 13.3b shows the same equipment connected to a Basic access ISDN line, which, in effect, is one telephone line onto which digitized data is multiplexed. Note that although up to eight devices can share access to the same ISDN Basic access line, only two devices can simultaneously operate at 64Kbps because a Basic access line offers only two B channels. The capability to transmit packet-switched data enables the D channel to be used to support such applications as the monitoring of a home alarm system and reading utility meters on demand.

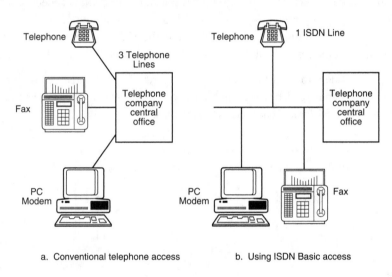

a. Conventional telephone access          b. Using ISDN Basic access

**FIGURE 13.3**

*ISDN Basic access versus conventional telephone access.*

## ISDN Primary Access

Primary access is a multiplexing arrangement whereby a grouping of Basic access users shares a common line facility. Primary access is designed to directly connect a PABX or high-speed networking devices, such as inverse multiplexers (described later in this chapter), to the ISDN network. This access method eliminates the need to provide individual Basic access lines when a group of terminal devices shares a common PABX that could be connected directly to an ISDN network via a single high-speed line. Because of the different methods used to multiplex digitized voice conversations between telephone company offices in North America and Europe, two Primary access standards have been developed.

In North America, Primary access consists of a grouping of 23 B channels and 1 D channel to provide a 1.544Mbps composite data rate. This data rate is more commonly known as the standard T1 carrier data rate, which is described in Chapter 6, "Multiplexing Techniques." The D channel in Primary access, and each B channel, operates at 64Kbps. Multiply 24 channels by 64Kbps, and you get a data rate of 1.536Mbps, which is precisely 8Kbps fewer than the T1 carrier's 1.544Mbps data rate.

A North American T1 carrier consists of 24 digitized voice channels. Each voice channel is sampled 8,000 times per second, and 8 bits are used to encode the digitized value of each sample. Thus, a 64Kbps data rate is required to transmit a digitized voice conversation. To permit synchronization of the T1 signal, a single bit, known as a *framing bit*, is added to the data stream. The framing bit represents 24 channels, as illustrated in Figure 13.4. Therefore, one sample of 24 channels of digitized voice is represented by 193 bits. Because the sampling occurs 8,000 times per second, the data rate of a T1 carrier is 19×8,000, or 1.544Mbps.

In Europe, the equivalent to the T1 carrier is the E1 carrier. The E1 carrier consists of 30 digitized voice channels and 2 separate signaling channels. Because each channel operates at 64Kbps, the resulting E1 carrier data rate is 2.048Mbps.

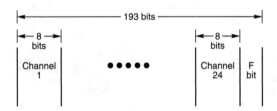

**FIGURE 13.4**
*The T1 frame.*

# ISDN Implementation Standards

ISDN implementation standards address the lower three layers of the OSI reference model described in Chapter 10, "WAN Architectures and Packet Networks." The ITU-T defined a series of standards that govern both basic and primary rate physical layer interfaces, as well as the D channel link layer and call setup procedures over the D channel that take place at the network layer level of the OSI reference model. Figure 13.5 shows the relationship of ISDN implementation standards to the OSI reference model. As indicated in Figure 13.5, two sets of standards, I and Q, govern the implementation of ISDN. The I standards govern the physical connection of ISDN-compatible equipment to ISDN circuits, and the Q standards govern the transmission of D channel setup data and information.

The Q.921 standard defines the frame structure for transmitting information on the D channel, as well as the contents of the fields of the frame. The Q.931 standard defines the call control procedures used for call setup and teardown, the message structure used to carry call procedure information, and the types of messages that can be transported at the network layer. If you want more specific information concerning call establishment procedures and data formats on the D channel, as well as on how the framing format is used to transport information on that channel, refer to ITU-T ISDN Q-series standards. ITU-T standards can be purchased from the ITU.

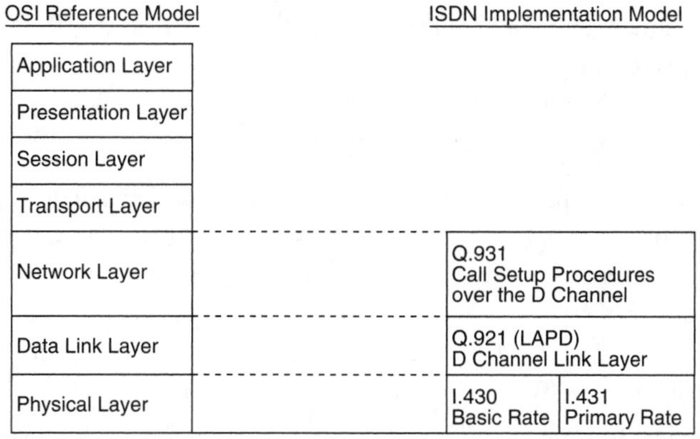

| OSI Reference Model | ISDN Implementation Model | |
|---|---|---|
| Application Layer | | |
| Presentation Layer | | |
| Session Layer | | |
| Transport Layer | | |
| Network Layer | Q.931 Call Setup Procedures over the D Channel | |
| Data Link Layer | Q.921 (LAPD) D Channel Link Layer | |
| Physical Layer | I.430 Basic Rate | I.431 Primary Rate |

**FIGURE 13.5**
*The relationship of ISDN to the OSI reference model.*

**13**

ISDN

# Network Characteristics

The following list outlines the primary characteristics of an ISDN network, which form the basis of businesses' and telephone companies' desire for the development of this new network:

- ISDN integrates voice, data, and video services.
- ISDN has a digital end-to-end connection that provides a high transmission quality.
- ISDN has improved and expanded services because of B and D channel data rates.
- ISDN is more efficient and productive.
- ISDN offers advances in device connectivity.

The digital nature of ISDN integrates voice, data, and video services, eliminating the need for subscribers to get separate facilities for each service. Because an ISDN network is designed to provide end-to-end digital transmission, pulses can be regenerated easily throughout the network, which means new pulses can be generated to replace distorted ones.

In comparison, analog transmission facilities use amplifiers to boost the strength of transmission signals, but they also increase any impairments in the analog signal. Because regeneration is superior to amplification, digital transmission has a lower error rate and provides a higher transmission signal quality than an equivalent analog transmission facility.

Basic access provides three signal paths on a common line, and ISDN, too, offers subscribers the potential for improvements and expansion to existing services. For existing services, current analog telephone-line bandwidth limitations preclude data transmission rates of more than 56Kbps downstream and, more commonly, a two-way rate of 33.6Kbps from occurring on the switched telephone network. In comparison, under ISDN, each B channel can support a 64Kbps transmission rate, and the D channel can operate at 16Kbps. In fact, if both B channels and the D channel were in simultaneous operation, a data rate of 144Kbps would be obtainable on a Basic access ISDN circuit, exceeding the current maximum analog circuit transmission rate by a factor of approximately three.

Because each Basic access channel consists of three multiplexed channels, different operations can occur simultaneously without requiring the subscriber to acquire separate multiplexing equipment. Thus, a subscriber could receive a call from one person, transmit data to a computer, and have a utility company read his or her electric meter all at the same time. With the ability to conduct as many as three simultaneous operations on one line, the subscriber gains efficiency and productivity. Efficiency should increase because one line now can support several simultaneous operations, and productivity can increase because of the ability to receive telephone calls and conduct a conversation while transmitting data.

Advances in device connectivity to the ISDN network occurred in two areas. At the physical interface, an eight-pin modular plug and jack provides a common interface that enables devices to be portable between jacks. This eliminates special cabling and, usually, additional telephone company installation charges for the movement of devices between offices. Digital telephones and other instruments can now be manufactured with an intelligent reporting capability. When a telephone is moved from one office to another, simply plugging it into a jack causes it to report its extension and location to a PBX. This enables employees who are moving within an organization to immediately receive telephone calls at their new locations without waiting for the company to reprogram the PBX.

## Telephone Equipment and Network Interface

A key element of ISDN is a small set of compatible multipurpose user-network interfaces developed to support a wide range of applications. These network interfaces are based on a series of reference points for different user terminal arrangements that define the interfaces. Figure 13.6 illustrates the relationship between ISDN reference points and network interfaces.

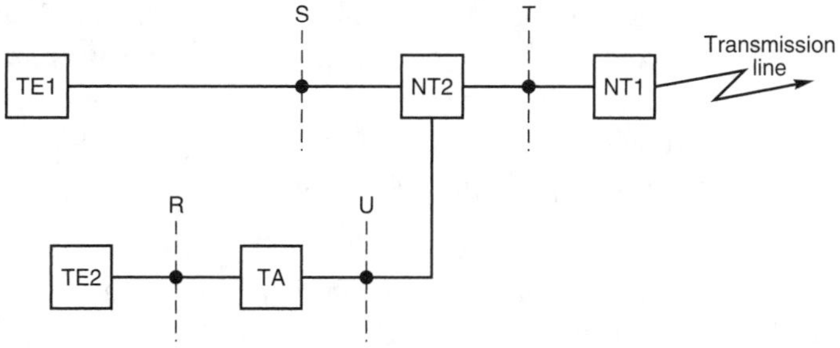

TE1   (Terminal Equipment 1) type devices comply with ISDN network interface.

TE2   (Terminal Equipment 2) type devices do not have an ISDN interface and must be connected through a TA (terminal adapter) functional grouping.

NT2   (Network Termination 2) includes switching and concentration equipment that performs functions equivalent to layers 1 through 3 of the OSI reference model.

NT1   (Network Termination 1) includes functions equivalent to layer 1 of the OSI reference model.

**FIGURE 13.6**

*ISDN reference points and network interfaces.*

The ISDN reference configuration consists of functional groupings and reference points at which physical interfaces can exist. The functional groupings are sets of functions that can be required at an interface, whereas reference points are employed to divide the functional groups into distinct entities.

The Terminal Equipment (TE) functional grouping is composed of TE1- and TE2-type equipment. Digital telephones, conventional data terminals, and integrated voice-data workstations are examples of TE equipment. TE1-type equipment complies with the ISDN user-network interface and permits such equipment to be connected directly to an ISDN "S" type interface that supports multiple B and D channels.

The TA (Terminal Adapter) plays a key role in the use of ISDN because it permits equipment with a non-ISDN interface to be connected into an ISDN network.

The NT2 (Network Termination 2) functional group includes devices that handle switching and data concentration functions equivalent to the first three layers of the OSI reference model. Typical NT2 equipment can include PABXs, LANs, terminal controllers, concentrators, and multiplexers.

The NT1 (Network Termination 1) functional group is the ISDN digital interface point. It is equivalent to layer 1 of the OSI reference model. Functions of NT1 include the physical and electrical termination of the loop, line monitoring, timing, and bit multiplexing. In Europe,

**13**

ISDN

where most communications carriers are government-owned monopolies, NT1 and NT2 functions can be combined into a common device, such as a PABX. In such situations, the equipment serves as an NT12 functional group. In comparison, in the United States, the communications carrier can provide only the NT1, whereas third-party equipment would connect to the communications carrier equipment at the T interface.

A word of warning is in order concerning the use of the NT1 interface in the United States. The Federal Communications Commission specified the implementation of ISDN in a manner that requires subscribers to supply the NT1 interface to which the line is connected. This specification causes the subscriber to be responsible for powering the NT1. This also means that if the NT1 loses power, the ISDN line will not be useable. In comparison, traditional analog telephone service requires only a telephone instrument as the terminating device, and the telephone instrument does not need an independent power source. This is because the telephone normally receives its power from the serving central office. That office typically has backup generators and batteries to enable phone service to continue during a power failure. This explains why your lights can go out during a storm and your pesky neighbor, Martha, can call you to ask if you have electricity! For this reason, many carriers recommend that ISDN should supplement and not serve as a replacement for analog telephone service.

The last interface that occurs at reference point U is a two-wire connection (Basic access) or four-wire connection (Primary access) between the customer premises (NT1) and the carrier's central office. From this reference point to the central office, data flows in a special compressed transmission format (2B1Q) in which two binary bits (2B) are encoded in one quaternary symbol (1Q). When transmission occurs in the 2B1Q format, up to four signal levels can occur, each of which defines the encoding of two bits of data. Table 13.1 indicates the relationships among the four allowed signaling states and the composition of the encoded pairs of bits. Figure 13.7 illustrates an example of 2B1Q coding (top) and the resulting relationship between the quaternary symbol and the encoded binary pairs.

**TABLE 13.1** The 2B1Q Relationship

| Quaternary Signal Level | Encoded Bit Values |
| --- | --- |
| −3 | 00 |
| −1 | 01 |
| +3 | 10 |
| +1 | 11 |

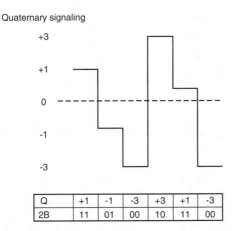

Quaternary signaling

| Q | +1 | -1 | -3 | +3 | +1 | -3 |
|---|----|----|----|----|----|----|
| 2B | 11 | 01 | 00 | 10 | 11 | 00 |

**FIGURE 13.7**

*A 2B1Q encoding example.*

Through the use of 2B1Q encoding, the Basic access 144Kbps data rate is achieved via a 4 kilobaud rate. This allows the large base of conventional copper pair wiring previously installed between customer premises and communications carrier central offices to be used to support ISDN transmission.

**13**

**ISDN**

> **NOTE**
>
> Refer to the ITU-T I recommendation series for detailed information about ISDN reference points and network interfaces.

With a set of standardized network interfaces, both pre- and post-ISDN terminals will be able to share the benefits of using ISDN. Pre-ISDN terminal devices will be connected to ISDN facilities by terminal adapters, which will convert the non-ISDN interface (R) into an ISDN interface (S).

# Growth and Adaptation of ISDN

During the late 1980s, a series of well-publicized field trials of ISDN were conducted in the United States and abroad. Although those trials proved the reliability of technology, it was not until the mid-1990s that ISDN began to acquire a degree of acceptance that could be equated to a few percent of the number of analog telephone lines installed in the United States. The delay in the acceptance of ISDN was based on various factors—of which, its availability was probably the major impediment to its use. In many cases, to display ISDN, telephone companies had to upgrade or replace older switches in their central offices. In fact, in the late 1980s and early 1990s, a map showing the availability of ISDN in the United States resembled a series of islands surrounding a few major metropolitan areas.

Gradually, over the years, ISDN deployment has been extended so that what appeared to be isolated islands on maps now appears as merged larger areas of availability. Although in late 2001 ISDN was still far from universally available, it was available in more than 90% of the United States.

Two additional problems that contributed to the slow acceptance of ISDN included problems associated with obtaining ISDN service and a lack of viable applications that could justify the use of this service. As you will learn shortly, both of those problems have, to a large degree, been rectified, resulting in a substantial increase in the installation of ISDN lines by the late-1990s.

## ISDN Service

Until recently, the actual installation of an ISDN line and connection of third-party vendor equipment to that line often resulted in the proverbial horror story. The horror story reflected hours or even days of trial-and-error settings and adjustments to make ISDN equipment work with telephone company lines. Until recently, all carriers issued their own Service Profile Identification (SPID) codes. The SPID represents a free-formatted numeric string between 3 and 20 characters in length. The subscriber is responsible for entering the assigned SPID into its ISDN terminal before the terminal can initialize at Layer 3. The SPID is transmitted to the serving telephone company switch and uniquely identifies the ISDN terminal at layer 3 of the D-channel signaling protocol. This code is also transferred between switches operated by different telephone companies to establish an ISDN call between subscribers of different communications carriers.

## Code Standards

A second significant ISDN problem involved the ordering of an ISDN line. Because of the lack of ISDN Order Code standards, users had to notify the carrier of the type of device they wanted to connect to an ISDN line, and the carrier had to make adjustments to its facilities to accommodate the equipment. With a lack of standards, it was often difficult for one carrier to correctly program the central office switch to support third-party ISDN hardware products and to coordinate an agreement for coding among carriers.

Recognizing the previously mentioned problems was far easier than fixing them. In February 1991, Bell Communications Research (Bellcore) issued a technical specification for what is referred to as *National ISDN* in an attempt to standardize services offered by the independent

Bell operating companies that were established by the breakup of AT&T. National ISDN-1 was finalized and adopted by the Bell operating companies during late 1996 and early 1997. Those companies, including Cincinnati Bell, GTE Corporation, and Southern New England Telephone Company, agreed to implement a uniform procedure to connect users' ISDN terminal equipment to their ISDN services. All those companies agreed to use the same SPID codes to connect ISDN terminal equipment to the ISDN switches. Under this agreement, SPID functionality moved from central office switches out to network switches by mid-1997, and SPID capability was totally automated by early 1998. This meant that the coding errors at the central office and between carrier switches that adversely affect interoperability were essentially relegated to the past. However, several inter-exchange carriers do not adhere exclusively to the National ISDN-1 specification, instead offering separate versions of what is generically referred to as *Custom ISDN*. This lingering compatibility problem was further alleviated with the appearance of National ISDN-2 and National ISDN-3 specifications that made slight changes to the manner by which ISDN operates.

## Ordering Codes

In addition to SPID standardization, National ISDN resulted in the development of ordering codes whose use greatly simplified ISDN ordering and line provisioning. To date, two types of ISDN Ordering Codes (IOCs) have been adopted by the Bell operating companies: generic IOCs and non-generic IOCs. Generic IOCs reflect a standard set of commonly used interface configurations for an ISDN Basic Rate Interface that is grouped into a series of 22 packages referred to as "Capability Package A through Capability Package V." Table 13.2 lists three examples of the 22 generic ordering codes.

In comparison to generic IOCs, non-generic IOCs are based on generic IOCs and represent tailored or customized versions. Equipment developers can register a non-generic IOC with Bellcore. For both generic and non-generic IOCs, industry-wide agreement on the functionality associated with a capability package or customized package simplifies the ISDN ordering and equipment provisioning process. Another benefit of standardization was the development of a common set of cause codes, which indicate the state of an ISDN call or call attempt.

## Cause Codes

Each ISDN call condition has an associated cause code. That code is a numerical message generated by telephone company switching equipment to the subscriber. The subscriber's ISDN adapter receives the cause codes and, depending on the software governing its operation, either displays the cause code and terminates its operation or performs another operation. Some ISDN adapter manuals might include an appendix listing cause codes and their meanings. Unfortunately, other manuals might not, which leaves some subscribers slightly puzzled when a message such as Cause Code 17 is displayed. To facilitate knowledge about ISDN call conditions, Table 13.3 lists currently defined cause codes and their meanings.

**TABLE 13.2** Examples of ISDN Generic Ordering Codes

| Ordering Code | Functional Description |
| --- | --- |
| Capability Package A | Basic D channel packet services. No voice capabilities are provided. |
| Capability Package B | Circuit-switched data on one B channel. No voice capabilities are provided, but basic voice capabilities are supported. |
| Capability Package N | Alternate voice/circuit-switched data on one B channel, circuit-switched data on a second B channel and D channel. Voice capabilities include three-way conferencing, call hold, call drop, and call transfer. |

**TABLE 13.3** ISDN Cause Codes

| Cause Class | Value | Number | Cause |
| --- | --- | --- | --- |
| 000 | 0001 | 1 | Unallocated (Unassigned number) |
| 000 | 0010 | 2 | No route to specified transit network |
| 000 | 0011 | 3 | No route to destination |
| 000 | 0110 | 6 | Channel unacceptable |
| 000 | 0111 | 7 | Call awarded and being delivered in an established channel |
| 001 | 0000 | 16 | Normal call clearing |
| 001 | 0001 | 17 | User busy |
| 001 | 0010 | 18 | No user responding |
| 001 | 0011 | 19 | No answer from user (user alerted) |
| 001 | 0101 | 21 | Call rejected |
| 001 | 0110 | 22 | Number changed |
| 001 | 1010 | 26 | Non-selected user clearing |
| 001 | 1011 | 27 | Destination out of order |
| 001 | 1100 | 28 | Invalid number format |
| 001 | 1101 | 29 | Facility rejected |
| 001 | 1110 | 30 | Response to status inquiry |
| 001 | 1111 | 31 | Normal, unspecified |
| 010 | 0010 | 34 | No circuit/channel available |
| 010 | 0110 | 38 | Network out of order |

**TABLE 13.3** continued

| Cause Class | Value | Number | Cause |
|---|---|---|---|
| 010 | 1001 | 41 | Temporary failure |
| 010 | 1010 | 42 | Switching equipment congestion |
| 010 | 1011 | 43 | Access information discarded |
| 010 | 1100 | 44 | Requested circuit/channel not available |
| 010 | 1101 | 45 | Preempted |
| 010 | 1111 | 47 | Resources unavailable, unspecified |
| 011 | 0001 | 49 | Quality of service unavailable |
| 011 | 0010 | 50 | Requested facility not subscribed |
| 011 | 0100 | 52 | Outgoing calls barred |
| 011 | 0010 | 54 | Incoming calls barred |
| 011 | 1001 | 57 | Bearer capability not authorized |
| 011 | 1010 | 58 | Bearer capability not presently available |
| 011 | 1111 | 63 | Service or option not available, unspecified |
| 100 | 0001 | 65 | Bearer capability not implemented |
| 100 | 0010 | 66 | Channel type not implemented |
| 100 | 0101 | 69 | Requested facility not implemented |
| 100 | 0110 | 70 | Only restricted digital information bearer capability is available |
| 100 | 1111 | 79 | Service or option not implemented, unspecified |
| 101 | 0001 | 81 | Invalid call reference value |
| 101 | 0010 | 82 | Identified channel does not exist |
| 101 | 0011 | 83 | A suspended call exists, but this call identity does not |
| 101 | 0100 | 84 | Call identity in use |
| 101 | 0101 | 85 | No call suspended |
| 101 | 0110 | 86 | Call having the requested call identity has been cleared |
| 101 | 1000 | 88 | Incompatible destination |
| 101 | 1011 | 91 | Invalid transit network selection |
| 101 | 1111 | 95 | Invalid message, unspecified |
| 110 | 0000 | 96 | Mandatory information element is missing |
| 110 | 0001 | 97 | Message type nonexistent or not implemented |
| 110 | 0010 | 98 | Message not compatible with call state or message type nonexistent or not implemented |

**TABLE 13.3** continued

| Cause Class | Value | Number | Cause |
| --- | --- | --- | --- |
| 110 | 0011 | 99 | Information element nonexistent or not implemented |
| 110 | 0100 | 100 | Invalid information element contents |
| 110 | 0101 | 101 | Message not compatible with call state |
| 110 | 0110 | 102 | Recovery on timer expiry |
| 110 | 1111 | 111 | Protocol error, unspecified |
| 1111 | 1111 | 127 | Interworking, unspecified |

## Pricing

When ISDN was first introduced, the cost of Basic access was, in many instances, relatively prohibitive in comparison to analog service. In addition to paying a monthly service charge that averaged $100, many subscribers were billed a usage charge of 6 cents/minute per B channel. If you surfed the Web for an hour at 128Kbps, you could incur a $7.20 usage charge, even if the call was local.

Recognizing that the disparity between ISDN and analog line pricing impeded residential acceptance of the technology, most carriers eliminated the per-minute local call charge by 1996. By 1998, the cost of residential ISDN service was approximately $30 per month to include 200 hours of free local calling.

## Applications

The growth in the use of video-conferencing, a substantial increase in the connectivity requirements for geographically separated LANs, and the literal explosion in the use of the Internet represent three key applications responsible for a significant increase in the use of ISDN.

Until the early 1990s, most video-conferencing systems were relatively expensive, requiring the use of 512Kbps or greater bandwidth, and were usually implemented on a point-to-point networking basis via the installation of T1 or fractional T1 leased lines. Although a company might use video-conferencing only an hour or two per day, it had to pay for the 24-hour-per-day use of the leased line. Recognizing this communications cost problem, as well as the requirement of many organizations to perform video-conferencing among many geographically separated locations, communications product manufacturers developed a product known as an *inverse multiplexer*, or a bandwidth-on-demand multiplexer.

The inverse multiplexer derives its name from the fact that it accepts high-speed input and subdivides the input into two or more output data streams. When the inverse multiplexer's output data streams are connected to an ISDN service, it becomes possible not only to perform video-conferencing on a dial-up basis, but also to adjust the bandwidth used for communications between two video-conferencing systems based on the bandwidth supported by each system and economics. For example, consider Figure 13.8, which illustrates the use of a video-conferencing system via an inverse multiplexer connected to an ISDN Primary Rate Interface (PRI) line operation.

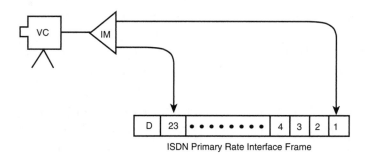

ISDN Primary Rate Interface Frame

Legend

VC    Video-conferencing system

IM    Inverse multiplexer

**FIGURE 13.8**

*Video-conferencing via an inverse multiplexer and ISDN.*

**13**

ISDN

Because an ISDN PRI line represents the multiplexing of 23 B channels and a D signaling channel, the inverse multiplexer could be used to support video-conferencing at data rates from 64Kbps using one B channel to 1.472Mbps using all 23 B channels. Due to advances in compression technology, most video-conferencing systems require the use of 4–6 B channels, in effect requiring four to six calls to be made via ISDN facilities from one video-conferencing location to another. Although carriers typically bill each call on a per-minute basis, it is often far more economical to pay for several switched dial-up ISDN hours per day than to install a high-speed digital leased line between locations. In addition, through the use of dial-up ISDN, each video-conferencing system in an organization can communicate with other systems by requiring the installation of a mesh structured series of leased lines to connect each system to every other system.

In a LAN connectivity environment, the traditional networking approach was to connect networks via the use of remote bridges or routers and increase the operating rate of the line when users complained about response time delays. Similar to the previously discussed video-conferencing application, inverse or bandwidth-on-demand multiplexers can be used either as a replacement or to supplement the use of leased lines. Concerning inverse multiplexers, if inter-LAN communications are infrequent, ISDN can be used periodically as a replacement for leased lines. One of the key attributes of ISDN is the fact that the time required to set up a call is relatively short in comparison to a call initiated over the analog switched telephone network. This means that transmission delays are more tolerable and do not adversely affect inter-LAN communications. Concerning the use of inverse multiplexers as a supplement to the use of leased lines, this method of communications is highly suitable when an increase in transmission requirements for short periods would otherwise require the installation of a higher-operating-rate and more-expensive leased line. Instead of incurring a higher monthly lease line cost when an increment of 64Kbps of bandwidth is required for only a small portion of the day, a subscriber could use an inverse multiplexer as an economical supplement to the use of a digital leased line.

A third application where ISDN provides a significant potential for benefiting subscribers results from a new feature introduced during 1998. Known as Always On/Dynamic ISDN (AO/DI), this version of ISDN continuously uses the 16Kbps D channel as a mechanism to transfer e-mail, stock quotes, and similar low-bandwidth requirement data transfers. If there is more data than the D channel is capable of handling, its signaling capability is then used to establish a circuit-switched call using one or both ISDN B channels. For example, an initial e-mail could flow over the D channel, which would then initiate a B channel connection to transfer a file containing a 5-Mbyte image attached to the e-mail.

The fourth major application that has significantly increased the use of ISDN is represented by the explosive growth in the graphics-based World Wide Web. The integration of digital voice, video clips, graphics, and text on Web pages forces Web servers to transmit hundreds of thousands to millions of bytes in response to a person clicking an icon on his browser's screen. Because analog modems are limited under the best of connections to a one-way data rate of 56Kbps, whereas ISDN access provides operating rates up to 128Kbps, the use of ISDN can provide a mechanism for viewing Web pages without irritating delays. Similar to the manner in which "plastics" was used as the all-encompassing word of the future in the popular 1960s movie *The Graduate*, ISDN was expected to be its replacement for the late 1990s.

Unfortunately for proponents of ISDN, competition in the form of digital subscriber lines and cable modems literally placed a damper on the growth of ISDN in the residential market. Instead, ISDN's growth is primarily in the business area, providing a mechanism for government, industry, and academia to obtain cost effective video conferencing and supplement the use of costly leased lines.

# What You Have Learned

- ISDN can be viewed as an evolutionary process because communications carriers have been converting their facilities to digital technology since the 1960s.
- Access arrangements to the ISDN network include Basic and Primary access.
- The multiple channels on one ISDN physical line are obtained through time division multiplexing.
- Multiple channels on one ISDN physical line permit multiple voice or voice and data transmission to occur at the same time on a common circuit.
- The Basic access D channel on which data is transmitted in packet form can be used for such applications as monitoring of home alarm systems and reading of utility meters, as well as for the transmission of signaling information to control the operation of the B channels.
- Non-ISDN equipment can be connected to ISDN lines through the use of terminal adapters.
- An NT1 interface requires power from the subscriber's premises; therefore, the ISDN line is unusable when a power failure occurs.
- The standardization of Service Profile Identification codes facilitates the connection of third-party ISDN hardware to ISDN lines.
- Such applications as the use of video-conferencing and inter-LAN communications, as well as the increase in the use of the graphics-based World Wide Web, are the driving forces behind the use of ISDN.

**13**

**ISDN**

# Quiz for Chapter 13

1. What is the data rate of the ISDN Basic access B channel?

    A. 32Kbps

    B. 64Kbps

    C. 144Kbps

    D. 192Kbps

2. What is the data rate of the ISDN Basic access D channel?

    A. 64Kbps

    B. 16Kbps

    C. 8Kbps

    D. 144Kbps

3. Which of the following equations defines the composition of an ISDN Basic access line?

   A. 2B + D

   B. B + D

   C. B + 2D

   D. 2B + 2D

4. Which of the following equations defines the composition of an ISDN Primary access line in North America?

   A. 30B + D

   B. 2B + D

   C. B + D

   D. 23B + D

5. What network interface permits equipment without an ISDN interface to be connected into an ISDN interface?

   A. TE1

   B. TE2

   C. TA

   D. TE

6. On what number of channels can different operations occur simultaneously on one ISDN Basic access line?

   A. One

   B. Two

   C. Five

   D. Three

7. Digital telephones and integrated voice-data workstations are examples of what type of ISDN equipment?

   A. TE

   B. TA

   C. NT2

   D. TP

8. The transmission of data on an ISDN line between a customer's premises and a carrier's central office is encoded using

   A. Quadrature amplitude modulation.

   B. 2B1Q encoding.

    C. Hexadecimal encoding.

    D. Octal encoding.

9. The Service Profile Identification code

    A. Identifies the type of ISDN service.

    B. Identifies ISDN equipment to telephone company personnel.

    C. Identifies ISDN equipment to telephone company switches.

    D. Is 12 alphabetic characters in length.

10. What are the two types of ISDN ordering codes?

    A. Ordinary and generic

    B. Generic and non-generic

    C. SPID and ISDN-1

    D. ISDN-1 and ISDN-2

11. The use of capability packages

    A. Simplifies the ordering of ISDN services.

    B. Is the responsibility of the FCC.

    C. Costs more than non-capable packages.

    D. Allows 122 types of services to be ordered.

12. The connection of an inverse multiplexer to an ISDN PRI line

    A. Requires three days for installation.

    B. Uses a SIDIC code.

    C. Enables the use of 1–23 B channels.

    D. Both A and B.

13. Always On/Dynamic ISDN is suitable for which of the following?

    A. Digitized voice transmissions

    B. Large file transfers

    C. Web surfing

    D. Obtaining stock quotations

14. What transmission rate can be attained by using four B channels for video-conferencing?

    A. 64Kbps

    B. 128Kbps

    C. 192Kbps

    D. 256Kbps

**13**

ISDN

15. What is the primary competition to ISDN in the residential market?

   A. Packet switching

   B. Leased lines

   C. DSL and cable modems

   D. Video conferencing

# Asynchronous Transfer Mode

CHAPTER

# 14

## IN THIS CHAPTER

This chapter focuses on a rapidly evolving networking technology that provides the capability to transport voice, data, video, and images. Commonly referred to by the acronym ATM, *Asynchronous Transfer Mode* provides the opportunity for both end users and communications carriers to transport virtually any type of information using a common format. In this chapter, you will examine the rationale for the development of ATM and its underlying technology.

# Evolution

Asynchronous Transfer Mode (ATM) represents a communications technology designed to overcome the constraints associated with traditional and, for the most part, separate voice and data networks. ATM has its roots in the work of a CCITT (now known as ITU-T) study group formed to develop broadband ISDN standards during the mid-1980s. In 1988, a cell switching technology was chosen as the foundation for broadband ISDN, and in 1991, the ATM Forum was founded.

The ATM Forum represents an international consortium of public and private equipment vendors, data communications and telecommunications service providers, consultants, and end users established to promote the implementation of ATM. To accomplish this goal, the ATM Forum develops standards with the ITU and other standards organizations.

The first ATM Forum standard was released in 1992. Various ATM Forum working groups are busy defining additional standards required to enable ATM to provide a communications capability for the wide range of LAN and WAN transmission schemes it is designed to support. This standardization effort will probably remain in effect for a considerable period due to the comprehensive design goal of the technology, which was developed to support voice, data, and video on both local and wide area networks.

# The Rationale for ATM and Its Underlying Technology

ATM can be considered to represent a unifying technology because it was designed to transport voice, data, and video (including graphics images) on both local and wide area networks. Until the development of ATM, networks were normally developed based on the type of data to be transported. Thus, circuit-switched networks, which included the public switched telephone network and high-speed digital transmission facilities, were primarily used to transport delay-sensitive information, such as voice and video. In comparison, on packet-based networks, such as X.25 and Frame Relay, information can tolerate a degree of delay. Network users can select a networking technology to satisfy a specific communications application, but most organizations support a mixture of applications. Thus, most organizations are forced to operate multiple networks, resulting in a degree of inefficiency and escalating communications costs. By combining the features from both technologies, ATM enables a single network to support voice, data, and video.

ATM is designed to be scalable, enabling its 53-byte cell to be transported from LAN to LAN via WAN, as well as for use on public and private wide area networks at a range of operating rates. On LANs, ATM support is currently offered at 25 and 155Mbps, whereas access to WAN-based ATM carrier networks can occur at T1 (1.544Mbps), at T3 (45Mbps), or via different SONET facilities at data rates such as 622Gbps, all based on the transportation of 53-byte cells. A key to ATM's ubiquitous transmission capability is its fixed 53-byte cell length, which remains static regardless of changes in media, operating rates, or framing.

The use of a fixed-length cell enables low-cost hardware to be developed to perform required cell switching based on the contents of the cell header, without requiring more complex and costly software. Thus, ATM can be considered to represent a unifying technology that will eventually become very economical to implement when its development expenses are amortized over the growing production cycle of ATM communications equipment.

Although many organizations merged voice and data through the use of multiplexers onto a common circuit, this type of merger is typically not end-to-end. For example, traffic from a router connected to a LAN might be fed into a port on a high-speed multiplexer with another connection to the multiplexer from the company PBX. Although this type of multiplexing enables a common WAN circuit to be used for voice and data, it represents an interim and partial solution to the expense associated with operating separate voice and data networks. In addition, the emergence of multimedia applications requiring the transmission of video can wreak havoc with existing LANs and WANs because of their requirement for high bandwidth for short periods. ATM represents an emerging technology designed to provide support for bandwidth-on-demand applications, such as video, as well as voice and data. A comparison of the key features associated with each technology can give you an appreciation for ATM technology in comparison to conventional data communications- and telecommunications-based technology. Table 14.1 compares nine features of data communications and telecommunications networks with those of an ATM network.

**TABLE 14.1**   Comparing Network Features

| Feature | Data Communications | Telecommunications | ATM |
|---------|---------------------|--------------------|-----|
| Traffic Support | Data | Voice | Data, voice, video |
| Transmission Unit | Packet | Frame | Cell |
| Transmission Length | Variable | Fixed | Fixed |
| Switching Type | Packet | Circuit | Cell |
| Connection Type | Connectionless or connection-oriented | Connection-oriented | Connection-oriented |
| Time Sensitivity | None to some | All | Adaptive |
| Media and Operating Rate | Defined by protocol | Defined by class | Scalable |
| Media Access | Shared or dedicated | Dedicated | Dedicated |

In a data communications environment, the network can range in scope from an Ethernet or token-ring LAN to an X.25 or Frame Relay WAN. Thus, although some features are common to both LAN and WAN environments, there is also some variability. In general, a data communications network transports data by using variable-length packets. Although many WAN protocols are connection-oriented, some are connectionless. Similarly, many LAN protocols are connectionless, whereas others are connection-oriented. Because data communications networks were designed to transport files, records, and screens of data, transmission delay or latency, if small, does not adversely affect users. In comparison, in a telecommunications network, a similar amount of latency that is acceptable on a data network could wreak havoc with a telephone conversation. Recognizing the differences among voice, video, and data transportation, ATM was designed to adapt to the time sensitivity of different applications. It includes different classes of service that enable the technology to match delivery to the time sensitivity of the information it transports.

One of those classes of service provides a constant bit rate (CBR) that guarantees delivery of cells without variation occurring between cells. CBR provides a built-in Quality of Service (QoS) that is required to transport real-time voice and video applications. In comparison, other technologies, such as the Internet Protocol (IP) use literally dozens of standards in an attempt to obtain a QoS capability that is available by default in ATM. You can gain an appreciation for how ATM accomplishes this by learning about its architecture.

# Architecture

ATM is based on the switching of 53-byte cells—in which each cell consists of a 5-byte header and a payload of 48 bytes of information. Figure 14.1 illustrates the format of the ATM cell, including the explosion of its 5-byte header to indicate the fields carried in the header.

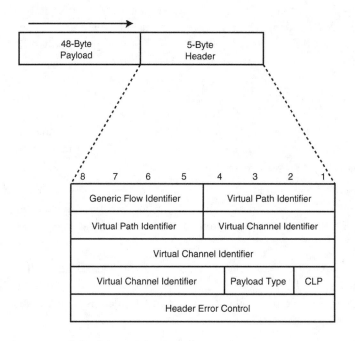

CLP = Cell Loss Priority

**FIGURE 14.1**

*The 53-byte ATM cell.*

The 4-bit Generic Flow Control (GFC) field is used as a mechanism to regulate the flow of traffic in an ATM network between the network and the user. The use of this field is currently under development. As we will shortly note, ATM supports two major types of interfaces:

Network-to-User (UNI) and Network-to-Network (NNI). When a cell flows from the user to the network or from the network to the user, it will carry a GFC bit value. However, when it flows within a network or between networks, the GFC field is not used. Instead of being wasted, its space can be used to expand the length of the Virtual Path Identifier field.

The 8-bit Virtual Path Identifier (VPI) field represents one half of a two-part connection identifier used by ATM. This field identifies a virtual path that can represent a group of virtual circuits transported along the same route. Although the VPI is eight bits long in a UNI cell, the field expands to 12-bit positions to fill the Generic Flow Control field in an NNI cell. It is described in more detail later in this chapter.

The Virtual Channel Identifier (VCI) is the second half of the two-part connection identifier carried in the ATM header. The 16-bit VCI field identifies a connection between two ATM stations communicating with one another for a specific type of application. Multiple virtual channels (VCs) can be transported within one virtual path. For example, one VC could be used to transport a disk backup operation, whereas a second VC is used to transport a TCP/IP-based application. The virtual channel represents a one-way cell transport facility. Thus, for each of the previously described operations, another series of VCIs is established from the opposite direction. You can view a virtual channel as an individual one-way end-to-end circuit, whereas a virtual path that can represent a collection of virtual channels can be viewed as a network trunk line. After data is within an ATM network, the VPI is used to route a common group of virtual channels between switches by enabling ATM switches to simply examine the value of the VPI. Later in this chapter, you will examine the use of the VCI.

The Payload Type Identifier (PTI) field indicates the type of information carried in the 48-byte data portion of the ATM cell. Currently, this 3-bit field indicates whether payload data represents management information or user data. Additional PTI field designators have been reserved for future use.

The 1-bit Cell Loss Priority (CLP) field indicates the relative importance of the cell. If this field bit is set to 1, the cell can be discarded by a switch experiencing congestion. If the cell cannot be discarded, the CLP field bit is set to 0. Thus, this 1-bit field is similar to the Discard Eligible (DE) bit in a frame relay frame.

The last field in the ATM cell header is the 8-bit Header Error Control field. This field represents the result of an 8-bit Cyclic Redundancy Check (CRC) code, computed only over the ATM cell header. This field provides the capability for detecting all single-bit errors and certain multiple-bit errors that occur in the 40-bit ATM cell header.

# Network Connections

ATM defines two sets of network interface specifications. The User-Network Interface (UNI) specification represents the specification that governs the manner by which an end-user connects to an ATM network. In comparison, the Network-Network Interface (NNI) specification governs the manner by which two ATM networks interconnect. Because both private and public ATM networks can be developed as well as interface one another, the user-network and Network-Network interfaces are further broken down into public and private specifications.

A public UNI specification governs the manner by which an ATM user interconnects with an ATM switch deployed in a public service provider's network. In comparison, a private UNI specification defines the manner by which an ATM user is connected to a private ATM switch. Figure 14.2 illustrates the relationship between public and private ATM UNIs.

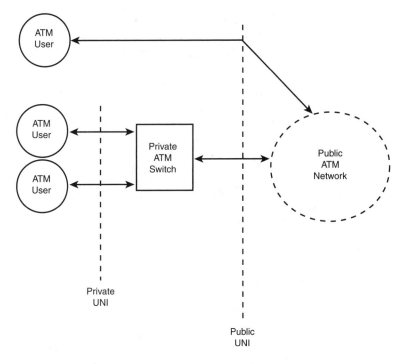

**FIGURE 14.2**
*ATM User Network Interface (UNI) options.*

**14**

ASYNCHRNOOUS
TRANSFER MODE

# Advantages of the Technology

The use of cell-switching technology in a LAN environment provides some distinct advantages over the shared-medium technology employed by Ethernet, token-ring, and FDDI networks. Two of those advantages are obtaining full bandwidth access to ATM switches for individual workstations and enabling attaching devices to operate at different operating rates. Those advantages are illustrated in Figure 14.3, which shows an ATM switch that could be used to support three distinct operating rates. Workstations could be connected to the switch at 25Mbps, and a local server could be connected at 155Mbps to other switches either to form a larger local LAN or to connect to a communications carrier's network via a different operating rate.

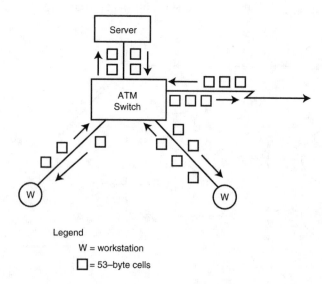

Legend

W = workstation

☐ = 53–byte cells

**FIGURE 14.3**

*ATM is based on the switching of 53-byte cells.*

The selection of a 53-byte cell length results in a minimum of latency in comparison to the packet length of traditional LANs, such as Ethernet, which can have a maximum 1526-byte frame length. Because the ATM cell is always 53 bytes in length, cells transporting voice, data, and video can be intermixed without the latency of one cell adversely affecting other cells. Because the length of each cell is fixed and the position of information in each header is known, ATM switching can be accomplished via the use of hardware. In comparison, on traditional LANs, bridging and routing functions are normally performed by software or firmware, which executes more slowly than hardware-based switching.

Two additional features of ATM that warrant discussion are its asynchronous operation and its connection-oriented operation. ATM cells are intermixed via multiplexing, and cells from individual connections are forwarded from switch to switch via a single-cell flow. However, the multiplexing of ATM cells occurs via asynchronous transfer in which cells are transmitted only when data is present to send. In comparison, in conventional time, division multiplexing, keep-alive, or synchronization bytes are transmitted when there is no data to be sent. Concerning the connection-oriented technology used by ATM, this means that a connection between the ATM stations must be established before data transfer occurs. The connection process results in the specification of a transmission path between ATM switches and end stations, enabling the header in ATM cells to be used to route the cells on the required path through an ATM network.

# Cell Routing

The actual routing of ATM cells depends on whether a connection was pre-established or set up as needed on a demand basis. The pre-established type of connection is referred to as a Permanent Virtual Connection (PVC), and the other type is referred to as a Switched Virtual Connection (SVC). Examine the 5-byte ATM cell header shown in Figure 14.1 and note the VCI and VPI fields. The VPI is 8 bits in length, whereas the VCI is 16 bits in length, enabling 256 virtual paths of which each path is capable of accommodating up to 65,536 ($2^{16}$) virtual connections.

By using VPs and VCs, ATM employs a two-level connection identifier that is used in its routing hierarchy. A VCI value is unique only in a particular VPI value, whereas VPI values are unique only in particular physical links. The VPI/VCI value assignment has only local significance, and those values are translated at every switch a cell traverses between endpoints in an ATM network. The actual establishment of a virtual path is based on ATM's network management and signaling operations. During the establishment of a virtual path routing table, entries in each switch located between endpoints map an incoming physical port and a Virtual Path Identifier pair to an outgoing pair. This initial mapping process is known as *network provisioning*, and the change of routing table entries is referred to as *network reprovisioning*.

Figure 14.4 illustrates an example of a few possible table entries for a switch, where a virtual path was established such that VPI=6 on port 1 and VPI=10 on port 8, representing two physical links in the established connection.

Next, we will examine the entries in the routing table shown in Figure 14.5, and note that the table does not include values for VCIs. This is by design because a VP in an ATM network can support up to 65,536 VC connections. Thus, only one table entry is required to switch up to 65,536 individual connections if those connections all follow the same set of physical links in the same sequence. This method of switching, which is based on the VPI and port number, simplifies the construction and use of routing tables and facilitates the establishment of a connection through a series of switches. Although VCIs are not used in routing tables, they are translated at each switch. To help you understand the rationale for this technique, you must focus on their use. As previously noted, a VCI is unique within a VP and is used at an endpoint to denote a different connection within a virtual path. Thus, the VPI/VCI pair used between an endpoint and a switch has a local meaning and is translated at every switch; however, the VCI is not used for routing between switches.

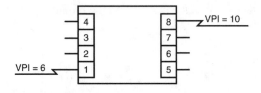

Routing Table Entries

| Received | | Transmit | |
|---|---|---|---|
| VPI | Port Number | VPI | Port Number |
| 6 | 1 | 10 | 8 |
| 10 | 8 | 6 | 1 |

**FIGURE 14.4**

*Switch operations based on routing table entries.*

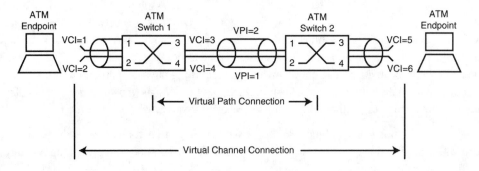

**FIGURE 14.5**

*Connections in an ATM network.*

The establishment of a connection between two end stations is known as a Virtual Channel Connection (VCC). To illustrate the routing of cells in an ATM network based on a VCC, consider Figure 14.5, which represents a small two-switch–based ATM network. The VCC represents a series of virtual channel links between two ATM endpoints. In Figure 14.5, one VCC could be represented by VCI=1, VCI=3, and VCI=5, which collectively form a connection between workstations at the two endpoints shown in the network. A second VCC could be represented by VCI=2, VCI=4, and VCI=6. The second VCC could represent the transportation of a second application between the same pair of endpoints or a new application between different endpoints served by the same pair of ATM switches.

As indicated by the previous examples, each VC link consists of one or more physical links between the location where a VCI is assigned and the location where it is either translated or removed. The assignment of VCs is the responsibility of switches during the call setup process.

# The ATM Protocol Reference Model

Three layers in the ATM architecture form the basis for the ATM Protocol Reference model, illustrated in Figure 14.6. Those layers are the Physical layer, the ATM layer, and the ATM Adaptation layer.

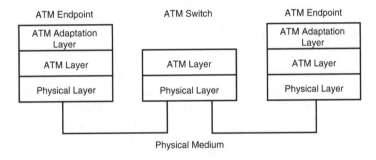

**FIGURE 14.6**
*The ATM protocol suite.*

# The Physical Layer

As indicated in Figure 14.6, the lowest layer in the ATM protocol is the Physical layer. This layer describes the physical transmission of information through an ATM network. It is not actually defined with respect to this new technology. The absence of a Physical layer definition results from the design goal of ATM to operate on various physical interfaces or media types. Thus, instead of defining a specific Physical layer, ATM depends on the Physical layers defined in other networking protocols. Types of physical media specified for ATM include shielded and unshielded twisted-pair, coaxial cable, and fiber-optic cable, which provide cell transport capabilities ranging from a T1 rate of 1.544Mbps to SONET rates of 622Mbps, 2.4Gbps, 4.8Gbps, or even 10Gbps.

# The ATM Layer

The ATM layer represents the physical interface between the ATM Adaptation layer (AAL) and the Physical layer. Thus, the ATM layer is responsible for relaying cells from the AAL to the Physical layer for transmission, and in the opposite direction from the Physical layer to the AAL for use in an endpoint. When transporting cells to the Physical layer, the ATM layer is responsible for generating the five-byte cell header for each cell. When receiving cells from the Physical layer, the ATM layer performs a reverse operation, extracting the 5-byte header from each cell.

The actual manner by which the ATM layer performs its relaying function depends on the location of the layer at a switch or at an endpoint. If the ATM layer is located in an endpoint, it receives a stream of cells from the Physical layer and transmits either cells with new data or empty cells if there is no data to send to the AAL. When located in a switch, the ATM layer is responsible for determining where incoming cells are routed and for multiplexing cells by placing cells from individual connections into a single-cell stream.

# The ATM Adaptation Layer

The ATM Adaptation layer (AAL) represents the top layer in the ATM Protocol model. This layer is responsible for providing an interface between higher-layer protocols and the ATM layer. Because this interface normally occurs based on a voice, data, or video application accessing an ATM network, the operations performed by the AAL occur at endpoints and not at ATM switches. Thus, the AAL is shown in Figure 14.6 to reside at ATM endpoints.

The primary function of the ATM Adaptation layer is format conversion. That is, the AAL maps the data stream originated by the higher-layer protocol into the 48-byte payload of ATM cells, with the header placement being assigned by the ATM layer. In the reverse direction, the AAL receives the payload of ATM cells in 48-byte increments from the ATM layer and maps those increments into the format recognized by the higher-layer protocol.

Because it is not possible to address the requirements of the diverse set of applications designed to use ATM within a single AAL, the ITU-T classified the functions required by different applications based on their traffic and service requirements. This classification scheme defined four classes of applications based on whether a timing relationship is required between end stations, the type of bit rate (variable or constant), and the type of connection (connection-oriented or connectionless) required. Table 14.2 summarizes the four classes of applications with respect to their timing relationship, bit rate, and type of connection.

**TABLE 14.2** The ATM Application Classes

| *Class* | *Timing Relationship* | *Bit Rate* | *Type of Connection* |
|---|---|---|---|
| A | Yes | Constant | Connection-oriented |
| B | Yes | Variable | Connection-oriented |
| C | No | Variable | Connection-oriented |
| D | No | Variable | Connectionless |

In Table 14.2, note that the timing relationship references whether one is required between end stations. Real-time services, such as the transportation of voice or video, represent two examples of applications that require a timing relationship. In comparison, a file transfer represents an application that does not require a timing relationship. When a timing relationship is required, clocking between two end stations must be aligned.

A constant bit-rate (CBR) application represents an application that requires an unvarying amount of bandwidth, such as voice or real-time video. In comparison, a variable bit-rate application represents "bursty" traffic, such as LAN data or transmission via a packet network.

The capability to support connection-oriented or connectionless applications enables ATM to support various existing higher-layer protocols. For example, Frame Relay is a connection-oriented protocol, whereas IP is a connectionless protocol. Through the use of different AALs, both can be transported by ATM.

Based on the four application classes, four different types of AALs were defined: AAL1, 2, 3/4, and 5. At one time, AAL3 and AAL4 were separate types; however, they had a sufficient degree of commonality to be merged. Figure 14.7 illustrates the relationship between application classes and ATM Adaptation layers with respect to the different parameters used to classify the application classes.



<table>
<tr><td>Application Classification</td><td colspan="2">Class A</td><td colspan="2">Class B</td><td>Class C</td><td>Class D</td></tr>
<tr><td>Timing Relationship</td><td colspan="4">Required</td><td colspan="2">Not Required</td></tr>
<tr><td>Bit Rate</td><td colspan="2">Constant</td><td colspan="4">Variable</td></tr>
<tr><td>Connection Mode</td><td colspan="5">Connection-Oriented</td><td>Connectionless</td></tr>
<tr><td>ATM Adaptation Layer</td><td>AAL 1</td><td colspan="2">AAL 2</td><td colspan="2">AAL 5, AAL 3/4</td><td>AAL 3/4</td></tr>
</table>

**FIGURE 14.7**
*Application classification and associated AALs.*

# AAL1

ATM Adaptation layers are distinguished from one another based on the method by which the 48-byte cell payload constructed as a data stream generated by a higher-level protocol is passed to the ATM layer. For example, consider a Class A application represented by a voice conversation. Because misordering cells can be viewed as being worse than losing cells, the payload is constructed to include a sequence number when Class A traffic is transported. Figure 14.8 illustrates the format of an AAL1 cell payload. Note that the Sequence Number Protection (SNP) field protects the Sequence Number (SN) field from the effect of bit errors occurring during transmission, in effect providing a forward error detection and correction capability.

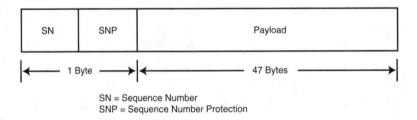

SN = Sequence Number
SNP = Sequence Number Protection

**FIGURE 14.8**
*AAL 1 cell payload format.*

AAL1 is designated for transporting continuous bitrate (CBR) data, such as real-time voice and video traffic. The AAL1 specification defines the manner by which a continuous signal is transported in a sequence of individual ATM cells. As indicated in Figure 14.8, the first byte in the normal 48-byte cell payload is used for cell sequencing and protection of the sequence number, limiting the actual payload to 47 bytes per AAL1-generated cell.

# AAL2

The purpose of AAL2 is to transfer variable bit rate, which is time dependent. To accomplish this task, AAL2 transmits timing information along with data, enabling a receiver to recover the timing relationship at the destination. This means that when there is no data to transmit, there is no need to transmit cells filled with nulls to maintain a timing relationship because AAL2 includes the timing relationship within its cell. Figure 14.9 illustrates the format of an AAL2 cell. Note the actual payload is 45 bytes. Because ATM can transport lengthy frames or packets that require transport by multiple cells, the length indicator (LI) functions as a payload positioning mechanism, indicating the number of bytes of the higher layer protocol that are included in the payload. The cyclic redundancy check (CRC) provides a mechanism to detect up to two correlated bit errors and uses the generating polynomial of $X^{10}+X^9+X^5+X^4+X+1$.

| Sequence Number | Cell Type | Payload | Length Indicator | CRC |
|---|---|---|---|---|
| 4 bits | 4 bits | 45 Bytes | 6 bits | 10 bits |

FIGURE **14.9**

*AAL2 cell payload format.*

## AAL3/4

Originally AAL3 was considered as a mechanism to transfer variable rate data, which is time independent in a connectionless mode of operation, whereas AAL4 would transport variable bit time independent data in a connectionless mode of operation. Because of the close relationship between AAL3 and AAL4, they were merged into a common ATM adaptation layer now referred to as AAL3/4. AAL3/4 supports both connectionless and connection oriented variable data rate transmissions. Figure 14.10 illustrates the AAL3/4 cell payload format. Note that the multiplexing identification field permits the multiplexing and demultiplexing of multiple payloads over a single ATM connection.

| Sequence Number | Sequence Number Protection | Information Type | Multiplexing Indentification | Payload | Length Indicator | CRC |
|---|---|---|---|---|---|---|
| 4 bits | 4 bits | 4 bits | 10 bits | 44 Bytes | 6 bits | 10 bits |

FIGURE **14.10**

*AAL3/4 cell payload format.*

One of the major problems associated with AAL3/4 is its high level of overhead. If you consider the fact that each ATM cell begins with a 5-byte header, AAL3/4 is reduced to transporting 44 bytes in a 53-byte cell, which results in a significant level of overhead. This resulted in the development of what was originally known as the Simple and Efficient ATM Adaptation Layer (SEAL) and which is now known as AAL5.

## AAL5

AAL5 was designed to provide an enhanced level of efficiency for the transmission of data traffic over an ATM network. To accomplish this, AAL5 treats a data flow as a transparent transfer of user-to-user information. This results in 48 bytes of payload occurring in every cell but the last one, which transfers a higher layer frame or packet. The last cell is used to transfer overhead fields for the prior n-1 cells and the last cell (n) that transfers the payload.

**14**

ASYNCHRNOOUS
TRANSFER MODE

Figure 14.11 illustrates the format of a sequence of AAL5 payloads. The payload field contains user data up to $2^{16}-1$ bytes, in effect up to 64Kbytes in length. Thus, a stream of 48 byte payloads with 5 byte headers would transport the higher layer packet or frame. The PAD field pads the higher layer physical data unit, such as a packet or frame, so that it fits exactly before the trailer in the last cell transporting the payload. The CPCS-UU field is used to indicate user-to-user information. The CPI (Common Part Indicator) field aligns the trailer to 64 bits, whereas the length field indicates the length, in bytes, of the payload that can reside over the prior n-1 cells. The maximum value of the Length field is 65535 bytes. A Length field value of 0 is used to indicate an abort condition. Finally, the CRC field protects the entire payload transferred as a sequence of cells.

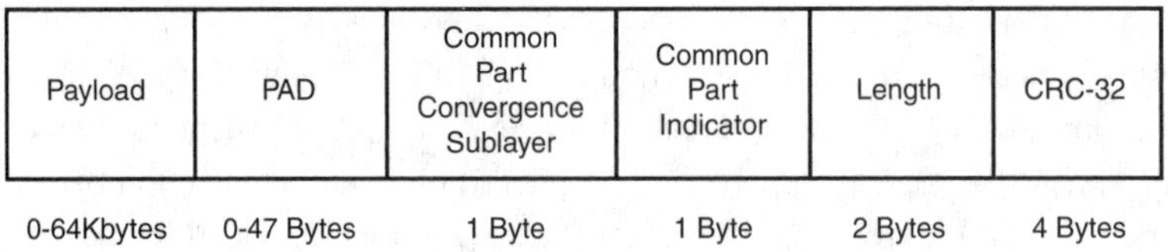

| Payload | PAD | Common Part Convergence Sublayer | Common Part Indicator | Length | CRC-32 |
|---------|-----|----------------------------------|----------------------|--------|--------|
| 0-64Kbytes | 0-47 Bytes | 1 Byte | 1 Byte | 2 Bytes | 4 Bytes |

**FIGURE 14.11**
*AAL5 payload sequence.*

One of the key uses of ATMs AAL5 is to transport multiple protocols over ATM. In fact, both the Internet community in the form of an RFC and the Frame Relay Forum in the form of an Implementation Agreement (IA) developed standards that define the manner by which IP and Frame Relay traffic flows over an ATM backbone network.

Although several aspects of different AAL operations remain to be specified, the use of different AALs provides the mechanism for the cell-based switching technology on which ATM is based to transport different types of information using a common cell structure.

## Service Definitions

Perhaps the major benefit of ATM is that it enables users to obtain a QoS for each class of service. The QoS represents a guaranteed level of service that can be based on such parameters as peak cell rate (PCR), sustained cell rate (SCR), cell delay variation tolerance (CDVT), minimum cell rate (MCR), and burst tolerance (BT). Each of these parameters is used with other parameters to define one of the five classes of service for which a carrier might offer cell loss, cell delay, and bandwidth guarantees. Those classes of service include Continuous Bit Rate (CBR), Variable Bit Rate–Real Time (VBR–RT), Variable Bit Rate–Non-Real Time (VBR–NRT), Unspecified Bit Rate (UBR), and Available Bit Rate (ABR).

Continuous Bit Rate and Variable Bit Rate–Real Time services generally correspond to Class A and Class B services, respectively. Variable Bit Rate–Non-Real Time is a less time-stringent version of VBR–RT.

Both UBR and ABR services are for transporting delay-insensitive traffic, corresponding to Classes C and D. UBR represents a best-effort delivery mechanism for which cells can be discarded during periods of network congestion. In comparison, an ABR service is allocated all the bandwidth required by the application that is available on a connection, with a feedback mechanism employed to control the rate the originator transmits cells to minimize cell loss when available bandwidth contracts. Table 14.3 provides a summary of the five types of ATM services.

**TABLE 14.3**   ATM Services

| Guarantees | ATM Service | Metrics | Loss | Delay | Bandwidth Feedback |
|---|---|---|---|---|---|
| Constant Bit Rate (CBR) | PCR, CDVT | Yes | Yes | Yes | No |
| Variable Bit Rate–Real Time (VBR–RT) | PCR, CDVT, SCR, BT | Yes | Yes | Yes | No |
| Variable Bit Rate–Non-Real Time (VBR–NRT) | PCR, CDVT, SCR, BT | Yes | Yes | Yes | No |
| Unspecified Bit Rate(UBR) | Unspecified | No | No | No | No |
| Available Bit Rate (ABR) | PCR, CDVT, MCR | Yes | No | Yes | Yes |

Legend:

PCR = Peak Cell Rate

CDVT = Cell Delay Variation Tolerance

SCR = Sustained Cell Rate

BT = Burst Tolerance

MCR = Minimum Cell Rate

**14**

**ASYNCHRNOOUS
TRANSFER MODE**

# LAN Emulation

Although numerous advantages are associated with the use of ATM, its use in corporate and government offices causes a degree of interoperability problems when it's used to support legacy LANs, such as Ethernet and token-ring networks. Figure 14.12 illustrates the interoperability problems associated with using ATM as a backbone to interconnect legacy LAN switches. In Figure 14.12, note that ATM uses virtual path and virtual channel identifiers for addressing. In comparison, legacy LANs that include Ethernet use MAC addressing. Another difference between the two is that ATM is a connection-oriented protocol, whereas Ethernet is connectionless. This means there is no direct equivalent to a legacy broadcast transmission capability.

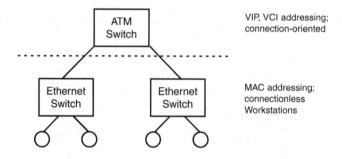

**FIGURE 14.12**

*Interoperability problems associated with using ATM as a backbone to connect legacy LANs.*

To obtain compatibility between ATM and legacy LANs, the ATM Forum developed a protocol called LAN Emulation (LANE). The goal of LANE is to provide a mechanism that enables ATM to interoperate with legacy LANs while hiding the ATM network from the legacy network. To accomplish this, the ATM LANE protocol emulates the characteristics of the legacy network.

LANE functions are performed on switches at the edge of an ATM network. As you might surmise, such switches are referred to as ATM *edge devices*. Four components are needed to provide LAN Emulation: a LAN Emulation Configuration Server (LECS), a LAN Emulation Server (LES), and a Broadcast and Unknown Server (BUS).

## The LAN Emulation Client

The functionality of an LEC is typically located in an ATM adapter card installed in a legacy switch. That card is configured with two addresses: an IEEE 48-bit MAC address and a 20-byte ATM address. The LEC is responsible for address resolution, data forwarding, and registration of MAC addresses with the LANE server (LES). It also communicates with other LECS via ATM virtual channel connections established across the ATM network.

# The LAN Emulation Configuration Server

The LANE Configuration Server maintains a database of emulated LANs (ELANs) and the ATM address of LAN Emulation Servers (LESs) that control the ELANs. When a LANE client needs an ATM address, it first searches its connections, called *Virtual Channel Connections (VCCs)*, that it previously opened. The LEC maintains a translation table of destination MAC addresses mapped to VCCs. If the destination address is in the table, the LEC can use the existing VCC to send the message. If not, the LEC must perform an address resolution procedure using the LAN Emulation Address Resolution Protocol (LE-ARP). To do so, it queries the LECS, which returns the ATM address that serves the appropriate emulated LAN. The LEC then uses that address to query the LES. The LECS database is defined and maintained by the network manager or LAN administrator and represents the only manual process in the entire emulation process.

# The LAN Emulation Server

The LES represents a central control point for a predefined group of LECs. The LES maintains a point-to-multipoint Virtual Control Channel to all the LECs it controls. When the LEC queries the LES, the LES verifies that the LEC can joint the ELAN. Assuming it can, it examines the request of the LEC to resolve a MAC to ATM address by searching its tables for the appropriate ATM address that provides a path to the desired MAC address. Those tables are formed by LECs registering their ATM-to-MAC address translations with the LES. If the address is in the LES's cache memory, the LES returns the ATM address to the LEC that uses that address to establish an ATM connection. If the LES does not have that address in cache memory, it uses the services of the BUS.

# The Broadcast and Unknown Server

The Broadcast and Unknown Server (BUS) functions as a central point for transmitting broadcasts and multicast messages. It is required because ATM is a point-to-point connection-oriented technology that lacks a broadcast or one-to-many transmission capability. If the LES does not have the address required by the LEC, it uses the services of the BUS. That is, the BUS transmits an address resolution request to all stations that make up the ELAN, and the station that recognizes its own MAC address returns its ATM address. The LES updates its cache memory and returns the ATM address to the LEC. The LEC can then establish a connection across the ATM network.

Although communications carriers have expended a significant amount of effort to develop an ATM infrastructure for transporting information between carrier offices, the expansion of this evolving technology to customer premises—as well as its common use on LANs—will probably take several years because, as with any new technology, the cost of ATM equipment is relatively high in comparison to the cost of older technology. Over the next few years, you can

**14**

ASYNCHRONOUS
TRANSFER MODE

expect several important standards to be promulgated, and you can also expect to see the cost of ATM equipment become more reasonable as development costs are amortized over a larger base of products. As this occurs, the use of ATM will expand considerably.

# What You Have Learned

- ATM represents cell-switching technology designed to transport voice, data, and video by using a common cell format on both local and wide area networks.
- ATM represents a scalable technology for which 53-byte cells can be transported at a range of operating rates from 25Mbps on LANs to 622 10Gbps on SONET.
- Recognizing the differences between voice and data transportation requirements, ATM is designed to adapt to the time sensitivity of different applications.
- The User-Network interface (UNI) specification governs the manner by which an end user connects to an ATM network.
- The Network-Network Interface (NNI) specification governs the manner by which two ATM networks interconnect.
- A two-part identifier consisting of a Virtual Path Identifier and Virtual Channel Identifier enables multiple connections to be carried on the same path.
- The ATM Protocol Reference model has three layers: the Physical layer, the ATM layer, and the ATM Adaptation layer.
- The routing of ATM cells between switches is based on Virtual Path Identifiers and port number routing table entries in the two switches.
- A Virtual Path Connection (VPC) represents a concatenation of virtual paths between switches; a Virtual Channel Connection (VCC) represents a connection between two end stations via a VPC.
- ATM users can obtain a guaranteed level of service referred to as a Quality of Service (QoS).
- LAN Emulation provides the mechanism for overcoming incompatibilities between ATM and legacy LAN addressing and their use of connection-oriented and connectionless operations.

# Quiz for Chapter 14

1. What is the ATM forum?
    A. A government agency that regulates the use of ATM
    B. An international consortium that promotes the implementation of ATM
    C. A branch of the ITU-T involved in the ATM standardization effort
    D. A debating society involving ATM operations

2. ATM scalability references the capability of the technology to support what?

   A. Different cell lengths

   B. Different wide area networks

   C. Different local area networks

   D. A range of operating rates using the same old format

3. Latency is a measure of

   A. LAN operations.

   B. Cell length.

   C. Transmission delay.

   D. WAN operations.

4. The Cell Loss Priority field indicates

   A. The loss of a cell.

   B. The priority of a cell.

   C. Whether a cell can be discarded.

   D. The capability of a cell to be prioritized.

5. What is the function of the Header Error Control field in an ATM cell?

   A. To protect user data

   B. To correct user data

   C. To indicate the occurrence of any possible error in the cell header

   D. To indicate the occurrence of certain types of errors in the cell header

6. Which of the following is an advantage of using ATM over using conventional LANs?

   A. Shared medium access

   B. Full bandwidth access

   C. Support of fixed operating rates

   D. Direct sharing of the medium

7. What is the lowest layer in the ATM protocol?

   A. ATM Adaptation layer

   B. Convergence layer

   C. ATM layer

   D. Physical layer

8. Which layer generates the five-byte ATM cell header?

   A. ATM layer

   B. Physical layer

   C. ATM Adaptation layer

   D. Convergence layer

9. The routing of ATM cells between switches is based on the

   A. Virtual Path Identifier.

   B. Port number.

   C. VPI and port number.

   D. Virtual Channel Identifier.

10. Which of the following is defined as a connection between two end stations?

    A. Virtual path

    B. Virtual Channel Connection

    C. Virtual link

    D. Virtual LAN

11. Which ATM layer is responsible for providing an interface to higher-layer protocols?

    A. Physical layer

    B. Convergence layer

    C. ATM layer

    D. ATM Adaptation layer

12. Which ATM application class requires a timing relationship, a variable bit rate, and a connection-oriented type of connection?

    A. Class A

    B. Class B

    C. Class C

    D. Class D

13. A constant bit rate application represents an application that requires

    A. An unvarying amount of bandwidth.

    B. File transfer capability.

    C. A varying amount of bandwidth.

    D. A connectionless type of connection.

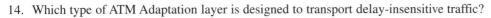
14. Which type of ATM Adaptation layer is designed to transport delay-insensitive traffic?

    A.  AAL1

    B.  AAL2

    C.  AAL3

    D.  AAL4

15. Which type of ATM Adaptation Layer has a very high level of overhead?

    A.  AAL1

    B.  AAL2

    C.  AAL3/4

    D.  AAL5

16. Which type of ATM Adaptation layer is designed to transport multiple protocols efficiently?

    A.  AAL1

    B.  AAL2

    C.  AAL3/4

    D.  AAL5

17. The Quality of Service represents

    A.  A guaranteed cell rate.

    B.  A guaranteed cell delay.

    C.  A guaranteed burst tolerance.

    D.  A guaranteed level of service.

18. Which LAN Emulation component has to be manually configured?

    A.  The LAN Emulation Client

    B.  The LAN Emulation Configuration Server

    C.  The LAN Emulation Server

    D.  The Broadcast and Unknown Server

19. Which of the following is the central control point for a group of LAN Emulation Clients?

    A.  The LES

    B.  The LECS

    C.  The BUS

    D.  The high-order MAC address

**14**

ASYNCHRNOOUS
TRANSFER MODE

20. Which component of ATM LAN Emulation transmits broadcasts and multicast messages?

   A.  The LES

   B.  The LECS

   C.  The BUS

# Wireless Transmission

## IN THIS CHAPTER

Earlier in this book, we briefly described and discussed the operation of several types of wireless transmission systems. In Chapter 3, "Messages and Transmission Channels," we discussed microwave radio, geostationary, and low Earth orbit satellites, and we took a quick look at cellular radio. In this chapter, we will considerably broaden our discussion of wireless transmission by focusing our attention upon three distinct wireless areas: mobile wireless, fixed wireless, and wireless LANs.

# Mobile Wireless

For the purpose of the book, mobile wireless will be equated to cellular communications. If you watch TV or read the newspaper, more than likely you cannot help but notice numerous advertisements for different cellular calling plans. Some vendors include wireless access to the Web or e-mail, or the ability to send and receive messages similar to a pager—all on one mobile telephone. If you read trade publications, you will become exposed to a literal alphabet soup of acronyms that describe how mobile wireless systems operate and the manner by which they support different features. Because it is easier to understand what such acronyms as AMPS, FDMA, TDMA, and CDMA mean by reviewing how mobile wireless communications evolved, let's do so. As we discuss the evolution of mobile wireless, we will note the features, functions, and capabilities that different generations of wireless communications provide so that you can sharpen your crystal ball to explore the future.

## Mobile Communications Evolution

During the 1970s, Bell Telephone Laboratories, which was then part of AT&T Corporation, developed the first wireless transmission system to provide service to mobile subscribers. That system consisted of three major components that continue to form the infrastructure for more modern mobile systems to this day. Those components include base stations, a mobile telephone switching office (MTSO), and cellular phones.

Although significant technological developments have occurred in the field of mobile wireless communications since the 1970s, the basic components of a cellular system retain the same infrastructural relationship. In addition, the basic concept behind cellular systems has remained the same. Thus, before we investigate the communications techniques that evolved, we will focus on the basic infrastructure.

## Basic Mobile Communications Infrastructure

In a mobile communications environment, a geographic area is subdivided into cells that support operations on distinct frequencies. To prevent interference between cells, the first type of mobile wireless communications system, which is referred to as the Analog Mobile Phone System (AMPS), employed a seven-cell pattern, as illustrated in Figure 15.1. The cell pattern shown in Figure 15.1 ensures that no adjacent cells operate on the same frequency. In actuality, each cell consists of a base station and antenna that supports operations over a wide range of frequencies. However, only one call can occur at one of the frequencies supported in a cell at any given time; the cell pattern is used to ensure that two adjacent cells do not use the same frequency at the same time.

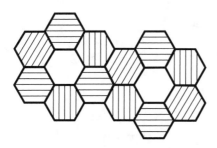

**FIGURE 15.1**

*Mobile wireless communications require a geographic area to be subdivided into cells that support operations on distinct frequencies. Under AMPS wireless communications, a seven-cell pattern is used.*

## Cellular Component Relationship

Each cell consists of a base station housing applicable electronics to support the wireless transmission method used and an antenna. As indicated in Figure 15.2, each base station is connected to an MTSO. The MTSO, in turn, is connected to the public switched telephone network and provides the interconnection mechanism that allows a mobile phone user touring downtown Chicago to wake up Aunt Tilly in Seattle.

As a mobile subscriber begins to leave the area of coverage of a particular cell, the base station notes a decrease in the level of signal strength of the subscriber. The base station of one or more other cells notes an increase in the level of power as the subscriber moves toward a new cell. Both the serving cell's base station and base stations adjacent to the serving base station communicate this information to the MTSO, which, in effect, functions as a traffic cop, selecting the base station with the strongest increase in signal power to receive a handoff of the subscriber from the existing cell's base station.

In performing the handoff operation, the MTSO checks its database to determine what frequencies are available in the cell the subscriber is entering. The MTSO then communicates this information to the base station that the subscriber is entering, referred to as the "gaining" cell. The base station in the gaining cell then adjusts its transmit and receive frequencies, and sends a message to the subscriber on its old receive frequency that informs the cell phone to adjust itself to the new frequency pair.

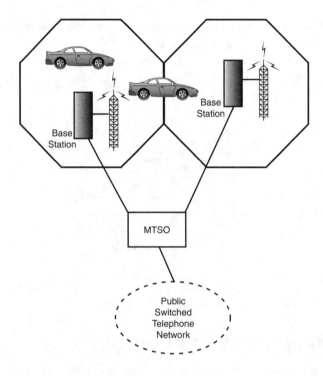

**Figure 15.2**

*The three components of a mobile wireless system include a cellular phone, a base station, and a mobile telephone switching office (MTSO).*

# AMPS

The analog cellular telephone system invented by Bell Laboratories can be considered to represent the first generation of wireless mobile communications. This system uses frequency-division multiple access (FDMA) as the network access technique. Figure 15.3 illustrates the use of FDMA.

Under FDMA, the 50MHz of frequency spectrum allocated by the Federal Communications Commission in the 800MHz band for AMPS operation was subdivided into distinct subchannels of 30KHz bandwidth, with each subchannel capable of supporting a single conversation. When the FCC allocated frequency to AMPS, it permitted two companies to offer service, referred to as the A-side and B-side carriers. Each carrier was allocated 25MHz, which, at 30MHz per channel, results in 832 cellular channels available per call. However, each 25MHz is subdivided into forward (base station to subscriber) and reverse (subscriber to base station) operations, referred to as transmit and receive operations. This action was required to provide support for full-duplex communications; however, it limits the number of full-duplex conversations that can occur within a cell to 416.

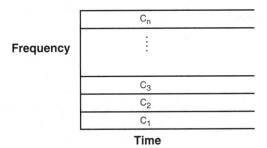

**Legend:** $c_1$ . . . $c_n$ channel 1 through channel n

**FIGURE 15.3**

*Under frequency-division multiple access (FDMA), the frequency band allocated for AMPS is subdivided into distinct channels, with each channel capable of supporting a voice conversation.*

As an analog technology, it is relatively easy to transmit data over AMPS. You can simply connect a modem to an AMPS-compatible cell phone. However, due to potential interference, you normally require a modem designed for over-the-air transmission that supports adjustable packet lengths and error correction. Because the 25KHz channel used by AMPS includes frequencies preassigned for special purposes, a data rate at 9.6Kbps is usually the highest that you can expect to achieve.

Until the turn of the millennium, AMPS had by far the most widespread coverage of all mobile wireless systems. Unfortunately, its success also resulted in the search for other network access technologies. As more users purchased AMPS-compatible cell phones, they began to experience an inability to make calls, especially in urban areas. This situation, referred to as blocking, occurs when call 417 is attempted with a cell whose maximum capacity is the support of 416 simultaneous calls. A second problem encountered by AMPS subscribers occurred when a cell lacked the capacity to assign a channel to a mobile user arriving in its area of coverage. This situation resulted in dropping a call in progress. Noting that fixed-cell analog couldn't support the growing base of subscribers, cellular developers introduced two new access methods. Those access methods are referred to as time division multiple access (TDMA) and code division multiple access (CDMA). Each access method supported an increase in the number of simultaneous subscribers that could use the transmission capacity of a cell.

# TDMA

Time division multiple access (TDMA) subdivides the frequency allocation of AMPS into time slots. Each AMPS channel is divided into a repeating sequence of three time slots, with a subscriber allocated to a frequency and time slot, as illustrated in Figure 15.4.

**15**

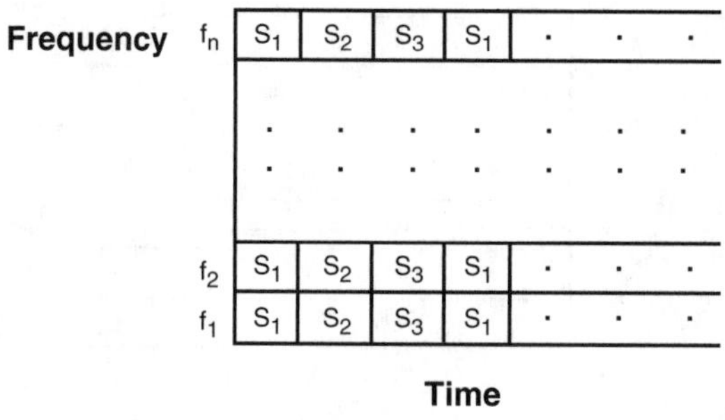

**FIGURE 15.4**

*Under time-division multiple access (TDMA), each AMPS channel is divided into a repeating sequence of three time slots.*

In North America, TDMA-based cellular systems operate at 800MHz or 1900MHz. When operating at 800MHz, TDMA can normally coexist with analog channels on the same network. This enables subscribers with a dual-mode phone to take advantage of AMPS or digital TDMA as they move about, a situation referred to as roaming. A second difference between TDMA and AMPS concerns the manner by which voice is transmitted. Under AMPS, which is an analog system, the 30–20000Hz range of human voice is first filtered to remove very low and high frequencies that are not important for understanding a conversation. Next, the remaining frequencies are frequency-modulated using a carrier in the center of the channel. In comparison, under TDMA voice is first encoded digitally at a low bit rate, typically using a hybrid coder that codes voice at a fraction of the 64Kbps PCM rate. Then the resulting digital data stream is modulated onto a radio signal. As a result of the digital coding of speech, the first version of TDMA that operated at 800MHz was also referred to as Digital Advanced Mobile Phone Services (D-AMPS).

## PCS

A second version of TDMA that operates at 1900MHz is referred to as the Personal Communications System (PCS). PCS systems operate at higher frequency than D-AMPS, and wavelength is proportional to the reciprocal of frequency, which results in the use of a shorter wavelength. The shorter wavelength associated with PCS results in a smaller cell diameter, which means that a 1900MHz system requires more cells per geographic area than an 800MHz system. This also explains why it's relatively easy to place a call using a PCS cell phone in urban areas or along an interstate highway. When you get into a rural area, however, your dual-mode phone more than likely uses AMPS to communicate.

Several types of PCS systems are in operation around the world. Examples of PCS systems include D-AMPS 1900 when it operates at 1900MHz, Global System for Mobile (GSM), and

CDMA. GSM is similar to D-AMPS 1900 in that it is based on the use of TDMA, whereas CDMA uses a completely different access technology.

The key advantage associated with PCS is the fact that a TDMA frame can be modified to support two calls instead of three for a specified period of time. When this occurs, time slots can be used to support what is referred to as a digital control channel (DCC). Through the use of the DCC, it becomes possible to transmit alphanumeric messages to and from PCS phones, a capability referred to as short message service (SMS). This permits a PCS-compatible cell phone to function as a pager.

The use of TDMA for D-AMPS and GSM permits cell phones to obtain an extended battery life in comparison to AMPS phones. The key reason for the extended battery life is the fact that the use of TDMA normally results in only one-third of the transmission time used in comparison to that of an AMPS phone. A second reason is based on the capability of a PCS phone in idle mode to periodically check the control channel to see if it has an incoming call. If a signal on the control channel is not found, the phone performs another Rip Van Winkle operation and goes back to sleep.

## GSM

GSM dates to the 1980s, when analog cellular systems in Nordic countries experienced rapid growth that resulted in the development of a new digital cellular standard. After five years of effort, 13 network operators and administrators signed a charter for the standardization of GSM. At that time, GSM was referred to by its French name, Group Speciale Mobile, but it is now known on a worldwide basis as Global System for Mobile Communications.

The European version of GSM operates in the 900MHz band, which was available in countries that are members of the European commission. Unfortunately, the 900MHz band in the United States was not available, so the 1900MHz band is used by GSM personal communications system in the United States.

GMS represents a TDMA version of PCS. As a digital technology, voice is first compressed using a hybrid coder at approximately 13Kbps before the data is modulated. With this digital technology, you can connect a data source directly to a GSM cell phone without the use of a modem. However, the highest data rate that you can expect to obtain will be approximately 14.4Kbps.

## CDMA

A third mobile wireless access technology is CDMA. Unlike AMPS and TDMA, which occur at one frequency, CDMA signals occur over an extended frequency band, referred to as broadband or spread-spectrum communications. The key advantage associated with spreading a signal is that, from Shannon's Law, channel capacity can be maintained at a lower power level. Thus, CDMA supports low-power operations.

Under CDMA, spreading occurs through the use of a pseudo-random (PN) digital code that spreads each bit. The PN signal is referred to as a code of chips, with each chip representing a data bit in the PN code. Each data bit to be transmitted under CDMA is first modulo 2 added to the PN code. The sequence of extended bits then is modulated over a 1.23MHz channel.

Figure 15.5 illustrates an example of the direct sequence spreading process. In this example, a 5-bit PN spreading code is used to spread a 3-bit message. This results in each data bit being transmitted five times, or once per chip operation. At the receiver, a modulo 2 subtraction process occurs to restore the data to its original composition. If a sequence of 5 bits (in this example) representing 1 data bit were corrupted because of transmission impairments, the receiver would select the most popular bit setting in the sequence. For example, if 4 bits were set to 1 and 1 bit was set to 0, the receiver would assume that the correct value of the data bit is 0.

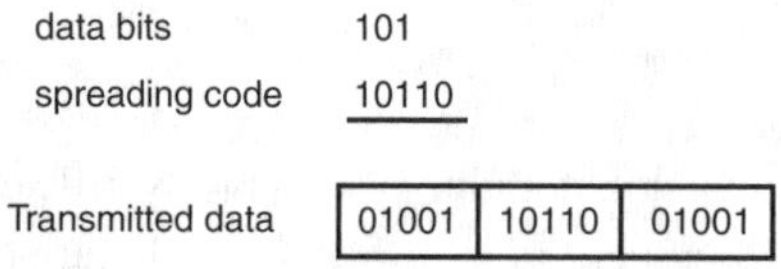

```
data bits          101
spreading code     10110

Transmitted data   | 01001 | 10110 | 01001 |
```

**FIGURE 15.5**

*Under direct sequence spread-spectrum transmission, each data bit is spread by its modulo2 addition with a PN code.*

Under CDMA, 1.23MHz of frequency spectrum accommodates one channel. Although this is significantly higher than with AMPS and TDMA, all available frequency spectrums under CDMA can be reused in each cell. In addition, by varying the PN code, it becomes possible for a CDMA system to support several times the capacity of a TDMA system. According to some studies, CDMA can support 10 times the capacity of a TDMA system, which, in turn, can support 3 times the capacity of an AMPS cell.

# Internet Access

In an attempt to find new uses for cell phones, a consortium of vendors founded the Wireless Application Protocol (WAP) forum. The WAP forum standardized an HTML-like protocol to provide subscribers with the capability to access the Internet. In actuality, WAP defines a protocol suite that includes a script language, a wireless version of HTML, security, and other functions. Because of the limited data-entry and storage capability of cell phones, the use of WAP requires a gateway to convert WAP into HTML and to perform hostname-to-IP-address-resolution functions. In addition, the limited screen display and relatively slow data-transfer rate of existing cell phones makes the use of the Internet via mobile wireless communications awkward. Although the screen size and keypad of cell phones are not expected to significantly change in the near future, a new generation of wireless communications may solve the slow data-transfer limitation of existing technology.

# 3G Networks

We can consider AMPS to represent the first generation of mobile wireless communications service, while TDM and CDMA represent second-generation services. Recognizing the need for supporting operations that would require higher data-transmission rates, the ITU launched a 3G project in 1986 referred to as IMT-2000. IMT-2000 represents a family of wireless systems intended to provide wireless access through satellite and terrestrial facilities for both fixed and mobile users. As such, it is entirely possible for emerging 3G systems to provide an alternative to wideband Internet access via DSL and cable modems.

Under the ITU's IMT-2000 roadmap, network services will include support for all existing PSTN services; voice message services such as paging, Teletex, and SMS; and high-speed multimedia. Both packet- and circuit-switched bearer services are intended to be supported under IMT-2000. Table 15.1 indicates the minimum data rates for different bearer services and different types of mobility.

**TABLE 15.1**   IMT-2000 Minimum Data Rates

| Bearer Service | Mobility | Data Rate |
|---|---|---|
| Packet | Vehicular | 144Kbps |
| | Outdoor to indoor and pedestrian** | 384Kbps* |
| | Indoor office | 2Mbps |
| Circuit-switched | Vehicular | 144Kbps |
| | Outdoor to indoor and pedestrian** | 384Kbps* |
| | Indoor office | 2Mbps |

* Minimum will be 144Kbps if vehicular technology is used.
**Asymmetric option results in lower reverse performance.

Until recently, it appeared that the efforts of cellular operators and product manufacturers in Europe and Japan would take a divergent path from North America in the development of 3G wireless systems. Initially, European and Japanese cell phone manufacturers and system operators selected the use of wideband CDMA (WCDMA), which is substantially different from North American CDMA.

In North America a CDMA development group branded the trademark CdmaOne to describe a complete wireless system to include the air interface, switch interconnection, and other aspects necessary to obtain a complete wireless system based upon CDMA. A standard approved by the Telecommunications Industry Association (TIA) in July 1999 referred to as 1XRTT addressed upgrading CDMA to 144Kbps in a mobile environment.

To move toward 3G in the United States, the TIA assigned the name Cdma2000 to identify the planned evolution of CDMA from a second-generation CdmaOne system to 3G services and features defined by the 1XRTT standard. On the road to 3G, it appeared that Europe and Japan would take a separate path from the United States. However, a June 1999 meeting of the ITU group of radio experts on IMT-2000 endorsed harmonization for the CDMA component of the IMT-2000 standard that will enable WCDMA and CDMA2000 phones to interoperate.

During 2000 and 2001, bandwidth was licensed in Europe for 3G operations. By 2004, it is expected that the first 3G systems and phones will be activated, permitting residential users to surf the Web at data rates of 2Mbps as well as send and receive information when mobile at a data rate of 144Kbps. Now that you have an appreciation for the manner in which mobile wireless can be expected to evolve to support both mobile and high-speed fixed voice and data transmission, let's conclude this chapter by looking at the operation and utilization of wireless LANs.

## Wireless LANs

Because of the growth in the use of e-mail, the expansion of Internet communications, and the mobility requirements of a growing number of persons in business, government, and academia, wireless LANs went from a niche product to a popular solution for many networking requirements. Part of the growth in the use of wireless LANs can be attributed to the IEEE 802.11b standard, which increased the data-transmission rate of wireless LANs to 11Mbps (now at 54Mbps), making them practical for use in homes, offices, and even hotels and airports. Because wireless LANs avoid the need of wires, they can be deployed quicker and in many instances faster than their wired cousins.

The use of wireless LANs dates to the mid-1980s, when several proprietary systems were developed to operate in unlicensed frequency bands. In 2000, the IEEE developed an initial standard for wireless LANs, referred to as 802.11. This standard defined wireless LAN access methods—infrared, frequency-hopping spread spectrum (FHSS), and direct sequence spread spectrum (DSSS). Each access method supports data transmission at either 1Mbps or 2Mbps.

The IEEE extended the 802.11 standard with its 802.11b specification that added operations at 5.5Mbps and 11Mbps using DSSS. A second extension to the 802.11 standard, referred to as 802.11a, extends data transmission to 54Mbps using a transmission method referred to as orthogonal frequency-division multiplexing (OFDM). Products compliant with the IEEE 802.11 standard and the IEEE 802.11b extension to the standard are actively marketed and operate in the 2.4GHz frequency band. Products compliant with the 802.11a extension to the standard will operate in the 5.0GHz frequency band and became commercially available during 2002.

## Transmission Methods

IEEE-compliant LANs support one of four transmission methods—infrared, FHSS, DSSS, or OFDM. Infrared communications support relatively short transmission distances and have never achieved a significant degree of use. Both FHSS and DSSS represent wideband transmission methods that were originally developed for the military to overcome jamming by the enemy.

Figure 15.6 illustrates the operation of FHSS communications. Note that the execution of the same algorithm by transmitter and receiver governs the manner by which frequency hops become compatible. Because each frequency is used for a relatively short period of time before the transmitter hops to a new frequency, this action minimizes the effect of jamming. In addition, because interference due to machinery, electronic ballasts, and other devices usually occurs within a small frequency band, FHSS minimizes the effect of interference upon transmission.

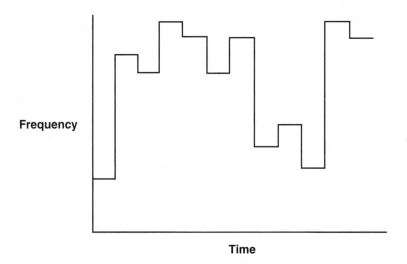

**FIGURE 15.6**

*Frequency-hopping spread spectrum (FHSS) minimizes the potential effect of electromagnetic interference.*

As previously noted in our discussion of CDMA, DSSS uses a pseudo-random (PN) code to spread a signal over a range of frequencies. The receiver uses the same PN code to recover the original data. Under the IEEE 802.11 standard, an 11-bit Barker code is used to spread each data bit into 11 bits that are then modulated. The receiver demodulates the data and compares the setting of each group of 11 bits, selecting the value assigned to 6 or more bits. For example, if a demodulated 11-bit sequence was 11011111101, the receiver would consider the two 0 bits as bit errors and would assign a value of 1 to the data bit represented by the 11-bit sequence. The third transmission method used by IEEE LANs is OFDM. Under OFDM, groups of bits are modulated using a series of subcarriers, as illustrated in Figure 15.7. Because each subcarrier is independent of other subcarriers, transmission is orthogonal. The IEEE 802.11a standard is based upon OFDM and uses 48 subcarriers and 4 pilot tones per channel.

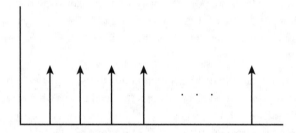

**FIGURE 15.7**
*Orthogonal frequency-division multiplexing uses multiple subcarriers, each independent of one another.*

## Network Types

Two types of networks are supported by the IEEE 802.11 standard—peer-to-peer and infrastructure. Peer-to-peer networking is referred to as ad hoc and permits two or more clients to communicate with one another directly. The top portion of Figure 15.8 illustrates an example of wireless LAN ad hoc communications.

The second type of network supported under the IEEE standard requires wireless LAN clients to employ the services of an access point. This type of wireless LAN networking is illustrated in the lower portion of Figure 15.8 and represents the infrastructure method of networking.

An access point can be considered to represent a bridge that connects wireless clients to a wired LAN. Wireless clients use a six-hex-digit Media Access Control (MAC) address similar to that of their wired clients. By constructing a port-address table that now reflects on the air and wired MAC addresses, the access point rapidly learns which frames on the wired LAN need to be broadcast over the air and which frames remain on the wire.

**Ad hoc**

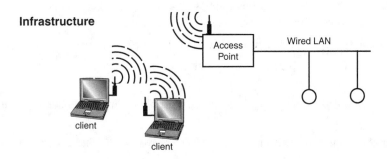

**Infrastructure**

Access
Point

Wired LAN

client

client

**FIGURE 15.8**
*Wireless LAN networking includes ad hoc and infrastructure networks.*

# Wireless LAN Service Sets

Similar to most networks, a wireless LAN needs an identifier. When you use a single access point, the identifier is referred to as a basic service set (BSS) and is normally the MAC address of the access point that is obtained over the air by each client. When you establish multiple access points within a building, each will have its own BSS identification and will act independently of the other access points. To permit clients to roam from one access point to another, an extended service set (ESS) must be established. An ESS is formed by configuring two or more access points with the same identification, which allows them to operate in conjunction with one another.

# Wireless LAN Applications

No discussion of wireless LANs would be complete without mentioning a few of the numerous applications that are the driving force behind its growth.

In the home or office, wireless LANs provide a quick and relatively inexpensive method to allow multiple users to access the Internet via a single connection, such as a cable or DSL modem line. At airports and hotels, you can expect to encounter Internet portals where 802.11b-compatible access points are installed that allow travelers to obtain high-speed access to the Internet from their laptops or notebooks. On college campuses, wireless LANs facilitate

**15**

WIRELESS
TRANSMISSION

such activities as class registration and sporting events, allowing LAN administrators to place computer equipment on gym floors and at other locations that previously would have required hours of recabling and necessitated taping cables to the floor to prevent tripping. As we move through the new millennium, wireless LAN applications are limited only by the imagination.

## What You Have Learned

- The three components of a mobile wireless transmission system include base stations, a mobile telephone switching office (MTSO), and cellular phones.

- Each wireless cell contains a base station housing applicable electronics and an antenna.

- AMPS uses a seven-cell pattern to prevent interference between subscribers communicating in adjacent cells.

- The three primary access technologies used by mobile wireless products include FDMA, TDMA, and CDMA.

- Digital-AMPS uses TDMA and encodes voice into a low bit rate prior to its modulation.

- The digital control channel obtained from a TDMA slot enables a short message service to be added to PCS.

- CDMA represents a wideband communications technology in which a signal is spread over an extended frequency band.

- WAP represents a suite of protocols that enables compatible cell phones to access the Internet.

- 3G systems will enable data transmission at data rates of 2Mbps from fixed locations, providing competition to cable and DSL modem access to the Internet.

- The IEEE 802.11 standard governs wireless operations at 1Mbps and 2Mbps, while the 802.11b extension increased the transmission rate of wireless LANs to 11Mbps. The second extension referred to as 802.11a will support data rates up to 54Mbps.

- IEEE wireless LANs support ad hoc and infrastructure networking.

## Quiz for Chapter 15

1. The assignment of a subscriber to a new cell is referred to as

    A. Power adjustment

    B. Handoff

    C. Falloff

    D. Conversion

2.  What is a gaining cell?

    A.  A cell in which a subscriber arrives from a different cell

    B.  A cell from which a subscriber exists the system

    C.  A cell with no occupants

    D.  A cell that has put on weight

3.  An example of the first generation of mobile wireless communications is

    A.  CDMA

    B.  TDMA

    C.  1XT34

    D.  AMPS

4.  What is the method of network access used by AMPS?

    A.  CDMA

    B.  TDMA

    C.  WCDMA

    D.  FDMA

5.  The number of simultaneous conversations supported in an AMPS cell is

    A.  832

    B.  416

    C.  1,296

    D.  Undetermined

6.  What does blocking represent?

    A.  The incapability to place a call

    B.  The incapability to receive a call

    C.  The incapability to roam

    D.  Making a call at a long distance from a base station

7.  The use of TDMA instead of FDMA increases cell capacity by what factor?

    A.  15

    B.  8

    C.  3

    D.  2

8. Which represents an example of a personal communications system?

   A. AMPS

   B. 800MHz D-AMPS

   C. GSM

   D. All of the above

9. What is the access method used by GSM?

   A. CDMA

   B. FDMA

   C. TDMA

   D. WCDMA

10. Assume that a CDMA receiver using a seven-chip PN code received the bit sequence 1011101. What would the receiver set the data bit value to?

    A. 1011101

    B. 0100010

    C. 0

    D. 1

11. What is the maximum operating rate of a wireless LAN using infrared communications?

    A. 1Mbps

    B. 2Mbps

    C. 5Mbps

    D. 11Mbps

12. What is the maximum operating rate of an IEEE wireless LAN using direct sequence spread-spectrum communications?

    A. 1Mbps

    B. 2Mbps

    C. 5Mbps

    D. 11Mbps

13. What is the type of wireless networking that allows two clients to communicate directly with each other?

    A. Ad hoc

    B. Infrastructure

    C. Roaming

    D. Blocking

14. What is the type of wireless networking that requires clients to employ the services of an access point?

    A. Ad hoc

    B. Infrastructure

    C. Roaming

    D. Blocking

15. Roaming in a wireless LAN environment requires

    A. Different service set identifiers.

    B. Blocking the old access point.

    C. Setting the BSS values sequentially.

    D. An extended service set.

# Network Security

## IN THIS CHAPTER

Although we briefly mentioned network security earlier in this book, we deferred an in-depth discussion of this topic until this chapter. In the wonderful world of data communications, security is essential for many computer-to-computer tasks we perform. Without security, it might be difficult, if not impossible, to expect consumers to place online orders for books, computers, and perfume. In addition, how many people would be tempted to send e-mail messages informing an associate of the price to bid on industrial equipment, an office building, or a consulting project without the ability to encode the message? About a hundred years ago, a member of the Foreign Service stated that "gentlemen do not read other person's mail." Unfortunately times have changed, and we not only have the threat of third parties attempting to read electronic mail but also altering the contents of the message. In addition, we live in a society in which some people obtain a strange perversion by defacing Web pages, breaking into corporate servers, and attempting to generate a large enough level of extraneous activity that legitimate users are blocked or denied service of their requests. In this chapter, we will commence with the basics of security and expand upon our knowledge of this important field. First, we will focus our attention upon access techniques to include authentication methods that can be used to gain access to network facilities. Other topics we will cover include public and private key encryption, the role of router access lists, firewalls, and digital certificates.

# Authorization, Authentication, and Accounting

One of the pillars of network security is commonly referred to as triple A or AAA as an abbreviation for authorization, authentication and accounting. The process of identifying an individual is referred to as *authentication*. A common method of authentication is based upon a username and password, requiring a person to enter a preassigned data pair to gain access to a network facility. This most basic form of authentication results in the transmission of a user ID and password in the clear (not encrypted)over a network. This method of authentication occurs via the *Password Authentication Protocol (PAP)* in which the data-pair is compared to entries stored in a table at the destination. Although the stored data is encrypted, the transmitted data is not, representing a weakness that can be exploited by a network monitor.

A more security conscious version of a challenge-response system is referred to as the *Challenge Handshake Authentication Protocol (CHAP)*. Under CHAP, an authentication agent, which is commonly a software module operating on a server, transmits a key to a client. The client uses the key to encrypt the user ID and password, which are then transmitted to the server. This action makes it much more difficult for an unauthorized user to determine the user ID and password of another user via monitoring network activity. In comparison, authorization is the process of providing persons with access to system objects based upon their identity. Thus, although a person might be able to gain access to a computer, router, or gateway, she might have only a limited ability with respect to performing functions once access occurs.

Because authentication literally unlocks the door into a system, a considerable amount of development effort has occurred beyond the entry of a user ID/password pair. One of the more common higher levels of authentication developed occurs using a smart card challenge-response system. Smart cards physically resemble a credit card with a 6-digit display that changes value every minute. Such cards are distributed to persons that need to access a computer. Each person is also provided with a four-digit secret *personal identification number (PIN)*. When a person accesses a computer that uses smart card authentication, she is prompted (challenged) to enter the six-digit value on her smart card as well as her PIN. The computer uses the same algorithm as electronic circuitry on the smart card to compare the six-digit code entered against the code that is applicable in the current one-minute period and verifies the PIN of the user. If both values are accepted, the user obtains access to the system.

Because the smart card is useless without the PIN, its loss does not compromise the system. However, if the user taped his or her PIN on the card, carelessness can compromise this system.

The third *A* in the triple A process is accounting. By logging access attempts, you can determine whether a third party is attempting to break into your system or an employee simply forgot her password. Thus, accounting can represent a mechanism to note when your organization is potentially under attack as well as serve as a warning to consider corrective action.

## Computer Lockout

During the 1980s, one of the favorite methods used to break into a computer system was to run the contents of an electronic dictionary against a user ID. Because many organizations simply used the first initial, middle initial, and last name as the user ID, any knowledge of persons who work at an organization provides a foundation for breaking into a computer. Recognizing this problem, computer software developers quickly added a lockout facility to the user sign-on module. The lockout facility is set by the administrator to prevent further access attempts once a specified threshold of unsuccessful attempts is reached. Most lockout software also enables the administrator to set a second threshold that governs the duration of the lockout. For example, an administrator might be able to set the lockout duration to 5, 10, or 15 minutes or permanently, with the latter requiring manual intervention by the administrator to overcome the lockout.

## Data Encryption

Two types of encryption systems are used in data communications—private key and public key. Under a private key encryption system, the sender and receiver of a message share a single, common key that is employed to encrypt and decrypt a message. In comparison, under public key encryption, a pair of keys is used. One is the public key whereas the other is a private key. A public key is known to everyone and is used to encrypt data. The private key is known only to the recipient of a message and through a complex mathematical relationship with the public key is used to decrypt the message.

Both public and private key systems employ modulo-2 arithmetic to encrypt and decrypt data. Through the use of a key a pseudo-random data stream is generated, which is modulo-2 added to clear text to generate ciphered or encrypted text. The top portion of Table 16.1 illustrates the encryption process. At the recipient the same key is used to operate upon the encrypted data to reconvert it back into clear or deciphered data. However, instead of modulo-2 addition, this reverse process requires the use of modulo-2 subtraction. The lower portion of Table 16.1 illustrates the use of modulo-2 subtraction.

**TABLE 16.1**  Both Private and Public Key Operations Use Modulo-2 Arithmetic to Encipher and Decipher Data

| A. | *Encipherment Using Modulo-2 Addition* | |
|---|---|---|
| | Data to be encrypted | 1 0 1 1 0 1 1 0 |
| | Key generated PN data | 0 1 1 0 1 1 0 1 |
| | Encrypted data | 1 1 0 1 1 0 1 1 |
| B. | *Decipherment using modulo-2 subtraction* | |
| | Encrypted data | 1 1 0 1 1 0 1 1 |
| | Key generated PN data | 0 1 1 0 1 1 0 1 |
| | Decrypted data | 1 0 1 1 0 1 1 0 |

In examining Table 16.1, note that the key generates a pseudo-random (PN) data string that is modulo-2 added to produce an encrypted data stream. At the receiver, the key must generate the same PN data, which is modulo 2 subtracted from the encrypted data to create decrypted or clear text data.

One of the key problems associated with a private key encryption system is key management and distribution. Because both transmitter and receiver must use the same key, the more persons who share the key increases the risk that the key will be compromised. If each pair of persons uses a separate key, both key management and key distribution can become increasingly complex. Due to this, private key encryption would be impossible to manage in a World Wide Web environment. Instead, public key systems permit any user accessing a secure Web site to retrieve the public key associated with the site. The client then uses the public key to encrypt data while the Web site uses its private key to decrypt data.

Private key systems are referred to as symmetric-key systems because the same key is used to encrypt and decrypt data. Although private key systems are relatively simple to operate and their computation effort is minimal, the distribution of keys represents a significant management problem. Either keys must initially be distributed in the clear or mailed or hand delivered to the other party. In comparison, public key systems permit the public key to be available to everyone, which eliminates the key distribution problem associated with private key systems. However, the mathematical relationship between the public and private key pair in the public key system is very complex, based on the use of prime numbers, and requires a considerable amount of time and processing power. Because of this, some applications combine the two. That is, a public key system is used to distribute a private key, which is then used to perform encryption.

# Digital Certificates

Because we need to ensure that the party we are communicating with is who he claims to be, we need a method to authenticate that party. Similarly, that party will want to verify the identity of the client. Providing this capability resulted in the development of a system of digital certificates and certificate authorities that are referred to collectively as a public key infrastructure (PKI).

A digital certificate can be considered to represent an attachment to an electronic message. The primary purpose of a digital certificate is to verify the person sending a message as well as to provide the receiver with a mechanism to send a reply. Note that, by itself, a digital certificate only represents a proof of identity and is not a permission to do anything.

A person or organization who wants to transmit an encrypted message that verifies the identity of the originator applies for a digital certificate from a Certificate Authority (CA). The CA issues an encrypted digital certificate, which will contain the applicant's public key and additional information. The Certificate Authority also makes its public key available so that the recipient of an encrypted message can use that key to decrypt the digital certificate attached to a message. This enables the recipient to verify that the CA issued the digital certificate. After the CA is verified, the recipient will obtain the originator's public key, which it will use to transmit an encrypted response.

The CA can be viewed as a trusted third party, which enables verification of third parties. The most widely used standard for defining digital certificates is the ITU-T X.509 Recommendation.

# Secure Sockets Layer and S-HTTP

To facilitate the growth in the use of browsers for electronic commerce, Netscape Corporation, now part of AOL, which merged with Time Warner, developed a protocol for transmitting encrypted data between Web browsers and Web servers. That protocol is referred to as *Secure Sockets Layer (SSL)*. Under SSL a public key is transmitted to the browsers over the SSL connection. The browser uses the key to receive a private key from the server. The private key is then used to encrypt data. Both Netscape's Navigator and Microsoft's Internet Explorer support SSL.

You can note an SSL connection in two ways. First, Web pages that require an SSL connection commence their URL with https: instead of http:. Second, an icon on the browser will change shape when you have a secure connection.

Figure 16.1 illustrates two Netscape browsers. The browser in the background has a secure connection to Waterhouse Securities. Note the closed lock icon in the lower left portion of the background window. In comparison, the browser's window in the foreground has a non-secure connection to the Netscape home page. If you carefully look in the left lower portion of the foreground window, you will note that the lock is open, signifying the use of a non-secure connection.

**FIGURE 16.1**

*Netscape uses a lock icon to denote the type of connection. The lock appears closed to indicate a secure connection and is shown open or unlocked to indicate a non-secure connection.*

A second protocol for transmitting data securely via the Web is referred to as *Secure HTTP (S-HTTP)*. In comparison to SSL, which creates a secure connection between a client and server, S-HTTP is used to transmit individual messages securely.

Through the use of Netscape Navigator, you can view a certificate associated with a Web page. To do so you would first select the Security Info display, which provides you with information about the page you are viewing as well as the ability to examine the certificate of pages that are encrypted. Figure 16.2 illustrates the Security Info display when I pointed my Web browser to the Salomon Smith Barney home page. Salomon Smith Barney is a full-line brokerage business that uses a digital certificate provided by VeriSign. We can view the digital certificate by clicking on the button labeled View Certificate, so let's do so.

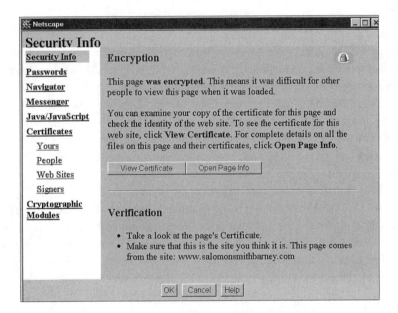

**FIGURE 16.2**

*The security information display provided by Netscape represents a focal point for obtaining security-related information to include viewing the digital certificate issued to a Web page.*

Figure 16.3 illustrates information displayed concerning the digital certificate issued to Salomon Smith Barney. Note that the display informs us that the certificate was issued by VeriSign. The display also shows the serial number of the certificate and the time period when it is valid. Because Citigroup, a very large financial organization, acquired Salomon Smith Barney several years ago, the certificate also indirectly includes the fact that Salomon Smith Barney is an operating unit of Citigroup by including the name of the parent organization on the certificate.

This Certificate belongs to:     This Certificate was
www.salomonsmithbarney.com issued by:
   Salomon Smith Barney              www.verisign.com/CPS
   Citigroup                         Incorp.by Ref. LIABILITY
   New York City, New York, US       LTD.(c)97 VeriSign
                                     VeriSign International
                                     Server CA - Class 3
                                     VeriSign, Inc.
                                     VeriSign Trust Network

Serial Number:
25:E0:EC:6C:60:16:DA:31:F5:37:6C:E0:F0:24:8B:AE
This Certificate is valid from Wed Nov 15, 2000 to Fri
Nov 16, 2001
Certificate Fingerprint:
   DE:9F:8E:AC:8D:4A:F8:40:EE:DF:65:BE:91:19:FC:E2

OK

**FIGURE 16.3**

*Viewing information about a digital certificate issued to Salomon Smith Barney, an operating unit of Citigroup.*

When working with digital certificates, your browser will occasionally leave the ultimate decision of whether to proceed up to the user. A common example in which the browser user must make a decision to proceed or terminate a secure connection occurs when the site you attempt to access has a certificate that does not match the site name. Figure 16.4 illustrates an example of the warning message displayed in the form of a dialog box labeled Certificate Name Check. In this example, I was attempting to access my CompuServe e-mail account via the Internet. Because America Online acquired CompuServe, accessing CompuServe results in a digital certificate issued to America Online being presented. In this situation, the browser informs us that the certificate for the site does not contain the correct site name. The dialog display then informs us that it is possible, but unlikely, that someone could be attempting to intercept our communications with the site we are attempting to access, and we must contact the site administrator if we suspect hanky panky. Because I, like millions of CompuServe users, know that America Online acquired this information utility: The fact that the certificate for CompuServe was presented by the other company is no cause for alarm. Thus, we would click on the button labeled Continue, which would accept the certificate. The result would be the establishment of a secure connection to my e-mail account on CompuServe.

Now that we have an appreciation for passwords, encryption, and the role of digital certificates, let's turn our focus to the use of two key network devices in enhancing security. Those network devices are routers and firewalls.

# Router-Based Security

The primary function of a router was and remains the movement of packets between networks. However, because a router represents the primary connection point between networks to include private networks and the Internet, it also represents a first line of network defense.

**FIGURE 16.4**

*When a digital certificate does not contain the same organization's name as the site being accessed, the browser will inform you of this fact.*

Although the Internet opened a literal endless source of information to tens of millions of users, it also opens up corporate networks to any person with access to the Internet. Those persons can include customers and potential customers, rivals, Web surfers, and, unfortunately, a group of unscrupulous persons referred to as *hackers*. Recognizing the fact that in any large population there are probably one or more unscrupulous persons, it becomes necessary to add a variety of security features to different types of network equipment as a means of protecting corporate networks. Because the router can literally provide the first line of network defense, one of the first areas of comprehensive network security occurred by the addition of access list processing as a router feature.

## Access Lists

Because a router represents the initial connection between networks, it also represents an organization's first line of defense. In this section, we will examine the use of access lists that enable organizations to perform packet filtering operations.

An access list can be considered to represent one or more statements that control the flow of packets through a router's interface. Many router manufacturers support two types of access lists, commonly referred to as standard and extended. A standard or basic access list represents one or more statements that include a source IP address and the keyword permit or deny. The keyword permit allows packets with the source IP address in the statement to flow through the interface to which the access list is applied. In comparison, the keyword deny results in packets with the source IP address matching the address in the access list being transmitted to the great bit bucket in the sky.

In a Cisco router environment, the format of a basic or standard access list is as follows:

```
access-list list # {permit|deny} IP address wildcard mask
```

The list number can be any value from 1 to 99 and identifies the access list as an IP access list. In addition, the list number also identifies a group of statements as belonging to the same access list. The `wildcard mask` serves as a special operator in a reverse manner to a `subnet mask`, identifying a specific IP address or a group of IP addresses. That is, a `wildcard mask` consists of 32 bits, specified in dotted decimal notation, that use a bit setting of 0 to denote a match and a bit setting of 1 to denote a don't care condition.

## Standard Access Lists

To better understand the use of a standard access list, let's assume that your organization's network is connected to the Internet at two geographically separated locations. At one location, the network address is 205.131.195.0. To enable only those computers on the 205.131.195.0 network to gain access to the second network, you would add the following access list to the router at the second network location:

```
access-list 1 permit 205.131.195.0 0.0.0.255
```

In examining the preceding statement, note that the wildcard mask is `0.0.0.255`. Because binary 0s indicate a match condition whereas binary 1s indicate a don't care condition, the first three bytes result in all packets to be permitted requiring the network address of the Class C network. The last byte has the value `255` decimal, which is equivalent to binary `11111111` and indicates that we do not care which computer address is on the network.

A second item to note from the prior example is the fact that although packets from the 205.131.195.0 network are permitted, we do not see any deny statement. In actuality, most routers to include those manufactured by Cisco operate their access lists by denying everything other than that explicitly permitted. In fact, an access list can be considered to have a "hidden" deny all statement at the bottom of the list.

To add a few additional examples of basic or standard access lists, let's assume that you only want to permit packets from the host whose IP address is 205.131.195.12. To do so you would code the access list as follows:

```
access-list 1 permit 205.131.195.12 0.0.0.0
```

Because it gets boring after a while to add a wildcard mask of `0.0.0.0` to a host address, Cisco uses the keyword `host` to replace the use of that mask. Thus, you could rewrite the preceding access list statement as

```
access-list 1 permit host 205.131.195.12
```

Similar to using the keyword host to replace a wildcard mask, Cisco also supports the key-word any as a mechanism to allow all IP addresses. Here the word any replaces the IP address wildcard mask sequence of 0.0.0.0 255.255.255.255.

# Extended Access List

The extended access list provides a significant level of additional packet filtering capability. This access list permits filtering on both the source and destination IP address, protocol (IP, ICMP, TCP, UDP) port number, and other metrics. The general format of the Cisco extended access list is shown as follows:

```
access-list list # {permit|deny} (protocol) source-
address wildcard-mask [source port] destination-address
 wildcard-mask [destination port] [optional parameters]
```

The list number for an extended IP access list must be between 100 and 199. Similar to a basic access list, the list number identifies the type of access list as well as the statements that make up a particular access list. Although only one access list can be applied at any one time to an interface in one direction, you can create multiple access lists and apply them as needed. You can also apply different access lists to the inbound and outbound directions on an interface. The inbound direction represents the flow of packets toward a router, whereas the outbound direction references the flow of packets outward from a router.

In a Cisco router environment, you can specify ports by their numeric number or mnemonic identifier. For example, to specify Web traffic, you could use 80 or http because both refer-ence the TCP port used to convey Web traffic.

Cisco's operating system, which is known as the Internetwork Operating System (IOS), sup-ports many optional parameters that can be added to an extended IP access list. One common example is the keyword log, which results in each match—resulting from a packet meeting the criteria of an access list statement—being logged to memory. Another example of an optional parameter is the keyword established. When used in an extended IP access list, this keyword only permits packets to flow through an interface that is part of an existing conversation. To do so, the packet examines the setting of the ACK or RST bit in the TCP header. This action enables hosts behind the router to limit the flow of packets to their IP address in response to TCP requests they generated. Unfortunately, UDP has no ACK or RST bit settings, so estab-lished does not work with that protocol. For additional information on the variety of access list keyword options, you should consider the book *Cisco Access List Field Guide*, coauthored by Gilbert Held and Kent Hundley and published by McGraw-Hill.

To illustrate an example of the use of an extended IP access list, let's assume that your organi-zation has the IP network address 205.131.175.0. Let's further assume that your organization operates a Web server whose IP address is 205.131.175.10 and a Telnet server whose IP address is 205.131.175.14. Last, but not least, let's assume that you want to allow users on the 205.131.195.0 network access to the Web server whereas only the manager on that network whose IP address is 205.1311.195.007 will have access to the Telnet server. To accomplish this "mission possible" scenario, you would create the following access list:

```
access-list 101 permit 205.131.195.0 0.0.0.255 host 205.121.175.10
access-list 101 permit host 205.131.195.7 host 205.121.175.15
```

The first statement in the preceding access list allows any host of the 205.131.195.0 network to access the host whose address is 204.131.175.10. The second statement in the access list requires the source IP address in a packet to be 205.131.195.7, whereas the destination IP address must be 204.131.175.15. Any other IP source and destination address combination is sent to the great bit bucket in the sky.

Prior to moving on, a few words concerning the processing of access list statements are in order. Access list statements are processed sequentially from the top down until a match occurs between the contents of a packet and access list statement parameters. Once a match occurs, the packet is either permitted or denied and there is no going back nor forward. Thus, it is important to consider both the contents of the statements in an access list as well as their order.

Although router access lists represent a valuable method of safeguarding corporate networks from intrusion, they are not infallible. IP addresses can be spoofed, which means that it is possible for a cracker to override the access list barrier unless everything is denied, defeating the purpose of having an Internet connection. In addition, access lists do not look into a packet to examine its contents. This means that it is possible for a person to attempt to access a closed user group on a server by repeatedly trying different passwords, a technique referred to as a "dictionary attack" when the person writes a program that cycles through every entry in an electronic dictionary. Because of those problems, a new type of network protection device referred to as a *firewall* was developed.

# Network Protection Via a Firewall

A firewall is often installed between a router and the network that is used to protect your internal network. From a physical perspective, the firewall is a computer with two LAN adapter cards. One card connects to what is referred to as a Demilitarized (DMZ) LAN hub, and the second adapter connects to a hub on the protected network. Figure 16.5 illustrates the previously described connection. Note that because only the router and firewall share access to the DMZ hub, all traffic to and from the Internet must pass through the firewall.

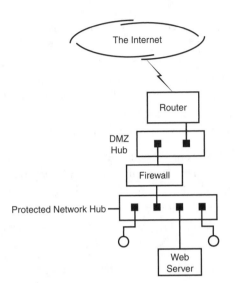

**FIGURE 16.5**
*A firewall is normally connected to a DMZ LAN to ensure that all traffic to and from the Internet flows through the device.*

A firewall is programmed to perform a number of security-related functions. Those functions can include stateful inspection, proxy services, encryption, authentication, and alert generation. Stateful inspection represents the examination of the contents of packets in a flow that has the same destination address. This enables suspicious activity, such as repeated logon attempts, to be noted. Depending on how the firewall is configured, subsequent packets might be barred, or the firewall administrator or other persons might be paged or e-mailed and alerted of the situation.

A proxy service is an intermediary between the service requestor and the desired service. A proxy service can be employed for FTP, Telnet, and other applications. Instead of packets directly flowing through the firewall to the desired destination, they are serviced by the firewall and then passed to the destination. In this way, the firewall handles connection requests for services, which means it operates as a proxy service. Through the use of a proxy, it becomes possible to place a greater level of control on the use of certain application services. For example, many FTP proxy services let you enable or disable certain FTP commands. One common use of an FTP proxy is to bar the use of the MGET command. This is because a person accessing an FTP server who either intentionally or unintentionally issues the command MGET *.*, which could cause every file in a directory to be downloaded, could saturate the outbound communications circuit from the organization to the Internet.

One of the more recent features added to firewalls is selective encryption. This enables data flowing over predefined Internet locations to be encrypted, whereas other data remains as is. Using selective encryption and authentication, you can create a logical tunnel through the physical structure of the Internet to connect two or more geographically separated organizational locations. This technique creates a *virtual private network (VPN)* and is gaining in popularity as a means of replacing expensive leased lines commonly used to interconnect businesses. Leased lines are normally billed on a monthly basis based on transmission distance.

In comparison, Internet access is billed on the line access rate and is transmission distance insensitive with respect to cost. This means that an organization with offices in New York and Los Angeles that might otherwise have to pay $4 per mile per month for a T1 connection between those locations for 2600 router miles might be able to pay $1,000 per location for T1 access to the Internet. Thus, the monthly cost of communications could decrease from $10,400 to $2,000.

However, before you run into your boss's office and suggest replacing a leased line network with the use of the Internet, it is important to note that, unlike in a private network, there is currently no method to guarantee bandwidth and data delivery through the Internet. Thus, real-time and time-sensitive applications are generally not well suited for conversion to a VPN. However, if your organization primarily uses a leased line network for file transfers and e-mail (both delay-insensitive applications), a VPN might be just what the doctor ordered.

## What You Have Learned

- One of the pillars of network security is authorization, authentication, and accounting, referred to as AAA.

- A higher level of authentication occurs using a smart-card challenge-response system instead of a user ID-password pair.

- The use of a lockout facility blocks further access attempts after a predefined number of invalid access attempts occur.

- A private key encryption system operates faster than a public key encryption system but requires careful thought concerning the distribution of keys.

- Public key encryption permits a person or organization to publish their public key that anyone can use to encrypt data. The user keeps her private key, which is used to decrypt messages.

- Digital certificates provide a mechanism to identify or authenticate a user or organization.

- Secure Sockets Layer represents a protocol that facilitates the encrypted transmission of Web pages from a server to a client.

- Two types of access lists are basic or standard and extended. Both use permit and deny statements to control the flow of packets through an interface.

- Both router access lists and firewalls can be used to protect organizational computer facilities connected to the Internet from hackers.

# Quiz for Chapter 16

1. The process of identifying an individual is referred to as

    A. Authorization

    B. Authentication

    C. Accounting

    D. Quality of Service

2. How is the password and user ID associated with a password transmitted under the Password Authentication Protocol?

    A. In the clear.

    B. Encrypted.

    C. The password is encrypted.

    D. The user ID is encrypted.

3. The use of a smart card represents a form of

    A. Password encryption

    B. User ID encryption

    C. Authorization

    D. Authentication

4. What effect does the loss of a smart card have on a smart card–based security system?

    A. Requires all smart cards to be replaced

    B. Requires only the master smart card to be replaced

    C. Requires the replacement of the last smart card

    D. Has no effect on the smart card security system

5. What is another name for a private key encryption system?

    A. An asymmetrical key system

    B. A symmetrical key system

    C. A dual key system

    D. An unbreakable system

6. Assume that a byte to be encrypted has the bit composition 10110110, whereas the pseudo random data used to encrypt the byte has the bit composition 10110000. What is the composition of the encrypted byte?

   A. 00000000

   B. 11111111

   C. 11111001

   D. 00000110

7. What is a key problem associated with private key encryption?

   A. Maintaining dual keys

   B. Modulo-2 addition

   C. Key management and distribution

   D. Modulo-2 subtraction

8. What is the organization that issues digital certificates called?

   A. Digital developer

   B. Digital authority

   C. Certificate developer

   D. Certificate authority

9. One method of noting a secure Web connection is the display of a URL with the prefix:

   A. SSL

   B. HTTPS

   C. HTTP

   D. S-SSL

10. In a Cisco router environment, the IP address and wildcard mask of 192.131.122.0 0.0.0.255 signifies

    A. 255 hosts on any network

    B. 192 hosts on the 255 network

    C. 131 hosts on the 122 network

    D. Any host on the 192.131.122.0 network

11. What function does the following standard access list perform:

    access-list 1 permit 198.146.12.1 0.0.0.0

    A. Allow packets with source address 198.146.12.1

    B. Allow all packets from the 198.146.12.0 network

    C. Allow all packets regardless of IP address

    D. Block all packets

12. The operating method most access lists follow is

    A. Unless denied all packets are permitted.

    B. Unless permitted all packets are denied.

    C. All packets are always allowed.

    D. All packets are blocked on holidays.

13. In a Cisco access list environment, the keyword `host` represents which of the following wildcard masks?

    A. 1.1.1.1

    B. 255.255.255.255

    C. 0.0.0.0

    D. 0.1.0.1

14. How many access lists can be applied to both directions on an interface?

    A. 1

    B. 2

    C. 3

    D. 4

15. An example of a firewall proxy service is

    A. Operating a DMZ.

    B. Enabling or disabling access lists.

    C. Enabling or disabling FTP commands.

    D. Checking user passwords.

# Network Design and Management

## IN THIS CHAPTER

A user's terminal device is the source and destination of all user data, but good network design and management is always necessary to make data communications networks usable and affordable. The term *network design* refers to the selection of different types of communications facilities and the selection and interconnection of various devices to accomplish design goals.

This chapter covers the goals, principles, and tools of efficient network design and management. Many of the administrative principles of network management, such as planning and budgeting, are similar to other kinds of management. The technical aspects to be discussed here include network design goals and throughput timing, networking devices, interconnection, fault isolation, fault correction, and quality assurance.

Any network, no matter how simple or complex, can be incorporated into a larger network. The approach of this chapter is to start with the principles of good network design for basic point-to-point networks, establishing a solid basis for these, and then to discuss some of the technologies for building and managing more complex networks.

## Network Design Goals

The greatest motivation for network design is cost. Cost includes a multitude of factors other than the prices of terminal devices and networks. For example, the costs of local area networks are usually justified on the basis of higher speed because the time of the people and computers that use these networks is valuable. In other situations, communications reliability is the basic cost justification. In many cases, the failure of a data communications system to function properly when needed can cost a business far more than the price of the system.

If price were no object, most data networks would be a collection of simple point-to-point channels. Indeed, if a point-to-point channel can be kept busy at a reasonably high bit rate for transmitting data that's worth sending, it might be the most cost-effective way to handle a particular data communications task.

On the other hand, many data applications cannot cost-justify dedicated channels because of insufficient quantity or priority of the data. In such cases, it is sometimes possible to combine data from more than one source into a single long-haul transmission path by using multiplexers and other networking devices. Although the use of such techniques might allow cost-justification of the application, the addition of equipment is likely to reduce reliability and to increase the time and effort required to find and correct a problem.

The underlying objective of data networking is to strike a satisfactory balance between the accurate, timely, and secure delivery of user data and total cost. The term *satisfactory* implies that the user or organization who is paying for the delivery system is satisfied with it.

# Transmission Accuracy

Previous chapters discuss the subject of accuracy in terms of error control. Not all data transmissions have to be error free. For example, electronic mail messages that contain human-language messages do not suffer loss of meaning if a word is occasionally misspelled. On the other hand, the transfer of accounting information between financial institutions requires a high level of accuracy.

# Timeliness

Timeliness involves four general aspects: the amount of data to be transmitted, the importance and priority of the information, the average rate of transfer of error-free data, and the availability of the network to the user. These aspects are discussed in the following sections.

## The Amount of Data

Obviously, the quantity and priority of data will have an impact on the throughput rate required, but cost must be considered when establishing these parameters. In some extreme situations, the amount of data might be so great that the best way to transfer it will be by physically transporting truckloads of magnetic tape! At the other extreme, a satisfactory networking solution might be a simple low-speed transmission over a dialed point-to-point telephone channel.

## The Priority of the Data

As a general rule, the importance and frequency of testing is directly proportional to the importance and priority of the data. An Italian proverb asserts, "Good things cost less than bad ones." Although this proverb doesn't apply universally to data communications, it does remind us that the best solution isn't always the cheapest. In numerous situations, for example in industrial process control and manufacturing, a total failure of a data link could cost a company more than $10,000 an hour. In such cases, reliability, testing, and planning for alternative methods obviously are of extreme importance.

It's important to recognize that the priority of data is based on a mixture of requirements, equipment, and transmission facilities that are upgraded or acquired based on those requirements, as well as on economics. For example, the transmission of data from an ATM machine to a bank's central computer complex might have an initial design goal of one second. However, because the customer will not change banks if the delay is increased to five seconds, the network designer's initial set of requirements could be changed if it was more economical to use a lower data rate to transmit the ATM request, even if it results in additional customer waiting time. However, in a LAN environment in which employees can intimate queries throughout the day, a five-second response time could result in a severe loss of productivity. Thus, you also need to consider productivity as well as customer satisfaction.

## The Information Throughput Rate

The information throughput rate, properly known as the *Transfer Rate of Information Bits (TRIB)*, is covered in detail in the next section. Basically, TRIB is the average rate of transfer of the actual error-free bits of user data, not counting overhead bits.

## The Availability of the Network

The availability of the network is determined by three factors: access time, mean time between failures (MTBF), and mean time to restore service (MTRS). For private lines and permanent virtual circuits, access time is of no concern; for dialed connections and virtual calls, the time delay for establishing the call might be significant in comparison with the transmission time if the amount of data is small. MTBF usually refers to the time between "hard" (permanent) failures, but if the error rate becomes high enough, the TRIB can nose-dive even though the connection still exists. MTRS might involve a temporary restoration, as in the case of dialed backup for a private line, or it might simply refer to repair time if no alternative service is available.

## Component Availability

We can also compute the availability of individual network components, such as modems, transmission lines, routers, and similar devices. Because MTBF + MTRS must equal unity, we can express the availability as a percent as follows:

$$A = MTBF + MTRS * 100$$

As an example of an availability computation, assume that a router is expected to fail once every two years. Let's also assume that upon failure it requires 48 hours to obtain a new part and restore the router to an operational state. A two year period consists of 24 hours/day * 365 days/yr * 2, or 17,520 hours. Thus, the availability of the router becomes

$$A = 17,520 + 48 * 100 = 99.72\%$$

If you consider the arrangement of components, you can determine the availability of a transmission system. For example, a router connected via a T1 line to a second router represents three components connected in series. Thus, if $A_1$, $A_2$, and $A_3$ represent the availability of the first router, the T1 line, and the second router, the system availability becomes

$$A_S = A_1 * A_2 * A_3$$

For additional information concerning the computation of component and system availability, you are referred to *Enhancing LAN Performance, Third Edition*, written by Gilbert Held and published by John Wiley & Sons.

# Security

Security is receiving increasing attention as data communications is used more and more for significant and important matters of everyday life. Many sources of information are now available that cover this area in detail. Besides the physical aspects of security, data communications security involves both privacy and authentication. Privacy refers to secrecy (use of codes) and protection from unauthorized access (use of passwords). Authentication has to do with ensuring that a data message hasn't been tampered with between source and sink, and verifying that the sender of the message is who he claims to be.

In certain kinds of transmissions, authentication is more important than any other aspect of networking mentioned so far. For example, a Swiss bank receiving an international telex from another bank containing instructions to transfer funds between accounts will be interested in knowing whether extra zeros have been added to the amount, whether account numbers have been modified, and whether the claimed source of the message is authentic.

In summary, data network design involves a complex series of interrelated judgments involving these and other factors:

- Cost of the delivery system
- Priority of the data
- Response time required
- Throughput rate
- Accessibility
- Availability
- Reliability
- Testing
- Contingency planning
- Privacy
- Authentication

# TRIB

As mentioned earlier, TRIB is sometimes called the information throughput rate. By definition, it is

> Number of information bits accepted by the sink or receiver divided by the total time required to get those bits accepted

Due to the burst nature of most data transmission, TRIB has meaning only as an average over a period. Although the data link bit rate has a lot to do with TRIB, other factors might at times have as much or more influence. For example, if the channel is noisy, a higher bit rate might increase the error rate to such an extent that the TRIB actually goes down.

TRIB is almost always less than the bit rate at the serial interface. (In a few sophisticated data compression systems, the TRIB might appear to exceed the actual interface bit rate because the receiver puts out more bits than were actually transmitted.) Two other parameters that usually affect TRIB are transmission overhead and delays. Both of these parameters are closely tied to the coding and blocking of the data and to the protocols used. For example, if the protocol requires that the acknowledgment of a block must be received by the sender before the next block is transmitted, round-trip delays are added to the denominator of the TRIB definition given previously. In such instances, block length and delays can have a substantial effect on TRIB. Besides bit rate, the following factors should be considered when estimating TRIB:

- Noninformation bits sent with the data. These include

    Start and stop bits if asynchronous transmission is used

    Parity bits if ASCII code is used

    Redundant (or "stuffed") zeroes if a bit-oriented link protocol (SDLC/HDLC) is used

    Filler bits used by teleprocessing system utilities to fill out partial data blocks, if any

- Noninformation characters in the message stream. Depending on the link protocol used, these might include

    Sync characters or flags

    Address characters

    Control characters (STX, ACK, and so on) or control bytes

    Error-checking characters (BCC or FCS)

    Transparency characters (DLE) and pads

- Noninformation messages required in the administration of the link protocol. These are the initialization, connect, disconnect, polling, and status messages, and so forth. They usually are not counted in TRIB calculations if the sessions are sufficiently long for them to have a negligible effect.

- Carrier turn-on delay. This is the period between request-to-send from the terminal and clear-to-send from the modem. It is also known as "modem turnaround time." It is required only when a modem is operating with a switched carrier on a circuit that cannot support the bit rate of the modem two ways simultaneously. It also applies to at least the remote (secondary) stations and sometimes to all stations on a multipoint circuit. The amount of the delay, if any, is programmed into the modem at the time of installation, based on the modem manufacturer's recommendations for the particular circuit type and bit rate. It can be from a few milliseconds to a few hundred milliseconds.

- Modem propagation delay. All synchronous modems operating on voice-grade circuits buffer the data on both transmit and receive. Depending on bit rate, the delay can be in the range of 2 to 10 milliseconds (ms) per modem.

- Circuit propagation delay. Microwave radio signals, including communication satellite signals and signals in optical fibers, travel nearly at the speed of light. Electrical signals in local wires and cables travel somewhat slower. Also, many local telephone systems contain buffers of various types. As a rule of thumb, estimate 6ms for local equipment on each end, and 1ms for every 150 miles of cross-country terrestrial circuit. This gives [12 + (miles/150)] milliseconds for terrestrial one-way delay. Depending on latitude and longitude, geostationary satellite signals travel 45,000 to 50,000 miles in propagating from one satellite earth station to another; they also are buffered in the satellite and in the earth stations. Generally, estimate 350ms from user to user (one way), including terrestrial links between respective earth stations and users.

- Propagation delays because of buffering. Most devices used to create complex networks for data communications store groups of received bits in buffers before retransmitting those bits on the next link. Multiplexers, concentrators, routers, remote bridges, and other types of communications processors are examples of such devices. Depending on the number of bits so buffered and the circuit length, the buffer delays in some systems can exceed all other propagation delays in the transfer of data. Buffer delays are normally included in the equipment specifications provided by the manufacturer.

- Computation time for response and other time delays. Although the time for data calculations normally wouldn't be considered in TRIB, the processing time required to check for transmission errors and fabricate an appropriate response should be included because this is a communications function. Also, systems that allow multiple blocks to be sent between acknowledgments often require time gaps or filler bits between successive blocks.

- Error rate. For blocked data, if the error rate is not large, it is usually sufficient to estimate TRIB by first assuming no errors and then making an adjustment based on the block error rate (BLER). For example, if 1% of the blocks contain an error, the block error rate is said to be 1%. This means that 1% of the blocks will need to be retransmitted; thus, the TRIB will be lowered by approximately 1% due to errors.

## Example of a TRIB Calculation

Problem: How long will it take to transmit 10,000 records a distance of 500 miles every day on a dialed connection at 9600bps using the half-duplex BSC protocol? There are 80 EBCDIC characters per record, and two records per block; thus, there are 5,000 blocks containing 160 characters. What is the TRIB?

Solution: Assuming that 9600bps half-duplex modems are used, there will be a carrier turn-on delay in each direction for each block (one for data, one for acknowledgment). From the modem manufacturer's recommendations, this is established as 100ms. Other delays include the following:

- Circuit propagation delay, which for a terrestrial 500-mile circuit would be about 15ms.

- Modem propagation delay, which according to the modem operation manual is 4ms.

- Computation delay, which according to measurements on the actual terminals is 10ms for the receiving terminal and negligible for the transmitting terminal.

Assume that each data transmission block includes the following items:

| | |
|---|---|
| 1 | leading pad character |
| 4 | sync characters |
| 1 | STX character |
| 160 | data characters (2 records at 80 characters each) |
| 1 | EOB or ETX character |
| 2 | character lengths of BCC |
| 1 | trailing pad |
| 170 | characters |

Thus, each block has 170 characters including overhead, but not counting DLE characters that would be sent if transparency is required. If each character requires 8 bits, the transmission time actually needed to send a data block at 9600bps can be figured with this formula:

$(170 \times 8)/9600 = 42\text{ms}$

Assume that each acknowledgment block includes the following items:

| | |
|---|---|
| 1 | leading pad character |
| 4 | sync characters |
| 2 | character lengths of ACK0/ACK1 |
| 1 | trailing pad character |
| 8 | characters (all overhead) |

The transmit time actually needed to send an acknowledgment block can be figured with this formula:

$(8 \times 8)/9600 = 6.6\text{ms}$

Including delays, this will be the round-trip time to send 1 block:

100ms near-end carrier turn-on

142ms data block transmission

4ms transmit modem propagation

15ms circuit propagation

4ms receive modem propagation

10ms sink terminal calculation

100ms far-end carrier turn-on

6.6ms acknowledgment block transmission

4ms transmit modem propagation

15ms circuit propagation

4ms receive modem propagation

403ms or 0.403 second round-trip time per block

The total time needed to send 5,000 blocks, excluding retransmissions because of errors, is $0.443 \times 5,000 = 2,215$ seconds, or 37 minutes. If we assume that 1% of the blocks will contain at least 1 bit in error, the time will be lengthened by about 1%. The actual number of information bits transmitted is 160 characters per block $\times$ 8 bits per character $\times$ 5,000 blocks = 6,400,000 bits. If errors are not counted, this is true:

$$\text{TRIB} = (6,400,000 \text{ bits})/2215 = 2889 \text{ bits/sec}$$

Note that the TRIB in this example is less than half of the modem bit rate of 9600bps! Major factors contributing to this poor result were the modem carrier turn-on delay (modem turn-around) and the fact that acknowledgment of each block had to be received before the next block could be transmitted. (Note that the total of these times accounted for almost 40% of the round-trip time.)

People who are unfamiliar with the type of calculation just illustrated often assume that the best way to improve throughput is to increase modem speed. To attempt such a remedy in this example would probably result in lower (not higher) TRIB because it is likely that the modem turnaround, modem propagation delay, and error rate would all be higher. Not only would the modem cost more, but also the dialing and redialing required to get a connection that would operate satisfactorily at a higher rate would be both time-consuming and frustrating to the operator—if it would work at all.

One possible approach to improving the TRIB in the example might be to eliminate modem turnaround entirely by installing full-duplex modems. Still another approach might be to change to a different protocol. SDLC is capable of allowing acknowledgment of up to seven frames with only one response. However, changing from BSC to SDLC link protocol would require different software and probably hardware modifications in both terminals.

The best way to improve the TRIB in this case would be to increase block length. Assuming that both terminals have sufficient buffer capacity, increasing block length from 2 records to 10 records would result in a total round-trip time of 1.619 seconds per block, and only 1,000 blocks would have to be sent. The total time needed would be 27 minutes, a daily savings of 10 minutes of long-distance calling. The new TRIB would be 3953bps, an increase of 37%.

> ## Caution: Block Length and Error Rate
>
> Increasing block length always increases the block error rate because there is a greater exposure to the probability of error in a long block. For a block length increase of 500 percent, the BLER will increase by roughly the same factor. In the example, if the block error rate had really been 1% before (very high for such a short block), it would be about 5% now. This would erode some of the time savings.

## Optimum Block Length

Figure 17.1 illustrates how block length affects TRIB when all other factors are equal. For very short blocks, the TRIB is low (as illustrated in the previous calculations) because overhead is a significant proportion of the total transmission. For very long blocks also, the TRIB is low because there is a significant probability of error within the block, and many blocks have to be retransmitted. Somewhere between the extremes, there is a block length, $B_L$, that yields maximum TRIB. Whether $B_L$ is optimum depends on several factors besides TRIB, including the following:

- If the error rate is low, the value of $B_L$ might be so large as to be impractical, particularly for an interactive data system in which fast response is more important than throughput.
- Quite often, the memory capacity of terminal devices might not be sufficient to handle a block length of $B_L$.
- The utility programs that actually perform the blocking of data usually won't allow a precise match with $B_L$.
- Long-term changes in error rates and delays make precise matching impractical anyway.

Regardless of these considerations, the network designer should make reasonable estimates of TRIB, be aware of the major impairments to faster TRIB, and ensure that the combination of factors is best for each situation.

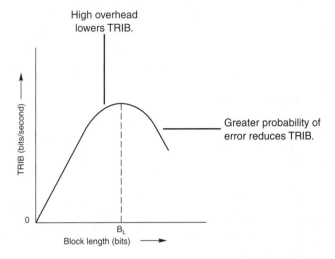

**FIGURE 17.1**

*The block length ($B_L$) for maximum TRIB.*

# Networking Devices

Several types of special-purpose devices exist for improving cost-effectiveness of data networks. The basic purposes and advantages of the main types are given in the paragraphs that follow. Refer to Chapter 6, "Multiplexing Techniques," for detailed information concerning the operation and utilization of multiplexers, and refer to Chapter 11, "Local Area Networks," for details about LAN internetworking devices such as bridges, routers, and gateways.

Multiplexers are devices that allow the combination of several data channels independently into one physical circuit. Data streams so combined can be separated and recovered at the opposite end of the system. There are two main types: frequency-division multiplexers (FDMs) and time-division multiplexers (TDMs). The advantage of FDM is that it can be used on multi-point circuits, but the individual channels usually must each be for start-stop data. TDM can be used if all channels are point-to-point. It generally allows faster bit rates and potentially more channels than FDM at less cost.

TDMs come in two types: classical (or dumb) TDMs and statistical (or smart) TDMs. Dumb TDMs should be used if the duty cycles (time spent filling time slots with actual data) of the data channels to be multiplexed are relatively high. A high duty cycle means that the channel is actually carrying bits most of the time. Because dumb TDMs send idle (marking) bits when a channel becomes inactive, they waste a lot of potential capacity when the duty cycles are low.

Whenever usage statistics show low duty cycles as the normal mode of utilization for most of the channels to be multiplexed, a statistical multiplexer system is usually a good choice. These devices send only data bits (no idle bits), so they can appear to have a higher total bit rate than the actual rate if a high percentage of idle bits are coming from the terminals.

## Modem Sharing Devices

Modem sharing devices (MSDs) do just that: They allow several remote terminals at one site on a common multipoint circuit to share a single modem at that site. MSDs do not multiplex; they simply provide a means of sharing the serial interface of one modem among several terminals.

When a modem sharing unit is used, transmission occurs via polling and broadcast. To understand the operation and utilization of a modem sharing unit (MSU), consider Figure 17.2, in which three terminals share access to a common modem via an MSU. Two popular names for MSUs are *control units* and *cluster controllers*.

## Line Bridging Devices

Line bridging devices allow two or more analog circuits to be shared as one. Bridges are not multiplexers. They allow one modem to be used with circuits to more than one destination. Telephone companies and users can use bridges to create multipoint analog circuits from point-to-point segments.

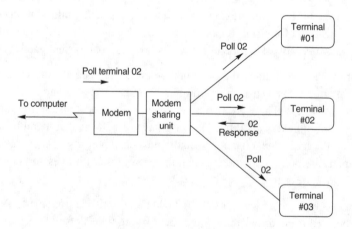

**FIGURE 17.2**

*A modem sharing unit enables transmission via polling and broadcasting.*

## Modem Eliminators

Modem eliminators are used to connect two DTEs directly. They also are called *null modems*.

## Protocol Converters

Protocol converters are microprocessors that convert data operating in one protocol (say start-stop ASCII) to another (say IBM BSC). A dial-up X.3 PAD for converting start-stop to X.25 is an example of a protocol converter.

Three communications devices have the primary operational function of interconnecting local area networks. Those devices are bridges, routers, and gateways.

## Bridges

Depending on the geographical relationship of LANs, you can consider using a local bridge or a pair of remote bridges to connect LANs. When LANs are in close proximity, you should consider using a local bridge to interconnect the networks. A local bridge consists of a processor, memory, and two LAN adapter cards, in which each adapter is connected to a separate network. The bridge operates at the data link layer of the OSI reference model, examining the source Media Access Control (MAC) address of each frame on the LAN to which it is attached. This enables the bridge to construct and periodically update a table of known addresses. By comparing the destination address in each frame to the table of known addresses on the LAN, the bridge can decide whether to forward the frame to the other LAN. That is, if the destination address matches a source address in the table of known addresses, the destination of the frame resides on the LAN, and the bridge will not forward the frame on to the other LAN.

In addition to forwarding frames, a bridge also filters and floods frames. If the destination address of a frame resides on the same port as its entry into the bridge, there is no need to forward the frame. Thus the bridge *filters* the frame, preventing it from flowing through the bridge. If the destination address of the frame has yet to be learned, the bridge forwards the frame onto all ports except that from which it was received, a process referred to as *flooding*.

Although flooding represents a valid technique for processing frames whose destination addresses are unknown with respect to a port on a bridge at a particular point in time, it reduces throughput on LANs connected to other bridge ports. Depending on the amount of flooding, such operations can degrade the performance of other LANs connected to bridge ports and serve as one of several reasons for performing routing as a mechanism to reduce flooding and LAN broadcasting overhead. Concerning broadcasts, many LAN servers advertise their facilities by broadcasting their location and type of service every 30 or 60 seconds. When broadcasts are restricted to one LAN, their overhead might be minimal; however, when broad-

17

NETWORK DESIGN
AND
MANAGEMENT

casts flow from one LAN to another via a bridge, the additional broadcast traffic can adversely affect performance.

A remote bridge operates much like a local bridge does; however, it is designed to interconnect geographically separated LANs via a wide area network. To accomplish this task, the remote bridge converts frames requiring forwarding into a suitable protocol for transmission via a WAN, such as SDLC or HDLC. Similarly, a remote bridge converts frames received via a WAN link into their appropriate LAN format. Figure 17.3 compares the use of local and remote bridges to interconnect LANs.

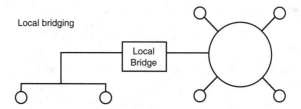

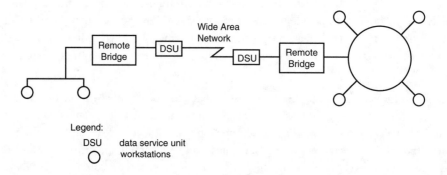

**FIGURE 17.3**

*Using local and remote bridges.*

Although flooding and broadcast traffic adversely affects LANs connected via a local bridge, their impact is much greater on a wide area network used to interconnect geographically separated remote bridges. This is because the data rate used to interconnect remote bridges is typically a small fraction of the operating rate of interconnected LANs. For example, an Ethernet LAN could operate at 10, 100, or 1000Mbps. In comparison, a wide area network connection typically operates at either 56/64Kbps, a multiple of 64Kbps up to 784Kbps that is referred to as a fractional T1 circuit, or at the T1 operating rate of 1.544Mbps.

# LAN Switches

A LAN switch can be considered to represent a multiport bridge that routes data on a frame-by-frame basis. The first series of LAN switches worked at the data link layer, routing frames based on their MAC address similar to a bridge. Improvements in very large scale integrated circuits and application specific integrated circuit (ASIC) design resulted in the ability to switch frames based on their network address and even the port in the TCP or UDP header carried inside a Layer 2 frame. Some switches that operate at the transport layer examining TCP and UDP port numbers in effect provide load balancing for organizations with popular Web sites and are marketed as "load director" or "load balancer." Figure 17.4 illustrates the employment of a load balancer to direct traffic to one of three Web servers.

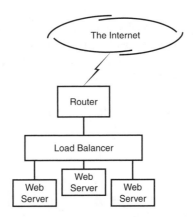

**FIGURE 17.4**
*Using a load balancer LAN switch to direct traffic to one of three Web servers.*

# Routers

In comparison to bridges, which operate at the data link layer, a router operates at the network layer of the OSI reference model. This means that routers make their forwarding decisions based on network addresses as opposed to the media access control (MAC) addresses used by the first generation of LAN bridges. Although installing routers normally requires more effort than installing bridges does, routers provide a significant increase in functionality and operational capability. For example, routers can be programmed to forward traffic via different paths through a network based on line availability, line utilization, and other parameters.

Another advantage associated with the use of routers is the fact that they limit broadcast domains. This means that Layer 2 broadcasts can be restricted to each LAN instead of being forwarded between LANs when bridges are used. In addition, because routers use explicit

Layer 3 addresses, they do not perform a flooding operation because frames with an unknown address are not processed.

Figure 17.5 illustrates the use of routers to interconnect three LANs. Note that data transferred from a workstation on LAN A to a workstation on LAN C can flow on the path A–C or the paths A–B and B–C. Thus, routers can be used to construct backup communications paths in case a primary path becomes inoperative.

## Gateways

A gateway represents a special type of protocol converter that operates at all layers of the OSI reference model. The primary function of a LAN-based gateway is to convert application data transported at the data link layer on a LAN for transmission to a mainframe computer. This conversion is twofold. First, application data generated by a workstation on the LAN is encoded into an application data stream used by a particular type of mainframe computer. Then the LAN-based data stream is converted into the transport protocol recognized by a mainframe computer. The actual transmission of data from a gateway to a mainframe commonly occurs via a serial transmission link, in which the gateway is connected to a LAN via a network adapter card. Thus, a gateway commonly provides a series of conversions from the physical layer through the application layer.

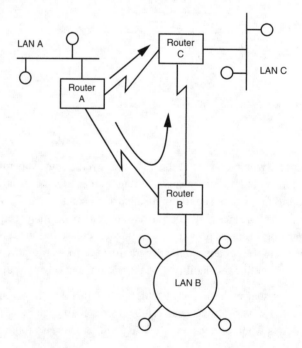

**FIGURE 17.5**

*Routers support the use of alternative paths on a dynamic or predefined basis.*

# Interconnection of Networking Devices

The preceding section contains only a partial listing of devices intended to interconnect different types of networks and network components. Space does not allow a discussion of the numerous possible alternative requirements in the actual interconnection of leads between devices, terminals, modems, and so forth.

Probably the best advice that can be given is to study the equipment manuals and the interface standards themselves. As an alternative, refer to the book *Data Communications Networking Devices, Fourth Edition*, by Gilbert Held, published by John Wiley & Sons, for specific information concerning the operation and utilization of more than 40 networking devices.

While you are selecting appropriate networking equipment, ordering necessary transmission lines, and developing an equipment installation schedule, you should also consider policies, procedures, and equipment you might need in order to maintain your network. Although they're often overlooked, testing, troubleshooting, and capacity planning are important network management issues that every network manager and administrator can eventually expect to face. Thus, this chapter concludes by turning the focus to different tests and test equipment that can be used to isolate network problems, procedures that can improve network operations, and two standards supported by many networking devices that facilitate the management of TCP/IP-based networks.

# Fault Isolation

The process of recognizing the failure of a device or circuit is commonly referred to as *fault detection*. Fault detection usually is pretty easy; fault isolation is more complicated. The first question is, "Is the problem in a terminal device or in the communications system?" Troubleshooting data terminals and LAN workstations is beyond the scope of this book, but one book you can refer to is *LAN Testing and Troubleshooting*, by Gilbert Held, published by John Wiley & Sons. If terminals and workstations pass self-test procedures but still will not communicate, chances are good that the problem is in the communications system.

## Loopback Tests

One of the basic techniques for isolation of faults in data communications is the loopback test. In a loopback, the output at the far end of a system or subsystem is connected to the input of the return path. Then the output of the return path is examined in relation to the input to the outgoing path.

Figure 17.6 illustrates how successive loopbacks can be used to isolate a fault on a single point-to-point data link that uses an analog circuit. The local modem is first self-tested using an analog loopback at its far terminals (point A). If it passes the test, the loop is removed from the local modem. Then the local modem and the analog circuit are tested together using a remote analog loopback at the near terminals (point B) of the remote modem. If that test also appears satisfactory, the remote analog loop is removed, and the entire data link is tested end-to-end round trip using a digital loopback at the far terminals (point C) of the remote modem. (Loopbacks at points B and C are useful only if the channel is full-duplex.) Using a process of elimination, the location of the fault can be narrowed to the local modem, the analog circuit, or the remote modem.

Loopbacks cannot determine which side of a path, outgoing or return, is faulty; only the person who has to repair it really needs that information. End-to-end tests can distinguish the direction of the fault, but that often requires at least modest training of a person at the remote site.

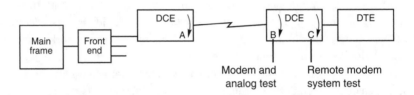

FIGURE 17.6
*Loopback test points.*

## Use External Tests, Too

Know what is being tested when you're performing a self-test on a device. As with terminals, no self-test ever tests all the circuitry. For example, Figure 17.7 shows that a self-test of a modem doesn't check data continuity through the line transformers and through the RS-232 interface circuitry. The latter problem can be very treacherous. Whenever practical, use external tests to be sure.

# Data Communications Test Equipment

Test equipment enables network technicians and users to observe the state of the DTE-DCE interface circuits, as well as the composition of data on a circuit. In this section, you will examine the operation and initialization of several types of test equipment.

Modem

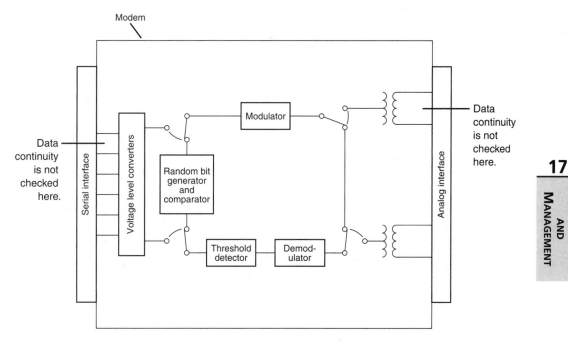

Data continuity is not checked here.

Data continuity is not checked here.

Switches are shown in self-test position.

**Figure 17.7**

*Some modem circuitry is not tested in self-test.*

## Automatic Gain

Most analog data circuits are designed to operate with a substantial drop in signal level from input to output; for example, there is a 16dB loss each way in a private-line voice-grade circuit to be used for data. When an analog loopback is performed at the remote end without gain being inserted at that point, the input signal for the return path is 16dB lower than it should be. Such a low-level signal can cause both the analog return path and the local modem receiver to operate improperly, perhaps giving a false indication. Many systems that provide for remote analog loopbacks automatically insert gain in the loopback path to avoid this problem. If the modems used in the test depicted in Figure 17.6 are not so equipped, a different procedure should be used. For example, perform a self-test on each modem, and then with an assistant at the far end, perform an end-to-end test.

## Amplifier-Monitor

The self-contained, battery-operated audio amplifier-speaker-monitor, sometimes called a "watergate box," is readily available at retail electronics supply stores for around $20 or less. Not only is it useful for detecting the modem carrier and changes in modem output signals, but it's also the easiest way to detect a noisy circuit or to tell whether a modem is putting out tone-dial or pulse-dial signals. It can also be used to monitor call progress and answer-back tones on dialed data links.

## The Breakout Box

The basic specialized data testing device is the breakout box, so named because it provides access to individual leads in the serial interface between a DTE (such as a terminal) and a DCE (such as a modem). Prices range from about $60 to $250 for breaking out the 25 leads of an RS-232 interface, to $100 to $500 or more for devices that test high-speed interfaces. Price depends on ruggedness, whether the unit is programmable (leads can be crisscrossed), and whether data activity can be observed directly without a voltmeter. The higher-priced units feature built-in battery power, full tri-state LED monitoring of leads, programmability, ruggedness, and DIP switches to open the circuits of individual leads. They might also provide positive and negative test voltages.

## The Bit Error Rate Tester

The next step up in acquisition of specialized data test equipment would be a bit error rate tester (BERT). RS-232 BERTs range in price from under $150 to around $500, depending on whether block error (BLERT) and error-second measurements are to be included, whether start and stop bit insertion/deletion is required (if asynchronous multiplexers are in the circuit), and whether various automatic indicator features are present. Some models also feature programmable message generators for checking out terminal devices. High-speed BERT/BLERTs in the multimegabit-per-second range can cost much more.

## The Decibel Meter

If analog voice-grade circuits are used extensively, a decibel (dB) meter is a wise investment for checking transmit and receive levels. A basic dB meter costs around $50 to $200. Anyone considering purchasing a dB meter should consider a combination unit. Excellent portable meters with digital display are available. Such a meter that can read dBm, relative dB, frequency, relative frequency, voltage, current, and resistance costs about $100 to $250. This expense is not recommended, however, unless testing on analog circuits is expected to be a common occurrence.

## Using an Oscilloscope

A multichannel oscilloscope (or *scope*) with x-y inputs can be used with a breakout box to observe serial interface signals or with a modem detect certain impairments on analog circuits.

Examples of the use of a dual-trace scope in the RS-232 interface would be to measure modem turnaround time, to check for crosstalk interference between timing leads, and to observe degradation of signals in long serial interface cables.

With synchronous modems having signal-space (constellation) pattern generators, an x-y oscilloscope becomes a powerful instrument for detecting phase hits, phase jitter, amplitude hits, harmonic distortion, dropouts, and impulse noise in analog circuits. With other modems, a scope can be used to observe eye patterns for harmonic distortion, phase jitter, and certain types of hits.

Scopes that are suitable for these purposes generally cost in the range of $500 to $2,000, depending on compactness, maximum data rate, and number of channels.

## Voice Frequency Test Set

For the really serious user of data over voice-grade analog circuits, a voice frequency test set is a device that can quantify the major parameters of a voice-grade analog circuit. Standard capabilities include frequency response (amplitude received versus frequency for constant amplitude transmitted), C-message noise in dBrnc, C-message notched noise (S/N) in dB, and audio monitoring. Prices start at $1,000, depending on the degree of automation in the tests and additional test functions provided. Although the less-expensive units do not provide for measurement of envelope delay distortion (one of the two parameters affected by C-conditioning), large amounts of delay distortion often are accompanied by large amounts of attenuation distortion, which is much easier to measure. Voice frequency test sets normally should be used in pairs to provide end-to-end testing.

## Data Link Content Monitor

Many large users of data communications have painfully discovered that the general purpose computer is not an efficient device for debugging data link and network protocols. Nor is it the best device for bit error rate testing of wideband data channels, T1 multiplexers, and the like. The computer time, programmer time, and other expensive resources saved in a single project often can pay for the purchase of test equipment to cover these areas.

One equipment category is the basic RS-232 data link content monitor. This device simply monitors and displays signals passing across the serial interface. The display is normally in terms of characters, if appropriate, or it can be in binary or hexadecimal in the case of uncoded data. Pricing varies with the number of codes, the type of display, the capability to trap (or freeze) and display specific sequences, the amount of memory, scrolling of trapped memory contents, speed of the device with and without recording in memory, and whether the conditions of various nondata leads in the serial interface are recorded with the data for later analysis.

17

NETWORK DESIGN
AND
MANAGEMENT

## Using a Simulator

Monitor devices are excellent for diagnosing protocol problems in data links, but they are not efficient for system development. This function is best handled by a simulator. Such a device can be user-programmed to simulate a computer port, remote terminal, or network gateway in order to "exercise" the hardware/software system being developed. Simulators are actually special-purpose computers utilizing easy-to-learn, high-level programming languages. They also can be programmed to operate effectively as content monitors, BERTs, and BLERTs. Prices range from $1,000 to $25,000, depending on protocols supported, speed, serial interfaces supported, amount of memory, type of display, ease of programming, and portability. The more sophisticated units provide simulation up through the packet level (OSI Level 3) of X.25/X.75 protocols or through all ATM layers.

## The Protocol Analyzer

The protocol analyzer is the most sophisticated type of data communications test equipment currently marketed. The protocol analyzer gets its name from the major function it performs: protocol analysis. The protocol analyzer monitors the bit stream flowing on a communications circuit or a LAN cable and decodes the bits into characters that represent the format and information content of the protocol. When designed explicitly for use on LANs, the protocol analyzer is usually referred to as a "LAN analyzer." When designed for use on LANs and WANs, the protocol analyzer is referred to as an "enterprise analyzer." For example, a protocol analyzer monitoring an HDLC transmission would convert the bit sequence 01111110 to a flag character and then indicate the start or end of a frame of information. Other features incorporated into most protocol analyzers include the capability to analyze several communications protocols, perform data simulation, and carry out BERT and BLERT testing.

Most protocol analyzers include a built-in breakout box, a keyboard, online storage, and a display in a common housing. Because of the almost ubiquitous status of personal computers, some protocol analyzer manufacturers designed their products as adapter boards that are inserted into the system unit of a PC. When acquired as an adapter board, the protocol analyzer uses the keyboard, online storage, and display of the computer, significantly reducing the cost of the analyzer. Prices of protocol analyzers range from $1,000 for devices manufactured on adapter boards for use in personal computers to more than $5,000 for standalone protocol analyzers designed to automatically determine the protocol being transmitted, and then decode the protocol.

Figure 17.8 illustrates a hand-held and very portable protocol analyzer manufactured by Frederick Engineering of Columbia, Maryland. Referred to as the "ParaScope 64M," this protocol analyzer can be cabled to any PC DOS computer's parallel port to use the processing power of the computer to execute the vendor's software, which turns the computer into a protocol analyzer.

The ParaScope 64M shown in Figure 17.8 can be used to monitor standard RS-232 communications at data rates up to 19200bps or V.35/RS-449 communications at data rates up to 64000bps. The light-emitting diodes and switches located in columns in the middle of the ParaScope 64M provide users with a breakout box capability to monitor and open and close circuits on a monitored interface. However, the primary use of the ParaScope 64M is as a protocol analyzer, providing users with the ability to monitor the flow of data, create programs to operate on the monitored data, and display the results of the execution of programs.

The Frederick Engineering ParaScope 64M was developed as an extension of that vendor's Feline series of protocol analyzers. The Feline series was developed as adapter cards designed for insertion into conventional PCs and laptop and notebook computers, as well as software that operated on each computer. A special hardware interface box, referred to as a *pod*, is cabled to the adapter card installed in the computer. The pod is very similar to the ParaScope 64M in that it contains connectors for monitoring the interface between a DTE and DCE and converts the voltage level of the monitored circuit to the transistor-to-transistor logic (TTL) voltage level used internally by computers. The ParaScope 64M differs from the Feline pod in that it incorporates the adapter card logic, alleviating the necessity to install an adapter card in a computer. This makes the ParaScope 64M ideal for use with modern notebook computers that lack an expansion slot to accommodate the insertion of an adapter card.

**17**

NETWORK DESIGN
AND
MANAGEMENT

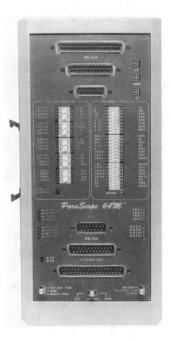

**FIGURE 17.8**

*The Frederick Engineering ParaScope 64M protocol analyzer.*

The integration of the Feline adapter card into the ParaScope 64M enables it to be used with Feline software. To understand the utility of the system obtained from the use of Feline software and ParaScope 64M hardware, take a look at some of the features of the software. Figure 17.9 illustrates a split-screen Feline display in which the upper portion of the screen defines information about the interface being monitored and the status of timers and counters. In the computer operating Feline software, timers and counters are considered memory locations that accumulate specific timing or counting values based on the execution of a program you create using Feline. In the next section, you will follow the creation of a small program and see its execution on monitored data. The lower portion of Figure 17.9 contains a window that indicates the DCE and DTE data flow across the monitored interface.

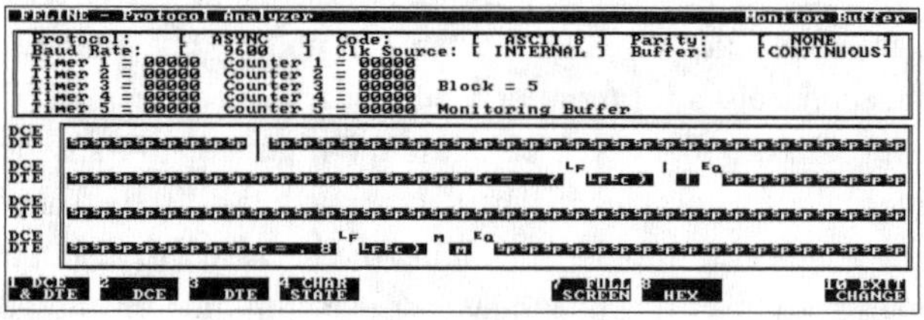

## FIGURE 17.9

*A Feline protocol analyzer software split-screen display.*

In Figure 17.9, note that control and nonprintable characters are indicated by mnemonics, such as LF for line feed and Sp for space character. The lower line across every Feline display screen indicates the function key values assigned to a specific screen. For example, to remove the split screen and display monitored data in a full screen, you would press the F7 key, which is assigned to the generation of a full-screen display.

## Feline Program Development

Figure 17.10 illustrates the creation of a program that counts the number of spaces encountered on the DTE side of a monitored interface. When you select Feline's program mode of operation, your display is initially filled with a series of blank steps and function key value assignments. If you press appropriate function keys when the cursor is placed in a step, you assign one or more program instructions to the step. In Figure 17.10 (step 1), the program waits until it encounters a space on the DTE side of the line, and then the program jumps to step 2. In step 2, counter 1 is incremented, and step 3 simply branches the program back to step 1. Thus, when data is monitored using this program, the value in counter 1 indicates the number of spaces encountered on the DTE side of the line.

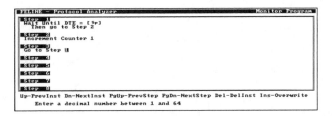

**FIGURE 17.10**

*Creating a program to count spaces on the DTE side of the line.*

Having created a program, you can monitor the line and examine the value assigned to counter 1. Figure 17.11 illustrates the Feline split-screen display as it looks when monitoring a 9600bps line that includes the program illustrated in Figure 17.10. Note that when the screen was captured for printing, a total of 2,810 spaces had been encountered on the DTE side of the line (which you know because that is the value assigned to counter 1). Although the program is not very sophisticated, it provides an indication of how you can create a program and use the program when monitoring a line. If users were reporting throughput problems on a particular circuit during a file transfer operation, you might consider developing a program to count negative acknowledgments (NAKs). Because each NAK causes the retransmission of a previously transmitted block, a high level of NAKs would indicate that retransmissions due to line errors are causing a low level of data throughput.

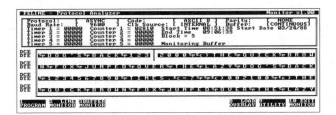

**FIGURE 17.11**

*Monitoring with a program that counts spaces on the DTE side of the line and assigns the number of spaces to counter 1.*

## Network Control System

Many companies that operate large, complex data networks have found the timely isolation of faults to be so important as to cost-justify the installation of a centralized network control system, as depicted in Figure 17.12. When based on the use of analog leased lines, such systems commonly use the low end of the frequency spectrum of the voice-grade circuit to carry a signal interrogation and reporting "side channel." Such systems add significantly to the cost of each modem in the system.

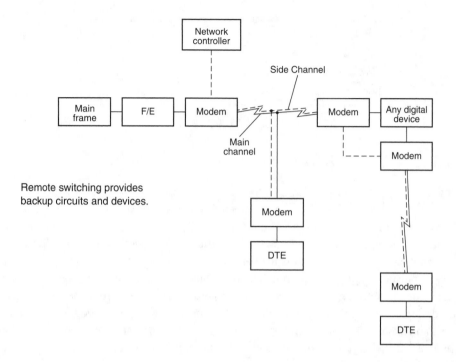

**FIGURE 17.12**

*A network control system.*

A modem that is addressed by the central unit can be commanded to perform certain tests and report the results back for display or recording. Such tests as continuity, level of received signal, and condition of an RS-232 lead can be accurately conducted without interrupting or modifying data flow. Other tests, such as self-tests and loopbacks, do interrupt data flow. Many of the more sophisticated systems can be programmed by the user to perform interruptive tests automatically during off-peak hours when actual interruption of data is unlikely. Test results can be automatically logged and compared with former test results to detect changes in circuit parameters.

When digital transmission circuits are used in a network device, control cannot be affected by the use of a side channel of frequency to convey control information and return statistics and device status data. Instead, both data and control information are transmitted on the same digital channel. This requires managed devices to interpret data and respond to recognized commands embedded in the data stream.

Although network control systems were originally developed for use with analog circuits, most modern systems are now produced to operate with digital circuits, and some systems support both types. Regardless of the type of transmission circuitry supported, the network control system can be characterized by the inclusion of a scheme for remote switching of circuits and devices to provide backup in the event of failures. The combination of remote testing and remote backup of data communications network control systems based on digital interrogation and reporting is now beginning to replace the analog systems.

## Software-Based LAN Analyzers

Today, network managers and administrators can select from a wide range of local area network analysis tools. In addition to hardware-based tools, a number of vendors developed software-based products that turn desktop, laptop, and notebook computers into LAN analyzers. Some software-based LAN analyzers are designed to provide users with traffic- and network-related error information, whereas other products are designed to decode packets and provide data important for isolating errors resulting from improper hardware or software configurations or application problems. To help you gain an appreciation for the functionality and capability of a software-based LAN analyzer, you will examine the use of TokenVision, a software product developed by Triticom, Inc., of Eden Prairie, Minnesota, for operation on IBM PC or compatible computers connected to a token-ring network.

TokenVision is a software product that turns an IBM PC or compatible personal computer into a LAN analyzer. Although the use of this product requires that the personal computer have a token-ring adapter card installed and connected to a token-ring network, you can use the PC for other applications when you are not analyzing the data flow on the network. Another product from Triticom is EtherVision, for which an Ethernet adapter card must be installed in a PC and connected to an Ethernet network. EtherVision provides a traffic monitoring and analysis capability for Ethernet LANs.

TokenVision operates at the data link layer, enabling a user to monitor traffic based on either the source or the destination address contained in MAC frames that flow on the network. Figure 17.13 shows the Triticom TokenVision Source Address Monitoring Screen display. Note that at the time the screen was captured, the program had identified 187 distinct network stations. To do so, the program constructs a table of source addresses in memory. As network stations become active, the program recognizes their source addresses in frames placed on the network, adds their addresses to the table, and increments a counter that defines the number of distinct network stations recognized at a particular point in time.

The main window of the source address monitoring screen display shown in Figure 17.13 contains four columns listing source MAC addresses that have been encountered and the number of frames containing that source address. Thus, the program provides a real-time count and display of locations originating traffic. When examining the MAC addresses shown in Figure 17.13, note that some addresses indicate the name of a vendor, whereas other addresses have the prefix Vend?. Because the IEEE assigns blocks of MAC addresses to different vendors, the program reads the first three bytes of the six-byte address to determine the vendor that manufactured the token-ring card. Those addresses with the prefix Vend? represent adapter cards produced by a vendor that received a block of MAC addresses from the IEEE after the program was developed.

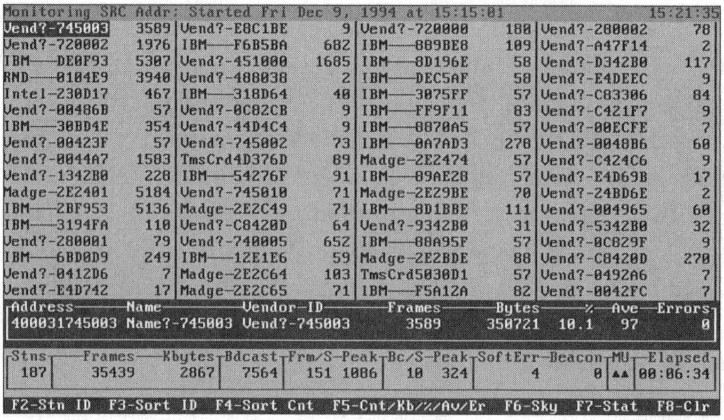

**FIGURE 17.13**

*A TokenVision source address monitoring screen display.*

By pressing the F4 key, you can sort MAC addresses by their count. Thus, from this screen, you can easily determine which stations are generating a large percentage of network traffic. This fact can be important if your LAN utilization is high and you want to investigate who is heavily using the network and what they are doing before considering a potential and probably costly network upgrade.

From the TokenVision station monitoring window, you can display network utilization on a percentage basis via a Skyline display. Figure 17.14 shows the network utilization Skyline display on a per-second basis. Note that during the 60-second interval shown in the figure, the maximum network utilization was 5%, which indicates that during the monitoring period visually shown onscreen, the network was not heavily used. Because a 60-second period represents a small amount of time on which to base a decision concerning network utilization, the program provides users with several methods for monitoring utilization and other parameters over a prolonged period. First, by pressing the F5 key, you can change the Skyline display to a per-minute basis, and the past hour of utilization is displayed.

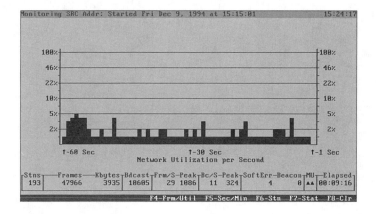

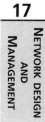

**FIGURE 17.14**

*A Triticom TokenVision Skyline display of network utilization.*

A second method you can use is to set a threshold that will generate an alarm when the threshold is exceeded. Thus, you can use the threshold method to determine whether during a certain period the utilization exceeded a predefined level. A third method you can use to track network utilization is obtained from the program's Statistics display, which is shown in Figure 17.15. By looking at the Statistics Screen display in the figure, you can see that in addition to denoting average, current (now), and peak utilization, the display indicates the time when the network utilization peak occurred. Also note that the display provides a distribution of frames based on their length or size. This information can be very important if you're attempting to determine the type of traffic carried on the network and whether a certain type of traffic is hogging network bandwidth. For example, small frames typically transport interactive traffic, whereas relatively long frames transport files. Thus, if the frame size distribution indicates a large number of relatively long frames and network utilization is very high, it could mean that one or more network users are transferring large files, which represents a major contributing factor to the use of network bandwidth.

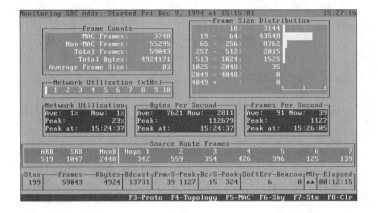

**FIGURE 17.15**

*A Triticom TokenVision statistics display.*

# Restoration of Service

Given enough planning and money, prompt and reliable restoration of data communications service is easy. But making it economical is a little harder.

If you're planning for data communications backup, you should consider the following questions:

- What is the frequency and length of downtime to be expected?

- Can steps be taken to decrease the frequency and length of downtime without incurring additional costs—that is, are you getting what you already are paying for?

- What extra costs will be incurred due to complete outage of the service for the frequency and duration indicated?

- Can these extra costs be reduced by a reduced-capability backup (for example, by backing up a T1 private line using a 9600bps dialed connection or a 64Kbps or 128Kbps ISDN dialed connection)?

- What are the actual costs of all relevant backup schemes? Include the cost of personnel time as well as the cost of backup. The cost of backup must include the operating costs, such as dialed connection charges, as well as initial investment and installation costs.

## Getting the Most Backup for the Money

Before your backup technique is designed and implemented, a review of current procedures might improve the frequency and duration of downtime:

- Is there ongoing positive communication not only with the people in the user's own organization, but also with suppliers of equipment and services?

- Do users have a thorough knowledge of the capabilities and limitations of all data communications system facilities, software, and hardware at their disposal, particularly the capabilities and limitations of self-contained test features?

- Are there well-designed restoration procedures that are agreed to in advance by all concerned and that are strictly followed?

- Are new systems benchmark-tested as they are placed in service and then tested on a regular schedule to detect changes in circuit parameters?

- Are exceptions (failures) documented, and are repeat offenders discovered?

- Is there an ongoing in-house training program to ensure that each individual in the organization can properly handle all appropriate parts of the preceding five points for those portions of the system within his purview?

## Rapport with Suppliers

Central to any cost-effective service-restoration program is a firmly established positive rapport with all major suppliers of equipment and services—especially with key individuals such as telephone company (telco) personnel. Many data-link failures can be traced directly or indirectly to a breakdown in people-to-people communications between vendors and users. For example, in the case of an organization like a telephone company in which many levels of personnel deal with the customer, the rapport between supplier and customer must exist at all levels: Data technicians should be on a first-name basis with telco testboard personnel, technician supervisors with testboard supervisors, the data communications operations manager with the telco network operations manager, and so on. When such rapport exists, several symptoms will be apparent:

- Employees on both sides will be more helpful and understanding, especially in high-pressure situations.

- Information on new testing and quality assurance techniques will flow easier. The user will gain a better understanding of the built-in test capabilities in the vendor's services and equipment. In fact, technicians on both sides will be eager to share their excitement over some new piece of test gear or a new discovery.

- Better confidence in one another's abilities will emerge and will give rise to more of a supplier-user team approach.

- The vendor employee will often render assistance above and beyond what is required and expected.

Data communications managers who succeed in cultivating this kind of rapport with their major vendors consider it among their greatest assets. In particular, they are careful to establish and follow good procedures for the testing of systems and to properly report problems to the vendor. Inherent in this process is the careful development of an escalation and reporting system.

## Escalation and Reporting Problems

Through meetings with all concerned, the data communications manager should develop a very specific escalation schedule. This schedule should show exactly who becomes involved at increasing levels of authority, what calls are placed, and at what levels when a particular type of problem fails to show progress toward resolution after a specific time lapse. All persons involved in this schedule should be involved in its development, should "sign-off" on it, should have a personal copy of the finished product, and should have a cause for negative feelings whenever it is invoked.

Before asking for help from higher levels or from the vendor, it is absolutely vital that the user exhaust all means at his disposal to make use of test facilities available to him—especially self-tests. Remember the story about "the little boy who cried wolf?" Nothing can damage credibility and rapport faster than blaming the vendor when the problem stems from another vendor or is caused in-house.

Personnel responsible for data subsystem and system testing must be thoroughly familiar with self-tests, the limitations of those tests, and the meaning of any other tests for which they have equipment. Troubles should be reported only after such testing has been adequately documented, and escalation should be invoked only after the lack of progress in problem resolution has been documented.

Such documentation of problems and their resolutions should be permanently recorded and reviewed with the vendor at regular intervals. This review helps you find areas of recurring difficulties and possibly degrading facilities and components so they can be serviced before a "hard" failure occurs. This is why the benchmarking of newly acquired facilities is important.

Finally, appreciation should be expressed when appropriate. Nothing will make the employee of a vendor work harder for a user than an appreciation letter to his boss for good work done on the user's behalf.

## Network Management Standards

As with other aspects of data communications, network management has both de facto and de jure standards. One popular example of a de facto standard is IBM's NetView product, which can be used to control and manage NetView-compliant products used in an IBM mainframe-based network. Two popular examples of de jure network management standards are the Simple Network Management Protocol (SNMP)—followed by SNMPv2—and Remote Monitor (RMON), both of which were developed to facilitate the management and control of TCP/IP-based networks. The following sections provide an overview of both standards.

# Simple Network Management Protocol

The Simple Network Management Protocol (SNMP) represents a de jure standard for managing TCP/IP-based networks. Developed by the Internet Engineering Task Force (IETF) as a mechanism for facilitating the management of multivendor products used in TCP/IP networks, SNMP uses a client-server architecture to monitor and control SNMP-compliant devices.

## Architecture

SNMP architecture is based on the interrelationship of three basic components: a manager, an agent, and a database.

The SNMP manager represents a software program that turns the computer executing the program into a Network Management Station (NMS).

The agent represents software or firmware residing in a managed network device, such as a bridge, router, or host. Each agent stores management data and responds to SNMP manager queries for one or more data items.

The third component of SNMP is the database, which is formally referred to as the *Management Information Base (MIB)*. In actuality, the MIB represents a collection of databases for the set of all managed devices supported by SNMP. This means that each agent has its own database of relevant objects for which it collects statistics and performs other functions.

Figure 17.16 illustrates the general relationship between an SNMP manager, an agent, and the agent's MIB. Although only one agent is shown in Figure 17.16, the SNMP manager can theoretically control an infinite number of agents.

The ability of a manager to control an agent is based on the use of two addresses. The first address is the IP address of the agent, which enables the manager to send requests to distinct agents. The second address represents the location in the MIB of an object to be set or the counter value to be retrieved. To facilitate the vendors' ability to develop products that interoperate with one another, objects in the MIB are assigned addresses based on a tree structure. Thus, a network manager developed by one vendor can set or retrieve information from an agent developed by another vendor as long as the user knows the agent's IP address and the location of the object in the MIB that's to be set or retrieved.

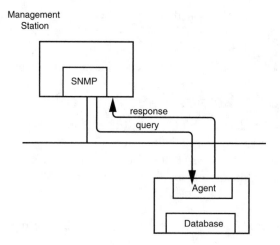

**FIGURE 17.16**
*The SNMP architecture.*

## The Naming Tree

The tree structure used by SNMP was jointly developed by the International Organization for Standardization (ISO) and the International Telecommunications Union (ITU). The result is a global naming tree, which provides a mechanism for assigning identifiers to objects that require naming.

Figure 17.17 illustrates a portion of the global naming tree that is applicable to TCP/IP. Note that the global naming tree provides both a labeling mechanism as well as an identifier mechanism because each object in the tree is assigned to a specific node under the root of the tree. The tree structure makes it possible to define an object by traversing the tree, commencing at its root, until the intended object is reached. Although several formats can be used to define an object, the most common method uses a sequence of integers separated by dots. For example, the system group object is identified by the integer sequence 1.3.6.1.2.1.1. Note that system represents one of 11 TCP/IP MIB groups, with a series of object identifiers located under each group. The system group contains seven objects, identified from .1 (dot one) through .7 (dot seven), that are used to describe configuration information about a managed device. For example, although not shown in Figure 17.17, the object identifier sysDesc (which contains a description of the managed device) is the first object identifier in the system group. Thus, its address in the tree becomes 1.3.6.1.2.1.1.1.

Each identifier has a specific access associated with it, such as read, write, or read/write. When you specify an IP address and a global tree identifier via an SNMP management platform, you gain the ability to read and write data to and from an MIB.

Network Design and Management

CHAPTER 17

681

17

NETWORK DESIGN
AND
MANAGEMENT

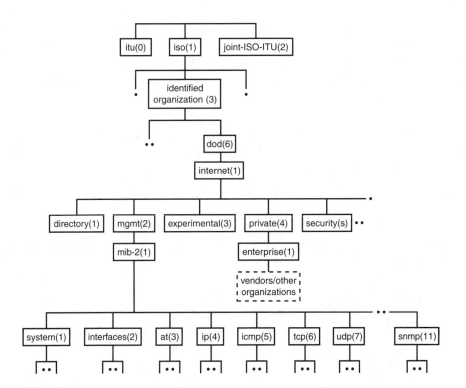

**FIGURE 17.17**

*A portion of the ISO/ITU global naming tree.*

Figure 17.18 illustrates the operation of SimpleView, an SNMP Manager program from Triticom, Inc. This program turns an IBM PC or compatible computer into a TCP/IP network manager. In the left portion of Figure 17.18, note two network map entries labeled Ethernet probe and Token Ring, with an IP address assigned to each entry. Here each entry represents a special type of agent known as a Remote Monitor probe, whose use you will learn about shortly. To set or retrieve an object associated with a selected agent, you need to specify the location of the object in the MIB. To do so, you can either directly enter a numeric sequence of digits and dots (which are hard to remember), or you can use the program's MIB Walk facility to locate a selected object. Using the window labeled MIB Walk, you can click on higher-level MIB entries referred to as groups to explode the objects stored in a particular group. For example, the System group contains seven objects, which were displayed by double-clicking on the system entry in the MIB Walk window. By moving a highlighted bar over a selected object and clicking the Select button, you cause the selected object to be used as the MIB Variable entry in a selected SNMP command.

If you compare the MIB Walk window shown in Figure 17.18 to the portion of the global naming tree shown in Figure 17.17, you will see the similarity between the two, as well as how SimpleView hides the complexity of the sequence of MIB object addresses. For example, the entry system shown in Figure 17.18 corresponds to the global naming tree address 1.3.6.1.2.1.1, and the entry interfaces corresponds to the global naming tree address 1.3.6.1.2.1.1.2. Because the Get command is shown selected in Figure 17.18, selecting the sysDescr object from the MIB Walk window and using that object in the Get command would result in the retrieval of the system description of the agent whose IP address is 198.78.46.41.

SNMP is based on the use of a limited number of commands. In addition to Get, SNMP supports the Get Next, Set, Get Response, and Trap commands. The Get Next command enables you to "walk" through an MIB one variable at a time. Agents provide results using a Get Response command. The Set Request command is used to alter the setting of an agent, such as a router table, and a Trap represents an unsolicited command that an agent sends to a manager after sensing the occurrence of a predefined condition, such as a line failure.

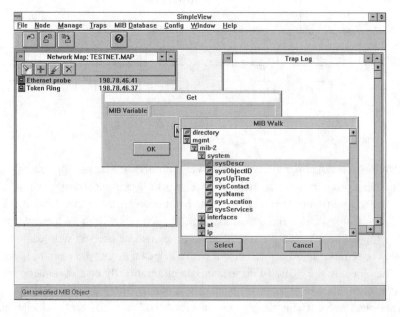

**FIGURE 17.18**

*Using SimpleView's MIB Walk window to select an object from an agent's database as the variable to retrieve.*

One of the major limitations associated with the original version of SNMP was its use of community names as a mechanism for providing an elementary form of security. A community name is a string of characters in which the default setting is the string public. When a command is issued to an agent, the agent compares the transmitted string to its configured string to determine if it should execute the command. Needless to say, a cracker could easily write a script program to use the contents of an electronic dictionary as a mechanism to Set a router to reboot or perform another unwelcome act that would raise the hair on the back of the head of a network manager or LAN administrator. Therefore, many vendors did not design SNMP-compatible equipment to respond to Set commands.

## SNMPv2 and SNMPv3

Recognizing the security limitation of SNMP as well as a few defects in its performance, the Internet Engineering Task Force (IETF) formed a working group to develop a new version of SNMP. That version, which is referred to as SNMPv2, fixed several limitations of its predecessor. However, because of divergent views of members of the working group concerning the method to implement security, the group deferred action on the addition of authentication and encryption. Instead, SNMPv2 added a feature enabling management stations to communicate with one another, providing the ability to develop a hierarchical series of management stations in which one station reports results to another up a "chain of command."

Other major enhancements to SNMPv2 included a GetBult operator that enables data to be retrieved more efficiently, better error handling capability, and the use of 64-bit counters instead of 32-bit counters. Concerning error handling, under SNMPv1, if an error occurred during data retrieval, the operation would terminate, and no data would be returned to the requestor. Under SNMPv2, all validly requested data would be returned, allowing a management station to obtain some—perhaps most—of the requested information. Concerning the use of 64-bit counters, this allows statistics to be maintained for long periods of time when monitoring Fast Ethernet and Gigabit Ethernet, whereas 32-bit counters caused the counter to fill much more rapidly.

Although SNMPv2 has many advantages over the initial version, it never obtained a significant base of implementation, perhaps because of its lack of security. In fact, in trade literature, SNMPv2 is commonly referred to as SNMPv2c, where *c* denotes the fact that community names are still used for security. Recognizing the need for security, a new working group was formed during 1998 to add security to SNMPv2. This effort produced a draft series of RFCs for SNMPv3, which was finalized during 1999. Although SNMPv3 has been available for several years, the vast base of existing products that support the original version of SNMP means that it will continue to be used for quite some time.

## Remote Monitoring

A *Remote Monitoring (RMON)* set of standards was developed by the IETF to facilitate the collection and retrieval of information on remote networks from a management platform. In an RMON environment, remote agents, known as probes, are configured to automatically collect predefined information about the operating characteristics of the network they are connected to. Information to be collected is defined by different RMON standards. For example, the RMON standard for Ethernet defines nine groups that an Ethernet RMON probe would be designed to support. An RMON probe maintains statistical tables for each group and can

**17**

NETWORK DESIGN
AND
MANAGEMENT

manipulate tables independently, which reduces the amount of data required to be transmitted between a probe and a manager. This feature can be extremely valuable, especially when LANs are interconnected by relatively low-speed 56Kbps circuits. Otherwise, if all traffic were passed from a probe to a distant manager, the management traffic could saturate the WAN connection between LANs.

The RMON standard for Ethernet defines nine groups, and a tenth group was added to the token-ring RMON standard. Table 17.1 lists the RMON MIB groups and describes the contents of each group.

Figure 17.19 shows the screen display of Network General's Foundation Manager when it was used to retrieve information from the statistics group of an RMON probe. Note that the top window contains eight bar charts that identify such performance elements as bytes/sec and frames/sec, and the lower window provides bar charts of the distribution of frames by frame length and by different error conditions. Foundation Manager isolates many SNMP and RMON details from the user by allowing most operations to be performed by a simple point-and-click operation. For example, clicking on different icons at the top of the screen displays values for different RMON groups.

**TABLE 17.1**   RMON MIB Groups

| Group | Description |
| --- | --- |
| Statistics | Provides information for quantifying the operation of a network, such as packets, octets, and different errors. |
| History | Provides historical data on Statistics group variables for trend analysis. |
| Hosts | Collects information for each host on the network. |
| Host Top N | Enables a user to define information about the most active hosts on the network. |
| Traffic Matrix | Provides traffic and error reports that occur between pairs of stations. |
| Alarms | Reports changes in network characteristics when a preset condition is reached. |
| Events | Generates SNMP traps based on the previously set Alarms group thresholds. |
| Filters | Allows selection of packets to be captured so that managers can isolate traffic for review based on a predefined criteria. |
| Packet Capture | Copies packets into the probe for transfer to the manager later. Packet capture is based on filtering specifications in the Filters group. |
| Token Ring | An extension to the basic RMON MIB to provide token-ring–specific information, such as ring station information. |

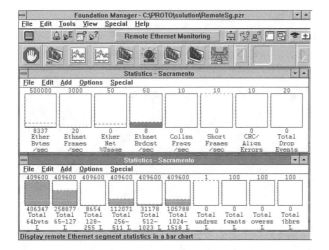

**FIGURE 17.19**

*Using Network General's Foundation Manager to retrieve statistical information from an RMON probe.*

Today, network managers and administrators can select from a wide range of network management products that can greatly facilitate the operation of national and international networks. By selecting appropriate network management products, you can isolate and rapidly correct network-related problems, as well as gain knowledge of potential problems before they become actual problems. Thus, SNMP and RMON can be used for network planning as well as problem isolation.

# What You Have Learned

- The underlying objective of data networking is to strike a balance between the accurate, timely delivery of user data and total cost.

- Any network, no matter how simple or complex, can be incorporated into a large network. A larger network cannot be optimized until its component parts are individually optimized.

- Information throughput rate involves many factors besides the modem bit rate.

- Classical time division multiplexers provide a powerful tool for combining data transmission link requirements into a smaller number of higher speed links. Statistical TDMs can be even more powerful if the duty cycles of individual links to be combined are low.

- Frequency division multiplexers can be useful if the links involve low-speed multipoint data transmission.

- Other useful networking devices include bridges, LAN switches, routers, gateways, sharing devices, modem eliminators, and protocol converters.

- Loopbacks are a common and simple technique for testing data communications components and networks.

- Test equipment for data communications falls into two generic categories: digital testing and analog testing.

- The capability to create programs that operate against monitored data can be used to isolate different types of communications problems.

- Good network design includes appropriate planning for contingencies and procedures for restoring service.

- Dialed backup is a common technique for restoring service on analog and digital transmission systems.

- SNMP and RMON are the network management standards that facilitate network planning and problem isolation.

- The global naming tree provides a mechanism for defining different managed objects.

- Two addresses are required to extract management information from a TCP/IP agent: the IP address and the global naming tree addresses of its managed objects.

# Quiz for Chapter 17

1. Which of the following is not considered a primary objective of data networking?

    A. Security

    B. Packet switching

    C. Timeliness

    D. Accuracy

2. Assume that the MTBF of a DSU is 320 days and its MTRS is 48 hours. What is its availability?

    A. 99.4%

    B. 44.7%

    C. 99.9%

    D. 100.0%

3. Assume that the availability of a router is 99.7%, whereas the availability of a T1 transmission line is 99.9%. What is the availability of a transmission system consisting of a pair of routers and the T1 line?

A. Cannot determine

B. 100%

C. 99.725%

D. 99.3%

4. On a point-to-point data channel using an analog circuit, TRIB is

    A. Higher than the modem bit rate.

    B. Equal to the modem bit rate.

    C. Lower than the modem bit rate.

    D. Not related to the modem bit rate.

5. The block length that gives maximum TRIB

    A. Increases as the error rate increases.

    B. Decreases as the error rate increases.

    C. Isn't related to error rate.

    D. Is called the optimum block length.

6. Smart TDMs

    A. Are always better than dumb TDMs.

    B. Are always better than FDMs.

    C. Are the same as modem sharing devices.

    D. Might be better than dumb TDMs if the data terminals have a low-duty cycle.

7. FDM devices can operate

    A. On multipoint analog data channels.

    B. More efficiently than dumb TDMs.

    C. More efficiently than smart TDMs.

    D. Like modem sharing devices.

8. Protocol converters are

    A. The same as multiplexers.

    B. The same as TDMs.

    C. Usually operated in pairs.

    D. Usually not operated in pairs.

17

NETWORK DESIGN AND MANAGEMENT

9. Null modems are a type of

   A. Modem eliminator.

   B. Modem.

   C. Multiplexer.

   D. Protocol converter.

10. Which of the following is a basic technique for isolating data communications faults?

    A. Calling the telephone company

    B. Performing a loopback test

    C. Calling the DTE service department

    D. Simulating the system on a special-purpose computer

11. Bridges operate at which layer of the OSI reference model?

    A. The data link layer

    B. The network layer

    C. The transport layer

    D. The application layer

12. At what layer of the ISO Reference Mode does a LAN switch that routes frames based on TCP or UDP port numbers operate?

    A. Physical Layer

    B. Data Link Layer

    C. Network Layer

    D. Transport Layer

13. Routers make forwarding decisions based on which of the following?

    A. MAC addresses

    B. Network addresses

    C. Source addresses

    D. MAC address tables

14. Which of the following devices can make forwarding decisions based on line availability and line utilization?

    A. Local bridge

    B. Remote bridge

    C. Gateway

    D. Router

15. What is the main purpose of a data link content monitor?

    A. Determine the type of switching used in a data link

    B. Determine the type of transmission used in a data link

    C. Detect problems in protocols

    D. Measure bit error rates

16. Which of the following is the most sophisticated type of data communications test equipment?

    A. Simulator

    B. Protocol analyzer

    C. DTE

    D. Breakout box

17. Which of the following is an example of a portable protocol converter?

    A. ParaScope

    B. Datascope

    C. UniScope

    D. UltraScope

18. Which of the following is an example of a protocol converter counter value?

    A. Bit delay

    B. ACK/NAK delay

    C. ACK/NAK count

    D. Data rate

19. Which organization assigns blocks of MAC addresses for use in network adapter cards?

    A. IEEE

    B. ITU-T

    C. CCITT

    D. AAA

20. Knowing the distribution of frames by their length is important in attempting to determine the

    A. LAN speed.

    B. LAN type.

    C. Type of traffic.

    D. Type of user.

21. The SNMP Management Information Base is

    A. Located in the network manager.

    B. Based on time.

    C. Based on the manager used.

    D. A database.

22. Which of the following must you have in order to set or retrieve data from an SNMP agent?

    A. The agent's IP address

    B. The address of the agent's object to be set

    C. An SNMP manager

    D. All the above

23. What is the global naming tree address of the IP group?

    A. 1.3.6.1.2.1.4

    B. 1.3.6.1.2.4

    C. 1.3.6.1.2

    D. 1.3.6.1

24. The RMON standard for Ethernet has how many groups?

    A. 9

    B. 10

    C. 11

    D. 12

# Glossary

**2B1Q**   An encoding technique used on ISDN lines in which 2 binary bits (2B) are encoded in one quaternary (1Q) symbol.

**10Base-2**   The 10Mbps version of Ethernet that operates on thin, RG58 coaxial cable.

**10Base-5**   The 10Mbps version of Ethernet that operates on thick coaxial cable.

**10Base-T**   The 10Mbps version of Ethernet that operates on Category 3 twisted-pair cable.

**10Base-T4**   The 100Mbps version of Fast Ethernet that operates on four pairs of Category 3, 4, or 5 unshielded twisted-pair or shielded twisted-pair wire.

**100Base-FX**   The 100Mbps version of Fast Ethernet that operates over two-strand 62.5/125-micron multimode fiber media.

**100Base-TX**   The 100Mbps version of Fast Ethernet that operates on two pairs of Category 5 unshielded twisted-pair cable.

**1000Base-CX**   The version of Gigabit Ethernet that operates on copper twin-axial shielded twisted-pair cable.

**1000Base-LX**   The version of Gigabit Ethernet that uses a 1300nm laser transmitting on single-mode or multimode fiber.

**1000Base-SX**   The version of Gigabit Ethernet that uses an 850nm laser transmitting on multimode fiber.

**1000Base-T**   The version of Gigabit Ethernet that operates on four pairs of Category 5 unshielded twisted-pair media.

**American Wire Gauge (AWG)**   A specification that defines the diameter and resistance of wire. The AWG gauge number is inversely proportional to the diameter of the wire.

**amplifier**   A device used to increase the strength of an analog signal.

**analog signal**   A signal, such as voice or music, that varies in a continuous manner. *See also* digital signal.

**ASCII (American Standard Code for Information Interchange)**   A 7-bit code established by the American National Standards Institute to achieve compatibility between data services. Equivalent to the international ISO 7-bit code.

**Asymmetrical Digital Subscriber Line (ADSL)**   A twisted-wire local loop that modems operate on to provide a data transfer rate of up to 8Mbps downstream and 1Mbps upstream.

**ATM adaptation layer**   The ATM layer responsible for translating higher-level protocol data into the 48-byte ATM cell payloads.

**ATM endpoint**   The location in an ATM network where a connection is either initiated or terminated.

**attenuation**   The difference between transmitted and received power due to transmission loss through equipment, lines, or other communication devices.

**backbone cabling**   Cable run between floors in a building or between buildings on a campus or industrial complex.

**balun**   A transformer used to connect coaxial or twin-axial equipment to twisted-pair cabling.

**bandwidth**   The frequency range between the lowest and highest frequencies that are passed through a component, circuit, or system with acceptable attenuation.

**baseband**   The frequency band occupied by a single or composite signal in its original or unmodulated form.

**baseband signaling**   A method of signaling in which only one signal occurs on the transmission medium at any point in time.

**basic access**   The method by which individual telephone instruments and terminals will be connected to a digital network.

**Basic Rate Interface (BRI)**   An ISDN line that provides up to two 64Kbps B channels and one 16Kbps D channel over an ordinary two-wire telephone line. B channels can transport circuit-switched voice or data, and D channels transport call-control signals and packet data.

**baud**   A unit of signaling speed equal to the number of signal events per second. Not necessarily the same as bits per second.

**Baudot code**   A five-element code that includes figure shift and letter shift characters that extend the number of characters supported by the code.

**Binary Coded Decimal (BCD)**   A system of binary numbering in which each decimal digit 0 through 9 is represented by 4 bits.

**Binary Synchronous Communications (BSC or BiSync)**   A communications protocol developed by IBM that has become an industry standard. It uses a defined set of control characters and control character sequences for synchronized transmission of binary-coded data between stations in a data communications system.

**bis**   Meaning "second" in Latin, this term is used as a suffix to denote a secondary version of a CCITT modem standard.

**bit**   (Contraction of "binary digit.") The smallest unit of information. A bit represents the choice between a 1 and a 0 value (a mark or space, in communications terminology).

**bit rate**   The speed at which bits are transmitted, usually expressed in bits per second. Not necessarily the same as baud rate.

**block**   A sequence of continuous data characters or bytes transmitted as a unit. A coding procedure is usually applied for synchronization or error-control purposes.

**bps (bits per second)**   A measure of the information transfer rate of a data channel.

**bridge**   A device that connects LANs at the ISO data link level.

**broadband signaling**   A method of signaling in which multiple signals share the bandwidth of the transmission medium by the subdivision of the bandwidth into channels based on frequency.

**buffer**   A storage device used to compensate for a difference in rate of data flow or time of occurrence of events when data is being transmitted from one device to another.

**byte**   A binary element string operated on as a unit and usually shorter than a computer word. Eight-bit bytes are common.

**carrier**   A signal suitable for modulation by another signal containing information to be transmitted. The carrier is usually a sine wave for analog systems.

**Category 3 cable**   A cable specification that supports transmission up to 16MHz.

**Category 4 cable**   A cable specification that supports transmission up to 20MHz.

**Category 5 cable**   A cable that supports transmission up to 100MHz.

**Category 5e cable**   Also referred to as enhanced Category 5, this twisted-pair cable specification supports transmission up to 100MHz and voice and data transmission up to 1000Mbps.

**Category 6 cable**   A cable specification that supports transmission up to 250MHz.

**CCITT (Consultative Committee for International Telephone and Telegraph)**   A standards-making body whose recommendations are more closely followed in Europe than in North America.

**cell**   A 53-byte-long transmission unit used by ATM. Each cell has a 5-byte header and a 48-byte payload.

**channel, voice grade**   A channel, generally with a frequency range of about 300 to 3400Hz, suitable for transmission of speech or data in analog form. Data transmission rates of 9600bps can be achieved by modulation techniques that produce a baud rate of 2,400.

**character**   A letter, figure, number, punctuation, or other symbol contained in a message or used in a control function.

**character set**   The characters that can be coded or printed by a particular machine.

**coaxial**   A single-conductor cable with a braided shield. Abbreviated as coax.

**code**   A set of unambiguous rules specifying the way in which characters can be represented.

**committed information rate**   The minimum operating rate supported by a Frame Relay service.

**common carrier**   A company that furnishes communications services to the general public and that is regulated by appropriate state or federal agencies.

**conditioning, line**   The addition of equipment to a leased voice-grade channel to improve analog characteristics to allow higher rates of data transmission.

**conductor**   A material that enables the flow of electrical current. Gold and silver are excellent conductors, and copper is a good, economical conductor commonly used in many electrical applications.

**connection-oriented**   A type of communications in which a connection must be established between the sender and receiver before transmission occurs.

**constellation pattern**   The pattern that results from plotting the location of each bit combination modulated by a modem through phase and amplitude changes.

**contention**   The facility provided by the dial network or a port selector that allows multiple terminals to compete on a first-come, first-served basis for a smaller number of computer ports.

**data communications equipment (DCE) (also data circuit-terminating equipment)**   The equipment that provides the functions required to establish, maintain, and terminate a connection, and that provides the signal conversion required for communication between data terminal equipment and the telephone line or data circuit.

**data terminal equipment (DTE)**   A computer or business machine that provides data in the form of digital signals at its output.

**dBm**   Decibel referenced to 1 milliwatt. Used in communications circuits as a measure of signal power. 0dBm equals 1 milliwatt into a specified impedance, often 600 ohms.

**decibel (dB)**   A logarithmic measure of the ratio between two powers, P1 and P2. The equation is dB = 10 log10 P2/P1.

**delay equalizer**   A corrective network that is designed to make the phase delay or envelope delay of a circuit or system substantially constant over a desired frequency range.

12

GETTING STARTED
WITH JAVASCRIPT

**delay, propagation**   The time required for a signal to travel from one point to another in a component, circuit, or system.

**delay skew**   The difference in propagation delay between the slowest and fastest pairs in a cable.

**demodulation**   The process of recovering data from a modulated carrier wave. The reverse of modulation.

**dialing directory**   A module in a communications program that enables telephone numbers and descriptions of those numbers to be entered. Selecting an entry in the dialing directory causes the program to dial the number associated with the entry.

**dial-up line**   A communications circuit that is established by a switched-circuit connection using the telephone dial network.

**dibit**   A group of 2 bits. In four-phase modulation, such as differential phase shift keying (DPSK), each possible dibit is encoded as one of four unique carrier phase shifts. The four possible states for a dibit are 00, 01, 10, and 11.

**digital repeater**   A data regenerator that, on the detection of the rise of a digital pulse's leading edge, regenerates the pulse.

**digital signal**   A discrete or discontinuous signal; one whose various states are identified with discrete levels or values.

**distortion, delay**   Distortion resulting from nonuniform speed of transmission of the various frequency components of a signal through a transmission medium. Also called group delay.

**distortion, harmonic**   The result of nonlinearities in the communication channel that cause harmonics of the input frequencies to appear in the output.

**distortion, linear (or amplitude)**   An unwanted change in signal amplitude such that the output signal envelope is not proportional to the input signal envelope, but no frequency-related distortion is involved.

**drop**   A reference to horizontal cabling in a work area in which a cable is installed from a hub to a workstation.

**echo suppressor**   A device that allows transmission in only one direction at a time. Echo suppressors are inserted in telephone circuits to attenuate echoes on long-distance circuits. They are not desirable in data-communications circuits because they increase the turnaround time.

**emulation**   The process of duplicating the attributes of another device, such as a terminal.

**entropy**   A measurement of the randomness of data.

**equalization**    The process of reducing the effects of amplitude, frequency, or phase distortion of a circuit by inserting networks to compensate for the difference in attenuation or time delay at various frequencies in the transmission band.

**ergonomics**    The process of dealing with the interaction between people and their working environment.

**Ethernet**    A 10Mbps bus-based local area network that uses the CSMA/CD access protocol.

**Extended Binary-Coded Decimal Interchange Code (EBCDIC)**    An 8-bit code that enables 256 characters to be represented.

**far-end crosstalk (FEXT)**    The unwanted noise coupled onto a receive pair from a transmit pair at the far end of a transmission line.

**Fast Ethernet**    A 100Mbps hub-based local area network version of Ethernet that uses the CSMA/CD access protocol.

**filter**    A network designed to transmit electrical signals having frequencies within one or more frequency bands and to attenuate signals of other frequencies.

**flow control**    The orderly regulation of the flow of data by the use of special characters (inband signaling) or control signals at the RS-232 interface (outband signaling).

**Frame Relay**    A packet-switched service that does not provide for error detection and correction, resulting in minimal routing delays.

**frequency-division multiplexer (FDM)**    A device that divides the available transmission frequency range into narrower bands, each of which is used for a separate channel.

**frequency response**    The change in attenuation with frequency relative to the attenuation at a reference frequency. Also called attenuation distortion.

**frequency shift keying (FSK)**    A form of frequency modulation commonly used in low-speed modems in which the two states of the signal are transmitted as two separate frequencies.

**full-duplex**    Refers to a communications system or equipment capable of simultaneous two-way communications.

**g.Lite**    A reduced operating rate version of an asymmetrical digital subscriber line (ADSL) that does not require splitters at the customer premise.

**gateway**    Hardware and software that enables devices located on a local area network to access the facilities of another network.

**12**

GETTING STARTED
WITH JAVASCRIPT

**geostationary**   The orbit of a satellite at a constant speed and in the same direction as the Earth's rotation, resulting in a fixed location with respect to the Earth.

**Gigabit Ethernet**   A 1000Mbps hub-based local area network version of Ethernet that uses the CSMA/CD access protocol.

**global naming tree**   A mechanism that enables unique identifiers to be assigned to objects that require naming.

**half-duplex**   Refers to a communications system or equipment capable of communications in both directions, but in only one direction at a time.

**handshaking**   Exchange of predetermined codes and signals between two data terminals to establish a connection.

**hub**   A network device that functions as a repeater. A hub is commonly installed in a wiring closet, and workstations in the office are cabled to the hub.

**inband signaling**   A method of flow control in which a device transmits one character (usually an XOFF) to inform another device to suspend transmission and then transmits another character (usually an XON) to resume transmission.

**interface**   A shared boundary defined by common physical interconnection characteristics, signal characteristics, and meanings of interchanged signals.

**intermodulation noise**   Spurious frequencies, such as sum and difference frequencies, that are the products of frequencies transmitted through a nonlinear circuit.

**IP address**   A 32-bit address that identifies the network and host in a network.

**ISDN (Integrated Services Digital Network)**   A future offering designed to provide a universal digital network that will enable the integration of voice and data on a common telephone company facility.

**jitter**   A tendency toward lack of synchronization caused by mechanical or electrical changes.

**Kilostream**   A digital network that operates in the United Kingdom.

**line**   1. A circuit between a customer terminal and the central office. 2. The portion of a transmission system, including the transmission medium and associated repeaters, between two terminal locations.

**link**   A circuit or transmission path, including all equipment, between a sender and a receiver.

**local area network (LAN)**   A communications network that is restricted to a small geographical area, usually within a building or on a campus, and that has cabling normally installed or controlled by the organization that operates the network.

**local loop**   The pair of wires between a customer terminal and the central office.

**loopback test**   A test of a communications link performed by connecting the equipment output of one direction to the equipment input of the other direction and testing the quality of the received signal.

**management information base (MIB)**   A collection of databases for the set of managed devices supported by SNMP.

**mark**   One of the two possible states of a binary information element. The closed circuit and idle state in a teleprinter circuit. *See* space.

**microprocessor**   A computer on a chip that contains millions of transistors etched into a square of silicon.

**modem (MOdulator/DEModulator)**   A type of DCE that, at the transmitting end, converts digital data to an analog signal for transmission on telephone circuits. A modem at the receiving end converts the analog signal to digital form.

**modulation**   The process of varying some characteristic of the carrier wave in accordance with the instantaneous value or samples of the intelligence to be transmitted. Amplitude, frequency, and phase are the characteristics commonly varied.

**multimode**   A type of optical fiber in which light travels in multiple paths from end to end. LEDs or lasers are used as the light source.

**multiplex**   To interleave or simultaneously transmit two or more messages on a single channel.

**multistation access unit (MAU)**   A device that enables workstations on a LAN to be cabled in a star configuration.

**near-end crosstalk (NEXT)**   The electromagnetic coupling between a transmit wire pair and a receive wire pair.

**network interface card (NIC)**   An adapter card installed in the system expansion slot of a PC that provides network connectivity.

**node**   A device connected to a network.

**noise**   Random electrical signals, introduced by circuit components or natural disturbances, that tend to generate errors in transmission.

**octet**   A group of 8 bits.

**outband signaling**   A method of flow control in which an RS-232 control signal (usually Clear to Send) is lowered to inform a device to suspend transmission and raised to inform a device to resume transmission.

**12**

GETTING STARTED
WITH JAVASCRIPT

**PABX (private automatic branch exchange)**   A device that is installed on a customer's premises and that enables a large number of telephones to automatically access the switched telephone network by using a smaller number of lines connecting the PABX to the telephone company network.

**PBX (private branch exchange)**   Telephone switching equipment dedicated to one customer and connected to the public switched network.

**permanent virtual circuit (PVC)**   A logical connection between endpoints in a network that remains in place until the network administrator tears it down.

**personal computer**   A computer with processing power based on a microprocessor and designed primarily for use by one person.

**personal digital assistant (PDA)**   A handheld computer.

**personnel communications service (PCS)**   A relatively new cellular service that operates in the 800MHz band.

**polling**   The individual selection of multiple terminals by a controller to allow transmission of traffic to and from all terminals on a multidrop line in an orderly manner.

**port**   An interface on a computer configured as data terminal equipment and capable of having a modem attached for communication with a remote data terminal.

**powersum FEXT (PSFEXT)**   The composite sum of all far-end crosstalk (FEXT) signals. PSFEXT is important in applications that use all cable pairs at the same time.

**powersum NEXT (PSNEXT)**   The sum of individual NEXT effects on each pair by the other pairs in a cable. PSNEXT is important in applications that use all cable pairs at the same time.

**primary access**   A multiplexing arrangement in which many ISDN Basic access subscribers can be connected to a digital network over a common line facility.

**Primary Rate Interface (PRI)**   A four-wire ISDN line that operates at 1.544Mbps and contains 23 64Kbps B channels and one 64Kbps D channel. The B channels can transport circuit-switched voice or data, while the 64Kbps D channel transports call-control signals and packet data.

**protocol**   The rules for communication between like processes, giving a means to control the orderly communication of information between stations on a data link.

**protocol analyzer**   A device that decodes a bit stream being monitored into characters that represent the format and information content of a transmission protocol.

**redundancy**   The portion of the total information contained in a message that can be eliminated without loss of essential information.

**Remote Monitoring (RMON)**    A set of Internet standards that facilitate the collection and retrieval of information on remote networks from a management platform.

**repeater**    A communications system component that amplifies or regenerates signals to compensate for losses in the system.

**RJ-11**    A six-position modular jack.

**RJ-45**    An eight-position modular jack.

**router**    A device that operates at the network layer of the ISO OSI reference model, examining the network address in packets as a mechanism to forward them on a route to their appropriate destination.

**serial transmission**    A method of information transfer in which the bits that compose a character are sent in sequence one at a time.

**Simple Network Management Protocol (SNMP)**    A standard for managing TCP/IP–based networks.

**single-mode**    A type of optical fiber in which light flows in a single path. It utilizes lasers as a light source.

**slow scan video**    The process by which still video images are transmitted frequently to provide the appearance of video motion.

**space**    One of the two possible states of a binary information element. The open circuit or no current state of a teleprinter line. See also *mark*.

**start bit or element**    The first bit or element transmitted in the asynchronous transmission of a character to synchronize the receiver.

**statistical multiplexer**    A multiplexer that uses the idle time of connected devices to carry data traffic from active devices.

**stop bit or element**    The last bit or element transmitted in the asynchronous transmission of a character to return the circuit to the at-rest or idle condition.

**switched virtual circuit**    A logical connection through a network established on a demand basis for a temporary period.

**symbol**    The graphical representation of some idea that is used by people. Letters and numbers are symbols.

**TA (terminal adapter)**    A device that is used to enable equipment with a non-ISDN interface to be connected to that digital network.

**12**

GETTING STARTED
WITH JAVASCRIPT

**TE1 (terminal equipment 1)**   Devices that comply with the ISDN network interface and that can be connected directly to the digital network.

**TE2 (terminal equipment 2)**   Devices that do not have an ISDN interface and must be connected by using a TA (terminal adapter) to the digital network.

**ter**   Meaning "third" in Latin, this term is used as a suffix to denote a third version of a CCITT modem standard.

**terminal emulation**   Software or firmware that enables a personal computer or terminal to duplicate the screen attributes of a specific terminal.

**time-division multiplexer (TDM)**   A device that allows the transmission of two or more independent data channels on a single high-speed circuit by interleaving the data from each channel on the circuit by time.

**transmission, asynchronous**   Transmission in which each information character is individually synchronized, usually by the use of start and stop elements.

**transmission, synchronous**   Transmission in which the sending and receiving instruments are operating continuously at substantially the same frequency and in which the desired phase relationship can be maintained by means of correction.

**trellis-coded modulation**   A modem-modulation process in which one or more redundant bits are added to each group of bits used to generate a signal change. The extra bit (or bits) allows only certain sequences of signal points to be valid, which lowers the error rate.

**turnaround time**   The actual time required to reverse the direction of transmission from sender to receiver, or vice versa, when a half-duplex circuit is being used. Time is required for line-propagation effects, modem timing, and computer reaction.

**UART (universal asynchronous receiver/transmitter)**   A device that performs asynchronous communications functions by converting parallel digital output from a DTE into serial bit transmission, and vice versa.

**Universal Serial Bus (USB)**   A PC bus that can support up to 12 devices and that provides a data-transfer capability up to 12Mbps. The USB supports Plug-and-Play operations.

**virtual channel connection (VCC)**   A concatenation of virtual channel links between two endpoints in an ATM network.

**virtual path connection (VPC)**   A concatenation of virtual path links between two or more switches in an ATM network.

**XMODEM**   A half-duplex file-transfer protocol limited to transmitting one file at a time.

**YMODEM**   A half-duplex file-transfer protocol that supports the transfer of multiple files.

**ZMODEM**   A full-duplex file-transfer protocol that supports the transfer of multiple files and enables a previously interrupted transmission to be resumed at the point of interruption.

# Bibliography

*A History of Engineering & Science in the Bell System: The Early Years (1875–1925).* Whippany, NJ: Bell Telephone Laboratories, Inc., 1975.

*Bell Laboratories Record.* Whippany, NJ: Bell Telephone Laboratories, Inc., November 1980.

Bellamy, John. *Digital Telephony.* New York: John Wiley & Sons, Inc., 1982.

Bigelow, Stephen. *Understanding Telephone Electronics, Third Edition.* Carmel, IN: Sams, a division of Macmillan Computer Publishing, 1983.

Black, Uyless. *Computer Networks Protocols, Standards, and Interfaces.* Englewood Cliffs, NJ: Prentice Hall, Inc., 1993.

Black, Uyless. *Data Networks.* Englewood Cliffs, NJ: Prentice Hall, Inc., 1989.

Black, Uyless. *Frame Relay Networks.* New York: McGraw-Hill Book Co., 1996.

Black, Uyless. *Sonet and T1.* Englewood Cliffs, NJ: Prentice Hall, Inc. 1996.

Black, Uyless. *TCP/IP and Related Protocols.* New York: McGraw-Hill Book Co., 1997.

Chirillo, John. *Hack Attacks Revealed.* New York: John Wiley & Sons, 2001.

Chirillo, John. *Hack Attacks Denied.* New York: John Wiley & Sons, 2001.

Doll, Dixon. *Data Communications: Facilities, Networks and Systems Design.* New York: John Wiley & Sons, 1978.

EIA Standard RS-232-C (and others). Electronic Industries Association.

Freeman, R.L. *Telecommunication System Engineering, Third Edition.* New York: John Wiley & Sons, Inc., 1996.

Freeman, R.L. *Telecommunication Transmission Handbook, Fourth Edition.* New York: John Wiley & Sons, Inc., 1998.

*General Information—Binary Synchronous Communications.* IBM Publication Nr. GA27-3004, IBM Systems Development Division, Publications Center.

*General Information—IBM Synchronous Data Link Control.* IBM Publication Nr. GA27-3093-2, IBM Systems Development Division, Publications Center.

Held, Gilbert. *Cisco Access Lists Field Guide.* New York: McGraw-Hill Book Co., 1999.

Held, Gilbert. *Data and Image Compression, Fourth Edition.* New York: John Wiley & Sons, 1996.

Held, Gilbert. *Data Communications Networking Devices, Fourth Edition.* New York: John Wiley & Sons, 1998.

Held, Gilbert. *Data Over Wireless Networks: Bluetooth, WAP & Wireless LANs.* New York: Osborne McGraw-Hill, 2001.

Held, Gilbert. *Dictionary of Communications Terminology, Third Edition.* New York: John Wiley & Sons, 1998.

Held, Gilbert. *Ethernet Networks, Third Edition.* New York: John Wiley & Sons, 1998.

Held, Gilbert. *Frame Relay Networking.* Chichester, England: John Wiley & Sons, 1999.

Held, Gilbert. *High Speed Digital Networking, Second Edition.* New York: John Wiley & Sons, 1999.

Held, Gilbert. *High Speed Networking with LAN Switches.* New York: John Wiley & Sons, 1997.

Held, Gilbert. *Internetworking LANs and WANs, Second Edition.* New York: John Wiley & Sons, 1998.

Held, Gilbert. *LAN Management with SNMP and RMON.* New York: John Wiley & Sons, 1996.

Held, Gilbert. *Protecting LAN Resources.* New York: John Wiley & Sons, 1995.

Held, Gilbert. *The Complete Modem Reference, Third Edition.* New York: John Wiley & Sons, Inc., 1996.

Held, Gilbert. *Voice over Data Networks, Third Edition.* New York: McGraw-Hill, 2001.

IEEE Transactions on Communications. IEEE Communications Society, August 1980, Vol. COM-28.

ITU-T Recommendations V.29, X.21, and X.25. ITU-T, Geneva, C.H.

Kreager, Paul. *Practical Aspects of Data Communications.* New York: McGraw-Hill Book Co., 1983.

Kumar, Vineet, Markku Korpi, and Senthil Sengodan. *IP Telephony with H.323.* New York: John Wiley & Sons, 2001.

Martin, James. *Local Area Networks: Architectures and Implementation.* Englewood Cliffs, NJ: Prentice Hall, 1994.

Martin, James. *Telecommunications and the Computer.* Englewood Cliffs, NJ: Prentice Hall, Inc., 1994.

Martin, James, and Joel Leben. *TCP/IP Networking: Architecture, Administration and Programming.* Englewood Cliffs, NJ: Prentice Hall, Inc., 1994.

**B**

UNDERSTANDING DATA COMMUNICATIONS

McNamara, John E. *Technical Aspects of Data Communications, Second Edition.* Englewood Cliffs, NJ: Digital Press, 1982.

Members of the Technical Staff and the Technical Publications Department. *Engineering and Operations in the Bell System.* Whippany, NJ: Bell Telephone Laboratories, Inc., 1977.

Members of the Technical Staff. *Transmission Systems for Communications, Revised 4th Edition.* Whippany, NJ: Bell Telephone Laboratories, Inc., 1971.

*Notes on the Network.* New York: American Telephone & Telegraph Co., 1980.

Owen, Frank E. *PCM and Digital Transmission Systems.* New York: McGraw-Hill, Inc., 1982.

*Parameters of Telephone Network Design.* New York: IBM Publication Nr. ZZ-11-3201-0, IBM World Trade Corp., January 1977.

Sherman, Kenneth. *Data Communications: A User's Guide, Third Edition.* Reston Publishing Co., 1989.

Stallings, William. *Data and Computer Communications, Fifth Edition.* Englewood Cliffs, NJ: Prentice Hall, Inc., 1996.

Stallings, William, and Richard Van Slyke. *Business Data Communications, Third Edition.* Englewood Cliffs, NJ: Prentice Hall, Inc., 1997.

Tanebaum, Andrew S. *Computer Networks, Third Edition.* Englewood Cliffs, NJ: Prentice Hall, Inc., 1996.

# Answers to Quizzes

# Chapter 1

1. D
2. B
3. A
4. C
5. C
6. C
7. B
8. B
9. A
10. C
11. C
12. B
13. C
14. C
15. B
16. B

# Chapter 2

1. C
2. A
3. B
4. B
5. C
6. C
7. C
8. C
9. D
10. A
11. A
12. B

13. C
14. C
15. C
16. A
17. B
18. C
19. D
20. A
21. C
22. B
23. A
24. C
25. A

# Chapter 3

1. C
2. A
3. B
4. A
5. C
6. B
7. D
8. D
9. B
10. B
11. D
12. B
13. C
14. D
15. B
16. A
17. A

18. A
19. A
20. B
21. B
22. C
23. D
24. C
25. C

# Chapter 4

1. C
2. A
3. B
4. A
5. B
6. B
7. B
8. C
9. B
10. C
11. D
12. C
13. C
14. B
15. A
16. C
17. B
18. C
19. C
20. C
21. C
22. B

23. D
24. B
25. B

# Chapter 5

1. D
2. B
3. C
4. C
5. D
6. C
7. A
8. C
9. B
10. C
11. D
12. D
13. B
14. B
15. D
16. B
17. B
18. C
19. C
20. A
21. B
22. D
23. A
24. C
25. B
26. C
27. C

28. C
29. B
30. C
31. D

# Chapter 6

1. B
2. C
3. C
4. C
5. A
6. D
7. B
8. B
9. C
10. D
11. B
12. A
13. A
14. C
15. D
16. A
17. B
18. A
19. D
20. A

# Chapter 7

1. A and C
2. C
3. B

4. D

5. A

6. C

7. D

8. C

9. D

10. B

11. C

12. A

13. C

14. C

15. C

16. B

17. C

18. D

19. C

20. B

21. B

22. C

23. A

24. F

25. A

26. C

27. B

28. D

29. B

30. D

# Chapter 8

1. A
2. C
3. C
4. D
5. C
6. D
7. D
8. B
9. C
10. C
11. C
12. B
13. D
14. C
15. B
16. B and D
17. A
18. B
19. C
20. D

# Chapter 9

1. A
2. C
3. B
4. D
5. D

6. B

7. D

8. C

9. A

10. B

11. B

12. D

13. A

14. D

# Chapter 10

1. C

2. B

3. A

4. A

5. D

6. B

7. C

8. D

9. C

10. D

11. A

12. B

13. A

14. B

15. C

16. A

17. D

18. B

19. A

20. C

21. C
22. C
23. D
24. D
25. C
26. D
27. A
28. C
29. A
30. B

# Chapter 11

1. C
2. A
3. D
4. A
5. B
6. C
7. D
8. A
9. B
10. C
11. A
12. B
13. B
14. B
15. B
16. A
17. B
18. D
19. D
20. A

21. C
22. B
23. B
24. A
25. B
26. D
27. D
28. C
29. D
30. A
31. B
32. C
33. C
34. D
35. B

# Chapter 12

1. B
2. B
3. C
4. D
5. C
6. A
7. C
8. B
9. B
10. C
11. A
12. C
13. C
14. C
15. D

16. B
17. B
18. A
19. B
20. D
21. A
22. C
23. B
24. D
25. C

# Chapter 13

1. B
2. B
3. A
4. D
5. C
6. D
7. A
8. B
9. C
10. B
11. A
12. C
13. D
14. D
15. C

# Chapter 14

1. B
2. D
3. C

4. C

5. D

6. B

7. D

8. A

9. C

10. B

11. D

12. B

13. A

14. B

15. C

16. D

17. D

18. C

19. A

20. C

# Chapter 15

1. B

2. A

3. D

4. B

5. D

6. A

7. C

8. C

9. C

10. D

11. B

12. D

13. A

14. B
15. D

# Chapter 16

1. B
2. A
3. D
4. C
5. B
6. D
7. C
8. D
9. B
10. D
11. A
12. B
13. C
14. B
15. C

# Chapter 17

1. B
2. A
3. D
4. C
5. B
6. D
7. A
8. D
9. A
10. B
11. A

12. D
13. B
14. D
15. C
16. B
17. A
18. C
19. A
20. C
21. D
22. D
23. A
24. A

# INDEX

## SYMBOLS

# X

# Y-Z